Transference and Its Context

Transference and Its Context

Selected Papers on Psychoanalysis

Leo Stone, M.D.

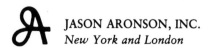

JASON ARONSON, INC.
New York and London

Copyright © 1984 by Jason Aronson, Inc.

10 9 8 7 6 5 4 3 2 1

ISBN 0-87668-655-2

Library of Congress Cataloging in Publication Data

Stone, Leo, 1904–
    Transference and its context.

    Bibliography: p.
    Includes index.
    1. Transference (Psychology)—Addresses, essays,
lectures. I. Title. [DNLM: 1. Transference (Psychology)
—Collected works. 2. Psychoanalysis—Collected works.
WM 62 S878t]
BF175.S69   1984   616.89′17   83-25807
ISBN 0-87668-655-2

Manufactured in the United States of America.

FOR MARTHA CARETHE

Contents

Preface

These selected papers are grouped largely around my own evolving conception of the psychoanalytic situation and process, and a broad construction of the dynamism of transference as the central propulsive force of the analytic process. The manifestation that opposes the movement of analytic work, known as resistance and regarded by Sigmund Freud as the other indispensable concept in defining psychoanalysis was, from early on, seen as one of the possible manifestations of transference. In my own extended paper on the subject of resistance, I view the transference as integral in the very origin and nature of resistance, apart from its clinical appearance in this form.

Beginning with "Psychoanalysis and Brief Psychotherapy" (1951), and continuing through "Widening Scope" (1954), "The Psychoanalytic Situation" (1961), and its "Postscript" (1967), the developing holistic perspective on the structure and general dynamics of the format, attitudes, and technical procedures of the work has been the leitmotiv of my theoretical position and thus of my practical inferences and applications. In all, the rule of abstinence, its relation to transference and the transference neurosis, and the special considerations in its application are of particular importance. Although these elements are always considered in relation to the standard technical procedures of psychoanalysis, it is the total dynamic situation and its integration with procedural theory that holds my special interest.

Although the trend of my interest and attitude is consistent, there is, of course, a palpable evolution of ideas. Even though my 1951 paper has some adumbrations of later ideas, its essential framework is traditional, with, I think, rational extrapolations to a psychotherapeutic structure. In "Widening Scope," I emphasize the cognitive and emotional "vacuum" inherent in the analytic situation. In "Psychoanalytic Situation" and "Postscript," I elaborate on previously incipient ideas and give them a theoretical substructure. Reactions to the archaic problems of separation and germane oral mechanisms, with the related and derived function of speech as a bridge to the primal object, provide the keystone of understanding.

Also included in this volume are papers not pertaining to this principal theme. Among them, the papers on aggression represent a significant theoretical divergence from the mainstream of classical psychoanalytic thought. The second of these papers also reconsiders the psychobiologic emergence of speech, as well as other intimately related hypotheses, for example, the anthropological-psychological role of fire.

Omitted from this selected group of psychoanalytic papers are some miscellaneous efforts: a couple of early papers, a review, a few discussions, and panel participations. In addition, one recent paper on depressive illness has not yet been published.

Part I

The Psychoanalytic and Psychotherapeutic Situations

Chapter 1
Psychoanalysis and Brief Psychotherapy
(1949–1951)

This paper was my first formal psychoanalytic communication regarding psychotherapy, a field that has never ceased to interest me. Yet I believe that psychotherapy has been neglected both clinically and theoretically in the evolution of psychoanalysis, not to speak of its self-evident practical importance in the life of the community. Obviously the preeminent issue would be the application of psychoanalytic theory and methodology to the increasingly rational and better organized psychotherapeutic methods. However, the possibilities of reflexive gains for psychoanalysis from the intimate scrutiny of its more humble (and primarily derivative) neighbor are not to be rejected.

Although this paper sometimes emphasizes formalism, which is modified in my later writings, the nuclear ideas are still, I think, useful. The main themes, as elaborated over a few decades, are represented in papers given in different contexts, e.g., at the Pre-Congress on Training of the International Psychoanalytic Association in July 1979 and at a Symposium sponsored by the Atlanta Psychoanalytic Society in October 1979. There are also brief references to psychotherapy in "The Widening Scope," "The Psychoanalytic Situation," and most pointedly in "Some Problems and Potentialities of Present-Day Psychoanalysis." These three papers are included in this volume.

It should be noted, with regard to the modest research effort mentioned in the paper, that the clinical records which resulted from it have not been systematically explored. The group involved in the work learned much from it as individuals, and the group work and discussions continued for a few years. However, various methodological problems and disagreements disqualified an overall systematic review. Thus the gains have remained in the sphere of personal observation and experience. To me, this was a great boon.

This paper, apart from the fact that it is "old," should not be construed as part of the current wave of unqualified enthusiasm for "brief therapy." (See Chapter 14) I do not know the later history of the young

3

male patient in the paper. The young woman, although much improved for a time, did have further trouble in the marital sphere at a later date, and ultimately needed more thorough treatment in another part of the country.

T he term *brief psychotherapy* is used in preference to *psychotherapy*—
which has the support of wide current usage—because the latter ignores
the historical fact that psychoanalysis is a special and relatively new
branch of psychotherapy. The adjective *psychoanalytic* has merit but facilitates
the blurring of distinctions. The adjective *nonanalytic* sharpens the distinction
from psychoanalysis but gives a negative inferential place, if any, to the psychoanalytic rationale, from the analyst's viewpoint, that any psychotherapeutic
technique may have. While the actual brevity of psychotherapy is highly variable,
the qualification connotes the effort to meet the current tremendous need and
demand for treatment, and the consequent prevailing tendency in research, i.e.,
toward diminution of the total time involved in treatment.

Psychoanalysis, as is any science, is full of unsolved problems (Glover et al.
1937, Oberndorf et al. 1948). However, it is a relatively well-defined and
systematized procedure, compared to this large and chaotic field, ranging from
simple suggestion to the procedure most usually referred to as *psychotherapy*,
which bears a superficial resemblance to psychoanalysis but which, because of
the inclusion of important variables, is very poorly defined, highly unpredictable,
and exceedingly difficult to evaluate. The only exception to this general charac-
terization lies in those few instances where the trained analyst treats a patient
at long but regular intervals and follows sound and well-defined psychoanalytic
precepts in his general management of the case. Here, there is only one important
immediately discernible variable, the infrequency of the visits. The analyst may,
from terminological scruples of his own, prefer to distinguish this work from
regular psychoanalysis, a borderline distinction which may indeed be importantly
justified, in the sense that we cannot assume a priori that the infrequency of visits
does not change the basic relationship and certain modalities of its expression.

The actual functional distinction between psychoanalysis and brief psychotherapy is, of course, really in doubt only in the area where there are certain
resemblances; but it is precisely in this area that it is most important that the
distinction be maintained. The tendency to dissolve the distinction has been
strongly manifested in the contributions of the Chicago Institute for Psychoanalysis in the last several years (Alexander et al. 1946, McLean 1948, *Proceedings* 1942, *Proceedings* 1944, *Proceedings* 1946). In Alexander's last book
(1948), however, the question is only briefly mentioned as a "matter of defini-

tion." I should like to affirm the importance of the definition and distinction and offer some reasons for their maintenance. For a long time psychoanalysis was conceded a special meaning even by some of the more radical deviant groups (Jung and Adler, for instance) and by most nonanalytic psychiatrists. What then is the advantage or motive for diffusing or vitiating the meaning of an accepted and explicit scientific term?

A real issue is the basis for definition. There is no doubt that in Knight's recent classification of psychotherapy as either "suppressive or supportive," or "expressive or exploratory" (1948), psychoanalysis, despite minimal admixtures of other techniques, belongs to the second group. However, this functional classification of separate technical maneuvers does not take into account the intricate and relatively constant configuration of techniques in psychoanalysis. In several contributions, Freud's statement of 1914, "Any line of investigation, no matter what its direction, which recognizes these two facts [transference and resistance] and takes them as the starting point of its work may call itself psychoanalysis, though it arrives at results other than my own," has been invoked for purposes of definition, although obvious assumed parenthetical extensions are sometimes recognized (Fenichel 1945, Gill 1951, Knight 1948). If one accepts authoritative permission as a basis for definition, one should also take into account the fact that Freud laid down elsewhere a considerable number of technical precepts for the practice of psychoanalysis, ranging from the basic rule to the number of hours per week that he treated patients. These were acknowledged by Freud to be incomplete; however, certain of the fundamental ones, such as the basic rule and the general tendency of the analyst's attitude were reiterated by him in 1938 (1949). Regardless of one's objective judgment of their value, these precepts, interpreted with varying degrees of flexibility or rigidity and with occasional modifications or elaborations for special reasons and the development of certain interpretative trends from ego and character analysis, have continued to provide the broad outlines of technical procedure for most analysts. Since this conception of psychoanalysis has been so influential, a more important factor than the invoking of authority enters: the simple fact that this is what the word means to most of us as a technique and that the great mass of psychoanalytic literature, except that known to be different by individual or group specification, may reasonably be assumed to be material acquired by this method. This has important methodological significance, for we must be aware of the relation of our data to our instrument, especially when we undertake to apply these data to other techniques which may involve highly influential variables. What I have in mind is whether clinically important dynamic phenomena such as transference, repression or other ego defenses, and free association can be assumed to have the same character and meaning or to be manipulable in the same way when important technical variables are introduced. Aside from transference and resistance, which are really powerful dynamic forces appearing in the psychoanalytic situation rather than maneuvers or deliberately planned conditions, one may list several important factors in the situation and technique from which scientific data have been derived, and on which specific technical variations have been built. These undoubtedly differ greatly in importance and constancy. Some are at times deliberately changed (Freud advocated certain "flexibilities"), but they have great weight as an ensemble in the accumulation of our knowledge, and we are not in a position to speak with broad systematic certainty of the relative importance of each factor: (1) practically exclusive reliance during the hour on the patient's free associations for communication;[1] (2) regularity of the time, frequency, and duration of appointments and a clearly defined financial agreement; (3) three to five appointments a week (originally six), with daily appointments the dominant tendency; (4) the recumbent position, in most instances, with some impediment to seeing the analyst directly; (5) confinement of the analyst's activity essentially to interpretation or other purely informative interventions such as reality testing or an occasional question (Loewenstein 1948); (6) the analyst's emotional passivity and neutrality ("benevolent objectivity"), specifically abstention from gratifying the analysand's transference wishes; (7) abstention from advice or any other direct intervention or participation in the patient's daily life; (8) no immediate emphasis on curing symptoms, the procedure being guided largely by the patient's free associations from day to day. In a sense the analyst regards the whole scope of the patient's psychic life as his field of observation.

These several enumerated features of the psychoanalytic situation form a fairly constant and unique ensemble. It seems paradoxical, but it is functionally true that with the patient's conscious and continuing voluntary cooperation, a psychological relationship is achieved that is reminiscent of—although far from identical with—the self-abandonment of hypnosis. This relationship is certainly important in the special phenomenology of the psychoanalytic situation.

Whenever reassurance, persuasion, manipulation of the environment, active therapeutic interest or other deviations[2] are included in therapy to any large degree, we should assume important alterations in the dynamics of the transference. While fully granting the primacy of understanding the patient, I would agree with Kubie's point of view (*Proceedings* 1942) about the importance of technical variables, rather than with those who feel that the psychoanalytic understanding of a problem is all that is necessary, the variations of technique being left to art or intuition, or even to planning which underestimates these complexities. Lest it be thought that such scientific rigidity would be tantamount to inhibiting the practice of brief psychotherapy, it should be emphasized that these considerations are purely in the sphere of critical scientific evaluation of process and result—of research. That the practice of brief psychotherapy justifies itself seems self-evident. But the sequel to the practice should be critical differential scrutiny, not rationalization or procrustean oversimplification. In this connection, Knight's comment about the facility of recollecting successful cases and forgetting the others (*Proceedings* 1942) has an important general significance in the selection of case material for publication.

One may also view the distinction in a purely practical clinical sense. Psychoanalysis for some time has been the treatment of choice for the neuroses. From Freud onward, critical minds have been conservative about therapeutic results, and there has recently been a strong movement toward their careful evaluation, largely stimulated by Oberndorf et al. (1948). Freud always regarded the transference neuroses as the chief, if not exclusive, indication for psychoanalysis (1904, 1949), and were this indication adhered to, the therapeutic results of psychoanalysis might remain grounds for enthusiasm. Driven by the stimulation of therapeutic success and the possession of the first rational and effective psychotherapeutic instrument, analysts have carried their work into the fields of severe character disorders, addictions, borderline conditions, and even psychoses and frank somatic disorders. In many instances explicit modifications in technique have been proposed. Further advances or modifications of psychoanalysis may make certain of these extensions more secure; however, it is possible that the tide of therapeutic optimism will recede in certain areas, leaving psychoanalysis closer to its original indications, and leaving large groups of illnesses to be better treated by techniques of "brief psychotherapy," "psychoanalytic psychiatry," or "modified psychoanalysis" yet to be established. An opposite type of extension has also occurred in the treatment of relatively acute reactive neuroses, or mild neuroses where less extensive methods might be adequate or more appropriate. As precise clinical indications become established with current research, the maintenance of as clear-cut categories of therapy as possible will be highly advantageous. This advantage can be first consolidated in the one well-defined and well-organized technique that we know. Such clear-cut categories would have obvious advantages over regarding the whole field of psychotherapy as an undifferentiated mass of psychoanalytic pathology and technology, entirely flexible in its application in any combination to each case according to individual judgment. Such technical flexibility is inherent in psychoanalysis, but to substitute flexibility for a tested instrument or series of instruments, rather than to maintain flexibility as a desirable *quality* of an instrument, may mean little more than a well-rationalized wholesale return to the eclectic, semi-intuitive so-called psychoanalytic psychotherapy which many or most of us practiced before we became psychoanalysts.

Another reason for the maintenance of a basic distinction is based on scientific necessity. If psychoanalysis as such is the source of all important knowledge and understanding in psychotherapy, we must keep the method alive to deepen and extend that knowledge; furthermore, maintenance of the distinction between psychoanalysis and other therapeutic techniques can provide mutual clinical controls and a possible profitable scientific exchange. Bandler's suggestion that psychoanalysis and other methods be tested clinically with the same types of cases is a relevant example (Oberndorf et al. 1948).

A final requirement for the maintenance of the basic distinction is that of training. Unless one rejects the whole principle of the personal preparatory analysis, it seems self-evident that this work must be thorough and deep in the "classical" sense.

Among students in training and practicing psychoanalysts, brief psychotherapy is employed usually with diminishing frequency and interest in proportion to experience. Some analysts, however, have for many years been especially interested in the application of psychoanalysis to brief psychotherapy, whether in hospitals or private practice, and feel some surprise to find it regarded as a new field of interest (Dunn 1947). In hospital practice, brief therapy is often regarded as imposed by necessity rather than as a technique of special scientific interest.

Except by the interested minority, this work is usually accorded a general position of inferiority. The lack of rules and boundaries gives rise to a situation in which either a sense of gratification or of frustration, or both, may participate. In general, among younger physicians the free intuitive play with psychoanalytic concepts, neglect of the analysis of resistance and specific ego defenses are frequent. On the other hand, among students in training one frequently hears the complaint that the therapist does not understand what has happened to his patient; and I have heard this complaint just as frequently when the patient has shown striking improvement. That physicians from the vantage point of psychoanalytic experience can more safely and effectively give play to intuition in atypical psychotherapeutic situations would, I think, be generally conceded because discipline and training seem to enrich the effectiveness of creative and intuitive tendencies in almost any science or art.

It is not the purpose of these observations to depreciate the importance of intuition in such a complex relationship as psychotherapy (Kris 1948); rather, the aim is to further the generally accepted principle of extension of the sphere of secure scientific knowledge as a necessary framework, with a special view to teaching. One may think of a continuum from the free play of human relationships in which there is no conscious psychotherapeutic intention—but which obviously play an enormously important psychotherapeutic role in the lives of relatively normal people—to the objective and precise relation between the surgeon and his patient, which Freud idealized. The well-defined psychoanalytic technique and brief psychotherapy are both far from either pole, and yet definitely removed from one another in these opposite directions. However, respect for the enormous but uncontrolled potentialities of brief psychotherapy is entirely compatible with the effort to maintain intellectual precision and objectivity and the striving for a working synthesis.

Established analysts, who could most safely and productively allow their intuitive technical tendencies free play, seldom practice brief psychotherapy; instead, they refer patients unsuitable for classical analysis to students in training. Much more difficult for the student is his patient who needs and wants psychoanalysis, which the physician believes to be the treatment of choice. The only subject about which he has any systematic knowledge is psychoanalysis, and he thinks of his patients along psychoanalytic lines. For these reasons it would seem logical that psychiatrists be permitted to practice psychoanalysis during the period of training in psychoanalysis, as a general practitioner may practice surgery without claiming thorough training or the status of specialist. A physi-

cian should not be forced to disavow what he knows; nor should he be forced
to absurd ritualistic denials of what he is doing; nor should he be forced to free
himself of a discipline before he has mastered it. As brief psychotherapy is not
a definite technique, it is logically a subject for advanced study and research or
practice by experienced therapists.

Although interest in the application of psychoanalysis to other forms of
psychotherapy is by no means new (Codet 1933, Freud 1919, Hann-Kende
1936), it was only during World War II that it assumed the proportions of a
movement. The Chicago Institute for Psychoanalysis greatly stimulated interest
in this direction, through the work of some of its most experienced members,
through conferences and extensive publications. Some pointed criticism of this
work appears in one of the Institute's own publications (*Proceedings* 1946) in
the discussion of two case reports. To this may be added Ernest Jones's comments (1946). With the exception of Grotjahn's presentation in the Proceedings
of the Brief Psychotherapy Council in 1942, and certain individual experiences
recorded in the Proceedings of the Second Council in 1944, I do not find any
important efforts to give quantitative evaluations of effectiveness or noneffec-
tiveness of brief therapies;[3] certainly there is minimal effort to demonstrate failures or errors in methods, the same being true of the scrutiny of clinical decisions inevitably made under pressure. That the selection of "successful" material
characterizes such reports in general has been mentioned; however, one expects
more from a large-scale group effort.

The general, persisting prejudice against the importance of the infantile
neurosis in human psychological development makes such formulations as the
adult "corrective experience" in the transference eagerly acceptable. While this
may well be a factor in therapy that deserves emphasis, it cannot replace, in
psychoanalysis, the reconstruction of the infantile neurosis—as recognized even
by Ferenczi and Rank (1925), who are credited with the inspiration for Alexander's later work. In such techniques there is a misleading appearance of facility
in controlling powerful dynamic forces, best exemplified in the impression given
that the transference can not only be distributed almost at will, but can be controlled in intensity by the frequency of visits.

In conceiving of a system of brief psychotherapy, based on psychoanalysis,
to meet the increasing demand one has to consider that it must be suitable for
all economic and intellectual levels, ages, physical conditions, religious affiliations, and so forth. It is unlikely that the "bottleneck" of outpatient psychiatric
care will ever be materially reduced as long as the principal type of psychotherapy
employed is that which imitates analysis, including its sense of "timelessness."
It is probable that to provide psychotherapy for all classes, a re-evaluation of
the potentialities of all psychotherapeutic methods for their maximum and most
efficient exploitation should be made. The interest of psychoanalytic writers in
"primitive" methods (Abraham 1926, Federn and Meng 1926, Jones 1923)
should be extended into objective research. Some of Masserman's experimental work touches on these subjects (*Proceedings* 1942). Hypnoanalysis and narco-

analysis have their own literature. Occasionally drugs are given orally to facilitate psychotherapy (Bellak 1949). Pedagogical therapy was a relatively early development (Zulliger 1940, 1941). Group therapy is a technique of increasing interest. However, the simple matter of consultation and advice has received little systematic attention among analysts. It does seem odd that the psychotherapists who rarely or never give advice are those who best understand human personality. This does not mean making critical, highly personal decisions for the patient, but it is not impossible that circumspect advice, kept within the bounds of special medical competence, may accomplish more through the influence of the transference than the provocation of relatively benign substitution neuroses (Fenichel 1945, Glover 1931). This method is mentioned by Levine (1942). A field of which Freud has dreamed (1949), that is the direct influence of chemical substances on the psychic apparatus, may conceivably come to life in our time, from the direction of endocrine research, in the sense of influencing libidinal and destructive attitudes. The problem here would be the integration in psychotherapy from a dynamic rather than a symptomatic point of view. Regardless of the technique, it seems a matter of fairly general agreement among psychoanalysts (Alexander et al. 1946, Berliner 1941, Dunn 1947, Fuerst 1938, Gitelson 1942, Hahn-Kende 1936, Knight 1937, Menninger 1940, Zulliger 1940, 1941) that a dynamic, sometimes genetic interpretation of the personality in psychoanalytic terms is an essential prerequisite to any rational psychotherapy. From my own point of view, this must be evaluated in connection with a broader estimate of the patient's intrinsic and situational resources and liabilities. In general, broad dynamic elements are more reliably estimated and more immediately useful than are preliminary genetic reconstructions.

The indications for psychoanalysis given, for instance, by Fenichel (1945) must yield to a brief psychotherapy the great numbers of patients who because of limitations of money or time cannot be analyzed. Others, for whom preferential indications have been advanced by various writers (Alexander et al. 1946, Berliner 1941, Codet 1933, Dunn 1947, Fenichel 1945, Fuerst 1938, Gill 1951, Hann-Kende 1936, Knight 1937, *Proceedings* 1942), including this writer, fall broadly into the following categories: (1) people who are sick mentally, or whose situation in life is so unpropitious, that the effort toward extensive revision of the personality is not justified, or might even lead to greater difficulties; (2) those whose illness is so slight that radical and lengthy procedures are not justified; (3) acute reactive disorders in those who have given evidence of healthy adaptation under reasonable circumstances, exacerbations of mild disorders, fulminating conditions, and incipient conditions in general; (4) transitional states as, for instance, the readaptation to civilian life of some veterans, or certain problems of adolescence; (5) preparatory preanalytic therapy for borderline patients or psychotics, and follow-up treatment for certain unresponsive patients who have had long or multiple analyses; (6) more specific indications, mentioned by individual writers, as certain masochistic marital problems, monosymptomatic impotence, "psychosomatic" illnesses, certain mild chronic neuroses, and certain schizoid personalities; (7) a high degree of secondary gain is mentioned by a few writers as a contraindication (Berliner 1941, Fuerst 1938, Gill 1951, *Proceedings* 1942), whereas a slight degree is believed a conceivable avenue of approach to a patient.

An initially modest project begun at the New York Psychoanalytic Institute is expected to require several years before yielding any tangible findings worth presenting. A study group, consisting of members of the institute and a few advanced students, see patients once a week as a basic frequency. Treatment is carried out according to the convictions of the individual physicians, derived from previous training, experience, and temperamental variations. The case load is minimal. The essential feature is detailed retrospective self-observation as to specific technical maneuvers and the immediate and long-term responses of the patients, with careful recording. The observation of technique ranges from the initial total plan to the exact wording and timing of interpretations, suggestions, or whatever other methods are used. The recording of responses ranges from the general therapeutic response through immediate details of response and relevant peculiarities of resistance or transference. A few examples of the many questions we should like to ask about a given case would be: Were ego defenses, character reactions, resistances, systematically analyzed? Were "deep" interpretations made early without analysis of resistances? What were the responses? Were manifest transference reactions discerned? Were they discerned in acting out, dreams, or symptoms? How were they handled? Were free associations used exclusively or partially, alternating with what other forms of communication? What was the basis for change of communication, if known? What special responses could be observed? Could any impact on transference or resistance of isolated or mixed noninterpretative techniques be observed or reasonably inferred, in specific instances, or in summation, for example, with suggestion, reassurance, advice, persuasion, etc.? Do the long intervals and the generally different expectation create discernible differences in the character of productions, in the evolution and manifestation of transference and resistance? A detailed uniform scheme of study is now in preparation.

Like many other questions, these are not easily answered, and even if confidently answered, we have no control treatment for the same patient (Oberndorf et al. 1948, *Proceedings* 1946). The intangible elements of the personal equation and especially hidden countertransferences are exceedingly difficult to evaluate. Aside from the wish to allow each physician to treat his patient to the best of his ability, it is felt that the evaluation of subtle and uncharted problems of psychotherapy lies in testing various personal techniques. Possibly, as time goes on, and with an increment of personnel with special technical preferences, some controlled experiments will spontaneously evolve. No one, for example, has shown any interest in using rational persuasion as a basic technique while studying the patient's dreams and other unconscious responses. In the conferences there is a thorough review and discussion of cases and, naturally, a certain amount of teaching, supervision, and mutual influence. Except where convictions about grave clinical issues are involved, there is minimal authoritative pressure on the therapeutic spontaneity of physicians. The important thing is to learn from what has been done and its results, and to test these wherever possible against the preliminary rationale and expectations.

One preliminary observation that emerges is the remarkable variety of therapeutic approaches to patients among physicians with a few to several years of psychoanalytic training: one actively engages the patient's attention to himself and the therapeutic relationship by leading questions and by prompt interpretations of the transference; another proceeds very much as in analysis; a third proceeds vigorously with id interpretations with or without transference emphasis; a fourth gives a great deal of advice about the conduct of life, but minimal interpretation except of a general didactic nature; and so forth. While most physicians of some years of analytic experience have certain tendencies in common, usually conservative, the results of other techniques, conscientiously recorded, must be highly instructive. Who knows that the "wrong thing to do" may not prove to have a special indication? And what several meanings may an interpretation or a trend of interpretations have for a patient, aside from the actual or intended function of making him aware of something about himself?

My own practice of brief interpretative psychotherapy includes the possible applicability in certain cases of almost any technique I have heard described. What follows are the principles I find most often effective, a precipitate from positive and negative observations of my own and others' work over several years.

One must depend on one's initial interpretation of the entire case more than is necessary in psychoanalysis. As with the working diagnosis of general medicine, it is important to decide which of the patient's dynamic problems are crucial, those whose alteration is most likely to affect the dynamics of his personality and illness and to act on that selection. One should avoid interfering with the patient's way of life unless it is unequivocally pathological, and avoid stirring up superfluous conflicts or interfering with useful defenses. With the tendency to localize the therapeutic effort, an atmosphere of temporariness and limitation of the relationship may usefully be communicated to the patient. The interviews center on the patient's actual personal relationships and events of his daily life. Observations are made by the analyst on the general dynamic role of the illness within this system and occasional interpretations given. This does not mean an emphasis on symptom analysis as such, nor does it resemble the "associative anamnesis" of Deutsch (1939, 1949), except possibly in the relative localization of the effort.

The patient is encouraged to express himself spontaneously and without reservation; however, the interviews are definitely guided or influenced, largely by questions. Free association (literal sense) is prescribed in special situations, for instance, in studying dreams. The patient usually sits facing the therapist, a feature emphasized by several writers. This is one of the several factors which minimizes the tension between reality and the patient's fantasy life, a tension which Hartmann regards as characteristic of the psychoanalytic situation, and that may be one of the factors involved in the distinctive character of the transference neurosis in psychoanalysis.

The general trend of interpretation is determined by the relevant and convincing character of material and the patient's state of compliant or negative transference. The tendency is always to keep interest centered on large and decisive dynamic issues rather than details of fantasy, and in close relation to immediate realities. Interpretations are made, as far as possible, in the patient's own idiom — or a reasonable compromise between it and the therapist's natural mode of expression. There is an effort to integrate in single simple communications material involving levels of varying psychic depth and different psychic structures, resolving contradictions and antagonisms, exploiting to a maximum the areas of overlapping in clarifying the patient's problems. Insofar as the psychic apparatus is dealt with as a closely integrated system and not revealed in layers as in psychoanalysis, one may theorize tentatively that certain simpler resistances may be avoided or perhaps minimized in this approach. It is interpretations of the id, the primary process, the infantile neurosis, that provide the greatest challenge. Here the therapist must exert his maximum skill, reconstructing in his own mind what is going on in the patient's unconscious, translating it into everyday language, and incorporating it in the synthesis mentioned. Similar techniques, I am sure, are practiced by many therapists who have not formulated their work in this way.

It may be argued that such a method can make no lasting change in the structure of a patient's personality. Only prolonged observation can settle the matter. Resistances vary in permeability among individuals and under differing conditions, for instance, between relatively "normal" individuals and those with severe neuroses, in the spontaneous exchanges of everyday life, or in the controlled exploratory situation of psychoanalysis. The varied phenomenology of everyday life, with its precipitations of illness and its vehicles of self-cure, testifies to the potential continuum of human personality from its outermost layers to its depths.

Glover's incidental remark, "It is obvious that many people cure themselves through their unconscious human contacts" (1937), was made in relation to Strachey's conception of psychoanalytic cure by the introjection of good objects into the transference. Also relevant is Nunberg's stress on the constant pressure of the repetition compulsion, contemporaneous with the tendency of the ego to extend its boundaries in alliance with the therapist in the positive transference (Glover et al. 1937). The integrative interpretative communication may here act as a temporary bridge over a narrowing chasm. From the observation of side effects of certain interpretations in psychoanalysis, and theoretical considerations of the nature of ego defenses, the "principle of multiple appeal" (Hartmann 1951) may also apply.

Infrequent interviews may prove to concentrate relevant dream associations and memories germane to current problems. Considerable reliance is placed on the forces within the patient tending to spontaneous cure and toward independence from treatment. Intensification of repression, transference cures, and even the phobic mechanism of displacement described by Glover (Glover 1931, Reider 1944) all have their place, as in the functioning of the socially integrated personality, so long as their nature is understood, and the total dynamic shift can be regarded as favorable (Berliner 1941, *Proceedings* 1942) in relation to the patient's situation and personal potentialities. The aim is always to achieve some degree of reorganization within a relatively intact personality, however modest, or that some support will have been given to the positive transference experience by a degree of reeducation. The transference, when the patient is seen infrequently in an atmosphere charged with current realities, may remain largely a potential or latent phenomenon in the therapeutic relationship, if the patient's illness is not weighted with pregenital regressive elements. While it remains integrated in a patient-doctor relationship of traditional form, operating unconsciously in its positive aspects, attention can be directed to the pathological multiple "transferences" that are evident in the patient's outside relationships. While there may be spectacular spontaneous exceptions, there is no reason to assume a priori that all of the patient's libidinal and aggressive conflicts are concentrated in the treatment situation. Experienced therapists, however, should be alert to disturbing trends of transference as expressed in dreams, manifest attitudes, symptom fluctuations, acting out, and avoid exacerbations by interpretation.

Since the primary emphasis is on demonstrable reality as a background for interpretation of emergent ego-dystonic fantasy, the stimulation of transference, whether by superfluous and repetitive "active permission" or excessive tendentious interpretation, enormously magnifies an error that can also occur in psychoanalysis, reflecting overzealous acceptance of the principles advanced in the brilliant monograph of Ferenczi and Rank (1925). This applies even more to the deliberate taking of roles by the physician (Alexander 1948, Alexander et al. 1946) insofar as the attitudes are not strictly germane to his role as physician. From an itellectual point of view, these techniques mean approbation and fostering of unreality where heightened appreciation of reality is the goal; emotionally, they stimulate fantasy or infantile attitudes, thus making them more difficult to interpret and work through, in contrast with the spontaneous evolution of transference or even the occasional occurrence of massive regression in psychoanalysis, where the controlled and stable realities of the situation usually make interpretation intellectually and emotionally at least feasible in the long run. It is also to be recognized that the entire structure, intensiveness, and potential duration of the psychoanalytic situation favor the actual concentration of the patient's "transferences" in the therapeutic transference. Hence, aside from purely empirical practical considerations, a potential psychic reality is involved in the anticipatory transference clarifications, which many or most of us recognize as indispensable, when judiciously employed. The stable realities of the situation are even more necessary in brief psychotherapy. Active transference techniques can be useful in certain cases and are apparently used with therapeutic effectiveness by experienced therapists. This, however, does not alter the general principle,[4] especially in teaching.

The transference may emerge as a problem in any therapeutic relationship and require interpretative intervention. It is possible that some accidental therapeutic successes are obtained by not recognizing it and, therefore, not "meddling" unnecessarily with a positive ego-syntonic transference — and lack of success due to failure to intervene when really necessary. When the transference is relatively simple and forthright, it may be interpreted to good advantage within the scope of a brief relationship. Simple rebellion against parental authority, sibling rivalry (in relation to other patients), erotic fantasies of mild or moderate intensity, and obvious clinging to the therapeutic relationship are instances.

An intelligent girl of nineteen was given twenty-two interviews during fifteen months. She had hysterical weeping spells and gastric disturbances while struggling to adapt herself to her first serious attachment to a young man, from a background of overintense attachments to girl friends and older women. The threat to this type of ambivalent mother-sister relationship was the chief subject of interpretative discussions, finally the ambivalent homosexual attachment itself. The patient developed a brief incestuous father transference to me, evident in her dreams. Interpretation was readily accepted. The girl is married and is said to be doing well at this time; however, this is neither as reliable nor as important as the technical fact that a relatively forthright and therapeutically available transference emerged in relation to the physician in the course of interviews devoted largely to the understanding and interpretation of the stormy "transferences" that were disturbing the patient in relation to her fiancé, friends, and family. Such isolated transference reactions, I believe, are more liable to occur in the atmosphere described than is the full-blown transference neurosis which characterizes psychoanalysis.

If in the initial interviews, one infers strong pregenital ambivalent tendencies, the patient ought to be in psychoanalysis or else be helped actively to strengthen his defenses, and extension and deepening of the transference avoided. Berliner (1941) regards all brief therapeutic contacts as potential first stages of psychoanalysis. Such an attitude might vitiate an important aspect of the atmosphere to be created for brief psychotherapy. However, the wisdom of a technique that is consistent with this possiblity cannot be doubted.

A closing example is from a clinic case, a young man who had reacted well to a short period of treatment for hypochondriacal fears. He had always been excessively jealous. He returned after an absence of ten months, acutely disturbed by jealousy. At an office party, a pleasant man named Bill (also the patient's name), with whom he had been drinking, had put his arm around the patient's wife in an innocuous way. The patient suggested that the therapist see his wife so that she might be more cooperative about his treatment. This was an actual problem to him, as she had a mildly derisive attitude about it. A reserved willingness to see his wife was expressed, with the expressed preference that he settle the problem himself. No interpretation of the implications in the transference was made, an important decision, made at the moment, obviously susceptible to discussion. Considerations stated earlier in the paper would be relevant. The patient returned without his wife, feeling much better and bringing a dream: a man called him from the office, addressing him as Bill, and said, "We couldn't help it, standing there, and I just kissed your wife." The patient started for the place, found himself with a blonde in an apartment, and had a seminal emission. He recalled that he had proposed a foursome date with Bill's and his wife. The man in the dream had the name of a girl whose picture in a bathing suit he had seen in the paper and who was to marry a senator. In addition to the projection of his own extramarital wishes, and jealousy as a reaction to something that he himself wished, the interpretation was given that he wished to share his wife with a man whom he obviously liked; that it could express his affection for this man; moreover, that it could be an avoidance of conflict and complications about the exclusive possession of a woman. Had he not previously recalled playing with his sister in bed on two occasions while his brother was in the next bed? Might it not be possible that (then and now) there was an impulse to share sexual guilt and avoid rivalry at the same time? The patient had been fond of his brother; also he had had a dream in which his wife and sister had been manifestly interchanged. During the following interview he related several instances from adolescence of making, with a friend, joint sexual overtures toward the same girl. A few weeks later he reported that he had eaten some good dinners at his brother's house, had enjoyed a party at which his friend Bill had been present and had shown a naïve competitiveness with his brother's wife, in tobogganing with his brother. These responses suggest that the interpretation was to some degree effective; however, it must be noted that his wife had quit working in this period, a change for which he had devoutly wished. The normality of this wish had previously been confirmed by the therapist, while interpreting his envy of certain features of the woman's role in life. The immediately relevant question is whether there is a special advantage in brief psychotherapeutic contacts in trying to integrate in a single interpretation, in a concept available to the personality from multiple points of view, and in acceptable language, elements of defense, aggression, and libido, including a clearly available genetic parallel.

Brief interpretative psychotherapy, based on psychoanalytic principles, is a field for empirical research by psychoanalysts to determine its therapeutic effectiveness, scope of applicability, and techniques.

NOTES

1. On this point, Glover (1940) was not satisfied with his inquiry. In any case, the fact that a majority "permit relaxation" does not, in my view, diminish the general importance of the prevalent mode of communication in psychoanalytic therapy.

2. Changes in form, such as active discussion instead of free association or sitting instead of lying, are, in my view, of profound dynamic importance.

3. The term *brief psychotherapy* was abandoned by the Chicago group after the Second Council.

4. The treatment of manifest psychotics presents a different problem of reality, hence a different technical problem. For the therapist to act the role of father or mother may be relatively real compared to the patient's delusions or hallucinations and thus conceivably, through a developing transference, a possible bridge to a more commonly accepted view of the facts. Similar considerations may apply to the character of the interpretations. Note the work of Dr. John Rosen.

REFERENCES

Abraham, K. (1926). Psychoanalytical notes on Coué's method of self-mastery. *Int. J. Psychoanal.* 7:190–213.

Alexander, F. (1948). *Fundamentals of Psychoanalysis.* New York: Norton.

Alexander, F., French, T. M., et al. (1946). *Psychoanalytic Therapy.* New York: Ronald Press.

Bellak, L. (1949). The use of oral barbiturates in psychotherapy. *Amer. J. Psychiatry* 105:849–850.

Benjamin, J. D. (1947). Psychoanalysis and nonanalytic psychotherapy. *Psychoanal. Q.* 16:169–176.

Berliner, B. (1941). Short psychoanalytic psychotherapy: Its possibilities and its limitations. *Bull. Menninger Clin.* 5:204–213.

Codet, H. (1933). Traitements d'inspiration psychanalytique. *L'Evolution Psychiatrique* 3, pt. 1.

Crank, H. H. (1940). The use of psychoanalytic principles in outpatient psychotherapy. *Bull. Menninger Clin.* 4:35.

Deutsch, F. (1939). The associative anamnesis. *Psychoanal. Q.* 8:354–381.

———— (1949). *Applied Psychoanalysis. Selected Objectives of Psychotherapy.* New York: Grune & Stratton.

Dunn, W. H. (1947). Psychotherapy in private practice. Address to New York Psychoanalytic Society. (Unpublished)

Federn, P., and Meng, H. (1926). Stellung der Psychoanalyse zur übrigen Psychotherapie. In *Das Psychoanalytische Volksbuch*, pt. 1. Stuttgart–Berlin: Hippokrates Verlag, p. 15.

Fenichel, O. (1945). *The Psychoanalytic Theory of Neurosis.* New York: Norton.

Ferenczi, S., and Rank, O. (1925). *The Development of Psychoanalysis.* New York: Nerv. and Ment. Dis. Publ. Co.

Freud, S. (1904). On psychotherapy. *S. E.,* 7.

———— (1905). Wit and its relation to the unconscious. In *The Basic Writings of Sigmund Freud.* New York: Modern Library, 1938.

———— (1914). On the history of the psycho-analytic movement. *S. E.* 14.

———— (1919). Turnings in the ways of psycho-analytic therapy. *S. E.* 17.

———— (1949). An outline of psycho-analysis. *S. E.* 23.

Fuerst, R. A. (1938). Problems of short-time psychotherapy. *Amer. J. Orthopsychiatry* 8:260.

Gill, M. M. (1951). Ego psychology and psychotherapy. *Psychoanal. Q.* 20:62–71.

Gitelson, M. (1942). The critical moment in psychotherapy. *Bull. Menninger Clin.* 6:182.

Glover, E. (1931). The therapeutic effect of inexact interpretation: A contribution to the theory of suggestion. *Int. J. Psychoanal.* 12:397–411.

————— (1940). *An Investigation of the Technique of Psychoanalysis.* Baltimore: Williams & Wilkins.

Glover, E., Fenichel, O., Strachey, J., Bergler, E., Nunberg, H., and Bibring, E. (1937). Symposium on the theory of the therapeutic results of psychoanalysis. *Int. J. Psychoanal.* 18:125–189.

Hann-Kende, F. (1936). Abbreviated psychoanalysis in clinical practice. Address to International Psychoanalytic Congress in Marienbad. (Unpublished.)

Hartmann, H. (1951). Technical implications of ego psychology. *Psychoanal. Q.* 20: 31–43.

Jones, E. (1910). The action of suggestion in psychotherapy. In *Papers on Psychoanalysis*, 3rd ed. London: Baillière, Tindall & Cox, 1923, pp. 340–381.

————— (1946). Review of *Psychoanalytic Therapy* by F. Alexander and T. M. French. *Int. J. Psychoanal.* 27:162–163.

Knight, R. P. (1939). Why people go to cultists. *J. Kansas Med. Society*, July, pp. 1–4.

————— (1937). Application of psychoanalytical concepts in psychotherapy: Report of clinical trials in a mental hygiene service. *Bull. Menninger Clin.* 2:99–109.

————— (1948). Psychoanalytically oriented psychotherapy. *Bull. Amer. Psychoanal. Assn.* 4(3):36.

————— (1949). A critique of the present status of the psychotherapies. *Bull. N.Y. Acad. Med.* 25:100–114.

Kris, E. (1948). Problem of interpretation. Bull. Amer. Psychoanal. Assn. 4(2):34.

Levine, M. (1942). *Psychotherapy in Medical Practice.* New York: Macmillan.

Loewenstein, R. M. (1948). Problem of interpretation. *Bull. Amer. Psychoanal Assn.* 4(2):31.

McLean, H. V. (1948). Treatment of the neuroses. *Cincinnati J. Med.* 29:545–555.

Meerloo, J. A. M. (1944). The difference between psychoanalysis and psychotherapy. Outline of presentation before Psychoanalytic Study Group, London. (Unpublished.)

Menninger, K. A. (1940). Psychoanalytic psychiatry: Theory and practice. *Bull. Menninger Clin.* 4:105.

Oberndorf, C. P. (1946). Constant elements in psychotherapy. *Psychoanal. Q.* 15: 435–449.

Oberndorf, C. P., Greenacre, P., and Kubie, L. S. (1948). Symposium on the evaluation of therapeutic results. *Int. J. Psychoanal.* 29:7–33.

Proceedings of the Brief Psychotherapy Council (1942). Chicago Institute for Psychoanalysis, October 25–26.

Proceedings of the Second Brief Psychotherapy Council (1944). Chicago Institute for Psychoanalysis, January.

Proceedings of the Third Psychotherapy Council (1946). Chicago Institute for Psychoanalysis, October 18–19.

Reider, N. (1944). Remarks on mechanisms of nonanalytic psychotherapy. *Dis. Nerv. Syst.* 5:1–4.

Zulliger, H. (1940, 1941). Psychoanalytic experiences in public school practice. *Amer. J. Orthopsychiatry* 10:824; 11:356.

Chapter 2
The Widening Scope of Indications
for Psychoanalysis
(1954)

This paper was originally presented as the opening statement for a symposium of the same name. The title was thus assigned rather than chosen. Dr. Edith Jacobson also presented a paper, "Transference Problems in the Treatment of Depressives," at the same meeting. Both papers were discussed by Anna Freud, among others. The paper was therefore an individual response to a historical movement already current in psychoanalysis, which had stimulated several papers by earlier authors (see Bibliography). Apart from the major position and various subthemes and obiter dicta, which do not require an introductory summary, there are certain specific ideas in the paper that, I feel, still are valuable and have found continued elaboration in my later contributions. Among these are the concept of the perceptual and emotional vacuum intrinsic in the psychoanalytic situation and its rule of abstinence, the idea of *resemblance* as a necessary condition of transference, the role of varying degrees of deprivation in facilitating regression, and the function of variable controlled and appropriate transference gratification in warding off the more profound (undesirable) grades of transference regression in the more severe illnesses.

Since the time of this paper, the concept of "borderline" has, of course, been greatly elaborated by several authors, notably Otto Kernberg and the Kris Study Group of the New York Psychoanalytic Institute. But this paper, which has continued to elicit some strong and mixed reactions in opposing directions (including a movement toward the "narrowing scope"!), is not, in my view, without some continuing messages of its own.

T he remarkable and steadfast conservatism of Freud regarding the therapeutic application of his discovery appears in several places in his writings. We may generalize briefly to the effect that Freud believed the true
indications for psychoanalysis to be the transference psychoneuroses and equivalent character disturbances. While temperately hopeful for the future treatment
of psychoses, the very expression, "some other plan better suited for that purpose" (1939), suggests how closely linked in Freud's thinking were the psychoanalytic technique and the basically reliable ego. We know from his writings
that Freud was far from rigid or static in his technical methods; however, he
was apparently not much concerned with developing and systematizing new
techniques, or in experimenting with remote nosological groups.

Yet it was still early in the history of psychoanalysis that Abraham (1927)
began to treat manic-depressive psychosis, and not too long before Simmel
(1929) opened a psychoanalytic sanatorium where he treated very severe
neuroses, incipient psychotic conditions, and addictions. Also early came the
psychoanalytic interest in character, beginning with Freud himself (1908), and
followed by the distinguished contributions of Jones and Abraham. However,
character analysis as a special technical problem was precipitated sharply into
the foreground of general interest by Wilhelm Reich's brilliant and stimulating,
although still controversial, book (Reich 1947, Sterba 1953). With Anna Freud's
book, *The Ego and the Mechanisms of Defense* (1936), one might say that a
movement toward the broadening and multiplication of the psychoanalytic
spheres of interest in the personality, and an appropriate complication of
psychoanalytic technique, found general and secure acceptance.

I trust that it is not superfluous on this occasion to mention child analysis
as an early special development in theory and technique, whose implications extend far beyond the immediate clinical applications. The application of
psychoanalytic knowledge in the treatment of delinquents, begun by Aichhorn,
continued in our own group by the Eisslers currently, has a similar importance.

Other psychiatric syndromes were rapidly brought within the scope of
psychoanalytic therapy: the perversions, including homosexuality; paranoia and
the schizophrenias; a considerable and growing variety of psychosomatic
disorders; and, of course, that vast, important, and heterogeneous group — the
"borderline" cases. One might say that in the last decade or two, at least in the

23

United States, any illness or problem which has a significant emotional component in its etiology has become at least a possible indication for psychoanalysis. In its extreme development, this indication includes not only conditions where this etiology is quite well established, but not infrequently, as in the psychosomatic disorders, only reasonably probable.

First, I should mention that this generally expanding scope of psychoanalysis, which I should judge is now on a sort of peak plateau, has more than one facet; furthermore, my own reaction to this expansion is divided, according to these facets. One element which should not elude our attention is the enthusiasm of that section of the informed public which is devoted to psychoanalysis. Among this group, not inconsiderable in size and influence in a city like New York, scarcely any human problem admits of solution other than psychoanalysis; by the same token, there is an almost magical expectation of help from the method, which does it grave injustice. Hopeless or grave reality situations, lack of talent or ability (usually regarded as "inhibition"), lack of an adequate philosophy of life, and almost any chronic physical illness may be brought to psychoanalysis for cure. It is a matter of serious interest to us that this phenomenon exists; it is of course even more important that this type of ambivalent worship not be allowed to influence, however subtly, the judgment of the psychoanalytic practitioner. A special development of this sort has occurred in the practice of general medicine. This I would regard as a small but definite public health hazard. One cannot question the tremendous scientific importance of research in psychosomatic medicine or its potentialities for improving preventive or therapeutic medical practice. The complete displacement of well-established medical methods by purely psychological methods, even when the psychological indications are reasonably practical and sound, is quite another matter. It is, however, in the field of diagnosis where one observes the most serious deterioration. The hospital resident who, on completing a negative physical examination in a patient with bowel complaints, immediately calls for a psychiatric consultation, then gets an X-ray report of carcinoma of the colon, is funny to his colleagues. However, under other conditions, the same orientation may occasion tragedy. I should emphasize that this tendency exists on the side of the public and the medical practitioners, *not* on the side of analysts as a group. My occasional discussions with medical practitioners in connection with the patients whom they refer to the Treatment Center (of the New York Psychoanalytic Institute) confirm this longstanding observation and conviction. Some subtle fault in the publicization of psychoanalytic findings may contribute slightly to this phenomenon. In any case, it is important to be alertly aware of, to try to understand, and, if possible, to remedy this situation; at very least, to resist any distortion of judgment in response to it.

I should also like, in passing, to mention a less immediately grave but intellectually disquieting feature of this spurious increase of psychoanalytic indications. There is sometimes a loss of sense of proportion about the human situation, a forgetting or denial of the fact that few human beings are without some troubles and that many must be met, if at all, by "old-fashioned" methods: courage, or wisdom, or struggle, for instance; also that few people avoid altogether and forever some physical ailments, not to speak of the fact that all die of illness in the end. Even if these illnesses all represent disturbances in the total psychosomatic complex (which, oddly enough, I believe to be the case), they are not all indications for psychoanalysis. The "psyche" is only half of the psychosomatic continuum, and it remains a practical empirical problem as to whether a drug or surgery or psychotherapy is most effective in a given illness. If a man is otherwise healthy, happy, and efficient, and his rare attacks of headache can be avoided by not eating lobster, for example, it would seem better that he avoid eating lobster than that he be analyzed. This takes us to another indication for psychoanalysis—not spurious—but one where delicate judgment is involved; I have in mind the very mild or incipient neurosis. Here, it seems to me, a careful general evaluation of the personality is especially imperative. For, if the personality illness were judged really slight (a matter which we know, does not necessarily parallel the severity of immediate symptoms), I would regard the indication for psychoanalysis as very seriously in doubt. For psychoanalysis represents a tremendous investment of many complicated elements by two people, and it should not be invoked for trivial reasons. Aside from the fact that many people can live with mild neuroses (I am certain that a good part of the population live long lives with various subclinical phobias, mild conversion symptoms, fragmentary compulsions, etc.), a simpler, less intensive form of psychotherapy may suffice for many such illnesses.

Before considering some of the more severe problems which are now being treated psychoanalytically, it may be well to say a few words about what we mean by psychoanalysis (as differentiated from psychotherapy), since it is in relation to the severe illnesses that important clinical alterations may be required. If we do not have some reasonable degree of agreement about this, there is little ground for discussion regarding indications, for few would dispute the helpfulness of some form of psychotherapy in any of these instances. Most psychotherapy practiced in the United States has been strongly influenced by psychoanalysis. Certainly, the psychotherapy practiced by psychoanalysts and candidates borrows so much from the original discipline that the boundary becomes obscure, and is sometimes defined on a rather arbitrary or ritualistic basis, which is quite unsatisfactory. Sometimes bad or slovenly or inadequate psychoanalytic tactics find both definition and privilege in being "not analysis, but psychotherapy." A few years ago, I wrote on this subject, and I do not wish to burden you with a repetition of that material (Stone 1951). Furthermore, I should prefer nowadays to place greater stress on the functional elements to which the formal factors are ancillary. The relevant point which I proposed was that the several formal factors which participate in the classical psychoanalytic situation—ranging from free association through the recumbent position to such matters as the character of the analyst's technical interventions and general attitude—constitute an ensemble which has much to do with the dynamics of the analytic process, and specifically with the evolution of the transference neurosis. Most important in the ultimate dynamic meaning of this ensemble is the relative emotional vacuum which the analysand must fill with transference impulses and fantasies, and the parallel reduction of reality-testing opportunity which facilitates the same process. In a sort of paradoxical tour de force, the very same set of factors provides the optimum background for the testing and interpretative reduction of the transference neurosis. Of the several technical instrumentalities which may be used purposively in any psychotherapeutic procedure—for instance, those listed last year by Bibring (1954)—it is interpretation which is ultimately relied on for the distinctively psychoanalytic effect. I put aside the many possible interpersonal meanings which interpretation may have for a patient and refer to the circumscribed function of communicating to a patient something true of him in a specific reference, which he has, before the interpretation, seen in a radically different light, or of which he has been quite unaware.[1] Without entering into the basic problems discussed in the Marienbad Symposium we can state in a very general descriptive way what wholly or partially occurs in analysis. We dissolve or minimize resistances, and make the ego aware of its defensive operations, ultimately of id and superego contents and operations. Through this accurate awareness, implemented by the process of "working through," we expect the effect of abolition or reduction of id and superego qualitative distortions and pathological intensities, the resolution or reduction or at least the *awareness* of intrapsychic conflict in general, and finally the extension of the ego's positive sovereignty over the instinctual life, with the freeing or facilitation of its synthetic, adaptive, and other affirmative capacities. In this process, the mobilization of the transference neurosis holds a central place. Whether one views this phenomenon theoretically as essentially a resistance to recall of the past or as an affirmatively necessary therapeutic phenomenon, toward which interpretation and recall are directed for the freeing of the patient from the analyst and thus from internal parental representations, is largely a question of emphasis, which in a pragmatic sense may vary from patient to patient. For, as Freud long ago observed, an adequate positive transference is necessary even to the *acceptance* of decisive interpretations. Furthermore, the sense of reality or vividness about the past is *largely* dependent on the therapeutic transference experience, and there are many instances where the dissolution of amnesias or of the emotional isolation of memories only follows adequate emotional experience in the transference. This is even more true of the reconstruction of very early experience, which may be quite inaccessible to adult memory or may indeed have played little or no part in childhood consciousness. In any case, the current dynamisms of personality (and thus, of neurosis) are to be brought so effectively into relation with their origins in the past, that the adult ego must perforce recognize their inappropriateness to current realities and thus free itself of the disturbances attendant on the burdening from the past. That this process includes, or is at least in part dependent on or relative to, reduction of disturbances in the id and superego is apparently implicit in, although not always explicit in, current formulations.

When Freud said that any procedure which utilized the principles of transference and resistance could be called psychoanalysis, whether the findings agreed with his own or not, he offered a permission, whose current acceptance or nonacceptance should be decided on a scientific rather than a factional loyalty basis. Freud at times used the term *psychotherapy* in its historical inclusive sense for psychoanalysis, or — when referring to "other" psychotherapies — for explicitly nonanalytic procedures. I do not know if he foresaw the growth of a medley of practices which are called *psychotherapy* in contradistinction to analysis, which borrow from its psychological formulations, and while often including many other formidable and uncontrolled variables, tend with varying degrees of purposive clarity and thoroughness to employ interpretation as their chief manifest technical tool. I do not believe it important to participate in power struggles, to which unfortunately the nature of our work lends itself, on the issue of definition. And I do not believe that patients should bear the burden, or sometimes the trauma, of our distinctions. However, I do think that the scientific progress of psychotherapy in its broadest sense, with psychoanalysis as its central science and technology, depends on an increasingly clear-cut knowledge of the conditions in which findings occur. This, of course, presupposes certain minimal basic terminological distinctions. I do not believe that the distinction between psychoanalysis and psychotherapy will remain adequate, aside from linguistic considerations, for psychotherapy is or should be a large and complicated field. But the reasonably clear delimitation of psychoanalysis from other psychotherapies, especially interpretative psychotherapies, is a necessary beginning. In our immediate context, some such general concept as "modified psychoanalysis" would be useful and, I believe, valid. For scientific progress, the careful study of the "modifications" and their effects will be necessary, whether we think of the given procedure as psychoanalysis, or as beyond its most elastic limits. Perhaps they will prove to be less important than some of us think. But this is a very unsound *a priori*.

I would view the idea of psychoanalysis as beginning with Freud's own basic requirement. To this, most of us would add, as indispensable technical and intellectual context, certain other basic elements of psychoanalytic observation and theory: the unconscious, of course, since it seems no longer inevitably implicit in the basic requirement; the libido theory; the power of infantile sexuality; possibly additional elements in instinct theory; certainly, the genetic principle, with the connotation of psychodynamic continuity with the remote past. One cannot divorce this initial context from subsequent phenomena of a real therapeutic process. We would, while acknowledging that other psychotherapeutic agents play an important role in the psychoanalytic process, assign to interpretation the unique and distinctive place in its ultimate therapeutic effect. We would, I think, require that the interpretations achieve this effect through the communication of awareness of facts about himself to the patient, with the sense of emotional reality that comes only with technically correct preparation, rather than through certain other possible effects in the transference-countertransference system, which occur so frequently in other psychotherapies. (Certainly, they occur also in psychoanalysis, but they are regarded as miscarriages of effort.) I would think that the mobilization of as full and undistorted a transference neurosis as may be possible and its ultimate dissolution (or minimization) by interpretative means, would be regarded as essential to a genuinely analytic outcome. Both for the mobilization of this neurosis *and* for its reduction by such means the essentials of the formal and emotional milieu which we associate with the classical psychoanalytic situation would usually seem necessary; these components of the milieu are then assumed integral parts of the definition. One cannot be rigid about the details of the definition; nor can one simplify it too much; the general functional meaning, with its formal requirements, can, however, be brought to discernible outlines. Probably all analyses include certain formal and subtle emotional deviations somewhere along the line, aside from the fact that no two analysts would ever give precisely the same interpretations throughout an analysis. We are therefore dealing with principles, outlines, tendencies. Indeed, my own clinical experience and observation lead me to believe that *too* great approximation to the mathematical ideal in certain references is antitherapeutic (in the sense of antianalytic). For example, some patients may not be able to do their "analytic work" in relation to exaggerated and artificial efforts or to personalities whose "neutrality" is tantamount to complete emotional detachment. Yet I am convinced that any considerable tangible deviation from the attitude of neutrality should be motivated and handled along the general lines which Eissler (1953) has described in his discussion of "parameters." Where the dividing line appears is impossible to specify quantitatively. From a qualitative point of view, I would speculate that the optimum exists where the patient feels that the analyst's neutrality is a self-imposed, purposive technical discipline (in fact, a technique), willingly accepted for good reasons and neither enjoyed as a personality gratification, nor rigidly embraced in panicky fear of rule-breaking. We must frequently remind ourselves that the analytic situation is an artificial situation, a drama in which both participants have "roles" imposed by the technique, differing from both their everyday human behavior and the inner primitive drama of the transference. We expect of the analysand a benign split of the ego, which enables him to experience while still observing. In the classical method, we exclude any *assumption* of a role in the transference by the analyst. However, the *complete* merging of the analyst as an individual and the analyst as technician may also be inimical to the analytic process. Is it not rational to assume that since these two aspects of the analyst's identity are in psychodynamic balance with the two phases of the patient's (technical) ego activity, a grave imbalance on one side may seriously affect the other? It might contribute, for example, to an excessive avoidance of transference fantasy, on one hand, or to overwhelming ego-syntonic transference reactions, on the other.

If we avoid involvement in other (interpretative) psychotherapies (for lack of time, not for lack of interest), we can go directly to the question: How far can the classical analytic method be modified and still be regarded as psychoanalysis, "modified psychoanalysis," if you wish, rather than another form of interpretative psychotherapy? I believe that any number and degree of parameters can be introduced where they are genuinely necessary to meet special conditions, as long as they are all directed to bringing about the ultimate purposes and processes of the analytic end requirements, as we have just described them; so long as these purposes and processes are rationally to be expected as sequellae and are brought about to the maximum extent which the patient's personality permits. (We must distinguish between a valid psychoanalytic effort which may be unsuccessful or only partially successful and an effort which is essentially different.) Ordinarily, this would presuppose the transition from any postulated previous psychotherapeutic methods to the classical psychoanalytic situation, without irreversible transference distortions. In an ideal sense, I think the requirements for acceptability of parameters given by Eissler, with one exception, are excellent. The exception is the one which requires that the parameter *must* terminate before the end of analysis — a requirement which, as the author states, automatically excludes the time-limitation parameter, which Freud used with the Wolf Man. While the discussion of this conflict between parameter and rule would provide technical, metapsychological, and logical interest, I must waive the disproportionate space which this would require. The practical value of retention of this maneuver as consistent with true analytic work outweighs the ideal requirement, even if it must be an exception. A patient may require this confrontation with reality, in the same sense that the phobic sometimes requires the intervention that is now a general and accepted practice. Aside from this issue, however, this rule seems altogether too severe. There are very sick personalities who, to the very end of analytic experience, may require occasional and subtle or minimal emotional or technical concessions from the analyst, in the same sense that they will carry with them into their outside lives, vestiges of ego defects or modifications, which, while not completely undone, are — let us say — vastly improved. If in such patients, the essential structure and relationship of analysis have been brought about, if a full-blown transference neurosis has emerged, if the patient has been able to achieve distance from it, if it has been brought into effective relation with the infantile situation, if favorable changes in the ego have occurred as a result of interpretation and working through, if the transference has been dissolved or reduced to the maximum possible degree, I would say that the patient has been analyzed.

With regard to the earlier deviant phases of such analyses, or atypical technical residues that may persist, I would state the broad and general opinion that most parameters can be deprived of their effects on the transference, so long as they are genuinely psychotherapeutic, i.e., maneuvers bound to the immediate reality, arising from, strictly limited by, and always compatible with, the role of *therapist* — as opposed to good father, or solicitous friend, or magician, or anxious husband, etc., in a patient whose reality testing and other ego functions are largely capable of the various rigors implicit in analysis, at the point we are discussing. An excellent example of how even affirmative or constructive use of wide deviations from the classical psychoanalytic situation can be made, where these deviations are necessary and rational, may be seen in Simmel's still fascinating paper about the Tegel Sanatorium (1929). I am inclined to agree with Eissler that the giving of a cigarette to certain patients, in a certain context, might create serious difficulty. In general, if this occurs as an *exception* to a general climate of deprivation, I would believe it more likely to cause trouble than, let us say, an appropriate expression of sympathy in a tragic personal bereavement — or even, circumspect competent direct advice in a real emergency which requires it — precisely because the giving of a cigarette, aside from its obvious susceptibility to unconscious symbolic countertransference interpretation — is, in ordinary practice with nonpsychotic patients, *always* unnecessary and *never* relevant to the treatment as such. Should the previous treatment methods provide insoluble transference distortions, which may well be required by the active phases of psychosis, I would agree with Eissler that a change of therapist may be necessary *unless* more is lost thereby than is gained by the uncontaminated transference. It may be that the person who has ministered to the acute psychotic is the only one who can elicit a strong attachment from the patient; since this is indispensable to initiate analysis. I would — to be a bit slangy — "settle" for the transference distortion, with the hope that this may in time come into better perspective. This is always possible, where even outright "mothering" may retrospectively be seen as having been dictated by actual therapeutic needs of the time. If not, we may have to accept a transference situation something like that described by Miss Freud for the child, without clear-cut transference neurosis. Where to classify this, I would not know; I would hesitate to exclude this from the modifications of adult psychoanalysis, if all other analytic purposes are maintained, if the modification is judged necessary, if the analysis of the transference is extended to its utmost possible limit.

A psychological treatment that does not seek to provide, to the maximum compatible with the situation, the conditions necessary for a full-blown, undistorted transference neurosis and therefore does not mobilize one, or which does not dissolve this neurosis or reduce it to the greatest extent which the patient's structure and the therapist's skill permit, ultimately by genetic interpretations, should not be called analysis, even if the necessary formal aspects of the analytic situation *are* reproduced. For without these important processes, the profound reorganization of the personality, which we associate with analysis and in which the cure of illness is, in a sense, an incidental part of general economic change, cannot occur. At this point, I should mention, as I have elsewhere — that, in certain well-managed psychotherapeutic situations, where many ordinary emotional needs of the patient are met, within the limits of the physician-patient relationship, significant *pathological fragments* of the transference relationship (i.e., those which cannot be met in any ordinary real relationship) may separate from integrated expression in this real professional situation, and be utilized to great and genuine interpretative advantage by a skillful therapist. Classification of such treatment situations would present problems. For the moment — since they are infrequent, since they are fragmentary rather than general and systematic, since they arise under atypical and uncontrolled auspices, and since unknown large areas of transference remain integrated and unanalyzed—we shall leave them in the broad heterogeneous field of "psychotherapy."

With some conception of what we mean by psychoanalysis in mind, we can move to an examination of the expanding scope of psychoanalysis, insofar as this originates legitimately from scientific development or practical technical experience, as opposed to irrational enthusiasm. First, a few words about those conditions which have the least part in usual analytic practice. In the psychoses, we have a tremendous range, extending from those who are not independently viable, or who require hospital restraint or protection, or who cannot or will not establish voluntary cooperative contact with a therapist, or specifically, with his therapy. From these, regardless of the particular type of psychotic expression, there is a continuous gradation down to the incipient or very mild psychotic who *complains* of his symptoms and seeks help exactly as a neurotic does; and perhaps in the very end zone of this continuum is the "borderline" patient, who is in fact neither medicolegally nor clinically psychotic. With patients who are floridly psychotic, the initial management requires extraordinary measures or techniques which, however influenced or guided by psychoanalytic understanding, are certainly removed from the scope of ordinary psychoanalytic office practice. Where patients, whether through spontaneous or therapeutically induced remission or subsidence of symptoms or the initial mildness of illness present themselves voluntarily for treatment, we may think of their problems as approximating to various degrees the problems which appear in the "borderline" cases.

In the addictions and perversions alike, the *immediate* criterion of accessibility to treatment would seem to lie in the degree to which the patient experiences the tendency as illness, plus the genuineness of this experience, i.e., the question of whether this view of the problem arises from its essential incompatibility with intrinsic elements in the patient's personality or from the impact of the police, a desperate wife, or a desperate employer. These two types of origin are, of course, not mutually exclusive, but they must be appraised quantitatively. A special difficulty in dealing with these illnesses derives from their special nature, i.e., they are sources of relief of painful tension, or of positive pleasure. Thus, instead of providing direct incentive for the psychoanalytic effort, as in the case of ordinary symptomatic suffering, they literally compete with it. To be sure, the moral suffering involved in these disorders or, in the highly developed patient, the realistic estimate of a life pattern may provide incentives of great power. That is what brings them within the scope of our work. In other respects, it would seem, these disorders lend themselves largely to a discussion of the general problems involved in the "borderline" cases, although the less severe perversions can often be treated without appreciable technical modifications. The more severe psychosomatic disorders, apart from their special physical problems, may present psychopathology of a potential severity equivalent to that of the psychoses, and must be handled accordingly; milder cases may often be treated quite conventionally.

In current private practice, at least in this area, the usual "borderline" cases are equaled in importance, perhaps exceeded, only by the character disorders. In the latter, loosely considered, are all manner of occupational maladjustments and inhibitions and marital problems of all types. In their more severe forms, the character disorders are indeed in the "borderline" group as to psychopathologic severity. Very frequently, the presenting neurotic or neuroticlike symptom which dominated the anamnesis quickly yields first importance in the therapist's eyes to a grave character distortion. The patient with one or more classical phobias who impressed one in an initial interview with his intelligence and sincere wish to struggle for health, quickly proves to be an irritable demanding Don Juan, megalomanic, externally submissive yet irrationally and diffusely defiant, rationalizing everything to suit his one-sided view of all personal relationships, driving everyone from him and complaining unremittingly that loneliness causes his illness, and (incidentally) taking about eight times the ordinary soporific dose of a barbiturate daily. Aside from the very severe character disorders as major complaints, or those which quickly assume this position, the tendency nowadays is to perceive sensitively the characterological aspect of every neurotic complaint. This is probably due to the recent tremendous growth of interest in ego psychology, especially in the individual nuances of character, and of defense in general. That this has enriched psychoanalytic technical resources cannot be doubted, especially in dealing with the more difficult character cases, or those in whom the defense aspects of the character have great economic importance. It is barely possible that overenthusiasm in this direction may unnecessarily complicate the management of simpler neurotic problems. One sometimes suspects this when a student, reversing the traditional pedagogical problem, still shudders after a year at the idea of interpreting anything other than a subtle and intricate ego attitude of the patient.

Cases whose principal complaints lie in the sphere of character range from those which are equivalent or nearly equivalent to neuroses — true "neurotic characters" — where awareness of the disorder is present from the beginning — up to those in whom the disorder — I agree with Knight (1953) — is more malignant than in most borderline cases, because it is so thoroughly ego-syntonic. One of the most difficult patients I have treated in recent years[2] was a talented chemist of extreme oral character — with work inhibitions, occasional excessive drinking, severe sexual disturbances, Don Juanism, general financial irresponsibility, pathological jealousy, a remarkable almost legalistic capacity for rationalizing all his behavior (alternating with masochistic self-castigation), severe depressions, and a few minor neuroticlike complaints. This patient was at times quasi-psychotic in his transference reproaches, rationalizations, and acting out. The analysis has been terminated — at least, for the time — with considerable genuine improvement. I am waiting to evaluate the ultimate effect of a nonterminated parameter, that of having allowed the patient to run up a very large debt while he dissipated his earnings elsewhere, borrowing money, ostensibly to pay me, and then not seldom spent it on carousing — simply because it was the only alternative to putting him out of the analysis prematurely, as he proposed a few times—to what I thought would be sudden or gradual self-destruction. The patient's illness prevailed, in this sphere, over my best interpretative efforts. A condition of analysis was established, in relation to which the interpretative effort continued—and not, I believe, without important analytic effect.

I think that the most common usage of the borderline designation would be in relation to those patients who present largely neurotic syndromes, sometimes quite conventional, who nevertheless induce in the clinician the conviction or strong suspicion of more grave illness. This may be because of psychotic fragments, or admixtures of vague, unclassified, suspiciously narcissistic phenomena (bodily, emotional, or intellectual),very severe character distortions or quasi addictions, the sheer massiveness and multiplicity of concurrent symptoms, the history of severe disturbances of behavior or personal relationships, or indeed by the patient's atypical reactions in the early phases of treatment (immediate primitive transference reactions, extreme rigidity, early archaic material, euphoric rapid "improvement," terror of the analytic situation, and many other more subtle considerations). The important clinical issue in these cases is that, according to the individual therapist's prognostic point of view—and according to individual severity—they may be judged unanalyzable, or possibly liable to psychosis under treatment, or liable to become generally worse under treatment, or to occasion interminable analyses, or perhaps to require very long, especially skillful analyses, with eventual minimal improvement. The broad common denominator in these patients and the common feature which allies them with the psychoses—Freud's "narcissistic neuroses"—is their narcissism, not seldom specifically oral in its tendency. One might say that the problems of their treatment are similar to those of the mild or incipient psychoses, except that the initial problem of establishing or maintaining distance between the patient and his psychotic symptom is often liable to appear, instead, in the arduous problem of placing the borderline patient's severe transference reactions in perspective for him.

This brings us to the question of narcissism and transference. I think that most of us would agree that true psychoanalytic therapy could not occur without transference. It would seem that apart from the specific vitiation of the therapeutic alliance by psychotic symptoms, the assumption of incapacity for transference in the narcissistic neuroses was originally held by Freud to be the reason for their therapeutic inaccessibility. Yet we know that very early Abraham began to treat psychotics: he speaks of the increments of positive transference in reaction to interpretations. (Interestingly enough, Abraham mentions Freud's personal communication regarding two melancholics whom he treated with good results.) The literature regarding the psychoanalytic treatment of schizophrenia has by this time grown quite formidable. In relation to our immediate problem, I should like to mention Waelder's case published in 1925. This patient might be regarded as "borderline." The case is of special interest because Waelder mentions his belief that the patient remained nonpsychotic because a union occurred between his intense narcissism and his object-libidinal sublimation, which was pure mathematics. Perhaps nowadays a great many highly intellectual and artistic "borderline" patients who present themselves for treatment are not frankly psychotic for similar reasons. Unfortunately, the problems of recognition versus frustration are unusually severe in most instances, to some extent in proportion to the degree of narcissism involved. A gifted mathematician is in an unusually favorable position, in the sense that the mechanisms are so largely "narcissistic"; yet the demonstrable reality value is very great. At the same time, the influence on events and persons is, in this era, very great, unlike that of certain comparable activities—for example, pure philosophy. I have seen a gifted woman composer, after several years of intermittent treatment, swing for a time from a highly personal and recondite musical idiom, which brought her little of the recognition which she so desperately needed, into a routine but secure effort, quite remote in character from her original work. Interestingly enough, this change paralleled efforts to establish a genuine relationship with her husband, which would occasionally collapse in wild outbursts of aggression, whenever something resembling love would begin to appear. These phenomena occurred in the atmosphere of a mildly friendly positive transference, experienced for the first time, instead of the medley of fear, hostility, and bizarre erotic fantasies which had usually dominated the therapeutic relationship. It would seem that the conception of narcissistic incapacity for transference rests to some extent on a terminological-historical basis. For it is true that the original transference love of the hysteric or the transference fear and aggression of the incest complex are different from the primitive phenomena of the narcissistic transferences, although all gradations between them may occur. The psychotic's transference is liable to invade or overwhelm his personality as his psychosis does, with an equal intensity, with an equal difficulty in perceiving the inappropriateness of his attitudes. I recall an intelligent ambulatory schizophrenic nurse, treated very early in my psychoanalytic career, who had made a painful oral suicidal attempt shortly before treatment was begun, who, after a few years of analysis, following some frustrations of quite impossible demands, abandoned her frequent and characteristic suicidal threats for the impulse to kill me. At this point, she dreamed of avoiding the police while she carried a pail of vomitus, which was the remains of her mother. The patient quite naïvely protested that she saw no point in analyzing this impulse, since the wish was to *do* it, and her gratification would be in doing it. Fortunately, there was enough positive transference to carry us through a difficult period, and the patient left the analysis a few months later. Incidentally, and this is not irrelevant to our general interest, this patient often complained that she felt somehow that I was a very warm person, but that she could get none of the warmth. The analysis was conducted along quite strictly conventional lines. In retrospect, as in a few related instances, I am impressed at how much was accomplished by these methods. This suggests to me how little more may be needed in unusual cases. A little less of the novice's fear to unbend, and a little less need to react against what I viewed as unconventional features in my own early training might have produced a true and thorough analysis of a relatively mild but genuine schizophrenic. At least, that is the way I tend to think of it.

To generalize further and briefly from personal experience, regarding narcissistic transferences: it would seem to be the sheer fear of their primitive intensity that forces certain patients to remain detached. In some patients a subtle but discernible aloofness, reservation, or superciliousness may play a similar role, while the patients for the most part "go through the motions." In one such instance, I have discerned and interpreted grandiose fantasies; in another, they were — in time — frankly and spontaneously stated. In both, the magical expectations and demands were not less strong because of these reservations. In those many instances in which the transference does break through, insatiable demands may appear; or the need to control or tyrannize over the therapist; or failing that, the polar alternative — to be completely submissive, passive, obedient, to be told what to do, or indeed whether things can be done, whether a symptom will appear or disappear, or the transference may be literally "narcissistic" i.e., the therapist is confused with the self, or is like the self in all respects; or, as emphasized by Stern (1938), the therapist must be omnipotent, omniscient, Godlike; or the therapist and patient — alternatively — are, in effect, parts of one another. Extreme ambivalences of simultaneous insatiable demand and destructive nullification are frequent. In the fantasy of the analyst's omnipotence, which affords intolerable anxiety should the analyst exhibit the slightest human frailty, it has been my impression that the guilt about primitive destructive agressions plays an important part. Weird specific phenomena may occur. A medical technician whom I treated for many difficult years would spend hour after hour of eerie indescribable fear and mistrust in my office, eyes popping, talking frantically from an endless store of historical detail, to control her fear, then leave my office to be seized with the terror that I had disappeared, that I was not real! This patient feared me and held me in contempt. Yet any suggestion that she leave me produced a superpanic which quickly settled the problem. This last attitude I should say is a not infrequent trend of "borderline" transferences. Unfortunately, I cannot go into detail about the background, symptoms, genesis, and fate of specific examples. The common factors are the primitiveness, the intensity — at times, the overwhelming quality — and, one should add, the relatively small quanta of genital object love. I think — from my own experience with a few very severe cases in recent years — that one may speak with justification of a transference psychosis, in the sense of a still viable variant of transference neurosis, in the extreme forms. The thin layer of observing, reality-testing ego and the thin thread of transference love and hope for love which enabled these patients to grow up in the first place, sustain the analytic situation.

Various recommendations have been made for the special management of these patients, for example: prolonged preliminary periods of supportive therapy; deliberate fostering and maintenance of the positive transference; avoidance of analysis of defenses or the dissolution of surface neurotic symptoms (Knight), long analytic periods in which the historical material is ignored for direct work with the painful distorted narcissistic transference reactions (Stern); similarly, bypassing of the incestuous conflicts until the narcissistic disturbances are worked through (Cohn, Stern). Zilboorg in his paper, "Ambulatory Schizophrenia" (1941), specifies psychoanalysis as the treatment, without suggesting technical modifications. Bychowski (1953) makes several technical suggestions for protecting and strengthening the ego, and avoiding regression. Greenacre (1941), discussing the treatment of borderline cases in the continuation of her work on the predisposition to anxiety, gives many detailed clinical suggestions. Outstanding are: strong emphasis on increasing the immediate reality hold of the patient, and strengthening of the patient's ego through education of his narcissism (with recognition that these may continue throughout the analysis); a general emphasis (with nuances) on holding the line against — or minimizing — outright concessions to the patient's demands for activity, with calmness, firm realism, and quiet competence being the effective agents in the analyst's attitude. The ultimate importance of analyzing the "essential neurosis" (as distinguished from the basic anxiety) is also stressed. In certain patients who produce abundant archaic fantasy material and ignore the actualities of their reactions to the analyst or the persons and events of their daily lives, I have found it useful to make this phenomenon itself a focus of patient, repetitive interpretation. Sometimes the fantasies themselves may be interpreted in their respective defensive meanings in this connection, or at times in their substitutive significance for the real ego or total personal conflicts, which they seek to evade. This type of "interpretation-back-into-reality" reverses direction, yet is allied to the "direct" maneuver advised by Franz Cohn (1940), in which the patient's bizarre symptom formation is quickly reduced to its origins in narcissistic bodily tensions. Each has its application according to the immediate indications, both tend to substitute more genuine experience for defensive symptom formation or fantasy evasion. In the case of the patient who "lost me" on leaving my office, the treatment was advanced when a dream about the African native workers who stole diamonds by swallowing them and recovering them from their stools, permitted an interpretation of her cannibalistic incorporation of me. The patient, incidentally, had had a childhood fear of a dragonfly which might fly up and attack her, from her stool in the toilet bowl. As an adult, the persistent mild phobia was dissociated from feces. However, the effect of interpretation in this instance, was not dramatic; I would regard its effect as dependent on other long and patient work, including reality testing, with the content of the tortured transference experience itself. If I were to review my general experience with such cases broadly, I would be impelled to say that — assuming adequate perceptiveness, knowledge, and technical skill — the decisive factor is the ability to stand the emotional strains of the powerful tormented and tormenting transference and potential countertransference situations which such cases are liable to present over long periods, without giving up hope, or sometimes, alternatively the severe "acting out" which borderline patients may exhibit as the other alternative to intercurrent clinical psychoses. Fortunately for one's development and unfortunately for the precise evaluation of one's work, neither one's intellectual equipment nor one's degree of emotional maturity — or vulnerability — is static. In general, I am surprised at how well most of these cases have gotten along, relative to the depth and severity of illness, considering that they were treated in rather conventional psychoanalytic fashion. I do not speak of striking total cures. Such patients, I think, are liable to return for occasional interviews, periods of psychotherapy, or reanalysis. My own "striking successes" have been in young persons with transference psychoneuroses and — occasionally — in persons of middle age with similar illnesses. A "borderline" patient whose recovery *apparently* remains excellent, was young and unmarried when she came to me; the same is true of a second patient who might also be classified in this group. In one or two instances of very severe illness, were I to do things over again, in reflection, I might consider not beginning an analysis, or I might consider discontinuing the work shortly after beginning, although I would probably be dissuaded from either course by further reflection on what would happen to these patients *without* psychoanalytic help. In each instance, I can think only of suicide or a sanitarium. It is possible, in a few instances, that simpler forms of psychotherapy based on maintained transference, broad didactic interpretations, and guidance might have been adequate, although I doubt it. In most it would have been inapplicable. In all instances that I recall, I would now institute what I regard as a minimally psychotherapeutic attitude — with the specific limitations that I associate with that attitude (Stone 1951, 1954) — to a degree and for a duration and with revivals as necessary, which would be determined as sensitively as I could, by the urgent need of the patient. I should stress that this would be a controlled-planned-purposive response, which is to be distinguished from a "countertransference" attitude. This would, to some degree, correspond to what is often called building up or maintaining a positive transference. This concept, I believe, originated with Abraham and has been stated in similar terms by several distinguished analysts since then. However, I believe this usage to be inconsistent with the progressively more exact interpretation of transference. I would rather think of it as building up security in an actual personal relationship, so that it can stand the strains of the hostile transference when it appears, as it inevitably *must* appear, if there is to be analytic effectiveness within the treatment itself. It also provides a degree and type of permissible emotional gratification, which would tend to minimize early regressive demands. I am prepared too, to understand that the real personal relationship can slant and at least quantitatively influence the true transference. We do not know all about the (dynamic) relationship between transference and reality. Resemblances have indubitable importance. To reduce this to an absurdity: except where narcissism and remembered perceptions are completely detached from objects, as in psychotic hallucinations, transference requires some degree of resemblance. One may develop a father transference to a man, perhaps a woman, but not to a rocking chair. Thus paradoxically, in relation to the question of transference and narcissism, one might say that the psychotic alone can experience *pure* "transference," entirely separated from the immediate object. The problem lies in the nature and conditions of reinvestment in the objects from whom he has fled. Franz Cohn (1940) speaks of transference as a specifically narcissistic phenomenon.

We know that opinions differ within our own society regarding the analytic treatment of psychoses and the so-called *latent psychoses*. This may be true to a lesser degree of the "borderline" cases. (Knight, in his recent paper, [1953] qualifies what at first sounds like an adverse opinion, by requiring an initial period of psychotherapy.) I have heard a respected colleague say in a seminar that he thought a patient in question was basically psychotic and that the analytic treatment would be harmful to him. I am prepared to accept the fact (indeed, I must at times!) that some patients are unanalyzable; that some (psychotic or nonpsychotic!) cannot even adapt themselves to the requirements of analytic treatment; that some have a very poor prognosis for cure or improvement; that some, if ineptly handled in a powerful dynamic situation, may be precipitated into trouble; that faulty diagnosis may lead to inept handling even in expert hands; and that, in many instances, the expectations may be so poor that the time, skill, and energies should be withheld for more likely application. However, I find it very hard to believe that the procedure in itself, if well managed (i.e., employed with sensitive individual adaptations where necessary) is harmful. Certainly, while I recognize the profound predisposition to psychosis, I do not believe that a fully preformed psychosis exists in latent form in the adult, to appear only because it is "uncovered." The psychosis may be on its way in response to everyday life stresses; it may possibly be expedited by certain formal factors of analysis and the routine emotional "vacuum" of analysis; in a sensitively modified situation, the interaction of archaic drives and potential psychotic defenses may come to a different solution in the transference. Nevertheless, this assumption of latency and inevitability is a point of view which is held, I am sure, by more than a few experienced colleagues. Aside from this point of view, since the nuances of technical approach depend on preliminary diagnosis, the problem of recognizing these patients beforehand, or at least in the very earliest phase of treatment, is extremely important. If we agree on the central importance of diagnosis, it is probable that we shall find many different methods for reaching this goal. In his 1938 paper Stern lists, and then discusses, several traits which distinguish these patients as to history, nature of their symptoms, and reactions in treatment: narcissism, "psychic bleeding," inordinate hypersensitivity, psychic and body rigidity ("rigid personality"), negative therapeutic reactions, deeply embedded feelings of inferiority, masochism, deep organic insecurity and anxiety, projection mechanisms, and disturbed reality testing in personal relationships. Knight (1953) in his recent paper, goes into some detail about objective psychiatric subtleties which may reveal the "borderline" psychotic elements. In setting aside the "free-association" interview as an adjunct to the formed or controlled conversational interview, Knight gives weight to psychological testing. Bychowski (1953) also values projective tests. Zilboorg stresses the subtle evidences of dereism in relatively normal-seeming personalities. With due recognition that one's own biases are not synonymous with best procedure, it is fitting to state one's own preference. I believe that we require longer (and often multiple) psychiatric examinations than we have usually employed. We need detailed histories, detailed observations of the patient's thought processes and language expression, and the opportunity to observe his postural, gait, voice, and mimetic reactions. Certainly, in these modalities, the patient may reveal to the sensitive observer psychotic fragments from a descriptive psychiatric point of view. Furthermore, in being allowed to talk spontaneously at times, in his choice of material, in his response or manner of response or nonresponse to questions, the patient may tell us much that might be expected to appear in a diagnostic "free-association" interview, often more, because certain questions cannot be evaded, at least from an inferential point of view. In his longitudinal history and in the current patterning of the patient's activities, one can learn much of the personality structure which underlies the symptoms. Most significant of all is the character and pattern of his relationships with people. Finally, as a strong personal preference, I believe that the patient's reactions to the examiner in the interview can be of great diagnostic importance. Irritability, detachment, shallowness, euphoria, and pompousness may sometimes mean more than do pages of symptom description. In the case of the lady who made me "disappear," a greater emphasis on her anxious pressure of speech, on her shallow, strained, and euphoric eagerness in the first interview, might have rendered me, if not prepared for it, at least less surprised by what so soon appeared. As for the psychological tests, I have no doubt that these should and can reveal data that are inaccessible to us in interviews, and that these data can in time become very valuable to us clinically. However, I do not feel that these tests, in their present state of development, can offer conclusions as to clinical diagnosis, accessibility to treatment, and prognosis, which are to be balanced *against* the results of careful clinical examination. That the data can be usefully integrated with clinical observations in the thinking of a clinician who knows these tests well, I do not doubt. But there is still much to be learned about the significance of the data themselves.

I should like to return at least briefly, before closing, to the basic question posed by our "widening scope," i.e., what *are* the true indications for analysis? If one reads the indications as given by a reasonably conservative authority like Fenichel (1945), it soon appears that practically every psychogenic nosological category can be treated psychoanalytically, under good conditions, although — obviously — they vary extremely in availability and prognosis. None of us would doubt that a true although severe hysteria in a young individual in a good life situation, with a reasonably competent analyst, has an infinitely better prognosis than — let us say — a mild but genuine schizophrenia in a similar setting, even with an analyst of extraordinary experience and skill. So we must acknowledge that, imperfect as our nosology is, it is still meaningful prognostically, at least in the sense that the "hypothetical normal ego," as recently discussed by Eissler (1953), is meaningful. However, the deceptiveness of a descriptively established hysteria was recognized early by Freud. Nowadays, we are groping toward recognizing and regrouping such problems in such conceptions as the "borderline" case or the "latent psychosis." This would still be an essentially (although improved) nosological approach. However, it is my feeling that there are elements of great importance which, while they may come to play a role in nosologies of the future, remain for the moment in a different sphere. I have in mind personality traits and resources, which we may try to assess from careful historical and cross-sectional evaluation of the personality. This general type of evaluation was stated succinctly by Freud in 1904. I add a few details. Has the patient talents, which may serve him for emergency releases of tension, or—more importantly—to give sublimated productive expression to large elements in his fantasy life? Has the patient certain simple but important capacities, such as courage, patience, deliberate purposive tolerance for unavoidable suffering (as distinguished from masochism)? Does the patient's ego participate in the primitive magical demands and expectations for cure which characterize his infantile transference? To what extent in general is the patient capable of self-observation or self-appraisal, as opposed to the tendency to rationalization, as differentiated from symptomatic self-depreciation and self-castigation? Then there are the questions of the patient's biological age, his occupational, social, and family milieu, the possible rewards of cure, his goals, his degree of independence of thought and action, and relative mobility or fixity of his situation in life. It is true that some of these matters may change with treatment. But some must be reckoned with as one does with the climate or with a patient's physical diathesis. What I am trying to say is that any few or several of these considerations may reverse or overturn, or at least profoundly modify, the nosological consideration. The "borderline" patient under certain special conditions may be a better patient in the long run, for all of the intrinsic difficulties, than the hysteric whose epinosic gains are too great.

Another consideration in our field is the analyst himself. In no other field, save surgery, with which Freud frequently compared analysis, is the personal equation so important. It is up to us to know our capacities, intellectual and emotional, even if we cannot always know one another as clearly in this respect. Again, special predilections, interests, and emotional textures may profoundly influence prognosis and thus—in a tangible way—the indications. I suppose one might generalize that apart from skills, a therapist must be able to love a psychotic or a delinquent, and be at least warmly interested in the "borderline" patient (whether or not this feeling is utilized technically), for optimum results. For in a sense, their "transferences" require new objects, the old ones having been destroyed, permanently repudiated, or nearly so, as they will be again and again in the transference neurosis (or psychosis). The true neurotic patient can probably get along with a reasonably reliable friendliness behind the analyst's technically assumed objectivity and neutrality and sometimes, apparently, with much less. For his transference has remained, after all, true to its original objects, whatever the dissatisfactions which he assigns to his life with them.

Now a few words in brief conclusion: the scope of psychoanalytic therapy has widened from the transference psychoneurosis to include practically all psychogenic nosologic categories. The transference neuroses and character disorders of equivalent degree of psychopathology remain the optimum general indications for the classical method. While the difficulties increase and the expectations of success diminish in a general way as the nosological periphery is approached, there is no absolute barrier; and it is to be borne in mind that both extranosological factors and the therapist's personal tendencies may profoundly influence the indications and prognosis. Furthermore, from my point of view, psychoanalysis remains as yet the most powerful of all psychotherapeutic instruments, the "fire and iron," as Freud called it. While it should be used only with skill, care, and judgment and supported by painstaking diagnosis, it is basically a greater error to use it for trivial or incipient or reactive illnesses or in persons with feeble personality resources than for serious chronic illnesses, when these occur in persons of current or potential strength. With this, paradoxically enough, there is some ground to believe that Freud would have agreed, although not necessarily in a nosological sense. I do not believe that it should be wasted if one is convinced of a very bad prognosis; certainly it should not be applied or persisted in if one is convinced that a personality cannot tolerate it. Some of us may be too quick to abandon efforts, some too slow; these are matters which only self-scrutiny can correct. However, psychoanalysts may legitimately be invoked, and indeed *should* be invoked, for many very ill people of good personality resources, who are probably inaccessible to cure by other methods and who are willing to accept the long travail of analysis without guarantees of success. There is always a possibility of helping, where all other measures fail. With progressively better understanding of the actions of psychotherapeutic admixtures or of large-scale parameters in the psychoanalytic method, now so largely intuitive in their application, we can hope that such successes will be more frequent.

NOTES

1. Bibring (1954) differentiates interpretation from clarification by confining the reference of interpretation to "repressed or otherwise warded-off unconscious material and its derivatives."

2. It is a long time since I have treated an actively psychotic patient; borderline cases and severe character disorders have been numerous.

REFERENCES

Abraham, K. (1927). Notes on the psycho-analytical investigation and treatment of manic-depressive insanity and allied conditions. In *Selected Papers on Psycho-Analysis*. London: Hogarth, pp. 137–156.

Bibring, E. (1954). Presentation in panel on psychoanalysis and dynamic psychotherapy — Similarities and differences. *J. Amer. Psychoanal. Assn.* 2:160–162.

Bychowski, G. (1953). The problem of latent psychosis. *J. Amer. Psychoanal. Assn.* 1:484–505.

Cohn, F. S. (1940). Practical approach to the problem of narcissistic neuroses. *Psychoanal. Q.* 9:64–79.

Eissler, K. R. (1953). The effect of the structure of the ego on psychoanalytic technique. *J. Amer. Psychoanal. Assn.* 1:104–141.

Fenichel, O. (1945). *The Psychoanalytic Theory of Neurosis.* New York: Norton.

Freud, A. (1936). *The Ego and the Mechanisms of Defense.* New York: International Universities Press, 1946.

Freud, S. (1904). On psychotherapy. *S. E.* 7.

_____ (1908). Character and anal erotism. *S. E.* 9.

_____ (1940). An outline of psycho-analysis. *S. E.* 23.

Greenacre, P. (1941). The predisposition to anxiety, pt. 2. *Psychoanal. Q.* 10:610–638.

Knight, R. P. (1953). Borderline states. *Bull. Menninger Clin.* 17:1–12.

Reich, W. (1947). *Character-Analysis.* New York: Orgone Institute Press.

Simmel, E. (1929). Psycho-analytic treatment in a sanatorium. Int. J. Psychoanal. 10:70–89.

Sterba, R. (1953). Clinical and therapeutic aspects of character resistance. *Psychoanal. Q.* 22:1–20.

Stern, A. (1938). Psychoanalytic investigation of and therapy in the borderline group of neuroses. *Psychoanal. Q.* 7:467–468.

Stone, L. (1951). Psychoanalysis and brief psychotherapy. *Psychoanal. Q.* 20:215–236. *Reprinted in this volume, Chapter 1.*

_____ (1954). Discussion in panel on psychoanalysis and dynamic psychotherapy — Similarities and differences. *J. Amer. Psychoanal. Assn.* 2:164–166.

Waelder, R. (1925). The psychoses: Their mechanisms and accessibility to influence. *Int. J. Psychoanal.* 6:259–281.

Zilboorg, G. (1941). Ambulatory schizophrenias. *Psychiatry* 4:149.

Chapter 3
The Psychoanalytic Situation
Excerpts
(1961)

I regret that certain practical obstacles prevented the reproduction of this work in its entirety. It does present a thorough summary of many of my intellectually "synergistic" views developed over a long period. However, I believe that the excerpts are sufficient to acquaint the reader with the essential trends of thought of this contribution. Some of my observations included in "Widening Scope" led to further reflection on the psychoanalytic situation, including the pattern of unconscious reactions to it, regardless of the patient's degree of illness. (The degree of illness, however, maintained its significance with regard to the depth of transference regression elicited by the situation as such.) The crucial function of the rule of abstinence is stressed both in its affirmative function in the development of transference and the transference neurosis, and in the potential complications that may arise from its overwrought and ill-considered application. I also propose the concept of legitimate transference gratification and discuss and delimit its proper — or optional — sphere. I consider a reduction of superfluous deprivations innocuous, often salutary and sometimes necessary, while maintaining, nonetheless, unyielding barriers in certain spheres. The basic primordial transference, directed against archaic separation, is defined; also its antithetical — complementary alternative, the "mature transference." The primary mother (of bodily intimacy) and the secondary mother (of separation) are given essential place in the unconscious dynamics of the psychoanalytic situation. The state of "deprivation-in-intimacy," bridged by the psychosomatic function of speech in early childhood, again in the psychoanalytic situation, provides the force for the primordial and the mature transferences, the regressive activation of the transference neurosis, and its clinical reduction. Essential in the process is the evolution of the functions of speech from the current derivatives of their primitive origins to the true representational-communicative sphere, appropriate to the phenomena of interpretation and insight.

This small volume was followed by an extended postscript, published six years later, which provides the next chapter in this book.

THE CLASSICAL PSYCHOANALYTIC SITUATION

I realize that the word *classical* has many meanings in ordinary usage. However, in relation to psychoanalysis, its essential meaning is quite clear. Insofar as there are connotations such as adherence to well-tested and established forms and the prestige of early origin and durability, I see no reason to disavow them. As Freud gave up the hypnotic technique and then the specific alternative method of head pressure and, with them, many traditional and manifestly medical practices, ranging all the way from physical examination to conventional attitudes toward fees, a new psychological situation emerged which is usually quite clearly crystallized in the minds of those who practice psychoanalysis in the classical sense. That there are many variations in individual technical inclinations, even in specifications of personal attitude toward the patient, was established (at least for the British Society) by Glover's questionnaire many years ago (1938). However, such variations radiate from a fairly well defined general conceptual structure, about which, except where there is stated or known group or individual dissent, agreement may quite usually be assumed. It may be objected that since analysts are in fact human and do vary in their practices, this has little importance. It must be pointed out, in response, that this conceptual structure has great influence and power, occasioning self-conciousness or even guilt, when its outlines are transgressed. It definitely provides the core of teaching (in relation to which "variations" may be discussed). It certainly represents the central theoretical outline for considerations of the psychoanalytic process. One may see this tendency in its extreme current development in Eissler's (1953) designation as a parameter of any technical action of the analyst except interpretation, with a more recent introduction (1958) of the concept *pseudoparameter*. Thus a rigidly outlined conception of the situation is, for an increasing number of analysts, as important as our fundamental metapsychological concepts. Furthermore, the theoretical conceptual structure of the analytic situation does undeniably exist as a sort of ideal, which many analysts actually try to embody in their clinical work, the "human" element appearing as a sort of conscious *détente*, reservation, or minimal forced concession. This crystallized conception is of composite origin: Freud's own statements of principle and explicit recommendations; the hardening of habit and tradition about selected elements in these recommendations (sometimes abetted by specific doctrinaire attitudes in influential colleagues); elements of convenience or facilitation for analyst or patient, of which some (the anterior and recumbent position of the patient, for example) have proved to have critical dynamic significance, outreaching by far the original manifest and immediate motivation for their establishment; and certainly the secondary affirmative elements deriving from the tests of practical experience, rational reflection, and deepening insight into the nature of established practice. There are also ambiguities or reservations in Freud's statements of certain fundamental principles, which have permitted exegetic treatment of varying clarity and rationale. This is notably true in a reference of special interest to us in this paper, i.e., the analyst's personal orientation to his patient. Whether this hazy area was a special reflection of Freud's general reluctance to lay down authoritarian technical rules or of certain problems of inherent contradiction to which I humbly address myself in this paper, I cannot say. Possibly both were involved. In any case, this situational structure, which arose largely to facilitate free association by the patient and the undisturbed, "evenly suspended" attention of the analyst, also to permit the transference to develop as a discrete and "uncontaminated" phenomenon, can now be understood as a dynamically formidable psychoanalytic instrumentality in itself. I refer to its role in facilitating, indeed, in contributing decisively to, the very existence of the transference neurosis. It exercises the silent cumulative function of promoting regression through its intrinsic and inevitable frustrations, anterior to the reductive interpretative interventions (my own usage!) (Panel Discussion 1956), which appear against its necessary and consistent background.

I shall not review in detail the descriptive features of the classical analytic situation. Several of its features contribute to what I have called elsewhere (1954b) the analytic (perceptual and emotional) "vacuum": the total or relative nonvisibility of the analyst during the hours; the relative confinement of his responses to interpretation, clarification, or other "neutral" maneuvers; the stereotypy of schedules and fees; the relative lack of even conventional emotional responses to the patient's personality and career; the lack of intervention in the patient's everyday life, whether through advice, persuasion, or purposive extra-analytic contact; the general "blanketing" of the analyst's personality, actively and passively, except as it appears inevitably or inadvertently. Another group of factors, closely intertwined with the others, albeit explicitly *voluntary* and *cooperative* on the patient's side (indeed, a part of the burden of heavy *adult* responsibility which he assumes), emphasizes in their manifest character the *formally* childlike role of the analysand. I emphasize the adult burden because, while it may be understood, it is sometimes submerged in the emphasis on the "child" element (for example, Waelder's introduction [1956] to the panel discussion on transference). Among these factors are free association as the sole or heavily preponderant means of communication by the patient, with abrogation of any "right" to suppress verbalization; the generally extreme one-sidedness of communication and thus of the gratification of curiosity, and an imbalance which allies itself with the extreme inequality of manifest emotional involvement. Not least in the structural configuration is the supine position of the patient, whose alteration (unless it derives from the clinical judgment of the analyst) tends to be technically resisted, in favor of verbalization of such impulses. On the patient's side the relative failure of cognitive gratifications blends with and augments, at every turn, the failure of gratifications in terms of ordinary exchange of feeling or the experience of demonstrable effective influence on another person, in the sense that these gratifications are always operative in the economy of relationships in everyday life or even — to a considerable extent — in relations with other physicians. I do not overlook the security and support, the high tolerance, and the sense of expressive freedom which are implicit for the patient in the psychoanalytic situation as such. However, I must state my conviction that a nuance of the analyst's attitude can determine the difference between a lonely vacuum and a controlled but warm human situation, which does indeed offer these gratifications, along with its undoubted rigors. The rigors of the analytic situation are subtle and cumulative, importantly operative, *whether evident or not*. It is one of the burdens of this presentation to suggest that the intrinsic formal stringencies of the situation are sufficient to contraindicate superfluous deprivations in the analyst's personal attitude.

In developing this altogether remarkable and largely unprecedented purposive human relationship, Freud stated a few broad principles, and occasionally, in keeping with his talent for strikingly vivid illustrative expression, utilized figures of speech, which have been widely and persistently influential. They are quoted frequently, although the weight or the qualitative interpretation given them may vary considerably. I should like to select for brief special mention at this point (1) the principle of abstinence, (2) the surgeon as model, and (3) the "mirror" reference. In Freud's "Transference Love" (1915a), the reference to abstinence is specifically in the sphere of erotic transference craving. Freud offers the basic generalization: "The treatment must be carried out in abstinence." The positive purpose in the general principle is to preserve the motivation for further genuine analytic change. Within this avowedly incomplete discussion, an important if somewhat vague qualification is made: "By this I do not mean physical abstinence alone, nor yet the deprivation of everything that the patient desires, for perhaps no sick person could tolerate this." One may only surmise that Freud still had in mind as the permissible gratifications, sympathy and respect (continuing "after the confession has been made") which he mentions as necessary motivating compensations for the patient, along with the invoking of his own intellectual interest (in the *Studies on Hysteria* [Breuer and Freud 1895, pp. 282–283]). In this early passage in the *Studies*, impressive in its simplicity and clarity, Freud mentions as affirmatively productive forces those elements in the psychoanalytic situation, deriving naturally from the doctor-patient relationship, and persisting in the realm of common sense, which with the passage of time have been crowded increasingly to the theoretical and operational periphery, to be regarded as reservations, exceptions, or minimal necessary concessions, sometimes as vaguely taken for granted or optional, or—a priori, in some quarters—as downright technical errors.

In his Budapest Congress paper (1919), Freud makes a similar general statement regarding abstinence. He also expresses the general reservation: " . . . nor do we mean what it popularly connotes, refraining from sexual intercourse; it means something else which has far more to do with the dynamics of falling ill and recovering." (We should note, incidentally, how frequently the disclaimer regarding sexual intercourse is ignored; see Eissler [1958]; also Scheunert [1961].) There then follows a brief passage, relatively simple in statement, but actually quite complex as to the principle stated. The symptoms are viewed on the one hand as substitutive satisfactions and on the other hand as providing the suffering motive power for further progress; the necessity for establishing other privations, if the symptoms subside too early, is mentioned. ("Cruel though it may sound . . . ") the analyst must require the patient not only to abandon harmful or dangerous satisfaction or solutions, but even *harmless* pursuits that have a (premature) substitutive value. And finally, the analyst must deny to the patient the transference satisfactions which he may seek to substitute for his neurosis. ("It is expedient to deny him precisely those satisfactions which he desires most intensely and expresses most importunately.") There is a characteristic reservation: "Some concessions must of course be made to him, greater or less, according to the nature of the case and the patient's individuality. But it is not good to let them become too great."

With regard to the surgeon as model, Freud (1912b) calls on his colleagues to "model themselves during psycho-analytic treatment on the surgeon, who *puts aside* [italics mine] all his feelings, even his human sympathy, and concentrates his mental forces on the single aim of performing the operation as skillfully as possible." After warning against therapeutic ambition (to impress others), he goes on to say: "The justification for requiring this emotional coldness in the analyst is that it creates the most advantageous conditions for both parties: for the doctor a desirable protection for his own emotional life and for the patient the largest amount of help that we can give him to-day."

The "mirror" reference appears in the same paper (1912b). This was directed specifically against the physician's attempting to overcome resistance by citing to the patient his own "mental defects and conflicts and, by giving him intimate information about his own life, enable him to put himself on an equal footing." Freud speaks of the closeness of this technique to suggestion, points out its basic inadequacy and technical hazards, and then asserts: "The doctor should be opaque to his patients and, like a mirror, should show them nothing but what is shown to him."

We should note in scrutinizing the statements concerning abstinence that, apart from the quantitative ambiguities in the "exceptions," there is little basis for inferring just *what* might be permitted or given the patient. In Freud's Budapest paper (1919), the negative reference to sexual intercourse is obviously a reference to extraanalytic gratification, whereas the less explicit and broadly inclusive succeeding phrase ("something else which has far more to do with the dynamics of falling ill and recovering") must deal largely with the transference situation. In the brief elaboration which follows it, practically any gratification which can be related to the effort to find relief for unconscious conflict is to be set aside, in the interest of propelling the psychoanalytic process. (The single qualification is prematurity.) Certainly, while this rather forbidding formulation is susceptible to discussion and certain reservations, especially as to practical application, the affirmative recommendations themselves, in their very inclusiveness if not explicitness of statement, become relatively unambiguous.

With regard to the surgeon analogy, I call attention to the words *puts aside,* inasmuch as they certainly imply that certain sympathetic attitudes exist, but must be subordinated to the requirements of skillful technical work. I see no reason, furthermore, why this must in any sense be construed as a directive regarding a general personal attitude, in the larger sense. It would seem specifically applicable to the analyst's only scalpel, his interpretations, which may indeed, at times, be painful. The "justification for requiring this emotional coldness" includes a statement connected with that facet of psychoanalytic practice (the analyst's needs and frailties) which Freud, with the inspiring frankness which characterizes his genius, never hesitated to mention, whether in relation to fees, to being stared at all day, or to less specific emotional hazards of the analyst's life. Even this (first) aspect of the "justification" might not elicit universal agreement; however, an adequate discussion of this point would take us too far afield. The "mirror" simile, like the surgical ideal, is open to interpretation, and the interpretation is of enormous theoretical and operational importance. While the "mirror" aphorism is unquestionably a forceful generalization of great vividness, we must note that (1) it derives from the rejection of a specific hypothetical treatment maneuver (as mentioned above) and (2) were it to be accepted as if intended in a truly general and crudely literal sense, it would represent an insoluble contradiction, incompatible with the essential nature of psychoanalysis. Our entire interpretation method involves the presentation of the analyst's *own* mental activity, which leads to the subjective transformation of what the patient has shown into something manifestly different, albeit latent or implicit in what was shown. One might say, following the frequent dreams of patients, that the work of taking, developing, and elucidating an X-ray film to the patient would be closer to the fact, in the same narrow figurative frame of reference. It is, therefore, entirely reasonable to assume that Freud referred very broadly (1) to the essential long-term purpose of the analysis, i.e., to elucidate the patient's own unconscious mental life to him, as opposed to the revelation of the (personal) contents of the analyst's mind to him; and (2) to the operational fact that the latter procedure, in most instances, and in the long run, interferes with the essential purpose. There is no evidence that "coldness" or "lifelessness" were directly or indirectly adjured in this particular recommendation; it is of purely cognitive-communicative reference. . . .

This theme is somewhat removed from the immediate question of acknowledging certain selected facts about oneself, but it is not unrelated. For a physician also has a life beyond his work; and the patient knows it. This too is quite frequently brought into relation both with direct transference fantasies and with the fantasied attitudes toward him, which the patient ascribes to his analyst. Sooner or later, to a varying degree, this extraprofessional life is a subject of "diagnosis," opinion, and fantasy. It is a matter for serious consideration as to whether some degree of correct external bodily outline, added to the vocational skeleton, would not only be innocuous, but in many instances positively helpful. First, it would serve as a reasonable corrective or, at least, a measuring rod for the strange misinformation, or fragmentary or distorted information, which is so often selectively acquired or retained by analysands and which more often supports tenacious transference-resistance convictions than the therapeutic alliance; second, I offer the suggestion that the regressive elements in the transference neurosis are subjected to less adventitious stimulation and are thus more amenable to interpretative intervention if commonplace curiosities are not *superfluously* and systematically frustrated than if they are. Furthermore, in the sense mentioned before regarding the object-as-pure-listener-and-interpreter, the general endopsychic pressure to create a person, an intelligible object, "out of whole cloth" (as an alternative to a pure "discharge" target) is diminished. It is a discharge target which analysts may unwittingly strive to represent in some instances. The very word *object*, like *resistance* and a few other essential words in our vocabulary, is perhaps unfortunate; however, I think it is less important that we change the words than that we avoid their subtle influence on our thinking—and our feeling. By "adventitious stimulation" of the regressive elements in the transference neurosis, I refer to the quanta of frustration which exceed the ego's sense of rational purposiveness and/or capacity for adequate adaptation, in the analytic situation. The resultant deepening or progressive infantilization of the transference neurosis, or its increasing pervasiveness and tenacity, are liable to go beyond "the service of the ego." Not due primarily or preponderantly to persistent and genetically anterior conflicts, which would require analytic resolution by their original and intrinsic nature, such phenomena present technical problems, for which interpretation alone is not always adequate. We know that the frustrations of human curiosity, erotic or otherwise, are rarely complete, from the beginning. We cover our genitals and the greater part of our bodies, except under special conditions; we do *not* usually cover our faces. One can imagine the general bewilderment and anxiety of the adult world (not to speak of the world of infants!) if we had to renounce this greatly esteemed (however unreliable) cue. Actually, of course, the patient *does* see the analyst's face at the beginning and end of each hour; it is the psychological "face" that we are prone to hide with what may often be overwrought persistence and zeal. An overemphasis on the wholesale suppression of innocuous details also fails to take into account the fact that the true transference tends to invest reality according to its own requirements, sometimes in a quasi-hallucinatory sense. Hence knowledge of the type we have in mind is usually of no more, or little more, specifically determinative importance than the physical details with which the patient is inevitably confronted, and which he invariably invests with his own interpretation or selective or distorted perceptions. However, this perceptual aspect, in turn, derives its real significance only from the original dynamic need which occasions it. Hence it is only a fact of the analyst's emotional attitude or his life which impinges effectively on the current of the patient's specific dynamic demands, which may importantly influence the accessible phenomenology and thus the relative "validity" of the transference neurosis. The actual countertransference attitudes may of course be decisive. The manifest factual information can attain, or approximate, equally serious proportions only when it has the capacity to stimulate or feed tenacious fantasy, which supports the transference resistance. It is not unreasonable to assume that this would, in general, apply only to important and intimate facts about the analyst's personal life. It was such optional information (and, in this reference, I concur without reservation with the prohibition) that Freud had in mind in stating the "mirror" principle, which I believe has had an understandable (but not desirable) spread of application. Information about one's sexual habits or preferences would, for (indisputable!) example, be clearly within this scope. As a *reductio ad absurdum*: I doubt that the evolution of the transference neurosis is often seriously disturbed by the patient's knowing whether one takes one's vacation in Vermont or Maine, or indeed (let me be really bold!) that one knows something more about sailing than about golf or bridge. I think that it is not seldom disturbed by a persistent or repetitive arbitrary refusal to answer such questions, after sufficient speculative fantasy, if there is no more *specific* or *adequate* reason than the general principle that the patient must not know anything about one, or that the analyst does not answer questions. It *can* be seriously disturbed, although not necessarily destroyed, by a sudden (perhaps inadvertently) tendentious remark about how (well!) one handled a certain difficult problem in one's early life, similar to one about whose handling in his own life the patient feels ashamed; or by stating ostentatiously and repetitively (albeit "objectively") the great value one assigns to an element in life, which the patient does not and will never enjoy and about whose great value he has long since and all too sadly been convinced. Or a repetitive tone of voice or nuance of choice in words in framing certain interpretations may introduce less concrete and demonstrable but nonetheless seriously disturbing factors. Or the subjective sense of belittlement experienced by the patient in reaction to one's absolute and supercilious invulnerability to his aggression or criticisms, rather than one's tolerance and understanding, may be conducive to superfluous regression. I feel that that is how many patients must really react to the "mirror" identity, if narcissistic responses in both cognitive and emotional spheres are not more directly invoked. And, finally, a selective failure to speak can accomplish almost any destructive purpose that statement or action can accomplish, can disarm the patient seriously, and saddest of all, will often elude the analyst's own self-critique, whether as an objective self-observing function or as the healthy reproach of conscience.

This brings me to the general question of *legitimate* "transference gratification." The very phrase, I realize, may stimulate initial protest. Nevertheless, it comprehends an indisputable system of facts. There is every reason to assume that anything which the analyst does or says impinges in some respect on all topographical levels, on the three psychic structures, gratifies (or otherwise) both rational and nonrational and current and infantile strivings in extremely varied and complex economic distribution. This of course includes specifically transference wishes, however broadly or narrowly construed. Thus, in following our basic technique, in listening to free associations and in making interpretations, we are gratifying transference wishes, whether in one of myriad possible archaic references, such as the wish for the tolerant acceptance of excreta or the desire to be given food, or, in my view, in gratifying a more "mature" wish of childhood, underlying and essential to the initial genuine viability of the analytic situation: a wish for tolerance and for sympathetic understanding, for help in mastering the baffling and challenging outer world of living and inanimate objects and forces, the pressures of somatically experienced discomforts and urges, and, most of all, the mastering and directing of a dark and mysterious inner psychic world. Without the support of this component of latent transference, I am skeptical that the adult rational clinical need, supported by unconscious irrational transference expectations and fantasies (so well described by Nunberg [1925]) could sustain many analytic situations against the clamor of ambivalent and vulnerable instinctual demands and disappointments. In gratifying this "mature" wish of childhood, there is also in the analytic situation, as in childhood, an acceptable form of love that, in an economic sense, may well contribute importantly to the incentive for mastery of unneutralized and unelaborated erotic and destructive drives. This may well be one of the primary conditions of psychotherapy in general (see Freud 1915b, p. 319). The whole great complex of instruction in the techniques of life by adults in early years is involved in this; in it, of course, the teaching of language in its representational-communicative function is of basic importance. And in the psychoanalytic situation, in which free association provides at least a near-equivalent for the experimental babbling of the infant, to be met with the specifying and illuminating effort of interpretation, this great developmental movement finds a potential symbolic repetition. Comprehending as it does an intricate synthesis of psychic elements, beginning with the instinctual urges toward the parents, this relatively "mature" wish of childhood (often subject in itself to major frustration) is, I believe, an important part of the transference complex. It may well be an early and fundamental, biologically determined condition for the general "principle of multiple function" (Waelder, 1930) in human development. I would say that this type of gratification can be extended to its reasonable limits, with advantage. Even the *reasons* for analytic deprivations and frustrations can be explained with full and patient care that they be understood. Questions which deal with significant realities of the analytic situation, which the patient cannot answer for himself, should probably be answered more often than they are; when it is judged better not to answer them, the explicit or latent question "why not?" *should* be met, until one can soundly assume that the continued ignorance is of dubious or disingenuous origin; at that point, a relevant interpretation or clarification is usually in order. (Naturally, I recognize that plain silence is *also* in order in certain instances!) What I have in mind in stressing such matters is that there is an element in analytic technique, however strictly interpreted, which does inevitably and legitimately provide transference gratification, and that there are, in addition, areas of option, where the choice lies between arbitrary authoritarianism and the engagement of rational cooperation based on understanding. With the rarest of exceptions, the latter is the more desirable course.

The economic factor in the emotional-cognitive exchange of analysis permits some variation in the actual depth of transference regression, or at least in the intensity and degree of primitiveness of the transference instinctual demands. While I do not believe that these phenomena can be controlled at given points in an individual analysis, by simple quantitative formalistic devices (see Alexander et al. 1946), I do believe that the general tendency toward transference regression can be influenced. Freud recognized and stated the necessity for such "regulation." In his *Outline*, for example (1938b, pp. 69–70), Freud says: "And, to prevent him from falling into a state in which he will be inaccessible to all evidence, the analyst takes care that neither the love nor the hostility reach extreme heights." This is, of course, the affirmative reciprocal of Freud's several earlier statements regarding the vague but necessary limitations of frustration. However, the method suggested, like most suggestions in the direction of the "exceptions" or "reservations," lacks the force and clarity of the affirmative classical precepts: "This is achieved by forewarning the patient in good time of these possibilities and by not overlooking the first signs of their appearance." The first, indeed, if not for the ambiguity introduced by the phrasing of the early remark, might be viewed as a contradiction to the comment in "Observations on Transference Love" (1915a, pp. 161–162). Menninger (1958) elaborates vividly the essential role of the "regression," stresses the basic position of the rule of abstinence, and yet also recognizes repeatedly the hazards of excessively severe frustration. However, the recommendations for avoiding such excesses run true to classical tradition in their relative ambiguousness. In returning to this problem in the section on "The Therapist's Interventions," Menninger mentions the value of nonspecific evidences of the analyst's "presence" and concludes: "All he [the patient] may have been needing, actually, is some indication that the analyst accepts him in a measure, accepts what he is saying, likes him a little bit in spite of his importunities and his infirmities." Waelder, in *Basic Theory of Psychoanalysis* (1960, p. 239), excludes, in effect, all gratifications "(beyond a minimum that may be necessary for the very continuation of the analytic treatment)." We must note, however, that an utter lack of gratification (except for the need to suffer) will also motivate certain patients to continue treatment. Waelder, following the tradition of presentation in this connection, mentions the great emotional requirements which may be involved in the treatment of psychoses (under that heading) (p. 233) and notes that this requirement "far exceeds anything necessary in the psychoanalyis of the neuroses in which personal investment of the analyst is limited to friendly interest, a strong desire to help, and careful attention to the patient's productions." When I refer to the "tradition of presentation," in this instance, I have in mind the statements in a subordinate clause, in a minimizing context, that by implication tend to obscure the affirmative importance of what is said. In this instance, what is said if read separately constitutes a decidedly useful statement. It has become indeed a sort of routine observance to invoke this "contrasting" comparison, even though the purpose be far from mere conventional invocation (see, for example, Sechehaye 1956 or Nacht 1949, 1958). I have in the past also utilized it (1954b). A critical subtlety is involved, for the statements in point usually serve important and affirmative immediate purposes; furthermore, the quantitative differential which is implied is usually quite genuine. What miscarries is the latent or implied message regarding the emotional requirements, in the unmodified analytic situation, of the "classical" neurotic patient. For he too legitimately requires something more than has hitherto been regarded as sufficient. I shall not compound our present problem by speculating on how frequently this (relatively) hardy individual appears in our respective clinical practices.

Superfluously remote and depriving attitudes (which may indeed engender tremendous awe and attachment in the patient) tend to promote an artifact element in the transference neurosis, in a sense similar to the regressive tendencies which can occur in children deprived of the complex integrated satisfactions which they may reasonably expect from their parents (play, affectionate demonstration, interest, teaching, etc.). The patient who boasts euphorically that "*his* analyst *never* answers a question," and excitedly questions the correctness of his friend's analysis, because the latter's analyst *did* answer one, and indeed even asked him how he felt after a serious operation, may be an "easy person to work with," but his emotional state is actually a cause for serious concern.

In oversimple terms there are three discernible patterns of relationship between analyst and analysand, no one of them ever obliterated (although it may be ignored), coexisting and intimately interrelated in contrapuntal fashion: the real and actual integrated personal relationship, which includes the basic vocational (essentially physician–patient) relationship: the transference-countertransference relationship; and finally the unique system of routinized activities, deprivations, and prohibitions which find origin in the requirements of analytic technique but which, *unlike* most other technical systems, must be "*lived out*" in a full personal sense. Unfortunately, these cannot be separated in fact, as they can be by a few lines in schematic representation, and error or lapse in one sector is reflected in all. There is, throughout the process, the presence of the patient as an integrated adult personality, larger than the sum of his psychic parts or functional systems. Whereas purely technical or intellectual errors can, in most instances, be corrected, a failure in a critical juncture to show the reasonable human response which any person inevitably expects from another on whom he deeply depends, can invalidate years of patient and largely skillful work. It is indeed my impression, from a few observations, that the invalidation can occur with equal effectiveness in *anticipation* of the work (in a preliminary interview, for example). As mentioned before, continuance, even enthusiasm, in analysis is by no means incompatible with profound resentment and mistrust, sometimes quite or relatively unanalyzable, because documented or felt to be documented in reality. Such continuance may, perhaps often does, provide the patient with the ready-made "acting out" of a profoundly neurotic element in his character structure. It is often true that the patient (in some instances, unconsciously) distinguishes between reactions due to faulty technical principle, relatively benign therapeutic anxieties, and more profound individual countertransference attitudes in the analyst; and that the responses show corresponding variations in severity. I believe that these groups of "human failure" are common, and that a different emphasis or mode of statement in the teaching of certain basic formulations can be an important affirmative step in both scientific and practical directions. . . .

If it is the entanglement with early objects which elicits the infantile neurosis and lays the ground for its later representation in the transference neurosis, it is the clinical neurosis, the usual motivation for treatment, which lies between them, and is related to both, in a sense a "resistance" both to genetic reconstruction of the former, or to current involvement in the latter. This is, to be sure, a variation of Freud's statement (1914, p. 154) regarding the transference neurosis as an accessible "artificial illness." Perhaps it is not extravagant to suggest that unconscious recognition of the unique transference potentiality of the psychoanalytic situation is intimately connected both with the violent irrational struggle against and the sometimes fanatical acceptance of analysis as therapy (i.e., the general and intrinsic fascination of a relationship to "the doctor who gives no medicine") by the patient to whom it is recommended (and by many, prior to the fact). What is *always* fundamentally wanted, in the sense of primal transference, with rare (relative) exceptions, is the original physician, who most closely resembles the parent of earliest infancy. The "doctor who gives no medicine" is unconsciously a priori the parent of the repetitive phases of separation. To what extent this unconscious constellation participated in the discovery or creation of psychoanalysis as such would be pure speculation. However, Freud's capacity for transferences in the attachments of daily life is abundantly evident (Freud 1887–1902, Jones 1953–1957); and the importance of the relationship with Fliess in his self-analysis has been explicitly stated (Freud 1887–1902, pp. 43, 212.) That it plays an important part in the emotional life of many contemporary working analysts is very likely, since all (at this time) have experienced the role of analysand (or analytic patient); the vast majority are physicians; all have been physicians' patients in a traditional sense; and, certainly, all have been dependent and helpless children. Ferenczi (1919) described the evolution of the general psychoanalytic countertransference in terms of initial excessive sympathy, through reactive coldness ("the phase of resistance against the counter-transference"), to mature balance. Lewin (1946a) in referring to this formulation (to contrast it with the sequences of traditional medical training) attributes the first phase to the *fact* of the analyst's having only recently been a patient himself. While Lewin carefully separates the cadaver (the student's first "patient") as an "object" (psychoanalytic sense) from its qualities, we may reasonably speculate that a species of retaliatory mastery of the parental object (perhaps in contrast with the role of helpless child) is sometimes involved in this gratification and that something of this quality is carried into the dialectic genesis of the psycho-analytic situation. Again, see Freud's contrast between the work of a "man of letters" and his "dissection" of Dora's mental state (although, to be sure, the reference is "surgical" rather than anatomical!) (1905, p. 59). (Also, again, see Fliess's special and interesting elaboration of this theme [1949].) When I refer to the "dialectic genesis" of the psychoanalytic situation, I refer to its genesis largely in the genius of a physician who experienced the training to which Lewin refers. The dialectic is epitomized exquisitely in the role of speech, the bridge for personal separation, rejected or distorted by children in their desperate cling-ing to more gratifying or more violent object drives, or, on the other hand, sought eagerly as the indispensable vehicle for alternative ego-syntonic developmental aspirations. (See Nunberg [1951] regarding the "Janus" quality of transference.)

The transference neurosis, as distinguished from the initial transference, usu-ally supervenes after the treatment has lasted for a varying length of time. Its emergence depends on the combined stress of the situational dynamics and the pressure of the interpretative method. The latter tends to close off habitual re-petitive avenues of expression, such as new symptom formation, acting out, flight from treatment, etc. The neurosis differs from the initial transference, in the sense that it tends to reproduce in the analytic and germane extraanalytic setting an infantile *dramatis personae*, a complex of transferences, with the various con-flicts and anxieties attendant on the restoration of attitudes and wishes paralleling their infantile prototypes. The initial transference (akin to the "floating" trans-ferences of Glover [1955]?) is a relatively integrated phenomenon, allied to char-acter traits, an amalgam or compromise of conflicting forces which has become established as a habitual attitude, the best result of the "multiple function" of which the personality is capable, in the general type of relationship that now confronts it. It differs from its everyday counterpart only in its relative separa-tion from its usual everyday context, in the relative lack of tangible provoca-tion, justification, or substantiation, and — sooner or later — in the failure of eliciting the gratifications or adaptive goals to which it is devoted. As time goes on, varying as to interval before and character of emergence, with the nuances of the patient's personality organization and the analyst's technical and personal approach, the unconscious specific transference attitudes will press for expres-sion against the defenses with which they have been hitherto integrated, in vary-ing mixtures of associational derivatives, symptomatic acts, dreams, often "acting out," and manifest feelings. At this point (or better, in this zone of a continu-um), conflict involving the psychoanalytic situation becomes quasi-manifest, and the transference neurosis as such is incipient. If I offer a brief and oversimple outline illustration it is only because there are various interpretations of these terms, and I should like to make clear my own rather simple usage.

A male patient may adopt a characteristically obsequious although subtly sarcastic attitude toward his older male analyst, quite inappropriate to the situation, but thoroughly habitual in all relations with older men. As time goes on, his wife and business partner become connected in his dreams with the analytic situation, his wife in the role of mother, the analyst as father, and his business partner as older brother, with corresponding and related anxieties and fluctuations of function in his business and sexual life. Violently hostile, sexually submissive, or guilty attitudes may appear in direct or indirect relation to the analyst, in the patient's manifest activities, or in the analytic material, in dynamic and economic connection with changes in the patient's other relationships. The entire development is often first announced in diffuse resistance phenomena in the analytic situation and processes (Glover 1955). The transference neurosis as such can, of course, be endlessly elaborated; when extended beyond the point of effectively demonstrable relevance to the central transference, its resistance function may well be in the foreground. It must be remembered that the whole array of strongly cathected persons in the individual's development, as well as the related variety of attitudes, are all distributed, so to speak, from a single original relationship, the relationship with a mother in earliest infancy. In all of them, there are elements of "transference" from this relationship, most conspicuously and decisively, of course, the shifting of hostile or erotic drives from the mother to the father. In a sense, then, the entire complex of the transference neurosis is a direct, although paradoxically opposed, derivative of the basic attachment and unrenounced craving, which arises in relation to the primal object, the more complicated drama relating to the original object attachment somewhat like that which Lewin (1946b) assigns to the elements of the manifest dream in relation to the dream screen. (This is, of course, not unrelated to Lewin's interpretation [1955] of the analytic situation in terms of dream psychology.) I stress this because in the analytic situation, the patient is again confronted with a unique relationship on which, via the instrumentality of communication by speech, all other relationships and experiences tend to converge emotionally and intellectually. In this convergence, however, there is a conspicuous differential, due to the intellectual or cognitive lag. In the latter sphere, the analyst's autonomous ego functions play a decisive operational role, via his interpretations. In the genesis of this lag, an important role must be assigned to the original (reverse) differential which may establish itself between the centrifugal distribution of primal object libido and aggression and the relatively autonomous energies of perception (the ego's "activity"). The detachment of libido and aggression from the primal object will of course be contingent not only on their original intensities but also on the special vicissitudes of early gratifications. If we consider the limitless panpsychic scope and potentiality of free association, we must assume that some shaping tendency gives the associations a form or pattern reasonably accessible to our perceptive and interpretative skill. It would seem likely that this is the latent inner preoccupation with the elements of the transference neurosis, the original transferences of which it is in itself composed, and finally the derivative vicissitudes of the primal object relationship itself, the primal transference. . . .

Any relationship between two people carries with it a potentiality ranging in intensity and quality from silent and blissful oral merger or cannibalistic incorporation or destruction, up to philosophical dialogue. In most adults the proximal conception of *physical* intimacy, acceptable if any is acceptable, takes the direction of either sexual union of varying degree and kind or fighting, their respective derivative variants in play or art, and, of course, the unique relationship with the traditional physician or surgeon or his representatives, most importantly the nurse. The latter may, of course, readily become the object of the *tender* components of the maternal transference.

Since the earliest physical urgencies intrinsically requiring the participation of another individual, and necessary both to life itself and to instinctual (i.e., libidinal and aggressive) development, find focal expression in the mouth, a few remarks concerning this unique sphere are in order. These urgencies are, of course, fraught with appropriately intense somatic reactions. In the sphere of aggression, except in desperate defense, the actual (nonpsychotic) use of the mouth and teeth by an adult is a relative rarity. Vampire fantasies are common, their materialization in any form, rare and dubious. The mouth is always important sexually (with a progressive cultural breakdown of oral-genital prohibitions); and the wish to eat one whom one loves is still a part of the affectionate talk of lovers and fond parents. The struggle with cannibalistic aggression, on the other hand, or indeed any sort of killing with the teeth, invokes a taboo of perhaps greater severity than the incest taboo. To be sure, the two are connected, via the totem feast, and anterior to that, the aggressive incorporative urges toward the mother. The taboo on cannibalistic aggression finds biological support in two important directions. One is the development of remarkably versatile, subtle, and skillful *hands* for motor action. The hands are also extremely sensitive and perceptive in tactile and stereognostic sense. They are importantly involved in erotic activity, are the most essential and effective organs in hostile action, and certainly are the essential intermediary organs for the myriad tools, instruments, and weapons which man has evolved. That the hands (and arms) can also participate importantly in a function usually associated with incorporation (of libidinal emphasis) has recently been stressed by Krapf (1956). The second source of support is the even more distinctively human function, *speech*, which enables man to code the whole evident universe and his reactions to it, and to make such material mutually transmissible, as an autonomous ego function. (In relation to the *superego*, note Isakower's emphasis on the auditory sphere [1939] and Waelder's somewhat earlier concept of the "formal functions" as preconditions of speech and culture [1937].) The development of speech also provides man with a potential shift in libidinal and aggressive economy of far-reaching consequences. In favorable development, this indispensable function facilitates a remarkable system of sublimated (or neutralized) expression for, and defense against, the primal oral-destructive aggressions and certain untenable anal and urethral impulses. The same is true of primitive oral-libidinal impulses and fantasies, which must be largely renounced: sucking directed toward living objects and the libidinal fraction of the drive to incorporate objects. There is also a species of undoing or reconstruction for the destructive aggressions, in the cultural role of speech, most concretely and durably in the (manually expressed!) form of printed books. A third factor supporting the taboo on oral destruction may be suggested. This is explicitly cultural in character, yet, as far as I know, so widespread among humans, that there is doubt about the existence of tribes who live without it. Among crucial uses and unconscious symbolic meanings of *fire* is its use in cooking. In its primitive sense, this process would specifically diminish the energic investment required for violent and prolonged biting and chewing, thus freeing such energies for displacement, more elaborate utilization, or neutralization. (See Arlow [1955], and Joseph [1960] for emphasis on the oral-aggressive *symbolism* of fire and its implications.)

The psychoanalytic situation is one in which two persons in the state of "intimate separation" which we have already emphasized, express the whole gamut of tensions that may arise between them almost exclusively through the medium of speech, sacrificing not only pedal locomotion but also that specifically human instrumentality which provides biologic relief of profound oral-aggressive tension, the use of the hands. To this extent, there is an obvious resemblance to some of the normal conditions for dreaming. Even major gesticulation, a type of language (see Needles 1959), is liable before long—like other symptomatic acts—to be brought rapidly into abeyance, to facilitate the verbal and analytic process. The intimate early developmental relationship between hand and mouth has been stressed by psychoanalytic writers, for example, Hoffer (1956) and Spitz (1957). Through the intensiveness of the psychoanalytic relationship (i.e., frequency and duration of sessions) an "everyday" consideration is added, which tends to support the primordial fantasy of a single original object as an alternative to the rest of the world. The struggle against separation (the fundamental *biological* factor in anxiety [Freud 1926]) constitutes one of the basic general problems of human development, defended against in primitive fantasy most summarily by oral incorporation or its derivative (perhaps cognate?) phenomena (Fenichel 1937), with varying proportions of hostility or libido. It is therefore not surprising that the pressure of such impulses often threatens the overburdened function of speech with lapses or prolonged interruption of this consistent and essential instrumentality of psychoanalytic work. It is, by the same token, not irrelevant that one of the very early (and perennially useful) discoveries regarding the impingement of transference on technique was the relationship between the "blank" silence and emergent transference material (Freud 1912a). There is, as described by Money-Kyrle (1956), the corresponding problem in the analyst, in which failure or obstruction of *understanding* is corrected by the introjection of the patient, or can lead to more complicated introjective-projective sequelae. When these constitute major countertransference crises, they must assuredly be regarded as different, at least economically, from the vestigial elements of empathic identification which probably play some role in all genuine understanding. To be sure, in keeping with the widespread dualism in human impulse, there is also, directed *against* the clinging to an original object, a nonpathological urge toward separation and individual development, profoundly bound up with biological maturation. To the extent that this is connected with a largely libidinal object relationship, one may think of this affirmative trend toward separation as the origin of the "mature" type of transference which I have mentioned before, which may well provide the ultimate basis for insight as an autonomous ego function, as opposed to its primitive transference or symptomatic functions, in the sense described by Ernst Kris (1956). The element in the therapeutic relationship to which I refer has, of course, long been recognized and referred to in a variety of terms or descriptive or differentiating phrases, from Freud (1912a) onward (for example, Lagache 1953, Macalpine 1950). My emphasis is on its (relatively) independent origin and power. One might indeed think of one aspect of the "good analytic hour," so admirably described by Kris (1956), as a shift of emphasis in the triphasic personal relationship, toward a view of the analyst that invests with libido his correctly perceived role as an actual person, and, more specifically, as an effective interpreter of the analysand's inner world, with a corresponding decathexis of the primitive therapeutic transference images, i.e., both its id and superego aspects. We should note that the immediate experience of true integrated insight usually includes an id (i.e., oral or grasping) component (Kris 1956). In the same sense, the affirmative maturational tendency and the transference expectation that accompanies it, provide a basis whereby the essential dialogue of analysis, i.e., free association and interpretation, may gradually assume a relatively autonomous functional significance. For the patient, this signals the potentiality for a genuine distribution of libido and aggression from a single object to the remainder of the world and a mode of communication with an appropriate object *about* the world, or indeed (and importantly) about himself. This would stand in contrast to a discourse, which in itself represents essentially a highly cathected mode of relationship to the transference object, with an implicit ultimate drive to substitute him for the world. I think of transference in the latter sense as originating in the insistent irredentist craving for union with the original object, the principal and general Anlage of the "transference resistance" and therefore opposed to the craving for understanding, instruction, and facilitation of the displacement of interest to the environment (see Nunberg 1951). It may be observed even in the infantile struggle with speech itself, in the persistent mannerisms and private habits of speech, which may vary extremely from child to child. The extreme instance, in severe illness, is literal mutism, a massive morbid representation of the minute paradigm of the "blank" analytic silence. The economic shift in clinical transference that I have mentioned may not be as easy to come by as we sometimes think. This was dramatized for me by the rather sudden direct statement of a very intelligent patient, who had returned for occasional brief periods of follow-up interviews over several years, subsequent to the termination of analysis. The patient was gratified that she could now regard me as an *analyst* and in a *positive sense*! It is also important to mention that this redistribution of aggression and libido which we have in mind is to be sharply distinguished in its genuineness from "acting out," where other objects are *perceptually* differentiated *substitutes* for the transference object, in a sense recapitulating the original disturbance. The failure of such actual and original distribution is, I think, one of the general and basic phenomena in the pathogenesis of the neuroses.

The role of speech in analysis, to which I have already made several references, has been the subject of relevant and important studies. I mention a few of special significance in relation to our present theme. In 1940, Sharpe, in a brief paper on metaphor, emphasized the instinctual contributions to the formation of speech: the concurrence of establishment of sphincter control with incipient speech, the capacity of words to represent bodily substances, with appropriate affects, and (one might say) the "return" of the original instinctual components in the use of metaphorical expressions in analytic free association. More recently, Fliess (1949) pursued the theme of speech further in a study of free association and the phenomenology of regressive analytic "silences." Among several interesting inferences in this paper, the following are relevant to our discussion: (1) that the regressive element in the speech of free association, which involves actual physiological energies, constitutes in itself a force tending to weaken repression and (2) that the "oral" silence may be regarded as a temporary "deprivation" of the speech function, in relation to the threatened emergence of archaic oral (including oral-incorporative) impulses. Lewin, in reinterpreting the psychoanalytic situation in the context of dream psychology (1954, 1955), has again stressed the analogies between the analytic situation and hypnosis, thus with the wish to sleep. The analyst, depending on the trend of his interpretations, becomes, in a sense, a waker (when he makes id interpretations) or the opposite (when he interprets an ego defense). Lewin does not stress the other elements of his "oral triad" in this reference, although one may assume their dynamic place in the formulation. From my point of view, insofar as speech is par excellence a mode of communication and thus of object relationship, it would be this element of cannibalistic incorporation, projective and introjective, which provides the primal transference substrate on which the entire phenomenology of speech or lack of speech (in this context) rests. Lewin (1954) speaks of the "blank dream" as paralleling literal sleep in the analytic hour. In relation to the concept of the analyst as a paternal "disturber," he mentions in passing a patient (with duodenal ulcer) described by me (1947), who fell deeply asleep whenever I began to talk. This was a profound, if evanescent, narcissistic regression in which libidinal and sadistic impulses coalesced and were turned inward, in a complicated overdetermined reaction to *my words* as penis or breast. I would postulate that the "wish to be eaten" was also present, my speech projectively reduced to its primal (cannibalistic) substrate. It was as though all of the complicated phenomena of the individual's mental and emotional life were at this point funneled into the conflict situation: (intrauterine or prenursing) sleep *versus* speech, with the cannibalistic impulses as the momentarily impassable bridge between them. One can imagine how — except as wholly or partially "worked through" in the analytic situation — such latent mechanism would seriously burden the entire superstructure of personality, in which the wide and profound ramifications of speech play so large a functional role. It is likely that in the depressive, possibly also in the catatonic, stupors, there are large-scale pathologic variants of the same miniature model. Speculations regarding possible relationship with the psychologic mechanisms of electroshock or insulin therapy, I must leave to those more familiar with them.

Loewenstein (1956) has devoted a paper to the role of speech in psychoanalytic technique. While he focuses mainly on the operational role of speech as an ego function, as communication in the adult psychological sense, he does emphasize the heightened subjective reality with which a memory or thought become invested in being communicated to the analyst. Elsewhere (1956), Loewenstein, in commenting on the essential dynamic role of verbalization as such in psychoanalytic treatment, mentions that "spoken words become objects created by the act of speaking." (A related, more primitive phenomenon may contribute to the effectiveness with schizophrenics of Sechehaye's "symbolic realization" [1956].) This phenomenon may well be connected, at least in part, with the intermediate status of speech between mental and somatic activity, between the insubstantial psychic world to which it contributes so decisively and the world of material objects that it is continually recreating in (at least initial) opposition to the destructive impulses, perhaps first and most spectacularly represented by the mouth and its activities. It is likely no accident that the aggressive functions of speech, as Loewenstein (1956) notes, can actually *exceed* in objective effectiveness the actions for which they substitute. Apart from the endless range of subtlety and nuance of speech as a distinct function in relation to uniquely effective aggression, we must recognize that aggressor and victim in a verbal attack share alike the archaic fantasies that derive from the mouth and teeth.

I mention my own paper on "The Principal Obscene Word of the English Language" only because I believe it illustrates what complicated moments of instinct and defense may be reconstructed concerning the genesis of a single word and thus at least suggests certain possibilities about the structure of language in general. In an obscene word, to be sure, the expressive and pleading elements are still far preponderant over its relatively objective referential significance, regardless of how it may be manifestly used. The slightest nuance of voice or semantic context can turn such words from a sexual direction to one of contempt or aggression. In the particular word considered, both this potentiality and the long journey from the oral-receptive to the phallic sphere are encompassed within its very derivation and structure. The impact of any obscene word has a hallucinatory evocativeness in which any or all of the senses may participate, as though there were physical action, physical contact. Yet, from this very vantage point, that of a discernible primitive emphasis, the study of such words may have much to contribute to our general linguistic knowledge and theory. For, apart from specific semantic content, however diluted or muted by linguistic change, the elements of action, contact, emission, reception, and hallucinatory imagery remain significant in speech and are exaggerated in the psychoanalytic situation, where other modalities of human relationship are minimized.

It is, of course, understood that speech is a function for which man has specific neurophysiological endowments, that it is an autonomous ego function. Nevertheless, as in all such functions, its autonomy is relative; it is susceptible to regression, to invasion by conflict. And it is, furthermore, in itself a vehicle of actual object relationship, which arises as the more intimate and direct bodily contacts with the mother are drawing to an end or becoming greatly attenuated. As an actual, if complicated, sensory relationship between two persons, speech can be utilized regressively as a whole, as a substitute expression for the more primitive bodily impulses, as well as for communication of the secondary mental processes, and the imagery and abstractions of the whole inner and outer environmental world. Thus the speech relationship has an important economic position in the transference relationship, for example. It can, if the individual be of appropriate disposition, play a demonstrable and large, if temporary, substitutive role in an analysand's sexual life. Of this I have seen striking and unequivocal examples in my own practice, in individuals of demonstrated adult sexual viability. On the other hand, to the extent that speech in its intimate alliance with thought, extending into the most elaborate integrations and abstractions, is actually a separate and distinct function. Thus it would not be comprehensively correct to equate outright the understanding of verbal communications, for example, with the introjection, or the phenomenology of acceptance of a mutative (transference) interpretation with the introjection of parts of a good object (see Strachey 1934, also his and Fenichel's comments in Symposium 1937). The same reservation would have to be borne in mind in relation to Money-Kyrle's illuminating contribution to the vicissitudes of understanding in the countertransference (1956). To make clear the continuum with, and the probable continued integrated participation of, primitive mechanisms as such is a valuable contribution; the same is true of awareness of the regressive potentiality, whether as pathological experience, or "in service of the ego." The latter would probably include the phenomenon of benign and transitory empathic identification, so important for understanding, where ordinary modes of communication prove not quite adequate (Fenichel 1937). However, the communication of insight as such, the neutralizing of instinctual energies, the conversion of primary-process elements into directed thought, and the extension of the integrating scope of the ego, are all mediated in good part through the indispensable function of speech, largely in its referential functions. Thus, if we think of normal individuals exchanging a sort of mutual psychotherapy, in accordance with one another's transference needs, we may view this (at least in part) as a matter of mutual introjection; but it should be clearly distinguished from the corresponding pathological mechanism (for example, that of a depression), in that the latter is archaic and preponderant as to libidinal and aggressive investment in relation to the object or the object's unconscious representation. One may accept understanding, love, admiration, help, and knowledge from one's friends and even absorb traits that one admires. However, it is precisely the preservation of the object and the basic libidinal object relationship which differentiates such relationships from their primitive counterparts. The preponderant mediation of the relationship through the neutralized energies of speech and allied modalities contributes decisively to this preservation. The archaic mechanisms persist, it is true, but in a usually minimal economic role, which is sometimes insignificant, in the same sense that the "normal" person dreams and his dreams (in my observation) may not be strikingly different from those of a severely ill individual. One may indeed sometimes see trends appearing with special clarity in dreams, precisely when their quantitative role in character or symptom has diminished to a remarkable degree. The same is true, in an even more elaborate sense, of the freedom of verbal expression of hitherto warded-off feelings and ideas. In regard to speech and thought versus primitive introjective mechanisms, it is likely, in addition to the economic factor in the general sense, that the question of the presence, nature, and degree of *original* destructive aggression directed toward primal objects is critically important and that this factor may, if it does not demonstrably inhibit, at least render vulnerable or precarious or less genuinely integrated, the more elaborate, later-developing mechanisms (see Flescher 1953). We are all familiar with individuals of great verbal facility and fluency, whose speech, however, exhibits a remarkable apparent independence from or shallow relation to the depths of thought and feeling. This phenomenon has a certain resemblance to the perceptual "differential" mentioned before. In such instances, the verbal facility so frequently prized in terms of analyzability (also professional analytic aptitude!) is deceptive, a formidable vehicle of resistance in itself and prone to yield early and striking oral transference improvement, with equally striking regression when ambivalence begins to assert itself. In such instances, the speech fluency is often parallel to a sucking (breast or fellatio) disposition, which serves as a regressive defense against profound oral aggression. It is as though the capacity to use the teeth for *food* is preserved, at the expense of depth, continuousness, and integration in psychic "dimension," as reflected in speech.

One aspect of the speech relationship in analysis, which has not been the subject of extensive comment, is its role in the instinctual economy of termination. We may think of the patient, in his transference neurosis, as engaged in the persistent vain effort to find gratification for regressed transference demands through the vehicle of speech, in any of its various functions, but quite usually, to some degree, through speech as a literal vehicle of "contact" in itself. When an analysis ends, there is, to be sure, the ending of a large and complicated relationship, involving many subtleties, but still one in which the psychophysiological function of speech has been preeminent. It is conspicuously "talking," marked by abundance, regularity, a unique framework of (voluntarily obligatory!) freedom, and a specific and constant object, which is interrupted when analysis is terminated. Since it is not only the conveyor of almost everything of which the human mind is capable but also an actual motor-sensory contact between two people, it lends itself all too readily to hidden trends of the transference resistance, to a sort of paradoxical "acting out" of primordial transference tendencies within the framework of the actual analytic work. It must indeed have become a largely autonomous ego function, like the insight in which it plays so important a role, if it is to be relinquished as such, without significant withdrawal reactions. I use the term *withdrawal* advisedly, because of its appropriately vivid physiological connotations. This is a change which varies greatly with individuals in its degree of actual achievement. Most are able to resolve the transference in a practical clinical sense. The established and actual energic (i.e., economic) role that this relationship attains in an individual's life by the sheer fact of its continued existence must be reckoned with in all patients, but especially in those individuals in whom the primal transference is a psychological (rather than a metapsychological) reality. Such patients, if able to involve themselves in the relationship at all, in a genuine sense, require a most resourceful combination of instruction, controlled gratification, and interpretation, to effect the gradual separation which was never genuinely achieved in infancy. It is my impression that the terminal diminution in frequency of analytic hours, which some patients require, whether on a planned and regular, or on an unplanned and irregular basis, not only has an obvious and important cognitive function but also constitutes a certain subtle (not always appreciated) "psychosomatic" process of attenuation. Within the scale of relative resolution of transferences, among other important variables, the readiness with which such resolution occurs bears an important relation to the readiness and genuineness with which the original working therapeutic transference can be established; for the borderline, the addict, and others of the more severe grades of illness dread this attachment, which for them seems to promise only a nightmare world to be dissolved or attenuated in anticipation, only at the cost of terrifying aggression and anxiety. The "mature" transference potentialities in such individuals are thin and wistful threads of aspiration that require a skillful type of cultivation, to which some have devoted special attention. For such patients, speech becomes a token and an evasion, however facile, or else a tenaciously required multiple system of regressed gratification. It is, indeed, in such patients that the primal type of attachment (as a "transference") is often "lived out" in everyday adult life as manifest impulse, or largely as defense, beneath a veneer or shadow-play of real involvement in the life about them. The therapeutic management of this type of total archaic relationship to the therapist has recently been discussed, in its technical interpretative aspects, by Stewart (1960).

Summary

I have stressed the broad psychobiologic sweep of the psychoanalytic situation, a potentiality derived from the state of relative physical and emotional "deprivation-in-intimacy" which it represents, and its mediation almost entirely through the complex psychosomatic activity of speech. In my view, it represents to the unconscious, in its primary and most far-reaching impact, the super-imposed series of basic separation experiences in the child's relation to his mother. In this schema, the analyst would represent the mother-of-separation, as differentiated from the traditional physician who, by contrast, represents the mother associated with intimate bodily care. This latent, unconscious continu-um-polarity facilitates the oscillation from "psychosomatic" reactions and prox-imal archaic impulses and fantasies, up to the integration of impulse and fan-tasy life within the scope of the ego's control and activities. The latter state is largely contingent on the development of true integrative insight and its ancillary phenomena (Kris 1956) as autonomous ego functions. With the important spe-cial field involved in the latter process, the problems of interpretation, we have not occupied ourselves in this presentation; our interest has been devoted to the equally indispensable and prior dynamic setting, in which interpretations can become effective. Anterior to the ultimately decisive question of the relative preci-sion with which the analyst's interventions illuminate the patient's dark inner world, the patient must react to these sometimes knifelike (perhaps toothlike!) intrusions into the hidden recesses of his personality, to an important degree, in accordance with the general emotional-intellectual context in which they are offered, apart from his intrinsic transference expectations. For here, as in other references, primitive transferences (and their illusory or hallucinatory sequelae) will tend to be superfluously activated or intensified, as the "mature" egosyn-tonic transference requirement is inadequately gratified. Underlying the entire dynamics and structure of the psychoanalytic situation, perhaps one of the in-spirations of its genesis, is the driving force of the primordial transference in its varying phase and conflict emphases, a phenomenon that is in itself derived from the successive states of separation from the mother. Opposed to it, and necessary to constructive analytic work, is what I have called (tentatively) the "mature" transference, a correlate of biological maturation, a phenomenon of integration of multiple function from the beginning.

The rudiments of the remarkable structure of human relationship which I have discussed arose in unequivocally medical situations. I have offered the hy-pothesis that the unique transference valence of the physician (no doubt intuitive-ly recognized in the traditional prohibition of sexual intimacies with patients) was more than an accidental fact in the genesis of psychoanalysis. It has been said that the neurotic patient, our original inspiration, not only suffers as a result of his specific transferences but also seeks insistently to cure himself through them (Ferenczi 1909). Insofar as the prolonged biological helplessness of the human infant and the contingent vicissitudes of the child-parent relationship remain of decisive and demonstrable significance in all optative aspects of human psychol-ogy, the medical origin of psychoanalysis is entirely consistent with the validity and the preeminent importance of the psychoanalytic contribution to general psychology. From the active and traditionally authoritarian physician-patient relationship, there has evolved a situation remote from the traditional medical relationship, in nearly all respects, except its ultimate purpose. Insofar as the primary unconscious configuration established by the situation is based on separation and deprivation of primitive gratification, in the context of verbal intimacy, the psychoanalytic situation has become a formidable instrument, both in the genesis of the transference neurosis and its subsequent analysis. A tentative reflection on certain gross biological elements in the situation impresses one with the considerable psychophysiologic tension implicit in it. On reexamination of original precepts and the development of traditional practices, one is confronted by an important question: may not the trend toward a schematic perfection in carrying out the principle of abstinence and allied technical precepts have overwhelmed awareness of the reservations supplied by common sense and intuitive wisdom from the beginning and thus subtly and inadvertently produced superfluous technical difficulties of paradoxical character? The tendencies I have in mind are the withholding or undue limitation of certain legitimate and well-controlled gratifications, which can provide a palpably human context for the transmission of understanding, which is, by general agreement, the central function of the analyst.

Deviations from the prevailing tendency have been left largely to individual intuitive judgment, a faculty which can, of course, never lose its important place in our work. Not seldom, I believe, in ordinary practice, deviations arise as miniature countertransference explosions of "humanness," facilitated by the analyst's own overwrought communicative abstinence. Occasionally, recommendations have been made for wide deviations of response, in relation to special pathologic requirements of certain patients (Freud 1954b, Stone 1954b, Panel Discussion 1958). The usual tendency, however, is to reiterate the applicability of the traditional "mirror" or allied attitudes for the "usual" neurotic patient. What I have in mind in this presentation is a subtle shift in the general base line of the classical psychoanalytic situation, applicable, throughout treatment, to *any* patient. This does not, of course, in any way exclude the wide excursions of attitude which may be necessary for special cases. Apart from artifact depth of regression and allied quantitative considerations, there is a further important question: is it possible that a relatively undistorted transference neurosis is *less* liable to arise where inevitable human resemblances to the original bearer of gratifications are systematically, indiscriminately, and superfluously blanketed, than in situations where this tendency is judiciously modified? In the former instances, I refer to the "blanketing" (1) which does not concern matters that impinge importantly on the central dynamics of the transference neurosis and (2) which is not invoked to avoid undesirable impedance of an important flow of free association at a given time, in both its cognitive and emotional significance. Here again, the unavoidable play of paradox enters. It has justly been emphasized that *too* great a resemblance to an original object can initiate an insuperable transference resistance (Bibring-Lehner 1936). In harmony with the general tendency of this presentation, it is my personal conviction that the countertransference, especially where it is ego-syntonic, would play an infinitely more important and frequent role in this connection than *surface resemblance.* Disqualifying resemblance, furthermore, is usually construed in relation to specific personal traits, rather than the general human and occupational traits that I have stressed. What may be forgotten is that the negative or deficit aspects of the analyst even in the general sense can, with probably greater frequency, because more poignantly painful, provide "resemblances" i.e., to the depriving or remote and bombastic parent of childhood, especially as castrated in fantasy or otherwise devaluated by infantile aggression. On the first part of this negative "resemblance," Ferenczi (1929, 1930, 1931, 1932) built the conception that the analyst must be experienced as different from the parent, a principle later elaborated by Alexander in a special direction. What I have recommended, in effect, is that the patient be permitted to experience his analyst's physicianly vocation (an integrated reality-syntonic representation of parental functions) as a stable and active reality of the relationship, to whatever degree may be necessary, without yielding any of the crucial issues of nongratification, in the sense of primitive transference wishes. In effect, it would be as if the patient were to feel that physician and analyst were really representations of the same object, rather than entirely distinct from one another, but employing changed instrumentalities of care and help. This would parallel in the unconscious the images of primary and secondary mother, the mother of bodily intimacy and the mother of relative separation. In both principle and practice, I regard this nuance as valid and important, sometimes decisive. Apart from the specific technical problems connected with this issue, there is an apparently remote, yet related, and not unimportant problem. I refer to the tendency toward the establishment of a new form of cultural transference-countertransference stereotype, in which the process of separation of psychological and somatic physician tends to reproduce too closely the original polarization of priest and medical man, investing the analyst with a priestly identity and authority, instead of that of the physician. In presenting a brief critique of the principle of unmodified "anonymity," which also participates in the intense psychophysiological tensions of the situation, I am aware that the affirmative issue, except in general principle, is less definitely crystallized in my experience and thinking, especially in the sphere of quantitative limitations and boundaries, and concrete technical precepts. I have tried to present these briefly in their present state of development, and I would hope to have something further to say on the subject in the future. In any case, it is my conviction that some experimental relaxation of stringency in this sphere can also be carried out not only without hazard, if reasonable judgment is exercised, but most often with appreciably heightened effectiveness for the psychoanalytic situation. I do not think that we can entirely eliminate the role of judgment and intuition from our work, in this any more than in other important references. In the classical psychoanalytic situation, we have an instrumentality of unique scientific productiveness, also of tremendous psychodynamic range and power. It can, however, be improved, not only as a therapeutic instrument but also in a genuinely scientific sense, if we accept confrontation with certain ineluctable — if not as yet well-formulated — psychological realities. For these are always by common agreement more important than formulations as such, however convincing the latter may seem in primary logical encounter and however valuable their actual historical contribution may have been and may indeed continue to be. Their continued, perhaps increasing, value may indeed rest on the openmindedness with which they are repeatedly tested against our realities and brought into conformity with them, as opposed to their arbitrary preservation as ideal standards, to which exigent realities must somehow be adapted.

REFERENCES

Alexander, F., and French, T. M. (with C. L. Bacon, T. Benedek, R. A. Fuerst, M. W. Gerard, R. R. Grinker, M. Grotjahn, A. M. Johnson, H. V. McLean, E. Weiss) (1946). *Psychoanalytic Therapy, Principles and Application.* New York: Ronald Press.

Arlow, J. A. (1955). Notes on oral symbolism. *Psychoanal. Q.* 24:63–74.

Bibring-Lehner, G. (1936). A contribution to the subject of transference resistance. *Int. J. of Psychoanal.* 17:181–189.

Breuer, J., and Freud, S. (1895). Studies on hysteria. *S. E.* 2.

Eissler, K. R. (1953). The effect of the structure of the ego on psychoanalytic technique. *J. Amer. Psychoanal. Assn.* 1:104–143.

_____ (1958). Remarks on some variations in psycho-analytical technique. *Int. J. Psychoanal.* 39:222–229.

Fenichel, O. (1937). The scopophilic instinct and identification. *Int. J. Psychoanal.* 18: 6–34.

Ferenczi, S. (1909). Introjection and transference. In: *Sex in Psychoanalysis.* New York: Basic Books, 1950, pp. 35–48.

_____ (1919). On the technique of psychoanalysis (Part IV — The control of the countertransference). In *Further Contributions to the Theory and Technique of Psycho-Analysis.* London: Hogarth Press, 1926, pp. 177–188.

_____ (1929). The unwelcome child and his death instinct. In *Final Contributions to the Problems and Methods of Psycho-Analysis.* London: Hogarth Press, 1955, pp. 102–107.

_____ (1930). The principle of relaxation and neocatharsis. *Int. J. Psychoanal.* 11:428–443.

_____ (1931). Kinderanalyse mit Erwachsenen. In *Bausteine zur Psychoanalyse* 3:490–510. Bern: Hans Huber, 1939. [Child-analysis in the analysis of adults. In *Final Contributions to the Problems and Methods of Psycho-Analysis.* London: Hogarth Press, 1955, pp. 126–142.]

_____ (1932). Confusion of tongues between the adult and the child (The language of tenderness and of passion). *Int. J. Psychoanal.* 13:225–230.

Flescher, J. (1953). The "primary constellation" in the structure and treatment of psychoses. *Psychoanal. Rev.* 40:197–217.

Fliess, R. (1949). Silence and verbalization: A supplement to the theory of the analytic rule. *Int. J. Psychoanal.* 30:21–30.

Freud, A. (1954). Problems of technique in adult analysis (with discussion by several others). *Bull. Philadelphia Assn. for Psychoanal.* 4:44–69.

Freud, S. (1887–1902). *The Origins of Psychoanalysis*. New York: Basic Books, 1954.

_____ (1898). Sexuality in the etiology of the neuroses. *Collected Papers* 1:220–248. London: Hogarth Press, 1924.

_____ (1905). Fragment of an analysis of a case of hysteria. *S. E.* 7.

_____ (1912a). The dynamics of transference. *S. E.* 12.

_____ (1912b). Recommendations to physicians practising psycho-analysis. *S. E.* 12.

_____ (1914). Remembering, repeating and working-through. *S. E.* 12.

_____ (1915a). Observations on transference love. *S. E.* 12.

_____ (1915b). Some character-types met with in psycho-analytic work. *Collected Papers* 4:318–344. London: Hogarth Press, 1934.

_____ (1919). Lines of advance in psycho-analytic therapy. *S. E.* 17.

_____ (1926). Inhibitions, symptoms and anxiety. *S. E.* 20.

_____ (1938). *An Outline of Psychoanalysis*. New York: Norton, 1949.

Glover, E. (1928). *The Technique of Psychoanalysis*. New York: International Universities Press.

Hoffer, W. (1956). Transference and transference neurosis. *Int. J. Psychoanal.* 37:377–379.

Isakower, O. (1939). On the exceptional position of the auditory sphere. *Int. J. Psychoanal.* 20:340–348.

Jones, E. (1953–1957). *The Life and Work of Sigmund Freud*, 3 vols. New York: Basic Books.

Joseph, E. D. (1960). Cremation, fire, and oral aggression. *Psychoanal. Q.* 29:98–104.

Klein, M. (1952). The origins of transference. *Int. J. Psychoanal.* 33:433–438.

Krapf, E. E. (1956). Cold and warmth in the transference experience. *Int. J. Psychoanal.* 37:389–391.

Kris, E. (1956). On some vicissitudes of insight in psychoanalysis. *Int. J. Psychoanal.* 37:445–455.

Lagache, D. (1953). Some aspects of transference. *Int. J. Psychoanal.* 34:1–10.

Lewin, B. D. (1946a). Counter-transference in the technique of medical practice. *Psychosom. Med.* 8:195–199.

_____ (1946b). Sleep, the mouth and the dream screen. *Psychoanal. Q.* 15:419–434.

_____ (1954). Sleep, narcissistic neurosis, and the analytic situation. *Psychoanal. Q.* 23:487–510.

_____ (1955). Dream psychology and the analytic situation. *Psychoanal. Q.* 24:169–199.

Loewenstein, R. M. (1956). Some remarks on the role of speech in psycho-analytic technique. *Int. J. Psychoanal.* 37:460–468.

Macalpine, I. (1950). The development of the transference. *Psychoanal. Quart.*, 19:501–539.

Menninger, K. A. (1958). *Theory of Psychoanalytic Technique*. New York: Basic Books.

Money-Kyrle, R. E. (1956). Normal counter-transference and some of its deviations. *Int. J. Psychoanal.* 37:360–366.

Nacht, S. (1949). Réflextions sur le transfert et le contretransfert. *Revue Fr. Psychoanal.* 13:367–380.

_____ (1958). Variations in technique. *Int. J. Psychoanal.* 39:235–237.

Needles, W. (1959). Gesticulation and speech. *Int. J. Psychoanal.* 40:291–294.

Nunberg, H. (1925). The will to recovery. In *Practice and Theory of Psychoanalysis*. New York: International Universities Press, 1961.

—— (1951). Transference and reality. *Int. J. Psychoanal.* 32:1–9.

Panel Discussion (1956). Problems of transference. *Int. J. Psychoanal.* 37:367–395.

—— (1958). Variations in classical psycho-analytic technique. *Int. J. Psychoanal.* 39: 200–242.

Scheunert, G. (1961). Die Abstinenzregel in der Psychoanalyse. *Psyche* 15:105–123.

Sechehaye, M. A. (1956). The transference in symbolic realization. *Int. J. Psychoanal.* 37:270–277.

Sharpe, E. F. (1940). Psycho-physical problems revealed in language: An examination of metaphor. *Int. J. Psychoanal.* 21:201–213.

Spitz, R. A. (1957). *No and Yes: On the Genesis of Human Communication.* New York: International Universities Press.

Stewart, W. A. (1960). The development of the therapeutic alliance in borderline patients. (Presentation before the New York Psychoanalytic Society.) Summarized (with discussion) in *Psychoanal. Q.* 31:165–167.

Stone, L. (1947). Transference sleep in a neurosis with duodenal ulcer. *Int. J. Psychoanal.* 28:18–32. *Reprinted in this volume, Chapter 9.*

—— (1954a). On the principal obscene word of the English language: An inquiry, with hypothesis, regarding its origin and persistence. *Int. J. Psychoanal.* 35:30–56.

—— (1954b). The widening scope of indications for psychoanalysis. *J. Amer. Psychoanal. Assn.* 2:567–594.

Strachey, J. (1934). The nature of the therapeutic action of psycho-analysis. *Int. J. Psychoanal.* 15:127–159.

Symposium (1937). On the theory of the therapeutic results of psycho-analysis. (E. Glover, O. Fenichel, J. Strachey, E. Bergler, H. Nunberg, E. Bibring.) *Int. J. Psychoanal.* 18:125–189.

Waelder, R. (1930). The principle of multiple function. *Psychoanal. Q.* 5:45–62, 1936.

—— (1937). The problem of the genesis of psychical conflict in earliest infancy, remarks on a paper by Joan Riviere. *Int. J. Psychoanal.* 18:406–473.

—— (1956). Introduction to the discussion on problems of transference. *Int. J. Psychoanal.* 37:367–368.

—— (1960). *Basic Theory of Psychoanalysis.* New York: International Universities Press.

Chapter 4

The Psychoanalytic Situation and Transference: Postscript to an Earlier Communication *(1967)*

The title of this paper is self-explanatory, though there is, I believe, somewhat more in the text than the title suggests. A summary of the original text is included, with some extension and elaboration of the original ideas in connection with the nature and origins of transference. There is also a brief response to what I felt to be misunderstandings or misinterpretations of positions that I stated in 1961. As well, there are discussions of two subjects not represented in the original contribution: (1) transference object and object representation and (2) the interplay of past and present and the role of illusion. This paper has a special (favorite?) position in my own overview of my work. I hope that others will find it useful.

what is trans of neurosis

In a lecture of May 1961, subsequently published in expanded form (Stone 1961), I sought to examine the Psychoanalytic Situation, the fundamental setting and field of force of our clinical work, in global fashion: historical, descriptive-clinical, and dynamic. In the interval, I have had the stimulating benefit of published reviews, and of a variety of other formal and informal responses to the contribution. Furthermore, entirely apart from the question of my own views on the subject, certain intimately related problems have continued to evoke thoughtful contributions. See, for especially relevant examples, the distinguished papers of Gitelson (1962), Zetzel (1965), and Greenson (1965). This long-delayed "postscript" was to give expression to the combined themes of response, comparison, clarification, and further reflection; however, it is clear that these cannot all receive adequate treatment in a single paper of reasonable length. I shall, therefore, emphasize certain selected issues, with the hope that other equally important matters may be dealt with at another time.

There are, in broadest perspective, two general themes in the original communication: a clinical review and point of view, with special attention to the overzealous and indiscriminate applications of the crucial and essential rule of abstinence; and an intimately related hypothesis regarding the underlying dynamics of the psychoanalytic situation as such. In my view of the psychoanalytic situation, transference assumed a pervasive and intrinsic importance, which I should like to review and elaborate somewhat further on this occasion. If my effort toward clarification sometimes broadens, deepens, and complicates matters rather than simplifying them, I offer apology which is not unequivocal; for this vast and relatively bypassed subject deserves reinstatement in its true and legitimately challenging confusedness.

However, before proceeding with this, in view of the fact that the technical aspects of the original book have occasioned the strongest reactions, usually as quite separate from its dynamic hypotheses, I should like to say a few words (in highly condensed fashion) in relation to occasional trends of misunderstanding or misinterpretation, which, it seems to me, would be readily dispelled by careful and nontendentious reading of the original text. For an outstanding and central example: the idea that the work proposes the bypassing of the transference neurosis seems inexplicable, in view of its intense concentration on the indispensability of that condition. What is true is that it proposes steps toward the avoidance of spurious iatrogenic regressions, whose tenacity may defeat the purposes for which the neurosis is invoked, i.e., that it be successfully analyzed. Certainly no "do-gooder" utopia, where kindness obviates skill, is suggested. The sophisticated developments of psychoanalytic technique are taken for granted; the decisive importance of interpretation is specifically stated. It is true that this complicated technical subject (Loewenstein 1957) is not dealt with as such in the book but is considered only in its total meaning in the dynamic situation. The question of the "scientific attitude," as evoked in this context, seems to me entirely specious. Science finds more decisive representation in the eye and mind of the participant than in a machine-imitating schema of response. The natural-historical method of observation is not outmoded; and it can better take account of inevitable, sometimes necessary or productive human variables, than methods which seek ostentatiously (and unsuccessfully) to eliminate them or to ignore their inevitable presence. Hippocrates was at least the scientific equal of most modern laboratory technicians. All of this is, of course, without reference to the indisputable fact that the conduct of a psychoanalysis must always place the therapeutic obligation to the patient before all other considerations. The subject of "legitimate gratifications," words which frighten some, if the relevant passages are not carefully read, comprises a tentative effort to codify to the extent possible, and to generalize the importance of, those reservations and exceptions to which Freud called attention from his first mention of the rule of abstinence. His concern about excessive regression was dramatically voiced in the *Outline* (1940), but the proposed remedies are somewhat unclear. With regard to a possible psychoanalytic "crypto-radicalism": if my views become more revolutionary, they will be stated as such. At this time, I regret that I cannot offer greater flamboyance. The problems of psychoanalytic technique remain dialectical, the principles of abstinence and firm general structure essential, and yet requiring a certain important and discriminating latitude in modification of the diagrammatic ideal of cognitive and emotional deprivation, lest the latter destroy or vitiate the very ends for which it is employed. There are, of course, other important questions. Some will be touched on, at least implicitly, in the following material.

THE PSYCHOANALYTIC SITUATION AND SPEECH

Can the psychoanalytic situation as such and in a general sense, be viewed as other than a special relationship between a patient and his doctor, exchanging, as Freud explains in the *Outline*, full and unreserved communication for full discretion and interpretative skill, based on knowledge of the unconscious?[1] Can it mean something different or more than this, unconsciously, to all patients?

Others before me have thought that the psychoanalytic situation and process as such have a general unconscious meaning, which reproduces certain fundamental aspects of early development. For example: in 1954 Greenacre and in 1956 Spitz offered concepts of the psychoanalytic situation and of the origins of transference, based largely on the mother-child relationship of the first months of life. Greenacre used the term *primary transference* (with two alternatives). Insofar as the concepts of Greenacre and Spitz emphasize the prototypic position of the first months of life, as *reproduced* in the current situation,[2] there are subtle but important differences from the view here presented. Nacht and Viderman in 1960 extended related ideas to their conceptual extreme, requiring metaphysical terminology.[3] One can readily conceptualize the regressive transference drive set up by the situation as having such general *direction* (i.e., toward primitive quasi union), a reservation which Spitz accepted and specified, in response to Anna Freud. It is indeed the activation of this drive and its opposing cognate which underlies my own construction of the psychoanalytic situation, which is seen primarily as a state of separation, of "deprivation-in-intimacy."[4]

With the prolonged, sequestered, and strictly abstinent contact of the classical analytic situation, there is inevitably for the patient, a growing and paradoxical experience of cognitive and emotional deprivation in the personal sphere, the cognitive and emotional modalities in certain respects overlapping or interchangeable, in the same sense that the giving of interpretations may satisfy to varying degree either cognitive or emotional requirements. The patient, we must note, also renounces the important expression of locomotion. If developed beyond a certain conventional communicative degree, even gesture or other bodily expressions tend, by interpretative pressure, to be translated into the mainstream of oral-vocal-auditory language. The suppression of hand activity, considering both its phylogenetic and ontogenetic relation to the mouth (Hoffer 1949), exquisitely epitomizes the general burdening of the function of speech, with regard to its latent instinctual components, especially the oral aggressions. I have emphasized that all of the great psychobiological tensions, actual, potential, and emergent, between two persons in a prolonged intimate relationship, are essentially concentrated in, find concrete and demonstrable expression in one great interpersonal vehicle, *the complex psychosomatic activity of speech* (Stone 1961). It is my conviction that, *without* superfluous deprivations, and whether or not the patient indicates it manifestly, the basic analytic situation is one of great primary austerity for the patient. With Macalpine (1950), Lagache (1953, 1954), and others, I believe that the reaction to this chronic deprivation is the regressive transference neurosis, based in its essential outlines on the patient's latent infantile neurosis.

From the objective features of this real and purposive adult relationship, one may derive the inference that "it represents to the unconscious, in its primary and most far-reaching impact, the superimposed series of basic separation experiences in the child's relation to his mother. In this schema, the analyst would represent the mother-of-separation, as differentiated from the traditional physician who, by contrast, represents the mother associated with intimate bodily care. This latent unconscious continuum-polarity facilitates the oscillation from "psychosomatic" reactions and proximal archaic impulses and fantasies, up to the integration of impulse and fantasy life within the scope of the ego's control and activities" (Stone 1961, p. 105).

Within this structure, the critical function of speech is seen in a similar perspective, (as a continuous telescopic phenomenon ranging from its primitive meanings as physiological contact, resolution of excess or residual primitive oral drive tensions, through the conveyance of expressive or demanding or other primitive communications, on up to its role as a securely established autonomous ego function, genuinely communicative in a referential-symbolic sense. To the extent that an important fraction of human impulse life is directed against separation from birth onward, the role of speech, which develops rapidly as the modalities of actual bodily intimacy are disappearing or becoming stringently attenuated (Sharpe 1940), has a unique importance as a bridge for the state of bodily separation. In the instinctual contribution to speech, considering it as a phenomenon of organic or maturational "multiple function" (Waelder 1936), the cannibalistic urges loom large; they, and more manifestly, their civilized cognates (to some degree, derivatives?), introjection, and the more complex phenomena of identification, exhibit their functional traces and their continuing potentiality for reemergence as such, at all times. In such view, the most primitive and summary form of mastery of separation, fantasied oral incorporation, is in a continuous line of development with the highest form of objective dialogue between adults. The demonstrable level of response of the given patient, in this general unconscious setting, will be determined (in ideal principle) by his actually attained level of psychosexual development and ego functioning in its broadest sense and by his potentiality for regression.

In relation to this view of the psychoanalytic situation, one may reconstruct two essential and original streams of transference, from which the various clinical and demonstrable forms are derived. I have called them (somewhat ineptly): (1) the primal or primordial transference (from now on, primordial)[5] and (2) the mature transference. Both are responses to the fundamental psychobiological fact of separation and eventual separateness.

SEPARATION, THE PRIMORDIAL TRANSFERENCE, AND THE OEDIPUS COMPLEX

The primordial transference as here considered would be literally and essentially derived from the effort to master the series of crucial separations from the mother, beginning with the reactions to birth, as noted by Freud, and, in his own inimitable way, much earlier, by the poet-prophet William Blake (1757–1827).[6] This I mention, in Freud's sense of original traumatic situation (1926) and with due cognizance of his and others' disavowal of the fallacious psychological adaptations of the concept, notably in the one-time therapeutic system of Rank. This drive is present thence forward, and participates importantly in all of the detailed complexities of each infantile phase experience, with their inevitable contexts of warmth, pressure, skin, special sense, and speech contacts, in the problems of object relationship, separation and individuation, the multiply determined crises of adolescence, the specific neuroses, and many of the "normal" involvements and solutions of the conventionally healthy individual. One may assume for it an important participation, even if nonmanifest, in castration anxiety, also in "aphanisis" (Jones 1929). The striving, in short, is to establish at least symbolic bodily reunion with the mother. Further, the striving is to substitute this relationship for the kaleidoscopic system of relationships which have, in good part and inevitably, replaced it. This is a transference to the extent that actual and concrete—later, intrapsychic—barriers prohibit even part or derivative manifestations of this drive, in relation to the mother, requiring that, in varying modes and degrees, it be displaced to other individuals, sometimes even there undergoing secondary repression or otherwise warded off. In the instance where the drive actualization remains attached to the person of the actual mother, it is a primitive symbiotic urge, only a potentiality in relation to transference. This does of course exist clinically in very sick children (Mahler 1952). It is rare, in its explicitly primitive modalities, in adults, although not at all infrequent in its psychological expressions. That such striving may eventuate in a narcissistic solution (or more primitive regressive state, such as autism or primary identification) is certainly true; then only fundamental anaclitic strivings will persist; in psychotic states, even these may disappear. For the moment, I ask indulgence for the tentative concept that both erotic and aggressive strivings may, in various ways, express, facilitate, or subserve this basic organismic striving, apart from the empirical fact that disturbances in these spheres may be observed to initiate or augment it.[7] One may think of the original urge as having an undifferentiated or oscillating instinctual quality, like the bodily approaches described for psychotic children (Mahler 1952), or it may find more mature expression in the relatively neutralized need for closeness which causes the normal toddler, at a certain point, to recoil from his own adventurous achievement (Mahler 1965). While it is a universal ingredient of human personality, in a tremendous range and variety of expressions, the quality and quantity of this reaction, apart from innate elements, will be decisively influenced by earliest vicissitudes, certainly in the neonatal experience with the mother, possibly in the organismic experiences of birth itself (Greenacre 1941, 1945). It exhibits itself in the neonate, in a particularly distinctive biological sense, in those requirements for human contact—body warmth, pressure, skin stimulation, manual manipulation, and allied modalities of closeness—without which ultimate illness, even death, may result, regardless of how adequately basic physiological and biochemical needs are met. See Ribble (1944), Spitz and Cobliner (1965), and others.

The primordial transference only rarely appears as such in our clinical work. When it does appear, it leaves an impression not readily forgotten. This is the case when the underlying (as opposed to symptomatic) transference of the psychotic patient appears, displacing his symptoms, if only transitorily, or at times in conjunction with them. However, in the usual neuroses or character disorders with which we work, even most so-called "borderlines," this transference is in the sphere of inference, closest to the surface in the separation experience of termination, or in earlier interruptions, or in periods of extreme regression. It may be inferred at times in inveterate avoidance of transference emotion, in extreme and anxious exploitation of the formalized routines of analysis, or in inveterate acting out. What we usually deal with, in the working transference and the transference neurosis, are the phase representations and integrations of this phenomenon, and the larger and more subtle complexes of emotional experience clustering around them. Only a type of psychological need (or rather, demand) which sometimes assumes resemblance to original anaclitic requirements (for example, to exhibit indirectly the wish—rarely, to state it explicitly—that the analyst, in effect, *think* for the patient) would seem not infrequent, and often demonstrably allied to the original struggle against separation.

In the great majority of instances, the operational transference will come to display an intimate and critical relationship to the Oedipus complex. Here the primordial transference finds an especially important phase specification. The oedipal transference reiterates, in terms appropriate to the child's state of psychophysiological maturation, the inveteracy, the urge to kill if need be, to cling to the original object as the source of a basic gratification, which comprehends residual elements of past libidinal phases in its organization as such, intimately blended with complex attitudes of object constancy in a larger sense. It is, of course, the infantile prototype of the most general and comprehensive adult solution of the problem of separation, i.e., the institution of marriage. That this usually eventuates in the birth of children tends to close a circle in unconscious fantasy, by way of identification with the children. Obviously, in the healthy parent, this plays a minimal economic role, comparable to that of the residual and repressed incest complex. That the oedipal striving must be given up, in varying degree, in submission to *force majeure*, is a matter of the most far-reaching consequences for either healthy or pathological development. The phrase, "in varying degree," refers to its persistent unconscious fraction, the major energic source of everyday dream and fantasy life, neurosis, or creative achievement. It is also relevant to the general thesis of this paper to suggest that the important position of the Oedipus complex in relation to unconscious mental activity and specifically to that universal proximal derivative of the unconscious, the dream, provides a link between this climactic experience of childhood separation and the most primitive psychophysiological separation. It has been shown that the neurophysiological phenomena which are the objective correlates of dreaming are of strikingly high development in the neonatal period (Fisher 1965). The recently established prevalence of dream erection (Fisher 1966) awakens memories of and further reflections on Ferenczi's *Thalassa* (1938), at least in its ontogenetic aspects. At this point, one may well ask: "What of the girl who, development being reasonably favorable, turns to her father with a comparable striving?" If we recognize the important element of biologically determined *faute de mieux* in the girl's psychosexual development (i.e., the castration complex) and the multiple intrinsic and environmental factors usually favoring heterosexual orientation, I would suggest that this represents one of the early focal instances of reality-syntonic transference, which becomes integrated in healthy development. This is the "other side of the coin" from the boy's displacement of unneutralized hostility from his mother, as the first frustrating authority (even in relation to his access to her person), to his father. In optimal instances (again, allowing for inevitable unconscious residues), such reorientations become the dominant conscious and unconscious realities of further development.

This type of reality-syntonic developmental displacement is to be distinguished from the primordial transference problem, which is ubiquitous in the very beginnings of relations to proto-objects, i.e., the question of whether perceptual and linguistic displacement (or deployment) is accompanied by merely "token" displacements of libido and aggression away from the psychic representation of the original object, as opposed to genuine and proportionate shifts of cathexis. In other terms, is the "new object" really a person other than the mother who is loved and hated (to put it oversimply), or is the other person literally a substitute for the original object, a mannikin for that object's psychic representation? In the latter instance, the father is given cognitive status as a father. What is sought and sometimes found in him is a mother. This may be strikingly evident in the oral sphere, and may indeed be maintained for a lifetime. This is true transference (of primordial type), not "transfer" (to borrow the word tentatively from Max Stern [1957]), or "normal developmental transference," or "reality-syntonic transference." This deficit of varying degree, in instinctual and affective investment of the new and presenting real object, finds its mirror-image problem in the analytic situation, where there is a cognitive lag, which must be repaired by the analyst's interpretative activity, especially in the anticipatory transference interpretation. By this latter activity, recognition of the persisting importance of the original object, rediscovered in the analyst, can be established in consciousness, in relation to his current or developing affective-instinctual importance.

It would be beyond the scope of this paper even to summarize those complicated elements in the mother-infant reciprocal symbiosis which may be thought to exacerbate the primordial transference tendency. One may find invaluable suggestions toward such understanding in the growing literature on early mother-child relationships (or their disruption) (for example: Benedek 1938, 1949; Bowlby 1960, 1964; A. Freud 1965, A. Freud and Burlingham 1944, Greenacre 1960, Hendrick 1951, Mahler 1965, Murphy 1964, Ribble 1944, Spitz and Cobliner 1965, Winnicott 1953, 1960). The matter remains complicated; oversimplification is to be avoided. The same is even more true of reconstructions from adult (or even child) analytic work. The analytic work does provide, however imperfectly, a certain access to the residues of *subjective* experience in the period of infancy. Probably the eventual synthesis of the two will permit more dependable clarification. Obviously the relationship to a mother has many facets, even within each developmental phase; each can, to varying degree, introduce further complications, sometimes new solutions; furthermore, the life of an individual, beginning very soon after birth, will include other individuals, conspicuously the father, usually siblings, often adult parental surrogates, who can decisively influence development for good or ill. However, these considerations do not disestablish the general and critical primacy of the original symbiosis with the mother. In relation to the primordial transference striving (in the sense that we have just discussed it), my relevant reconstructive inferences from adult analyses point with general consistency only to the persistence of a variety of anaclitic needs and diffuse bodily libidinal needs (or rather, demands) accompanied by or permeated with augmented aggressive impulses and fantasies.[8] These, apart from innate infantile disposition, would seem often to be associated with maternal failures in necessary early bodily contacts, gratifications, and stimulations, as described by several authors. It would seem not unlikely that something like the Zeigarnik Effect, stressed by Lagache (1953) regarding transference in general, operates from earliest infancy. Thus the mother who responds inadequately, or who interrupts gratification prematurely or traumatically, is sought again and again in others, in the drive to settle "unfinished business." That an opposite or very different tendency may sometimes appear to have prevailed in certain segments of relationship (overstimulation, seduction, satiation, and sudden disappointment, for example) or may be demonstrable in complex spheres of the object relationship (parental possessiveness, undue demands, capricious harshness, failure to meet maturational developmental requirements, or myriad subtle variants) testifies only to the challenging complexity of the problem. Certainly, the phenomenon of regression, on the one hand from the oedipal conflicts, or — possibly more often than realized — from parental failures to meet the complex problems of relatively "neutralized" spheres of development, often contributes importantly to the clinical manifestations. Still, the anterior elements must be conceded at least a logical priority in shaping the child and his contributions to the pattern of later conflict.

In any case, the degree to which there is actual deployment of cathexis from the original object to other environmental objects, including the inanimate, determines (inversely) the power and tenacity of the primordial transference and probably has much to do with the basic predispositions to emotional health and illness, respectively. In other words, if there is true transfer of interest and expectation to the environment, with its growing perceptual (and ultimately linguistic) clarity, it exists for the infant largely in its own right, along with the primary object, the mother, whose unique importance is never entirely lost, in the development of most individuals. That there is also an organismic drive toward the outer environment is most assuredly true; and this contributes to what I have called the "mature transference," which I shall discuss later. On the basis of resemblances which progress from extreme primitiveness to varying grades of detail, the original object or part objects are sought by the primordial transference and often "found" in other aspects of the environment. It may well be that this urge provides an important dynamic element in primary process, and in the mature universal symbolic faculty. In any case, it is the actual power of this regressive drive, fraught at every step with conflict and anxiety, down to the ultimate fear of loss of "self," which can determine (in the light of other factors) whether the transference neurosis, indeed the given Oedipus complex itself, or the involvement in life in general, is a play of shadow-shapes or a system of relatively genuine reactions to real persons, perceived largely in their own right. I have compared this latent (dyadic) side of the transference neurosis—its "primordial transference" aspect—with Lewin's "dream screen" (1946), which really achieves full ascendancy only in the "blank dream."

It is important to emphasize that the primordial transference includes the actual or potential duality of body and mind within its own scope, and the distinction is of great psychodynamic, sometimes nosologic importance. However well the therapeutic transference (a specification, a derivative of the primordial transference) may have been analyzed, there is, for practical purposes (at least, I have never seen or known an unimpeachable exception), an inevitable residue of longing, of search for the equivalent of an omnipotent, omniscient, all-providing, and enveloping parent. The important issue for the individual's health and productiveness is that the critique of accurate perceptions and other autonomous functions be as actively participant as possible and that the social representations of this urge be as constructive and as consistent with successful adaptation as possible. The capacity to translate original bodily strivings into mental representations of relations with an original object, as literal needs are met in other ways, at least opens the endless realm of symbolic activities for possible gratification of the residual and irreducible primordial transference strivings. The anterior requirement, with regard to affirmative viability, is that such strivings, in their literal anaclitic reference, be detached from literal transference surrogates and carried over to functionally appropriate materials, processes, individuals, and transactions, the responsibility for their direction or execution essentially assumed by the individual himself, in early ego identification with the original object. With regard to sexual gratification, the persistent clinging to the primordial object or to literal transference surrogates (in the sense previously specified) leads through the pregenital conflicts to the peak development of the Oedipus complex, and (apart from other more specific factors) to its probable failure of satisfactory resolution.

Assuming that sexual interest is genuinely deployed to other objects, even in terms of unconscious representations, to the extent usually achieved, it remains nevertheless an important fact that bodily gratification is sought, usually by both individual and social preference, with another person who, at least in a generic organic sense, resembles the original incestuous object, most often including cultural-national "kinship." This holds a dual interest: (1) the general acceptance of the principle of symbolic "return" to the original object, if no father (or mother) must be thereby destroyed, or such aggression suggested by close blood kinship and (2) the paradoxical relation to the centrifugal tendency of the taboo on cannibalism. The latter, of course, with the advance of civilization, finds persistent representation only in symbolic ritual. In relation to the actual eating of flesh, the taboo *tends* to spread, not only to protect human enemies but also to include other animals with whom man may have an "object relationship," conspicuously the dog and horse. "Vegetarianism," of course, includes all animal life. There is no reason to doubt that the mother is the original object of cannibalistic impulse and fantasy, as she is the first object of the search for genital gratification. In the infantile cannibalistic impulse, the physiological urge of hunger, the drive for summary union, and the prototype of relatively well-defined oral erotic and destructive drives may find conjoint expression. That energies and fantasies derived from this impulse contribute importantly to the phallic organization was an early opinion of Freud (1905), which I believe to be profoundly correct. Except where severe pregenital disturbances have infused the phallic impulse as such with impulses (subjectively) dangerous to the object, the latter is not only not menaced with destruction (as in the cannibalistic impulse), but preserved, even enhanced. No doubt the critical difference in the cultural evolution of the two great taboos lies in the problem of the preservation of the object, as opposed to his or her destruction.

The Oedipus complex, in a pragmatic analytic sense, retains its position as the "nuclear complex" of the neuroses. For reasons mentioned earlier, it is a climactic organizing experience of early childhood. Apart from its own vicissitudes, it can under favorable circumstances provide certain solutions for pregenital conflicts, or in itself suffer from them, in any case, include them in its structure. Only when the precursor experiences have been of great severity is it a shadowy, organically determined new "frame of reference," which hardly has independent and decisive significance of its own. In any case, its attendant phallic conflicts must be resolved in their own right, in the analytic transference. From the analyst (or his current "surrogate" in the outer world), thus from the psychic representation of the parent, the literal (i.e., bodily) sexual wishes must be withdrawn and genuinely displaced to appropriate objects in the outer world. The fraction of such drive elements which can be transmuted to friendly, tender feeling toward the original object or to other acceptable (neutralized?) variants, will of course influence the economic problem involved. This genuine displacement is opposed to the sense of "acting out," where other objects are perceptually different substitutes for the primary object (thus for the analyst). This may be thought to follow automatically on the basic process of coming to terms with ("accepting") the childhood incestuous wish and its parricidal connotations. Such assumption does not do justice to the dynamic problems implicit in tenaciously persistent wishes. To the extent that these wishes are to be genuinely disavowed or modified, rather than displaced, a further important step is necessary: the thorough analysis of the functional meaning of the persistent wishes and the special etiologic factors entering into their tenacity, as reflected in the transference neurosis. Thus, I cannot subscribe, in principle, to the literal accuracy of the concept phrased by Wilhelm Reich (1933), "transference of the transference," as the final requirement for dissolving the erotic analytic transference, even though the clinical discussion, which is its context, is useful. This expression would imply that the object representation which largely determines the distinctive erotic interest in the analyst can remain essentially the same, so long as the actual object changes. Though a semantic issue may be involved to some degree, it is one which impinges importantly on conceptual clarity. I have often wondered what would have happened if an old popular song had remained current in the days when psychoanalysis became an important element in popular culture. The first line was—"I want a girl just like the girl that married dear old dad." The man who sang it in the dormitory shower would surely have suffered psychological lynching. Yet the truth is that the fortunate "average man," who has, even in his unconscious, yielded his sexual claim to his mother to his father's prerogative, can, if he very much admires his mother's physical and mental traits, seek some-one like her. The neurotic cannot do this, and may indeed fail in his sexual striving (in its broadest sense), even when the subject is disguised by the other appearance of remote race or culture.

Some Intercurrent Reservations

I am aware that such definite conceptualization of one basic element in the phenomenon of transference may be, indeed should be, subject to the reservations appropriately attaching themselves to any very clear-cut ideas about remote and obscure areas of observation and inference. On the other hand, I do believe that this view is not only relatively simple and well defined but also consistent with the clinical concept of transference, its clinical derivation, and its generally accepted place in the psychoanalytic process. Furthermore, it does encompass an important and intrinsic purpose of the psychoanalytic process, however imperfectly achieved. Such concepts are, however, always subject to further reflection, study, and—if need be—revision. This is also relevant to the general problem of transference versus therapeutic (or working) alliance. Whereas the "positive" transference was often in the past confused grossly and amiably with affirmative elements in the adult personal relationship or the therapeutic alliance, the tendency of recent years has been to make the distinction increasingly clear-cut (see, for example, A. Freud 1954, Greenson 1965, Stone 1954, Zetzel 1965). Here, too, the sharp distinction is clinically very useful, and represents an important advance over the loose and blurred terminology of the past. The view of the transference as distinct from the "real relationship," I have stated more than once (1954, 1961). However, the clear-cut, rigidly established distinction does not necessarily encompass all details of the reality. It is ineluctably true that certain real relationships or real personalities facilitate the development of transference in certain patients; others impede it, or the emergent transference is differently "slanted" in different instances. I have stressed the element of variable but necessary "resemblance" to the original object (1954, 1961) in the emergence of the transference response. This does not refer to "pure" (i.e., latent) transference, as it may be demonstrable in dreams, with or without therapy, or indeed autoplastically, in neurosis, for here the object is an old intrapsychic representation. Rather, it refers to that clinical transference which surges through defenses toward a real object of distinctive character, under special conditions, i.e., the analyst. It is also true that the therapeutic alliance includes certain elements of transference, as described earlier. Among these are the "mature transference," which (when genuine) is largely ego syntonic. The patient's character, even, to some degree, those epiphenomena deriving from cultural and family standards and values, cannot be dissociated from the mode of emergence, the expression, and the fate of the clinical transference. The degree of conscious acceptance, and thus the general economic distribution, of erotic or aggressive strivings will have much to do with such considerations. Or, the obstinate insistence on the carrying out or at least the indefinite maintenance, of erotic impulse and fantasy will probably be more often a function of widespread character traits than of the strength of the particular transference urge under consideration, as isolated from such interrelationship. Nor can such *quantitative* manifest reactions be separated easily and immediately from the qualities and traits of the analyst—his youth, quick wittedness, and physical attractiveness (or otherwise) —for single simple example. In the well-defined, relatively accessible forms of neurotic character, the adult ego-syntonic system of object relations is often dominated by the unresolved Oedipus complex, not seldom in manifestly nonerotic contexts, such as occupation. It is true that in such instances the connections with the incest complex of childhood can often be reestablished, that this theme will appear in the clinical transference, and that the germane character traits are not beyond reasonable modification. However, it is to be expected that the pregenital and other factors which have contributed to creating a neurotic character instead of a neurosis will have a widespread and tenacious place in the adult personality with whom one must deal in the analysis, regarding his transference, among other analytic problems. This is, of course, particularly relevant to the problem of "acting out."

The "nonneurotic" character, with a neurosis, is a compound of "transfers" (distinguished from "transferences" in the sense mentioned early in the paper) of ego-syntonic integrating identifications (beginning with the earliest identifications in the ego but including the important institution of the superego), clustered about and pervading the biologically determined maturational-developmental tendencies of the ego and the drives, in a relatively stable dynamic and economic interrelationship. His "transferences," the conflictual (unneutralized?) elements in his basic object relations, forced to operate through or across the (weakened) repression barrier, find expression in his neurosis. This would be assumed to include in a central position, in one form or another, the elements of the irredentist unregenerate Oedipus complex. The thrust of the dynamic wish would be (again, in "overclear" statement): "I want my mother sexually. Not just another desirable woman whom I can love, not even a woman just like my mother. *Only* my mother! Therefore I want to kill my father!" The next step in this idealized conception of transference is that any woman who excites desire is "perceived" unconsciously as the patient's mother, and any real (or fantasized) male rival, as his father, with a possible variety of predictable consequences. Clearly, the nonneurotic portion of the patient's personality has evolved in relation to the same critical early family objects as have the neurotic elements, and has the same biological core. It is unlikely, therefore, that they are permanently and rigidly disconnected from one another, except where (in principle) isolated traumatic elements have been consigned to repression. The neurotic character may often in the course of improvement, develop a neurosis. But even the individual "non-neurotic" character is in (less obvious) continuum with his neurosis, with his "transferences." The spontaneous onsets, fluctuations, or remissions of neuroses (and more subtle spontaneous alterations of character) are germane to this continuum. The affirmative aspect of this connectedness has been emphasized by Loewald (1960). If one keeps in mind the reservations mentioned earlier about clarity of conceptualization, the explanatory discussion of Kohut (1959), and Kohut and Seitz (1963), with accompanying diagram (p. 136), is a very useful contribution to the understanding of this complicated problem. Both Loewald and Kohut make important, although different use of one of Freud's three conceptions of transference, i.e., the "transference" from the unconscious to the preconscious (1900, pp. 562–564).

FURTHER COMMENTS ON PRIMORDIAL TRANSFERENCE

To the extent that the primordial transference includes, at least potentially, a largely psychological ("mental") component, the concept "transference of the transference" would be applicable to this component. For it does appear that certain aspects of the search for the omnipotent and omniscient caretaking parent are, for practical purposes, inextinguishable. As suggested earlier, there are indeed important qualitative and quantitative distinctions in the mode of persistence of such strivings. However, even to the extent that they are detached from the analyst and carried into some reasonably appropriate expression in everyday life, they retain at least a subtle quality which contravenes reality, one which derives from earliest infancy and remains — to this extent — a transference. Santa Claus lives on, where one might expect to meet him, whether as a donor of miracle drugs or of far more complex panaceas.

If one assigns to this parasymbiotic transference drive a true primordial origin, it is necessary to take cognizance of certain important concepts dealing with the earliest period of life. If we assume a powerful original organismic drive toward an original "object," a "striving" to nullify separation from the beginning, how does this square with concepts such as "primary narcissism," or the "objectless phase," or "the primal psychophysiological self" (Jacobson 1964)? (We note in passing that there are those who do not accept these as usually construed. See Balint [1937], for example, or Fairbairn [1963, Sullivan et al. 1963], or — conspicuously — Melanie Klein and her students [1952, Segal 1966]). These are states, variously defined or conceived, which apply to the earliest neonatal period in which mental life, to state it oversimply, exists only as potential, in physiological processes. Since there is (we postulate) no clear awareness of a self separate from the mother, there can be no "mentally" represented or experienced drive to obliterate the separation (referring to a self and object, conceived of as separate, in a continuing sense). There are, of course, discharge phenomena, the precursors of purposive activity; and there are urgent physiological needs, directed toward fulfillment or relief, rather than toward an object as such. However, in relation to these physiological needs as archaic precursors of object relationships, it must be noted that in all, except respiration and spontaneous sphincter relief (even in these instances, not without exception or reservation), the need fulfillment must be mediated by the primordial object (or her surrogate). There is also, of course, the uniquely important requirement for "holding" (Winnicott 1960), in a literal expression, from the outset. (The maternal partner in human symbiosis here supplies what the neonate cannot seek by "clinging"? See Bowlby [1960, 1964], Murphy [1964], and others.) In that sense, from the very beginning, there must be experience of physiological ebb and flow of tension (even if restricted to the coenesthetic), connected with a peripheral sensory registration, which is the protophase of the recognition of separation from the object (or nonpresence of the object) as a painful experience, her presence or apposition the converse. That the general context may be one in which the sense of unity is preponderant, or, more accurately, that there is no general awareness of "separateness" as such, means that the drive for union does not exist in a general psychological sense. It is, so to speak, satisfied. That object constancy, with its cognate "longing," is a later and quite different experience from the urgencies of primitive need fulfillment is true; however, regardless of what may be added by maturational and developmental considerations, instinctual and perceptual, there is no reason to assume other than a core of developmental continuity from the earliest needs and their fulfillment to the later state and indeed some continuing degree of contingency based on them. There is a very rough parallel in the way certain analytic patients, before a firm relationship with the analyst is established, signal certain primitive experiences and tendencies in special reactions to the end of the hour, to the nonvisibility of the analyst, to interruption of their associations, to failure of the analyst to talk, and similar matters. We must note that in the basic formation of the ego itself, there is evidence of primitive reactions to separations (Freud 1923, p. 29), in the form of very early identifications, based on caretaking functions (Hendrick 1951). Certainly in the very development of autonomous ego functions, not only the matter of specific training, but the quality and quantity of the mother's investment in them, have a decisive role in the character of their development. And in the case of object constancy, in its connotation of libidinal cathexis (Hartmann 1964, p. 173), where no need whatsoever (emotional or otherwise) is met for prolonged periods, the importance of the object is, to put it mildly, liable to deteriorate, or to suffer complicating aggressive change. Probably the characteristic features of the later developing relation to the object (love and the wish for love), as separable if not always separated from demonstrable primitive need fulfillment, have a special relationship to those "ancillary" aspects of neonatal nurture, mentioned earlier, whose lack has been shown to be an actual threat to life in some instances, not to speak of sound emotional development. So that from the first, regardless of the assumed state of libidinal (and aggressive) economy, or the assumed state of psychological nondifferentiation between self and potential object, there are critical precursive phenomena, objectively observable, and probably prototypic subjective experiences of separation, which are the forerunners of all subsequent experiences of the kind. One may generalize to the effect that, with maturation and development, secondary identification, and the various other processes of "internalization" in its broadest sense, the problem of separation and its mastery becomes correspondingly more complex, and changes with the successive phases of life, but never entirely disappears.

In the view of the psychoanalytic situation described earlier, the latent mobilization of experiences of separation stimulated by the situational structure awakens the driving primordial urge to undo or to master the painful separations which it represents, usually embodied in the various forms of clinical transference with which we are familiar. One legitimate gratification which tends to mitigate superfluous transference regression is the transmission of understanding. And this leads us to a consideration of what I have called the "mature transference."

THE MATURE TRANSFERENCE

It is sometimes thought that by the "mature transference" I mean, in effect, the "therapeutic alliance" or a group of mature ego functions which enter into such alliance. Now, there is some blurring and overlapping at the conceptual edges in both instances; but the concept as such is largely distinct from either one, as it is from the primitive transferences, which we have been discussing. Whether the concept is thought by others to comprehend a demonstrable actuality is a further question; this question, of course, can only follow on conceptual clarity. What I have in mind is a nonrational urge not directly dependent on the perception of immediate clinical purposes, a true "transference" in the sense that it is displaced (in currently relevant form) from the parent of early childhood to the analyst. Its content is not antisensual but largely nonsensual (sometimes transitional, as in the child's pleasure in so-called dirty words) (Ferenczi 1911) and encompasses a special and not minuscule sphere of the object relationship: the wish to understand, and to be understood; the wish to be given understanding, i.e., teaching, specifically by the parent (or later surrogate); the wish to be taught "controls" in a nonpunitive way, corresponding to the growing perception of hazard and conflict; and very likely the implicit wish to be provided with and taught channels of substitutive drive discharge. With this, there may well be a wish, corresponding to that element in Loewald's description (1960) of therapeutic process, to be seen in terms of one's developmental potentialities by the analyst. No doubt, the list could be extended into many subtleties, details, and variations. However, one should not omit to specify that, in its peak development, it would include the wish for increasingly accurate interpretations and the wish to facilitate such interpretations by providing adequate material; ultimately, of course, by identification, to participate in or even be the author of, the interpretations.[9] The childhood system of wishes which underlies the transference is a correlate of biological maturation, and the latent (i.e., teachable) autonomous ego functions appearing with it (Hartmann 1939). However, there is a drivelike quality in the particular phenomena, which disqualifies any conception of the urge as identical with the functions. No one who has ever watched a child importune a parent with questions, or experiment with new words, or solicit her interest in a new game, or demand storytelling or reading, can doubt this. That this finds powerful support and integration in the ego identification with a loved parent is undoubtedly true, just as it is true of the identification with an analyst toward whom a positive relationship has been established. That "functional pleasure" participates, certain specific ego energies perhaps, very likely the ego's own urge to extend its hegemony in the personality (Waelder 1936), I do not doubt. However, I stress the drive element, even the special phase configurations and colorations, and with it the importance of object relations, libidinal and aggressive, for a specific reason. For just as the primordial transference seeks to undo separation, in a sense to obviate object relationships as we know them, the "mature transference" tends toward separation and individuation (Mahler 1965) and increasing contact with the environment, optimally with a largely affirmative (increasingly neutralized) relationship toward the original object, toward whom (or her surrogates) a different system of demands is now increasingly directed. The further consideration which has led me to emphasize the drivelike element in these attitudes as integrated phenomena, as examples of "multiple function" rather than as the discrete exercise of function or functions, is the conviction that there is a continuing dynamic relation of relative interchangeability between the two series, at least based on the response to gratification, a significant zone of complicated energic overlap, possibly including the phenomenon of neutralization. That the empirical "interchangeablity" is not unlimited goes without saying, but this in no way diminishes its decisive importance. In my previous communication, I mentioned that the excessive transference neurosis regression, which can so seriously vitiate the affirmative psychoanalytic process, finds a prototype in the regressive behavior and demands of certain children, who do not receive their fair share of teaching, "attention," play, nonseductive affectionate demonstration, nonexploitative interest in development, and similar matters, from their parents. In the psychoanalytic situation, both the gratifications offered by the analyst and the freedom of expression by the patient are much more severely limited and concentrated practically entirely (in the everyday demonstrable sense) in the sphere of speech; on the analyst's side, further, in the transmission of understanding.

Whereas the primordial transference exploits the primitive aspects of speech, the mature transference urges seek the heightened mastery of the outer and inner environment, a mastery to which the mature elements in speech contribute importantly. I have elsewhere stressed that the most clear-cut genetic prototype for the free association–interpretation dialogue is indeed in the original learning and teaching of speech, the dialogue between child and mother. It is interesting to note that just as the profundities of understanding between people often include — "in the service of the ego" — transitory introjections and identifications, the very word *communication* representing the central ego function of speech, is intimately related etymologically, even in certain actual usages, to the word chosen for that major religious sacrament which is the physical ingestion of the body and blood of the Deity. Perhaps this is just another suggestion that the oldest of individual problems does, after all, continue to seek its solution in its own terms, if only in a minimal sense and in channels so remote as to be unrecognizable.

The mature transference is a dynamic and integral part of the "therapeutic alliance," along with the tender aspects of the erotic transference, even more attenuated (and more dependable) "friendly feeling" of adult type, and the ego identification with the analyst. Indispensable, of course, are the genuine adult need for help, the crystallizing rational and intuitive appraisal of the analyst, the adult sense of confidence in him, and innumerable other nuances of adult thought and feeling. With these giving a driving momentum and power to the analytic process — always by its very nature a potential source of resistance — and always requiring analysis, is the primordial transference and its various appearances in the specific therapeutic transference. That it is, if well managed, not only a reflection of the repetition compulsion in its baleful sense, but a living presentation from the id, seeking new solutions, "trying again," so to speak, to find a place in the patient's conscious and effective life, has important affirmative potentialities. This has been specifically emphasized by Nunberg (1951), Lagache (1953, 1954), and Loewald (1960), among others. Loewald (1960) has recently elaborated very effectively the idea of "ghosts" seeking to become "ancestors," based on an early figure of speech of Freud (1900, p. 553n.). The mature transference, in its own infantile right, provides some of the unique quality of propulsive force, which comes from the world of feeling, rather than the world of thought. If one views it in a purely figurative sense, that fraction of the mature transference which derives from "conversion" is somewhat like the propulsive fraction of the wind in a boat sailing close-hauled to windward; the strong headwind, the ultimate source of both resistance and propulsion, is the primordial transference. This view, however, should not displace the original and independent, if cognate, origin of the mature transference. To adhere to the figure of speech, a favorable tide or current would also be required! It is not that the mature transference is in itself entirely exempt from analytic clarification and interpretation. For one thing, like other childhood spheres of experience, there may have been traumas in this sphere, punishments, serious defects or lacks of parental communication, listening, attention, or interest. In general, this is probably far more important than has hitherto appeared in our prevalent paradigmatic approach to adult analysis, even taking into account the considerable changes due to the growing interest in ego psychology. "Learning" in the analysis can, of course, be a troublesome intellectualizing resistance. Furthermore, both the patient's communications and his reception and utilization of interpretations may exhibit only too clearly, as sometimes in the case of other ego mechanisms, their origin in and tenacious relation to instinctual or anaclitic dynamisms; greediness for the analyst to talk (rarely the opposite); uncritical acceptance (or rejection!) of interpretations; parroting without actual assimilation; fluent, "rich," endlessly detailed associations without spontaneous reflection or integration; direct demands for solution of moral and practical problems entirely within the patient's own intellectual scope; and a variety of others. It may not always be easy to discriminate between the utilization of speech by an essentially instinctual demand and an intellectual or linguistic trait, or habit, determined by specific factors in their own developmental sphere. However, the underlying essentially genuine dynamism which I have been discussing remains largely of a character favorable to the purposes and processes of analysis, as it was to the original processes of maturational development, communication, and benign separation. I agree with Lagache (1953, 1954) on the desirability of separating the current unqualified usage, "positive" and "negative" transference, as based on the patient's immediate state of feeling, from a classification based on the essential effect on analytic process. In the latter sense, the mature transference is, in general, a "positive transference."[10]

ARCHAIC FORERUNNERS OF TRANSFERENCE

The clinical fact of the interaction of drive, defense, and autonomous ego (sometimes superego) (Freud 1936, Nunberg 1951) in matters of perception, is indisputable, easily demonstrable in everyday life, where people so often "see what they want to see," occasionally even "what they *must* see," sometimes with strange combinations of both.[11] This tendency has an archaic Anlage. Very early in the history of specific interpersonal reactions is the three-month smiling response to any bearer of a moving face, without regard to individual traits (Spitz and Cobliner 1965). It may be quite reasonably assumed that this requires some degree of psychic organization, at least the existence of memory of gratification, and the capacity to associate this with an object in the outer world. What is striking is the rudimentary nature of the perceptual stimulus (two eyes, nose, forehead, and motion straight on) and the corresponding interchangeability of the objects (or object precursors). This is, in other words, a primitive "transference" response of a sort, a "prototransference"; at the very least, it is an Anlage of the capacity for displacement and generalization based on rudimentary (but nevertheless indispensable) resemblance, in this instance, limited to a "sign Gestalt," which will later appear in the transference phenomenon of adult life.[12] It is reasonable to assume that the question of sheer clarity, i.e., neurophysiological efficiency of perception, is fundamental in the (perceptual) aspect of the phenomenon. However, the response is definitely to a sign Gestalt associated with the bearer of security or gratification. It is not, therefore, beyond our consideration that neurophysiological immaturity and relative strength of drive are synergistic in this phenomenon, the prototype of much later, much more complex situations in which the "balance of power" among perceptual functions, defense, drive, and internalized prohibitions or demands may also modify perception or interpretation of perception, toward the heightened importance of the "common denominator." Only a few months after the smiling response (between six and eight months), the variously adverse reaction to unfamiliar persons appears. Again, since this is a sharp change in behavior, we may assume that it is, at least in great part, dependent on a sharply accelerated maturation of perceptual capacity. It may well be that the memory traces are richer in detail, and "unfamiliar" is correspondingly more nearly accurate. However, one must observe that even though the mother (or her surrogate) is uniquely favored, there is still some degree of displacement from the original nurturing or caretaking person to others in the immediate environment, and that the common features now have an important added dimension of "resemblance," the common denominator of "familiarity." Further, the distinctly negative reaction ("stranger anxiety") obviously includes something more than mere categorization as nonfamiliar. The stranger is bad, frightening, at least, in some way, distressing. Spitz explains this essentially on the basis of the child's recognition that the stranger is not his mother, that his mother "has left him." However, it is well to recall the view of Freud that the infant tends to externalize the source of his pains, discomforts, tensions. In the light of an established "good object" and a related coterie of "familiars," is it not likely that the unhappy stranger is the logical object for investment with hostility and fear, derived from the infant's own inner tensions and his inevitable negative experiences with the intimates, whom he is beginning to love. Xenophobia of varying degree is, of course, a reaction which is never lost in adult life; and Freud (1922) makes explicit reference to the proximity of the concepts "stranger" and "enemy" in relation to the paranoid mechanism. Possibly, in the Kleinian system (Klein 1952, Segal 1966), this phenomenon would be assigned to the "depressive position," the "nonmother" evoking the anxiety (or guilt) that the mother has been destroyed? Obviously, the question of what constitutes resemblance, of what is adequate for symbolism, condensation, and displacement, changes with the growing accuracy of perception and the richness of its associative background, with the increasing importance of reality testing, and of impulse control, which develop *pari passu* with general ego development, and the growing ascendancy of the "secondary process." With this development, the conditions facilitating transference evolve in rough correspondence, gradually including considerations of greater functional significance. (See Jacobson's 1964 discussion of this complicated evolution, in a different context.) There are individuals to whom complex human character traits or functions seem all but inextricably linked to physique. However, in line with maturation of discernment and the capacity for thinking in nonconcrete terms, the functional aspects of parents and the traits which accompany or influence parental functions, usually become increasingly important: the nurturing or caretaking and the inevitable disciplinary functions, in their satisfactory or unsatisfactory role in the child's

life. In any case, to most adults, the transference "tag" of the parentallike function is at once a stable, dependable, nonseductive reality and at the same time
a stimulus, through deep archaic reverberation, of the anaclitic, and still more
profound symbiotic, elements in the struggle against separation, which find representation in the various shades of the therapeutic transference. Furthermore,
to the extent that this is integrated in the adult reality of the analytic situation,
i.e., the analyst's physicianly commitment, no violence need be done to the patient's sense of reality or emotional requirement, currently or in the future prospect. Basically determined by the genetic aspects of the pathology, the economic
balance of the two streams of transference will nonetheless be influenced, as it
was in the original states of separation, by the nuances of the analyst's attitude,
i.e., by whether the successive "weanings" to understanding are truly "weanings to" (i.e., to other "food") in the original sense, or whether the emphasis
of the term is, as it is largely used nowadays, essentially in the sphere of deprivation, of giving up something.

Comments on the Transference Neurosis and Transference Interpretation

A few remarks about clinical considerations in the transference neurosis and
the problem of transference interpretation, may be offered at this point. The
whole situational structure of analysis (in contrast with other personal relationships), its dialogue of free association and interpretation, and its deprivations
as to most ordinary cognitive and emotional interpersonal strivings tend toward
the separation of discrete transferences from their synthesis with one another
and with defenses, in character or symptoms, and with deepening regression,
toward the reenactment of the essentials of the infantile neurosis in the transference neurosis. In other relationships, the "give-and-take" aspects—gratifying,
aggressive, punitive, or otherwise actively responsive, and the open mobility of
search for alternative or greater satisfaction—exert a profound dynamic and economic influence so that only extraordinary situations or transferences of pathological character or both, occasion comparable regression.[13].

It is a curious fact that whereas the dynamic meaning and importance of the
transference neurosis have been well established since Freud gave this phenomenon a central position in his clinical thinking, the clinical reference, when the
term is used, remains variable and somewhat ambiguous. For example, Greenson, in his excellent recent paper (1965), speaks of it as appearing "when the
analyst and the analysis become the central concern in the patient's life." I do
not wish to repeat in detail my own previous remarks in this connection (1961).
But I think that it is worthwhile to specify certain aspects of Greenson's definition, for the term *central* is somewhat ambiguous, as to its specific reference.
Certainly the term would apply to the analyst's symbolic position in relation to
the patient's experiencing ego (Sterba 1934) and the symbolically decisive position which he correspondingly assumes in relation to the other important figures

in the patient's current life. Although the analysis is in any case, and for many reasons, exceedingly important to the seriously involved patient, there is a free-observing portion of his ego, also involved, but not in the same sense as that involved in the transference regression and revived infantile conflicts. And there is, of course, always the integrated adult personality, however diluted it may seem at times, to whom the analysis is one of many important realistic life activities. I think it is rare then, although it certainly does occur, that the analysis actually exceeds in importance the other major concerns, attachments, and responsibilities of the patient's life; nor do I think it desirable that this should occur. On the other hand, if construed with proper attention to the economic considerations as mentioned, the concept is important both theoretically and clinically. In the theoretical direction, I refer to the assumption that there is a continuing system of object relationships and conflict situations, most important in unconscious representations but participating to some degree in all others, deriving in a successive series of transferences from the experiences of separation from the original object, the mother. In this sense, the analyst is indeed, to a uniquely important portion of the patient's personality, the portion that "never grew up," a central figure. In the clinical sense, I refer to the importance of the transference neurosis as outlining for us the essential and central analytic task, providing by its very currency and demonstrability a relatively secure cognitive base for our work. By its inclusion of the patient's essential psychopathological processes and tendencies in their original functional connections, it offers in its resolution or marked reduction, the most formidable lever for analytic cure. The transference neurosis must be seen in its interweaving with the patient's extra-analytic system of personal contacts. The relationship to the analyst may indeed influence the course of relationships to others, in the same sense that the clinical neurosis did, except that the former is alloplastic, relatively exposed, and subject to constant interpretation. It is also an important fact that, except in those rare instances where the original dyadic relationship appears to return, the analyst, even in the strictly transference sphere, cannot be assigned all the transference roles simultaneously. Other actors are required. He may at times oscillate with confusing rapidity between the status of mother and father, but he is usually predominantly in one of these roles for long periods, someone else representing the other. Furthermore, apart from "acting out," complicated and mutually inconsistent attitudes, anterior to awareness and verbalization, may require the seeking of other transference objects: husband or wife, friend, another analyst, and so forth. Children, even the patient's own children, may be invested with early strivings of the patient, displaced from the analysis, to permit the emergence or maintenance of another system of strivings. Physicians, of course, may find in their patients their own strivings, mobilized by the analysis, even experience the impulses which they would wish to call forth in the analyst. The range is extensive, varied, and complicated, requiring constant alertness. Transference interpretation therefore often has a necessarily paradoxical inclusiveness, which is an important reality of technique. There is another aspect, and that is the dynamic and economic impact of the intimate and actual *dramatis personae* of the transference neurosis on the progress of the analysis as such and on the patient's motivations, as well as his real-life avenues for recovery. For the persons in his milieu may fulfill their "positive" or "negative" roles in transference only too well, in the sense that an analyst motivated by a "blind" countertransference may do the same. Apart from their roles in the transference drama, which may facilitate or impede interpretative effectiveness, they can provide the substantial and dependable real-life gratifications which ultimately facilitate the analysis of the residual analytic transferences, or their capacities or attitudes may occasion overload of the anaclitic and instinctual needs in the transference, rendering the same process far more difficult. In the most unhappy instances, there can be a serious undercutting of the motivations for basic change.

There is also the fundamental question of the role of the transference interpretation. At the Marienbad Symposium (1937), most of Strachey's colleagues appeared to accept the essential import of his contribution (1934, Symposium 1937) and thus the unique significance of the transference interpretation, despite the various reservations as to details and emphases on other important aspects of the therapeutic process. Nevertheless, there are still many who, if not in doubt regarding the great value of transference interpretations, are inclined to doubt their uniqueness and to stress the importance of economic considerations in determining the choice as to whether transference or extratransference interpretations may be indicated. Now, apart from the realistic considerations mentioned in the preceding passage (in a sense, the necessarily "distributed" character of a variable fraction of transference interpretation), there is the fact that the extraanalytic life of the patient often provides indispensable data for the understanding of detailed complexities of his psychic functioning, because of the sheer variety of its references, some of which cannot be reproduced in the relationship to the analyst. For example, there is no repartee (in the ordinary sense) in the analysis. The way the patient handles the dialogue with an angry employer may be importantly revealing. The same may be true of the quality of his reaction to a real danger of dismissal. There are not only the realities but also the "formal" aspects of his responses. These expressions of his personality remain important, even though his "acting out" of the transference (assuming this was the case) may have been even more revealing and, of course, requiring transference interpretation. Furthermore, these expressions remain useful, if discriminatingly and conservatively treated, even if they are inevitably always subject to that epistemological reservation, which haunts so much of analytic data. Of course, the "positive" transference facilitates such interpretations: it is what enables the patient to listen to them and take them seriously!

In an operational sense, it would seem that extratransference interpretations cannot be set aside or underestimated. But the unique effectiveness of transference interpretations is not thereby disestablished. No other interpretation is free, within reason, of the doubt introduced by not really knowing the "other person's" participation in love, quarrel, criticism, or whatever the issue. And no other situation provides for the patient the combined sense of cognitive acquisition, with the experience of complete personal tolerance and acceptance, that is implicit in an interpretation made by an individual who is an object of the emotions, drives, or even defenses, which are active at the time. There is no doubt that such interpretations must not only (in common with all others) include personal tact but also must be offered with special care as to their intellectual reasonableness, in relation to the immediate context, lest they defeat their essential purpose. It is not too often likely that a patient who has just been jilted in a long-standing love affair and is suffering exceedingly will find useful an immediate interpretation that his suffering is due to the fact that the analyst does not reciprocate his love, even though a dynamism in this general sphere may be ultimately demonstrable, and acceptable to the patient. On the other hand, once the transference neurosis is established, with accompanying subtle (sometimes gross) colorations of the patient's life, then more far-reaching often anticipatory, transference interpretations are indeed indicated; for, if all of the patient's libido and aggression is not, in fact, invested in the analyst, he has at least an unconscious role in all important emotional transactions; and, if the assumption is correct that the regressive drive, mobilized by the analytic situation, is in the direction of restoration of a single all-encompassing relationship, specified pragmatically in the individual case by the actually attained level of development, then there is indeed a dynamic factor at work, importantly meriting interpretation as such, to the extent that available material supports it. This would be the immediate clinical application of the material regarding the "cognitive lag," mentioned earlier.

TRANSFERENCE OBJECT AND OBJECT REPRESENTATION

In considering more broadly the function of the transference in the psychoanalytic process, one is confronted by the apparently naïve but nonetheless important question of the role of the actual (current) object as compared with that of the object representation of the original personage in the past.[14] We recall Freud's paradoxical, somewhat gloomy, but portentous concluding passage in "The Dynamics of Transference" (1912): "This struggle between the doctor and the patient, between intellect and instinctual life, between understanding and seeking to act, is played out almost exclusively in the phenomena of transference. It is on that field that the victory must be won—the victory whose expression is the permanent cure of the neurosis. It cannot be disputed that controlling the phenomena of transference presents the psychoanalyst with the greatest difficulties. But it should not be forgotten that it is precisely they that do us the inestimable service of making the patient's hidden and forgotten erotic impulses immediate and manifest. For when all is said and done, it is impossible to destroy anyone *in absentia* or *in effigie*" (p. 108).

Both object and representation are made necessary by the basic phenomenon of original separation. Indeed, the existence of an image of the object, which persists in the absence of that object, is one of the important beginnings of psychic life in general, certainly an indispensable prerequisite for object relationship, as generally construed. Whether this is viewed as (or at times demonstrably is) an unstable introject, which is always subject to alternative projection, or an intrapsychic object representation clearly distinguished from the self representation, or a firm identification in the superego or in the ego itself, these phenomena are in various ways components of the system of mastery of the fact of separation, or separateness, from the originally absolutely necessary anaclitic or (in the very earliest period) symbiotic "object." In the light of clinical observation, it would appear to be the relatively stable (parental) object representation, at times drawing to varying degree on the more archaic phenomena,[15] at moments, even in nonpsychotic patients, overwhelmed by them, sometimes a restoration from oedipal identification, which provides the preponderant basis for most demonstrable analytic transferences, in neurotic patients. The transference is effectively established when this representation invests the analyst to a degree—depending on intensity of drive and mode of ego participation, which ranges all the way from wishing and striving to remake the analyst, to biased judgments and misinterpretations of data, and finally to actual perceptual distortions.[16]

However richly and vividly the old object representation as such may be invested and however rigidly established the libidinal or aggressive cathexis of the image may be, this as such can become the actual and exclusive focus of full instinctual discharge, or of complicated and intense instinct-defense solutions, only in states of extreme pathological severity. This is consistent with the usual and general energy-sparing quality of strictly intrapsychic processes. For the vast majority of persons, viable to any degree, including those with severe neurosis, character distortions, addictions, and certain psychoses, the striving is toward the living and actual object, even at the cost of intense suffering. In a sense, this returns us to the beginning, to the state in which the psychological "object-to-be" (if you prefer) has a critical importance never again to be duplicated, except in certain acute life emergencies, even if the object is not firmly perceived as such, in the sense of later object relations. And it does seem that trace impressions from the earliest contacts in the service of life preservation, plus the associated instinctual gratifications, and innumerable secondarily associated sensory impressions, are activated by the specific inborn urges of sexual maturation. These propel the individual to renew many of the earliest modes of actual bodily contact, in connection with seeking for specific instinctual gratification. Or, to look away from clear-cut instinctual matters to the more remote elaborations of human contact: few regard loneliness as other than a source of suffering, even when self-imposed, as an apparent matter of choice; and the forcible imposition of "solitary confinement" is surely one of the most cruel of punishments.

I mention these few generalities because I think that they have some important implications. No reaction to another individual is all transference, just as surely as no relationship is entirely free of it. There is not only the general maturational-developmental drive toward the outer world but also the seeking for a variety of need and pleasure satisfactions, learned or stimulated in relation to the primordial object but necessarily and inevitably transferred from this object to generically related things and persons in the expanding environment. These may be used or enjoyed without penalty, if the distinction between the original and the new is profoundly and genuinely established (with due respect for the quantitative "relativism" of such concepts). The range of such inevitable displacements ("transfers") is endless in all spheres — sexual, aggressive, aesthetic, utilitarian, intellectual. More immediately relevant to the lives of those whose development has been relatively healthy, are those individuals whose vocations provide similarities or parallels, however rarefied, to the caretaking functions of the original parents: teachers, physicians, clergymen, political rulers, and occasionally others. Again it must be noted that such persons perform real functions, that the adult individual's interest in them, his specific need for them, often greatly outweighs similar reactions to parents, who retain their unique place for a complex and variable combination of other reasons. For such surrogate parents perform for the adult what his parents largely performed for him in earliest years; and the psychological comparison is with an old object representation, or with an early identification, to which such latter-day parent surrogates may indeed add important layers or elaborations. It is on the basis of such functional resemblances that persons in these roles have a unique transference valence. The analyst is first perceived as a real object, who awakens hope of help and who offers it on the basis of his therapeutic competence. This operates in the patient's experience at all levels of integration, from that of actual and immediate perception, evaluation, and response, to the activation of original parental object representations and their cathexes. That the analyst becomes invested with such representations, in forms ranging from wishes or demands to functional or even perceptual misidentifications, comprises the broad range of phenomena which we know as the therapeutic transference. Thus, the complicated structural phenomena of conflict are activated in relation to a real object, and such activation is uniquely dependent on the participation of this object, in a situation whose realities revive, with their affirmative associations, the memories of old and painful frustrations. In this situation, the continuing and prolonged contact, under strictly controlled conditions, is an important real factor, which has been elaborated previously. Without these actualities, dream life, or — in instances of greater energic imbalance between impulses and defense — neurosis, will be the spontaneous solutions, while everyday "give-and-take" object relations are, at least on the surface, maintained as such. Occasionally, neurotic behavior, where "transferences" dominate the everyday relationships, will supervene.

Interpretation, recollection or reconstruction, and, of course, working through, are essential for the establishment of effective insight, but they cannot operate mutatively if applied only to memories in the strict sense, whether of highly cathected events or persons. For it is the thrust of wish or impulse, or the elaboration of germane dynamic fantasies, and the corresponding defensive structures and their inadequacies, associated with such memories, which give rise to neurosis. It is a parallel thrust, which creates the transference neurosis. When memories are clear and vivid, through recall or accepted as much through reconstruction and associated with variable, optional, and adaptive rather than rigidly "structuralized" response patterns, the analytic work has been done.

This view does place somewhat heavier than usual emphasis on the horizontal coordinate of operations, the conscious and unconscious relation to the analyst as a living and actual object, who becomes invested with the imagery, traits, and functions of critical objects of the past. The relationship is to be understood in its dynamic, economic, and adaptive meanings, in its current "structuralized" tenacity, with the real and unreal carefully separated from one another. The process of subjective memory or of reconstruction, the indispensable genetic dimension, is, in this sense, invoked toward the decisive and specific autobiographic understanding of the living version of old conflict, rather than with the assumption that the interpretative reduction of the transference neurosis to gross mnemic elements is, in itself and automatically, mutative. At least, this view of the problem would seem appropriate to most chronic neuroses embedded in germane character structures of some complexity. That neurotic symptoms connected with isolated traumatic events covered by amnesia may, at times, disappear with restoration of memories with adequate affective discharge, regardless of technical method is of course indisputably true, even though the details of process, including the role of transference, are probably not yet adequately understood. Psychoanalysis was born in the observation of this type of process. Indeed, the role of the transference in the early writings of both Freud and Ferenczi seemed weighted in the direction of its resistance functions (i.e., as directed against recall), although its affirmative functions were soon adequately appreciated and placed in the dialectical position, which has remained to the present day. This last is well illustrated by the quotation from Freud in the beginning of this section.

THE INTERPLAY OF PAST AND PRESENT AND THE ROLE OF ILLUSION

However, even if it is insufficient for exclusive reliance, in relation to the complicated neurotic problems we are largely called on to treat, it would be fallacious to assign to the recall and reconstruction of the past an exclusively explanatory value (in the intellectual sense), important though the function be, and difficult as its full-blown emotional correlate may be to come by. There is no doubt that, even in complicated neuroses, with equivalently complicated transference neuroses, the genuinely experienced linking of the past and present can have, at times, a certain uniquely specific dynamic effect of its own, a type of telescoping or merging of common elements in experience, which must be connected with the meaninglessness of time in unconscious life, as against its stern authority in the life of consciousness and adaptation to everyday reality. Contributing decisively to such experience, to whatever degree it occurs is of course the vivid currency of the transference neurosis and, central in this, the reincarnation of old objects is an actual person, the analyst.

Thus, an allied problem in the general sphere of transference is the fascinating and often enigmatic interplay of past and present. If one wishes to view this interplay as a stereotyped formulation, the matter can remain relatively uncomplicated—as a formulation! Unfortunately, this is too often the case. The phenomenon, however, retains some important obscurities, which I cannot thoroughly dispel but to which I would like to call attention. To concentrate on the dimension of time, I omit references to the many complicated and intermediate aspects of technique, however essential. For example, we can assume that the transference neurosis reenacts the essential conflicts of the infantile neurosis in a current setting. If a reasonable degree of awareness of transference is established, the next problem will be the genetic reduction of the neurosis to its elements in the past, through analysis of the transference resistance and allied intrapsychic resistances, ultimately genetic interpretations, recollections and reconstructions, and working through. As the transference is related to its genetic origins, the analyst thereby emerges in his true, i.e., real, identity to the patient, and the transference is putatively "resolved." To the extent that one follows the traditional view that all resistances, including the transference itself, are ultimately directed against the restoration of early memories as such, this is a convincing formulation. Indeed, in its own right, it has a certain tightly logical quality. However, we know that all this is not so readily accomplished, apart from the special intrapsychic considerations described by Freud in "Analysis Terminable and Interminable" (1937). Although in a favorable case, much of the cognitive interpretative work can be accomplished, there remains the fact that cognition alone, in its bare sense, does not necessarily lead to the subsidence of powerful dynamisms, to the withdrawal of "cathexes" from important real objects. For, as mentioned a short while ago, the analyst is a real and living object, apart from the representations with which the transference invests him, and which are interpretable as such. There is often a confusing interrelation and commingling of the emergent responses due to an old seeking, and those directed toward a new individual in his own right. Both are important, and furthermore, there are large and important zones of overlapping. Apart from such considerations, even the explicitly incestuous transference is currently experienced (at least in good part) by a full-grown adult (like the original Oedipus), instead of a totally and actually helpless child. To be sure, the latter state is reflected subjectively in the emergent transference elements of instinctual striving, but it is subject to analysis, and the residue is something significantly, if not totally, different. It is these residual sexual wishes, presumably directed toward the person of the analyst *as such*, which must be displaced to others. If, as generally agreed, the revival of infantile fantasies and strivings in the biologically mature adolescent (Jacobson 1964) presents a new and special problem, one must assume distinctiveness of experience for the adult, although it is true that in the majority of instances, adequate solution is favored by the adult state. There is, in any case, a residual real relationship between persons who have worked together in a prolonged, arduous, and intimate relationship, which, strictly speaking, is not a transference; but there may be mutual coloration, blending, and some confusion between the two spheres of feeling. The general tendency is, I believe, to ignore this dual aspect; in continuing professional relationships, probably both components are gratified to some degree. Above all, there is the ubiquitous power of the residual primordial transference, the urge to cling to an omnipotent parent, to resist the displacement of its "sublimated" anaclitic aspects, even if the various representations of the wishes for bodily intimacy have been thoroughly analyzed and successfully displaced. The outcome is largely the "transference of the transference" mentioned earlier, in a different context. For everyday reality can provide no actual answer to such cravings. In this connection, note Freud's genial envy of Pfister (Freud and Pfister 1963). If the man of faith finds this gratification in revealed religion, others in a wide range of secular beliefs and "leaders," the modern rational and skeptical intellectual is less fortunate in this respect. Presumably free, he is prone to invest even intellectual disciplines or their proponents with inappropriate expectations and partisan passions. I have mentioned elsewhere that our own field does not provide exception to this tendency (1961).

Of unequivocal importance, and I think largely overlooked, is the sheer fact of current continued physical proximity, as dynamic and economic factor of great importance in itself, in the prolongation of transference effects. The flood of neurophysiological stimuli occasioned by the analyst's presence causes an entirely different intrapsychic situation from that prevailing in his absence, regardless of how one conceptualizes the difference. Thus, the gradual "weaning" to independence, via reduction of hours, is very useful in many instances; in some, it may be that the dissolution of the transference (in a practical sense), if well analyzed, occurs, as Macalpine (1950) suggests, only after regular visits cease. There are a number of patients who will never show a terminal phase (or incipient adaptation to the idea of termination as a reality), without a relatively arbitrary setting of a termination date. Even though it has been tendentiously misunderstood in one or two instances, I shall reiterate my suggestion (1961) as worthy of trial, that a predismissal period of varying duration following what would ordinarily be regarded as termination be devoted to vis-à-vis interviews, at reduced frequency, dealing in integrated fashion with whatever preoccupations the patient is impelled to bring to such valedictory. The vis-à-vis element adds the further advantage of testing tenacious transference images against the actuality.

The urge toward actual instinctual gratifications and allied satisfactions, the need to be rid of burdens of time and expense, and the sheer urge toward independent functioning often participate importantly in the dynamics of ultimately successful separation. Certainly, the analyst's own gentle but firm inaccessibility to the patient's residual transference wishes (however expressed), coupled with the conscious and unconscious wish to set him free to develop his individual potentialities, also contribute to this important development.

Apart from and anterior to the indubitably important ancillary elements in the dissolution of clinical transference, mediated in the sphere of reality, the restoration of the past in gross mnemic units, whether by recollection or reconstruction, finds specifying and augmenting support toward effectiveness in the increasingly detailed technical exploitation of the transference neurosis, in the sense of the analysis of the dynamic nuances which it presents. In other words, if the exposure of a man's Oedipus complex, or indeed his passive homosexual solution of its vicissitudes, is an important step in the analytic work, the further understanding of the determinants of the pathological augmenting elements in the incestuous fixation or the specific determinants of the choice of solution in the crosscurrents of the childhood setting, is most liable to be accessible in a useful way in the details of the transference neurosis, where they lend themselves to reconstruction, which is often far more useful than the gross units of spontaneous recollection. In proceeding to such further analysis, such concepts as the universality of the Oedipus complex or intrinsic bisexuality become only the more helpful, rather than suffering degradation to the position of stereotypic impediments. Such processes, in common with respect for the realities of the analytic (and extraanalytic) setting, serve not only to facilitate the genuine recollection and reconstruction of the past but also to provide a context in which recall and reconstruction can more often "cast the balance," i.e., provide the mutative or at least catalytic element in insight which is distinctively psychoanalytic. Whether or not it serves to resolve the transference neurosis entirely, it contributes something not be dispensed with, toward its adequate understanding and resolution.

Other views of the role of transference in therapeutic change have grown up, often in direct relationship and adjacency to the original schema and sometimes deviating rather widely from it. I shall not review these, at this time. Horney (1939), for example, omitting all detailed considerations, presents a view whose logic is, in a sense, antithetical to that of the classical view. While not discarding the etiological importance of the early past, the principal emphasis is on the transference as a current interpersonal relationship involving the patient's adult character, whose pathological devices are to be exposed and resolved or changed, as such. The prompt resort to interpretation of the past by the analyst is viewed as a facilitation of the patient's resistance to facing the current confrontations, and a tendency to leave the essential dynamic issue unaltered. I think it is a commonplace of intelligent conservative analytic technique to be aware of such resistance flights into the past, and to incorporate that awareness in the interpretative schema. It is furthermore quite usually agreed that the analysis of current dynamisms (including first, the resistances) takes precedence over genetic reduction. However, unless the current conflict can be met *only* in direct confrontation, i.e., unless evasion is the only neurotic reality, we assume that, ultimately, the genetic analysis of this conflict — in our immediate reference, the transference neurosis — will accomplish a type of understanding not otherwise available, which facilitates the stripping of transference illusion away from the person of the analyst. By this we mean apart from the obscure dynamism implicit in the subjective time dimension, an explanatory source beyond the general and rational, and the referents established by scientific observation, in the sense that it rests on exquisitely personal subjective experience. This can of course be integrated with current experience along the lines which are part of standard technique. It is also difficult to gainsay the assumption that, in general, the alterative power of original experience is greater to the extent that it has occurred in an early developmental, i.e., formative period, and that the data recalled or reconstructed (under proper technical conditions, including proper evaluation and critique) may be assumed to have created the special potentialities for the current experience under consideration. Now this genetic reconstruction, like the evolution of the manifest transference in the first place, requires the benign ego splitting emphasized by Sterba (1934), for the psychological realities connected with the past and present, respectively, are far from naturally congruent. It is indeed on this basis, although it presents its own problems of energic distribution, that the logic of our view rests. Nevertheless, even though the concept of a "transference" (Horney did minimize the importance of the term, as such) dealt with essentially in current terms, in relation to current realities, is perplexing and, from our point of view, *a priori* fallacious, there is a certain stark hard-headed (even if wrong-headed) consistency in the view that the individual must necessarily work out his problems with the other individual with whom he is actually involved, in the situation which creates the confrontation, without distraction by the "past." At least, it places in bolder relief certain problems of our own assumptions.[17]

To come closer to the continuing mainstream of psychoanalytic thought, let us look at the concept of the transference interpretation and its implications, to whatever degree it is regarded as specifically "mutative," whether in more general usage or in the specific sense postulated by Strachey (1934, Symposium 1937). Strachey's view lends itself readily to examination because it is so clear-cut. I wish to make it clear that I do not regard the mechanisms described by Strachey as the central and inclusive mechanisms of therapeutic change or even, in the form described, as necessarily constituting the comprehensive actualities of mutative effect in transference interpretation. However, I do not doubt the importance of superego modification in analysis and its role in facilitating or permitting necessary processes of modification in the ego; nor do I question the uniqueness of impact of the transference interpretation. In common with most of his colleagues at the Marienbad Symposium, I find much that is phenomenologically valid in Strachey's contribution, the introjective details at least interesting, and the explanatory effort in itself worthwhile. The introjective processes may indeed play a variable role in the impact of interpretation, as in other special spheres of communication, in the complex sense mentioned earlier. At the very least, Strachey's view may be taken as a tangible and clear-cut construct of a phenomenon which presents paradigmatically certain problems of the "past and present." These are present, however they are viewed, or included implicitly in other explanatory efforts, even if no more spectacularly than in terms of the benignly tolerant "psychoanalytic atmosphere." (See, for example, Bibring [Symposium 1937], even if in a different context of explanation and with important reservations; or Nunberg's reference [1960] to the projection of the patient's superego on the analyst and the modification of his superego through identification with the analyst.)

It appears to me that the "transference interpretation" as elaborated by Strachey or as used in the current psychoanalytic vernacular refers not so much to the genetic interpretation of the current transference attitude, as it means a concise direct statement to the patient of an attitude toward the analyst which is at the moment active but unconscious or, possibly more often, preconscious. Strachey indeed specifies that genetic material may follow promptly, and Glover (1955, p. 121) specifies that the interpretation is incomplete, until the genetic aspect is included. Strachey's original reference was to hostility. Let us say the interpretation is "You wish to kill me." From the impact of such interpretation, there ensues, putatively, a series of changes in the superego, in which introjections of the analyst as a good (i.e., nonaggressive) object are gradually substituted for the archaic fantasy objects. The whole process takes origin by virtue of the analyst's power "(his strictly limited power) as auxiliary superego."

Whether or not one views the impact of such interpretation in this or another framework (note Bibring's and Fenichel's comments at the symposium [1937]), there is no doubt of its important effect (when it is correct and well timed). The same is, of course, to some extent true of the analyst's genuine acceptance of the patient's conscious aggressions, especially (in apparent paradox) when these do not have to do with such gross matters as killing, rape, devouring, or attacks of equivalent primitiveness. For, given a reasonably mature patient, both analyst and patient readily take distance from such impulses or fantasies. This is not always true of personal criticisms, derogations, snidely contemptuous comparisons, for example, especially if they find some resonance in vulnerable aspects of the analyst's self-image. Analysts vary as much in their capacities to handle such aggressions as they do in their interpretative skills, and they are not one whit less important! That the impact of interpretation of an impulse or wish, which has not been clearly in awareness, is greater than the acceptance of conscious verbal aggressions is, however, true. The experience is unique, and includes factors beyond the exchange of archaic for good object, especially where the wish or impulse has been genuinely unconscious. Apart from the surprise of discovery, there is (for single example) the provision of words for the hitherto wordless, permitting the decisive intrapsychic "transference" to the preconscious, with its important general implications. With those which are generally accepted, I would submit my personal conviction that this important process bears some obscure relation to the very origins of speech, i.e., the biological translation from the instinctual contributions to these origins, specifically the cannibalistic aggressions.

In any case, to return to the central question: how can we—or can we—in the light of our present psychology and metapsychology, understand such effects? We expect the patient to maintain a clear picture of who the analyst really is. According to Strachey, the ego of the patient, at the moment of emergence of the aggression, perceives the differences between the analyst and the archaic fantasy object. But is he not aware of this difference, as a *condition* of the emergence? Presumably the superego reaction to the "wish to kill" is either archaic in a pregenital sense, or derived from the Oedipus complex, in either case, from a remote situation, in the remote past. The analyst is a professional person, engaged and remunerated by the patient to help him, largely by understanding him, and, in turn, by giving him that understanding. It is at the analyst's behest and under his explicit guarantees that the patient follows the basic rule, and accepts the regressive transference fantasies which are mobilized by the analytic situation. To phrase it as a naïve bystander might: "What then is so remarkable about his (the analyst's) being tolerant? He is supposed to be! Besides, it's only talk." (This last is, of course, the condition which makes the whole transaction possible for both patient and analyst.) How then does the analyst's attitude influence that of the fierce internalized parent image of the past, reacting punitively or vengefully to the child's murderous wishes? Strachey warns against the analyst playing the good parent lest he become confused with the opposite (i.e., the good archaic) fantasy object. It is imperative that the patient's sense of reality not be strained in either direction, lest the analyst be introjected as a good or bad fantasy object. But even if this pitfall is avoided, there remains, and all the more vividly thereby, the problem of the noncomparable objects. (Actually and, from my point of view, paradoxically, Strachey makes a special issue of just this difference; indeed, it is the implicit cornerstone assumption of his essential argument.) I am not speaking of the genetic interpretation as such, which may follow on the other or the spontaneous recovery of genetic material, facilitated by the transference interpretation, for these, at least in principle, disestablish (or at least diminish or modify) the hostility, by creating awareness of its past origins, thus, its probable current inappropriateness. This is a different effect, closer to the original schema; in schematic-cognitive principle, it remains unquestionably clear.

But let us return to the more direct transaction between analyst and patient. A unique aspect of the technical work of analysis is the involvement of the analyst's whole personality. In short, to be totally "objective" would require a sort of de-personalization. The patient knows that some things must hurt at times. So it is, by greatly oversimplified analogy, as if one were an orthopedist, and told a child to exercise his sick muscles by kicking one in the shins, and then, to his surprise, did not become angry, when the instructions were followed with wholehearted enthusiasm. "Look, he really meant it!" But this would be in the sphere of the integrated real relationship. What about the less readily demonstrable provinces of the mind? Does something of the sort described by Strachey occur, despite the noncongruent contexts involved? Within the regressed sphere of transference illusion, which does not, however, encompass the entire functioning ego, a transaction at least analogous to that described by Strachey may well occur. But this requires that another latent transference illusion be unconsciously available, also investing the analyst, albeit tacitly, as background for the immediate aggressive fantasy, given a sense of body, vividness, and reality by his living presence, i.e., the representation of a good object, not essentially a fantasy object, from an equivalent past. It is then as if the analyst were a good mother (or a good father) saying: "You wish to kill me, but I still accept you and wish to help you!" For we may assume that all, except those whose early vicissitudes have been at the remote pole of severity, have preserved images of (actual) good objects and that these, perhaps augmented in some by wistful fantasy (*faute de mieux*), may well include the capacity to love (a child) in the face of destructive aggression. Apart from idealized fantasy objects (in the archaic Kleinian sense), this wish and corresponding fantasy would seem to be clinically demonstrable in many patients. But what of the observing portion of the ego? It is there to join with the actual (i.e., "nontransference") analyst in understanding all this, in placing it where it belongs, in the genetic past. Can important structural changes, as opposed to purely transference effects, occur without its participation? I do not believe so. If I must speculate (and I can do little more), I would say that it participates in, at least acquiesces to, the powerful force of illusion. However, if I may, for a moment, talk with tongue in cheek, yet gravely, it does this from a somewhat less naïve and "involved" point of view than its other functional portion, in the same sense that it acquiesces, at least temporarily, to the vagaries of the creative imagination or other productive inconsistencies of human psychic life. It is as if there is an awareness that what is being tested in the present is veritably "what might have been," and that furthermore if the analyst, as a person, has met the acid test of unconscious probing, he may indeed, all the more convincingly, wear the robes of a good and "timeless" unconscious image from the past, to give them life and meaning (a "taste of blood") (Freud 1900, Loewald 1960), in the sphere of illusion, while structures within the psyche undergo some degree of modification on that basis.

In Winnicott's admirable contribution on "Transitional Objects and Transitional Phenomena" (1953), he places strong emphasis on the role of illusion, deriving from the child's omnipotent reactions to good mothering, and the subsequent enduring and pervasive role of illusion in human mental life. It is the inevitable ("normal") breaches of this perfection of maternal response which establish the primordia of the experience of separation but which may contribute nonetheless, if in a different sense, to the illusory feeling of omnipotence, as a larval organismic striving for mastery of separation, and thus to the genesis of the primordial transference. The "transitional object" is itself an important transference object, with unique features which derive from its usually being inanimate (albeit usually invested with suggestive body qualities, such as odor). And there is, of course, an important element of illusion, in the sense of conjuror's magic, in the psychoanalytic transference, mediated by the subordination (or to varying degree, the acquiescence) of adult mental functions. The patient does, after all, "invoke" mother or father in the person of the analyst, as Aladdin invoked the genie. The living presence of the analyst perhaps obviates the lamp-rubbing! One might say that the observing portion of the ego, identified with the adult (the analyst), takes a tolerant attitude toward the childlike portion's experimentation with its hitherto unconscious images, similar to that which the sensible parent takes toward the child's dependence on his "transitional object." I have, in my earlier communication (1961) mentioned the quality of "serious play acting" which is implicit in the psychoanalytic situation and process. This refers to that tacit agreement between the analyst and the persistently adult portion of the patient's ego, to take seriously those emotions and fantasies, which the patient will experience in the unfolding of his transference neurosis. If one includes in this the mutative interplay between present transference and past experience, the role of illusion extends further, i.e., into the deeper intrapyschic processes of the patient himself.

I believe that there are other considerations and phenomena which support and give greater validity and power to this illusory process. For just as the child is assisted by the transitional object in his gradual progression to an object relationship which will provide what he (in an "average expectable" sense) will require,[18] the transitional but living analytic illusion, in much more complex fashion, readies him for reasonably available real relationships, with a revised organization of internal images. The analyst, outsider and "hired hand" though he be at the outset, does perform a therapeutic function, which, in its best development, calls on sound and benevolent parental identifications. This is a part of the ongoing process between patient and analyst, integrated in the current realities of the situation. One may be certain that the patient tests these and that on the outcome of such testing depend many critical nuances of the therapeutic alliance. Although both adult patient and analyst are relatively firm psychic compounds in reality, there is an ineluctable difference between the psychic and concrete, which with the "timelessness of the unconscious" permits images, fantasies, impulses, identifications, to live, in effect, in individual psychic actuality, not just as analytic potentialities, like the elements of chemical compounds, but concurrently with their existence in adult integrations. Thus, Glover's remark in the Marienbad Symposium regarding the "*attitude* [his italics], the true unconscious attitude of the analyst to his patients" (Symposium 1937) may be invested with additional meaning. The patient's real wishes and his transference alike seek out this remote sphere of feeling, impinge on it, and react to it. In the sense that this includes somehow the attitudes and wishes of a genuinely benign parent,[19] apart from the literal instrumentalities of professional function, the patient finds an answering reverberation to his transference testing, which, in psychic reality, supports his operational illusion.

All of this is not irrelevant to recent attempts to construe or interpret the psychoanalytic situation itself and transference as implicit in it, in terms of very early and general infantile experience; in other words, to view the situation in terms of a spectrum range between its adult actualities and purposes and the perennial, if only partial, wish, to restore the infant's relationship to his first and most important object. In any such effort, there is, I would think, the implicit assumption that whatever the form of the manifest clinical transference, it is a variant, a specification, of a phenomenon latent and implicit in the situational structure, which tends to deviate from the forms of the ubiquitous "give-and-take" transference of everyday life. The latter tend by the very fact of mobile seeking and elicitation of responses to maintain a relatively fixed and integrated level, barring unusual pathology, or unusual frustration, or both. Whatever the developmental phase or level of integration which finds expression in the transference, there are at least unconscious reverberations between the two persons involved which include self and object images (or their earliest precursors in physiological experience), ranging from the anaclitic or symbiotic beginnings to the integrated elaborated representations of adult years. These thus play a role in the realities of the relationship, in transference, and in their interaction. Whereas in my original presentation, my stress was on the technical modification of the analytic attitude and general responses, in the direction of more discriminatingly selective implementation of the essential rule of abstinence, I have, on this occasion, sought to examine further, under the pressure of my own perplexities, some unclear elements in the participation of clinical transference in the therapeutic process. Such reflections, insofar as they may deal with processes which largely remain unconscious, do not thereby diminish in any sense the importance of the manifest technical exchanges between patient and analyst, which are indeed also the principal carriers of the nonmanifest. However, they draw further attention to the necessary and productive, if sometimes silent, role of illusion in the psychoanalytic process. Paradoxically, at the same time, the importance of the analyst as a real object is heightened, in the sense of that vague but certainly critical sphere, the participation of what the analyst really is, in the depths of his unconscious life, in the contrapuntal course of the development and involution of transference illusion. I hope that, if I have not brought notable clarification to these subjects, I have at least excited renewed interest in their intellectual challenges.

SUMMARY

The paper, a delayed "postscript" to an earlier communication, *The Psychoanalytic Situation: An Examination of its Development and Essential Nature*, seeks to reiterate, in some instances amplify, and clarify, certain underlying dynamic constructs of the original work, with special reference to the pervasive functions of transference. There are further comments, mostly clinical in nature, on the transference neurosis and transference interpretation. In the interest of space, there is minimal condensed response to selected criticisms or misunderstandings of the clinical implications of the earlier work. The subject of comparison and possible integration with germane contributions of recent years is largely deferred. In the sense of "further reflection" by the author, two subjects are discussed: (1) transference object and object representation, and (2) the interplay of past and present and the role of illusion.

Notes

1. See page 173 of the *Outline* for the paragraph which defines the analytic situation. The sentence given is a paraphrased excerpt.

2. (a) Greenacre (1954): "I have already indicated that I believe the matrix of this *is* a veritable matrix; i.e., comes largely from the original mother-infant quasi-union of the first months of life. This I consider the basic transference; or one might call it the primary transference, or some part of primitive social instinct" (p. 672). It is possible, of course, that I read this brief introductory passage too literally. There is a partial reiteration, of slightly different elaboration, on p. 674. Most of the paper is devoted to other considerations.

(b) Spitz (1956): "It is not the objectless phase which returns in the transference of the patient. It is the analytical setting which reproduces many of the elements of this phase. Through this reproduction the analytical setting pulls, funnel-like, the patient's transference in the direction of the objectless phase" (p. 383).

3. "But the analytic situation as a whole goes beyond the elementary dynamic of transference, perhaps to include the original, primitive experience of Being and to express its essence. From this point of view it is legitimate to describe the analytic situation as an ontological experience" (p. 386).

4. In the views quoted, sometimes in more remotely related instances, it is difficult to be certain how much the differences are verbal or to what degree there are real differences in fundamental premises. If I seem to stickle on this question, it is because (a) the idea of separation as an excitant of transference phenomena is of fundamental importance in my views; and this has not always been understood, even by intellectually sympathetic readers. (b) Great as is my emphasis on the *unconscious* meaning and power of the analytic situation, I do not believe that its concrete and manifest realities actually reproduce early situations to the degree that is sometimes thought. There are certain resemblances, and there is the tremendous power of transference illusion; to these there may be added important supporting elements from the analyst's emotional participation. This question reappears in the final section of the paper.

5. In using this term, I should note that the meaning intended is quite different from that of Ferenczi, who, in his pioneer paper of 1909, used the term *primordial transferences* for the first object love and the first object hate, as transferred from autoerotic feelings.

6. "Infant Sorrow," in *Songs of Experience*.

7. The justification for asking this indulgence lies in the empirically established importance of this striving, normal or pathological, and its obvious connections with either or both of the great instinctual drives, from the beginnings of life to its end, including the "fear of death" itself. It has an old position in psychoanalytic thought. (See Freud (1905, p. 224.) Throughout this paper, I deal with "separation" in its broadest and most inclusive sense. It seems inescapable that the growing interest in the role of separation in development (Mahler 1965), in separation anxiety (Bowlby 1960), in possible specific instinctual components in attachment phenomena (Bowlby 1960), and the question of the primary or secondary character of the latter phenomena (Bowlby 1960, 1964; Murphy 1964) will ultimately occasion a general reexamination of the theory of drives and of anxiety.

8. The complexities of instinct and anxiety theory do not lend themselves to facile disposition. However, a clinical impression derived from reflection on total experience over many years is probably not without *some* significance. With regard to female pa-

tients in whom *unconscious* homosexual urges are singularly tenacious and pervasive, the background of one form or another of severe maternal deprivation (in some instances with noteworthy harshness, in others, quite subtle) has been conspicuous (regardless of other factors). To my surprise, this brought with it the afterreflection that the same was true of males with inveterate incestuous fixations to the mother (again apart from other complicated considerations). Assuming that one does not set aside such impression (for any of myriad methodological reasons), there are many possible inferences. My own, which seems to accumulate supporting rationale and observations through the years, is in the following direction: that, apart from its instinctual sources, the aggression aroused by such relationships can take the form of "irredentist" insistent and coercive tenacity, the urge to force or extort what has not been given and to punish the object for the delinquency at the same time. In the instances under consideration, such impulses can be fused with the erotic impulses and thus contribute to the "fixation." It has long been my conviction that a miniature of the same phenomenon is intrinsic in the structure of the "normal" phallic phase and Oedipus complex. Note the infancy history of Sophocles' Oedipus!

9. This explicit apposition of the role of technique and of "mature transference" wish is, I think, appropriate and useful in further diminishing the (apparent) gap between the two essential and interacting systems of psychoanalytic process, the emotional and the cognitive.

10. Again, we are considering "transference" as not identical with, although importantly related to, "therapeutic alliance." The question is whether "positive" or "negative" are to be derived from the current descriptive quality of the infantile elements in the personal relationship or from the dynamic effect on the analytic process (Lagache 1953, 1954). It would be better that the former be stated in frankly descriptive terms, i.e., hostile or erotic, with specifying variants. The primordial transference is intrinsically and inevitably ambivalent. It is a truism that an erotic transference can conceal severe hostilities, and, even when "pure," can occasion obstinate resistances; a hostile transference (even assuming its genuineness), if accepted and verbalized, in the context of an active "mature transference," may be compatible with excellent analytic progress. Note Kris's incidental remark in describing the "good analytic hour" (1956, p. 447).

11. In Hans Christian Andersen's justly treasured and richly meaningful story "The Emperor's New Clothes" (a story which Freud [1900] has examined, from a different point of view), the people only pretend to see the clothes of the naked king. In our time, which has seen repeatedly the spectacular rise and fall of political tyrants, it would seem that actual perception of the ruler's virtues and capacities (his "clothes") has often undergone radical change, in susceptible personalities, with the fling in either direction of the hero's fortunes.

12. In these and subsequent remarks (regarding the "eight-month anxiety"), I take considerable interpretative liberty with the work of Spitz and his coworkers, omitting all observational and conceptual refinements so carefully presented in Spitz's and Cobliner's recent book (1965). Needless to say, I am greatly indebted to these remarkable contributions.

13. There is a problem connected with the central importance of the transference neurosis in current clinical psychoanalytic thought, which would really merit a separate communication in its own right. However, it can be mentioned at this point. It is, in fact, a specification of a problem that Freud deals with in "Analysis Terminable and Interminable" (1937) and especially relevant to the importance of the present and living object in the analytic process. I refer to individuals who have had apparently satisfactory

analyses, yet suffer severe relapses, sometimes after a latent period of some years. Particularly in mind are those whose secondary symptoms are of great severity, of a type apparently unsuspected — or at least not clearly discerned — in the original analytic experience. In my own observation of a few such instances, I have every reason to infer that the deepest problems of object relationship and the associated erotic-aggressive phase problems did not enter actively into the transference neurosis in the original analysis. To put it more accurately: those severe transference problems which seemed nuclear in the severe secondary illness were apparently not emotionally active in the first analysis, except possibly in "acting out," to whose more profound motivations access was not obtained. Interpretable "material" was not lacking in these instances, in the first analysis; what later erupted in the form of severe illness was not unfamiliar to the patient in verbal-intellectual terms. I am forced to assume that the personality guarded itself tenaciously against the emotional reemergence in the transference of what had been sequestered in early childhood, "grown around" so to speak, in a sort of epipersonality (albeit, in some cases, forceful and effective). The catastrophic aspect lies in the fact that, in such instances, the vicissitudes of "real life," sometimes combined with the end results of cumulative neurotic behavior or "acting out," do produce the demands, disappointments, threats, and the extreme anxious-hostile responses in the patient which were automatically and primitively feared and avoided in the therapeutic situation. As always, it is difficult to specify the balance between pathology and technique, in every case. By technique, I mean, of course, the question of interpretations which were clearly indicated. Certainly, one must join in Freud's (remarkably tolerant) pessimism (1937) regarding any effort to elicit by personal activity the latent transference conflicts. One inevitably thinks of some connection with Winnicott's concept of true and false selves (1956) in certain cases; this connection may well exist. However, I cannot, at this point, verify the very early reconstructive elements, nor the technical phenomena, which he specifies (except, of course, the need to make adaptations to severely regressed patients), at least as major generalizations about these cases.

14. This is, of course, a complicated matter, both metapsychologically and empirically. I am aware that all psychological transactions — cathexis, for example — are held to refer necessarily to a representation rather than to the actual object in the outer world. Furthermore, the analyst himself, as himself, gives rise to an internalized representation, which presumably becomes increasingly clear and important, in comparison with the parent image which invests his own, in the transference, as the analysis progresses. In this passage, I am, as stated, interested essentially in the dynamic function of the analyst as a currently real and living object in the revival and solution of problems in the remote past. I suppose that one can view his role as mediated by his intrapsychic representation in the patient, the representation continuously receiving "nutriment" through the influx of perceptual data, because of his living presence. (See Gaarder [1965] in this connection, also Rapaport [1958]). However, Freud did not often make an issue of the distinction, and Hartmann could oppose "one's own person" to "object representation" on the same page on which he suggests the usefulness of referring to representations in both instances (1964, p. 127). I mention this only because of my inference, no doubt subjectively colored, and possibly quite unjustified, that there is a persistent interest in the distinctive meaning of the "self" and the "object" psychologically apart from and in addition to their representations. At any rate, that is my own tendency. Also, at this moment, my interest is essentially empirical and clinical, with constructs invoked only as immediately necessary. With regard to the early object whose representation is preserved in the un-

conscious, there can be no doubt of its exclusively psychological nature. However, the relation between such representations and the internalized perceptual experience of later transference objects is indeed complicated. (See, for example, the problems implicitly posed in this sphere by Pfeffer's study [1963]). The question of the original roles of physical and psychological traits of the object, respectively, and their relation to one another in forming persistent "representations" is equally complex, and, further, probably varies considerably with the individuals under consideration.

15. In the view of Melanie Klein (1952), not only do the origins of transference lie in the earliest neonatal period, with its complicated system of internal and external objects, commingling of real and fantasy elements, projection and introjection, and other germane mechanisms, but these must be dealt with in the analytic transference. (Klein does, however, also emphasize the importance of later developments, and their integration with the phenomena of the very earliest period.) While one sees these phenomena at times and one can keep an open mind about their genetic position in others, I cannot verify their frequent appearance or accessibility in the transference of most adult patients.

16. In relation to one of the patients mentioned by Nunberg (1951), the author uses the term *transference readiness* to specify reactions in which the patient *wishes* that he were like her father, and is constantly displeased with his failure to be like him, as opposed to the situation in which the patient reacts as though the analyst *were* the patient's father. I understand the effort toward semantic-conceptual clarity regarding the term transference, however, I am not convinced that the adjacent concept of readiness fulfills such a criterion. Is the difference really not in the sphere of certain qualities of the ego in its response to warded-off impulse and fantasy, or, as mentioned earlier, in the economic sphere, the "balance of power"? Is this type of "transference-ready" patient ever going to have a transference, in the sense of transference illusion, or is this her particular and painful mode of expressing her transference?

17. In a relatively recent paper by Szasz (1963), exceedingly ingenious in its dialectic, although (to me) not persuasive in its interpretation of certain important facts of process and scientific history, the defense elements in the concept of transference, on the *analyst's* side, beginning (in the author's view) with its very discovery, are stressed, although the brilliance and indispensability of the discovery are acknowledged. While it is true that a real relationship can mistakenly be viewed as transference, this problem has been under active scrutiny and discussion for some time. The possibility of such error in no way diminishes the critical importance of the transference. Its opposite counterpart remains the more frequent and serious problem. Szasz does not, in this paper, propose a new system of technique, only the overriding importance of certain personal qualities in the analyst, a requirement with which very few would disagree.

18. Pollock (1964) has employed a similar analogy.

19. Some germane considerations deserve brief mention here. The first is the hazard of sentimentalizing this concept, or further, of contributing to a "mystique" regarding unconscious curative powers. No one can cure with the adequate unconscious attitude alone. The patient requires the pabulum of good technical method, just as certainly as a child needs certain concrete ministrations, even from the best parent in the world! Second, just as surely as it is true that the practice of analysis is a remarkably exacting profession in many ways (see Greenson 1966), so is it probably true that an appropriate unconscious attitude toward patients is not the exclusive property of an anointed few. It exists, at least potentially, in most reasonably decent people. What is intended in this passage is to postulate an important process which occurs in analyses. It is, of course,

true that some individuals may fail in this respect, as in others or, any of us may fail or be inadequate with certain patients, sometimes without being aware of the lack or failure. The general problem lies more in having analyzed thoroughly the distortions in this all-important sphere of one's unconscious life and in the continuing analysis of the specific "countertransference neurosis" (see Tower 1956) with each patient. Beyond this, there is the ability to accept without conflict a benevolent disposition toward one's patient, with the concomitant ability to distinguish between such genuine disposition, as implemented by the technically correct instrumentalities of psychoanalytic procedure, and an attitude which presses for extraanalytic expression, which tends toward "spoiling," overindulgence, overanxious concern, and other obviously distorting modalities of expression. One can reasonably assert that the latter is not the expression of an uncomplicated benevolent attitude in a well-schooled analyst, any more than it is in an intelligent parent.

REFERENCES

Balint, M. (1937). Early developmental states of the ego: Primary object love. In *Primary Love and Psycho-analytic Technique*. London: Tavistock, 1965, pp. 74–90.

Benedek, T. (1938). Adaptation to reality in early infancy. *Psychoanal. Q.* 7:200–215.

_____ (1949). The psychosomatic implications of the primary unit: Mother-child. *Amer. J. Orthopsychiatry* 19-642–654.

Bowlby, J. (1960). Separation anxiety. *Int. J. Psychoanal.* 41:89–113.

_____ (1964). Note on Dr. Lois Murphy's paper (with reply by Dr. Murphy). *Int. J. Psychoanal.* 45:44–48.

Fairbairn, W. R. D. (1963). Synopsis of an object-relations theory of the personality. *Int. J. Psychoanal.* 44:224–225.

Ferenczi, S. (1909). Introjection and transference. In *Sex in Psychoanalysis*. New York: Basic Books, 1950, pp. 35–93.

_____ (1911). On obscene words. In *Sex in Psychoanalysis*. New York: Basic Books, 1950, pp. 132–153.

_____ (1923). *Thalassa: A theory of genitality*. Albany, N.Y.: The Psychoanal. Quarterly, Inc., 1938.

Fisher, C. (1965). Psychoanalytic implications of recent research on sleep and dreaming. *J. Amer. Psychoanal. Assn.* 13:197–303.

_____ (1966). Dreaming and sexuality. In *Psychoanalysis — A General Psychology*, ed. R. M. Loewenstein, L. M. Newman, M. Schur, and A. J. Solnit. New York: International Universities Press, pp. 537–569.

Freud, A. (1954). The widening scope of indications for psychoanalysis: Discussion. *J. Amer. Psychoanal. Assn.* 2:607–620.

_____ (1965). *Normality and Pathology in Childhood: Assessments of Development*. New York: International Universities Press.

Freud, A., and Burlingham, D. (1944). *Infants without Families*. New York: International Universities Press.

Freud, S. (1900). The Interpretation of dreams. *S. E.* 4 and 5.

_____ (1905). Three essays on the theory of sexuality. *S. E.* 7.

_____ (1912). The dynamics of transference, *S. E.* 12.

_____ (1916). Some character-types met in psycho-analytic work. *S. E.* 18.

_____ (1922). Some neurotic mechanisms in jealousy, paranoia and homosexuality. *S. E.* 18.

_____ (1923). The ego and the id. *S. E.* 19.

_____ (1926). Inhibitions, symptoms and anxiety. *S. E.* 20.

_____ (1936). A disturbance of memory on the Acropolis. *S. E.* 22.

_____ (1937). Analysis terminable and interminable. *S. E.* 23.

_____ (1940). An outline of psychoanalysis. *S. E.* 23.

Freud, S., and Pfister, O. (1963). *Psychoanalysis and Faith: The Letters of Sigmund Freud and Oskar Pfister* (1909–1939), ed. H. Meng and E. L. Freud. New York: Basic Books.

Gaarder, K. (1965). The internalized representation of the object in the presence and in the absence of the object. *Int. J. Psychoanal.* 46:297–302.

Gitelson, M. (1962). The curative factors in psycho-analysis: 1. The first phase of psychoanalysis. *Int. J. Psychoanal.* 43:194–205, 234.

Glover, E. (1955). *The Technique of Psycho-Analysis.* New York: International Universities Press.

Greenacre, P. (1941). The predisposition to anxiety. In *Trauma, Growth and Personality.* New York: Norton, 1952, pp. 27–82.

_____ (1945). The biological economy of birth. In *Trauma, Growth and Personality.* New York: Norton, 1952, pp. 3–26.

_____ (1954). The role of transference: Practical considerations in relation to psychoanalytic therapy. *J. Amer. Psychoanal. Assn.* 2:671–684.

_____ (1959). On focal symbiosis. In *Dynamic Psychopathology in Childhood*, ed. L. Jessner and E. Pavenstedt. New York: Grune & Stratton, pp. 243–256.

_____ (1960). Considerations regarding the parent-infant relationship. *Int. J. Psychoanal.* 41:571–584.

Greenson, R. R. (1965). The working alliance and the transference neurosis. *Psychoanal. Q.* 34:155–181.

_____ (1966). That "impossible" profession. *J. Amer. Psychoanal. Assn.* 14:9–27.

Hartmann, H. (1939). *Ego Psychology and the Problem of Adaptation.* New York: International Universities Press, 1958.

_____ (1964). *Essays on Ego Psychology.* New York: International Universities Press.

Hendrick, I. (1951). Early development of the ego: Identification in infancy. *Psychoanal. Q.* 20:44–61.

Hoffer, W. (1949). Mouth, hand and ego-integration. *Psychoanal. Study of the Child* 3/4:49–56.

Horney, K. (1939). *New Ways in Psychoanalysis.* New York: Norton.

Jacobson, E. (1964). *The Self and the Object World.* New York: International Universities Press.

Jones, E. (1929). Fear, guilt, and hate. In *Papers on Psycho-Analysis*, 5th ed. Baltimore: Williams & Wilkins, 1949, pp. 304–324.

Klein, M. (1952). The origins of transference. *Int. J. Psychoanal.* 33:433–438.

Kohut, H. (1959). Introspection, empathy, and psychoanalysis: An examination of the relationship between mode of observation theory. *J. Amer. Psychoanal. Assn.* 7: 459–483.

Kohut, H., and Seitz, P. F. D. (1963). Concepts and theories of psychoanalysis. In *Concepts of Personality*, ed. J. M. Wepman and R. W. Heine. Chicago: Aldine, pp. 113–141.

Kris, E. (1956). On some vicissitudes of insight in psycho-analysis. *Int. J. Psychoanal.* 37:445–455.

Lagache, D. (1953). Some aspects of transference. *Int. J. Psychoanal.* 34:1–10.

_____ (1954). La doctrine Freudienne et la thèorie du transfert. *Acta Psychother.* 2: 228–249.

Lewin, B. D. (1946). Sleep, the mouth and the dream screen. *Psychoanal. Q.* 15:419–434.

Loewald, H. W. (1960). On the therapeutic action of psycho-analysis. *Int. J. Psychoanal.* 41:1–18.

_____ (1962a). Internalization, separation, mourning and the superego. *Psychoanal. Q.* 31:483–504.

_____ (1962b). The superego and the ego-ideal: II. Superego and time. *Int. J. Psychoanal.* 43:264–268.

Loewenstein, R. M. (1957). Some thoughts on interpretation in the theory and practice of psychoanalysis. *Psychoanal. Study of the Child* 12:127–150.

_____ (1963). Some considerations on free association. *J. Amer. Psychoanal. Assn.* 11: 451–473.

Macalpine, I. (1950). The development of the transference. *Psychoanal. Q.* 19:501–539.

Mahler, M. S. (1952). On childhood psychoses and schizophrenia: Autistic and symbiotic infantile psychoses. *Psychoanal. Study of the Child* 7:286–305.

_____ (1965). On the significance of the normal separation-individuation phase, with reference to research in symbiotic child psychosis. In *Drives, Affects, Behavior*, ed. M. Schur. New York: International Universities Press, Vol. 2, pp. 161–169.

Murphy, L. B. (1964). Some aspects of the first relationship. *Int. J. Psychoanal.* 45:31–43.

Nacht, S., and Viderman, S. (1960). The pre-object universe in the transference situation. *Int. J. Psychoanal.* 41:385–388.

Nunberg, H. (1951). Transference and reality. *Int. J. Psychoanal.* 32:1–9.

Pfeffer, A. Z. (1963). The meaning of the analyst after analysis: A contribution to the theory of therapeutic results. *J. Amer. Psychoanal. Assn.* 11:229–244.

Pollock, G. H. (1964). On symbiosis and symbiotic neurosis. *Int. J. Psychoanal.* 45:1–30.

Rapaport, D. (1958). The theory of ego autonomy: A generalization. *Bull. Menninger Clin.* 22:13–35.

Reich, W. (1933). *Character-Analysis*. New York: Orgone Institute Press, 1945.

Ribble, M. A. (1944). *The Rights of Infants*. New York: Columbia University Press.

Segal, H. (1966). *Introduction to the Work of Melanie Klein*. New York: Basic Books.

Sharpe, E. F. (1940). Psycho-physical problems revealed in language: An examination of metaphor. *Int. J. Psychoanal.* 21:201–213.

Spitz, R. A. (1956). Transference: The analytical setting and its prototype. *Int. J. Psychoanal.* 37:380–385.

Spitz, R. A., and Cobliner, W. G. (1965). *The First Year of Life: A Psychoanalytic Study of Normal and Deviant Development of Object Relations*. New York: International Universities Press.

Sterba, R. (1934). The fate of the ego in analytic therapy. *Int. J. Psychoanal.* 15:117–126.

Stern, M. M. (1957). The ego aspect of transference. *Int. J. Psychoanal.* 38:1–12.

Stone, L. (1954). The widening scope of indications for psychoanalysis. *J. Amer. Psychoanal. Assn.* 2:567–594. *Reprinted in this volume, Chapter 2.*

_____ (1961). *The Psychoanalytic Situation. An Examination of Its Development and Essential Nature*. New York: International Universities Press.

Strachey, J. (1934). The nature of the therapeutic action of psycho-analysis. *Int. J. Psychoanal.* 15:127–159.

Sullivan, C. T. (1963). Freud and Fairbairn: Two theories of ego-psychology. In *Doylestown Foundation Papers*. Doylestown, Pa.: Doylestown Foundation.

Symposium on the Theory of the Therapeutic Results of Psycho-Analysis (1937). (E. Glover, O. Fenichel, J. Strachey, E. Bergler, H. Nunberg, E. Bibring). *Int. J. Psychoanal.* 18:125–189.

Szasz, T. S. (1963). The concept of transference. *Int. J. Psychoanal.* 44:432–443.

Tower, L. E. (1956). Countertransference. *J. Amer. Psychoanal. Assn.* 4:224–255.

Waelder, R. (1936). The principle of multiple function. *Psychoanal. Q.* 5(1936):45–62.

Winnicott, D. W. (1953). Transitional objects and transitional phenomena. *Int. J. Psychoanal.* 34:89–97.

—— (1956). On transference. *Int. J. Psychoanal.* 37:386–388.

—— (1960). The theory of the parent-infant relationship. *Int. J. Psychoanal.* 41:585–595.

Zetzel, E. R. (1965). The theory of therapy in relation to a developmental model of the psychic apparatus. *Int. J. Psychoanal.* 46:39–52.

Chapter 5

On Resistance to the Psychoanalytic Process: Some Thoughts on Its Nature and Motivations *(1973)*

This long and complicated paper was born of my own struggle to understand the nature of resistance beyond its phenomenology. I believe that the paper's most distinctive feature is the integration of the phenomena of transference and resistance, in the sense that the responses to the transference, whether latent or in awareness, invoke the richly varied manifestations of resistance. I also tried to substitute for the concept of the Death Instinct as the ultimate resistance, the primordial struggle against separation. For some time this paper received relatively little attention, possibly because it appeared in an annual volume rather than a journal. Interest in it, however, has increased perceptibly in the last few years.

I t is important to mention at the outset that, (whereas resistance is, in certain fundamental references, an operational equivalent of defense, its scope is really far larger and far more complicated.) It utilizes an array of mechanisms which sometimes defy classification in the way that fundamental genetically determined defenses, derived from important and common developmental trends, can be classified. From falling asleep to brilliant argument, there is a limitless and mobile spectrum of devices with which the patient may protect the current integrations of his personality, including his system of permanent defenses. In fact, resistances of a surface, conscious type, related to individual character and to educational and cultural background, often present themselves at the patient's first confrontation with a unique and often puzzling treatment method. While some of these phenomena are continuous with deeper resistances, others must be met at their own level. These considerations are obviously very important. However, I must leave them for now for the much-neglected faculty of informed and reflective common sense, and move on to the less readily accessible and explicable dynamisms, which inevitably supervene in analytic work, even if these initial surface resistances have been largely or wholly mastered. Nor shall I attempt to discuss the specific influence of the immediate cultural climate, especially the general attitudes of many young people (A. Freud 1968) toward the psychoanalytic process and its goals.

When Freud gave up the use of hypnosis for several reasons, beginning with the personal difficulty in inducing the hypnotic state and culminating in his ultimate and adequate reason—that it bypassed the essential lever of lasting therapeutic change, the confrontation with the repressing forces themselves—he turned to the method of waking discourse with the patient, in which insistence, with a sense of infallibility, accompanied by head pressure and release, were the essential tools for the overcoming of resistances (Breuer and Freud 1893–1895). Although various forms of resistance (general sense) had been observed before (for example, inability to be hypnotized, total and willful rejection of hypnosis, selective refusal to discuss certain topics under hypnosis, adverse reactions to testing for trance), it was the effectiveness of insistence in inducing the patient to fill memory gaps or to accept the physician's constructions which led Freud to a first and enduring formulation: since effort—psychic work—by the physician was required, it was evident that a psychical force, a resistance which was opposed to the pathogenic ideas, becoming conscious (or being remembered), had to be overcome. This was thought to be the same psychic force which had initiated the symptom formation by preventing the original pathogenic idea from achieving adequate affective discharge and establishing adequate associations—in short, from remaining or becoming conscious. The motive for invoking such a force would be the abolition (or avoidance) of some form of psychical distress or pain, such as shame, self-reproach, fear of harm, or equivalent cause for rejecting or wishing to forget the experience. Such defensive effort was attributed to the constellation of ideas already present, later clearly the ego and especially the character. It was thought important to show the patient that his resistance was the same as the original "repulsion" which had initiated pathogenesis. The step thereafter was short to the essentially equivalent and permanent concept of defense at first repression. What I have said is, I believe, a brief but essentially sound amalgam of quotation, paraphrase, and condensation (Breuer and Freud 1893–1895). Although Freud gave tremendous weight to the effectiveness of the hand pressure maneuver he saw it essentially as a way of distracting the patient's will and conscious attention and thus facilitating the emergence of latent ideas (or images). From a present-day point of view, one cannot but think of the powerful transferences excited by an infallible parental figure in a procedure only one step removed from the relative abdication of will and consciousness involved in hypnosis, and that this quasi-archaic qualitative pattern of relationship was actually more important to effectiveness or failure than were the exchanges of psychic energy postulated by Freud. In this sense, the "laying on of hands" granted its effect on attention, was probably even more significant in inducing transference regression than in the role which the great discoverer assigned to it.

What is of the first importance, however, is the establishment of a viable scientific and working concept of resistance to the therapeutic process as a manifestation of a reactivated intrapsychic conflict in a new interpersonal context. This in its essentials persists to this day in psychoanalytic work, in the concept of ego resistances.

Pari passu with this development, less explicitly formulated but often described or implied, was a more nearly total rejecting or hostile or unruly attitude of the patient, sometimes evoking spontaneous antagonistic reactions in the physician. In occasional direct references in the early work and in the choice of figurative phraseology for years thereafter, Freud recognizes this "balky child" type of struggle against the doctor's efforts. One need only recall Elizabeth von R., who would tell Freud that she was not better, "with a sly look of satisfaction" at his discomfiture (Breuer and Freud 1893–1895, pp. 144–145). When deep hypnosis failed with her, Freud "was glad enough that on this occasion, she refrained from triumphantly protesting 'I'm not asleep, you know; I can't be hypnotized'" (p. 145). I mention this category of resistance phenomenon because it represents a type of ego-syntonic struggle with the physician which remains potentially important in the course of any analysis, when the patient is motivated by what we call (in shorthand) the negative transference, regardless of its particular nuances of motivation. This is, of course, a manifestly different phenomenon from the earnest effortful struggles of the cooperative patient whose associations fail him, or who forgets his dream, or who comes at the wrong hour, to his extreme humiliation. Yet there is an important dynamic relationship between the two sets of phenomena, that I shall touch on again later.

Even in the period of experimentation with techniques strikingly different from those now employed, Freud made the analysis of resistances the central obligation of analytic work and proceeded from primitive beginnings, with rapidly increasing sophistication, both technical and psychopathologic, to concepts which remain valid to this day: that conscious knowledge transmitted to the patient may have no, or an adverse, effect in the mobilization of what is similar or identical in the unconscious;[1] that the repressing forces, the resistances, are more like infiltrates than discrete foreign-body capsules in their relation to preconscious associative systems; that the physician must begin with the surface and proceed centripetally; that hysterical symptoms are more often serial and multiple than mononuclear; and that resistances participate in all productions and must be dealt with at every step of analytic work; and other matters of equal significance (Breuer and Freud 1893–1895).

Freud always maintained the central concept of resistance stated before, and bequeathed it (reinforced later by the structural theory) to the generations of analysts who have followed him. But as the years went on he elaborated the general scope of resistance far beyond the basic concept of intrapsychic defense, recognizing that a great variety and range of mechanisms could impede psychoanalysis as a recognizable process or, beyond this, nullify or reverse expected therapeutic responses, or extend indefinitely the patient's dependence on the analyst. When extended beyond its direct equation with the anticathexes of defense, the variety of sources — not to speak of manifestations — of resistance multiplied rapidly. To mention only a few which were recognized very early: secondary gain of illness (Freud 1905); "external" resistances, for example, the hostility of the patient's family to the treatment (Freud 1917a, pp. 458–461); persistence of illness, with detachment, superciliousness, and mechanical compliance as a weapon for frustrating the analyst, as in the case of the homosexual girl (Freud 1920b); gratification from the dependent aspects of the transference (Freud 1918); sense of security in the symptom as a primary mode of conflict solution (Freud 1910a, p. 49); and most crucially, the complicated, subtly evolving concept of the "transference-resistance" in its oscillating pluralistic sense (for example, Breuer and Freud 1893–1895; Freud 1912a, 1917a). In his last writings, conspicuously in "Analysis Terminable and Interminable" (1937), in considering several possible factors in human personality which might obstruct or render ineffectual the successful termination of the analytic procedure, Freud offered a variety of psychodynamic considerations which could be fundamental in the extended or broadened concept of resistance: the question of the constitutional strength of instincts and their relation to ego strength; the problem of the accessibility of latent conflicts when undisturbed by the patient's life situation; (briefly but pointedly) the impingement of the analyst's personality on the analytic situation and process; the existence of certain qualities of the libidinal cathexes— especially undue adhesiveness or excessive mobility; rigid character structure; the existence of certain sex-linked "bedrock" conflicts which Freud regarded as biologically determined (insoluble penis envy in the female, and the male's persisting conflict with his passivity). Finally and most formidably, there was the cluster of dynamisms and phenomena which Freud, beginning with *Beyond the Pleasure Principle* (1920a) and *The Ego and the Id* (1923), attributed consistently and with deepening conviction to the operation of a death instinct. I refer to the "unconscious sense of guilt" and need for punishment, the repetition compulsion, the negative therapeutic reaction, and the more general operations of the need to suffer or to die or to seek outer or inner destruction. In an earlier presentation (Stone 1971) I have examined critically the theories of primary masochism and the death instinct in their relation to aggression. In the course of this paper I hope to offer, incidental to other comments, some simpler and somewhat more proximal, although similarly general, explanations of the deeper strata of resistance to the analytic process and their synergistic sources than the effects of primary masochism. I do this not because I believe it an imperative to be "optimistic" (Freud justifiably rejected the imputation of "pessimism" in this connection) but because, in my view, it may more closely tally with the clinical facts and because it may be clinically more useful. It remains an inexorable truth that the resistances inherent in the nature of certain cases or certain limitations implicit in the nature of psychoanalytic work, are at times invincibly formidable and cannot be disestablished by a theoretical position any more than they can be thus created.

The varied clinical manifestations of resistance are dealt with extensively throughout Freud's own writings, in many individual papers of other analysts, and also in comprehensive works on analytic technique, for example, those of Fenichel (1941), Glover (1955), and more recently Greenson (1967). I shall therefore make only selective and occasional references to their kaleidoscopic variety.

When free association and interpretation displaced hypnosis and derivative primitive techniques, psychoanalysis as we now construe it came into being. To the extent that free association was the patient's active participation, it was in this sphere that his "resistance" to the new technique was most clearly recognized as such. Cessation, slowing, circumlocution, lack of informative or relevant content, emotional detachment, and obsessional doubt or circumstantiality became established as relatively obvious impediments to the early (no longer exclusive but still radically important) topographic goal: to convert unconscious ideas largely via the interpretation of preconscious derivatives into conscious ideas. Only with time and increasing sophistication did it become evident that fluency, even vividness of associative content, indeed tendentious "relevancy" itself could, like overcompliant acceptance of interpretations, conceal and implement resistances which were the more formidable because expressed in such "good behavior."

One may define resistance (and in so doing include a rather liberal and augmenting paraphrase of Freud's own most pithy definition [The *Interpretation of Dreams* 1900, p. 517]) as anything of essentially intrapsychic significance in the patient that impedes or interrupts the progress of psychoanalytic work or interferes with its basic purposes and goals. In specifying "in the patient" I do not underestimate the possibly decisive importance of the analyst's resistances; rather, I separate the "counterresistance" as a different matter, in a practical sense, requiring separate study. One may concur in general with Glover's statement (1955, p. 57) that "however we may approach the mental apparatus there is no part of its function which cannot serve the purposes of mental defence and hence give rise during the analysis to the phenomena of resistance." One may also concur with his formulation that the most successful resistances (in contrast with those employing manifest expressions) are silent (p. 54) but disagree with the paradoxical sequel: " . . . and it might be said that the sign of their existence is our unawareness of them." For the absence of important material is in itself a sign, and it is necessary to become aware of such an absence, if possible.

Freud, in his technical papers and in numerous other writings, despite his reluctance in this direction did lay down the general and essential technical principles and precepts for analytic practice. We must note, however, that the clear and useful technical precepts are largely in what I would regard as the "tactical sphere", i.e., they deal with the manifest process phenomena of ego resistances. Other resistances, those largely subsumed in the "silent" group (for example, delays or failure of expectable symptomatic change, omission of decisive conflict material from free association or [more often] from the transference neurosis, inability to accept termination of the analysis, and allied matters), I would think of as in the "strategic sphere," relating to the depths of the patient's psychopathology and personality structure and to his total reactions to the psychoanalytic situation, process, and the person of the analyst. My use of the terms *strategic* and *tactical* I should note, differs from their use by others, for example, Kaiser (1934). While I do not presume to offer simple precepts for the ready liquidation of the massive silent resistances, I would hope to contribute something, however slight, to understanding them better and thus, potentially, to their better management. Some of these considerations, for example, iatrogenic regression, I have dealt with in other contexts (1961, 1966). In the "stategic" sphere of resistance, so often manifested by total or relative "absence," it is the informed surmise regarding the existence of the silent territory, by way of ongoing reconstructive activity, which is the first and essential "activity" of the analyst. Beyond this lie the subtle potentialities of the shaping and selection of interpretive direction and emphasis and the tactful indication of tendentious distortion or absence.

Because of a possible variety of factors, beginning with the strange magnetism which the verbal statement of unconscious content exerts on analysts and patients alike (in itself a frequent resistance or counterresistance), the priority of the analysis of resistance over the analysis of content, as discretely separate, did not readily come to full flower. This may well have been owing to the difficulties of dealing with more complicated resistances or developing an adequate methodology in this sphere, or even to the fact that a well-timed and tactful reference to content (or its general nature) sometimes seems the only way of mobilizing (reflexively) and thus exposing the corresponding resistance for interpretation and "working through," an echo of Freud's early, never fully relinquished biphasic process (1940a, p. 160).

Since this is not a technical paper, I must omit an extended discussion of the evolution of views on methods of resistance analysis, even though such views are inevitably related to our immediate subject matter. I have in mind approaches that range from the strict systematic analysis of character resistances of Wilhelm Reich (1933) or the absolute exclusion of content interpretation of Kaiser (1934), to the special efforts toward dramatization of the transference of Ferenczi and Rank (1925) or Ferenczi's own experiments with active techniques of deprivation and (on the other hand) the gratification of regressed transference wishes in adults (for example, 1919, 1920, 1930, 1931, 1932). Developments in ego psychology (for example, Anna Freud's classic contribution on the mechanisms of defense [1936]) brought the variety and importance of defense mechanisms securely into the foreground of analytic work, and the subsequent more widely accepted priority of defense analysis has indeed rectified a great deal of the original (and not entirely inexplicable) "cultural lag" in this fundamentally important, if not exclusive, sphere of resistance analysis. Concomitant with a more widespread functional acceptance of the essentiality and priority (in principle) of resistance analysis over content interpretation, there is in general a more flexible view of the technical implementation of the essential precepts, permitting interpretive mobility, in accordance with intuition or judgment between the psychic structures, somewhat in accordance with Anna Freud's (1936) principle of "equidistance." Resistances may sometimes be dealt with other than by discrete specification of them, apart from the intrinsic conceptual difficulty in the latter intellectual process, i.e., the specifying of a resistance without indicating that against which it is directed (Waelder 1960). There is also a general broadening of the scope of interpretive method. Witness, for example, Loewenstein's "reconstruction upward" (1951) and my own differently derived but somewhat allied conception, the "integrative interpretation" (1951), both of which recognize that resistance may indeed be directed "upward" or against the integration of experience, rather than against the explicitly and exclusively infantile or against the past. Similar considerations are also reflected in Hartmann's "principle of multiple appeal" (1951).

It is noteworthy that, while the emphasis on resistance in Freud's early clinical presentations is in general proportionate to his theoretical statements, his methods of dealing with the concealed and more formidable resistances are not very clear, except in certain very active interventions, such as the magical intestinal prognosis in the "Wolf Man" (1918), or the "time limit" in the same case, or the principle that at a certain point patients should confront phobic symptoms directly (1910b, p. 145), or the suggestion of transfer to a woman analyst, in the case of the homosexual girl (1920b). In these maneuvers and attitudes it is recognized that (1) interpretation, the prime working instrument of analysis, may often reach an impasse in relation to powerful "strategic" resistances; and (2) an implicit recognition that elements in the personal relationship of the analytic situation, specifically the transference, may subvert the most skillful analytic work by producing massive although "silent" resistances to ultimate goals, and that in some instances, where energic elements are formidable, they may indeed have to be dealt with directly and holistically, in the patient's living and actual situation.

Freud's own interest in active techniques (see above) stimulated Ferenczi to extreme developments in this sphere (1919, 1920), later combined with his oppositely oriented methods of indulgence (1930). As time went on, noninterpretive methods, especially those involving gratification of transference wishes, whether libidinal or masochistic, were set aside with increasing severity, in recognition of their contravention of the indispensability of the undistorted transference and the unique importance of transference analysis in analytic work. The same has been largely true of tendentious, selective instinctual frustrations (Ferenczi 1919, 1920). However, there is no doubt that the use of interpretive alternatives (sometimes suggestions for the deliberate control of obstinate resistance phenomena in this sphere) has been sharpened by — to some degree colored by — the earlier experiments in prohibition, whose transference implications were not fully apparent at the time of their introduction. The type of active intervention introduced by Freud (the time limit, the confrontation of symptoms), confined in actuality to the sphere of the demonstrably clinical relationship, has retained a certain optional place in our work, although the potential transference meaning and impact of such interventions, with corresponding variations or limitations of effectivenes, are increasingly understood and considered. The broad general principle of abstinence in the psychoanalytic situation, stated by Freud in its sharpest epitome in 1919, remains a basic and indispensible context of psychoanalytic technique. The nuances of application remain open to, in fact require, continuing study (Stone 1961, 1966).

In addition to important developments in ego psychology and characterology (for conspicuous examples: A. Freud 1936, Kris 1956, Hartmann 1951, Loewenstein 1951, Waelder 1930), the principal factor in deepening, broadening, and complicating the conceptual problem of resistance, and thus modifying the strict layerlike sequential approach (Reich 1933) to the analysis of resistance and content respectively, even in principle, has been the progressive emergence of transference analysis as the central and decisive task of analytic work. For, to state it oversuccinctly, and thus to risk some inaccuracy, the transference is far more than the most difficult implementation of resistances and (at the same time) an indispensable element in the therapeutic effort. Given the mature capacity for working alliance, it is the central dynamism of the patient's participation in the analytic process and, at the same time the proximal or remote source of all significant resistances, except those manifest phenomena originating in the conscious personal or cultural attitudes and experiences of the adult patient or those deriving from the inevitable cohesive-conservative forces in the patient's personality, for which we must still summon briefly the Goethe-Freud "witch," metapsychology (Freud 1937, p. 225n.). Later on I shall comment further on the relationship between transference and resistance.

In relation to the "tactical," i.e., process, resistances, a general view of what is immediate and confronting for example, the threatened emergence of ego-dystonic sexual or aggressive material, may be adequate. However, in order to gain access to what I have called the *strategic* sphere of resistance, one must have a tentative working formulation of the total psychic situation in mind, including an informed surmise regarding large and essential unconscious trends. Such suggested procedure is, I know, open to discussion on more than one score, and it does involve one immediately in some of the basic epistemological problems of psychoanalysis. Unfortunately, we cannot become involved in this fascinating sphere of dialectic in the course of a brief paper on a large subject. In his early work Freud relied enthusiastically on his own capacity to fill primary gaps in the patient's memory through informed inferences from the available data, and then, with an aura of infallibility, actively persuaded the patient to accept these constructions. However, with the further elaboration of psychoanalysis as process, in the sense of the increasing importance of free association, of the analyst's relative passivity, and other characteristics of the process as we now know it, there have inevitably been some important modifications of the attitudes reflected in such procedures. While, as far as I know, Freud never revised or repudiated his view that the resistances are operative in every step of the analytic work, I know that there exists in many minds a paradoxical mystique to the effect that the patient's free associations as such, unimpeded (and uninterpreted), could ultimately provide the whole and meaningful story of his neurosis, in the sense of direct information. This is, of course, manifestly at variance with Freud's basic assumptions about the role of resistance, and the germane roles of defense and conflict in the origin of illness.

In any case, in Freud's "Recommendations" (1912b, p. 114) is his advice against attempting to reconstruct the essentials of a case while the case is in progress. Such a reconstruction, he assumes, would be undertaken for scientific reasons. The caution, however, rests on both scientific and therapeutic grounds, on the assumption that the analyst's receptiveness to new data and his capacity for evenly suspended attention would be impaired by such an effort. It is true, of course, that rigid preoccupation with an intellectual formulation can impair these capacities. But it is also true that the "formulation" or structuring of a case can and largely does proceed preconsciously, in some references even unconsciously, and usually quite spontaneously. One must assume at the very least that some such process enters into the analyst's first perception of a "resistance."

I do not believe that Freud would have disagreed with using such a process. In any case, its use, whatever the form, is in my view a necessity, and, at times, it requires and should have the hypercathexis of conscious and concentrated reflection. One may, of course, assign the more purposive intellectual processes to periods outside of hours, and thus better preserve the other equally important response to the dual intellectual demand of psychoanalytic technique. The "voice of the intellect," however, should not be deprived of this essential place in analytic work. It goes without saying that it must never be allowed to foreclose mobile intuitive perceptiveness or openness to unexpected data. Nor must ongoing formulations in the mind of the analyst be allowed to cramp the spontaneity of the patient's associations. They should remain "in the analyst's head." To epitomize the technical situation: Strategic considerations require varying degrees of reflective thought, possibly outside of hours. Except for the perspectives and critiques they silently lend to understanding, they should not influence the natural and spontaneous, often intuitive, responses of the trained analyst to the endlessly variable nuances of his patient's "tactics." In relation to any category of clinical psychoanalytic problem, it is the structure of the transference neurosis and its unfolding, with the adumbrative material in characterology, symptom formation, personal and clinical history and the clues from specific data of the psychoanalytic process, taken as an ensemble, which provide the most reliable basis for general tentative reconstruction and thus for the understanding of resistances. While we must marshal our entire body of data, theory, and technology to see the transference neurosis as an epitome of the patient's emotional life, our comprehension of it is nonetheless based essentially on something which is right before us. Again: The total ensemble is essential, and the objectively observable phenomena of the transference neurosis are of crucial and central valence.

In the background data, the large outlines of life history are uniquely important because they do represent, or at least strikingly suggest, the patient's gross strategies of survival and growth, of avoidance and affirmation; and one may reasonably infer that they will be invoked again in the confrontation with the analyst, in his pluralistic significance. Allow me a few oversimplified and fragmentary illustrations. Chosen occupational commitments with children and the mood in which they are carried out, with the general character of manifest sexual adaptation, can certainly contribute to rational surmise about whether neurotic childlessness is based predominantly on disturbances of the Oedipus complex, on an original inability to achieve an adequate psychic separation from parent representations, or on the vicissitudes of extreme sibling rivalry. It must surely illuminate illness and analytic process if one knows that a patient lives, by choice, the breadth of an ocean removed from parents and siblings with whom there has been no evident quarrel, when this is not a crucial matter of occupational opportunity or equivalently important reality. Certainly a male patient's gross psychosexual biography helps us to understand which "side" of the incestuous transference is more likely to be surfacing in his first paroxysm of heterosexual "acting out." While it is true that dreams, parapraxes, and other traditionally dependable psychoanalytic material may dramatically reveal the ego-dystonic directions of impulse and fantasy life, and also the specific nature of opposing forces, it is only the composite historical and current picture which reveals the prevailing or alternative defenses, the large-scale economic patterns, and the preferred or relatively stable, i.e., most strongly overdetermined, trends of conflict solution.

Tactical problems of resistance were earliest observed largely in disturbances of free association, which, in frequent tacit assumption, would, or in principle could, lead without assistance to the ultimate genetic truth. This truth was construed to be the awareness of hitherto repressed memory (or the acceptance of convincing and germane constructions). As time went on, in Freud's own writing, terms of conative import appeared—such as "tendency" or, more vividly, "impulse." But the critical etiological and (reciprocally) therapeutic importance of memory has, of course, never really lost its importance. What has changed is its significance, a matter which I have discussed elsewhere (Stone, 1966). For, while the recovery of traumatic memories, with abreaction, is still dramatic in its therapeutic effect, for example, in war neuroses or equivalent civilian experiences and occasionally in isolated sexual experiences of childhood or adolescence, neuroses of isolated traumatic origin are actually rare in current psychoanalytic experience. Traumata are usually multiple, repetitive, often serving to crystallize, dramatize, and fix (sometimes even "cover") more chronic disturbances, such as distortions or pathological pressures in the instinct life, against the background of larger problems of basic object relationships. Actually, Freud was already becoming aware of the complex structure of neuroses when he wrote his general discussion for the *Studies on Hysteria* (Breuer and Freud 1893–1895). Thus, to put it all too briefly, when hitherto structuralized impulses or general reaction tendencies can truly be accepted in terms of memory, i.e., as matters of the past, other than in a tentative explanatory sense, much of the analytic work with the dynamics of the transference neurosis has necessarily been accomplished. One does not readily give up a love or a hatred, personal or national, only because one learns that it is based on a crushing defeat of the remote past.

The manifest communicative phenomena of resistance remain very important, just as the common cold remains important in clinical medicine. It will never cease to be important to be able to tell a patient that he is avoiding the emergence of sexual fantasies, that his blank silence covers latent thoughts about the analyst, or (somewhat more sophisticated) that glib and enthusiastic erotic fantasies about the analyst conceal and include a wish to humiliate or degrade him. However, we can be better prepared, even for these problems, on the basis of ongoing holistic reconstruction. Certainly we shall be better prepared for the formidable resistances of patients who apparently do "tell all," or even "feel all," in a most convincing fashion and in all sincerity, yet may finish apparently thorough analyses without having touched certain nuclear conflicts of their lives and characters or (more often) having failed to make effective contact with them in the transference neurosis, with a sense of affective reality. I do not, in this comment, refer to the instances described by Freud (1937) in which such conflicts remain dormant because current life does not impinge on them, but rather to those in which the "acting out" in life or the solution in severe symptoms is desperately elected by the personality in apparently paradoxical preference to the subjective vicissitudes of the transference neurosis (Stone 1966, pp. 31–32n.).

Having worked backward, or perhaps in circular fashion, I may at this point state a brief tentative formulation of the respective natures of the two general groups of resistance phenomena. These are, I believe, ultimately and fundamentally related and exist in varying degree in all analyses. However, one or the other is usually of preponderant importance and are, in a practical and prognostic sense, quite different: (1) Those manifested largely in discernible impediments of the psychoanalytic process in its immediate operational sense. These are usual in the neuroses, in persons who have achieved relatively satisfactory separation of the "self" from the primary object but whose lives are disturbed by the residues of instinctual and other intrapsychic conflicts in relation to the unconscious representations of early objects and thus to transference objects. (2) Those which may be similarly manifested at times but may indeed be relatively or even exaggeratedly free of them, where the essential avoidance is of the genuine and effective biphasic involvement in the transference neurosis, with regard to fundamental and critical conflicts, and thus of the potential relinquishment of symptomatic solutions and the ultimate satisfactory separation from the analyst. Here, among other phenomena, there may be large-scale hiatuses in (biographically indicated) analytic material in the usual experiential sense, or there may be a striking absence of available and appropriate cues of connection with the transference, or failure of significant reaction to pointing out fleeting but vivid cues. In some instances, this complex of phenomena may repeat an original disturbance in "separation and individuation," to use Mahler's terminology (1965). Or other severe disturbances in early object relationships or related pregenital (especially oral) conflicts can have given rise to tenacious narcissistic avoidance of transference involvement, to façade involvement, or to the alternative of inveterate regressed and ambivalent dependency. Dependable and largely affirmative secondary identifications have usually not been achieved originally, and this phenomenon, related to basic disturbances of separation, contributes importantly to the variously manifested fears of the transference.

Certainly, the phenomena of the two groups may overlap. There may indeed be deceptively benign "epineurosis" in the more severe group. In the troublesome phenomenon of "acting out," for example, one may deal with a relatively transitory resistance to an emergent transference fragment, in some instances due to a delay of effective interpretation, or one may be confronted by a deep-seated, variably structuralized, and sometimes even ego-syntonic "refusal" to accept the verbal mode of communication with an unresponsive transference parent in dealing with exigent and disturbing affects and impulses.

Some Remarks on the Relevance of
Structural and Topographic Concepts

Whereas the ego and the Cs.-Pcs. (as a system) were once thought of as practically coextensive in their struggle with unruly instinctual strivings, the more refined observations of phenomena have clarified their essentially different natures and references (Freud 1923, Arlow and Brenner 1964). Conflict as such is now considered to exist largely between the psychic structures or elements within them. "Conscious," "preconscious," and "unconscious" are viewed principally as qualities, conditions, or states of certain psychic processes. However, it is possible that such undoubted advances have given structural concepts and their role in conflict and process a dominant position in psychoanalytic thought which tends to overshadow topographical considerations to a disadvantageous degree. For example, the merit of the psychoanalytic goal of ego change—let us say the abandonment or relative abandonment of a pathological defense, or the extension of ego control over certain elements in the id, or a revised relationship with the superego—cannot be questioned. However, the process of making all the psychic components of such processes conscious is of the first importance; furthermore, the fact of persisting availability to consciousness, i.e., the preconscious state, is probably an important functional element in the relative permanence of ego change. It would seem that the topographic consideration is indispensible to the pursuit of the goal epitomized in Freud's aphorism: "Where id was, there ego shall be" (Freud 1933, p. 80). The reason is, at least in part, quite clear. With consciousness comes access to the voluntary nervous system, thus the capacity for action and thus the mobilization of special dangers inherent in certain gratifications, or the seeking for them.

Germane to this simple nuclear fact is the fact that the conscious wish in itself involves responsibility, and thus guilt of a more pervasive type than that involved in unconscious mechanisms. Everyday morality, religion, and the law give crucial significance to this distinction, which is still importantly related to the distinction between a person's "It" and his "I." However, this "I" is more exactly the "self" rather than an objectively conceived structure, the ego. The person struggles, even consciously, to maintain freedom from the manifest subjective guilt that comes with full consciousness. "It's only a dream, after all!" However, in view of the subterranean but all-too-real life of the unconscious, where the wish is more thoroughly at one with its magical powers, he can rarely exculpate himself fully by this device—i.e., free himself from endogenous suffering—as society does exculpate him in the everyday sense. Just as speech, even in the psychoanalytic situation, is closer to action than is thought, that it is, indeed, the patient's only psychoanalytic "action," it is fraught with even greater guilt or anxiety than is its precursor, conscious thought. Thus resistance does indeed have a special function in the relationship between the Ucs., and Pcs.-Cs. systems, and the process of change between them, even though this be anterior or precursive to the more radical process of lasting structural change. It is to avoid these subjective dangers in the transference—or anterior to the awareness of transference—from the patient's own superego, the original (now internalized) punitive parent. That the emergence may lead to new solutions is known to the analyst and (presumably and tenatively) to the adult portions of the patient's ego, but not necessarily to the intimidated child in the patient, a child who has, furthermore, never quite given up his ancient and original goals. Unless one views the ego resistance directed against the specific idea as becoming conscious exclusively as an inborn tendency of ego function, one must look for its further meaning in a larger functional concept of resistance as a dynamism.

We must note the pathological instances of relative failure of structure formation, or reversible pathological regressions of structures, as in psychoses, exceeding those normally occurring in sleep, not to speak of the massive transitory revisions which may occur under the stresses of group dynamics (for example, riots, revolutions, wars, or regressive ideologies). One may therefore assume that, granted the primary constitutional endowment, the development of structures is in good part a sustained dynamic response to powerful dynamic elements in the human situation: to the prolonged biological helplessness of the human infant and to the indispensable and germane environmental influences of kinship and the human family (Fries 1946). Related to these factors are the evolution of the instinct life in practically exclusive relation to parents and siblings, before either executive capacities in this sphere or their acceptance by the adult environment are established (not to speak of the permanent barriers to incest and murder), and the complexly related (primary and secondary) struggles against separation. The mental capacity for permanent representations and the processes of identification—indeed internalization in general—facilitate (and in turn are perhaps to some degree derived from) structure formation. Certainly the earliest ego functions themselves include identifications with the caretaking mother (Freud 1923, Hartmann, Kris, and Loewenstein 1946, Hendrick 1951).

The original tendency of the infant organism is to react as a whole. The striving of the adult organism is to do the same. However, it can do so, or rather preserve the subjective illusion of doing so, only with the aid of an elaborate unconscious system, various compromise formations (ranging from dreams to well-marked symptoms or pathological character traits), and, paradoxically, through the operations of the underlying tripartite structural system. These structures and dynamisms respond, in their cooperation and conflict, to the need for a consistent sense of self, for a consistent sense of identity, which can at the same time permit survival, growth, and the likelihood of certain basic gratifications in external reality. The "principle of multiple function" formulated by Waelder (1930) is, in effect, a statement of the tendency to react as a total "self" in terms of already-established divisions within the mind. There is no need to postulate a basic and intrinsic antagonism among structures as such. The superego that can torture, even murder (or command the murder of), the self in melancholia can contribute to the calm of a "quiet conscience" in the healthy person and facilitate his social adaptation. The ego that defends itself vigorously against persisting incestuous or destructive fantasies and impulses (lest the person himself be castrated or destroyed) facilitates and implements acceptable aggressive or sexual impulses. It is indeed indispensable for the external conveyance of "drive" in the human. As Hartmann emphasized (1948), it replaces, with its myriad perceptive, adaptive, and conative capacities, the relative stereotypy of instinctual response in other animals. If the human infant is confronted with the special stimulations and frustrations, as well as the "privileges," attendant on its prolonged physical helplessness, and then the psychological extensions of the same state in the protective and hierarchical structure of the human family, the adult will live in a further modified elaboration of the same general milieu in one form or another in the extended human community, especially his tribe or nation.

The earlier passing reference to sleep and the corresponding changes in the structures reminds us of certain quasi resemblances of elements in the psychoanalytic situation to those in sleep (see Lewin 1954, 1955). In our present context we should note that in the light of the latent transference, the obligatory character of free association tends, like the hypnotic command, to reduce energies invested in defense or at least permits their reduction. Also, the inhibition of motor activity (although voluntarily assumed)—that the psychoanalytic work is in effect confined to "words," though not as "safe" as pure subjective visual imagery—does tend in itself to reduce the ordinary ego and superego resistances, as compared with their defense correlates in "everyday life." It may also give substance to another radically different form of resistance, which has been mentioned in the literature (Kaiser 1934) but has not stimulated sufficient concern and thought, i.e., the separation of the analytic work from the processes and demands of everyday life and the consequent heightening of its regressive attraction for certain persons.

Both the restraints and conveniences of human social organization intensify the potential discreteness of structural development. However, as Waelder has emphasized (1960, p. 84), Freud himself was not at all inclined to the conceptual sharpness of demarcation that has sometimes been expressed. Apart from the question of interstructural "shading," the relatively direct connection between the presumed instinctual reservoir in the id and the severe aggressive activities of the superego in certain persons appears to outweigh, in its archaic power, the role of identification with actual parents in superego formation. An allied theoretical conception, less accessible empirically, would be the assumption that the energies of defense derive, at least in good part, from aggression (Hartmann 1950, pp. 131ff.). In both instances, often clearly demonstrable with regard to the superego, the incipient aggressive responses evoked by parents would have been turned against the self or its instinctual strivings in the interest of improved object relationships and adaptations.

In intense conflict, the antagonistic aspects of these groups of functions (i.e., the structures) do become conspicuous and in extreme instances can overshadow the essential integrative tendency. Where such conflict arises in the infantile period or in very early childhood, when both executive and adaptive capacities are few or nonexistent, the invocation of ego defenses leads to a species of structuralization of the conflict itself, due in part to sequestration and banishment from consciousness. It is certainly rendered largely inaccessible, by these mechanisms, to the direct modifications and influences of maturation, education, favorable experience, and allied phenomena. The development of neurotic symptoms or ego-syntonic character distortions permits the relative reestablishment of a consistent sense of self, of integrated voluntary behavior, in relative safety from attack or deprivation by parents or their intrapsychic representations. The adjective *relative* is important, for with the unconscious gratification afforded by symptoms, punishment is also sustained, thereby permitting the gratification. However, the investment of psychic representations, sometimes embodied in the subject's own person, rather than original objects, and above all the sequestration of the entire process from consciousness, permit the "relative safety" of which I have spoken. A crude parallel would be the self-reproaches, anxiety, or guilt connected with masturbation, with repressed incestuous fantasies, compared with the punishment envisaged for actual incest and parricide (see Freud 1908 and Arlow 1953). In more severe illnesses, such as melancholia, where the demands, reproaches, and latent violence toward the internalized primal mother are the issue, in intense and primitive energic terms, the penalty for the patient may indeed be his death.

The process of punishment, of course, includes the internalized image of the early parental disciplinarian, the superego, which, with the rarest of exceptions, remains an integral and indispensible part of human personality, an especially eloquent testimony to the irredentist struggle against separation as well as a unique way of dealing with it. In this immediate context of our discussion, the emergence of ego-dystonic material is "resisted" by the infantile "experiencing" portion of the ego, in the relative materialization of speech (one of Freud's earliest conceptions of "transference": from unconscious [imagery] to preconscious [words] [1900, p. 562]), because of fear of superego punishment, anterior to the investment of the analyst with the superego functions. It is also resisted, to some degree by the entire ego, as disruptive to the conscious integrated sense of self and, secondarily, its narcissistic overevaluation as such. With this, in a more functional and objective sense yet related to the subjective sense of self, there is a "struggle" to maintain, against disorganizing intrusion, the economies of interstructural balance, i.e., the character, developed in accordance with the "principle of multiple function" (Waelder 1930).

If we think of the long-term aspects of the psychoanalytic situation, expressed in structural concepts, in relation to the assumption (for me, the conviction) that the earliest relations with objects decisively influence both the qualitative and economic characteristics of psychic structures (evolving from the "givens" of constitution), we must assume the powerful impact of the transference on the activities of all three. Insofar as this impact permeates all details of process it is, of course, a critical and complicated influence in the general pattern of resistances. For while the patient's ego reacts to the analyst always, to varying degree, in terms of the perceived and immediate realities, these reactions also receive impetus from the sphere of regressed genetically early experience in object relationships. To the patient's id, the analyst is primarily an object for love, aggression, and any of their nuances. In relation to the superego, he is a parental surrogate, eminently suitable for investment as an alternate with potential punitive, disciplinary, or allied more temperate functions. Each plays its respective role in facilitating or impeding the psychoanalytic process, as traditionally recognized, and each is susceptible to modification by the mood and structure of the psychoanalytic situation and by its interpretive interventions. A priori, and probably in actual statistical incidence, the superego, the initiator of the sense of guilt, would seem readiest for such change. However, for reasons mentioned before (the relation to the patient's own reservoir of destructive aggression, later subsumed in Freud's more forbidding views of the negative therapeutic reaction [1920a, 1923]), this is not always achieved so readily as we would hope or even expect in the light of the identificatory aspects of superego origin. However, that prolonged "working through" does sometimes produce such modifications in ego or superego when despair has almost supervened and impedes the ready acceptance of rigid etiological views of such phenomena, for example, the role of the death instinct (see above). In general, we may say that the degree of structural plasticity and its responsiveness to involvement and analysis in the transference neurosis is one of the important elements in both the limitations and potentialities of genuine change occasioned by the psychoanalytic process.

THE RELATIONSHIP OF RESISTANCE TO TRANSFERENCE

Several decades ago Freud (1925, pp.40–41) pointed out that everything said in the analytic situation must have some relation to the situation in which it is said. This is, of course, consistent not only with reflective common sense but also with the theory of transference and the current view of the central position of the transference neurosis in analytic work. Furthermore, despite his earliest view of the "false connection" as pure resistance (Breuer and Freud 1893–1895) and the continuing high estimation of this aspect of transference, Freud early established the (nonconflictual) positive transference as the analyst's chief ally against resistances. Thereafter he never stinted in his appreciation of the primitive driving power of the transference and its indispensable function of conferring a vivid and living sense of reality on the analytic process (Freud 1912a, for example). In my own view, elaborated in past communications, the transference is indeed the central dynamism of the entire psychoanalytic situation; and the transference neurosis certainly provides the one framework which gives essential and accessible configuration to the potentially panpsychic scope of free association (Stone 1961, 1966). In this frame of reference the irredentist drive to reunion with the primal mother, as opposed to the benign processes of maturation and separation, underlies neurotic conflict in its broadest sense and is the basis of what I have called the *primordial transference*, whose striving is toward renewed physical approximation or merger. Speech, which is the veritable stuff of psychoanalysis, serves as the chief "bridge" of mastery for the progressive somatic separations of earliest childhood. The "mature transference," in continuum, alternative and contrast, is that series and complex of attitudes contingent on maturation and benign predisposing elements of early object relationships (conspicuously, the wish to be understood, to learn, and to be taught) that enable increasing somatic separation in a continuing affirmative context of object relationship, as later reflected in the psychoanalytic situation. In this interplay, speech—our essential working tool—plays an oscillating, curiously intermediate role, ranging from the threat of regression in the direction of its primitive oral substrate to its ultimately purely communicative-referential function linked with insight (Stone 1961, 1966).

In general, however, the origin of the "transference" as we usually perceive it clinically, and as the term is traditionally employed, is in the primordial transference. Be it essentially the classical triadic incestuous complex or an oral drive toward incorporation or toward permanent nursing dependency or a sadomasochistic anal striving toward a parent, it will be reexperienced in the analytic situation, in good part in regressive response to its deprivations (Macalpine 1950), and give rise to the central, and ultimately the most formidable, manifest resistance, the transference-resistance.

The "transference-resistance," while sometimes used in varying references, meant originally the resistance to effective insight into the genetic origins and prototypes of the transference, expressed in the very fact of its emergence (originally, the "false connection" described by Freud [Breuer and Freud, 1893–1895, especially pp. 302–303]). Thereafter, as the transference became established in its own autochthonous validity, the same resistance could be viewed as an obstruction to genetic understanding of the transference, and thus putatively to its dissolution. I say "putatively" because empirical experience has not often shown that simple awareness of such origins is adequate for the dissolution of the transference.[2] Rather, such dissolution (using this word in a relative and pragmatic sense) is contingent on much germane analytic work, on analysis of the dynamics of the attitude as represented in the transference neurosis, on working through, and on complicated and gradual responsive emotional processes in the patient (Stone 1966). Nevertheless, this genuine genetic insight is indispensable for the demarcation of the transference from the real relationship and for the intellectual incentive toward its dissolution within the framework of the therapeutic alliance.

Before going further, we should comment on the intimately related (although apparently opposite) "resistance to the awareness of transference." While there are patients whose confrontation with the analyst is characterized by the immediate emergence of intense (even stormy) transference reactions, most patients experience these emergent attitudes as essentially ego dystonic, except in the sense of the attenuated derivatives which enter into (or vitiate) the therapeutic alliance or in the sense of chronic characterological reactions which would appear in other parallel situations, however superficial and approximate the parallels might be.

The clinical actualities of emergent transference require analysis in its usual technical sense, including the prior analysis of defense. Transference may appear in dreams long before it is emotionally manifest; in parapraxes, in symptomatic reactions, in acting out within the analytic situation, or—most formidably—in acting out in the patient's essential life situation. Except in cases of dangerous acting out, or very intense anxiety or equivalent symptoms, which can constitute emergencies, the technical approach involves the same patient centripetal address to the surface that is prescribed for analysis in general. However, in this connection, I would suggest a modification of the classical precept that one does not interpret the transference until it becomes a manifest resistance. At that point, the interpretation is obligatory. The resistance to awareness should be interpreted, and its content brought to awareness, as soon as the analyst believes that the libidinal or aggressive investment of the analyst's person is economically a sufficient reality to influence the dynamics of the analytic situation and/or the patient's everyday life situation.

It is useful to strip the matter of nuances, reservations, and exceptions, for the purpose of clarity in an essential direction. The avoidance of awareness of transference derives from all of the hazards that accompany consciousness: accessibility of the voluntary nervous system, hence heightened "temptation" to action; heightened conflict in relation to the sanctions and satisfactions of impulse materialization; the multiple subjective dangers of communication of "I-you" impulses and wishes or germane fears to an object invested with parental authority; heightened sense of responsibility (thus guilt) connected with the same complex; and, very far from least, the fear of direct humiliating disappointment—the narcissistic wound of rejection or, perhaps worst of all, no affective response at all from the analyst. In "acting out," sometimes so destructive in the patient's life situation, amid a great range of important determinants, this need for response, the avoidance of this particular helplessness of impact, plays an important part. There is also the exceedingly important fact that the transference conflicts remaining outside awareness retain their unique access to autoplastic symptomatic expression, in compact and narcissistically omnipotent, if painful, solution, without the direct challenge and confrontation with alternative (and essentially "hopeless") solutions.

Why, then, if such fears weigh heavily against the analytic effort and the ultimate therapeutic advantages of awareness, does the patient cling tenaciously to his view of the analyst and the system of wishes connected with this view, once it has become established in his consciousness? In the earliest view, where the cognitive elements in analysis were heavily preponderant, not only in technique but also in the understanding of process, such clinging to transference attitudes was thought to be, as our traditional term implies, a resistance to recall (or reconstruction) as such, since the latter was indeed the essential goal of the analytic effort and was thought to be, in itself, the essential therapeutic mechanism. But why is the patient not willing, like the historian Lecky's dinner partner, to "let bygones be bygones"? Unless one accepts this aversion to recall or reconstruction, a preference for "present pain," as a primary built-in aversion, in itself an unexplained fact of "human nature," one must look further. In my view, the situation is more nearly the reverse. The patient rejects these elements of "insight" because they vitiate or diminish both the affective and cognitive significance of this central object relationship, which is a current materialization of crucial unconscious wish and fantasy, hitherto warded off. If it is to be given up, why was it pried out of its secure nest in the unconscious? Such resolution is always felt, at least incidentally, as an attack on the patient's narcissism and on his secure sense of self, secondarily reestablished. Moreover, to the extent that there is a genuine translation of the subjectively experienced somatic drive elements into verbal and ideational terms related to past objects, there is an inevitable step toward separation from the current object which parallels the original and corresponding developmental movement.

An essential dynamic difference from the past lies in the different somatic and psychological context in which the renewed struggle is fought. Old desires, old hatreds, old irredentist urges toward mastery, have been reawakened in a mature and resourceful adult, in certain spheres still helpless subjectively but no longer literally and objectively, a fact of which he is also aware. It was pointed out by Freud (1910a, p. 53) that this great quantitative discrepancy between infant conflict and adult resources makes possible and facilitates therapeutic change, through insight. In many important respects, this remains true. However, the remorseless dialectic of psychoanalysis again asserts itself. Truly effective insight requires validating emotional experience, which is only rarely achieved through recollection alone. The affective realities of the transference neurosis are necessary (sometimes inevitable!), and with this experience comes the renewal of the ancient struggle, in which, with varying degrees of depth, the maturity and resources of the analysand often play a role at variance with his capacity for understanding.[3] This is true not only of the subjective quality and experience of his strivings but of the resources which support his resistances, in either phase of the transference involvement. Whether the wish be to seduce, to cling, to defeat and humiliate, to spite, or to win love, mature resources of mind—sometimes of body!—may be invoked to implement this purpose, including what in some instances may be an uncanny intuitiveness regarding the analyst's personal traits, especially his vulnerabilities.

The persistence of old desires for gratification and the urge to consummate them, or indeed the urge to restore and maintain an original relationship with an omnipotent (and omniscient) parent, are intelligible to everyday modes of thought. That the tranference, like the neurosis itself, may also entail guilt, anxiety, frustration, disappointment, and narcissistic hurt is another matter. If it gives so much trouble, why does it reappear? Freud's latter-day explanation involved the complex general theory of primary masochism and the repetition compulsion. One cannot, in a brief discussion, enter into disputation which has already occasioned voluminous writing. In ultimate condensation, the operational view to which I adhere is that all painful elements may be understood as (1) accompanying the renewed unregenerate drive for gratification of hitherto warded-off wishes, whether libidinal or aggressive, based on the presentation of an actual object who bears significant functional "resemblances" to the indispensable parent of early childhood, in a climate and structure of instinctual abstinence and/or (2) based on the latent alternative urge to understand, assimilate, perhaps alter parental response, or otherwise master poignantly painful situations as they were actually experienced in a state of relative helplessness in the past. Both may be viewed as independent of adult motivations, although the power of the first may at times importantly subserve such motivations, and the second may often be phenomenologically congruent with them. Implicit in both, in contrast with the experiential plasticities and varieties of mature ego development, is the persistent and continuous theme of adhesion to the psychic representation of the decisive original parent figure or a perceptually variant substitute. Inasmuch as I have stated my conviction that the fractional but profoundly important struggle against original separation from the primal mother, with its potential phase specifications, as opposed to the powerful urges toward independent development, provides the underlying basis for developmental and later, neurotic conflict, I must observe that these conflicting tendencies, in the sense of the profundity which I assign to them, provide a certain parallel to the Thanatos-Eros struggle which assumed a decisive role in Freud's final contributions. In a recent study of aggression (Stone 1971), I have examined Freud's views on this subject. Although — in seeming paradox — I find the existence of a profound "alternative" impulse to die at least conceptually tenable and susceptible to clinical inferential support, it is my conviction, from both observation and inference, that aggression as such is an essentially instrumental phenomenon (or cluster of phenomena) capable of serving self-preservation and sexual impulses alike, and that it is thus, in its original forms, pitted against a postulated latent impulse to die, as it is against external threats to life. These urges and instrumentalities find primal organismic expression and experience in the phenomenon of birth and the immediate neonatal period, the biological prototype of all subsequent specifications, elaborations, and transmutations of the experience of separation. At the very outset the "conflict" may find expression in the delay of breathing or, shortly thereafter, in the disinclination to suck. There is thus an intertwining of the two conceptions of basic conflict. It may be that time will validate Freud's latter-day views of the fundaments of human conflict. For the time being, however, I can only adhere to and present what I believe to be an empirically more accessible and a heuristically more useful view of the ultimate human intrapsychic struggle. Thus the originally unmastered or regressively reactivated struggle around separation, revived by developmental conflict, would in this schema represent the "bedrock" of ultimate resistances, although never — at least in theory — utterly and finally insusceptible to influence. If we assume that the vicissitudes of object relationships, initiated by the special relationship of the human infant to his family, are fundamental in the accessible processes of personality (thus, structural) development and thus of neuroses, and that, in "mirror image," the transference and thus the transference-resistance have a comparable strategic position in the psychoanalytic process, can we extend these assumptions into the detailed technical phenomenology of process resistance in its endless variety of expressions? I believe that this extension is altogether valid.

We may first, however, devote a brief detour to certain important phenomena of personality integration. The latter include the relative consistencies of character and identity and, further, the hard-won sense of optimal effectiveness in adaptation and drive gratification, in the light of available modes of spontaneous conflict solution, deriving from what we may call the established "parts" of the personality. The continuing and actual biological unity of the self, the psychological principle of "multiple function," and the postulated role of the libido in maintaining syntheses (Freud 1920a, Nunberg 1930) are objectively conceived elements in the tenacity of established personality manifestations. These in themselves pose a conservative obstacle to change. There is indubitably a "sparing of psychic energy" involved in fixed, relatively structuralized modes of reaction. Far from minimal in invoking struggle against incipient or "threatened" change is the inevitable and essentially healthy narcissistic investment in the secondary neurotic "self."

Furthermore, whether or not one thinks of it as "motivation" in its usual sense, one can without extravagance postulate an even more intense cohesiveness at the first signal of that stimulus which contributed to the establishment of the organization and its basic strategies in the first place, i.e., the analyst as transference object. In the subjective sense, the regressive trend of the transference, stimulated by the total structure of the psychoanalytic situation (i.e., the basic rule of free association and the systematic deprivations of the personal relationship) confronts the patient with one who is perceived ultimately as his first and all-important object, the prototypical source of all gratification, all deprivation, all rejection, all punishment—the object involved in the primordial serial experiences of separation (Stone 1961). This may seem an exaggeratedly magniloquent way to view a practitioner who sits in an armchair, listens, tries to understand, and then interprets, when he can, toward a therapeutic end. To a large portion of the adult patient's personality, the "observing" portion of his ego, the portion that enters into the therapeutic alliance, that is just what he is and what he should remain. To another portion, largely unchanged from its past, sequestered in the unconscious but powerfully influential albeit in derivative and indirect ways, he is indeed a formidable object. It is in this field of force that, along with the drive toward better solutions, the range of clinical transferences as we know them is awakened. I have already mentioned that in a broad sense, the entire effort to translate the patient's view of drives for reunion and contact, whether libidinal or aggressive, into genuine language, insight and voluntary control (or appropriate conative implementation elsewhere) is "resisted," as it was originally, as an expression (or at least precursor) of separation, thus repeating aspects of the original developmental conflict. It is, however, also true that the later and clinically more accessible vicissitudes of childhood create more accessible resistances within the postulated metapsychological context created by the infant-mother relationship just described. I refer to those patients in whom the phenomena of general bodily unity or approximation have been largely renounced, not only as physical *faits accompli* in perceptual and linguistic fact but also in terms of deployment of cathexis among other essential intrapsychic representations. Such changes remain subject to regression or to the primary investment of certain phase strivings, conspicuously the Oedipus complex, in excessive libidinal or aggressive cathexis. Such strivings, paradigmatically the incest complex, are in themselves the narrowed, potentially adaptive, maturational expressions of the basic conflict aroused by separation. If the analyst is, to this infantile portion of the patient's personality, an indispensable parent because cognition is, in this reference, subordinate to drive, it follows that the analyst becomes the central object in the complicated infant system of desires, needs, and fears which have hitherto been incorporated in symptoms and character distortions. The patient must, furthermore, tell these "secrets" to the very object of a complex of disturbing impulses. This is a new vicissitude, not usually encountered in childhood and indeed guarded against, even within the patient's own personality, by the very existence of the unconscious. Ordinarily he does not even have to "tell himself" about them, in the sense that he is to a considerable degree identified with his parents, originally in his ego, then, in a punitive or disciplinary sense, in his superego. To be sure, the adult "observing" portion of his personality, except where matters of adult guilt, embarrassment, or shame interfere, usually cooperates with the analyst. It can at least try to maintain the flow of derivative associations, which provide the analyst with material for informed inferences. The tolerant and accepting attitude of the analyst tested by all of the patient's rational and intuitive capacities, even more decisively his interpretative activity, which suggests to the unredeemed child in the patient that he, "knows (or at least surmises) already," gradually overcome the patient's fear of his own warded-off material and finally the fear of its frank expression.

There are, then, three broad aspects of the relationship between resistance and transference. Assuming technical adequacy, the proportional importance of each one will vary with the individual patient, especially with the depth of psychopathology. First, the resistance to awareness of the transference and its subjective elaboration in the transference neurosis; second, the resistance to the dynamic and genetic reductions of the transference neurosis and ultimately the transference attachment itself, once established in awareness; third, the transference presentation of the analyst to the "experiencing" portion of the patient's ego, as id object and as externalized superego simultaneously in juxtaposition to the therapeutic alliance between the analyst in his real function and the rational "observing" portion of the patient's ego. These phenomena give intelligible dynamic meaning to resistances ordinarily observed in the cognitive-communicative aspects of the analytic process. These are the process or "tactical" resistances, largely deriving from the ego under the pressure or threat of the superego.

In this connection, a word about "working through." Sometimes, as Freud (1914) mentioned, the structure yields only when a peak manifestation of resistance has apparently been achieved. The patient appears to require time, repetition, and a sort of increasing familiarity with the forces involved for real change to occur. Also, Freud originally thought of the energy transactions as having some relation to the phenomenon of abreaction in the earlier methods. One is indeed impressed with the insistent recurrence of transference affects, conspicuously irrational anger in essentially rational patients, as though the structuralized tendency from which they derive can give way only on the basis of repetitive reenactment and gradual reduction of affect. Insofar as circumscribed symptom formations or equivalent forms of neurotic suffering (and gratification) play an ongoing and inevitable economic role in the psychoanalytic situation and process, apart from usually having been the basis for its initiation, one might assume that they bear an important relationship to working through. Even when extinguished for shorter or longer periods under the influence of the transference, their continued latent existence (or potentiality) is opposed to the vicissitudes of the current transference neurosis or its gradual relinquishment via working through. This is true whether one thinks of the symptom in the quasi-neurophysiological sense of Breuer's early formulation of pathways of "lowered resistance" (Breuer and Freud 1893–1895) or in a more empirical sense as a perennially seductive regressive condensation of impulse, gratification, and punishment. A useful and well-grounded concept, allied with the struggle against separation, is the relationship of working through to the process of mourning (Freud 1917b). (See also Greenson's [1965] comprehensive paper, with references to several other authors.)

While from the adult point of view the gratifications may be small and the suffering great, the symptom is nevertheless autoplastic, narcissistic in an isolated sense, already structuralized, and subject to no outside interference (except by the analysis!), an expression of localized infantile omnipotent fantasy, however large or small this fantasy kingdom may be. By the same token, in the sense mentioned earlier, with regard to unconscious processes in general, the symptom affords protection from both the challenges and sanctions of the world of reality, and from the temporary disruptive intrusions of new elements into the narcissistically invested conscious personality organization. In working through, there is the biphasic and arduous problem of restoring original or potential object cathexes in the transference neurosis, reducing their pathological intensities or distortions, and then deploying them in relation to the outer world. One may thus think of "working through" as opposed to the renewal of symptom formation and as repeating some of the postulated vicissitudes of one of the earliest conceptions of "transference," the infantile transition from autoerotism to object love (Ferenczi 1909). In this sense, the clinging to the incestuous object, represented in the clinical transference, would represent an intermediate process.

There is thus a tenacious reluctance to bow to the threat of the "quiet voice" of the intellect which, with the cooperation of the "observing" ego, might seduce the involved portion from its inveterate clinging to the actual transference object or to its autoplastically equivalent symptomatic representations. The postulated two portions of the ego (Freud 1940b [with earlier adumbrations], Sterba 1934, in different references) are, after all, "of the same blood," to put it mildly, and the urge to reunion in integrated function, the libidinal (synthetic) bond, is indeed strong. This same affinity between ego divisions may, of course, take an opposite and adverse turn, a triumph of the "resistance." I refer to those instances of chronic severe transference regression, where the adult segment of the ego is "pulled down" with the other and remains recalcitrant to interpretative effort (Freud 1940a). While this is, of course, often contingent on the depth of manifest or latent illness, it may be facilitated by iatrogenic factors, such as excessive and superfluous deprivations in inappropriate and essentially irrelevant spheres. With these considerations, of whose importance I am increasingly convinced with the passage of time, I have dealt at length in the past (Stone 1961, 1966).

A Word about Certain Special Sources of Resistance

It is important to mention, even if briefly, that certain special factors, sometimes extrinsic to analysis as such, may indefinitely prolong apparently satisfactory analyses. Real guilt, for example, may not be faced. Emotional distress based on real-life problems may not be confronted and accepted as such. A person of the type described by Freud (1916) as an "exception," who feels himself to have been abused by Fate, even if in other respects not more ill than others, may consciously or unconsciously reject the psychoanalytic discipline or the instinctual renunciations derived from its insights. Fixed and unpromising life situations or organic incapacities may permit so little current or anticipated gratification that the attractiveness of the regressive, aim-inhibited analytic relationship is strong in comparison with the barrenness of the extraanalytic situation. The last general consideration is, of course, always an essential (if silent) constituent of the psychoanalytic field of force, especially in relation to the dissolution of the transference-resistance (Stone 1966, p. 34). Or, more accessibly, the "rules of procedure" of analysis itself may be consciously or unconsciously exploited by the patient. He may, in "obedience" to a traditional rule, delay certain decisions to the point of absurdity, invoking the analytic work in support of his neurosis and sometimes in contempt of important obligations in real life. Financial support of the analysis by someone other than the analysand can provide a basis for chronic, concealed "acting out." In general, the analysis itself can, on occasion, become a lever for subtle evasion of the obligations, vicissitudes, and contingent gratifications of everyday life, and thus, paradoxically, become a resistance to its own essential goals and purposes. It may indeed become *too much* like the dream, to which it bears certain dynamic resemblances (Lewin 1954, 1955). The analyst's perceptive and tactfully illuminating obligation is no less important in these spheres than in other sectors of his commitment.

A Few Words about Ego-Syntonic Resistances

Where resistance is a sustained conscious rebellion against the authority and methods of the analyst or a fear or mistrust of him in reality, or appears as another full-blown interpersonal difficulty of the same order (assuming, of course, that there is no basis for such attitudes in reality), we are dealing with a special category of resistance based on early disorders of object relationships and germane character problems, which may require long-term preanalytic preparatory work or may, indeed, make actual analytic work impossible. That such phenomena may occur in the usual period of preliminary interpersonal testing or episodically, with transference crises, in many patients, is well-known; the phenomena remain in the sphere of technical skill and personal resourcefulness, including its emotional components.

In such ego-syntonic "resistances" the patient is, in a subjective sense, really defending himself against a seducer, a deceiver, a cruel or punitive or unloving parent—ultimately and unequivocally, one who will, in the end, certainly put him aside. The patient fears to tell the analyst his secrets and fears even more deeply to become emotionally involved with him. These and secondary fears of the objective process components, are not essentially different in a qualitative sense from the unconscious, largely ego-dystonic resistances of the more mature and cooperative patient who is capable of the twofold (ostensibly "split") ego reaction which is indispensable to analytic work. The critical economic difference lies in the fact that the participation of the more difficult patient's ego in object relationships is controlled by his transferences in a total and unitary sense; sometimes even his autonomous perceptual functions are subordinated to them, in critical references and junctures. Certainly, unless and until the patient's personality undergoes certain necessary preliminary changes—preeminently some degree of benign identification with the analyst, which permits a therapeutic alliance, with some distance from and conflict with, his infantile self—the challenge of placing in hazard the personality integrations so painfully established in dealing with the analyst's prototypes in the past cannot even be seriously entertained. It is really in the sphere of intrapsychic conflict that the phenomena which we usually have in mind in speaking of "resistances" come into play, although never entirely unrelated to the primitive and unhappy paradigm to which I have just referred. All human beings have inevitably experienced some degree of deception, desertion, and rejection at the hands of their parents, at least subjectively; fortunately, most have also experienced love, protection, and understanding to a degree which permits or facilitates affirmative development. In the patient more suitable for analysis in the primary sense (with regard to the above referent, not traditional nosological considerations), the analyst is largely and firmly accepted in his actual functions, however tinged this acceptance may be by derivatives of repressed transferences.

One may legitimately ask, in response to this generally gloomy disquisition on one major force in the analytic process: Where is the other side, the will to recovery? The forces which support it? The patient's adult personality? The therapeutic alliance? The upward thrust from the id? And other attitudes and processes of an affirmative dynamic thrust? These are, of course, what makes psychoanalysis a therapy instead of a bitter struggle between patient and analyst. We have been speaking of the resistance, the force which is manifestly inimical to the analytic process, although based on an integral and essential element in human personality. Furthermore, we must note that even this dynamism, apart from its indigenous and integral functional dignity, has, like the skin, muscle, and fascia that oppose the surgeon, its affirmative aspect, even within the scope of psychoanalytic process.

SOME AFFIRMATIVE ASPECTS OF RESISTANCE

Even if we put aside adult and rational "resistances" such as intellectual skepticism and critique, the phenomena of resistance are largely if not exclusively of self-protective, conservative orientation. That their purposes are usually irrational in derivation, and largely ego dystonic, renders them amenable to analytic work. It must be recalled that they exist, in a subjectively purposive sense, to protect the encapsulated unconscious aspects of the personality, and, reciprocally, to protect the adult functioning personality syntheses from the potentially disruptive intrusions and demands of hitherto unconscious content. I mentioned earlier the "blood brotherhood" of the adult "observing" ego and the regression-prone "experiencing ego." Thus the resistance can arise just as importantly, although from subtly variant or even opposite motivation, from the "rational" ego as from its more thoroughly infantile counterpart, i.e., from the dread of its own regression. We all know the deceptively stilted "ultrarealistic" reactions and communications of the ego which doubts its own strength and reliability. If I may be permitted a brief obiter dictum: It is my conviction that this "blood kinship" between the two portions of the ego is an important factor both in the economic limitations of analytic cure in many instances and in its potentiation in others, where the "threat" (based on corresponding vicissitudes of development) is less severe. Unfortunately, analysis cannot actually repeat development, nor can it "imitate" it too closely without serious trouble. Where the economic problem is not too severe for the potentialities of the psychoanalytic situation, there is the opportunity for the two ego sectors to come to terms, in their respective modes, with the id and with the superego and thus with one another. In this event, the synthetic function of the ego can be restored to its primary place in the personality, as differentiated from the driven need for symptom formation.

In another direction: We are both intuitively and rationally skeptical, sometimes alarmed, about the patient who appears to show no "ordinary" resistances early in the analytic work. We suspect a serious lack of firm organization in his personality. Why does he seem to have no amnesias for early experiences; why does his transference fulminate in ego-syntonic form? We fear that impossible symbiotic fantasies, demands, and impulses, or the psychotic defenses of delusion and hallucination, will appear. Such unhappy developments are not, of course, inevitable, but it is, by common agreement, sound practice to be alert to their possibility. There is, to be sure, a disturbing cognitive deficit in a person who wholeheartedly develops prompt, violent, and inappropriate attitudes toward a person whom he hardly knows. But apart from this important observation, we expect a personality to be integrated, to be "stuck together," whether with the libidinal glue of the ego's synthetic function, metapsychologically considered, or on the basis of other functional tendencies such as the economies of structuralization or from more explicitly narcissistic motivations or the anxieties and natural guardedness against change which derive from these considerations. The current folk phrases—"coming apart," "falling apart," and, in contrast, "well put together"—are not without their intuitive perceptiveness.

The resistances, insofar as they assume an essentially intrapsychic form, i.e., if a viable therapeutic alliance has been established, oppose themselves to the suggestibility deriving from the positive transference (see Freud 1917a, p. 453). The resistances permit, indeed require, the testing of the analyst, both as to his perceptive and interpretative skill and as to his actual personal reliability, including latent countertransferences. They support—to some degree express— the healthy aspects of the "I'm from Missouri" reaction, as well as its impeding effect. In the same sense, they pace the development of the transference neurosis according to the personality's intuitively perceived ability to sustain it and to bring it to a more satisfactory resolution than that of the antecedent infantile neurosis. It would seem productive that the affirmative functional aspects of the resistances be appreciated by the analyst, and also their contingency on his general traits and methods beyond the ad hoc accuracy of his interpretations. The same is true of the structure and mood of the psychoanalytic situation, whether in its individual nuances or in its basic elements. To put this last in more blunt terms: the dissolution of resistances is as much an affective as an interpretative-cognitive process. Every interpretation, in fact—in content, mood, and timing— impinges on both spheres in the patient. This was, in effect, recognized even by such a die-hard "resistance analyst" as Kaiser (1934). It was recognized by Freud from the earliest period of his work onward. The positive transference, in its nonconflictual sense, can render a seemingly accusatory or irrelevant interpretation acceptable, at least for serious consideration. There are patients for whom the psychoanalytic situation in its basic essentials is intolerable and others for whom a changed nuance of mood and method can permit or restore its viability and usefulness (Stone 1961). The quality of the resistance may announce either one to the analyst.

And now for some concluding remarks, without the expedient of orderly recapitulation. Resistance, whether practically or conceptually considered, is not really identical with defense, although intimately related to it. This fact was emphasized by Jacobson in a recent panel discussion (1968). In the ultimate "showdown" in relation to an established transference, a resistance may be practically coextensive with a major defense, for example, in relation to a powerful instinctual impulse. However, anterior to this confrontation, it may strongly interfere with the analyst's first efforts to make the patient aware that a given trait or process *is* indeed a defense. For example, a patient who deals with powerful sadistic impulses by reaction formation, especially if the latter is an integral part of his character and thus of his adult sense of self, will struggle with all his resources against the awareness that his exaggerated pity or solicitude is not exclusively motivated by love or compassion, however tactful the analyst's approach may be. Resistance is a dynamism specifically directed against the psychoanalytic process and its goals. This process, to be sure, seeks to reactivate, reconstruct, or recall many important factors in personal development, as a necessary step toward potential affirmative change, but by way of a specific method and in a special and highly disciplined context. It cannot actually recapitulate development; it is at best neodevelopmental, in a partial and special sense.

The first — and continuing — struggle of the patient is to maintain personality cohesion and narcissistic pleasure in the self, in the specifications mentioned earlier. With this struggle, related to it from the beginning but conceptually separate and ultimately of more profound dynamic significance, is the struggle to avoid the awareness of basic infantile conflict in a new and powerfully dynamic interpersonal context. The functional significance of awareness as such, anterior to "working through," and in recent years overshadowed theoretically by the ultimate importance of structural change in therapy, is not to be underestimated in the genesis of process resistances. Implicit in the attainment of all technical aims and intrinsic in the nature and dynamics of the psychoanalytic situation, is the tendency toward the development of the transference neurosis, which occasions, in varying proportions, a hingelike process of resistance: avoidance of effective involvement in the relationship and — ultimately — the avoidance of its resolution in separation. In this sense, the analyst is from the beginning experienced as a threat by the infantile aspect of the ego, and in some instances even by the relatively more mature sectors. To hide from him, in this sense, is like the hiding of the hurt and mistrustful child from a deceitful and treacherous parent. Not only may the essential methods of analysis (free association, for traditional example) but also its intermediate and larger goals may be the targets of resistance. The latter resistances, for example the concealed avoidance of important issues, are in the strategic sphere, the resistances of choice in more severe disorders. It is an important fact, however, that resistances originating in the general personality motives and tendencies described earlier and implemented by any of the adult personality's deficits or resources — from new symptom formation to highly developed autonomous ego functions — may find expression in *any* of the broadly conceived areas of psychoanalytic process and goals.

Whatever form or direction the resistance takes, it interferes actively or by default in the broad, inclusive, and complex operational synthesis of effective analytic work. In a remote but real functional sense, this complex synthesis corresponds to the very organization of personality which "the resistance" seeks to defend. At the heart of this synthesis are, of course, the analytic situation and process as such, with intrinsic dialectic, balance, and integration of past and present, thought and feeling, communication and resistance in free association, transference and reality, and the analyst's interventions and the immediate or remote responses to them. Inextricably interrelated with this complex is the patient's everyday reality: the obligations, gratifications, sufferings, limitations, and potentialities inherent in his life situation and its dramatis personae, including the roles of these persons in reality and as conscripted participants in the transference neurosis. These inevitably present the requirements for confrontation with important realities and for dealing with them as such: the exertion of sheer will, effort, and endurance, where necessary, and the continuing acceptance of legitimate personal responsibilities. The latter considerations, to be sure, also obtain within the scope of the analysis proper. The chronic passive expectation of ultimate magical intervention by the analyst can disqualify the most richly productive analytic process.

It is the synthesis and continuum of these briefly sketched and merging components of psychoanalytic field and process, in its larger sense, against which the resistances in general are directed. For it is the synthesis which confers ultimate life and meaning on individual components, and facilitates the integrations of cognitive and emotional experience that are the most effective in analytic change. This synthesis finds its accessible epitome in the analysis of the genetically determined transference neurosis (and its extraanalytic ramifications) (Stone 1966). Exterior to specific correlation with certain characteristic defenses, resistances will in general be motivated by the dynamics of transference, personality cohesion, structural conflict, and other factors which have been described, always in the light (or darkness) of the ubiquitous topographic consideration. However, the mode and the site of operation of resistances will derive not only from habitual defensive and characterological tendencies but also from the patient's autonomous ego functions, even specific gifts or specific lacks, in interaction with the routine requirements and procedures of psychoanalytic work, the individual qualities of the immediate psychoanalytic situation, and often the personal traits and interests of the analyst, including, of course, his interpretive style, his countertransferences, and his counterresistances. Verbal fluency, scholarship, "psychological giftedness," talents as a raconteur, real or spurious obtuseness, dialectical superiority, and myraid other possible endowments (or lack of them) can be employed by the patient in the maintenance of the status quo.

An essential problem for the analyst, apart from the demonstrable process phenomena, is to become aware of what is omitted, hidden, or kept from asserting its genuine proportions. Comparable to the holistic scope of the analytic process and the analytic view of personality, the patient's involvement in analysis is in relation to all of his life activities, past and current. We assume that this fact is reflected in what I have called the *panpsychic scope* of his associations, shaped into ultimate meaningfulness by his transference neurosis (Stone 1961, p. 77). However, we can only be truly aware of the gaps and distortions in the communications of our single informant by keeping in mind not only the challenging and taxing details of analytic material but also the larger biographical background of the patient, his consistencies (and inconsistencies) of character, his system of current relationships and activities, his talents and sublimations, and his modes of symptomatic solution, to which the details of analytic data and process are always intimately related. For the patient may often in his larger strategies of resistance, tend to repeat both the exaggerated affirmations and the evasions or concealments which have characterized his life history. If we cannot, as Freud (1937) pointed out, artificially mobilize a transference conflict which is dormant in the patient's life context, we may at times, by tactful interpretive address to its analytic "absence" and in an affective climate which permits the patient to accept a second confrontation, to some degree mobilize a conflict which is indeed active but, because of archaic dread of the transference, moving toward delayed but severe symptomatic solution or unhappy large-scale materialization in the patient's everyday life (Stone 1966).

NOTES

1. This principle, however, always remained subject to some reservation. See Freud (1920b p. 152), for example, or the *Outline* (Freud 1940a, p. 160).

2. This experience began to assert itself quite early: See Freud (Breuer and Freud 1893–1895, p. 303): "Strangely enough, the patient is deceived afresh every time this is repeated."

3. See Freud's quotation from Diderot, which is indirectly but nonetheless pointedly relevant to this idea (Freud 1917a, pp. 337–338).

REFERENCES

Arlow, J. A. (1953). Masturbation and symptom formation. *J. Amer. Psychoanal. Assn.* 1:45–58.

_____, and Brenner, C. (1964). *Psychoanalytic Concepts and the Structural Theory.* New York: International Universities Press.

Breuer, J., and Freud, S. (1893–1895). Studies on hysteria. *S. E.*, 2.

Fenichel, O. (1941). *Problems of Psychoanalytic Technique.* Albany, N.Y.: The Psychoanalytic Quarterly.

Ferenczi, S. (1909). Introjection and transference. In *Sex in Psycho-Analysis* and (with O. Rank) *The Development of Psycho-Analysis.* New York: Dover 1956, pp. 30–79.

_____ (1919). Technical difficulties in the analysis of a case of hysteria. In *Further Contributions to the Theory and Technique of Psycho-Analysis.* London: Hogarth Press, 1926, pp. 189–197.

_____ (1920). The further development of an active therapy in psycho-analysis. In *Further Contributions to the Theory and Technique of Psycho-Analysis.* London: Hogarth Press, 1926, pp. 198–216.

_____ (1930). The principle of relaxation and neo-catharsis. *Int. J. Psychoanal.* 11: 428–443.

_____ (1931). Child analysis in the analysis of adults. In *Final Contributions to the Problems and Methods of Psycho-Analysis.* London: Hogarth Press, 1955, pp. 126–142.

_____ (1932). Confusion of tongues between the adult and the child. (The language of tenderness and of passion.) *Int. J. Psychoanal.* 13:225–230, 1949.

_____, and Rank, O. (1925). *The Development of Psychoanalysis.* New York and Washington, D. C.: Nervous and Mental Disease Publishing Co.

Freud, A. (1936). *The Ego and the Mechanisms of Defense.* New York: International Universities Press, 1946.

_____ (1968). *Difficulties in the Path of Psychoanalysis: A Confrontation of Past with Present Viewpoints.* New York: International Universities Press, 1969.

Freud, S. (1900). The interpretation of dreams. *S. E.* 4 and 5.

_____ (1905). Fragment of an analysis of a case of hysteria. *S. E.* 7.

_____ (1908). Hysterical phantasies and their relation to bisexuality. *S. E.* 9.

_____ (1910a). Five lectures on psycho-analysis. Fifth lecture. *S. E.* 11.

_____ (1910b). The future prospects of psycho-analytic therapy. *S. E.* 11.

_____ (1912a). The dynamics of transference. *S. E.* 12.

_____ (1912b). Recommendations to physicians practising psycho-analysis. *S. E.* 12.

_____ (1914). Remembering, repeating and working through. (Further recommendations on the technique of psycho-analysis II.) *S. E.* 12.

_____ (1916). Some character types met with in psycho-analytic work. *S. E.* 14.

_____ (1917a). Introductory lectures on psycho-analysis. Part III. *S. E.* 16.

_____ (1917b). Mourning and melancholia. *S. E.* 14.

_____ (1918). From the history of an infantile neurosis. *S. E.* 17.

_____ (1919). Lines of advance in psycho-analytic therapy. *S. E.* 17.

_____ (1920a). Beyond the pleasure principle. *S. E.* 18.

_____ (1920b). The psychogenesis of a case of homosexuality in a woman. *S. E.* 18.

_____ (1923). The ego and the id. *S. E.* 19.

_____ (1925). An autobiographical study. *S. E.* 20.

_____ (1933). New introductory lectures on psycho-analysis. *S. E.* 22.

_____ (1937). Analysis terminable and interminable. *S. E.* 23.

_____ (1940a). An outline of psycho-analysis. *S. E.* 23.

_____ (1940b). Splitting of the ego in the process of defence. *S. E.* 23.

Fries, M. E. (1946). The child's ego development and the training of adults in his environment. *Psychoanal. Study of the Child* 2:85–112. New York: International Universities Press.

Glover, E. (1955). *The Technique of Psycho-Analysis,* rev. ed. New York: International Universities Press.

Greenson, R. R. (1965). The problem of working through. In *Drives, Affects, Behavior,* vol. 2, ed. M. Schur. New York: International Universities Press, pp. 277–314.

_____ (1967). *The Technique and Practice of Psychoanalysis,* vol. 1. New York: International Universities Press.

Hartmann, H. (1948). Comments on the psychoanalytic theory of instinctual drives. In *Essays on Ego Psychology.* New York: International Universities Press, 1964, pp. 69–89.

_____ (1950). Comments on the psychoanalytic theory of the ego. In *Essays on Ego Psychology.* New York: International Universities Press, 1964, pp. 113–141.

_____ (1951). Technical implications of ego psychology. In *Essays on Ego Psychology*. New York: International Universities Press, 1964, pp. 142–154.

_____, Kris, E., and Loewenstein, R. M. (1946). Comments on the formation of psychic structure. *Psychoanal. Study of the Child* 2:11–38. New York: International Universities Press.

Hendrick, I. (1951). Early development of the ego. Identification in infancy. *Psychoanal. Q.* 20:44–61.

Jacobson, E. (1968). In Panel on Narcissistic Resistance. Fall Meeting of the American Psychoanalytic Association. 1968. *J. Amer. Psychoanal. Assn.* 17:941–954, 1969.

Kaiser, H. (1934). Probleme der Technik. *Internationale Zeitschrift für Psychoanalyse* 20:490–522.

Kris, E. (1956). On some vicissitudes of insight in psycho-analysis. *Int. J. Psychoanal.* 37:445–455.

Lewin, B. D. (1954). Sleep, narcissistic neurosis, and the analytic situation. *Psychoanal. Q.* 23:487–510.

_____ (1955). Dream psychology and the analytic situation. *Psychoanal. Q.* 24:169–199.

Loewenstein, R. M. (1951). The problem of interpretation. *Psychoanal. Q.* 20:1–14.

Macalpine, I. (1950). The development of transference. *Psychoanal. Q.* 19:501–539.

Mahler, M. S. (1965). On the significance of the normal separation-individuation phase, with reference to research in symbiotic child psychosis. In *Drives, Affects, Behavior*, vol. 2, ed. M. Schur. New York: International Universities Press, pp. 161–169.

Nunberg, H. (1930). The synthetic function of the ego. In *Practice and Theory of Psychoanalysis*. New York: International Universities Press, 1961, pp. 120–136.

Reich, W. (1933). *Character Analysis*. New York: Orgone Institute Press, 1945.

Sterba, R. (1934). The fate of the ego in analytic therapy. *Int. J. Psychoanal.* 15:117–126.

Stone, L. (1951). Psychoanalysis and brief psychotherapy. *Psychoanal. Q.* 20:215–236. *Reprinted in this volume, Chapter 1.*

✓ _____ (1961). *The Psychoanalytic Situation. An Examination of Its Development and Essential Nature*. New York: International Universities Press.

_____ (1966). The psychoanalytic situation and transference. Postscript to an earlier communication. *J. Amer. Psychoanal. Assn.* 15:3–58. *Reprinted in this volume, Chapter 4.*

_____ (1971). Reflections on the psychoanalytic concept of aggression. *Psychoanal. Q.* 40:195–244. *Reprinted in this volume, Chapter 11.*

Waelder, R. (1930). The principle of multiple function. *Psychoanal. Q.* 5:45–62, 1936.

_____ (1960). *Basic Theory of Psychoanalysis*. New York: International Universities Press.

Chapter 6

Notes on the Noninterpretive Elements in the Psychoanalytic Situation and Process
(1981)

This paper was written for a panel of the American Psychoanalytic Association. It states several of my long-standing convictions about psychoanalytic process in condensed integrated form. Perhaps for this reason it has elicited more than average interest among my writings. I believe that its clear title and content make any further introductory remarks unnecessary.

I n presenting these notes, I should first set aside any impression that the effort is "partisan," i.e., intended to derogate the role of interpretation in analytic work. I do indeed believe interpretation to be the essential and distinctive technical activity of the analyst's functional role. As to whether it operates effectively without certain prior and continuing activities, attitudes, and contextual conditions, one may say flatly "No!" As to whether it is, in every particular instance, the decisive analytic element—this may be open to reflection, discussion, possibly to debate. While I shall avoid significant incursions into the intellectual territory of interpretation as such, it is evident that I cannot avoid occasional references to the roles of interpretation and insight in the globally viewed psychoanalytic process and situation.

First, the general auspices of the psychoanalytic undertaking. The patient comes to the analyst for help with suffering. Whether he be a physician or lay analyst, the analyst is, in the old-fashioned lay vernacular, his "doctor." Omitting the rare instances of persons induced to participate in analysis for research purposes, the only other numerically significant group of analysands (to use the jargon) are candidates in training. Among the latter, it is indeed rare that some form of suffering (gross or subtle) is not present as an additional motivation. If this motive is not present, I am skeptical that a genuine psychoanalytic process will ensue, even though some insights may be established and some general benefits obtained. In other words, I am skeptical that resistances to the emergence of a true transference neurosis are likely to be overcome where it is not exchanged for prior neurotic suffering. In principle, the transference neurosis should follow on the acceptance of and sufficiently extended participation in the traditionally exercised analytic rule of abstinence in its widest sense, and the usual procedures of the psychoanalytic situation, conspicuously free association. However, my own empirical observation is that without important highly personal motivation, such participation, even when honest, is skin deep—with a corresponding depth of effectiveness. This is aside from the fact that—even where severe underlying pathology may exist—"normality" often constitutes the most impregnable form of defense (with corresponding process resistances). I do not, of course, go into the special peculiarities of the "training analysis" and its institutional context. At this moment, I am interested only in the basic initial orientation of analysand to analyst, which includes the need and wish for help.

With his need as motivation, the patient presents himself for analysis. That the "positive" parental transference is close to the surface in the reasonably viable neurotic patient one may expect in response to the inevitable functional "resemblance" of the analyst to parent figures (which I have mentioned in the past [1954]). Apart from severe intrinsic personality disturbances, this "resemblance" can be invalidated only by a tenacious commitment to the computer identity. The patient is then introduced to the "psychoanalytic situation," which—in shorthand—usually includes recumbency (with visualization of the analyst severely curtailed or absent), the obligation of free association (and behind it or underlying—possibly overlying—it), the separate "pledged" obligation of the "fundamental rule" (stressed by Kanzer 1972, 1979), the essential confinement of the analyst's manifest responses to interpretation and a very few ancillary techniques and—pervasively—the general rule of abstinence. The last, of course, applies to both participants, a not unimportant dynamic fact; but the greater intrapsychic burden is borne by the patient, and it is to his responses that we shall give our attention. (The old hymn, to the obliquely contrary notwithstanding, it is easier—if not better—to "not give" than to "not receive.").

According to the rule of abstinence, no gratifications other than those intrinsic in the situation and process, either affective or cognitive, are to be given the patient by the analyst. This rule, which attained its peak expression in Freud's Budapest Congress paper (1919), was offered in the sense of preserving the incentive for serious involvement in the psychoanalytic work. Thus it included the interdiction of emergency discharge processes or other expressions of the search for extra-analytic sources of symptomatic relief. But even more to the point, Freud mentions the necessity to deny the patient that which he most strongly desires—and that this lies explicitly in the sphere of the transference. While the rule of abstinence (although facilitated by other factors) became the principal dynamism of the transference neurosis, it was not so conceived by Freud. It remained for Macalpine (1950) to clarify the role of the analytic abstinences in the development of transference (and thus of the transference neurosis).

The diminished visual input (sensory deprivation, if you will), the recumbent posture and, of course, the significance of free association itself support the adaptation by regression that characterizes the evolution of transference and the establishment of the transference neurosis, which have become the crux of the analytic process. (That some now deny, in an inevitable swing of the historic pendulum, the essentiality of the transference neurosis in every analysis, I am well aware.) (See Gill 1979b and Modell 1979, for example.)

With regard to free association—neglecting, for the immediate issue, its special communicative function—I have mentioned in the past that its obligatory character (even if often honored in the breach) involves the sweeping renunciation of control of utterance in relation to another individual (a fundamental "civil right," so to speak), and is thus, if continuously required, tantamount to a significant regression in itself, or at least a voluntary functional facsimile of such a state. The paradoxical spiral of its voluntary, yet obligatory, commitment to an extreme and literal form of verbal "freedom," while vastly different in several critical respects, is certainly related to the voluntary relinquishment of control of consciousness which occurs in hypnosis, the more primitive technical ancestor of free association. Intrinsic in the successful achievement of either phenomenon is the investment of the analyst with a positive parental transference. In relation to free association, it is important to note that—with its organ keyboard range of communication of content and resistance, which I treasure as must any analyst—it can, as a totality, become an evasive habit, in some, a sort of addiction. The patient who never stops free-associating may require one of our infrequent noninterpretive interventions: the observation that free association in itself is not enough and that occasional pauses for reflection and assimilation are equally necessary. One may sometimes see patients analyzed many years before, who cannot state a current complaint without lapsing promptly into free association. That resistances may also dominate the course of rich and fluent free associations is an observation too old to require elaboration (Stone 1973). These may, of course, be evident and interpretable. But others must be sought in the extrinsic sphere: the patient's biography and the broad pattern of his daily life.

Germane to the general analytic context and process is the benign split of the ego, described by R. Sterba (1934), into an experiencing portion and an observing portion, the former involved in the transference and the latter cooperating with the analyst in his work and identified with him in this function. From this split evolves the patient's later interest in the intellectual process, including his free associations (an interest which was greatly valued by Freud) and ultimately, the variable capacity for self-analysis. Anterior to this therapeutic split is the split implicit in the very existence of neurosis, which, in the viable individual, must involve only a portion of the ego (although varying in magnitude), as an ego-alien phenomenon composed of ego-dystonic conflictive components.

At this point it may be useful to turn attention briefly to the processes of analysis and their intermediate operational purposes, both as classically conceived and as some have been modified with time. The recovery of memories of forgotten events was important in the very beginnings of analysis and never lost its importance to Freud. Witness the paper on "Constructions" (1937a). Originally, it was, with emotional abreaction, regarded as the curative process. The latter, of course, except in its supportive or "documenting" contribution to genuine insight is no longer regarded as intrinsically curative. The transference, which Freud (1912a) later elevated to an indispensable technical position first appeared in the role of a resistance to recall; and there has always remained a fascinating dialectical relation between the two aspects of the same phenomenon. I doubt that many of us would currently believe that the dissolution of amnesias in itself, except in the instances of isolated traumatic events in an otherwise relatively intact personality (whether in war or civilian life), would be therapeutically effective in a lasting sense. Certainly it is not true of the chronic psychoneuroses, where pathogenesis is far more complicated. Indeed, beginning with Freud himself, then enormously emphasized by Rank and Ferenczi (1925), the role of emotional experience in the transference gradually but insistently moved into the center of analytic work — with the recovery of memories or the establishment of constructions viewed as sequels of adequate transference interpretation, sometimes largely explanatory in their value, at times, when especially dramatic or vivid, accomplishing something allied to this function instantaneously through the ineffable simultaneous impact of temporal congruity and incongruity, without intermediate steps. Despite the occasional demurrals of some distinguished colleagues nostalgic for older emphases and methods, the trend toward the operational preeminence of the current, especially the "here-and-now" of the transference continues. However, the unique significance of reinstatement of the individual's past into his psychic life has never been disestablished. Gill (1979a, 1979b), for example, whose emphasis on the "here-and-now" in the transference extends it to its extreme technical limits, does not suggest exclusion of the historical element. He would, however, view its claim as secondary to that of the "here-and-now." For most analysts, including the writer, the individual genetic past remains the indispensable explanatory solvent of the irrational and inappropriate distortions of the present.

Now, to limit this already too discursive reference to matters adjacent to — but not within — my original subject, we can epitomize the essential questions. Whatever the direction or emphasis or order of one's approach, or one's emphasis as to ultimate analytic goals, certain operational elements persist in our work, e.g., to bring essential and relevant unconscious conflicts into the conscious sphere; to permit more adequate adaptive solutions; and to place, ultimately, irrational elements of personality in rational perspective by exposing their remote and no longer appropriate genesis. Thus the recollection or reconstruction of the past will facilitate the emergence and then the interpretive reduction of the transference neurosis, which will both outline the essential trends of conflict and give them meaningful and accessible life in the present. That there is an important trend of resistance to awareness of transference and of the transference neurosis is one of the primary interpretive tasks of the analyst in many — by no means all — instances. In regression-prone patients, the transference may provide an immediate confrontation (Stone 1954, 1973). Ultimately, the analytic reduction of the transference neurosis meets with the powerful and fundamental "transference resistance." Freud (1914) spoke of the functional recognition of transference and resistance as the indispensable criteria of analytic work (p. 16). In my view the two phenomena are inextricably related from the beginning (1973).

Now the past, we know, may be restored by recollection or by the analyst's constructions. The process of recollection is one of the special contributions of the patient's free association, sometimes dramatic in its quality. In either case the phenomenon of resistance — which Freud originally named as the reciprocal of the psychic force required of the analyst to overcome it — must be encountered and dissolved before such insight can be genuinely integrated in the patient's mind. The process would then be continued in the form of "working through" to render its establishment secure and inclusive. For the primitive actualities of (psychological) "force," there was substituted with time the subtle intellectual influence of interpretation or construction, for resistance as well as for unconscious content. The indispensable uses of the past, we have already acknowledged, but "insight" is a broader concept (curiously enough, it does not appear in the general index of the *Standard Edition!*). It includes a possible broad range of genetic, dynamic, economic, structural, and adaptive elements, ultimately in their interrelatedness and interaction. Note Blum's (1979) comprehensive paper on this subject. Interpretation is also a broad technical concept. It is designed to tell the patient what a manifest phenomenon means. In the strict sense (Bibring 1954), in distinction from clarification, it applies only to the unconscious meaning of manifest material. Interpretation may apply to the nature and direction of resistances, the nature of permanent defenses, the content of wishes or fantasies, the nature of warded-off impulses, punitive (or other) superego reactions, identifications, and similar matters.

Clarification is probably the most widely and deeply useful of the noninterpretive interventions. While, with other lesser techniques (which I shall not discuss separately) it is ultimately ancillary to interpretation, its skillful and patient employment can bring about the objectification and sequestration of occult symptoms, habitual responses, and pathological character traits, with accompanying perspective and sense of proportion, which are indispensable for effective involvement in the analytic pursuit of their reduction. Reality testing often falls within its scope or is implicit in it. "Confrontation" is often a brief and dramatic variant of the gradual process of clarification. While sometimes strikingly effective because of the primitive affective "force" implicit in sudden compressed perception and communication, there is a greater potentiality for massive transference impingement than in other interventions. For this reason, it should be invoked only with great circumspection in analytic work. In general, while clarification is addressed to the conscious-preconscious system in the latter's own terms, its impact on the basis of "the principle of multiple appeal," is often of greater scope than is usually assumed to be the case. Thus it is often more "synergistic" than merely "preparatory" in relation to interpretations of the unconscious. And when its effect is largely confined to the conscious-preconscious system, it contributes importantly to mobilizing the patient's capacities for self-interpretation and spontaneous insight.

There are, of course, other noninterpretive interventions whose judicious use is of high technical importance — for example, occasional well-timed questions or the considered exercise and interruption of silence. And always operative in analysis, to some degree — often subtly or silently or minimally — are the various procedures and mechanisms discussed by Bibring (1954) in relation to all psychotherapy. These do not exclude suggestion and manipulation, albeit in forms quite different from those usually invoked and most often implicit in other technical maneuvers rather than invoked "in their own right." All are preparatory or ancillary to mutative interpretation.

In previous communications I have dealt at length with the psychoanalytic situation (1961), with transference in relation to the situation and certain of its essential processes (1967), and with the nature of resistance (1973). I shall not summarize these lengthy papers. Before I continue with my immediate subject, however, I shall briefly state my views of the essential nature of the psychoanalytic situation and process. The basic "psychosomatic" function of speech (the central vehicle of psychoanalysis) I regard as the original bridge over separation between mother and infant, continuing in adult relationships, largely replacing the original bodily intimacies. The primordial transference[1] I view as the irredentist urge toward bodily reunion, extending through all of the libidinal phases as its focal manifestations. The "mature transference" includes the relative acceptance of bodily separation, with the wish for controlled tender interest, play, understanding, instruction, and communication. The first gives powerful impetus to the psychoanalytic process and, alternatively, powerful resistances. The second may provide irrational (in the sense of transference) energic components to the therapeutic alliance, occasionally its own resistances, and contributing, for example, to intellectualization or prolixity. In the archaic sphere, manifest only in the severest illness but a reasoned metapsychologic assumption if not a demonstrable dynamism in the transference psychoneuroses, is the continuum between oral incorporation and speech, expressed in the very words communion, communicant, and communication. The act of interpretation or construction is parallel—and in some respects functionally analogous—to the mother's giving words to the inchoate sounds, feelings, and protothinking (with apology for the neologism) of the infant. The important functional notion is that with each genuine acceptance of correct interpretation there is an actual or potential loosening of the somatic bond (or its alternative of oral incorporation in fantasy). Thus the mourning significance which has been attributed to "working through" may have a foundation in the gradual compensatory acceptance of constructions or insight (in any of its references). Now, it is obvious that this is an archaic, quasi-biological formulation of our work. We must postulate that it is continuous with the vast, endlessly complicated epigenetic structure of the mental life we experience and with which we largely deal. However, it does render intelligible the sheer biological power of the "talking treatment," and the depths of the transference-neurotic experience and transference attachment it can mobilize and resolve.

Others before me—for example, Spitz (1956a), Gitelson (1962), Greenacre (1954), Winnicott (1965)—have thought that the psychoanalytic situation has an infantile unconscious meaning to the patient. Broadly speaking, the essential differences between my views and theirs (if I understand them correctly) reside in two spheres: (1) I do not observe or infer that the most profound infantile fantasies excited by the psychoanalytic situation are actually gratified by or mediated in its structure; these fantasy investments follow on the abstinence-induced regression of the transference neurosis. (2) I regard the phenomenon of separation—bridged by speech (I have called it "deprivation-in-intimacy")— as the chief excitant of conflictive transference activity in the situation and process. This is not to disregard or minimize the gratification implicit in the psychoanalytic situation, whether in terms of adult reality (freedom of expression, genuine tolerance, unconditional acceptance, steadfast reliability) or in Winnicott's concept of the implicit infant response to "holding" and allied affirmative fantasies. These include the initial positive transference—as usually construed—essentially, the general expectation or assumption of renewed parental protection, interest, and care under whose benign umbrella the painful conflictive elements may be brought to new solutions. These elements, with the hope of relief of suffering, sustain the patient in treatment. But the more complicated transferences evolve in the climate and field of separation and abstinence.

It is probably clear from what I have said so far that the psychoanalytic situation is, in my view, a unique relationship, a dynamic situation, in which interpretation and ancillary activities are but parts (albeit important parts) of an integral psychological complex, fraught with important intrinsic energies of its own. The rule of abstinence facilitates regression, whose depth depends on (1) intrinsic manifest (or latent) illness and (2) the degree of rigidity and arbitrary inclusiveness with which the rule is applied. Whatever the initiation in a given instance, the regression that remains within the immediate or potential mastery of the rational observing ego is an indispensable integral component of the analytic process. Where the depth and energic cathexis of such regression threatens mastery (established in cooperation with the analyst), a formidable complication must be confronted. That greater-than-average regression may be consciously sought for therapeutic purposes in special instances and in skilled hands, should be noted, however. (See, for example, Ferenczi 1930 and Peto 1961).

Putting aside the subject of interpretive method and content, what are some other consciously practiced contributing elements in this situation and process (in addition to the tangible arrangements mentioned previously)?

1. The analyst's attitude: I refer especially to what has been called the "classical" attitude (the adjective sometimes fanaticized to "orthodox"). While I think this has largely (if not completely) emerged from the caricature status which was frequently adopted, taught, and admired some decades ago, it still retains (necessarily) certain essential and austere features. The analyst maintains "anonymity." Except for certain inevitable actualities of his identity and role, the patient is given no information or access to significant information about him. In general, the analyst does not answer questions. He gives no affective response to the patient's material or evident state of mind or opinions or direction, not to speak of active interest, advice, or other allied communications. Some of these elements were epitomized in the renowned "surgical" and "mirror" analogies (Freud, 1912b). Since, in 1961, I offered a detailed summary and critical analysis of this complex, I shall not extend this brief epitome to their further consideration.

The question of the functions and impact of this attitude does deserve a few words. The essential original purpose was to avoid "contamination" of the transference, so that it could emerge in relatively "pure culture." As with other important elements in the psychoanalytic situation — for example, the recumbent posture, or indeed the entire rule of abstinence — the original stated purposes of genius did not tell the whole story (although possibly unconsciously intuited). The affective and cognitive nonresponsiveness of the analyst provides the keystone of the entire system of abstinence, which is the chief stimulus for the adaptive regression of the transference in its conflictive and ambivalent form and thus of the transference neurosis. Not unimportant in the complex of abstinence is the renunciation — albeit voluntary — of the conscious control of utterance and of large-scale motor activity. And overall there is the sense of being unable to elicit the evidence of demonstrable personal impact on the analyst.

In this sense, the classical attitude performs an essential function in the psychoanalytic process. To the extent that it does not become equated with coldness, aloofness, arbitrary withholding, callousness, detachment, ritualization, or panicky adherence to rules for their own sake, it is an integral, indeed central element in the rule of abstinence, without which there is no analysis. However, it must be of a character which the ego of an intelligent adult can understand as rational and appropriate. Where the deprivation goes beyond the intelligibly rational or becomes merged with aversive, rejective, or clearly detached qualities, it can stimulate iatrogenic regressions in the transference which present a remarkable resistance to interpretive reduction (see Freud 1940). One might say that the rational observing portion of the ego, unsupported by the analyst's rationality (and perhaps resentful?) goes down with its other half, with which it is, after all, continuous and of identical origin (Stone 1967). It was in relation to this contingency that I proposed in 1961 a reasoned and measured reduction of the rigors of abstinence in all spheres and, above all, their restriction to spheres essential and relevant in the development of the transference neurosis. For ultra-simple example, if a patient asks, "Are you seeing patients on Christmas Day?" I do not believe that failing to answer will further the analytic purposes. Nor will wishing him well on the eve of a major surgical operation hinder these purposes. I realize that these examples will seem absurd to some; yet I know that there are others to whom my view is unacceptable.

2. Germane to the general analytic attitude is the tone, rhetorical quality, and implicit direction of verbal interventions. *Neutrality* is a favored term, often qualified as technical or interpretive. *Objectivity* is another term. *Benevolent objectivity*, sometimes neutrality, was, I believe, Loewenstein's preferred term. *Compassionate* has also been used in modification or adjacency (Greenson 1967). I believe that these substantive terms are really intended to represent attitudes toward elements in the patient's intrapsychic conflicts, something like the observing equidistance from structures proposed by Anna Freud, also the avoidance of any interference, however subtle, in the patient's life. It cannot, of course, mean that one is just as interested in the patient's adversaries as in him. It does mean that a balanced consideration of the issues will be more useful

to him than joining the fight. The qualifying adjectives are no doubt reflections of the increasingly evident necessity to establish the fact that the true analytic attitude is compatible with human friendliness and warmth. This is assuredly true. The danger (still not completely banished) has been that the seductive comforts of general personal neutrality and objectivity, perhaps (although rarely) their potential sadistic gratifications, will dominate the analytic attitude to a degree that merges them with the type of detachment mentioned before. To the extent that neutrality with an affirmative affective tone is genuinely achieved, it is an excellent contribution to both the legitimate principle of abstinence and to the high tolerance and acceptance which characterize the analytic work in its best sense.

While unreservedly depriving attitudes are usually viewed as "classical," there is some doubt about the authenticity of this usage. I have often thought (and sometimes said) that they might more properly be viewed as "neoclassical".[2] That they derive from or are elaborated from certain of Freud's precepts, there is no doubt. That he (or other pioneers) practiced the personality "masking" which evolved later is not only open to considerable doubt but was probably very rarely the case. Those who have been treated by Freud (even after 1912) testify to the naturalness and general expressive freedom that characterized his analytic work. Freud's common sense is never excluded from his reservations and exceptions regarding the application of the more severe "deprivations." His awareness that certain (limited) "concessions" may be necessary is explicit (1919, p. 164). He makes passing (somewhat ambiguous) reference to the limitations of deprivation: "nor yet the deprivation of everything that the patient desires, for perhaps no sick person could tolerate this" (p. 165). His awareness of the possibility of an inaccessible refractory transference neurosis if the analyst fails to take care "that neither the love nor the hositility reach an extreme height" is also explicit (1940, p. 177), although his prophylaxis is not convincing. Perhaps the most elegant codification of what I would call the neoclassical point of view is that of Eissler (1953), in which the hypothetical (or fictive) "normal ego" is susceptible to favorable change by interpretation alone; any variant is regarded as a "parameter," subject to strict rules for its employment and dissolution. Apart from the fact that this is a structure of metapsychological assumptions, there would be doubt in my mind that even a "hypothetical normal ego" would respond to interpretation alone, except, of course, as this response is a required fiction of definition. For Freud early pointed out that interpretations are ineffective (or adversely effective) before a bond of positive transference is established (1913, p. 129); the advent of hostile transference would, in effect, blow away many cognitive insights. Thus, the priority of the affective bond is clearly apparent, as indeed it is in development.

Apart from Freud's own recognition of the need for elasticity, including, for example, the need for educational admixtures in the treatment of childlike patients (1940, p. 175), there have, of course, been recommendations of a radical nature, for example Ferenczi's imaginative attempt to give to patients the

demonstratively accepting or responsive love of which they had been deprived
in early childhood (1919a, 1919b, 1930, 1931). This, he thought, would be
the most effective method of overcoming resistances. The attempt failed intrinsically and in its impact on the analytic world, for good reasons. However, it
may have a more successful spiritual descendant in Kohut's (1977) efforts to provide the empathy not provided by the maternal "self-object" of infancy. Since
empathy is an integral part of analytic technique in any case, to which an adult
can respond affirmatively without regression, this effort, whether or not it
remedies definitively a deficiency of the past (a response not currently claimed
by Kohut or his followers), may have a better fate than the effort to provide
parent-infant love as such. At the very least, it provides a climate and rapport
that have a profoundly positive influence on the therapeutic alliance.

Alexander's efforts of the early 1950s to revise analysis in the direction of
a "corrective emotional experience" via the analyst's assumption of attitudes contravening the patient's pathogenic developmental experience, have passed from
the analytic scene (Alexander 1956, Stone 1957). In my view, these experiences
were unsoundly based in the first place, and thus their passing is, so to speak,
logical and inevitable. One cannot give to the elaborately organized personality
of an adult what he missed as an infant or young child, in the original form in
which the lack occurred, and expect it to repair the defective structuralized
developments occasioned by its lack. Furthermore, the assumption by a physician
of an attitude of posture or function which is not naturally integrated in his
professional capacity, aside from its artificiality, promises something which —
unlike his professional functions — cannot be sustained in the future.

It should be noted as a matter of interest, and in line with our principal subject, that Ferenczi (1919b), who was an oscillating partner of Freud in general
matters of abstinence and "activity," also introduced ad hoc "deprivation" techniques into the conduct of analyses, along with "forced fantasies." These too
were largely abandoned as the transference impacts became better understood.
However, just as the "giving of love" has rational (and greatly transformed)
derivatives and descendants today, the techniques of ad hoc deprivation, in attenuated form better integrated with the fundamental movement of the analysis,
remain as sometimes useful elements in our noninterpretive analytic armamentarium, along with such major issues as the suggested confrontation of phobias
or the time limitation in treatment. "Why not see if you can dispense with that
routine brushing of the couch before you lie down for each hour?" (For commonplace "innocuous" example!)

Now, a few words about Lipton's (1977, 1979) papers on Freud's technique.
These are to be valued for their bold forthrightness, whether or not one agrees
entirely with the author's point of view. In a sense, they condense and try to
systematize what has long been inferred about the climate of Freud's analyses.
The principal (1977) paper is based largely on Freud's treatment of Lorenz, the
so-called Rat Man, and includes the herring repast Freud shared with his patient
and other allied matters. One has, of course, heard these and other "unorthodox"

behaviors of Freud severely criticized. Lipton's point — to condense it extremely — is that Freud usually established a living personal relationship with each patient, albeit a restricted one, which he thought did not interfere with the technical process but one in which he was nevertheless quite thoroughly himself, and his personal identity was quite accessible to his patients. This, according to Lipton, he regarded as separate from the technical relationship on which he based his case reports and his published precepts as to technique. Freud was aware, of course, that the patient might react to the personal relationship or his behaviors within the analysis and stood ready to interpret such reactions, but he did not inhibit the naturalness of behaviors he considered appropriate to everyday contingencies. In other words, as Lipton points out, Freud did not extend "technique" to include all aspects of the adult personal relationship. The preservation of this real object relationship, Lipton feels was advantageous, even for investiture with transference. This original position, Lipton feels, was modified by Freud's followers after his death, and personal responses became severely and technically routinized. This I have mentioned as a "neoclassical" position. Certainly, anyone who lived through — and participated in — the intellectual turmoil and debate occasioned by Alexander's proposals of the "fifties" would understand how the reaction to them, however understandable, may have gained a momentum which carried it beyond the desirable. It would be out of place here to invoke the truly extensive writing of the period. Since several of Lipton's arguments (at least as critique) are related to my own of 1961, albeit from a different angle, I shall not pursue this brief epitome further. One might infer from his papers (as some have done) that (1) the technical and personal relationships can be discretely separated or (2) that a purely spontaneous personal relationship is necessarily superior to a controlled professional relationship. Neither is, I believe, true. The personal relationship is always subject to important transference investiture and is thus — to some extent — an inevitable part of the analysis, whether the illness is a transference psychoneurosis or a narcissistic disorder.[3] An unrestricted personal relationship is not in question, nor do I believe it was with Freud (for example, 1913, p. 139). What I would assert, however, is that if one had to choose, one would do better to choose Freud's early latitudes and naturalness over the robotlike "anonymity" of our own neoclassical period, when it reached absurd heights. However, such a choice is not necessary. We can do our work within professional limitations — reasonable and liberal, but very strict at certain points — and thus avoid overstimulation or excessive gratification as well as irrational deprivation. I have tried to outline such boundaries in the past (1961). I have no doubt they can be greatly improved on.[4]

During the long period of hypertrophied formalism and ritualism, there were writers who with varying degrees of purposive emphasis (sometimes only by casual or incidental, almost inadvertent mention) disagreed with this tendency. Occasionally, their emphasis was on judgment in the particular instance. Most were analysts who could not in the remotest sense be regarded as "deviationists."

Loewenstein (1958), for example, spoke of having shocked a supervisee by telling him he ought to have accepted a gift offered by the patient in a specific instance. Nacht (1958) wrote of the occasional need for a "reparative gift" (psychological, of course) by the analyst or the occasional desirability of his emerging as a well-defined "presence" (a subject that merits a paper in itself!). Most such contributions were without modification or addition to the well-established views of psychoanalytic process. With Spitz (1956a) and then Gitelson (1962), the "diatrophic" element in the psychoanalytic process gained emphasis, and, implicitly, the emotional attitude of the analyst. Loewald (1960), in stating a fresh and imaginative view of dynamic elements in the psychoanalytic process, including the affirmative vitalizing dynamic thrust of the transference germane to the patient's search for a "new object," also called attention to the importance of the analyst's view of the patient's potentialities and thus, implicitly, to the function of this view in the analyst's work. The "holding" action (based on the literal "holding" of the infant in the adult's arms), as conceptualized by Winnicott (1965), has exercised important and increasing influence in understanding the initial phases of establishing analytic rapport. In the analytic situation, it is expressed largely in the evidence of understanding and empathy for the patient's profound anxieties. By many, this is construed as the action of the unmodified classical stance, even with regressed patients. This was largely Winnicott's own view. Winnicott, however, did not minimize the extent of unconventional participation he might invoke with certain patients in the early effort to make effective emotional contact with them, if necessary. Modell (1976, 1979) emphasizes this phenomenon (without "parameters") in the first ("cocoon") phase of his treatment of narcissistic personality disorders. Whether or not the postulated infantile prototype of this holding process is actually intrinsic in the analytic experience, the concept does express an analytic attitude, however conveyed to the patient, which may, after a time, permit him to go ahead with analytic work and to sustain its rigors.

Prominent in recent years is the impact of the thought of Kohut (1977) and his followers. Whether or not one accepts Kohut's views on the separate line of development of narcissism and the separate pathology of the "self" (with corresponding treatment techniques), there is no question of the value of the emphasis on the "self," and even more on the importance of the analyst's "empathy." To be sure, like most of our valued ideas, this interest in empathy began with Freud, to whom it was the primary basis of *any* understanding of another human mind. It participates in the evolution and crystallization of every intervention of any subtlety and in the end is usually assimilated into more conventional cognitive processes (see, for example, Arlow's 1979 paper or the early paper by Ferenczi [1919b], in which such thought was almost literally anticipated [p. 189]). But even more important than the heightened awareness of the indispensability of empathic (and thus introspective) processes in all interventions is the awareness of the empathic process as expressed in the attitude toward the patient, in the quality of listening, as manifested in the fluctuations of silence, and the content of its (noninterpretive) interruptions. This is also true of the importance of allowing certain processes to develop and evolve for extended periods without interpretive intervention. This does not apply only to the "grandiose self." Throughout analytic technique, the exploitation of empathic withholding of interpretive interruption is important, apart from the standard cognitive and transference rules governing the timing of interpretations. While I do not believe that the analyst's mirroring empathy can make up for the mother's empathic deficits, it can make for a much better analysis. I do not, for the present, accept the need for separate conceptual systems of illness and of therapy for the "self" on the one hand, and for the neuroses of structural conflict on the other. Except in the most deeply fixated or regressed illnesses, both are present, or potentially present, in all patients, in varying degree, as are varying degrees of narcissistic pathology. In this last, I am in agreement with Rangell (1979a, 1979b).

In all nuances of technical method, the attitude of the analyst is of critical importance. And beneath the descriptive fact, there is always the dynamic motivation of the attitude: general characterologic response, sense of rational appropriateness, intuitive or empathic sense of the situation, specific countertransference, and others less clearly defined. And it should never be forgotten that an absence of response may have a similar range of possible motivations. There are, no doubt, important elements of truth in various (sometimes—in the abstract—conflicting) suggestions, and one may recommend itself more clearly than others in a given situation. It is for the clinical perceptiveness, the intuition, and the empathy of the analyst to guide him in the flexible emphases and adjustments that may be required. The exchange of gaze with the patient by Fleming (1975), cited as problematic by Erle and Goldberg (1979), or the preliminary "Kleenex" intervention of de la Torre (1977) are passing examples of what need not be settled by arbitrary rules of procedure. One might, for example, have chosen otherwise or similarly—in either situation—were all the facts at hand. The question of qualitative and quantitative impact on the transference would, of course, have to be weighed against the communicative function and the impact on the "nontransference" relationship. But I do not believe that an arbitrary fixed and tendentious principle would properly be invoked in either instance, except perhaps the general principle of "minimization," and the commitment to afterinterpretation.

Most important attitudes are imparted nonverbally—by the timing and duration of silences, by tone of voice and rhetorical nuances in interventions, by facial expression at the beginning and end of hours, and by the mood in which realities are dealt with: hours, fees, absences, intercurrent life crises, or other important matters. The same is true of the ubiquitous countertransference, a never-absent dynamism in the analytic field. In the sense of Gitelson's (1952) distinction between countertransference (i.e., response to the specific transference) and transference to the patient (as such), it is probably the former that more often gives difficulty in sustaining the tormenting transferences of the borderline patient (Stone 1954; Kernberg 1979; Modell 1979), whereas transference to the patient as such may be more frequently operative with the neurotic patient. In any case, while the cliché obsessional preoccupation with the countertransference is to be avoided (certainly the fantasy of its "panetiologic" or "panexplanatory" position), its importance for good or ill must not be underestimated and its day-to-day analysis and reduction is one of the crucial obligations of the analyst. Indeed, in its controlled manifestation, in the light of adequate insight, the "positive" countertransference can make an important contribution to the basic physicianly attitude (Spitz 1956b). The actual personality and behavior of the analyst as a factor in the analysis was always intuitively recognized by both analysts and patients but for a long time sidetracked from scientific discourse. In 1954 I mentioned its role as distinct from the evolution of transference. Greenson (1967, 1971) has since elaborated on and advanced this subject considerably.

Long ago (1936), Glover[5] mentioned the importance to the patient of the analyst's attitude toward him, in the depths of his (the analyst's) personality. These are not easy matters! In my 1967 paper, I attempted a metapsychologic reconciliation of the respective actions of the transference and this search for a personal reality. More work in this subtle and profound sphere is necessary. The role of the analyst as a new object was also mentioned in 1954, in specific relation to the destruction or degradation of old object representations by patient's suffering from narcissistic neuroses (Freud's sense) or by those with severe ambivalent pregenital fixations. Self-evidently, the analyst (as such) is a new object but can be fully perceived as such only when the transference has been largely reduced. That his real identity is in constant interaction with the transference in the patient's mind only compounds our problem.

The "indestructibility" of the analyst is another important factor in the psychoanalytic situation (Winnicott 1969). In the long run, coupled with mutative interpretations of aggression (Strachey 1934), it may be decisive. In the short run, with intensely hostile narcissistic patients, it may stimulate acting out, because of the immediate frustrations involved. Whether the analyst's invulnerability is a manifestation of his patient and devoted commitment to his task or a supercilious statement of the patient's "insignificance" may weigh subtly but definitely in such effects.

Interpretation is not my topic. But I do feel that its position in relation to my topic merits a few words. It can serve as a conveyance for any of the analytic attitudes previously mentioned. Furthermore, it can be viewed as a giving or a feeding by the analyst in the light of primitive transference, just as the free associations may be similarly regarded, the latter perhaps more often as excretory. In Sechehaye's *Symbolic Realization* (1951) something intermediate between language and actual oral transference gratification was achieved.[6] In the light of the transference, interpretations may be reacted to as reprimands, criticisms, narcissistic humiliations or encroachments, instructions, praise, or even a "holding" lullaby. Thus an interpretation is not always an interpretation, pragmatically speaking. In the crowning achievement of analysis, a correct and decisive interpretation by the analyst is accepted and utilized as such by the patient and followed by working through. He will now (we hope) be able to confront the germane and actual conflict and make whatever new adaptations are within his capacities (about the contingencies of this last step, see Rangell [1979b] and, in a specific, restricted sense, Stone [1973, p. 62]).

Such acceptance and utilization of interpretation require a positive affective context, usually epitomized in the concept of positive transference—probably also an affirmative attitude toward the analyst as a real individual and the analysis in its real purpose and significance, as these move gradually into the foreground. Most analysts have the natural endowments to meet the patient's requirements, if not disturbed by specific countertransferences or artificially assumed personal attitudes (Stone 1961, 1967). To bring the particulate elements of insight into relation with one another and ultimately into relation with large and inclusive concepts is as important in resistance analysis as the anterior, more literally analytic function that exposes the particular elements (Stone 1973). When a patient, after a long period of parrotlike acceptance of interpretations finds apparent rescue (usually short-lived) in the truly commonplace (the formulations of a popular magazine article or the magniloquent diagnoses of a fictional television psychiatrist), his hostility may include (1) resistance to more poignant insights; (2) mockery for the analyst's pedantic attention to detail or for his lack of common-sense critique or intellectual integration (which the patient may crave and seriously need), or (3) sheer mocking antipathy for insensitive and unempathic lack of understanding for the patient's real suffering, and (4) a variety of other ingredients which I shall not try to detail.

In Brenner's critique (1979) of the concepts of therapeutic alliance and working alliance (as differentiated from transference), there are many cogent observations and a correct linear (i.e., diagrammatic) presentation of the essential classical view of the psychoanalytic relationship and process. However, no weight is given to the responses of the two participant adults as such, to the sometimes ineffable modes of expression and perception of attitude, intention, interest, and allied matters that exist between them. And it is overlooked that a real grievance, even though germane to individual personality structure (as are all responses), cannot be equated with a pure transference response and similarly reduced. The admission and correction of the analyst's error or of his failure of prior adequate explanation of a deprivation might, in some instances, render such an interpretation effective or at least restore such a possibility for the future. How a patient listens to interpretations, how he utilizes them, indeed the entire complex matter of his will to recover, are influenced by such considerations, as they are by the state of transference with which the adult attitudes are in constant, if fluctuating, interaction. But it must not be ignored that it is between the two adults that it all begins and ends. "What sort of person is this to whom I am entrusting my entire mental and emotional being?" It is striking testimony to the need for perennial dialectic that Brenner's and my own therapeutic and consultative experience lead to divergent, if not opposite, conclusions. In relation to Brenner's critique of my own putative overconcern about avoidance of patient's suffering, I must correct a frequent misunderstanding he appears to share. My essential position is directed against the superfluous iatrogenic regressions attendant on superfluous deprivations, whether or not the patient is aware of suffering as such. None of us would wish to court or provoke suffering, but—like Brenner—I recognize that it may sometimes be an inevitable accompaniment of benevolently purposive processes. I believe the powerful effects of the basic principle of abstinence are operative, whether or not there is manifest reaction to them by the patient.

Conclusion

The psychoanalytic situation and process, in the sense described earlier, have a powerful dynamic thrust of their own. I would speculate that with no interpretations, a transference neurosis of a sort would occur (in the sense that the infantile neurosis originally emerged). But without experiment I cannot guess what it would be like. Our system of interpretation (based on our adequate knowledge of our science and our clinical knowledge of the individual patient) does enable us to interfere with resistances and thus to give productive shape to the process. It would be naïvely fallacious to believe that the patient's free associations alone would enable him to reveal his basic warded-off conflicts to the listener and to himself. Biological data, even certain spontaneous minor insights—yes, but not the essential constituents of unconscious conflict. Free associations are governed fully as much by the resistances, which are integral in personality structure, as by the surge of warded-off material toward the verbal preconscious. Resistance is a large and complex subject. There is no doubt that interpretation is the dependable and teachable mode of approaching it. But here again other modalities are involved and may even be decisive. To overcome resistances a patient must want to do so and must want to do so in relation to the person who treats him, both as to the state of transference and the emergent perceptions of reality. Obviously, multiple factors within him (including the predetermined nature of his transferences) are usually decisive, but other factors may cast a precarious balance. Even the patient's capacity for "basic trust" may have evolved in relation to adequate considerateness, reliability, empathy, and a controlled but manifest friendly interest. If Ferenczi failed to dissolve resistances by indulgences of infantile love, there may still be a residue of truth in his ideas. The "love" implicit in empathy, listening and trying to understand, in nonseductive devotion to the task, the sense of full acceptance, respect, and sometimes the homely phenomenon of sheer dependable patience, extending over long periods of time, may take their place as equal or nearly equal in importance to sheer interpretive skill.

I should like, however, to make clear my position on two scientific issues. Just as surely as I do not believe that Ferenczi could alter repressed infantile needs by his methods, I do not believe that empathy, the "holding" attitude, or the diatrophic attitude are curative (in themselves) for the disorder of early genesis in their own technical impact. But their impact on the adult (if properly construed and administered) is in itself favorable and facilitating and may affect with special poignancy those current elements in ego structure that represent early deprivations and injuries in the total ego integration. Furthermore, in the sense of the "principle of multiple appeal," they may indeed set up reverberations in all topographic and structural distributions. In other words, while they cannot substitute for analytic work in the traditional sense, they may provide the best possible introduction and context for it—in some instances, a critically indispensable component of the ongoing analytic work as such, to the very end.

It is evident that, in a very general way, my position regarding the analyst's emotional orientation to the patient has important elements in common with those of Spitz (1956a, 1956b), Gitelson (1952), Greenson (1967), Zetzel (1966, 1970), and others who have written along similar or related lines. There are, of course, lesser or larger differences among these authors. By the same token, my own view of the total situation may be differentiated from theirs. I do believe that the patient must feel the analyst's support, sympathetic understanding of his painful predicament, and long-term physicianly commitment to the therapeutic task, despite the stringent limitations of expression imposed by technique on a unique personal relationship. There is no specific mode of communication for such attitudes. They may range from the largely nonverbal to more explicit statements for those more desperately needy. Nor indeed is there a specific genetically determined message that should be communicated. It is addressed to an adult, by an adult. That the patient responds to these attitudes in interaction with the climate of abstinence—or indeed (and more strikingly) to their absense—in specific transference patterns, determined by individual developmental vicissitudes, within a broad and universal archaic framework, and based on the early mother-child relationship, is my conviction. The range in patterns of such transference responses may extend in depth from the Oedipus complex to the most profound disturbances of ego and self formation (with corresponding expectable variations in the patient's operational needs). In general, Freud's original precepts would still remain centrally useful if interpreted with his own common sense: if reasonable and controlled responsiveness is not hidden to the point of imperceptibility by neoclassical masking; if a slavish and overliteral adherence to the "mirror" and "surgical" analogies is avoided, while their kernal of operational usefulness is preserved; and if empathic sensitivity to individual needs is given its appropriately indispensable position.

Actually, my own special interest, beginning with a 1954 paper, has been directed largely to the climate of abstinence and the psychological vacuum it establishes, in the dual potentiality mentioned earlier. In 1961, this interest was generalized and (I hope) refined, in extension from the treatment of more severe cases to the basic psychoanalytic situation. Thus the relative naturalness of the analyst's attitude (within well-defined professional boundaries) and the considered relaxation of superfluous nonrational deprivations, cognitive and affective, become, in my view, even more important than prescribed diatrophic attitudes (other than those implicit in the physicianly role in the context of analytic technique), granted that the absence of the latter to the degree appropriate for a given patient may often be a severe impediment in the initiation and productive continuance of a psychoanalytic process.

Notes

1. My usage differs from Ferenczi's (1909), who used the term to signify the original turning from autoerotism to object love.

2. I note that Valenstein (1979) uses this term for the change in analytic method, following Anna Freud's (1936) basic contribution, to include the analysis of ego mechanisms within its scope. This is obviously different from my own use of the word.

3. Modell (1979) feels that the separation of personal relationship and technique is reasonable in the neuroses, but not in the "narcissistic personality disorders," because—in the latter—the analytic situation itself becomes the central and confronting issue of the analytic work. My own experience would cast the emphasis in the opposite direction. It is precisely the narcissistic or otherwise regressed patient who must recoil the more deeply from a machinelike human being with whom he is expected to form a profound and viable relationship. In my own mind, there has been a series from early on, with regard to the (relative) stringencies of required (and effective) "abstinences": (1) "classical" (not neoclassical) analysis; (2) modified analysis (with more severe disorders [Stone 1954 and others]); (3) interpretive psychotherapy (in which the basic structure is decisively altered [Stone 1979]).

4. In the sense that I do not fully accept Lipton's inferences, while sympathetic with certain elements in them, I agree with Kanzer's (1979) observation that Freud's technique evolved and changed with his clinical and theoretical development (how could it be otherwise?). However, it seems to me that available testimony supports the idea that he did not assume the robotlike anonymity esteemed, in America at least, three or four decades ago, even long after his technical recommendations were established. Nor indeed, judging by several of my acquaintances, was this attitude prevalent among older analysts of the generation close to his. Again, it would seem to me that Freud's genius would not permit such a distortion of his own teaching. More than one patient has written of experiences with Freud (see, for example, Doolittle 1956).

As I have said, I have clear conceptions of the limits of the professional relationship in the light of its specific psychoanalytic purposes. It would be cumbersome to repeat them here. Suffice it to mention that I would not think it right to eat with a patient or to raise money for him, or to get involved in physical examination or treatment (short of an unequivocally compelling emergency). Strangely enough I would never even think it proper to eat (or take coffee) during a patient's hour—a "rigidity" which would make me seem more strict than some esteemed colleagues of a few decades ago. In mentioning the meal and the fund raising, I am of course indicating that I do not believe that all of Freud's pioneering behaviors are to be accepted as precedents. But in rejecting them (as he would have done), I would stick to the fact that we must take extreme care lest we throw out a healthy and promising baby with the bath! The core conception of a natural, friendly, appropriate adult relation to another adult (the patient) within the prescribed professional limits, remains, I believe, of decisive importance.

5. "This would suggest that in the deeper pathological states, a prerequisite of the

efficiency of interpretation is the *attitude*, the true unconscious attitude of the analyst to his patients" (p. 131).

6. I omit extended consideration of this work as well as the methods of treating psychotics of John Rosen (1953) and Gertrud Schwing (1954).

REFERENCES

Alexander, F. (1956). *Psychoanalysis and Psychotherapy.* New York: Norton.

Arlow, J. A. (1979). The genesis of interpretation. *J. Amer. Psychoanal. Assn.* 27(suppl.): 193–206.

Bibring, E. (1954). Psychoanalysis and the dynamic psychotherapies. *J. Amer. Psychoanal. Assn.* 2:745–770.

Blum, H. P. (1979). The curative and creative aspects of insight. *J. Amer. Psychoanal. Assn.* 27(suppl.):41–69.

Brenner, C. (1979). Working alliance, therapeutic alliance, and transference. *J. Amer. Psychoanal. Assn.* 27(suppl.):137–157.

de la Torre, J. (1977). Psychoanalytic neutrality: An overview. *Bull. Menninger Clin.* 41:366–384.

Doolittle, H. (1956). *Tribute to Freud.* New York: Pantheon.

Eissler, K. R. (1953). The effect of the structure of the ego on psychoanalytic technique. *J. Amer. Psychoanal. Assn.* 1:104–143.

Erle, J. B., and Goldberg, D. A. (1979). Problems in the assessment of analyzability. *Psychoanal. Q.* 48:48–84.

Ferenczi, S. (1909). Introjection and transference. In *Sex in Psychoanalysis.* New York: Basic Books, pp. 35–93.

—— (1919a). Technical difficulties in the analysis of hysteria. In *Further Contributions to the Theory and Technique of Psychoanalysis.* New York: Basic Books, 1952, pp. 189–197.

—— (1919b). On the technique of psychoanalysis. In *Further Contributions to the Theory and Technique of Psychoanalysis.* New York: Basic Books, 1952, pp. 177–189.

—— (1930). The principle of relaxation and neocatharsis. *Int. J. Psychoanal.* 11:428–443.

—— (1931). Child analysis in the analysis of adults. *Int. J. Psychoanal.* 12:468–482.

Fleming, J. (1975). Some observations on object constancy in the psychoanalysis of adults. *J. Amer. Psychoanal. Assn.* 23:743–759.

Freud, A. (1936). *The Ego and the Mechanisms of Defense.* New York: International Universities Press, 1946.

Freud, S. (1912a). The dynamics of transference. *S. E.* 12.

—— (1912b). Recommendations to physicians practising psycho-analysis. *S. E.* 12.

—— (1913). On beginning the treatment. *S. E.* 12.

—— (1914). On the history of the psycho-analytic movement. *S. E.* 14.

—— (1919). Lines of advance in psycho-analytic therapy. *S. E.* 17.

—— (1937a). Constructions in analysis. *S. E.* 23.

—— (1937b). Analysis terminable and interminable. *S. E.* 23.

—— (1940). An outline of psycho-analysis. *S. E.* 23.

Gill, M. (1979a). The analysis of the transference. *J. Amer. Psychoanal. Assn.* 27(suppl.): 263–287.

_____ (1979b). Psychoanalysis and psychotherapy. Presented at Symposium, Atlanta, October 20, 1979.

Gitelson, M. (1952). The emotional position of the analyst in the psycho-analytic situation. *Int. J. Psychoanal.* 33:1–10.

_____ (1962). The curative factors in psycho-analysis. *Int. J. Psychoanal.* 43:194–206.

Glover, E. (1936). On the theory of the therapeutic results of psycho-analysis. *Int. J. Psychoanal.* 18:125–132.

Greenacre, P. (1954). The role of transference. *J. Amer. Psychoanal. Assn.* 2:671–684.

Greenson, R. R. (1967). *The Technique and Practice of Psychoanalysis.* New York: International Universities Press.

_____ (1971). The "real" relationship between the patient and the psychoanalyst. In *The Unconscious Today,* ed. M. Kanzer. New York: International Universities Press, pp. 213–232.

Kanzer, M. (1972). Superego aspects of free association and the fundamental rule. *J. Amer. Psychoanal. Assn.* 20:246–266.

_____ (1979). Freud's "analytic pact"—the standard therapeutic alliance. *This volume,* pp. 69–87.

Kernberg, O. (1979). Character structure and analyzability. *Bull. Assn. Psychoanal. Med.* 19:87–96.

Kohut, H. (1977). *The Restoration of the Self.* New York: International Universities Press.

Lipton, S. D. (1977). The advantages of Freud's technique as shown in his analysis of the Rat Man. *Int. J. Psychoanal.* 58:255–273.

_____ (1979). An addendum to "The advantages of Freud's technique as shown in his analysis of the Rat Man." *Int. J. Psychoanal.* 60:215–216.

Loewald, H. W. (1960). On the therapeutic action of psycho-analysis. *Int. J. Psychoanal.* 41:1–18.

Loewenstein, R. M. (1958). Remarks on some variations in psychoanalytic technique. *Int. J. Psychoanal.* 39:202–210, 240–242.

Macalpine, I. (1950). The development of transference. *Psychoanal. Q.* 19:501–539.

Modell, A. H. (1976). "The holding environment" and the therapeutic action of psychoanalysis. *J. Amer. Psychoanal. Assn.* 24:285–308.

_____ (1979). Character structure and analyzability. *Bull. Assn. Psychoanal. Med.* 19: 97–103.

Nacht, S. (1958). Variations in technique. *Int. J. Psychoanal.* 39:235–237.

Peto, A. (1961). The fragmentizing function of the ego in the transference neurosis. *Int. J. Psychoanal.* 42:238–245.

Rangell, L. (1979a). Contemporary issues in the theory of therapy. *J. Amer. Psychoanal. Assn.* 27(suppl.):81–112.

_____ (1979b). From insight to change. *J. Amer. Psychoanal. Assn.* 29:119–141.

Rank, O., and Ferenczi, S. (1925). *The Development of Psychoanalysis.* New York and Washington, D.C.: Nerv. & Ment. Dis. Publ. Co.

Rosen, J. N. (1953). *Direct Analysis: Selected Papers.* New York: Grune & Stratton.

Schwing, G. (1954). *A Way to the Soul of the Mentally Ill.* New York: International Universities Press.

Sechehaye, M. A. (1951). *Symbolic Realization.* New York: International Universities Press.

Spitz, R. A. (1956a). Transference: The analytical setting and its prototype. *Int. J. Psychoanal.* 37:380–385.

_____ (1956b). Countertransference. *J. Amer. Psychoanal. Assn.* 4:256–265.

Sterba, R. F. (1934). The fate of the ego in analytic therapy. *Int. J. Psychoanal.* 15:117–126.

Stone, L. (1954). The widening scope of indications for psychoanalysis. *J. Amer. Psychoanal. Assn.* 2:567–594. *Reprinted in this volume, Chapter 2.*

_____ (1957). Review of *Psychoanalysis and Psychotherapy* by F. Alexander. *Psychoanal. Q.* 26:396–405.

_____ (1961). *The Psychoanalytic Situation.* New York: International Universities Press.

_____ (1967). The psychoanalytic situation and transference: Postscript to an earlier communication. *J. Amer. Psychoanal. Assn.* 15:3–57. *Reprinted in this volume, Chapter 4.*

_____ (1973). On resistance to the psychoanalytic process. *Psychoanal. Contemp. Sci.* 2:42–73. *Reprinted in this volume, Chapter 5.*

_____ (1979). The influence of the practice and theory of psychotherapy on education in psychoanalysis. Opening address, Pre-Congress on Training, International Psychoanalytical Association, New York, July 26, 1979.

Strachey, J. (1934). The nature of the therapeutic action of psychoanalysis. *Int. J. Psychoanal.* 15:127–159.

Valenstein, A. F. (1979). The concept of "classical" psychoanalysis. *J. Amer. Psychoanal. Assn.* 27(suppl.):113–136.

Winnicott, D. W. (1965). *The Maturational Processes and the Facilitating Environment.* New York: International Universities Press.

_____ (1969). The use of an object. *Int. J. Psychoanal.* 50:711–716.

Zetzel, E. R. (1966). The analytic situation. In *Psychoanalysis in the Americas,* ed. R. E. Litman. New York: International Universities Press, pp. 86–106.

_____ (1970). The analytic situation and the analytic process. In *The Capacity for Emotional Growth.* New York: International Universities Press, pp. 197–215.

Chapter 7
Some Thoughts on the "Here and Now" in Psychoanalytic Technique and Process
(1981)

This paper was stimulated by the recent controversial ferment on the position of early and active transference interpretations. In it I seek to examine critically the merits of this approach and to broaden the scope of the "here and now" so that it includes recognition of the patient's reality problems. The economic factor (energic sense) in selecting an interpretive approach is stressed. At the same time, the ultimate and unique importance of genetic understanding is reaffirmed.

T hese reflections are stimulated by what might be regarded as naïve surprise at the impact of the renewed emphasis on the "here and now"[1] in our technical work during the last few years, including the early interpretation of the transference. This emphasis has been urged most vigorously by Gill and Muslin (1976) and Gill (1979a, 1979b). It has at times been reacted to, in my impression, as if it were a technical innovation. This is, of course, not so, at least in a qualitative sense. Gill and Muslin (1976) and Gill (1979a), for example, explicitly recognize the well-established position of ongoing transference interpretation and refer to the earlier literature in this connection, including my own views (1967, 1973). It is clear, however, from the persistence and reiteration which characterize Gill's contributions, that he believes the "resistance to the awareness of transference" to be a critically important and neglected area in psychoanalytic work, thus deserving of further emphasis. This may indeed be true in selected instances. In Gill's latest contribution of which I am aware (1979b),[2] he concedes (as before) that the recall or reconstruction of the past remains useful but that the working out of conflict in the current transference is the more important (i.e., should have priority of attention). In view of the centrality of this issue and its interesting place in the development of psychoanalysis, a few remarks about special problems in the tendency (or countertendency) under consideration may be in order. The work of Gill and Muslin (1976) and Gill (1979a) presents a subtle and searching review and analysis of Freud's evolving views on the interrelationship between the conjoint problems of transference and resistance and the indications for interpretation. It would therefore be superfluous for me to repeat this painstaking work. My own references are therefore confined to those contributions which are immediately relevant to my own view. What I might have to say that differs from the ideas of these authors will appear in the course of the ensuing text, which—while stimulated by their work and the responses to it—is not intended principally as a critique of their contributions, with which in certain essential areas I am in broad agreement, as suggested by my previous writings (1967, 1973). My purpose is to state briefly my own views on transference and nontransference interpretation and beyond this to sketch briefly and tentatively certain further implications and potentialities of the "here and now."

In a sense, the current emphasis may be the historical "peaking" of a long and gradual, albeit fluctuating, development in the history of psychoanalysis. We know that Freud's first encounter with the transference, the "false connection," was in its role as a resistance (Breuer and Freud 1893–1895, pp. 302–303, and elsewhere). While Freud's view of this complex phenomenon soon came to include its powerfully affirmative role in the psychoanalytic process, the basic importance of the "transference resistance" remained. In *The Dynamics of Transference* Freud (1912) stated in dramatic figurative terms the indispensable current functions of the transference: "For when all is said and done, it is impossible to destroy anyone *in absentia* or *in effigie*" (p. 108). In fact, to some of us, the two manifestly opposing forces are two sides of the same coin. In my view (1973), the relationship is even more intimate, in the sense that the resistance is mobilized in the first place by the existence of (manifest or — often — latent) transference. It is a spontaneous protective reaction against loss of love, or punishment, or narcissistic suffering in the unconscious infantile context of the process.

Historically, the effective reinstatement of his personal past into the patient's mental life was thought to be the essential therapeutic vehicle of analysis and thus its operational goal. This was, of course, modified with time, explicitly or in widespread general understanding. It became increasingly evident that the recollection or reconstruction of a past experience, however critical its importance, did not (except in relatively few instances) immediately dissolve the imposing edifice of structuralized reaction patterns to which it may have importantly contributed. This (dissolution) might indeed occur — dramatically — in the case of relatively isolated, encapsulated, and traumatic experiences, but only rarely in the chronic psychoneuroses whose genesis was usually different and far more complex. Freud's (1914) discovery of the process of "working through," along with the emphasis on its importance, was one manifestation of a major process of recognition of the complexity, pervasiveness, and tenacity of the current dynamics of personality, in relation to both genetic and dynamic factors of early origin. Perhaps Freud's (1937, pp. 216–217) most vivid figurative recognition of the pseudoparadoxical role of early genetic factors, if not understood as part of a complex continuum, was in his "lamp-fire"[3] critique of the technical implications of Rank's (1924) *Trauma of Birth*. I say *pseudoparadoxical* because the recovery of the past by recollection or reconstruction — if no longer the sole operational vehicle and goal of psychoanalysis — retains a uniquely intimate and individual explanatory value, essential to genuine insight into the fundamental issues of personality development and distortion.

When Ferenczi and Rank wrote *The Development of Psychoanalysis* in 1924, they proposed an enormous emphasis on emotional experience in the analytic process, as opposed to what was thought to be the affectively sterile intellectual investigation then in vogue. Instead of the speedy reduction of disturbing transference experience by interpretation, these authors, in a sense, advised the elicitation and cultivation of emotional intensities. (As Alexander pointed out in 1925, however, the method was not very clear.) These alone could lend a vivid sense of reality and meaningfulness to the basic dynamisms of personality incorporated in the transference (see also De Forrest [1942] and Thompson [1943] on Ferenczi's personal psychoanalytic technique). Now it is to be noted that in this work, *too*, there is no "repudiation" of the past. Ultimately, genetic interpretations were to be made. The intense transference experience, as mentioned above, was intended to give body, reality, to the living past. Indeed, the ultimate significance of construction was invoked, in the sense of "supplying" those memories which might not be spontaneously available. It was felt that the crucial experiences of childhood had usually been promptly repressed and thus not experienced in consciousness in any significant degree. Therapeutic effectiveness of the process was attributed largely to the intensity of emotional experience, rather than to the depth and ramification of detailed cognitive insight. The fostering of transference intensity, we can infer, was rather by withholding or scantiness of interpretations (as opposed to making facilitating interpretations) and, at times (as specifically stated), by mild confirming responses or attitudes in the affective sphere; these would tend to *support* the patient's transference affects in interpersonal reality (Ferenczi and Rank 1924, pp. 43–44).[4]

This is, of course, different from the recent emphasis on "early interpretation of the transference" (Gill and Muslin 1976), which is a process in the cognitive sphere designed to overcome resistance to awareness of transference and thus to mobilize the latter as an active participant in the analysis as soon as possible. What they have in common is an undeniable emphasis on current experience, explicitly in the transference. Also, in both tendencies there is an implicit minimization of the vast and rich territories of mind and feeling, which may become available and at times uniquely informative if less tendentious attitudes govern the analyst's initial approach. Correspondingly, in both there is the hazard of stimulating resistances of a stubborn, well-rationalized nature by the sheer tendentiousness of approach, and by the same token transference distortions may be stimulated. This is, of course, true of any hypertrophic tendency pursued assiduously by the analyst.

The question of the moments entering into a sense of conviction in the patient (a dynamically indispensable state) is, of course, a complex matter. But I think that few would doubt that immediate or closely proximal experience ("today" or "yesterday") occasions greater vividness and sense of certainty than isolated recollection or reconstruction of the remote past.[5] Thus the "here and now" in analytic work, the immediate cognitive exchanges and the important current emotional experiences, can, under favorable conditions, contribute to other elements in the process (e.g., recovery or reconstruction of the past) a quality of vividness deriving from their own immediacy, which can infuse the past with life. Obviously, it is the experience of transference affect which largely engages our attention in this reference. But we must not ignore the contrapuntal role of the actual adult relationship between patient and analyst, which is indeed the actual biological constellation that brings the transference itself into being. At the very least, a minimal element of "resemblance" to primary figures of the past is a sine qua non for its emergence (Stone 1954).

Thus far, one might say, we are discussing considerations that originated in or were inspired by Freud's work and were epitomized in the celebrated figure of speech of 1912, referred to earlier. The long chain of contributions since then was perhaps most strikingly (if controversially) propelled by Strachey's (1934) paper and Ferenczi and Rank's (1924) work, representing different directions of emphasis: "interpretation" versus "dramatization." These contributions— up to and including Gill's and Muslin's (1976) and Gill's (1979a, 1979b) recent papers—did not introduce alterations in the fundamental conceptions of psychopathology and its essential responses to analytic techniques and process. There are, of course, varying emphases—largely quantitative—and corresponding positions as to their respective effectiveness. In the case of Strachey, there is an approach to actual substantive modification in the keystone position assigned to introjective superego change as the essential phenomenon of analytic process— and possibly in the exclusive role assigned to transference interpretations as "mutative."

A related or complementary tendency may be discerned in Gill's (1979a) proposal that "analytic situation residues"[6] from the patient's ongoing personal life, insofar as they are judged transferentially significant in free association, be brought into relation with the transference as soon as possible, even if the patient feels no prior awareness of such a relationship. It is as if all significant emotional experiences, including extraanalytic experiences, could be viewed as displacements or mechanisms of concealed expression of the transference. That this is very frequently true of even the most trivial-seeming actual allusions to the analyst would, I think, arouse only rare demurral. However, the thoroughly extraanalytic references constitute a more subtle and difficult problem, ranging from dubiously interpretable minor issues to massive forms of destructive acting out connected with extreme narcissistic resistances and utterly without discernible "analytic situation residues." The massive forms are, of course, analytic emergencies, requiring interpretation. But such interpretation would usually depend on an awareness of the larger "strategic" situation (Stone 1973), rather than on a detail of the free association communication (granting the latter's usefulness, if present—and recognizable). This will merit some remark later on. Important at the moment is the fact that however intense these emphases on the present or the immediate are, the significance of the past or the historical is never entirely abandoned or nullified, even though the role assigned to it may be pale or secondary. That the preponderant emphasis on concealed transference may ultimately, in itself, constitute a "de facto" change in technique and process, with its own intrinsic momentum, is, I believe, true.

The Ferenczi and Rank technique included, in effect, a deliberate exploitation of the transference resistance, especially in the sense of intense emotional display and discharge. While the polemical emphasis of these authors is on (affective) experience as the sine qua non of true analytic process—the living through of what was never fully experienced in consciousness in the past (with ultimate translation into "memories," i.e., constructions)—the actual techniques (with a few exceptions) are not clearly specified in their book. For a detailed exposition of the techniques learned from Ferenczi, with wholehearted acceptance, see the paper of De Forest (1942), which includes the deliberate building up of dramatic transference intensities by interpretive withholding and the active participation of the analyst as a reactive individual. Also included is the active directing of all extratherapeutic experience into the immediate experiential stream of the analysis. See also the critical, although appreciative, more conservative comment of Clara Thompson (1943), another devoted pupil of Ferenczi. The extreme emphasis on affective transference experience became at one time a sort of vogue, appearing almost as an end in itself and measured by the vehemence of the patient's emotional displays. In Gill's own revival of and emphasis on a sound precept of classical technique (preceded by the 1976 paper of Gill and Muslin), fundamentally different from that of Ferenczi and Rank in its emphasis, one discerns an increment of enthusiasm between the studied, temperate, and well-argued paper of (1979a) and the later paper of the same year (1979b), which includes similar ideas greatly broadened and extended to a degree which is, in my view, difficult to accept.

Now, what is it that may actually be worked out in the present—(1) as a prelude to genetic clarification and reduction of the transference neurosis or (2) as a theoretical possibility in its own right without reliance on the explanatory power or specific reductive impact of insight into the past? First some general considerations. Whether or not one is an enthusiastic proponent of "object-relations theory" in any of its elaborate forms, it seems self-evident that all major developmental vicissitudes and conflicts have occurred in the context of important relations with important objects and that they or their effects continue to be reflected in current relationships with persons of similar or parallel importance. We assume that the psychoanalytic situation (and its adjacent "extended family") provide a setting in which such problems may be reproduced in their essentials, both affectively and cognitively.

There is something engaging, a priori, in the idea that an individual must confront and solve his basic conflicts in the immediate setting in which they arise, regardless of their historical background. Certainly this is true in the patient's (or anyone else's) actual life situations. A possible and sometimes stated corollary of this view would be that the preponderant resort to the past, whether by recollection or reconstruction, would be largely in the service of resistance, in the sense of a devaluation of the present and a diversion from its ineluctable requirements. It would be as if the United Kingdom and Ireland would undertake to solve the current problems in Ulster essentially by detailed discussions of Cromwell's behavior a few centuries ago. Granted that the latter might indeed illuminate the historical contribution to some aspects of the current sociopolitical dilemma, there are immediate problems of great complexity and intensity from which the Cromwell discussion might indeed by a diversion, if it were magnified beyond its clear but very limited contribution, displacing in importance the knotty social-political-economic altercations of the present and the recent clearly accessible and still relevant past. As with so many other issues, Freud himself was the first to note that resort to the past may be invoked by the patient to evade pressing and immediate current problems. In conservative technique, it has long been noted that a judicious alternation of focus between past and present, according to the confronting resistance trend, may be necessary (for example, see Fenichel 1945). However, it was Horney (1939) who placed the greatest stress on the current conflict and the greatest emphasis on the recollective trend as supporting resistance.

Now, from the classical point of view, the emphasis is quite different. The original conflict situation is intrapsychic, within the patient, though obviously engaging his environment and ultimately—most poignantly and productively— his analyst. This culminates in a transference neurosis which reproduces the essential problems of the object relationships and conflicts of his development. Thus, in principle, the vicissitudes of love or hate or fear, etc., do not require, or even admit of, ultimate solution in the immediate reality, perceived and construed as such. The problem is to make the patient aware of the distortions which he has carried into the present and of the defensive modes and mechanisms which have supported them. Obviously, the process ("tactical") resistances present themselves first for understanding; later there are the "strategic" resistances (i.e., those not expressed in manifest disturbances of free association) (Stone 1973). Insofar as the mobilization of the transference and the transference neurosis is accorded a uniquely central holistic role in all analyses, the "resistance to the awareness of transference" (Stone 1973) becomes a crucial issue, the problem of interpretive timing a controversial matter from early on. Ultimately the bedrock resistance, the true "transference resistance," must be confronted and dissolved or reduced to the greatest possible degree. Such a reduction is construed as largely dependent on the effective reinstatement of the psychological prototypes of current transference illusions, with an ensuing sense of the inappropriateness of emotional attitudes in the present and the resultant tendency toward their relinquishment. In a sense, the neurosis is viewed as an anachronistic but compelling investiture of the current scene with unresolved conflicts of the past. When successfully reduced, this does appear to have been the accessibly demonstrable phenomenology. Some further technical considerations will be mentioned later.[7]

What then may be carried into the analytic situation from the "hard-nosed" paradigm of the struggle with everyday current reality, with advantage to the process? We have already mentioned the sense of conviction, or "sense of reality"—affective and cognitive—which originates in the immediacy of process experience. It is our purpose and expectation that, with appropriate skill and timing, this quality of conviction may become linked to other, less immediate phenomena, at least in the sense of more securely felt perceptions, including first the fact of transference and ultimately its accessible genetic origins. What further? Insofar as the transference neurosis tends toward organic wholeness, a sort of conflict "summary" by condensation, under observation in the immediate present, one may seek and find access in it, not only to the basic conflicts mentioned earlier, but to uniquely personal modes of defense and resistance, revealed in dreams, habits of free association, symptomatic acts, parapraxes, and the more direct modes of personal address and interaction which are evident in every analysis. Further, in my view, although not always as transparent as one would wish, this remarkable condensation of affect, impulse, defense, and temporary conflict solution adumbrates more dependably than any other analytic element (or grouping of elements) the essential outlines of the field of obligatory analytic work in a given period of the patient's life. In it is the tightly knotted tangle derived from the patient's early or prehistoric life enmeshed in the actualities of the analytic situation and his germane and contiguous ongoing life situation.

Also, in the sphere of the "here and now," and of far-reaching importance, is the role of actualities in the analytic situation. Whether in the patient's everyday life or in the analytic relationship, the even-handed, open-minded attention to the patient's emotional experience (especially his suffering or resentment) as to what may be actual, as opposed to "neurotic" (i.e., illusory or unwittingly provoked) or specifically transferential, is not only epistemologically an a priori; it is also a contribution to the affective soundness of the basic analytic relationship and thus of inestimable importance. At the risk of slight—very slight!—exaggeration, I must say that, excepting instances of pathological neurotic submissiveness, I have not yet seen a patient who wholeheartedly accepted the significance of his neurotic or transference-motivated attitudes or behavior if he felt that "his reality" was not given just due. Further, even the exploration and evaluation of complicated neurotic behavior must be exhaustive to the point where a spontaneous urge to look for irrational motivations is practically on the threshold of the patient's awareness. Again, one must stress the impact of such a tendency on the total analytic relationship. For, in the last analysis, not only the quality and mood of utilization of interpretations, but ultimately the subtleties of transition from a transference relationship to the realities of the actual relationship depend, to a greater degree than has been made explicit, on the cognitive and emotional aspects of the ongoing experience in the actual sphere. Greenson (1971, 1972, Greenson and Wexler 1969) devoted several of his last papers to this important subject. The subject, of course, includes the vast spheres of the analyst's character structure and also his countertransferences. But more than may be at first apparent can reside in the sphere of conscious considerations of technique and attitude in relation to a basic rationale.

However, apart from the immediate function of painstaking discrimination of realities and the impact of this attitude on the total situation, there remains the important question of whether important elements of true analytic process may not be immanent in such trends of inquiry. The vigorous exploration and exposure of distortions in object relations, via the transference or in the affective and behavioral patterns of everyday life, including defensive functions, can conceivably catalyze important spontaneous changes in their own right. To further this end, the traditional techniques of psychoanalysis will, of course, be utilized. As an interim phenomenon, however, the patient struggles to deal with distortions, as one might with other errors subject to conscious control or pedagogical correction. It is my personal conviction that such a tendency may be productive (both as such, and in its intrinsic capacity to highlight neurotic or conflictive fractions) and has been insufficiently exploited. However, there is no reason that the specific dynamic impact of the past be lost or neglected in its ultimate importance, in giving attention to a territory which is, in itself, of great technical potentiality.

It is noteworthy that practitioners and theorists such as Horney (1939) or Sullivan (1953) who established deviant schools did not reject entirely the significance of the past, even though its role and proportionate position, both in process and theoretical psychodynamics, was viewed differently. The persisting common features in these views would be a large emphasis on sociological and cultural forces and the focusing of technical emphasis on immediate interpersonal transactions. With regret, I must omit detailed discussion here. See, for example, Alexander (1940) regarding Horney, and Jacobson (1955) regarding Sullivan.

Granted that various technical recommendations of both dissident and "classical" origin, including those on the nature and reduction of the transference, sometimes appear to devaluate the operational importance of the genetic factor, this devaluation is not, I believe, supported by the clinical experience of most of us; nor, indeed, does close scrutiny reveal it as part of the *confessio fidei* of major deviationists. Certainly, both in theoretical principle and in empirical observation, this essential direction of traditional analytic process remains of fundamental importance. Granted the power and challenge of cumulative developmental and experiential personality change and the undeniable impact of current factors, it remains true that the uniquely personal, decisive elements in neurosis, apart from constitution, originate in early individual experience. How to mobilize such elements into an effectively mutative function is a large technical problem in itself, and—in seeming paradox—relies to a considerable degree on the skillful handling of the "here and now." The purposive technical pursuit of the past has not been clinically rewarding. That the ultimate effort to recover and integrate early material in dynamic understanding may not always be successful, especially in severe cases of very early pathogenesis is, of course, evident (see, for example, Jacobson 1971, p. 300). In such instances, while our preference would be otherwise, we may have to remain largely content with painstaking work in the "here and now," illuminated to whatever degree possible by reasonable and sound, if necessarily broad, constructions dealing largely with ego mechanisms rather than primitive anatomical fantasies. In other cases, sometimes after years of painstaking work, even large and challenging characterologic behavioral trends which have been viewed, clarified, and interpreted in a variety of current transference, situational (even cultural) references will show striking rootedness in early experience, conflict, and conflict solution whose explanatory value then achieves a mutative force which remains unique among interpretive maneuvers or spontaneous insights. To this end, the broader aspects of "strategic" resistance (Stone 1973) must be kept in mind, as must subtle elements of counter-transference and counterresistance.

I may at this point state in summary my view of the current ferment regarding the "here and now." Granting any number of valuable critiques and theoretical and technical suggestions which may help us to improve analytic effectiveness, it would seem that the emphasis on the "here and now" remains not only consistent with but also ultimately indispensable for genuine access to the critical dynamisms deriving from the individual's early development. Nor is this, reflexively — assuming adequate technical sophistication — inconsistent with the understanding and analysis of continuing developmental problems, character crystallizations, and the influence of current stresses as such. Adequate attention to the latter as a complex interrelated group permits the clear and useful emergence into the analytic field of significant early material, as defined by the transference neurosis. At this point, I should note an important if subtle difference in emphasis between my own technical approach and that of Gill (1979a, 1979b), apart from certain larger issues. Whereas Gill would apparently recommend searching out the "day residues" of probable transference in the patient's responses to the analysis or analyst and in his accounts of his daily life and offer possible alternative explanations to the patient's direct and simple responses to them as self-evident realities, I would rely first on the acceptance and exploration of the patient's "reality," with the possibility that this will incidentally favor the relatively spontaneous precipitation of more readily available transference material. This general principle does not, of course, obviate or exclude the other alternative as sometimes preferable.

Consideration of the interaction between the two adult personalities in the analytic situation requires a mixture of common sense and interest in self-evident (although often ignored) elements, on the one hand, and rather abstruse psychological and metapsychological considerations, on the other. I shall not try to enter into the latter at this moment, and I shall be optimistic enough to take for granted a reasonable inclination in the former direction (in relation to my immediate purposes).

Thus, if we set aside from immediate consideration questions regarding the "real relationship" and accept as a "given" the self-evident fact that the entire psychoanalytic drama occurs (without our question or permission) between two adults in the "here and now," the residual issue becomes the management of the transference, which has been a challenging problem since the phenomenon was first described. Let us assume, for purposes of brevity, that few would now adhere to the principle that the transference is to be interpreted only when it becomes a manifest resistance (Freud 1913, p. 139). (See the recent extended discussion by Gill and Muslin [1976] and Gill [1979a].) It is in fact always a resistance and at the same time a propulsive force (Stone 1961, 1967, 1973). It has long been recognized that an undue delay of well-founded transference interpretation (regardless of the state of the patient's free associations) can seriously hinder progress in analysis, and further, it can augment the dangers of acting out or neurotic flight from the analysis by the patient. The awareness of such danger has been clearly etched in psychoanalytic consciousness since Freud's (1905) insight into the termination of the Dora case.

Apart from the hazards inherent in technical default, however, there has developed over the years with increasing momentum, perhaps in some relation to the increasing stress on the transference neurosis as a nuclear phenomenon of process, the affirmative active address to the transference, i.e., to the analysis—or sometimes the active interpretive bypassing—of the "resistance to the awareness of transference." While this has occasionally become a travesty, which is further distorted by excessive operational emphasis on the countertransference, the tendency—in rational form and proportions—must be regarded as an important integral component of a progressively evolving psychoanalytic method. That individuals vary in their acceptance of or technical devotion to this tendency is to be noted (as indicated earlier), but its widespread practice by thoughtful analysts cannot be ignored. By the same token, it should not be ignored that there is also a nostalgic countertendency among analysts, which would tend to restore an earlier emphasis on a more direct approach to early historical material and the avoidance of early or "excessive" transference interpretation.

A few words about my own views on the relatively circumscribed problem of transference interpretation. It is my long-standing conviction that the economic aspects of transference distribution are critically important, although largely ignored. I have sought to utilize this consideration in a broad general sense, by distinguishing between the potential transferences of the analytic situation and those of the typical psychotherapeutic situation (and beyond that, the transferences of everyday life) (Stone 1951, 1954, 1979). These vary in their degree of emergence and their special investment of the transference object with the intensiveness of contact, with the structured elements of deprivation, and with the degree of regression attendant on the operation of the rule of abstinence, which is, of course, most highly developed and consistently maintained in the traditional psychoanalytic situation (Stone 1961). Thus, although subject to constant informed monitoring, the transferences can be assumed in the analytic situation to be, at least latently, directed ultimately toward the analyst (as against other important persons in the environment).

Now, under what conditions and with what provisions should the awareness of such transference potentialities be actively mobilized? Obviously, the original precept regarding its emergence as resistance still holds true in its implied affirmative aspect, but it is no longer exclusive. Further, there are, without question, early transference "emergencies" that must be dealt with by an active interpretive approach: for example, the early rapid and severe transference regressions of certain borderline patients or the less common but sometimes seriously impeding erotic or hostile transference fulminations in neurotic patients. These are special instances in which the indications seem clear and obligatory.

The central situation, which we discuss, however, is the "average" analysis (with apologies!), where the latent transferences tend to remain ego-dystonic, warded off, developing slowly over long periods, and manifesting themselves by a variety of derivative phenomena of variable intensity. Surely, dreams, parapraxes, and trends of free association will reveal basic transference directions very early. But when should these be interpreted to the patient if he is affectively unaware of them? Again, "all things being equal," an old principle of Freud's suggested for all interpretive interventions (as opposed, for example, to clarification), is applicable: that unconscious elements be interpreted only when the patient evidences a secure positive attachment to the analyst. This would not obtain in the face of the "emergencies" mentioned above or in the light of growing erotic or aggressive intensities, certainly if "acting out" is incipient. The disturbing complications (even in the "erotic" sphere) occur most often when basic transferences are ambivalent (largely hostile) or colored by intense narcissism. Therefore, in relation to Freud's valuable precept, it may be understood that in certain cases, the interpretation of ambivalent or hostile transference may be an obligatory prerequisite to the establishment of the genuinely positive climate which he required. In such instances of obligatory intervention, the manifestations that require them are usually quite explicit.

Again, then, what about the relatively uncomplicated case, the chronic neurotic, potentially capable of relatively mature relations to objects? Here it is not the coping with complications, but the procedures best suited to furtherance of analytic process which are in question. There are, I believe, a few essential conditions and one cardinal rule. First the patient's sense of reality and his common sense must not be abruptly or excessively taxed, lest, in untoward reaction, his constructive imaginative capacities become unavailable. Preliminary explanations and tentative preparatory "trial" interventions should be freely employed to accustom him to a new view of his world. The traditional optimum for interpretation (when the patient is on the verge of perceiving its content himself [Freud 1940, p. 178]) is indeed best, although it must sometimes be neglected in favor of an active interpretive approach. Second, as indicated earlier, the patient's sense that the vicissitudes and exigencies of his actual situation are understood and respected must be maintained.

Beyond these considerations, the essential principle I propose is quite simple. If it is assumed that—in the intensive, abstinent, traditional psychoanalytic situation (as differentiated from most psychotherapeutic situations)—the transference (ultimately the transference neurosis) is "pointing" toward the analyst (and adjacent figures), it must also be assumed that although the unconscious trend is heavily weighted in this direction, there is still a manifest element of movement toward other currently significant objects.[8] Thus a latent economic problem assumes clinical form: essentially, the growing magnitude of transference cathexis of the analyst's person, as withdrawn to varying degree from important persons in the environment with whom most of the patient's associations usually deal. There is a point, or rather a phase, in the evolution of transference in which analytic material (often prior to significant subjective awareness) indicates the rapidly evolving shift from extraanalytic objects to the analyst. In this period (early in some, later in others) the analyst's interventions, whether in direct substantive form or aimed at resistances to awareness of transference, often become obligatory and certainly most often successful in mobilizing affective emphasis into the "here and now" of the analytic situation. The vigorous anticipatory interpretations suggested by some may be helpful in many instances (at least as preparatory maneuvers) if (1) the analyst is certain of his view, in terms of not only the substance but the quantitative (i.e., economic) situation; (2) the patient's state is soundly receptive (according to well-established criteria); (3) neither the patient's realities nor his sense of their reality are put to unjustified question or implicit neglect; (4) a sense of proportion regarding the centrality of issues, largely as indicated by the outlines of the transference neurosis (or their adumbration), is maintained in active consideration. This will avoid the superfluous multiplication of transference references that, like the massing of scattered genetic interpretations (familiar in the past), can lead to a "chaotic situation" resembling that against which Wilhelm Reich (1933) inveighed. This will be more striking with a compliant patient who can as readily become bemused with his transferences as with his "Oedipus" or his "anality."

Once the affective importance of the transference is established in the analysis, a further (hardly new) question arises, with which some of us have sought to deal in the past. Even if one agrees that transference interpretations have a uniquely mutative impact, how exclusively must we concentrate on them? And further: to what degree and when are extraanalytic occurrences and relationships of everyday life to be brought into the scope of transference interpretation? With regard to the concentration of transference interpretation alone: it is obvious that a large, complex, and richly informative world of psychological experience is lost if the patient's extratherapeutic life is ignored. Further, if the transference situation is unique in an affirmative sense, it is also unique by deficit. To rail at the analyst, for example, is a different experience from railing at an employer who might "fire" the patient or from being snide to a coworker who might punch him (Stone 1967; see also Rangell 1979). Such experiences are also components of the "here and now" (granted that the "here" aspect is significantly vitiated), and they do merit attention and understanding in their own right, especially in the sphere of characterology. Certain complex reaction patterns cannot become accessible in the transference context alone.

Now it is true that many spectacular extraanalytic behaviors can and should be seen as displacements (or "acting out") of the analytic transference or in juxtaposed "extended family" relation to it (especially where they involve consistent members of an intimate dramatis personae). While such "extratherapeutic" transference interpretations (often clearly germane to the conflicts of the transference neurosis) can be indispensable, the confronting vigor and definiteness with which they are advanced (as opposed to tentativeness) must always depend on the security of knowledge of preceding and current unconscious elements which invest the persons involved.

Finally, there are incidents, attitudes, and relationships to persons in the patient's life experience who are not demonstrably involved in the transference neurosis, yet evoke important and characteristic responses whose clarification and interpretation may contribute importantly to the patient's self-knowledge of defenses, character structure, and allied matters. Furthermore, such data may occasionally show a vitalizing direct relationship to historical material. It would not seem necessary or desirable that such material be forced into the analytic transference if the patient does not respond to a tactful tentative trial in this connection: for example, the "alternative" suggestion proposed by Gill (1979a). For the economic considerations mentioned earlier always obtain, and it may be that certain concurrent transference clusters, not readily related to the mainstream of transference neurosis, retain their own original extratherapeutic transference investment. In some instances, a closer, more available relationship to the transference mainstream may appear later and lend itself to such interpretive integration. This, I believe, is more likely to happen if obstinate resistances have not been stimulated by unnecessary assaults on the patient's sense of immediate reality, or his sense of his actual problems. In terms of metapsychology, one may recall also that all relationships, following varying degrees of developmental and conflict vicissitudes, are derived to an important degree from the original relationship to the primal object (Stone 1967), even if their representations are relatively free of the unique "unneutralized" cathexes that characterize active transference ("transfer" versus "transference" [see Stern 1957]).

Now it is clear, as mentioned above, that the "here" of "here and now" is vitiated in material which relates to extratherapeutic experience, whether this is seen "in its own right" or as displaced transference. The direct transference experience occurs in relation to an individual who knows his own position, i.e., knows "both sides" as in no other situation. (Even where there are interfering countertransferences, these are at least susceptible to self-analysis.) This can never be true in the analysis of extratherapeutic situation, as there is an inevitable cognitive deficit. For this we must try to compensate by exercising maximal judgment, by exploiting what is revealed about the patient himself in sometimes unique situations, and by being sensitive to the growing accuracy of his reporting as the analysis progresses. Epistemologic deficits are intrinsic in the very nature of analytic work. This is but one important example.

SUMMARY

The effort in this paper has been to examine the recently revived emphasis on the "here and now" in analytic method. The concept is not only self-evidently valid and intrinsic conceptually in the nature and phenomenology of analytic work but also has a long history of authoritative support in reference to the transference, beginning with Freud. However, a few important questions arise in this connection. First, does the legitimate technical emphasis on the "here and now" devaluate the importance of the past in pathogenesis or in analytic process? With due regard for difficulties which may occur in the adequate recollection or reconstruction of the past and for the fact that changes in methods of approach have occurred, the opinion is offered that despite special attention to the "here and now," the essential importance of the past remains unquestionable, not only in psychogenesis, but also in the need for its technical reinstatement to the degree reasonably and effectively possible. Second, is analytic work conceivable without resorting to the influences and impacts of infancy and early childhood? It is thought that while such effort might provide productive experiment and be capable of certain useful therapeutic effects, it would be severely (and unnecessarily) limited by its omission of ultimately decisive factors in the understanding of current distortions. While the immediate or direct potentialities of such effort may have been underestimated in the classical view, it would still seem that one of its most effective functions resides in the matrix which it provides for genuine access to the critical pathogenic influences of early development. Third, should the methodology of adequate emphasis on the "here and now," construed as the mobilization of transference awareness, be implemented by direct and intellectually forceful measures to this end? It is thought that several considerations and corresponding circumspection are important in implementing this tendency, which may, in selected instances, be desirable. Some suggestions in this connection are offered. These suggestions originate in the recognition that the current situation ("here and now") encompasses more than the existence of transference, granted the latter's unique importance. Included are certain basic considerations of analytic technique, the recognition of the adult relationship between patient and analyst, and due respect for the sometimes critically important significance of the patient's extraanalytic activities and relationships as such. The economic significance of transference distribution is given weight, and its estimation in the timing and mode of expression of transference interpretation is recommended. The same is true of the general configuration and intensities of the transference neurosis as a guide to the interpretive field. Attention to the patient's spontaneous struggle with his immediate and actual problems is thought to be important in more than one reference, including the maintenance of necessary trust and rapport in the adult analytic relationship, but not least in its possible (paradoxical?) facilitation of genuine transference awareness and ultimately the recovery of the past.

NOTES

1. The quotation marks in my text derive from the frequent use of Gill's expression (1979a, 1979b).

2. Presented at an Atlanta Symposium on Psychoanalysis and Psychotherapy, the paper was a widely ranging critique of past and current views on the subject, with statement of the author's more recent ideas. Since these are emphatically stated, interesting, and (to me) controversial, it would be intellectually unjust to summarize them briefly. The paper should be read when published. The "here and now" theme is a keystone con-

cept (essentially, the patient's experience of the relationship with the therapist), but the paper ranges far beyond this in various (often related) references.

3. Freud's sarcastically trenchant remarks were directed at Rank's belief that a few months of analysis would suffice to uncover the primal trauma (of birth) and thus obviate the entire neurosis deriving from it. Freud compared this to a fire brigade that, called to a house on fire, removed the overturned lamp from the room in which the blaze had started and regarded its work as finished.

4. Later, Alexander (1956) was to propose an opposite tendency, albeit inspired by this work, i.e., the "corrective emotional experience." In that method the "here and now" was invoked to contravene, to disarm the past (Stone 1957).

5. There is a specific exception to this statement: the disturbance of recent memory in diffuse organic brain syndromes, occasionally with remarkably vivid retention of remote memory. This is conspicuous in senile brain atrophy. However, these conditions are very uncommon among analytic patients.

6. The term *day residue* borrowed from the theory and technology of dream interpretation, underlies Gill's ingenious phrasing for the possibly unimpressive or incidental-seeming element in the patient's associations, which may, if its potentialities are skillfully presented to the patient, prove to be a useful link to awareness of ongoing but warded-off transference activity. Needless to say, the analyst's selection would, in such instances, require validation by the patient's responses. The dream "day residue" is, of course, a part of the patient's associative response to his own dream, granted that it may, on occasion, be elicited by the analyst's question.

7. If there is a mood of reservation in the phrasing of some of these remarks, it does not derive from significant doubt about what is stated. Rather, it reflects my continued preoccupation with the psychobiological substrata of the traditional mechanisms. These have been described or briefly summarized in various earlier publications; so I shall not restate them here. They involve considerations of the primordial transference, the mature transference, and the psychobiological role of speech (thus, interpretation) as the "bridge of separation" from the primal mother and ultimately from the analyst (Stone 1961, 1967). It is true that in the majority of analyses (not all!), these important considerations remain entirely or largely in the metapsychological sphere. But one element in this consideration is ubiquitous in its functional and conceptual presence; that the élan of transference does not derive from an exclusive role as resistance.

8. In this brief discussion, "objects" are referred to as such, instead of their mental representations, to avoid rhetorical awkwardness.

References

Alexander, F. (1925). Review of *Entwicklungsziele der Psychoanalyse* by S. Ferenczi and O. Rank. *Int. J. Psychoanal.* 6:484–496.

———— (1940). Psychoanalysis revised. *Psychoanal. Q.* 9:1–36.

———— (1956). *Psychoanalysis and Psychotherapy. Developments in Theory, Technique, and Training*. New York: Norton.

Breuer, J., and Freud, S. (1893–1895). Studies on hysteria. Part IV, the psychotherapy of hysteria. *S. E.* 2.

de Forrest, I. (1942). The therapeutic technique of Sandor Ferenczi. *Int. J. Psychoanal.* 23:120–139.

Fenichel, O. (1945). *The Psychoanalytic Theory of Neurosis.* New York: Norton.

Ferenczi, S., and Rank, O. (1924). *The Development of Psychoanalysis.* New York: Nerv. and Ment. Dis. Publ. Co., 1925.

Freud, S. (1905). Fragment of an analysis of a case of hysteria. *S. E.* 7.

_____ (1912). The dynamics of transference. *S. E.* 12.

_____ (1913). On beginning the treatment (further recommendations on the technique of psycho-analysis I). *S. E.* 12.

_____ (1914). Remembering, repeating and working through (further recommendations on the technique of psycho-analysis II). *S. E.* 12.

_____ (1937). Analysis terminable and interminable. *S. E.* 23.

_____ (1940). An outline of psycho-analysis. *S. E.* 23.

Gill, M. M. (1979a). The analysis of the transference. *J. Amer. Psychoanal. Assn.* (Suppl.) 27:263–288.

_____ (1979b). Psychoanalysis and psychotherapy—1954–1977. Symposium on Psychoanalysis and Psychotherapy—Similarities and Differences—A 25-Year Perspective. Atlanta, October 20. (Unpublished)

_____, and Muslin, H. L. (1976). Early interpretation of transference. *J. Amer. Psychoanal. Assn.* 24:779–794.

Greenson, R. R. (1971). The "real" relationship between the patient and the psychoanalyst. In *The Unconscious Today. Essays in Honor of Max Schur,* ed. M. Kanzer. New York: International Universities Press, pp. 213–232.

_____ (1972). Beyond transference and interpretation. *Int. J. Psychoanal.* 53:213–217.

_____, and Wexler, M. (1969). The non-transference relationship in the psycho-analytic situation. *Int. J. Psychoanal.* 50:27–39.

Horney, K. (1939). *New Ways in Psychoanalysis.* New York: Norton.

Jacobson, E. (1955). Sullivan's interpersonal theory of psychiatry (book review essay). *J. Amer. Psychoanal. Assn.* 3:149–156.

_____ (1971). *Depression. Comparative Studies of Normal, Neurotic, and Psychotic Conditions.* New York: International Universities Press.

Rangell, L. (1979). Contemporary issues in the theory of therapy. *J. Amer. Psychoanal. Assn.* (suppl.) 27:81–112.

Rank, O. (1924). *The Trauma of Birth.* New York: Brunner, 1952.

Reich, W. (1933). *Character-analysis. Principles and Techniques for Psychoanalysts in Practice and Training.* New York: Orgone Inst. Press, 1945.

Stern, M. M. (1957). The ego aspect of transference. *Int. J. Psychoanal.* 38:146–157.

Stone, L. (1951). Psychoanalysis and brief psychotherapy. *Psychoanal. Q.* 20:215–236. *Reprinted in this volume, Chapter 1.*

_____ (1954). The widening scope of indications for psychoanalysis. *J. Amer. Psychoanal. Assn.* 2:567–594. *Reprinted in this volume, Chapter 2.*

_____ (1957). Review of *Psychoanalysis and Psychotherapy* by F. Alexander. *Psychoanal. Q.* 26:397–405. *Reprinted in this volume, Chapter 8.*

_____ (1961). *The Psychoanalytic Situation. An Examination of Its Development and Essential Nature.* New York: International Universities Press.

_____ (1967). The psychoanalytic situation and transference: Postscript to an earlier communication. *J. Amer. Psychoanal. Assn.* 15:3–58. *Reprinted in this volume, Chapter 4.*

_____ (1973). On resistance to the psychoanalytic process: Some thoughts on its nature and motivations. *Psychoanal. Contemp. Sci.* 2:42–76. *Reprinted in this volume, Chapter 5.*

――― (1979). The influence of the practice and theory of psychotherapy on education in psychoanalysis. Address, Opening Session, Pre-Congress on Training, New York, I.P.A., July 26. *Published in this volume, Chapter 15.*

Strachey, J. (1934). The nature of the therapeutic action of psycho-analysis. *Int. J. Psychoanal.* 15:127–159.

Sullivan, H. S. (1953). *The Interpersonal Theory of Psychiatry*, ed. H. S. Perry and M. L. Gawel. New York: Norton.

Thompson, C. M. (1943). "The therapeutic technique of Sándor Ferenczi": A comment. *Int. J. Psychoanal.* 24:64–66.

Chapter 8
Review of Alexander's Psychoanalysis and Psychotherapy: Developments in Theory, Technique, and Training
(1957)

A few decades ago, the revisions of psychoanalysis proposed by Alexander and his followers initiated a storm of controversy. In retrospect, it is difficult to imagine the amount and intensity of the discussions and writing on both the organizational and scientific—polemical aspects of these proposals. My own limited participation was but a sample. Indeed, many others strongly opposed the new doctrines. Kurt Eissler and Maxwell Gitelson voiced their opposition well before I did. Nevertheless, each of us wrote from his or her own specific position, and this review, like my participation in a panel of the "American" in Los Angeles in the 1950s, represents my own view on a situation which, although faded from controversy, assumed rather large historical proportions at the time.

I n his latest book, dedicated to the memory of Freud, Alexander presents his own and related psychoanalytic contributions of the last two decades. The form, however, is that of a comprehensive text, and the content ranges, with varying degrees of thoroughness, over the whole field, historical and current, suggested by the title. The book is, in general, characterized by its conspicuously modest interpretations of the author's own contributions, its measured attitude toward past criticisms, and its elaborate and considered arguments in defense of certain of the author's ideas. However, unless the process of attenuation, circumspection, and conservative reservation is to be construed as tantamount to depriving the proposals of mutative significance, one must deal in certain important references with essentially the same debatable issues which have consumed much space and time in the past.

While Alexander's keen and pervasive awareness of the limitations (and the failures) of the traditional psychoanalytic method is no doubt founded on certain observed clinical occurrences, one must recognize that his overall orientation toward the method and its potentialities, whatever the origin of this orientation, is a special one. He appears to see it as one of many possible applications of psychoanalytic knowledge, one which has acquired a certain traditional prestige, rather than as a painstakingly forged instrument of unique power and rationale, deeply related to every known element in the body of science which he unreservedly esteems. The latter relationship he appears to value for its historical contribution; the research interest he criticizes as a current motivation vitiating therapeutic effectiveness. (If Ferenczi and Rank did have a basis for this criticism at the time of their monograph, one wonders how many analysts would agree that Alexander has reason for postulating this as an interfering motive in the therapeutic work of competent contemporaries.) In any case, this view of the conservative method lends itself readily to cliché conceptions such as the *principle of flexibility*. Who does *not* believe in flexibility? A surgeon can use a scalpel in many ways, for a great variety of surgical illnesses; he can use its point, its cutting edge, even its handle. However, it must remain a scalpel, necessary and precise in its form. Furthermore, a surgeon is not devaluated because he deals largely with surgical illnesses (apropos of the monotonous and specious complaint that analysts select patients to suit their method!). Most analysts, quite aware of the limitations and contraindications of their method, are more impressed with what it *can* do than what is can *not* do. They prefer to use their basic well-tested instrument in a variety of flexible applications and to continue to learn more about it, perhaps modify it gradually, than to turn to an amorphous mass of conceptual molten iron to forge a new instrument for each case. They are justly cautious about hurried extrapolations. Right or wrong, this conservative view cannot be ignored. Alexander is especially concerned that the *middle period* of the analysis is often unduly prolonged because the analyst, in his putative search for pregenital material, often fails to distinguish between regressive evasion (of the incest conflict) and the need to resolve or master a genuine early fixation to a traumatic conflict. This is a legitimate criticism of certain individual efforts; it is not a valid criticism of a method or of a group orientation. In relation to fixed frequency of hours, a typical bête noire, is this something which, in itself fosters regressive evasion and pathological dependency, or is this type of transference neurosis usually a reflection of the patient's essential psychopathology, requiring a reasonable degree of transference experience verification and working through in the analysis, as do other important latent transferences? In Alexander's refreshing rejection of the glib tendency to place the responsibility for failure invariably on the patient, he appears only to reverse the direction of the traditional error. In any case, the remedies for the errors and failures, putatively due to traditional methods, are the more effective interpretation of regressive evasion in regard to the current situation and the well-known specific technical precepts dealing with quantitative factors. It is specified, in line with the general mood of the text, that the latter are intended as additional methods, not substitutes, for interpretation.

The principle of flexibility is thought to solve the problem of the great number and variety of clinical problems which do not lend themselves to traditional analysis. While most would feel that traditional analysis is far wider in its applications than Alexander believes, few would disagree that many illnesses come outside its optimum indications, and only a rare analyst would not agree that it is an important obligation of psychoanalysis to contribute to the development of other rational psychotherapeutic methods. The scientific reasons for preferring, where possible, to maintain terminological distinctions have often been argued; this is not the place to repeat such arguments. It may be mentioned that a common body of knowledge does not of itself render methods identical; nor do comparable good results; nor do certain external resemblances. Regarding the inner psychological processes—not enough is as yet definitely known.

Alexander's remarks about the importance of discerning variations in the required depth of analysis (or interpretative intervention), the matter of circumscribed conflicts, the importance of studying scientifically the "rapid" cures, and the scientific importance of the divergences between the theoretical model of technique and actual psychoanalytic practice do point, without question, to certain crucial and fertile issues of the future, for psychoanalysis and for other psychotherapies. One demurs only to the suggestion that we are now ready for important innovations in basic psychoanalytic method derived from impressions gained in these spheres.

In reviewing the development of psychoanalytic technique, Alexander finds Two Main Trends: Emotional Experience — Ego Analysis. He makes clear his own current belief in the preponderant therapeutic importance of transference emotional experience. "At the same time recognizing and experiencing this discrepancy between the transference situation and the actual patient-therapist relationship is what I call the *corrective emotional experience.*" This is thought "more important even than interpretations which but spell out in words what the patient feels." He would regard himself as differing from Freud only in the use of his own explicit term. The "corrective emotional experience" is thought to serve as a natural challenge to the ego to find a new solution to old conflicts. In seeking to establish the fundamental position of this principle, Alexander suggests that the importance of the diminished *intensity* of transference experience compared to the actual experience of the past, and the comparative maturity of the ego reexperiencing infantile conflict have been emphasized, with corresponding neglect of the crucial role of the *difference* between the past and the therapeutic situation. We may state at the outset than many would not accept the fact that this sense of difference is the decisive therapeutic factor in analysis. That it is a necessary condition for the complicated processes which follow is self-evident. In his acknowledgment that recall of the past as such has some perplexing therapeutic value, Alexander appears to ignore the fact that unresolved infantile conflicts can only be disavowed or modified as such if the patient becomes aware of them in their infantile context, whether through direct recall or sound reconstruction. That they may be subject to other forms of therapeutic modification is quite true; and this may well be the case in transferences dealt with on an exclusively current basis. It is a matter of incidental interest that Alexander, who experienced some perplexity on this score in 1925, speaks without reservation of Ferenczi and Rank as if they proposed to ignore the past utterly, in a technical sense. Actually, while their preponderant emphasis on current emotional experience as the indispensable and anterior phenomenon is quite clear, they *repeatedly* emphasize the need to restore the past (largely through reconstruction) before a genuine analysis can have been consummated, i.e., to substitute remembering for the repetition compulsion as expressed in the transference.

Alexander's principal explicit technical recommendations in this text are: variation in frequency of hours, planned interruptions of treatment, and "control of the interpersonal climate of treatment." The latter is proposed by Alexander, following a lengthy preliminary discussion, with a few case illustrations. He specifies that this is not the *playing of a role.* Nevertheless, it is rooted in the idea of being *different* in attitude from the decisive historical personage who dominates the transference, to the extent that the "corrective emotional experience" is sharpened. A major argument for the specific *climate* is the fact that analysts' personalities vary and inevitably impinge on the transference situation, both in the real and countertransference sense, so that the complete neutrality of the analyst is only a theoretical fiction. Instead of subscribing to the purely *negative* prescription that the analyst analyze and master his *interfering* countertransferences, or accepting Tower's interesting suggestion of a specific countertransference neurosis for each case, Alexander, in a tour de force of logic, recommends that the variety of human attitudes present in analysts be bent to specific attitudes toward their patients, while at the same time believing that the classical analytic attitude is impossible to attain.

The methods of variation of frequency and planned interruptions do, of course, contain the seeds of a quantitative *reductio ad absurdum*. Furthermore, the temptation to substitute a xylophonic simplicity of method for the orchestra of psychoanalytic interpretative nuances is already adumbrated, not only by Alexander's difficulty in understanding the special role which Bibring assigns to interpretation in the hierarchy of techniques utilized in psychoanalysis, but even more by his implied suggestion that it requires more resourcefulness to vary the frequency of hours than to conceive, time, and express an alternative and effective interpretation. As adjunctive devices, for final resort, when interpretation may in certain instances be overwhelmed by the economic and dynamic elements of the neurosis as integrated in the psychoanalytic situation, many analysts have used and do use one or another form or variant of these methods. They do not, in themselves, contravene basic psychoanalytic principles, and they are, of course, legitimate subjects for further exploration as to effectiveness.

In the matter of the specific planned "interpersonal climates," however, the reviewer must enter unreserved and deep disagreement as to the basic principles involved. In the first case, in which Alexander showed his impatience and finally admitted his dislike (unlike the patient's father), the general inference which the author draws is not justified. The reviewer, for example, has often discussed a case where momentary "loss of patience" terrified a patient, struck her as *identical* with a critical early experience with her father—and provided a dramatically favorable turning point in the analysis. Problems of communication, of the meaning of tangible dramatization, of specific needs of certain personalities cannot be so readily simplified and generalized. In the second case, which includes an everyday type of countertransference error, one must ask whether adequate management of the countertransference, with realistic adjustment of the fee, would not have accomplished all that was accomplished by transfer to a "tough" colleague (or the hypothetical arbitrary adoption of attitudes resembling his).

In following correct precepts, in doing what is technically appropriate at a given time, in assuming an attitude required by the particular medical specialty which he practices, the analyst does assume a role, in the realistic sense that all adults assume specific adult occupational responsibilities. Whether this is carried out with greater or lesser ease, its impact cannot be "artificial," in the sense that this must be true of the assumption of attitudes or the creation of climates which are to be measured against inherently noncomparable situations, i.e., the patient's early life with parents, siblings, and other intimates. An individual cannot seriously and consistently maintain a comparison between the behavior and attitudes of a professional expert whom he, in a sense, employs—and that of his mother or father or siblings in early childhood—unless he is very seriously ill. To the extent that transference illusion is an even more tenacious, contrapuntal, and pervasive phenomenon in the lives of "normal" and neurotic people than it is commonly thought to be, it is possible that patients, for varying periods, subjectively compare the new good father, for example, with the old bad father, or the new "tough" father with the old overindulgent father, instead of the present physician with an aspect of the original actual father whom they have engrafted on him. If so, the treatment situation must be so arranged that it can ultimately dissolve this illusion too! Any attitude not directly derived from or germane to the therapist's role is, perforce, less unlike the patient's past experience than the classical analytic attitude, which, as Alexander explicitly recognizes, *is* different from all other human attitudes, past and present.

As for the nuances of analysts' personalities and the fact that they inevitably do play a subtle role in the analysis—if we eliminate personalities who hate their patients, or who seduce or exploit them, or otherwise betray the high essential responsibilities of the relationship—it is better that we continue to *try* to understand them than to coerce them prematurely to oversimplified technical recommendations. The same is true of the play of intuition, controlled by sound principles. Where occasional disturbing reactions arise in otherwise well-qualified analysts in regard to individual cases, self-analysis, or analysis by a colleague still seems best. In any case, if Alexander does not believe that most individuals can successfully adopt the standard analytic attitude, toward which their entire training is rationally directed, how will they fare with personal attitudes specifically prescribed for specific individuals? How does the patient's reality sense deal with the change from the pretransference neurosis neutrality (which is admittedly necessary) to the tendentious attitude adopted after its establishment? In his combined "role" as analyst, as physician, as friendly human being, there is a considerable reservoir of attitudes with which the analyst may appropriately and unaffectedly respond, to the degree *proved necessary* by the diseased ego with which he deals, without illusory or artificial historically specified "oppositeness". Otherwise, and indeed in most instances, he does better to adhere, to the best of his ability, to that tested technical attitude which alone permits a relatively uncontaminated transference neurosis to arise, and to be resolved.

Alexander feels that the relatively warm reception accorded to psychoanalysis in the United States has facilitated its diffusion throughout psychiatric thought and practice and has tended to render anachronistic the isolation of analysts from other psychiatrists, especially those who teach in universities. Both in methods of practice and in methods of teaching, Alexander feels that analysts perpetuate a tradition born in their bitter struggle for acceptance in Europe. He believes that the return to the university and the merger with general psychiatry are inevitable. He thinks that the questions are largely those of tempo, and he recognizes that these may vary in different situations. There is no question, however, of Alexander's enthusiasm for these trends. A long, able, and generally interesting discussion of the theoretical (and sometimes operational) continuum of psychoanalysis and other psychotherapies, as now practiced, leads inevitably to the conclusion that, in effect, all psychotherapists should receive basic psychoanalytic training, of which the keystone is personal analysis. This would then place the crucial problem in the sphere of selection, whose criteria are very soundly and lucidly discussed. The question of specialization in "standard" psychoanalysis or other psychotherapeutic methods would then develop as a matter of individual inclination. With this general ideal formulation few analysts would disagree. However, it is recognized that the practical difficulties involved in this approach necessitate the current maintenance of separate training in psychoanalysis as a special technique, regardless of the auspices. This poses the problem of the kind and degree of theoretical psychoanalytic instruction to be offered to residents who are *not* candidates in psychoanalysis, specifically whether or not it should differ from that offered to candidates. This is one of the important questions addressed to representative teachers of psychiatry in a questionnaire. The chapters devoted to this inquiry deserve careful reading by psychoanalysts, for multiple reasons. Alexander's own *tendency* in this reference appears to be consistent with his general attitude favoring the dissolution of barriers wherever possible. In the face of practical observation of the grotesque interpretative habits of residents who have had lectures and seminars in theory, excerpted without extreme didactic care from the training context of practical experience, the reviewer would feel, as do some of Alexander's respondents, that methods of teaching the two groups must be different.

Alexander's historical reminiscenses covering the Berlin Institute are of course valuable and interesting; the same is inevitably true of his intimate knowledge of the history and the training methods of the Chicago Institute, however controversial certain elements in the latter may be.

This book is readable, interesting, certainly always stimulating, but highly uneven in quality. In places, the good and exceedingly well-stated psychoanalytic common sense seems so obvious from the point of view of accepted good practice (for example, "Two Forms of Regression and Their Therapeutic Implications") that one almost wonders to whom the message is addressed. In a few places, where some detail of refined psychoanalytic argument appears, as in the extended discussion of resistance analysis or the interesting if inevitably selective sallies into the actual content of ego psychology, the material is in itself usually well put and decidedly worthwhile, but inner connections and the relevance to main themes are not always clear. In general, Alexander's devotion to simplicity (explicitly stated in "The Psychoanalysis of the Total Personality") tends to appear in this work as oversimplification, most conspicuous in the important theme of the *corrective emotional experience*, and the ancillary *control of the interpersonal climate*. One wishes that Alexander's engaging geniality and tolerance toward intellectual adversaries were not vitiated by patronizingly understanding argument via motive analysis (against which Alexander legitimately protests early in the book!). A footnote apology, implying that all other arguments have been invalidated and that it remains only to explain their heat (on the other side, of course!), does not undo the effect.

To expound on the limitations, shortcomings, and failures of classical psychoanalytic technique, to call for the development of new methods, to emphasize the public health need for the treatment of incipient cases, is indeed an important function in the analytic world, and in this connection many join with Alexander and acknowledge his important role. The great expense in time and money of the *classical* procedure (which Alexander does not elaborate) is a source of deep concern to many analysts, no less than to the public at large. To many, this is an even more pressing motive for developing modifications and derivative procedures than the problems of intrinsic clinical effectiveness or applicability. To confuse the two issues can obscure scientific realities and rather retard than accelerate advance. Alexander's recent contributions to this advance are stimulating, always at least of heuristic value; their intrinsic or substantive merits remain debatable, or at least *sub judice*. His enthusiasm, vigor, persuasiveness, optimism, the general *direction* of his strivings are usually admirable. This is true whether he deals with new psychotherapeutic techniques, the need for maintaining a genuinely scientific spirit, or the wish to establish psychoanalytic training in the university. Such enthusiasm, however, may also color one's views of formidable realities. The chapter on "Psychoanalysis in Western Culture," which is in general well considered and interestingly written, reflects in one or two places this excessive optimism. It may not be irrelevant (however right or wrong Alexander may be) that Alexander, who once fully accepted the idea of the death instinct and even recently at least discussed it as a philosophical formulation, no longer even mentions it seriously — in a chapter which deals extensively with the crisis of western man, a crisis whose social events surely threaten even more than "to extinguish his individuality." The occasional looseness of argument, excessive facility, lapse in strict textual accuracy, and the more frequent oversimplification, to which enthusiasm may perhaps contribute, are also less laudable than Alexander's ultimate purposes. They enjoin very careful discrimination in reading and laborious afterreflection on what has been read. With such injunctions in mind, all analysts can read this interesting book with profit.

Part II

Current Problems in Psychoanalysis and Psychotherapy

Chapter 9
Transference Sleep in a Neurosis with Duodenal Ulcer
(1947)

I have suggested the inclusion of this paper in this volume although it was published many years ago. It presents analytic case material in considerable detail. Some of the technical procedures carried out in it were subjected to intense methodological criticism by Dr. Robert Langs in our "Dialogue" published in 1980. Naturally, my technical methods have been modified over almost four decades. But the issues of general principle remain essentially as I debated and defended them in the "Dialogue". The case is of even greater interest in certain other fundamental (and independent) references: (1) The psychosomatic elements in peptic ulcer, (2) the relationship between ulcer and depression (in the broader context of primitive orality, (3) the central pervasive position of the transference in analytic process, (4) the enigmatic but compelling interrelationship of sleep, primitive orality, and–ultimately–speech itself. The latter consideration was only larval in my mind at the time of the paper, but as evident in later writings, it came to occupy a very large place in my thinking.

W hile psychiatric interest in the problem of peptic ulcer has continued at a high level (Dunn 1942, Saul 1946), relatively few detailed psychoanalytic studies of ulcer patients have been reported (Garma 1944, van der Heide 1940) since the work of the Chicago group (Alexander et al. 1934).

In this field, recent physiological studies, often combined with psychiatric examinations and anamneses (Mittelman et al. 1942, Wolff 1943a, 1943b, Wolff and Wolf 1942), have contributed impressively to a knowledge of the role of emotion in normal and pathological gastric function and thus toward belief in the emotional etiology of peptic ulcer. Nevertheless the study of this disease as of other fields of "psychosomatic" research continues to demand detailed scrutiny of material, toward the increasingly certain establishment of the very fact or estimated proportion of psychogenesis in the illness. The accumulation of further psychological detail would certainly seem desirable before general formulations regarding the psychogenesis of peptic ulcer can be securely established.

For these reasons, it is felt that the following case merits special report. This is executed with apology for the difficulty of finding a meaningful path between the convenient conciseness of a sound but inevitably influential interpretative system and the mass of unorganized biographical and psychoanalytic detail that would result, were an interpretative system to be ignored entirely. In this connection, emphasis on the phenomenon of obstinate transference sleep during analytic hours may provide an axial basis for communication, aside from its special place as an objectively observed clinical phenomenon.

The account is based on the detailed review of 776 analytic hours with a married business man of about forty when work was begun. The patient (Mr. Roland S.) was seen in three separate periods of analysis, each successively shorter, and the first constituting most of the total at five hours a week with the last only thirty-six hours at three hours a week. The patient resumed analysis on each occasion after an interval of a few months because of symptomatic difficulties, the second time predominantly depression and the third time for acute gastric disturbances. On each occassion except the last, the patient had "terminated" the analysis himself, against advice, in strong reaction against what he regarded as unhealthy, unnecessary, and intolerable dependency. In the second period, the device of "tapering," even to one visit a week, was employed

211

in an effort to control and possibly analyze this type of acting out. In the third period, a similar effort was made by way of an agreement that the patient would continue to visit the analyst at least one month after he felt completely symptom-free. Possibly because the patient was deeply improved at this time, he was able to agree to this and to carry it out. At the time of writing, a few years have passed. The patient has continued in excellent health, generally comfortable and successful in his life situation, including a greatly improved marital relationship.

The patient was a real estate broker. His complaints, present most of his adult life, had been increasingly severe since the financial disaster of 1929. There was excessive, sometimes entirely unjustified, anxiety about fluctuations in income and the expenditure of money. The patient often experienced severely depressed moods on the same basis, with mild perennial depression. He worried habitually. He was unable to enjoy and develop social relations with people despite an apparent ease in attracting friends. He was greatly concerned lest he be defeating himself in business, even in inexplicable neurotic losses at cards, which were frequent. He suffered from chronic constipation, a familial symptom. The diagnosis of duodenal ulcer had been unequivocally established both clinically and radiologically about four months before the beginning of analysis, the symptoms having appeared three months earlier.

Although duodenal ulcer was not stated initially as a reason for seeking analysis, the patient said later that this had been the determining factor in leading him to seek a treatment which he had considered for a long time. The idea of being treated psychologically for an organic disease was partly a result of the patient's intellectual level and milieu and partly neurotic. By the latter, I mean that it was determined by infantile strivings for painless and effortless relief and the wish to deny severe illness. The patient had had and continued to have much trouble with his teeth; he had had many sore throats and a tonsillectomy in 1928. There had been one attack of Vincent's angina. A severe food infection had occurred approximately within the year before analysis.

In the initial interview, I was impressed with the patient's apparent eagerness for analytic help and his drive to get well. A certain uncritical naïveté about the procedure seemed allied to this enthusiasm; both were later better understood in connection with the powerful passive transference demands. A strong and obvious self-critical attitude gave a preliminary and deceptively benign impression, which might be described as "intellectual honesty." A curious vagueness of complaints, uncertainty about details and dates, and even gross amnesia for certain important episodes of adolescence and early maturity, not to speak of advanced childhood were later repeatedly and tenaciously manifested in the analysis, wherein they very gradually lent themselves to a considerable degree of dynamic understanding. Depression was not objectively manifest. Intelligence seemed adequate. The patient's personality as described by himself and as it appeared in early interviews seemed bound by compulsive habit patterns and marked by considerable rigidity of both thinking and affect, yet tormented by the awareness of enormous demands on life and people, and the utter inability to express these demands even on a social level, not to speak of securing their fulfilment. There was also an utter inability to give anything of himself to others, with appropriate violent self-reproaches. For all these failings, whether within himself or in the gratifications afforded by the world, the patient felt a diffuse envy of other people of indescribable intensity. A striking detail in this envy was the early frank inclusion of the traditional occupational and financial role of the female.

Diagnostically the patient did not fit readily into a simple psychiatric category. He was a man of rigid personality, with compulsive character traits, frequent symptomatic reactions (especially depression and anxiety), and somatic disorders, constipation and duodenal ulcer, which played an important role in the composite personality structure.

The patient came from a West Coast family of successful and smug business people. The family was American of Anglo-French extraction on both sides. The father was of narrow intellectual scope and in the insurance business. He was tyrannical, on rare occasions (in the patient's childhood) violent toward his sons and rigid with his wife in money matters. He was extremely oversolicitous and overprotective toward his daughter. His strong tendency to suppress initiative in his sons carried with it an extended paternalistic protection and patronage even in their advanced adult years.

The patient's mother was physically active and of buoyant disposition. She was apparently overindulgent toward her sons in all spheres and antagonistic toward her daughter. In the patient's prepubertal or early pubertal period, she had a vaguely mentioned brief depression, with bowel symptoms.

Her "cool soft hands" had provided an incentive to illness and malingering in childhood, both frequently gastric. In early childhood, the patient had had frequent nightmares of being attacked and eaten by large animals. These nightmares brought his mother to his bedside. (Dreams of sharks were very common in the analysis.) The patient and his brother came into the mother's bed at least until the patient was nine and when the father took one of his frequent business trips, there was often frank rivalry concerning the alternation in sleeping with her. Her tastes were luxurious. The patient felt that he was manifestly in love with his mother until the time he married, after which, under the domination of his wife, he became resentful and finally apathetic and forgetful toward her. That the patient also envied some features of his mother's life was indicated by occasional experiments with her cosmetics in early boyhood. At puberty, he used her powder to cover the rings under his eyes ascribed to masturbation or attendant sleeplessness, but comments that he often succeeded in getting only a clown-like effect, a quality sometimes suggested in the analysis, in the patient's repetitious and mournful but self-derisive complaints. The patient noted that his mother used devious methods to extract money from his father. Later his wife showed him, to his disgust, how his mother had cheated subtly in an amateur business project.

The patient protested repeatedly that he was his mother's favorite child and his father's favorite son. He spoke with mingled contempt, pity, guilt, and irritation of his brother John, one and a half years older than he. The brother was and always had been utterly unsuccessful at anything he tried, including his father's business, in which he still remained on a small unearned salary. He had lived at home, with a few brief excursions, directly dependent on his parents financially, physically, and emotionally — suffering from occasional vague gastric symptoms and transitory attacks of depression. The patient had always been ashamed of him; neither he nor his friends accepted him. Lacking the patient's facility in argument and lying in childhood, his brother had been the principal butt of his father's punishments. On one occasion after a joint escapade in early childhood, the brother was struck so severely by his father that his nose bled. The patient was terrified. Nevertheless the brother was also the patient's scape-goat. At the slightest provocation, the patient would literally jump on his brother and beat him up unmercifully. Once when he "almost killed" him, he drew from his aunt an ominous pronouncement about "a bad end," which frightened him. Even very late in the analysis, the patient had difficulty understanding these attacks on his brother, except that he was "so greedy that he didn't want either his brother or his sister to have *anything*." His brother did have prettier hair, which the patient often seized, and he excelled in a few minor personal talents.

The patient's sister Minerva was born when he was five. The patient vividly remembered his discomfort over his father's preference for the girl child and the special indulgences accorded her in the household. (The "disappointment" with his mother was submerged beneath this, in conscious memory.) This continued during the analysis, since the sister, then a matron, still received a regular month-ly allowance from her father. She had been, furthermore, an exacting, ill-tempered child, crying readily and given to tantrums when frustrated. The patient was also almost as ashamed of her socially as he was of his brother, because of her ineffectuality. The sister was a doting, indulgent mother, especially toward her son. She was a strikingly pretty, small blonde woman. Incestuous attitudes toward her, like homosexual attitudes toward the brother appeared only in dream material.

The patient grew up in a midwestern metropolis and graduated from a midwestern university. His university career was punctuated by punishment for a spectacular isolated and impulsive academic deviation allied to "cribbing," whose peculiar character made discovery certain and whose transitory apparent disturbance of consciousness, or at least responsible thinking, had deep ramifica-tions in the patient's psychopathology and symptoms, which cannot be elabo-rated here. The episode itself precipitated in the patient a severe loss of self-esteem and an involution of overt aggressiveness of any type. He tended to ascribe the foundations of his adult character to this episode and to the subsequent unhappy experience of sudden unexplained rejection by his closest college chum.

Following a brief independent business experience, the patient worked for his father's firm for eight years. Here he was discontented with his subordinate position, and because he could not or would not openly fight his father (and instead covertly supported the opinions of other malcontents in the firm), he made a brief effort in another business venture but had to return to his father's firm for several years. Thereafter, he joined a large real estate firm, where he remained. It was noteworthy that he had originally intended to go into the same business as his father and to compete with him. The patient always earned a living for his family, but he was never free of a deep sense of inadequacy and insecurity in connection with it. He was also harassed by the feeling that his expenditures were always ahead of his income, a phenomenon which he attributed with intense resentment to his wife who was the dominant marital partner in all spheres. He would have wished to get along by extreme economy, his wife had always driven him to try to meet their needs by increasing his income.

The patient married in his twenties. His wife Louise came from a family similar to his own in general background. She was well educated, intelligent, and capable but harshly critical and exacting toward her intimates, especially her husband. She had been analyzed several years before the patient.

The patient had two adolescent daughters, Mary and Beatrice. Mary, the older daughter, was thought by his wife to resemble in many of her personal traits the patient's brother and sister and certain undesirable features of the patient's own personality. When these resemblances were mentioned by his wife, the patient suffered acutely. The younger girl, the wife's favorite, was said to be warm, outgoing, attractive, and especially attached to her mother. The patient too felt himself more strongly attracted to the younger girl, and he often described her position in the family as similar to his own in childhood. The patient was always excessively concerned with the danger of "father fixations" and thus strained to avoid any sort of physical intimacy with the girls.

Aside from the malingering, the patient, unlike his brother and sister, was frequently ill as a child, his illnesses including pneumonia and mastoiditis before puberty. At ages variously stated from two to four, he had had an operation on his penis, which he spoke of as his "second circumcision." There was some degree of hypospadias; the patient thought of the ventral orifice as operatively induced. He recalled clearly the intense pain while urinating after this operation. A "first circumcision," before two, was an occasional questionable memory. His brother's normal penis was an unequivocal point of superiority. Up to the age of at least nine or ten, the patient suffered from nocturnal enuresis ("sometimes lazy, half-awake") and occasionally wet his trousers during the day. He recalled, without a sense of motivation, the perverse habit of crossing his legs in order to retain by violent effort, urine or feces (more often the former) and thus avoid leaving his play to go to the toilet. His appetite was ravenous, especially in the period before puberty, but he never gained weight. He was grasping, inordinately competitive, and domineering as a child, and a glib liar to adults. He searched out hidden candies relentlessly, and very early began to steal change from his mother's purse and later from his father's trousers pockets. On one occasion, the mother punished both boys by forcing them to pace up and down the front porch of their home, each one placarded "I am a thief." The patient never forgave his mother for this severe punishment, which she later denied.

As a child, the patient was defiantly sloppy, rebelling against his father's compulsive neatness. As an adult he was as rigid in his habits as his father. As an example of his early perverseness, he described rolling in the mud in his new white sailor suit, to spite his mother for discontinuing a streetcar ride which he was enjoying.

His earliest clearly recalled sexual play was in the form of alternate "free show" (pulling up of nightgowns) with a girl cousin whom he later adored respectfully, while he suffered on hearing of her intimacies with other boys. This woman (a person of many "affairs") appeared in his adult social life, frequently in his dreams, and was at one time so intimately fond of his wife that he became intensely jealous of both of them. At least once in his early years, he exhibited and played with his penis before a woman teacher in school, but he could not recall the consequences, except that she "told him to stop."

At twelve to fourteen, in a public toilet, the patient submitted to the squeezing of his testicle by a homosexual, with momentary pleasure followed by pain, then flight to his father who threatened to kill the man. At the age of sixteen, the patient impulsively threw an attractive girl acquaintance on the bed, literally jumped on her, and ejaculated.

Between twelve and fourteen, the patient became aware that a young man was particularly attentive to his mother when his father was away. On several occasions he listened to conversations by an extension telephone. The patient confronted his mother with her "unfairness" and threatened to tell his father if the relationship did not cease. Apparently it was discontinued. In approximately the same period, the patient accidentally discovered masturbation and began from that point on, a terrific struggle with the "habit" ("like dope"). Each episode was followed by severe guilt and self-reproaches, later stated as "more pain than pleasure." (Note the similarity to later dietary indiscretions.) At times, in his effort to diminish the ill-effects, he would try to suppress ejaculation, permitting only seepage, and in so doing would lose or seriously diminish the pleasure of orgasm. He often bathed his genitals in cold water in an effort to diminish his passion. He felt that a later testicular atrophy (mumps orchitis at seventeen or eighteen) was connected with masturbation, also his smaller-than-average penis, about which he felt intense inferiority. Probably most severe was a spontaneous and persistent conviction that his supply of semen was strictly limited and that he would exhaust it prematurely as a result of masturbation.

At the age of fifteen or sixteen, the patient was taken by his mother to see Brieux's *Damaged Goods*. This, supported by his mother's books and gossip about veneral disease in friend's families, was the essential direct sexual threat of his adolescence. The patient was celibate until his marriage at twenty-three. He literally fled from the occasional prospect of sexual intercourse. He knew and went about with many girls and indulged at times in very passionate "necking." The flight phenomenon presented itself consciously as an unusually strong sense of taboo about respectable girls and as fear of disease from loose girls. There was also intense sensitiveness regarding a possible rebuff and an intense fear that he might not meet the girl's expectations.

During the patient's college career, he became involved in an alternating triangular love relationship, which repeated vividly the essentials of both phases of the Oedipus situation. The essential situation was that of an intense (sublimated) mutual attachment to the man and a brief interlude of passionate flirtation with his friend's sweetheart in his friend's absence. To the patient, the tragedy lay in his sense of inexplicable rejection by the man. Only very late in the analysis did the woman seem to have been of other than secondary (or reactive) importance, as an obstinate blurred distortion of the time that relations tended to right themselves.

When the patient married (at his wife's suggestion), his principal motive was to flee masturbation which he thought would ruin him. The patient's sexual attempts in the first days of marriage were unsuccessful, the failure ascribed to mutual clumsiness and ignorance of sexual technique. Thereafter, for a few years, sexual relations were satisfactory. However, after this period, there were occasional brief periods of partially disturbed erectile potency, as well as long periods of sexual apathy. There was a tendency to premature ejaculation early in marriage, which the patient suppressed by effort of will, a suppression which heightened his self-righteous resentment against his wife for what he regarded as her inconsiderateness in intercourse. While extremely courteous toward other people and generally submissive in really important matters, the patient was often singularly offensive toward his wife in terms of infantile bodily expressions, in that he had a special disposition to belch in her presence, even to pass flatus in bed, with no apparent effort at restraint. The same was true of sundry noises, especially joint cracking associated with stretching. Nose picking was an allied problem. Early in marriage, he felt that his wife was too passive in intercourse, that she "let him do all the work." Later he felt that she was too much concerned with her own physical comfort and that she was especially loathe to vary coital positions. After almost two years of analysis, the patient stated as a special grievance against his wife that she would never allow him to kiss her during intercourse.

In the belief that he had made a serious mistake in omitting premarital sexual experience and in the strong conviction that variety would restore his flagging sexual powers, the patient yearned for a fantasized extramarital indulgence all the time. These fantasies could be equated with his masturbation. On two occasions he had conducted brief actual flirtations of this kind, once consummating unsatisfactory intercourse with his partner, a married woman of his own social circle, with prompt flight thereafter. At about the same time, the patient was annoyed and told his wife of his annoyance (as he had once told his mother), because she often accepted with pleasure the admiration of a neighbor, who continued to frequent their house. The patient's florid extramarital fantasies during the analysis centered chiefly on a waitress in a famous restaurant.

The patient's infant feeding history is not known. Food had been a matter of extreme importance all of the patient's remembered life, and he could recall ruminating on how terrible it must be to be uncertain of one's next meal. The patient himself felt he was pathologically stingy with money. The expenditure which he made most willingly was for excellent food for himself. His parental family all were interested in fancy cooking but finicky in their tastes. His mother always served large quantities of rich and highly flavored foods. It was a passion with him, at times a querulous necessity, that his food be served very hot. This preponderant interest colored the patient's dream language persistently, often when other interests were obviously more important.

The patient received a promised gift of a few thousand dollars from his father on attaining his majority, supposedly for not having indulged in smoking until that age. Actually the patient had smoked quite frequently, but not when it might be seen and reported. The patient never sought to smoke during the analytic hour, and it was only after several months that the analyst learned that he was smoking quite steadily on the outside.

In speaking of the history of his gastric illness, it appeared that he had had a severe sore throat about seven months before beginning the analysis, about three months before the diagnosis of his ulcer. At this time he ceased to smoke. During his abstinence, he began to suffer from abdominal "rumbling" and pain. He also became so intolerably irritable that his wife persuaded him to resume smoking. His irritability diminished, but the pain persisted and led to a thorough medical examination and the diagnosis of ulcer. After more than a year of analysis, the patient, having long resisted the advice of his physicians, decided rather suddenly to give up smoking. At this time, it should be noted, his older daughter Mary began to smoke. The cessation was followed by a period of intense irritability and verbal aggressiveness. However, there was unmistakable symptomatic improvement in connection with the ulcer pain. The patient himself was perplexed by the paradox of onset and relief in this connection. It seemed to me that there was a strong connection among the content of his anamnestic fragment, the "sleeping" paradox (to be described later), the bipolar financial exacerbations of the ulcer pain, and the patient's own repetitious lamentations that he always "blocked" himself from getting what he desired. In other words, the painful constellation of feelings involved in oral deprivation (castration) would be importantly involved in the symptoms attendant on renewed gratification. The importance of child-as-sibling is also to be noted.

An allied fragment in the background of the transference was the patient's relationship with his personal physician (also a friend), who was a surgeon. This man had made the diagnosis of duodenal ulcer and instituted treatment. He had operated on the patient's hemorrhoids, and once or twice, he had suggested that the patient's inguinal hernia be repaired. The patient feared, however, that he was "too eager to operate." For a long time (although with decreasing intensity) the patient did not want his doctor-friend to know that he was being analyzed. In a certain sense, the patient was fleeing his sadistic father and his own inclination to submit to him, in coming to the magic breast of psychoanalysis, which — for many months — he apparently regarded, because he so earnestly wished it to be so, as an intellectually more acceptable version of Christian Science. (The word *breast* is used here and subsequently as a symbol for the actual organ or any substitutive device for the sucking nourishment intimately connected with a female object.)

The patient began the analysis in the rigidly compulsive manner that characterized the conduct of his daily life. Free association or freedom of emotional expression rarely occurred. The patient was as careful of his rhetoric as of his clothes. Aside from the element of anal orderliness, this was bound up with the patient's intense need for admiration and love, his fear of risking them, and his deep narcissism. Another conspicuous if contrasting phenomenon in the early period of the analysis was a remarkable pseudostupidity, a difficulty in understanding or remembering his own dreams (often pellucidly clear), interpretative remarks of the analyst, and important dates or events of his own life. This reaction diminished considerably as the analysis progressed, its functions absorbed by the "sleeping" reaction to be discussed below. Beside frustrating the analyst obstinately, this pseudostupidity was admirably designed to try to prick him to greater activity, even forcefulness. That there was a masochistic wish to provoke angry criticism or abuse such as his brother so often suffered was suggested later by strong feelings of identification with his brother. This was partly from guilt because of his own treatment of him and partly from the envy of his passive dependent relationship to his father (achieved via castration) and (more deeply) his permanent relationship with the seducing mother.

Since the analyst would not grant him the abuse or criticism which he often succeeded in getting from his harshly critical wife, the patient zealously reviled and heaped contempt on *himself*, for his infantilism, femininity, dependency, obstinacy or anything else that seemed even remotely appropriate.

After a year of analysis, on a few occasions in connection with particularly exasperating pseudostupid reactions, once with transference drowsiness, the patient was observed crossing his extended legs in scissors fashion above the knees. The resemblance to the sphincter phenomenon that he himself had described was unmistakable.

Aside from these symptomatic phenomena, the patient expressed passive demands and expectations of remarkable intensity and naïveté. There was literally an assumption of striking relief within the *first few weeks* and intense stated disappointment that it was not forthcoming. The question of how this was to be accomplished or just what the patient wanted from the analyst was not clear. Some relatively early dreams illuminate the preponderant character of the patient's unconscious demands. In one dream, the British navy manned by *women*, revolted against a frightened England. Instead of attacking all of England, they seized two small outlying islands. The patient wondered at their stupidity, comparing them with males. He was "against" them. The associations were with his wife's domination, his own wish to revolt, the recent war events, and most strikingly an article read the night before about the weakening of the English people through malnutrition since the era of Queen Victoria. The patient associated himself with this weakened state. In this dream, aside from current marital animosities, the resentment about his own weaning, his reactive cannibalistic aggression, and an envious fantasy of his sister's (and children's) nursing experience were strongly indicated. The enuresis theme was also suggested by the navy. The dream was followed by a severe stomachache.

In another dream, the patient lay on the couch talking about a business in which he had been involved and in which he had failed. As he spoke, he became "completely hysterical" with his worry about repeated failures. The analyst thereupon leaned over and kissed him gently on the mouth. Some spray from the analyst's mouth went into his mouth and quieted him down. He had been explaining how he always traveled a certain distance toward success, then lost his interest or ability and began to slide downhill. This episode was preceded by a vague fragment of which he remembered nothing, except that it had to do with Hitler and the German police. The associations were with mothers caring for babies, the chasteness of the kiss, the spray as a measure to "make things grow" (as he wished to be made to grow up), and his wish to evoke the analyst's affection and sympathy. In connection with the stated business, the patient recalled the early invitation by a relative with the surname of his mother's admirer to invest in such a business, his own wish to do it, and his father's refusal to permit it. Aside from the obvious passive oral wish, there is a basis for assuming the importance of regression from the genital level, because of castration fear, i.e. in the reference to Hitler and to his father's prohibitive role. Within a few months after the second dream, the patient did become quite upset on the couch, in a manner closely resembling that described in the dream. However, the basis for the reaction was severe epigastric pain, and the demand that the analyst do something remained, as usual, unclear, as compared with the specific wish in the dream. The absence of a breast or breast symbol in this dream, despite the "spray," foreshadowed the general trend of the analysis. Food and drink as such appeared often in dreams. Only toward the end of the analysis did the breast itself appear as an object of strong interest in dreams or associations. One may think of this restoration as accompanying the diminution of destructive oral aggressions.

In another multiply determined dream in which oral sadism and cannibalism were unmistakable, the Oedipus complex was also discerned. (See Abraham's emphasis [1924] on this combination, with disappointment in relation to melancholia.) The patient was to assist a trained nurse to do an emergency appendectomy on an unknown woman on a card table while the patient's phlegmatic husband stood by. A conspicuous feature was the presence of a large bowl of oyster stew, of uncertain purpose but most likely for the dipping of the patient. Aside from the protested resentment against the woman's (wife's) domination, the chief associations were that nurses perform midwifery, not surgery; his own feeling of being "cut up" at the bridge table by his wife; an emergency operation performed on his mother in the country in his early childhood; his love for oyster stew; his association of oyster stew with genital potency; his wife's confidential discussion of the night before with a young woman whom she was persuading to be analyzed.

The ulcer pain, with insistent demands for its cure, soon began to play an important role in the analysis and the patient's evaluation of his progress, despite the original concealment. The patient was intensely defiant about his mild dietary restrictions. He would frequently tempt and suffer pain by indulging in a cocktail, a cup of coffee, or a spicy food of which he was especially fond. If he missed the pain, he was delighted and used this to support his rationalization that since the genesis of the ulcer was "mental," dietary precautions were really superfluous. All of this was in significant contrast with a late analytic recollection that he enjoyed tremendously the very frequent feedings of milk and cream at the outset of his treatment. It was also very difficult to keep him in touch with his surgeon friend, who did not know of his analysis. When the patient did have pain, he regarded this solely as a demonstration that he "wanted to suffer" — ignoring entirely the obvious aspect of defiant insistence on pleasure.

The pain came especially frequently at times not connected with diet; for instance, when business was bad, sometimes when business was very good, similarly when he lost heavily or occasionally won heavily at cards, when he was disappointed, when he was impotently antagonized, when he was impatient or delayed, and when he felt discriminated against or unloved. Late in the first analytic period, as the pain greatly diminished after attaining an apparent peak about a year after the beginning of analysis, a relationship with the analytic hour was often apparent. The pain often began shortly before the patient was to come for his hour, but it usually disappeared during the hour. He sometimes said that this was because he must leave urgent business, the making of money, for the intangible (but indispensable) gains of analysis. However, this was also clearly dependent on the increasing concentration of all the patient's major emotional demands and conflicts in the analytic relationship. On going home in the evening, he very frequently felt the pain, occasionally depression, before dinner. This was connected for a long time with his essentially unhappy relationship with his wife and daughters. Here too it was only very late in the analysis that the pain was felt as something adventitious in relation to potential pleasure in returning to his "three women."

TRANSFERENCE SLEEP

Although there was an early tendency to drowsiness, this became a symptomatic reaction of extreme intensity and tenaciousness about ten months after the beginning of the analysis. One might say that its development overlapped the peak of the "ulcer" complaint of the first period, rapidly reached its maximum, and gradually and irregularly subsided, reappearing rarely and slightly even toward the end of the analysis.

With increasing frequency, until it became a regular phenomenon, the patient would become heavy lidded as soon as the analyst uttered a word. If he spoke more than a clipped sentence, the patient apparently became heavily unconscious, certainly he heard nothing. Yet he usually shook himself and awoke as soon as the analyst stopped talking. This, he protested, distressed him beyond all words and was utterly beyond his control or understanding. He reported no fantasies or dreams, if left undisturbed. Slowly and painfully, under the constant pressure to try to verbalize his feelings when the reaction was beginning, the patient made certain direct and relevant communications.

1. There was awareness of his continuing urgent wish that the analyst talk and make interpretations.

2. There was obviously some need or wish to exclude the voice and interpretations from his consciousness.

3. This did not diminish the demand for cure or his resentment over its delay.

4. There was acute awareness of the socially hostile nature of the reaction, as when a friend fell asleep while he was talking.

5. There was often a feeling that the analyst's voice had a pleasant "soothing" effect on him.

6. Interpretations were often resented as attacks, as painful criticisms, or as the aggressive searching out of matters which the patient wished to conceal from himself and from the analyst. Sometimes there was contemptuous inner questioning of the scientific validity of interpretations, as though they were based largely on the analyst's need to "show off." These feelings occasioned an uncontrollable tendency to *a priori* rejection.

7. The attitude which seemed to assume the greatest importance as time went on was that of hostility and envy that the analyst knew more than the patient did, that he could not make similar interpretations for himself. The consequence was that he wished the analyst to fail in his efforts.

8. There was also the tendency of which the patient became increasingly aware, to evade the analyst's (and putatively his own) intention to resolve his dependency (his "leaning on the analyst") and to cause him to "grow up," a process which he judged would be furthered by accepting the interpretations. (In this, the fear of identification through cannibalistic aggression probably played an important unconscious part.)

9. The "falling asleep" device also had a certain resemblance to the peculiar avoidance of responsibility implicit in the patient's enuresis and in derivative character phenomena, which cannot be discussed in detail here.

During a period of considerable rumination concerning this phenomenon, the patient had a fleeting dream, mentioned as though it were an inane fragment, about a "dagger in his anus." When pressed for associations, the patient could recall only his hemorrhoid operation, which he said (with annoyance) that his surgeon-friend had performed without a general anesthetic, in contrast with the good fortune of an aunt who had received such an anesthetic. Thus he too wished to submit to an overpowering male by the anal route, but painlessly and without awareness. That there might be a wish to submit to a punishing sadistic father, to be hurt, the patient was only too ready to agree. The possible erotic aspect was less immediately meaningful to him (Ferenczi 1914).

In another dream, the patient was with Dr. X (associated with the man who had admired the patient's mother when he was a boy) who was part of the government in a strange country, where the patient was only a visitor. Hitler invaded the country. He was at first abusive only toward Dr. X but suddenly turned on the patient, seized him violently by the ears, spun him about, face forward, and then bent him over. As though to assert doubly the intense submissive feminine element in this dream, blending and conflicting with the hidden original longing for the mother, the patient's own chief association aside from conventional references to Hitler, was the occurrence of lower abdominal pain wherewith he had gone complaining to a local doctor (the man in the dream), thinking that an operation might be suggested, his *wife* having had an abdominal operation during her analysis. The matter of the ears was also spontaneously associated with the sleeping symptom in the analytic relationship (and, by the analyst, with the original "listening in" on the telephone).

In contrast with these passive attitudes toward his father, the patient recalled overt early competitive and highly contemptuous estimates of the ability and intelligence of his father and his father's friends, compared with his own. The patient's deep competitive envy and hostility toward the father, masked by submissive "good will," were clearly reflected in dream material, at times almost naïvely expressing the patient's wish that he fail in the sexual act.

The patient's hostilities and consequent anxieties were not directed exclusively toward men. The patient married a phallic woman who quieted his intense castration anxiety and allayed his sense of guilt by fulfilling a certain paternal role, even to inducing chronic resentment beneath habitual submissiveness in addition to her feminine and maternal functions. His wife (like his mother) then bore children, ceased to nurse him (by ceasing to earn money, by diminution in her own parental wealth), accepted admiration from another man, and then turned to a surrogate parent in being analyzed. She was left, thereafter, with intensified dependent feminine needs and her cruelly critical sarcasm.

In a dream, the patient was in the street with his wife. She became ill and spouted a great mass of tomato aspic from her mouth, making a solid ridge across the sidewalk. The patient was embarrassed and tried to get her away from the place. Angered by his efforts, she turned and spouted it at him. By this time, however, it was a very disagreeable maroon liquid. He ran away, ducking, but she pursued him. The essential associations were as follows: he had had a bad weekend with his wife. There had been much quarreling. Her "vituperation" (especially toward the children) had been severe (a "barrier" between them). He had had much gastric pain. Tomato aspic is a spicy food, not good for his ulcer. Blood was also suggested, but not menstruation (when the analyst mentioned it), unless it was the wish for menstruation as a barrier to intercourse. He had had intercourse unwillingly the night before. He felt that he had tired of his mother as she grew older and had turned to his wife and that he now wished to turn away from his wife on the same basis. The orally represented castrative wish toward his wife, the relation between eating and speech, the reversed sadistic impulse (need for punishment?), the connection of castration with forbidden food, and the characteristic oral-genital confusion were features of the dream.

In extremely lucid dream material, the patient exhibited his wish to flee from the castrated feminine object to the phallic analyst. In a dream of decapitated women, the first association with the decapitation was that the women would be unable to talk.

From a symptomatic point of view, it should be noted that the patient had had a transitory period several years before, in which, in the subway, he had "inadvertently" felt women at the waist for a corset or girdle. If it were absent there was a feeling of heightened sexual excitation. This inverted fetishistic fragment was undoubtedly related to the problem of his multiply determined anxiety in relation to a castrated object.

As hostile rivalry and narcissistic pride were more freely expressed, with some diminution of intensity, there was a growing awareness of a vaguely defined but intense dependence on the analytic relationship itself, leading to a few bouts of manifest anxiety and nocturnal insomnia when the patient felt the relationship threatened, for instance, when his wife was objecting to its duration or, in another instance, very pointedly, when he was feeling unusually well and this became the subject of rather extravagant observation and comment. From the untoward reaction to these incidents, the patient evolved the interpretation that he did not wish to get well (in other words, to get from the analyst what he so strenuously demanded), because he would thus lose the analysis and the analyst.

Related to, but deeper than the question of rivalry in an ordinary sense, was an apparent need to be able to carry out *all* functions himself — to be completely independent, a narcissistic attitude of complicated and multiple genesis which probably made a primary contribution to the need to rival all other objects, including children and women (sister and mother) and definitely including the function of maternal nursing. It is likely that the nursing fantasy underlay the obvious fellatio fantasy and the autofellatio fantasy incorporated in his masturbation. A dream illustrating the ambivalent fellatio and autofellatio fantasy follows: the patient was in a sailboat fishing with P. L. The patient told P. L. to "pull his line in and out." Close to shore, P. L. drew his line in and caught a huge fish. He grabbed the fish close to the head and removed the hook. The patient pulled his own line up and down and caught a huge but strange fish. He was uncertain whether it was a dogfish or an "eating" fish. The patient awoke with an erection and a feeling of sexual excitement not present in the dream. The man in the dream was a rich man's (and woman's) son, extremely selfish and apparently not likeable even to his own children, with an inexplicable aversion for sexual intercourse with his attractive wife. The patient spontaneously described his companion's grip on the fish as similar to the manual grasp of an erect penis. The sailboat suggested that he was giving up that sport for the summer, as a matter of economy, a procedure unnecessary to P. L. whose two successive inheritances the patient had frankly envied the night before, at dinner at P. L.'s house. (The emphasis on the death of both parents should be noted.) Also, the patient ate excessively in an almost conscious effort to allay his anxiety about business. After several such associations, the patient thought of the dream largely in terms of his "sleeping symptom."

A little more than a year after the beginning of the analysis, the patient began to express the conviction that a major purpose of the analysis was for the patient to become able to *analyze himself* in the future, implying that the need for such treatment would never terminate. With this belief came the later manifestly avowed rivalry with the analyst, the deep sense of failure, the persistent sense of need, and the hostile oral urge for identification: in short, the factors that rendered the patient at times unable to accept the analyst's help at all. Toward the end of the first period of analysis, as the "sleeping" phenomenon became rare, one might think of the patient as in a period of attempted transition from the rejected but persistent passive wishes implicit in it, with preponderant father transference, to an oral clinging to the analyst as a mother, his wife the threatening father, with tentative genital wishes and castration fear. Sibling rivalry, often expressed in earlier dreams (especially the birth or "entry" of his sister), came conspicuously into the foreground with material in relation to other patients.

The following dream occurred in a period of restlessness and depression following a brief spring vacation taken after considerable conflict. The patient had also been ruminating with some resentment on pressing and imminent expenses for his daughters. To the patient's amazement, he had not had "stomach trouble" during either the vacation or the transitory depression following it. One night when the patient could not sleep, he rose and took one capsule from an old phial of sedatives to which he had not resorted for a long time. On returning to bed, he dreamed that he was looking at the bottle from which he had just taken the sedative. There was one capsule in it, which seemed slightly chewed. To his dismay, the chewed appearance was due to two small worms in the bottle, which had heads like little rag dolls. He immediately became concerned lest he had done himself harm by ingesting something contaminated by worms. The patient, on the basis of past interpretations but with considerable conviction, related the insomnia, the actual taking of a sedative, and the dream sedative to a breast fantasy. The worms he associated with biting into an apple, and the two dolls' heads he associated with the rag dolls his sister had kept on her bed as a youngster. He accepted for consideration the analyst's suggestion that his fear of disastrous consequences from the dream sedatives was connected with his hostility toward the prototypes of "worms" (his sister, his own children) and toward the breast that fed them. This dream was brought on an extra Saturday visit, which the analyst had proposed in place of granting the patient's urgent wish for a prescription for a sedative.

The problem of the patient's paradoxical "sleeping" symptom was further illuminated by a dream during the period of its subsidence. The patient was trying to have intercourse with his younger daughter Beatrice. His penis was at her vagina but did not enter; instead it pushed her up bodily toward the ceiling ("Like a little girl on his knee"). He awakened with an erection and a "slight" ejaculation, which he had been resisting. The patient had been missing his daughter, who was away at camp. He remarked on her great charm and attractiveness and his wish to be loved by her as she loved her mother. He recalled "jiggling" her as a baby on his foot. He remarked on his frequent rigidity and irritability toward this daughter, because she reminded him of *himself* when he was young, especially in her charm, attractiveness, and defiant sloppiness.

In connection with the coital attempt, he mentioned only that he did not wish to *hurt* his daughter. In connection with his nonpenetration and restraint of ejaculation, he recalled his early difficulty in coital penetration and his earlier efforts to diminish the ill effects of his masturbatory addiction. He made no spontaneous mention of, but accepted with interest, the analyst's remarks that the same daughter had been equipped with a penis in a previous dream and sexually active in relation to him (as though he were the mother and the daughter were he), that he had been aware of his strong passive rivalry with his own sister for his father's love, and that the difficulty in penetration paralleled closely the position in which he placed the doctor in connection with his rejection of interpretations by falling asleep. The latter, the patient thought, was especially appropriate.

In this manifest dream of incest, obviously multiply determined, the patient turned toward his child as he would have wished his father or his mother (with a penis) to turn to him. The frustration was a defense against injury (anatomic or punitive) for both participants, but this seemed clearest in this dream on the feminine receptive side. The sexual frustration desired for the parents was also achieved by identification.

ORIGINAL SUMMARY

On the basis of the objectively observed transference phenomena and germane analytic material, a tentative reconstruction of the essential unconscious tendencies was attempted in the second half of the first long period of analysis. It was felt that there was a powerful passive receptive wish of mixed character (involving both libidinal and destructive elements), directed at the analyst and thus originally at the parents. Underlying and determining the vague and mixed character of the expressed demands was the original passive infantile wish for the parental breast and later the penis, ranging from the wish for immediate gratification to the total incorporation of the object.

There seemed ample evidence that the mother-breast transference was primary. The submissive, more obviously treacherous positive father transference hid the former and was motivated by guilt and need for punishment, as well as the principle of *faute de mieux*. Either a breast was sought in the guise of the penis, with pain and humiliation, or the latter was desired because there was no hope of the former, which was now also hated. In attempting feebly to make the transition from passive to active libidinal gratification, the patient was and apparently had been driven back into submission by intense castration fear. To the latter, the unconscious memory of his own cannibalistic oral aggressions seemed at least to have contributed strongly (with more immediate and "conventional" factors), when preexisting psychic constellations had to be shifted to new zones of biological emphasis. In view of the type of oral anxiety exhibited in the transference, one could not say with certainty that the threat or barrier to genital activity was more or less important in leading to permanent and strong orality and general functional passivity than was the primary voracious, anxious, and ultimately hostile oral fixation and its inhibitions (Klein 1945). In a strong feminine identification with passive homosexual wishes, an effort was made to compromise the numerous conflicting needs and fears, the object, and the bodily zone. This compromise, however, brought up the need to be castrated and revived the old wish to castrate the object, with guilt and inhibition and the classical narcissistic fear and rejection of the patient's own castration.

The patient's intense fantasy confusion between oral and genital activity (probably due to original unresolved oral wishes) readily permitted a "displacement upward" (perhaps a "restitution upward"), so that the prohibited food (or drink) became the penis (as well as the breast) and gastric symptoms the constant reminder of the threat of castration (perforation or hemorrhage—as in the case of his wife in the dream). Aside from this, the symptoms seemed also to represent in suffering the insistent original passive wish and need (for the breast) with the several complicated and severe reactions dependent on anxiety, deprivation, disappointment, and sibling rivalry. Whether influenced by a primary narcissism or the anxiety-driven identification with the parent, the same type of pathology appeared in masturbation (and in dream material) and in enuresis. In the passive dependent wishes toward an object there was only a moderate and fluctuating degree of spontaneous ego rejection of the wishes by this patient; in the case of the autofellatio fantasy, the concept was insufficiently developed in the patient's awareness to permit evaluation. Even the hostility, rivalry, and fear toward the "donor" of breast or penis—apparently the major barrier to consummation— seemed to be based mostly on repressed infantile (id) factors rather than on an adult form of repudiating dependency, as such.

The barriers to the consummation of the patient's insistent passive wishes toward an external object were condensed in the curious "sleeping" symptom which arose in the transference. It was thought that this symptom was or was very nearly the equivalent of the patient's gastric symptoms, in terms of an object relationship based largely on verbal communication, and that like the gastric symptoms, it fused and epitomized the patient's pathological infantile relationship with both parents. It was felt that the deepest elements in this symptom, which most often occasioned its rare recrudescence, pertained to the narcissistic representation of the same fantasies in withdrawal from the analyst.

INTERVAL AND FIRST RETURN

Toward the end of the first period of analysis, the patient on a few occasions brought out his disappointment and active resentment toward the analyst with manifest angry emotion. He also noted spontaneously that his tendency to sleep in the hours might be related to the control of his violent rage, a problem that seemed of increasing importance later on, for instance, in his urge to "press" his clients or, as he once epitomized it, to "knock people down and wrest sustenance from them." In this period he had, as though on the other side of the coin, a frank dream of turning into a woman, with accompanying wistful desires to own a restaurant or become an innkeeper, later a frank pleasure in cooking and doing housework, and in jokes at home about how a man could even have a baby if constructed properly. The analysis as a soporific became equated on one occasion with his mother's massage in childhood, the masseuse having appeared more than once in his dreams. In this period too, the patient was awake at night on several occasions, with compulsive rumination about his business. On one occasion, this was associated with an urgent wish to quit the analysis and with a whirling in his stomach. Significantly, on one occasion, there was an alternation with fantasies of leisure and pleasure and on another, a dream or fantasy involving drinking. The patient insisted on terminating the analysis, on the basis of an apparent surging need to be "independent." Clearly, this need was related to the intolerable factors in either the manifestly aggressive attitudes or the passive feminine fantasies or their combination.

In a single interval visit and on return after a few months, depression was the major symptom, with fleeting suicidal rumination. Nocturnal wakefulness and "stewing" were conspicuous. It is important to note that stomach pains were relatively inconspicuous toward the end of the first period of analysis, in the interval, and in the early part of the second analytic period, that is, when *depression* was most highly developed. The sense of defeat and failure in business and the analysis were strong, with numerous "escape" fantasies, especially in the occupational sphere. In these, the element of feminine identification was strong. Again there was a sense of grievance, reproach and disappointment about the analysis, but now usually not acknowledged as active anger, except in occasional assent to persistent interpretations of the deep hostilities autoplastically implied in the depression, directed toward the analyst (Freud 1917) and the patients (siblings) who remained with him.

Throughout this period, the patient's struggle with symptomatic passivity was severe. There was often nocturnal awareness of the inclination to stay home in the morning, "just not work," side by side with the active obsessive rumination. On one occasion the (not unusual) frank wish that his parents die and that he have his full inheritance came up in the same connection. The advantages of such acquisition over gifts from the living were discussed seriously by the patient. A urinary urge was frequent with the nocturnal ruminations; there was occasional impulse to go to the bathroom to drink water; there were occasional headaches or dizziness. (Nocturnal dizziness had occurred occasionally before the analysis.) In general, the stomachache soon became the predominant nocturnal problem, with the biphasic obsessive rumination.

In this period, with more frank expression of diffuse deathwishing envy, hostility, and grasping impulses, with corresponding inhibition and passivity, their objects ranging from wife and parents through analyst and business associates, there was a deeper analytic working through of these attitudes.

A long period of extreme sexual apathy inevitably evoked more detailed attention to sexual problems. The early (second) operation was recalled more vividly, with memories of sitting on the pot with a "big bandage" on his penis. The patient recalled intense pain for two to three days, during which he would *much rather have suppressed urination.* This came into association with a dream in which he was able to watch his penis through his wife's transparent abdominal wall, as though to reasssure himself of its presence. The pain in urination was further associated (by the analyst) with the tears which the patient recalled in his early voluntary mechanical suppression of bladder impulse. Frank sexual comparison and rivalry (genital structure, size and noise of urinary stream) with the father appeared in dream material and childhood memories, as well as their rivalry for his mother in other dreams. The father's attack on the brother also reappeared, as well as the stated recollection that the patient had concealed his interest in his mother from his father thereafter. Of childhood or infantile masturbation, only the schoolroom episode was recalled. However, the memory of his brother's punishment was revived in an hour in which adolescent masturbation was reviewed in some detail. The unconscious effort to reconcile opposing psychic tendencies was vividly expressed in dream material in which, for instance, a threatened jibe in a sailboat became a normal tack without change of direction or, even more pointedly and naïvely, in a dream of coitus in which both the patient and his wife were flat on their backs. In a pithy dream expressing the essential nonspecificity of his passive wishes, the patient received a packet of bonds with which to "make his fortune." The donor was his mother, then his father, and then alternating; and then the patient was uncertain about the identity.

The patient spoke often of the "killer instinct of true males," which he illustrated by a dream of wheeling two criminals strapped to a carriage, who were trying to get at him with murderous intent with their mouths. This was associated with the analytic situation. He spoke of probable impulses to assault women sexually, in line with previous dream material. He mentioned his father's annoying requests for confidences about women and his injunctions about controlling natural sexual "brutality" toward them. The manifest violent wish to tyrannize his wife and daughters frequently emerged.

Toward the close of the second period, a few developments in the patient's actual life were of special importance. His wife resumed remunerative work. His own business showed remarkable improvement, partly because of changes in him and partly from purely external accidental factors. His sister moved to his near vicinity, mobilizing many attacks of pain and much material about her, which was worked through.

Of special importance was the patient's disclosure, after long concealment with great guilt, that his earnings had been very large, out of all proportion to the small fee he was paying on a partial credit basis. The patient had been practicing the same characteristic concealment in relation to his father, lest he "lose out" to his two siblings. The patient liquidated his debt and gladly arranged a moderate increase in fee. He showed marked symptomatic improvement in all spheres. But, he again forced the termination of the analysis in an uncontrollable burst of "independence," although he was in much better condition than on the previous similar occasion.

Third Period

When the patient returned for the last analytic period of a few months, his complaint was a severe gastric upset of several-days duration, with belching, nausea, pain, and a few attacks of vomiting. This had been precipitated by a literal fight with his wife connected with her vituperative contemptuous attacks on him when he defended his older daughter against her criticisms. The patient could not eat at home. He wondered whether he loved his wife, in fact expressed loathing provoked by her verbal vehemence. The patient was X-rayed again by his physician, who stated in telephone conversation that the findings were those of an old duodenal ulcer, with typical deformity of the bulb, partial healing, and recent exacerbation of symptoms.

The patient was in a generally more aggressive mood than in the past. He was insistent that his wife cease her verbal attacks, accept him as master of the house, and accept the changes in him due to psychoanalysis. He was aware of the literal violence of his attitude toward her at times and of the role this played in his gastric symptoms. Characteristically, although he had returned for help, he seemed to resent what he regarded as the *analyst's* assumption that he wanted further systematic work, and he "sat up" for several hours to express this attitude. He became more actively critical of his parents, justifying his own apathy toward them. He stressed especially his father's intellectual inferiority to him, his self-absorption, and his tendency to give and entertain solely for his own pleasure. To the previous arraignment of his mother, he added that her interest in him was of a prying morbid quality. It is very likely true that both father and mother, aside from their individual traits, together contributed to an incapacitating liberal materialism, repudiated by the patient intellectually but perhaps adding to the depth factors in an anxiety that often led him to measure his security in the amount of money he had in his pocket, rather than in the bank or in securities, not to speak of intangible and remote values. In this period, the patient dreamed of shooting birds in flight, who then turned into a man and a beautiful woman, the woman dying in convulsions.

In the general context, these seemed clearly related to the patient's mother and father in their sexual relationship and to his original intolerable hostility against the analyst in his biparental role, a factor undoubtedly contributing to the patient's successive flights from the analysis. (It should be noted that although there were dream material, indirect or inferential material, and screen memories, actual primal scene memories were not available.) In connection with the initial covenant of this period, the patient spoke of his impulse to "rush to the analyst whenever he had a stomachache"; otherwise he felt no reason to come. When asked why his family physician would not serve as well for this purpose, he responded that that would be "only a palliative." The patient had remarkable difficulty in seeing the grotesque inconsistency in this formulation. Certainly in his going and coming, sometimes at the analyst's considerable inconvenience, there was at one level the testing of a parent and the working through of an old fear of arbitrary rejection, beneath the apparent arrogant independence. However, in view of the later manifest material, the shooting dream, and the remark about the stomachache, the patient seemed to be pleading passively for love and help. In a state of suffering, he felt he must flee the violent consequences that he feared would ensure: the destructive fraction of the dynamics of his pain to turn again toward the original object or objects, not bound by "sleep," depression, chronic physical suffering, or characterological incapacitation.

The patient improved rapidly in this period and maintained his agreement. It was thought at once an important sign and expression of deep reorganization in the patient's emotional life that he ended his brief analytic period with a strong plea that his hours be given to a young woman of his family, toward whom in the past he would have directed only self-absorbed querulousness, who represented a considerable financial responsibility to him, and who often appeared in his analytic productions as a surrogate for his violently envied sister.

FURTHER DISCUSSION

In the light of further material and retrospective review, a few considerations may be noted in addition to those previously outlined. The sharply etched nocturnal bouts seem to state clearly the coexistence and struggle between insistent receptive passivity and obsessively represented activity (male-female, parent-child), the diffusion of an uneasy alliance. The capacity for a more genuine parental identification in the male role seemed to result from the analysis and working through of the untenable aspects of pathological passive wishes, better opportunity for and capacity to accept normal gratification of passive wishes, and finally the analysis of the residual exogenous castration fears.

Early in the patient's long analysis passivity was the pervasive attitude in the patient's actual life and in the transference; the movement toward the end was steadily in the other direction. One cannot assess conclusively the factors entering into the profound passivity, i.e. as to those basically constitutional or physiological, or fixed as such by early experience, or the result of the severe inhibition of aggressiveness. Anamnestic data, interpretative material, and transference reactions point at least to the great importance of the need to inhibit violent aggressiveness. In several spheres—manual, oral, verbal, genital—the tendency is toward violent forbidden expression, with recoil under severe penalty, probably taking earliest origin and impetus from the cannibalistic oral hostilities of infancy. Again, the well-known factor of violent aggressiveness as a reaction against passive helplessness, or an effort to break through severe anxiety or inhibition, cannot be ignored, perhaps as part of a circular or alternating system of impulses. The character of the parents and the early history render it likely that seduction and surfeit in biological gratifications would give rise to intense expectant dependency or its violent (oral or prehensile) implementation when necessary and that capricious punishment or threat or deprivation would engender hostilities, complete inhibition, or their alternation.

The importance of masochism, at least in the sense of the inturning of destructive attitudes, cannot be doubted. The patient on several occasions felt sudden relief of pain after an outburst of verbal sadism and, in a few instances, after crude manual sadism (for instance, throwing an orange). One aspect of his transference sleep was to protect the analytic situation from such outbursts. When the sleeping, the pain, and the depression were all absent, the impulse was precipitous flight ("independence").

The appearance of urinary urgency and water drinking with the nocturnal anxious biphasic rumination suggest a threefold significance of the childhood genito-urinary trauma and its sequelae: (1) An early (genital) castration threat of great severity. (2) Severe persistent pain associated with primitive bodily ejective experience, favoring retention (note the adolescent ejaculatory inhibition). (3) A general prototype of bodily pain in essential gratification. These are especially pertinent insofar as urinary elements (enuresis) were present in early self-nursing (autofellatio) fantasies. (See Eisler's interpretation [1922] of his patient's micturition and drinking during sleep as resembling intrauterine phenomena.)

Anal data have not been given in detail, for reasons of condensation. These touched on homosexuality, birth fantasies, narcissistic overevaluation of feces, and resentment of enforced control. (In relation to his wife, the cessation of enemas because of her jeering was especially important.) Those that seemed most relevant to the main theme indicated an intensification of constipation with increasing oral anxiety, usually in the economic sphere, and the converse. On one occasion, the patient reported a large easy bowel movement after anxious overeating the night before. On one of the rare occasions when he got drunk "with the boys," he enraged his wife by having a large bowel movement in bed.

If the related problems of transference sleep and insomnia are now reconsidered, further inferences may be gained. The former was part of the complex manifest struggle with the dependent transference and may be viewed as the narcissistic equivalent or corollary of the refusal or inability to nurse at the breast, whether primary or secondary to disturbed nursing (Ribble 1943, Wolff and Wolf 1942) and thus equated with Freud's prototypic intrauterine sleep (1916). The insomnia supervened on an established passive transference equivalent to the condition in infancy in which oral gratification is necessary to sleep (Fenichel et al. 1942, Lewin 1946, Isakower 1938). Here the separation or threatened separation from the oral object, especially as active (including genital) wishes began to appear, produced insomnia, since the only viable alternative was the identification with the object by introjection. With the patient fulfilling both roles, the required oral gratification at night (Lewin 1946) would meet the same complex barriers existing in the analytic situation and there guarded against by the very fact of the transference sleep.[1] This consideration would seem deeper in level than were more obvious factors, among them guilt and self-punishment in insomnia for the hostile frustration of the analyst (parent or parents) implicit in the transference sleep or for the erotic (masturbatory) fantasy expressed in the sleep. The occasional stupor of melancholia and its very frequent and severe insomnia may be compared with the sleep phases described in our patient. It should be noted again that the patient's acute depression tended to displace his duodenal symptoms during the course of the analysis. The disturbed sleep (with nocturnal hunger pain) so frequently connected with the duodenal variety of peptic ulcer need not be thought of as exclusively somatogenic. (See the occasional observations of Mittelman, Wolff, and Scharf [1942] in which the curve of gastric secretion and motility continued to rise in sleep, following disturbing interviews.)

RELATION TO OTHER FINDINGS

The first systematic psychoanalytic studies of peptic ulcer were carried out by Alexander and his coworkers at the Chicago Institute for Psychoanalysis (1934). In summarizing this work, Alexander states that the peptic ulcer is more common in one personality type than others, but there are exceptions. The essential characteristic lies in the *conflict situation*, which may occur in different personalities. One phase of this conflict is the wish to remain in the infantile situation, to be loved and cared for. This conflicts with the pride and aspirations of the adult ego for independence, accomplishment, and self-sufficiency. Many ulcer patients are excessively aggressive, ambitious, and independent to an exaggerated degree, while underneath, the old passive unconscious longings persist, intensified by denial, and lead to ulcer. The reasons for rejection of these infantile wishes are thought to be (1) narcissistic injury and sense of inferiority and (2) guilt and fear (especially in connection with aggressive oral wishes). To be fed is regarded as the primordial symbol of being loved. When the adult ego rejects the wish to be loved, there is regression to the constant wish for food, leading to a chronic stimulation of the stomach (independent of physiological hunger) and thus, putatively to the pathogenesis of ulcer. Alexander grants the lesion no psychological meaning, it is only an end result. In the original Chicago series, there were nine gastric cases, of which six were ulcers (three active, all duodenal) and three were gastric neuroses. In discussing the variation in genesis and personality Alexander mentions that in two cases, the passive cravings were less severely repressed than in others and that in these instances, there was a history of extreme and early deprivation in childhood.

The later study of Carel van der Heide (1940) includes two analyzed cases of ulcer, both males. In the summary, van der Heide says: "An oral regression, following earlier female identification and a sudden renunciation of aggressive tendencies were found to have been of definite importance for the development" (of the ulcers).

If we now evaluate our material against Alexander's original formulations, the following may be stated. The patient did present the extreme wish to be loved and cared for in a passive manner, and also the inhibited severe oral aggressions, which are included in the formulation. Denial of the purely passive attitudes was, however, only partial and often very weak. This relative failure of denial, as in van der Heide's case, was apparently *not* based on *gross* early deprivation. (The deprivation may have been very subtle and intangible, based on a characterological lack in the parents.) On the other hand, as evidenced in dream material, behavior, and transference reactions, severe interference with the passive wishes occurred on the basis of multiple unconscious conflicting impulses, of which narcissistic self-sufficiency (and appropriate anatomic fantasies) of very deep infantile genesis, similarly determined rivalry with and hostility towards the donor, the defense against cannibalistic and castrative wishes, and displaced genital castration fear were most conspicuous. Harsh superego development and perhaps an early orientation toward direct suffering may have influenced the choice of this disease instead of a possible alternative, such as alcoholism, which was common in dreams.

Van der Heide's statement (1940) of the common large features of his two cases could almost equally well include the patient described in this report. Of special relevance in van der Heide's cases, is the statement of "strong narcissism" in one patient, and the occurrence of enuresis in both patients. In putting the emphasis on the submissive withdrawal from (male) sexual competition, passive feminine identification, oral regression, and reaction formation, there is a relation to the statistical observations of Draper and Touraine (1932). These mechanisms occurred in our patient, with the exception of the reaction formation. It must be reiterated that far more primitive mechanisms than reaction formation or denial interfered with our patient's wishes.

A strong impression from this case would be that the fear of violent oral hostilities and their projections contributed preponderantly to the patient's suffering in and failure to establish an effective passive receptive role and that they contributed importantly to the severity of the genital castration fears (Klein 1945), in which there was also a not inconsiderable component of seductive excitation and danger in the Oedipal situation, including severe genitourinary pain. In this connection it should be noted that recent laboratory studies at least establish the fact that hostility (among other emotions) *can* invoke the gastric physiological conditions predisposing to ulceration (Mittelman et al. 1942, Ribble 1943, Wolff 1943a, 1943b). A fusion of the eating and destructive impulses in the sense of devouring has been suggested as a possible prototype for these conditions (Mittelman et al. 1942).

In this connection, Garma's emphasis (1944) on the forced internalization of biting impulses is relevant. His report is based on the common features of four cases. He stresses the importance of infantile oral fixation to the mother and the ulcer as a "wound of separation from the protecting mother." To the patient's own internalized aggression is added the acceptance of external aggression, a tendency also determined by infantile experience. Garma also emphasizes the neurotic tendency to reestablish situations unfavorable to the illness, hence the special importance of deep psychotherapy.

The biphasic problem of sleep strongly suggests that the Anlage of this patient's psychophysiological disease lay in the sadomasochistic and libidinal borderland between the intrauterine type of sleep and the need to establish normal sleep through the sucking of a breast. Such a depth consideration would be of importance in relation to Alexander's statement that the ulcer has no symbolic significance. (Garma's inference was that the lesion was definitely meaningful, like the vasomotor disturbances of hysteria.) It could legitimately be argued that the ulcer might achieve psychological meaning only after the fact. However, if its potentiality lay in the earliest experiences and dynamics of life (Stone, 1938), this Anlage might well be anterior to ordinary symbolic thought and thus importantly germane to the development of all further symbolic tendencies. The material in this case at least suggests such a possibility.

NOTES

1. A striking example of the apposition of the intrauterine and oral fantasies of sleep occurred in a dream during the second analytic period. The patient was swimming alone. He emerges from the water and then ran into it backwards. Immediately thereafter, he was lying on an oblong structure, just short of the waves. The structure was larger than, but otherwise just like, a coffin. The associations dealt with his wife's birthday, stomach pains, camp expenses for his daughters, the "structure" as the analytic couch, and most strikingly the sarcastic remark of a wealthy uncle in relation to the patient's troubles: "Take an overdose of my sleeping medicine any time you want." His mother's pregnancy and the birth of his sister as important factors in stimulating the patient's own fantasy of rebirth and infantile feminine identification were reflected in a brief dream in which two people were pushed beneath a ferry boat and emerged walking on their hands, feet in air. This occurred during a period where there was extremely frequent discussion of the sister and her current relation to their parents. The immediate association, however, was with the patient's childhood tendency to stand on his head so frequently as to occasion joking about "wearing his hair off, instead of having to cut it."

REFERENCES

Abraham, K. (1924). A short study of the development of the libido, viewed in the light of mental disorders. In *Selected Papers on Psycho-Analysis*, London, 1927, pp. 418–501.

Alexander, F., Bacon, C., Wilson, G. W., Levey, H. B., and Levine, M. (1934). The influence of psychologic factors upon gastro-intestinal disturbances, a symposium. *Psychoanal. Q.* 3(4)398.

Draper, G., and Touraine, G. A. (1932). The man-environment unit and peptic ulcer, *Arch. Int. Med.* 49: 615.

Dunn, W. H. (1942). Gastroduodenal disorders: An important war-time medical problem. Reprinted, with additions, from *War Medicine*, vol. 2, p. 967, in *Contem-

porary Psychopathology by S. Tomkins, Cambridge, Mass.: Harvard University Press, p. 175.

Eisler, M. J. (1922). Pleasure in sleep and disturbed capacity for sleep. *Int. J. Psychoanal.* 3:30–42.

Fenichel, O., Windholz, E., Olden, C., Deri, F., Maenchen, A., Berliner, B., and Simmel, E. (1942). Symposium on neurotic disturbances of sleep, *Int. J. Psychoanal.* 23:49–68.

Ferenczi, S. (1914). On falling asleep during analysis. In *Further Contributions to the Theory and Technique of Psycho-Analysis*, London, 1926, p. 249.

Freud, S. (1916). *A General Introduction to Psycho-Analysis.* (Riviere translation of revised edition). Garden City, N.Y.: Doubleday, 1943, p. 249.

_____ (1917). Mourning and melancholia. In *Collected Papers*, vol. 4. London: Hogarth Press, 1934, pp. 152–170.

Garma, A. (1944). Psychogenesis of peptic ulcer, *Rev. de Psicoanalisis*, vol. 2, 1945, p. 602, in *Psychosom. Med.* 8(3):217.

Isakower, O. (1938). A contribution to the patho-psychology of phenomena associated with falling asleep. *Int. J. Psychoanal.* 19:331–345.

Klein, M. (1945). The Oedipus complex in the light of early anxieties. *Int. J. Psychoanal.* 26:11–33.

Langs, Robert and Stone, Leo. (1980). The Therapeutic Experience and Its Setting. A Clinical Dialogue. New York: Jason Aronson, Inc.

Lewin, B. D. (1946). Sleep, the mouth and the dream screen. *Psychoanal. Q.* 15:419.

Mittelman, B., Wolff, H. G., and Scharf, M. (1942). Emotions and gastroduodenal function; experimental studies on patients with gastritis, duodenitis and peptic ulcer. *Psychosom. Med.* 4:5–61.

Portis, S. A. (1941). *Diseases of the Digestive System.* Philadelphia: Lea and Febiger, pp. 206–226.

Ribble, M. A. (1943). *The Rights of Infants.* New York: Columbia University Press, chap. 9.

Saul, L. J. (1946). Psychiatric treatment of peptic ulcer patients. *Psychosom. Med.* 8(3):204.

Stone, L. (1938). Concerning the psychogenesis of somatic disease. *Int. J. Psychoanal.* 19:1–14.

Van der Heide, C. (1940). A study of mechanisms in two cases of peptic ulcer. *Psychosom. Med.* 2(4):398.

Wolff, H. G. (1943a). Disturbances of gastro-intestinal function in relation to personality disorders, *Ann. New York Acad. Sci.* 44:567–568.

_____ (1943b). Emotions and gastric function. *Science* 98:481–484.

Wolff, H. G., and Wolf, S. (1942). Studies on a subject with a large gastric fistula. Changes in the function of the stomach in association with varying emotional states. *Trans. Assn. Amer. Physicians* 57:115–127.

Chapter 10
Two Avenues of Approach to the Schizophrenic Patient
(1955)

Although essentially a critical review and evaluation of the work of others, I have felt that this review may engage those readers who are interested in the psychological treatment of the severest grades of psychiatric illness. Furthermore, they may find in the work of Schwing and Rosen some illumination of the quintessential importance of the establishment of affective contact with the narcissistically detached patient. Neither method alone can be depended on for long-term and radical cures, but much can be achieved in a preliminary sense by these two radically different approaches to the patient: the tender "motherliness" of Gertrud Schwing, and the forceful entry into the patient's emotional life (even delusional system) of John Rosen. Rosen's own "direct" interpretive methodology need not obscure the importance of his primary forceful and dramatic entry into the patient's life and psychosis, whether or not one places high value on the interpretive system. With the growing interest in narcissistic pathology and borderline syndromes, including the increasingly sophisticated interpretive orientation toward them, it may be productive to reflect again on the importance of affective contact with the patient, as illustrated by more primitive approaches.[1]

W hile psychoanalysis was invoked very early in its history for the understanding of psychoses, its therapeutic application to these disorders was thought impracticable because of the psychotic's narcissistic incapacity for transference. However, since Abraham (1908), who originally shared this attitude toward schizophrenia, published his work on the manic-depressive psychosis (1911), efforts to psychoanalyze psychotics, especially schizophrenics, have become increasingly frequent. A considerable group of writings on this subject deals with these efforts in relation to schizophrenics or (more often) with less strictly defined psychotherapies in which psychoanalytic ideas play an important part. (See Brody, 1952, Hinsie 1927, 1929, Redlich 1952 as examples of early and recent reviews.) It merits special statement that Abraham himself, in 1916 mentioned the analysis of a case of schizophrenia simplex.

Thus the first obstacle to be overcome was the inhibiting pessimism regarding therapeutic contact with schizophrenics; soon thereafter came the published demonstration of actual and effective transference relationships with a certain number of schizophrenic patients. However, the apparent mastery of the sine qua non in certain cases left us with other no less formidable problems: Can such relationships be established with large numbers of severe cases, and if so, how? What are the essential nature, meaning, and remote effects of these relationships? Finally, do we have sufficient data with which to make valid generalizations regarding the actual *analysis* of the schizophrenic in the current sense of the term, i.e., including the decisive peculiarities of the psychotic ego?

The two books under discussion, while they both invoke analysis as indispensable for the secure recovery of schizophrenic patients, do not describe these analyses. They are therefore largely contributions to the still important residual problem of therapeutic *contact* with the more severe groups of schizophrenic patients. Schwing restricts her interpretation of her work to that sphere, although she postulates far-reaching effects. Rosen, who describes a much more elaborate method, regards his work as a definite system of treatment for the manifestly psychotic phase of the illness. In the great variety of personal approaches, techniques, and environmental manipulations which have proved effective in manifest schizophrenic psychosis, the common denominator of effectiveness would seem to be this "contact," the reestablishment of some form of object relationship, on which may well be contingent the reestablishment of repression and other basic phenomena (Hartmann 1953, Nunberg 1921, 1930). We do not therefore take this phenomenon lightly.

Few writings could more clearly demonstrate the wide divergences of personal approach which may lead to working contact with schizophrenic patients than these two books, which nonetheless approximate each other in certain important respects. Something of the essence of the differences is reflected in the modes of the authors' emergence on the American psychiatric scene. Although Rosen's first paper appeared in 1946, his work was at first (at least to many) propagated largely by spectacular word of mouth. The tone of such reports ranged through incredulity, amazement, enthusiastic admiration, amusement, and supercilious dismissal. Varying with the individual reporter, different trends or details might be emphasized: wrestling with the patients on the floor, rough and racy language, nursing with a bottle alternating with vigorous strong-arm attitudes, calling patients "crazy," or sniffing between a given patient's toes to show how ill-founded was a delusion of obnoxious odors. However, more papers followed the first, and as time went on, Rosen gained the opportunity to demonstrate and explain his work directly before learned societies and remote hospital staffs; his work has been seriously appraised by many and followed as a method by some. Certainly, it is known to all. Mrs. Schwing's little book appeared in German in 1940: many influential colleagues from Europe have known her and her work directly, and many more have read of it. She is occasionally mentioned by writers on schizophrenia, usually in a laudatory sense. Yet her work is little known, and seldom discussed. In the books themselves—the "books as books"—the differences are also reflected. Rosen's book is historically raw;[2] he is strongly opinionated; much patient building of the past is seemingly ignored while sweeping personal—sometimes commonly accepted—views are advanced. The tone is at times naïve, at times grandiloquent, at other times humble, occasionally pathetic and moving, and rarely even heroic. Shrewdness, humor, unvarnished roughness, rationalization, crude power and courage, and many less obvious ingredients are curiously commingled in this unusual book. On the other hand, an almost classical simplicity and restraint of expression[3] distinguish Schwing's book—from the nontechnical title (with its slightly mystical overtones) through the brief clinical descriptions, the scant theoretical affirmations, to the (preponderantly) tragic catamneses. Her single-minded emphasis on devoted "motherlness" is consistent with Schwing's background as a nurse, a nurse in the ideal tradition, passionately devoted to the relief of suffering from her early childhood. In this sense of passionate dedication there is a link with Rosen's attitude. There is indeed in both books an obvious primacy of feeling and intuition, whose instrumentalities the authors then seek to understand and formulate.

Direct Analysis consists of nine papers, of which only the first ("Direct Analysis, General Principles") was prepared for this book. The others are literal or revised versions of papers previously given or published (1946–1952).

The term *direct analysis* was suggested to Rosen by Paul Federn's discussion of his second paper. Great stress is placed on the classically stated analogy between dream and psychosis: "Once the psychosis is stripped of its disguises, will not this dreamer too awaken?" *All* are said to be potentially subject to psychosis, with varying thresholds. Psychotic and neurotic syndromes are viewed as successive stages of defense down to "deep psychosis." The author would, indeed, set these categories aside and determine the intensity of illness by the degree of judgment preserved, which would be in inverse proportion to the degree of invasion by the unconscious. The "neoneurosis" following direct analytic therapy is thought to differ favorably from the prepsychotic state, because of the intercurrent psychosis and treatment; the reaction to regular analysis is better. In the sphere of basic psychopathology, the author recounts his progress to his present position: "Just as the concept of neurosis as an Oedipal problem becomes the cornerstone of analysis, so the concept of psychosis as an oral problem becomes the cornerstone of direct analysis."

Rosen's basic therapeutic techniques rest on the following considerations: "The governing principle of direct analysis is that the therapist must be a loving omnipotent protector and provider for the patient." That this is the good mother (who is also capable of vigorous aggression or restraint, to protect the patient against retaliation or his own guilt) is soon clear. That the patient's own mother is the devil of the piece, the specific cause of his illness, is made increasingly clear (to reader and to patients) as the book progresses. "Direct" interpretations are thought to implement the general attitude and to be effective in their own right. These are given without preparation in relation to speech, movements, or postures: the psychotic patient is thought to absorb them without resistances. Sometimes, when patients deny their psychoses, the therapist may even pretend that he too has been "crazy"; in other instances, he must accept the patient's psychotic reality. In assuming various roles in the psychosis, the author believes that the essential underlying role is always that of the omnipotent mother. A number of shrewd technical tricks are described within this general framework, including special devices for the period of return to reality; limitations of space exclude their systematic presentation here. One should note the author's special employment of the term *transference interpretations*. Under this heading, Rosen often illustrates his vigorous assumption of the parental role and responsibility, with direct injunctions, commands, or wishes directed against what he feels to be the patient's pathological fantasies.

"A Method of Resolving Acute Catatonic Excitement" was the paper in which Rosen reported his first benevolent and reassuring assumption of roles which had been terrifying in the patient's psychosis. The results in cases apparently doomed to death by exhaustion were remarkably successful. Noteworthy is Rosen's assurance to the reader that the later relations of these patients with him as a doctor were in no way vitiated by these experiences. "Direct" interpretations appeared in this early work; also, conspicuously, the characteristic therapeutic device of spending enormous periods of time with the patient.

In "The Treatment of Schizophrenic Psychosis by Direct Analytic Therapy," there is an impressive table of detailed data regarding the apparently successful treatment of thirty-seven subacute or chronic schizophrenics. An addendum to the original paper deals with their fate when the traditional five-year period (mentioned by Paul Hoch in the discussion) has passed "almost twice." There is also the clinical description of the successful treatment of a middle-aged male schizophrenic, manifestly ill since 1922. Even though the statistical table is based on selected (i.e., successful) cases, one is impressed by the high frequency of persistence of social recoveries. (Thirty-one were doing well, several in responsible situations in life.) One may illustrate the author's "direct interpretations" from the case history:

Patient: "You are a son of a bitch. Cock-sucker. Your father put his cock in your mother's mouth, and that is how you were born. I had a feeling stronger than ever to throw myself under an elevated train."

Analyst: "Father will fuck you in the ass. The train is a big powerful penis, and you wish to lie under it." Somewhat later, in relation to the patient's crying over father's inviting mother (with whom the patient slept) into his bedroom:

Analyst: "No wonder you hate your father. No wonder you hate your mother."

Patient: "But my father was nice to me."

Analyst: "Then the way to get close to father is to be a woman like mother?"

The dramatic incident in which this patient threatened to cut the physician's throat with a spring knife should be read. In this instance, the impression of courage and intuitive resourcefulness outweighs all considerations of accuracy or consistency of interpretations.

In "The Perverse Mother," Rosen develops a thesis adumbrated earlier: "A schizophrenic is always one who is reared by a woman who suffers from a perversion of the maternal instinct." In relation to the delusion of poisoning: "Poisoning always come from the perverse mother who is not gifted with the divine attunement that makes her understand what her baby is crying for and allows her to return it to a world of omnipotent contentment." Without presuming to judge whether the author is right or wrong about the specificity of this so indubitably fundamental pathogenic experience, one finds both the clinical evidence and the logical inferences inadequate for demonstration.

In "The Survival Function of Schizophrenia," Rosen's thesis is "When a wish for something is so important that it involves a matter of life and death, then, and only then, does the unconscious part of the psychic apparatus spring into action and provide the necessary gratification with an imagination." (*Imagination* is a patient's term.) The fear of actual death is extended to include "biological" death, i.e., castration and, of course, to the psychotic's fear of what he conceives to be a death—threatening deprivation. The point of departure for the author's inferences is the traditional phenomenon of the desert mirage. An interesting and characteristic clinical account of treatment of a young woman is given. Again without questioning the crucial position of the idea of death in schizophrenia, whether as fear, suicidal wish, somatic alternative, or subjective experience (see Eissler 1951, 1953b or Pious 1949, for example), one is not impressed with either the methods of demonstration or the particular form of the basic thesis.

"The Prognostic Outlook in Schizophrenia" is based on one hundred cases treated over six years, of which twenty-seven responded with unusual speed. Accessibility was unfavorably influenced by shock treatment, by the "usual manner of incarceration," and to an impossible degree by psychosurgery. Diagnostic categories were found to be irrelevant; the level of regression was significant. It is suggested that "deterioration" may be largely man-made. The capacity for verbal communication, however bizarre, is favorable. That three successful cases were treated by two colleagues is thought to establish the fact that the method is *not* one of exclusive personal magic. It is in this paper, in the course of treatment of "Mary," that the patient fainted when the therapist told her pointedly that her mother had not visited her once in three weeks. (The mother had stayed away on the doctor's orders.) Despite this form of shock treatment, we learn later that "her family reports enthusiastically on her present adjustment."

"Discussion of Treatment Techniques" reviews, elaborates, and illustrates principles and techniques given before. Certain technical tours de force—for example, "You know damn well that I burned down St. Anne de Beaupré!" (p. 147) deserve reading.

In "An Initial Interview," three important purposes are stressed: (1) to show the patient that one is thoroughly on his side; (2) to show that one understands him, can speak his language—especially the language of the primary process; (3) to let the patient know that the therapist regards him as mentally ill—as "crazy." Here Rosen is not at his inspired best; at times, the going is labored.

In "Some Observations on Bleuler's Conception of Dementia Praecox," Rosen affirms his appreciation of Bleuler's contribution, reiterates his disbelief in the organic nature of schizophrenia, and rejects conventional nosology.

To proceed to Schwing's book, the Translators' Introduction to *A Way to the Soul of the Mentally Ill* mentions the highly personal childhood origins of Schwing's role of rescuer. Noteworthy also is the fact that Schwing was allowed to undertake psychoanalytic training because of her special talents, although she had no university degree. Paul Federn, to whose memory the English translation is dedicated, played an important role in Schwing's training, in her career, and in her psychiatric thinking (1934, 1943).

In the first chapter ("How is the Relationship Established?") there are (with one longer exception) brief, almost fragmentary notes on beginning contacts with five female patients, their illnesses ranging from complete catatonic withdrawal to dangerously destructive excitement. The "technique" is that of gentleness, patience, and the wish to understand and help—whether in silent companionship or a brief word of tenderness or the offer to make the patient more comfortable. The effects in several instances are spectacular. "Motherliness" (Chapter 2) is Schwing's central principle. Decisive primal conflicts, she feels, are always connected with the mother. The tendency is for regression to deepen until the period before these conflicts is reached; the deepest would be the intrauterine phase. The only way to establish the indispensable positive transference is to give the patient "that motherliness which he lacked as a child and which the patient, without knowing it, has searched for all of his life." She believes that, in one form or another, "motherlessness" has characterized the development of all of her patients. Their craving is to be distinguished not only from incest wishes but from the wish or need for that which is called "mother love." The latter is essentially instinctual, similar to the parallel phenomenon in animals: the child is loved not as an object but as part of the mother. Motherliness is "the product of sublimation resulting from the original mother functions and from the woman's natural preparedness for devotion." This involves an almost complete conversion of ego libido into object libido. Schwing speculates that motherliness enables the child to master the oedipal conflict and the interval between the attainment of sexual maturity and permissible full sexual activity. She classifies the mothers who occasion motherlessness, apart from gross deprivation. Furthermore, whenever material is available, she finds that these mothers of schizophrenic patients are usually "motherless" themselves. Only therapists whose personalities are deeply oriented in this motherly direction can reach deeply regressed patients; this capacity, Schwing feels, may exist "in certain bisexual men." In a series of generally agreed distinctions between the needs of psychotic and neurotic patients, Schwing presents the view (held by Federn and others) that negative transference is incompatible with continued treatment of the psychotic. The "slightest unmotherly reaction" may destroy all hope for success with the psychotic. The psychotic, whose ego is grossly disturbed, must be helped—like the growing child—to establish the differentiation and respective functions of the psychic structures and the separation of the self from the outer world. Force, even constructive discipline, are limited in effect, as apparent obedience may cover severe illness. Only in response to motherliness can the subordination of the id demands to the maturing personality be accomplished without damage.

In Chapter 3, "The Therapeutic Effect of Motherliness," Schwing describes the relationship with the patient Frieda in her severe mixed catatonic state and emergence. In the drama of the first contact, there is no ignoring the charismatic personal element. An urgently wished for kiss was added to the usual method. Work with the hands and finally the patient's quasi-nursing relationship with other patients (in positive identification) were useful. Even before the patient left the hospital, the relationship began to change into normal friendship.

Chapter 4, "Unconscious Communications—The Process of the Illness—Unmotherliness," is a simple and pithy statement of some of Schwing's theoretical convictions. Like Rosen, she believes in the necessity for unconscious communication to the patient—promising the fulfillment of his longing for motherliness. The limitations of motherliness based on "attempts to overcome one's own privations" are recognized, especially if true analytic work is attempted. Reviewing the absence of interpretive work with Frieda, Schwing states that she confined her efforts to being a "mother." The ensuing libidinous tie was used to get the patient to take responsibility for herself and to promote abreactions. The principle of ignoring the frank psychotic id material is discussed: "As the patient's ego develops strength in its ability to love, the patient is led slowly into an identification with the psychotherapist. Only this identification will bring about the quiet disappearance of the undesired guest."

In "Technical Aspects of the Treatment of Psychoses," certain previously stated principles are reemphasized. *Complete attention* is obligatory. Food gifts and other substitute instinctual gratifications are thought useful. Absolute honesty is advised. Reality education based on unavoidable interruptions of treatment is helpful. Taking notes is banned. Noninterference with irrational behavior and speech is advised, because of their useful cathartic effect.

Chapters 6 and 7, "The Psychological Aspects of Insulin-Coma Therapy" and "Case Reports of Two Patients Treated with Insulin-Coma Therapy" are devoted to Schwing's belief that patients receiving psychotherapy respond more favorably to coma therapy and that conversely, the insulin coma facilitates the patient's turning to and availing himself of psychotherapy. One may accept Schwing's impressions in this connection, even some of her reasoning. The case material, however, does not convincingly demonstrate the second proposition.

In Chapter 8, "The Clinical Courses of the Patients Treated," Schwing reviews the later courses of the patients previously described. Since these patients were treated in a university clinic, her contacts were frequently limited by the requirements of transfer. In other instances, the requirements of the therapist's own life — an extended absence, for instance — occasioned insurmountable complications. Indeed, in this poignantly honest chapter, tragedy predominates; in the case of Frieda, it was suicide by drowning. Chapter 9, "The Results," is a direct sequel. Schwing feels that the results show that this work is only a preparatory phase of necessary treatment. The changes in response to motherliness facilitate transfer to a foster home. The patient is now capable of transference and thus of being analyzed. If this is unavailable, the patient's precarious ego must be constantly supported. If this is impossible, or limited, we must count on possible regressions and, because of new disappointments, on possible suicide. Because of adverse local conditions, the author could go beyond the preparatory period to some degree with only two cases. These patients were in satisfactory states of adjustment after three years; the question of "cure" is left to the future. Based on experience with one of these cases, Schwing lists the advantages of dividing the treatment between a female helper and a male analyst. The value of family care as a substitute for the original traumatogenic family is discussed. The author proposes a "mother house" in charge of an analyzed motherly woman, where patients could be prepared for psychoanalytic treatment and foster home placement.

Chapter 10 is a thoughtful and appreciative postscript by Dr. Hans Christoffel of Basel. An "Author's Bibliography" follows. The translation is in general readable, and conveys well the quiet seriousness of the book. However, cursory comparison of certain passages with the German uncovers some minor inaccuracies of translation. For unknown reasons, the author's excellent little glossary is omitted; one author is omitted entirely from the Bibliography; and there are several important omissions of material in Dr. Christoffel's postscript.

The intentional assumption of a position within the psychosis was Rosen's first striking maneuver. By giving substantial and independent life to the creatures of the patient's narcissistic world, he provided what may well have been an indispensable bridge of transition to an object relationship in certain desperately ill patients. We accept Rosen's assurance that the reality of his identity in the manifest relationship was not thereafter vitiated by these early maneuvers, but it would nevertheless be of profound scientific interest to know the nonmanifest effects, to know the actual data of later analytic work. Perhaps this transition has a prototype in that utterly inaccessible period when persons as such first begin to impinge perceptually on the narcissism of the newborn. Insofar as a psychotic patient can establish a transference without the expedient of purposive reality distortion, one would feel this to be a superior method. However, strict theoretical methodology must concede something to the real requirements of therapy. In desperate illnesses, especially those with which Rosen first coped, where the patient is almost literally locked in a death struggle with narcissistic adversaries, one may think of this benign embodiment and manipulation of a psychotic fantasy as a useful technical tour de force, susceptible to further skillful development and exploitation and probably not altogether without rationale in genetic psychology. In the later manifestation of this technical tendency, to which Rosen usually refers as "transference interpretations," the forthright "role" as such is apparently dropped, and the physician-as-himself assumes magically authoritarian attitudes. In the case of the young man who imagined that he was "about to be married by the holiest father, even the Pope," the physician forbade the patient to marry anyone but him, then added "I want you to be my son." Here the physician in his permanent role still competes actively and forcefully with the persons of the psychotic play. The psychotic, requiring an actual parent more urgently than others and possessed of a more feeble reality sense, probably finds an especially prized gratification in this dialectical incarnation of reality and fantasy. Again one feels that if methods calculated to strengthen the patient's reality sense in the transference sphere, as in others, can be utilized effectively, they are vastly more desirable. The active cultivation of a viable and benign transference psychosis, as a lesser evil than the clinical psychosis, would then be reserved for cases whose chronicity is as desperate as the acuteness of Rosen's first catatonic cases.

Rosen's interpretative system, on which he relies heavily for "unmasking" the psychosis and awakening the "dreamer," is based essentially on the direct and vigorous presentation to the patient of id interpretations: (1) the homosexual and heterosexual aspects of the incest complex and accompanying castration complex and (2) the oral complex with the allied conception of the inevitable "bad mother." These, with the "transference interpretations," the arbitrary insistence on the historical occurrence of deprivation of maternal love, and the offering of the therapist himself as an all-loving, all-powerful authoritarian parent, seem to comprehend pretty well the general themes of verbal communication by the therapist. The interpretations often have little immediate basis in the material, in the usual sense, they seem to be offered largely on the basis of the conviction that they are there and because combinations of words and gestures can always be found to support this *a priori* conviction. Others have used interpretations in a manner which, to varying degree, might be regarded as "direct" but in more obviously meaningful relation to material and experience (See Brunswick 1929, or Rosenfeld 1952, 1954 in the framework of Melanie Klein.) Furthermore, while it is true that the productions of psychotics usually exhibit infantile sexual themes with remarkable transparency, and psychotic patients may, accordingly, accept such interpretations with great facility, we are not justified in assuming that these represent the patient's essential disturbances. It is more likely that these preoccupations are in themselves part of the psychotic's system of defense — a caricature of normal development — arising in the effort to deny or to master his real struggle, which always involves the withdrawal from (perhaps the annihilation of) the object. When Rosen states his growing conviction that the oral complex is the nuclear complex of the psychoses, he moves closer to the period of life and the type of object relationship which determines or at least strongly modifies the very nature of the individual's psychic structures and his instinctual life and thus their catastrophic fate in psychosis. However, the logical appeal of the shift in point of view is still remote from the proof that the oral complex has a consistent and specific etiological role in schizophrenic psychosis. In bypassing the problem of ego structure and function, to emphasize the *content* of the "dream," Rosen displays a tendency in which he is not alone. He does not elaborate on the crucial question of why the individual lives in a waking dream. One must also note in Rosen's theoretical statements the strong general drive toward oversimplification, toward the common denominator so ubiquitous in intellectual striving. This is only half of the problem of true understanding; the questions of difference and differentiation are equally important. The profound truth of the resemblance between dream and psychosis can become a diversionary truism if too little attention is given to the differences. The same is true of the universality of susceptibility to psychosis and also the question of nosological categories.

If we assume that Rosen's interpretations play an important role in his therapeutic effects, we can only speculate at this time about the mechanisms involved. Certainly they usually express a sort of psychological "blank check" to the patient's infantile sexual strivings, whether these be affirmative or defensive. "Usually" is a necessary qualification: When the therapist in his "transference interpretations" insists or demands that the patient remain a boy or a girl, as the case may be, the authoritarian tendency objectively overshadows the permissive acceptance, however benevolent the intention. In any case, this flood of interpretations expresses a fulsome acceptance of the existence of a complex of drive, conflict, and brooding of enormous and generally taboo importance in childhood, which in the patient's struggle with narcissistic regression assumes a pervasive and augmented importance. Insofar as regression to earlier ego states has occurred, Rosen — as Federn saw it — enters the patient's traumatogenic world and "fights the complexes" directly. The direction and the terms of the battle are not always clear and well defined; that the therapist fights, however, is always unmistakable. This may mean more to the embattled psychotic patient than accuracy of interpretations, or — in some instances — than the question of whether the interpretations are really relevant to his basic conflict or not. That the patient's "omnipotent mother" speaks in a language which is repellent and largely taboo to the Philistine world from which he has fled, may in itself be a profound and strong basis for residual ego contact, especially where that language can never be entirely alien to the patient. That this interpretative repartee often resembles a dialogue in terms of the primary process may provide a basis for contact which may be especially effective (Eissler 1951). Where the interpretations are not accurate, something allied to Glover's effect may be accomplished. In the light of the schizophrenic's dereism and proneness to the cathexis of words as such, the vigorous administration of these words by an avowedly omnipotent parent may be especially effective. At times, the sheer "shock" impact of these interpretations would seem to have a dynamic effect on the patient but we cannot at this time speculate on the therapeutic effects of shock, whether psychic or somatic. Finally, given the fairly diffuse validity of Rosen's interpretations and the impression that he is gifted with considerable perceptiveness in the sphere of the id, there must be interpretations to which the patient responds with sharp recognition. There is every reason to believe that the patient's belief in the uncanny understanding and omnipotence of his therapist must be enormously augmented on each such occasion.

In Rosen's technical "governing principle," there are certain implications that he does not sufficiently elaborate. In addition to the benign all-protective mother role that he feels the therapist must assume, he also stresses the attitude of omnipotence. Both aspects are extended, when necessary, to include victorious physical combat, restraint, or the threat of retaliation. It does not seem remote to assume that the matter of omnipotence reflects for the patient at one time the earliest view of the mother as object and the patient's own megalomania and that these facilitate the therapist's competition with the patient's delusional world. In the insistence on control or mastery of the patient a parallel potentiality is exploited. Here the primitive nucleus of a superego and its function in relation to aggression — so important in the hypothesis of Pious (1949), reflected in the work of Wexler (1951a, 1951b), and an implicitly important fraction in Knight's handling of a young male patient (1946) — may well be an essential gift to the patient from Rosen's technique. A distinctive feature in the work, as presented, is the primitiveness of the exchange between patient and therapist in the two great spheres of the id and superego. A pertinent feature is the apparent ignoring of the ego, except in one large sphere of reality testing, i.e., early or late, depending on intuitive evaluation of the patient's needs, the patient is confronted forcefully with the fact that he is "crazy." It is as though the ego is left to differentiate itself and grow again on the basis of a sort of friendly neglect. The same would appear to be true of the personality and its outer conflicts, insofar as it is or was an integrated entity.[4]

Insofar as Rosen *supplies* something lacking in the patient's past, it would seem to be something resembling that primitive "mother love," which Schwing disavows for the more complex offering of "motherliness." How then do both make dramatic contact with psychotic patients and facilitate emergence from psychoses? Are the patients who respond to them, as groups, radically different in their nonpsychotic personalities? Is it possible that Rosen's patients are more ill, more deeply regressed, have suffered traumatic deprivation at an even more archaic level than Schwing's patients? The "bad mother"—Rosen's "perverse mother"—as the etiologic agent of schizophrenia—has a certain immediate plausibility. No one doubts the profundity and severity of such pathogenic experience; by this time its general pediatric position has been made secure by direct observation. However, is it always present in schizophrenia? May it not occur in the background of other severe illnesses—psychosomatic illness, addictions, delinquency, criminality—at times in less severe illness and at times in the history of persons without demonstrable illness? Just how does it impinge on psychological development? Which of the myriad facets of such a broadly conceived agency has the specific relation to schizophrenia? To what extent might a relatively normal woman "fail" a baby whose instinctual requirements reflected the hypothetical schizophrenic constitution, to which Rosen gives only limited and grudging recognition? Apart from these and other relevant questions, there is the fundamental practical issue of the active application of such a hypothesis or conviction to treatment. While Schwing seeks only to supply the motherly love which she feels her patients did not get, Rosen feels impelled to convince his patients that they were not loved by their actual mothers, before any convincing material to this effect appears. Indeed, in the transcribed "first interview," where a patient does say something about wishing to return to his first or second year, when he had his mother's love, Rosen hastens to disabuse him of this idea, and assure him—in effect—that he was then worse off than ever. It is, of course possible that Rosen is right in his theoretical assumptions. In that case, he tells his patients what is generally true, in this sphere, as in relation to their fears of castration. Rosen's terse dramatic explanation of his technical maneuver, in the case of the girl who fainted, is an extreme development of practicality. It would be fascinating to speculate on the dynamics of the girl's faint in the alternating contingencies of whether Rosen's psychopathologic postulate was right or wrong. In any case, however, since other methods of treating schizophrenia are often effective, many of us, I think, would prefer to eschew this type of "fighting fire with fire," pending proof of its general validity.

If one seeks what seems most unquestionably effective in Rosen's work, one finds first the therapist's general personal attitude (which was stressed by Eisenbud in his discussion of the case presentation). This is a rare capacity for wholehearted empathy with the psychotic patient, for feeling his point of view against his environment while fighting his "crazy" imaginations (with no holds barred). Further than this there is an unreserved, uninhibited involvement with the patient, fearless, exuberant, loving, authoritarian, at times combative and punitive, but always strong and affirmative. If the terms and references of discourse seem stereotyped and primitive, without reference to the variety of patients' personalities, and often gratuitously so, we must remember: first, that the substructure of all of us is primitive and that in those of us who recoil from the relationships, values, and whole frame of reference in relation to which we ordinarily live and aspire this simple raw version of life may come as a hint of a possible new start; second, that even the most cloistered and previous savant, if sinking inexorably away from life, will not likely be offended by the primitive discourses that come with a brawny friendly hand that reaches into the darkness to save him. He may find, at least temporarily, virtue in their difference from those of the world which he is relinquishing.

From Rosen's methods to Schwing's there is a long step, despite the connecting links. It should be noted that all the patients whom Schwing mentions in this book are women; nevertheless, the difference in tone, vocabulary, and content of the dialogues with the patients is striking, even where the patients are violently disturbed. Certainly, schizophrenics vary in their spontaneous trends of vocabulary, too, their discourses are shaped to some extent by the attitudes of the therapist with whom they accept contact. A question for which we have no basis for answer at this point is that of the personal equation. To what extent do certain patient personalities respond exclusively to certain therapist personalities and their preferred technical instrumentalities? While this question is by no means irrelevant in the neuroses, it is critically important in the psychoses, where the establishment of vivid and genuine personal contact is an immediate necessity. For the moment, since we have no answer, we must proceed, with full knowledge that there exists a possible very large factor of error, on the assumption that the nosological or other clinical attributes of the patient and the methods of the therapist are essential determinants of the outcome.

Schwing's limited effort, the small number of cases included in the book, and the absence of male patients are, of course, not nearly as impressive from the point of view of therapeutic statistics as is Rosen's presentation. Nevertheless, there is enough in this small volume to establish a few important and relevant points. It seems clear that effective contact can be established with severe psychotics, even under routine ward conditions, by no other method than the attitude and tentative words or acts of motherly gentleness, which Schwing describes. This can be done without telling the patient of one's role, without making interpretations, with no tendentious attitudes toward the patient's family or previous environment, with no effort to restrain or command the patient, and in the rare brief allusions to discussions of the patients' personal problems, integrated and currently real, rather than infantile considerations predominate. Furthermore, it seems clear that contact can be established, and at least the temporary emergence from psychosis can be facilitated, on the same basis.

Schwing offers a few technical and theoretical convictions which merit our attention. When Mrs. Schwing speculates that it is "motherliness" which facilitates the mastery of the oedipal conflict and the control of adolescent sexual impulses, her speculation is plausible. In a sense, this view is germane to the basic nature of psychotherapy in the psychoanalytic sense. For, in the broadest view, we expose the patient to the pressure of his primitive wishes in the transference and offer him in return for their gradual renunciation only our *understanding*, which is certainly a rarefied derivative of that "motherliness" of which Schwing speaks. Both in her observation about the motherlessness of these pathogenic mothers and the fact that "the mother was also lacking in many neurotically ill patients," Schwing disestablishes any idea that this type of deprivation necessarily results in schizophrenia. Schwing states rather strongly that the "slightest unmotherly reaction" will instantly destroy the therapeutic situation. To this, with Fromm-Reichmann, we must demur. On the other hand, if stated affirmatively in a more specific direction, i.e., if made contingent on the emergence of buried chronic hostility or callousness, for example, one might assent to the general principle.

That the mobilization of the positive transference by actively establishing a positive relationship with the psychotic is a major task is generally agreed. That this relationship, transference and real, is in itself capable of producing far-reaching psychodynamic effects would probably also be largely agreed. It is quite possible that the impact of true motherliness in itself may bring about some of the detailed changes which Schwing specifies, even in the regressed adult; this would be more likely true, of course, if the relationship were to be maintained indefinitely in its original (i.e., motherly) form. Even if maintained on the therapist's side, however, the patient's potential negative transference could not for long be entirely denied. In the psychotic, we may assume, this is of extreme destructive severity. That these destructive dynamisms can endure without destroying the bearer, and without some outlet toward the person of the therapist who comes to represent the principal original love object, does not seem likely, in the light of ordinary analytic experience and theory. Perhaps with an associate therapist, some diversion (acting out) of both demand and aggression can be accomplished. It would seem that this might seriously vitiate, although not necessarily totally exclude, the analysis of the incompatible and violent emotions directed toward a single object. (This technical difficulty does not, of course, disqualify an expedient which may have much to offer toward lightening the well-nigh insupportable personal burdens of treating severe psychotics.) Certainly, milder cases do not require suppression of negative transference or the unlimited prophylactic administration of transference gratification, for the continuation of work. Experience shows that certain more severe cases can be handled without this technical effort. (See, for example, Rosen's cases or Rosenfeld's [1952, 1954].) In any case, we must distinguish between the powerful effects of the therapeutic relationship itself, the role of the relationship in permitting or facilitating the initiation of analysis as a technique, and finally the relationship with the therapist as it becomes a central theme in the course of the analysis as such. The first two could be subserved to varying degrees by the various techniques which may enter into fostering a positive relationship; in the last, they would militate against the progress of the true analytic phase, to the extent that they could not be translated, however, gradually, into matters of analytic insight rather than of direct gratification. The goal of the analytic work would be to undo the effects of early pathogenic experience through understanding, including the pathological emotional requirements generated by the experience; the effect of the therapeutic relationship is to diminish pathogenic pressure by gratifying the requirements, whether they be secondary or — as Schwing believes — a restoration of originally unsatisfied requirements in regression. Up to a certain point in the severely ill, the gratifications support and enable the analytic process; beyond that — and one hypothetical boundary could well be the suppression of negative transference — they must vitiate the analysis proper.[5] It should be noted that Schwing is entirely aware of the value of occasional disturbing reality intrusions in the management of psychotics; she is also aware of the partial role of pent-up transference aggression in the relapse of patient Lillie (even though this in itself was thought contingent on diminished visiting because of the therapist's lack of time). Our earlier question based on the differences of method under immediate consideration only gains in significance if we recognize that many other less dramatic approaches can also be successful. Sullivan (1931a, 1931b) achieved good results by a general sociopsychiatric atmosphere of friendly tolerance and understanding and a similar psychotherapeutic ("modified psychoanalytic") contact with an individual physician; Fromm-Reichmann (1952) advocates an effort to keep in contact with the more adult remnants of the patient's personality in analytic work, avoiding the extreme indulgences or precautions which would establish him as an infant. Wexler (1951a, 1951b) starting on the basis of extreme indulgent tolerance with a female patient, suddenly experienced a favorable surge in the treatment when he ranged himself on the side of the severely disciplinary elements in the patient's psychic structure; Knight (1946) had excellent success with a young male patient through persistent friendly interest, patient and persistent intrusion on his autism, and firm disciplinary pressure when indicated. Nunberg (1921, 1930) very early, described *no* distinctive attitude; he even took notes! (see Schwing), yet a strong (and therapeutically operative) transference was established. Rosenfeld (1952, 1954) approximates the usual psychoanalytic attitudes as closely as possible. Eissler (1951) has emphasized the therapist's deep inner confidence of success and the contact with the patient via the therapist's own primary process.

Certain common factors in these representative approaches exist explicitly or implicitly. There is undoubtedly a "massing of contact in all of them, whether in Rosen's sheer personal forcefulness and large expenditures of time, Schwing's promise of endless understanding and helpful availability, or the patient and silent sitting and waiting of others. In all, there is also, we may assume (risking an error of moralistic origin) a palpably strong wish to understand and help. However, the actual trends of discussion are strikingly different. We could assume that the contents of discussion make no difference to the psychotic as long as they provide a vehicle for intensive personal contact. Or they may, as mentioned before, vary in importance with the specific individuals involved and the psychological compounds that their personalities form. Neither view is entirely incompatible as a qualifying force with a third view which the reviewer believes is important. The schizophrenic, in common with other humans, is susceptible to a variety of approaches, representing important economic patterns, and may form a variety of deep attachments. No psychic structure operates independently of the others; the principle of "multiple functions" (Waelder 1936) may operate in many different alternative directions, as long as the economic requirements are met, depending on subtle or gross outer conditions and the quantities of certain basic energies, for example, nonneutralized aggression (Hartmann 1953). If Hitler swayed millions, so did Gandhi. Thus, when Eissler states that the spectacular responses to Schwing's motherly attitudes may have been dependent on an antecedent lack of loving attention in the prevailing hospital atmosphere of the time, he makes a reasonable estimate of a predisposing historical factor. He does not thereby exclude the specific and high potential power of the saintly attitude, as love experienced by the object and as a model in the eternal human struggle to find a viable solution for the conflict between love and aggression.

Since both Rosen and Schwing detail only the first phase of contact with patients, we can only speculate on the remote effects of these contacts. Rosen's work with the patient involves an active role-taking invasion of his life reality; therefore we must assume that a complicated personal relationship ensues, whether or not this is manifest when the psychosis subsides. It is difficult to see this as playing other than a large role in subsequent analysis, whether with the same or another therapist. Insofar as clinical cure results without further treatment, we may assume that this whole relationship is repressed en masse, in its complex intertwining with the patient's infantile history and that an actual or fantasy relationship with the therapist is a necessary condition of the cure. There are several reasons why Schwing's contact with patients may be assumed to have somewhat less complicated sequellae than Rosen's do. The motherly love which Schwing gives to the patients is given without qualification as to her identity. She remains the nurse—or therapist—in her address to the patient. Furthermore, what she gives is simple and consistent; it cannot be confusing; and it is traditionally compatible with the role of nurse (or physician), at least in the idealized sense. Schwing's work no doubt appeals with special poignancy to our moral sensibilities. Indeed, both Rosen and Schwing in their respective passionate drives to provide the mothering, which psychotics presumably lack, appeal to a latent general moral indignation—which should not cloud the scientific or technical issue. For the sober scientific fact is that the smaller the concession is to fantasy in content or affect which will permit a working contact with the psychotic patient (or any other patient), the better will be the chance of genuine analytic work.

This reaches beyond literal technique, far into the everyday actualities of human relations. A physician or a nurse can be devoted to patients far beyond the call of ordinary duty; still this devotion is far from what a devoted parent offers to a child. To cultivate the fantasy that the two are interchangeable, whether by indoctrination (Rosen), or by giving rise to an expectation (Schwing), is to cultivate authoritatively a transference fantasy which may indeed be far better than a psychosis but which is far from optimal. Schwing, in several places in her little book—and certainly in her ultimate withdrawal from her work (because of her marriage and children), shows her awareness of the incompatibility of the enormous responsibility she willingly assumed with the ordinary movements of life. Rosen does not express such an awareness.

However, we cannot so readily resolve the dilemmas posed by the psychoanalysis of schizophrenia. We must, of course, try to establish or verify an etiologic concept of schizophrenia. Only objective genetic and psychoanalytic studies can be of decisive importance in this connection. (For some complexities of the genetic approach, see Coleman, Kris, and Provence 1953.) Certainly the numerous therapeutic approaches to the psychotic phase, including the two that we have been discussing, can only make suggestions, which must be painstakingly scrutinized in themselves and on a comparative basis, lest they be grossly misleading. A twin problem is the question of the best therapeutic approach to schizophrenia. If we recognize that neither "direct analysis" nor motherliness is a thorough treatment for the basic disease, we must also recognize that extraordinary personal involvements (fortunately, often less spectacular than those described by our authors) are usually required to establish the contacts necessary for psychoanalytic effort. In other words, we must usually sacrifice a basic technical requirement to make our procedure at all possible. Insofar as we try to psychoanalyze schizophrenics genuinely, it remains obligatory that we minimize these unrealistic and complicating involvements to that point necessary for the establishment and maintenance of psychoanalytic contact. Two intimately interrelated problems arise immediately in connection with these considerations. As the number of published genuine psychoanalytic efforts with schizophrenics accumulates, we shall have to grapple with the question of whether they *can* be really cured by analysis with any frequency or consistency—as Eissler (1953a) puts it, "in the sense in which we commonly say neuroses can be cured." (Sechehaye [1951] arrived at her method, which has certain resemblances to those of our authors, in addition to its distinctive emphasis on symbolic gratification, after deciding that analysis was not adequate.) Was Freud after all prophetically, if paradoxically, right? If we no longer feel that schizophrenics cannot establish transference relationships, is it possible that the desperate quality of such transferences in itself excludes serious psychoanalytic work, which must always ultimately be directed against the transferences? Germane to this question is the variation in severity within the schizophrenias. There are schizophrenics (beyond the "borderline") with whom only minimal distortions are necessary for the establishment of contact, and—by the same token—whose transference intensities are largely compatible with true analytic work. From these we may range outward in severity to those who would respond only to Schwing's motherliness; finally, there are those whose narcissistic world could be invaded only by the unrelenting aggressiveness of Rosen's method or its equivalent. Thinking in crude diagrammatic terms, the degree of availability to genuine analysis would, from the beginning, vary inversely with the intensity of fantasy and emotion of the required personal approach.

We do not question Rosen's affirmation that following his treatment, thorough analysis occurred. But since criteria of analysis vary greatly, we must reserve the right to judge this for ourselves on the basis of actual analytic data. There may well be many schizophrenics who are susceptible only, if at all, to one or another variant of the "transference cure," some whose cures are of mixed origin, and others who can, to varying degrees, be analyzed.

If we accept Eissler's strict critique of current attitudes in psychotherapy as valid in principle (1951, 1953a), we need not thereby renounce Sullivan's observation that we are far too early in time to belittle the value of social recoveries from psychosis (1931b). Clear thinking, free of tendentiousness, can permit advance and cooperation in both directions. From true psychoanalytic efforts (perhaps with strictly controlled modifications) and objective study in the nursery, we must accumulate data indispensable to the future treatment of the psychoses, whether this be intensive and individual, preventive, or conducted on a large-scale sociopsychiatric level in public institutions. Wherever an unusual therapeutic effectiveness seems to reside in a given individual approach, however limited in application this may appear to be, the closest analysis and scrutiny of this effort is required, with a view to uncovering both its relation to the common therapeutic denominator and whatever may be unique in its character. While neither Schwing's nor Rosen's work recommends itself to this reviewer as a generally applicable method of approach to the psychotic patient, each teaches something about psychotic responses, and each offers suggestions whose patient study and development may yield significant additions to our general armamentarium in dealing with the schizophrenias.

Notes

1. *John N. Rosen, Direct Analysis: Selected Papers.* New York: Grune & Stratton, 1953.

Gertrud Schwing, A Way to the Soul of the Mentally Ill (Monograph Series on Schizophrenia No. 4). Translated by Rudolf Ekstein and Bernard H. Hall. Foreword by Frieda Fromm-Reichmann. New York: International Universities Press, 1954.

2. "So self-evidently promising did this hope of Freud's seem to me in my earlier days that I was surprised to learn that none of my psychoanalytic colleagues had attempted a systematic application of Freudian doctrine to the psychoses." One must assume that the author referred to his immediate colleagues.

3. "I do not claim a scientific status for my work. I only wish to demonstrate a simple method of intuitive treatment, with the hope that here, as so often occurs elsewhere, intuition may serve as a guide to science."

4. Exceptions occur of course; but they appear almost incongruous in relation to the other material.

5. We use the term in its usual sense. Federn felt that his technique with psychotics came within the scope of Freud's basic definition (Federn 1934, 1943).

REFERENCES

Abraham, K. (1908). The psycho-sexual differences between hysteria and dementia praecox. In *Selected Papers*. London: Hogarth Press, 1927, pp. 64–79.

_____ (1911). Notes on the psycho-analytical investigation and treatment of manic-depressive insanity and allied conditions. In *Selected Papers*. London: Hogarth Press, 1927, pp. 137–156.

_____ (1916). The first pregenital stage of the libido. In *Selected Papers*. London: Hogarth Press, 1927, pp. 248–279.

Brody, E. B. (1952). The treatment of schizophrenia: A review. In *Psychotherapy with Schizophrenics*, ed. E. B. Brody and F. C. Redlich. New York: International Universities Press.

Brunswick, R. M. (1929). The analysis of a case of paranoia. *J. Nerv. & Ment. Dis.* 70:1–22, 155–178.

Coleman, R. W., Kris, E., and Provence, S. (1953). The study of variations of early parental attitudes. *Psychoanal. Study of the Child* 8:20–47.

Eissler, K. R. (1951). Remarks on the psycho-analysis of schizophrenia. *Int. J. Psychoanal.* 32:1–18.

_____ (1953a). The effect of the structure of the ego on psychoanalytic technique. *J. Amer. Psychoanal. Assn.* 1:104–143.

_____ (1953b). Notes upon the emotionality of a schizophrenic patient and its relation to problems of technique. *Psychoanal. Study of the Child* 8:199–250.

Federn, P. (1934, 1943). Psychoanalyses of psychoses. In *Ego Psychology and the Psychoses*, ed. E. Weiss. New York: Basic Books, 1952, pp. 117–165.

Fromm-Reichmann, F. (1952). Some aspects of psychoanalytic psychotherapy with schizophrenics. In *Psychotherapy with Schizophrenics*, ed. E. B. Brody and F. C. Redlich. New York: International Universities Press, pp. 89–111.

Hartmann, H. (1953). Contribution to the metapsychology of schizophrenia. *Psychoanal. Study of the Child* 8:177–198.

Hinsie, L. E. (1927). The psychoanalytic treatment of schizophrenia. *Psychiatric Q.* July:1–15.

_____ (1929). The treatment of schizophrenia, a survey of the literature. *Psychiatric Q.* January:1–35.

Knight, R. P. (1946). Psychotherapy of an adolescent catatonic schizophrenic with mutism; a study in empathy and establishing contact. *Psychiatry* 9:323–339.

Nunberg, H. (1921). The course of the libidinal conflict in a case of schizophrenia. In *Practice and Theory of Psychoanalysis*. New York: Nervous and Mental Disease Monographs, 1948, pp. 24–59.

_____ (1930). On the catatonic attack. In *Practice and Theory of Psychoanalysis*. New York: Nervous and Mental Disease Monographs, 1948, pp. 3–23.

Pious, W. L. (1949). The pathogenic process in schizophrenia. *Bull. Menninger Clin.* 13:152–159.

Redlich, F. C. (1952). The concept of schizophrenia and its implication for therapy. In *Psychotherapy with Schizophrenics*, ed. E. B. Brody and F. C. Redlich. New York: International Universities Press.

Rosen, J. N. (1953). *Direct Analysis: Selected Papers*. New York: Grune and Stratton.

Rosenfeld, H. (1952). Transference-phenomena and transference-analysis in an acute schizophrenic patient. *Int. J. Psychoanal.* 33:457–464.

——— (1954). The psycho-analytic approach to acute and chronic schizophrenia. *Int. J. Psychoanal.* 35:135–140.

Schwing, G. (1954). *A Way to the Soul of the Mentally Ill*. New York: International Universities Press.

Sechehaye, M. A. (1951). *Symbolic Realization*. New York: International Universities Press.

Sullivan, H. S. (1931a). Environmental factors in etiology and course in the treatment of schizophrenia. *Med. J. Record* 133:19–22.

——— (1931b). The modified psychoanalytic treatment of schizophrenia (with discussion). *Am. J. Psychiat.* 11:519–540.

Waelder, R. (1936). The principle of multiple function. *Psychoanal. Q.* 5:43–62.

Wexler, M. (1951a). The structural problem in schizophrenia: The role of the internal object. *Bull. Menninger Clin.* 15:221–234.

——— (1951b). The structural problem in schizophrenia: Therapeutic implications. *Int. J. Psychoanal.* 32:1–10.

Chapter 11
Reflections on the Psychoanalytic Concept of Aggression
(1968, 1971)

Given as the Brill Lecture of the New York Psychoanalytic Society in 1968 and published in 1971, this is a nonconformist paper. Though accepting the sexual drive as such, I question the existence of a primary aggressive or destructive drive. I argue that aggression is essentially a pluralistic, instrumental phenomenon, possibly originating as a system of archaic ego functions, subserving sexual and / or self-preservative instincts and more subtle needs or urges. Curiously, this view is much closer to Freud's original view of aggression than his final Dual Instinct Theory. Although the Death Instinct, or phenomena suggested by the phrase, has always seemed valid, I cannot now view it as the continuous or direct origin of aggression. Rather, the occurrence of externally directed aggression is a manifestation of the urge to survive, thus opposed to the need to seek repose at any cost. I am aware that this distinction could be reconciled metapsychologically if it were assumed that quanta of specifically psychic energy are involved, rather than accessible psychic realities. But this would be an assumption that requires proof.

The metapsychological elegance implicit in the Dual Instinct Theory, and its corresponding intellectual attractiveness, impeded my own trend of thought from the beginning. I may still experience such seductions at moments. However, they are overcome by hard empirical thought and by the more compelling logic immanent in such thought.

This paper has not revolutionized current psychoanalytic thought, but it has had its impact. It has been highly esteemed by some individuals.

One latent concept in this paper has been modified with time. The distinction between predatory and "social" aggression, set aside in this paper, is later given a significant place in my thinking, in relation to major unconscious representations.

One type of reaction to this paper has amused me, an amusement, sometimes blended with responses of a different character. An inclusive

sample condensation would be: "Stone does not believe in aggression."
It is as if one's conviction that pneumonia is caused by bacteria rather
than by foggy air meant that one did not "believe" in pneumonia! Such
"know-nothing" attitudes are not likely to advance psychoanalysis . . .
whether I happen to be right or wrong!

I n this widely-ranging essay I offer a few thoughts about the idea that aggression, whether or not it is linked to the death instinct, is a primary drive, one of the poles of the dual-instinct theory. This is a concept which may only too readily lapse into a state of comfortable assumption or even dogma. My approach to it is largely empirical and deliberately naïve and, for the most part, is not based on the fundamental explanatory theory itself. Rather, I address the phenomena that may give rise to theory.[1]

I view the phenomenon of aggression and its psychological functions and representations as the aggregate of diverse acts, having diverse origins and bound together, sometimes loosely, by the nature of their impact on objects rather than by a demonstrably common and unitary drive. In psychic development, the indispensable components of wish, intention, or purpose are secondarily assimilated to the consequences. This does not mean that certain elements of aggression do not have an instinctual origin or affiliation; nor do I deny the existence of a latent drive to die (pragmatically considered), even if my view of such a drive and its relationship to aggression differs from Freud's.

Some writers such as Bibring (1941) and Hartmann, Kris, and Loewenstein (1949), have tended to examine the explanatory adequacy of Freud's theory more thoroughly than its empirically derived soundness, although they have explicitly recognized the importance of the latter. Moreover, the question of the death instinct or the polarity of Eros and Thanatos is often placed beyond psychoanalytic examination as a theory of the second order, as a biological or philosophical construct, as a dual biological tendency, or as a regulatory principle of the psyche to be set apart from the study and discussion of instinctual drives as such. This is even true of Waelder (1956) whose critique of the theory of aggression is essentially empirical. In contrast with such methodological strictness, Federn in "The Reality of the Death Drive" (1931) sought to demonstrate the death instinct largely by the phenomenology of true melancholia—unconvincingly, but with imaginative grandeur and intuitiveness. Federn mentioned the tendency of analysts to ascribe the death instinct theory to Freud's entry into old age, as well as the delay due to Adler's original emphasis on aggression in 1908 (see also Hitschmann 1947).

In my view, the explanatory value of a theory, its parsimony, and allied considerations are only half the problem. Theory must also be adequately rooted in empirical observation and proximal inferences. Without this we could end up, for example, with certain theological principles which could comprehend and explain all observable phenomena. Bernfeld (1935) remarks on the too-great convenience of "physiognomic" classification of phenomena, and thus of conflict, as one of the undesirable by-products of the then new theory of the death instinct, substituting broad instinctual configurations for detailed psychoanalytic data.

One may object to how Freud's theory of the death instinct has been intellectually "kicked upstairs." Freud took the Eros-Thanatos polarity seriously, explained important clinical and social phenomena by it (1930), and thought that a revision of the basic concept of psychic conflict in this light might be in order (1937). It seems to me that when he described Eros and Thanatos, Freud may have had in mind their actual instinctual representatives rather than certain remote biological or even philosophical principles. Brenner has pointed out that the theory of the death instinct fulfilled for Freud what he had insistently sought—a source for a theory of instinctual drives originating in a discipline outside psychoanalysis (but see Bernfeld 1935). In Freud's later thought it seems that the concept of primary aggression was inextricably bound to the idea of the death instinct, or primary masochism. Hence, it is imperative that we continue to examine the death instinct.

Bernfeld (1935) notes that the difficulties of considering the nature of instinct were acknowledged several hundred years ago and that modern biologists continue to be troubled by it (Beach 1955, Clemente and Lindsley 1967, Panel 1968). But for practical purposes the definitions given by Freud and reiterated by him with some variations and amplifications from 1915 until 1938 are entirely adequate. In his *Outline*, Freud says: "The forces which we assume to exist behind the tensions caused by the needs of the id are called *instincts*. They represent the somatic demands upon the mind. Though they are the ultimate cause of all activity, they are of a conservative nature; the state, whatever it may be, which an organism has reached gives rise to a tendency to re-establish that state so soon as it has been abandoned. . . . we have decided to assume the existence of only two basic instincts, *Eros* and *the destructive instinct*." He then equates the destructive instinct with the death instinct by way of its aim "to lead what is living into an inorganic state" (1940, p. 148). The essential questions, in my view, refer to the presumed inborn, primarily somatic origin of the urge, its spontaneous and continuing pressure, its seeking an object for its own purposes of discharge of tension, and the nature of its basic aim, in so far as these are demonstrable.

Human aggression has much in common with aggression in other species; yet in many respects it is distinct and unique. It is made so not only by facts of physical anthropology and neurophysiology but also by derived, yet autonomously powerful, factors originating in human social organizations. The relative stereotypy that characterizes much of the instinctual behavior of animals does not characterize that of the human being; man's behavior, even when it palpably originates in "drives," is of great range and variety—a fact which contributes to the growing preference for the term *drive* rather than *instinct*. Beres (1968) has discussed these distinctions. Hartmann (1948) pointed out that the ego in man bears a selective and directing relation to behavior which, to a great extent, is fixed by instinctual patterns in other species. The complexity of human behavior is determined by the obvious and far-reaching importance of the complex structure and functions of the human cerebral cortex; by the role of the hands; by the functions of speech and language; and, in my view, by the explicitly cultural but practically universal purposive use of fire (1961).

Aggression ranges far in psychoanalytic thought. It may include manifest bodily or verbal action; conscious or unconscious wishes and tensions; a specific qualitative type of psychic energy, and the final broad and inclusive idea of the death instinct — Thanatos, whose struggle with Eros putatively determines all the manifest phenomenology of life. The idea of the death instinct is a much later development in psychoanalysis than that of the libido, and many who follow Freud closely in other respects do not do so with regard to the death instinct. But among the distinguished proponents of this view of the origin and nature of aggression are Federn (1931), Nunberg (1932), and Weiss (1935).

Aggression unquestionably exists and is only rarely ambiguous. However, it is less clearly demonstrable in its assigned position as a primary instinct than is the sexual instinct, at least in man; this is so whether it is studied as the death instinct or in its manifest, externally directed form. Aggression has no specific anatomicophysiological apparatus devoted exclusively or even primarily to its specific purposes, and there is no conclusive evidence of a universally occurring and discrete pattern of spontaneous urgency in aggression. It does not evidence one of the most important criteria for instinctual drives stated by Freud in 1915 — operation as a constant force (1915a). Furthermore, the range and variety of processes which may be subsumed under the concept aggression, whether from the point of view of perpetrator or object, exceed the variety of processes that are subsumed under sex, or libido. (This opinion, of course, is contrary to some views of aggression as relatively fixed and rigid [Rosen 1969].) There are varying degrees and varying forms of aggression: for instance, when a hoodlum shoots an enemy, when an overprotective mother refuses to allow her child to go swimming with his peers, when an inveterate Don Juan accomplishes habitual, loveless seductions, or when a person deliberately omits to greet an acquaintance. This great range and scope of expression, including the phenomenon of omission, also is found in the basic and original physical prototypes of aggression, although it is not self-evident that they are of a common derivation.

In our initial considerations, let us set aside the more remote psychic representations of aggression, its presumed role as a special form of psychic energy, the problem of the repetition compulsion, the theoretical role of aggression in the mechanisms of defense (Hartmann 1950), and the more intricate problem of self-directed aggression, to deal with the nuclear elements of the concept.

What do we mean by the word *aggression*, which we use so freely and frequently in psychoanalysis? In the Oxford dictionary, the definition emphasizes attack and the initiation of hostilities in the sense of the military paradigm. The glossary recently published by the American Psychoanalytic Association (1967) generalizes the meaning, gives some suggestion of its variety of expressions, and places it in the dynamic psychoanalytic context. What Freud meant is not always unambiguous. In his earlier formulation of general conflict,—i.e., the ego instincts as opposed to the sexual instincts (1915a), the instinct of self-preservation included various separable grades or categories of impulse, including modalities of aggression. The participation of aggression in the manifestations of the sexual instinct, subject to excessive development at times, was recognized very early by Freud (1905, 1909a). The shift of the function of self-preservation to the broad canopy of Eros was a major change (1920), although this function was still allocated to the ego. Later, aggression was separated from its original, largely instrumental place in the ego instincts and moved to a place of psychic origin in the id (1937) as a separate primal instinct. In 1940, Loewenstein offered a penetrating critique of the new theory and also made some suggestions to bring order to the new conceptual confusion. Certainly this structural transposition would require a better integrated and more coherent meaning for the psychoanalytic term and concept, aggression than is now available. In his 1924 paper on masochism, for example, Freud speaks of "the destructive instinct, the instinct for mastery, or the will to power" (p. 163). In 1937, in connection with the death instinct, Freud speaks of the instinct of aggression or of destruction according to its aims. These are not inevitably congruent ideas; they are not necessarily serial ideas, although this may be the case; as alternatives, they may diverge widely.

The presumptive factor that would permit linkage of such concepts as death, destruction, and the instinct for mastery would lie in the phenomenon of fusion, requiring varying degrees of admixture of libido (Freud 1923). However, as Waelder (1956) points out, the impulse to master would be an inevitable part of ego function, whether or not derived from the putative instinct of destruction. Hendrick (1942, 1943) described a separate instinct to master as one of the "ego instincts." The Oxford dictionary notes an obsolete meaning of the word *aggress*: "to approach, march forward." Greenacre uses this derivation, "a *going at* or *towards*, an *approaching*" (1960, p. 578), in relation to the pseudopodal activities of unicellular organisms and incidental to discussion of the embryonic precursors of aggression. One also notes this meaning in the sense that we think of aggression as one type of approach to an object, whether the object be in the outer world or in the self (Schur 1966). This, of course, is unequivocally opposed to flight, whether from fear or aversion. Flight, nearly always a potential organismic alternative to aggression, finds little place in most theories of aggression, at least since the latter was detached from the function of self-preservation and placed in opposition to it.

Deliberately, habitually, or inadvertently we use the term aggression in psychoanalysis to cover the gamut of intentional or purposive harm[2] to the object, ranging from the inflicting of pain or humiliation to death or annihilation.

I omit the benign meanings of aggression, as we do not refer to them in our work except in specifying or implying sublimation, neutralization, fusion, or an allied mechanism. While such meanings are important, their relation to the central concept is no less unclear than that of mastery or the will to power. Elements in benign aggression (somatic or psychic) may be identical with those present in the destructive form and may indeed have a common origin, but it is the specific impact on objects and the evolution of such an impact as motivation that give rise to the ultimate and important distinction.

The idea of death as the final abolition of instinctual tension became central in Freud's later theory. Hartmann, Kris, and Loewenstein (1949) mention that "it has been said" that the aim of aggression is the total destruction of objects, animate or inanimate, subject to restriction, but they feel that the question of these aims cannot at this time be answered and do not feel that an answer is essential. They prefer to classify the aims according to the degree of discharge of aggressive tension which they allow and according to the means utilized in discharge. This seems to imply the primary assumption of the existence of a special form of psychic energy, presumably aggression, without intrinsic aim.[3] The doubt about empirical or logical support for such a concept underlies many of the considerations summarized below.

Certainly to inflict pain is a clear, outstanding, and unequivocal aggression in the mind of the young child. He learns this through his own experiences of pain and he learns of his capacity to inflict pain by accidental or experimental behavior, for example, biting himself or others.[4] Allied to pain in its ordinary sense are deprivation experiences such as suffocation, hunger, thirst, enduring cold or wetness, or sheer aloneness. This negative aspect of the perpetration of suffering, this "not doing" is a characteristic early parental aggression associated with power and is in striking constrast with the violent aggression, or aggresive impulse, of infantile helplessness. And finally, we know that the emergence in the child's development of object love as something different from the simple need for satisfaction provides a whole new system of vulnerability to aggression.

Adults, whether aggressors or victims, know that aggressive actions often cause pain, loss of bodily integrity, or death and that these are often closely interrelated or integrated. Does knowledge of this potential integration influence the original conceptual development of each component of the aggressive complex? We cannot assume that it does, unless we suppose that the primary aggressive drive is associated in the infant with some sort of innate awareness of these consequences and their potential integration.

The conventional representation of the peak effect or purpose of aggression is death of the object. One may conceivably prefer to disgrace, dishonor, humiliate, or torture another individual or his loved ones, thus causing a result "worse than death." Yet to kill remains the continuing general conception of the ultimate aggression toward an object. I stress this because the very concept to kill has multiple origins, facets, and relations to the lesser aggressions, usually forgotten in adult semantics.

The fear of pain has an obvious basis in experience. Freud, who took nothing important for granted, sought to understand the fear of death, calling attention to the fact that it is a remarkable instance of the fear of something that has no place in previous subjective experience. His suggestion (omitting the more complex reference to the ego-superego system) was that the prototypic basis is the experience of separation from objects and that fear of death is allied to the fear of castration in its broadest sense (1923, pp. 58–59). Aside from the possible occurrence of extreme suffering in the process of dying, there are objective elements that contribute to the sophisticated dread of death: the "passivity," "vulnerability," "helplessness" of the cadaver; the phenomenon of decomposition, including the presence of foul odors and the banishment of the cadaver by burial, fire, or more attenuated processes, paralleling the psychological disappearance from family, friends, and the living environment in general.

If we accept death in the sense of its biological finality for the victim, as the ultimate result of aggression, the question of the primitive motivation to kill and the immediate and remote meanings of the impulse are not clear and unitary. An oral incorporative urge, if it could be consummated, would mean destruction of the object without the slightest awareness in the infant of implications of death or killing. Even with a gradually progressive awareness of what such incorporation must mean in physical terms, its real meaning to the object as empathically perceived by the subject would be long delayed. To a child or an adult, to kill may mean to remove or conclusively incapacitate another individual who is a rival or impediment in getting something urgently needed or, similarly, to take from him in a definitive way what the attacker urgently wants or, conversely, to prevent permanently a similar attack upon the attacker. What is urgently needed may be air, water, food, territory, or a love object. One kills (in these hypothetically pure instances) in the service of a pressing or essential purpose. How one kills and the consequences for the victim may be unimportant (except as to efficiency of the method) or may be matters of intense guilt or anguished concern. Under primitive conditions, in criminal behavior or in the accepted conventions of tribal or national warfare, killing may be regarded as a realistic implementation of need—an ego function, so to speak—and the best way of protecting or advancing the interests of the individual or group.

Other important adult motivations for killing range from the complicated impulse toward vengeance (socially expressed in the *lex talionis*), through considerations of honor (for instance, the reaction to certain types of insults or other humiliations), to the desperate reaction to anxiety induced by the object (such as extreme castration fear). In contrast with these are, for example, an honest impulse to euthanasia in the presence of extreme and hopeless suffering, the obligatory killing of a soldier, or the professional killing of a criminal by an official executioner.

Let us now consider aggression in which the *object* of hopeless passion is killed instead of the *rival*. The mother is originally the person who decides whether her own love is to be given (for example, in the form of bodily care of the child) or withheld; in this way she is herself the "owner" of the object and thus equivalent to a rival long before the father comes into his unique position in the phallic phase.[5] In the fantasy of active, especially murderous, rape, there is a regressed and dim though genuine adumbration of the oedipal striving, even though the differences are, of course, great. When the love object is dead, all hope of gratification is at an end, save in fantasy. There is a kind of mastery in rendering the love object dead that lends itself to fantasies of permanent possession through incorporation, necrophilia, or more complicated acts of the imagination, which may be an important motive for killing. The loved one who is dead cannot turn away from the lover. No doubt the Anlage of this attitude lies in the oral phase. Freud reiterated this view of early "erotic mastery" in 1920. "During the oral stage of organization of the libido, the act of obtaining erotic mastery over an object coincides with that object's destruction; later, the sadistic instinct separates off, and finally, at the stage of genital primacy, it takes on, for the purposes of reproduction, the function of overpowering the sexual object to the extent necessary for carrying out the sexual act. It might indeed be said that the sadism which has been forced out of the ego has pointed the way for the libidinal components of the sexual instinct, and that these follow after it to the object" (p. 54).

Thus far we have viewed the impulse to kill largely in its adult or protoadult significance—the impulse as it includes a relatively organized and reality-syntonic conception of death. It is important, therefore, to recall that the linguistic concept "to kill," and to some extent the imagery it evokes, may readily be assimilated by earlier impulses and wishes that have no relation to the actual words or concept. Of course, under certain circumstances there may ultimately be genuine congruence instead of superimposition. To cause to vanish, to be nonexistent, readily finds expression in a death wish. Such a wish may be temporary and remain so even in adult consciousness, entirely apart from the sense of inappropriateness or the reproach of the conscience.

The earliest visual, auditory, and tactile impressions of absence are profoundly and poignantly related to the mother. The child, who is utterly incapable of a meaningful death wish, may fail to recognize his mother when she returns after a long absence; his oversimplified formula is "If you are going to go away too long, don't come back!" We may suppose that a negative hallucinatory satisfaction is achieved here, based on the experience that things can vanish and perhaps related to oral incorporative fantasies. This exclusion of painful situations or persons from consciousness is a common phenomenon in the adult patient, and at times it is referred to as a "psychological killing."

Destruction and annihilation can apply to the inanimate and thus are conceptually independent of a death instinct or an impulse to kill. The dependence of life itself on destructiveness—both in the inanimate sphere and in relation to living organisms—lends itself all too readily to paradox and *reductio ad absurdum* in relation to the dual instinct theory. However, the idea of the destructive energies in the service of the instinct of self-preservation (or Eros), by way of the devouring impulse, yet subject to regression to intestinal hatred, is given serious and challenging form in Simmel's 1944 paper. The fundamental and concrete position of the oral urges in the concepts of destruction, annihilation, and death should be emphasized. Especially notable is the holistic quality of the oral urge; in it the life-preservative necessities, as well as aggression and libido, are tightly integrated. The oral-gastric sphere maintains a place of basic importance in mimetic expression, even in contrasting emotions, as noted by Darwin (1872).

It is important to mention the problem of modes of killing as expressions of the "principle of multiple function" (Waelder 1936). I have in mind the frequent importance of specific infantile motivations in adult aggression. Bernfeld, in his 1935 methodological essay, suggested that practically all instinctual manifestations, if classified by the "psychoanalytic" criterion, as opposed to the "physiognomic" criterion, would show important connections with the erogenous zones. Choice of methods of killing such as poisoning, incendiarism, explosion, drowning, hanging, strangling, or defenestration may have important specific infantile and symbolic meanings as well as important aggressive motivations of specific genetic origin. The same elements are also important in suicide.

A radically different category of killing is the activity of a hunter who must kill animals for food. He does what the beast of prey does except that his activity is a conglomerate of all his ego functions in the service of his need for food, instead of a relatively stereotyped, largely hereditary series of sensory and muscular responses. Indeed, even with regard to these stereotyped responses we must bear in mind that Elsa the lioness had to be coached back into the "frame of mind" and movements necessary for making her kill, so attached was she to the feeding by her human foster parents (Adamson 1960). In contrast with killing for food, winning or putting to flight has an important place in the animal kingdom, often ritualized and mutually accepted—for example, in sexual competition or in the all-important territorial conflicts that characterize certain species (Barnett 1967, Eibl-Eibesfeldt 1967, Lorenz 1966, Woolpy 1968). This is also extremely important in human activities, even in war, where the concession of defeat usually ends the physical conflict. It may well be that the exterminations that occurred in early human warfare were as often a result of appropriate ego functioning in a primitive context as of unbridled instinctual drive. Man recognized that the killed opponent does not challenge again. A similar phenomenon can occur as an expression of revenge, hatred, or psychopathological cruelty or destructiveness. As I mentioned, flight has been neglected as a subject for study. It is always an alternative to combat within a species or among different species, and this fact is in itself an a priori difficulty in the concept of a primary destructive drive.

We must also recognize that fighting itself has been regarded as an instinct. Surely, such a view is at least as reasonable as the view that death or destruction are in themselves instinctive primary goals. If one studies the behavior of schoolboys, as Bovet did (1923), one might establish such a conviction. But such fighting often serves a purpose and is likely to be reactive; moreover, it is in part a discharge of surplus sexual, especially homosexual, energy. For these reasons such a proposition seems dubious. Social requirements or sanctions are also important factors. I do not doubt that fighting as such provides important functional musculoskeletal pleasure, as it involves certain combat patterns with strong phylogenetic background (Clemente and Lindsley 1967, Darwin 1871), or relief in the discharge of genetically determined and displaced hostilities, or pleasure in the secondary gain of applause and admiration (Bovet 1923, Durbin and Bowlby 1950). Athletics, like the aggressive play of animals (Porter 1967), provide similar functional pleasure with the additional incentives of winning and spontaneous admiration. Among certain primitive peoples (Matthiessen 1962), the actual waging of war for no significant territorial purpose becomes a sort of game with minimal, yet sometimes lethal, casualties, short battles, and continuing hostility toward the enemy tribe. One may speculate that besides the individual functional pleasure of combat and the spontaneous general esteem for fighting prowess, there may be a nonexplicit or unconscious social purpose. Both primitive and more advanced peoples may need to keep alive the skills and high prestige of the warrior lest this ultimate form of decision making elude the powers of the people should a critical need arise.

AGGRESSION AND SOCIAL STRUCTURE

Since human social structure has a decisive role in defining aggression and in administering it, some discussion of its relevant aspects is in order. I shall state without elaboration what I regard as certain salient and relevant features of the general topic.

1. In return for its physical protection of the individual, the state in effect arrogates to itself the exclusive right to physical violence as well as the exclusive right to punish the individual for transgressions in this sphere. Furthermore, it retains the right to conscript the individual for combat in its armed services when the governing agencies deem it necessary.

2. In becoming relatively pacific in everyday life, the individual delegates to the state, whether or not he is aware of it or actively wishes it, the protection or aggrandizement of his economic opportunity and certain primitive aspects of his narcissism, matters to which much of his energy would have been devoted in his "brutish" past. With this, he similarly delegates to the state the primitive morality that once governed his behavior and continues to govern the behavior of states: the killing in warfare, spying, intrigue, dissimulation, and allied activities. These he may resume only in the service of the state, and in case of war he may be forced to do so. A certain degree of psychopathology, reflected in national (i.e., official) attitudes, invites participation by the average, relatively healthy individual in a sense not readily condoned in relation to other individuals. From the primitive magical attitudes of the head hunter to the relatively sophisticated rationalized, grandiose, or paranoid attitudes of modern states (Durbin and Bowlby 1950, Rosen 1969), such tendencies may play a major motivating, facilitating, or overdetermining role in the initiation of war. The role of these

facts in the mental life of the average citizen remains somewhat obscure and has been insufficiently studied.

3. While the prevailing social organization, be it a tribal or national state, is an outgrowth of human needs and conflicts, it becomes vis-à-vis the individual a dynamic external fact of his existence. The chauvinist or active pacifist cannot alone initiate or terminate the waging of war; this is a matter of governmental decision. Officers of government, although varying importantly in individual reaction, are themselves largely bound by the obligations of office and the forces of history. "The king is the slave of history" (Tolstoy 1931, p. 565). Although some individuals love battle, there are probably millions who fight only because they must, under legal or psychological coercion. Thus aggression can be obligatory, and the majority of men are happy to lay down their arms when allowed to do so.

4. The terrifying nuclear stockpiles are evidence of the growth of wealth and scientific manpower in the superstates, products of the same Zeitgeist that produced prodigious advances in benign areas of human technology. While their threat is a perennial and horrible emergency and must be dealt with as such by appropriate and immediate methods, they are not, any more than the historical repetitiveness of war itself, evidences of innate destructiveness. Rather, they are evidences of (a) the transition of the belligerent functions from the pitiful individual to the endlessly resourceful superstate and (b) the persistence of nationalism as the last viable stronghold of primitive narcissism.

AGGRESSION AND NARCISSISM

Aggression may be construed as a pure accumulation of a special type of psychic energy without intrinsic direction (a "scalar" as G. S. Klein put it [1967]). In becoming functional it must have a target, whether it be the subject's own ego (or self), an external object, or the ego's projection. The phenomenon of narcissism, the lever for externalization of aggression, is thus critically important. It contributes decisively to the sense of differentiation of the self from the outer world and later, in its balance and interaction with object love, to the modes, directions, and degrees of externally directed aggression. In the second phase of Freud's dual instinct theory, beginning with the introduction of the concept of narcissism (1914), narcissism was thought of as the libidinal aspect of egoism, a concept that left its trace in a later (rare) usage: "ego instincts and object instincts" (1926). In 1915 Freud emphasized the priority of indifference or hatred toward the outer world in the earliest neonatal period, with libido developing later in its connection with crucial self-preservation phenomena (1915a). Most striking and well defined in this connection is the function of feeding in which physiologic need is obvious and the patterns that we designate as libidinal and aggressive respectively are clearly immanent. Indeed, the infant's need for sucking will speedily demonstrate itself, strikingly when the nutrient flows too quickly to give him sufficient sucking time.

Hartmann, Kris, and Loewenstein (1949), in an effort to reconstruct speculatively the earliest provocation of aggression, invoke Freud's assumption that the neonate tends to project all discomforts and tensions to the outer world and to assign all gratification or pleasure to the self. In the evolution of infantile narcissism, the ego ideal is one of the acceptable repositories for suplus libido. In group formation this may be externalized in the person of the leader (Freud 1921). In any case, subject to the vicissitudes of individual human development, there is a persistent underlying feeling in the human individual—perhaps only latent, yet having a remarkable range of intensity—that the self and its acknowledged extensions are a priori good and lovable and that others are bad, the objects of suspicion and potentially the natural objects of violent attack, especially if they create tensions or fail to gratify. This feeling is, of course, largely mitigated by the development of object love, by autonomous ego functions especially in the perceptual sphere, and by the development of the superego. However, the fundamental role of this attitude in human psychology is not thereby uprooted, whether its manifestations be in the "stranger anxiety" of infants (Spitz 1965) or the universal though variable xenophobia of adult individuals and groups.

We may reasonably assume that the process of being born represents a radical change in organismic economy in every sphere, even though the neonate is presumed to be biologically prepared for such change at term. This preparedness and the usually gradual transition from the uterus to the outer world (Greenacre 1945) presumably combine to establish extrauterine viability. Still, the process of being born is a critical test for the neonate as well as the mother. The first moments of emergence from the birth canal produce gross environmental changes, including the substitution of an "air and hands environment" for mucous membrane and physiologic fluids, usually unstable or at least inexact temperature matching, a flood of shifting light stimuli and sound stimuli, and most conspicuously the need to breathe. This, with the germane first cry, must occasion a massive and unique flood of sensory stimuli. The occasional uncertainty as to whether an apparently healthy newborn will breathe indicates the delicate balance in which the claim of intrauterine modes of adaptation and the necessities of extrauterine life are suspended. But certainly one may assume that infantile drive is at this point unitary and global, whether expressed in motor activity, such as respiration, or in manifestly passive need.

The critical self-preservative requirements for air, water, food, and protection from cold are integral with the germane libidinal needs and with potential aggression. These are more critically urgent than the need for handling, body contact, warmth, odors, and the oral stimulation of sucking. Deficiency in these latter needs, however, can cause very serious disturbances and possibly contribute to the fatal outcome of various infantile disorders (Ribble 1965). Assuming the availability of the critical necessities, which substitute for those delivered automatically through the umbilical cord,[6] the striving also is to achieve as nearly as possible the gratifications of the stable and undisturbing amniotic milieu in the extrauterine environment. In this connection the various bodily contacts involved in the maternal care of the infant are important. However, lung aeration and respiratory gratification must be supplied by the infant himself. Proximity to the object may at times be an impediment, for example, when the nose gets buried in the breast. Pleasure in free movement is assuredly the infant's own initiative if not impeded from the outside. Withdrawal into sleep, away from the congeries of external stimuli, is his own act, although it can be pleasantly facilitated from the outside by rocking and lullabies and is usually dependent on the precondition of adequate feeding. The infant can touch his own body and can from the very beginning suck his thumb. (It is said that an occasional infant is born with thumb in mouth: indeed, it has been stated that thumb sucking can occur in utero [Kanner 1966]). It is certain that there are infants who show a primary inclination to reject the breast, so great is the attachment to an earlier "way of life" (Lehman 1949).

The wish to sleep, to withdraw from the maternal object before nursing, to reproduce by an antiphysiological tour de force an imitation of intrauterine life, represents a tendency that is far from identical with a drive to die but does closely resemble and suggest such a drive. If not met with countermeasures, whether in infancy or in its resurgence in later years, it can bring about death. In this sense, it can be construed as an aggressive parallel to narcissism, perhaps to some degree a merger with it: the "primary masochism" of Freud's later constructions (1924). When a biological hesitation to institute breathing occurs, one may at least speculate that the physiologic Anlage of the same attitude is involved. The panicky search for air in the case of external impediment, possibly with convulsive movements, or the hyperpneic effort that may occur if there has been excessive delay, must then represent the countervailing and saving aggressive impulse and, at the same time, the libidinal gratification of filling the lungs with air. Primitive efforts to avoid forced occlusion due to excessive bodily proximity may represent the extension of the same urge in direct connection with the mother's body. Note the later motor expressions of "againstness" described by Greenacre (1960). The mother, of course, provides the gratifying and later reassuring smells of intimate bodily contact. These join the general stream of exogenous libidinal gratification.[7] In a sense, then, the vital function of respiration has in it the seeds of a dynamic narcissism and demonstrable aggression and is conspicuously independent of the first object. In this context, I employ the concept of narcissism in an objective dynamic sense, including but extending beyond the idea of libidinal, purely psychic energy invested in the ego. This is similar to Greenacre's usage in certain of her contributions (1945). One can speculate that it is the earliest prototype of aggressive riddance of the object—as distinguished from affirmative maturational and libidinal strivings toward the nonmaternal environment—of the interest in "open space," of "room to breathe," of "elbow room." (Perhaps also one aspect of Lebensraum?).

The second great focal need for food and water can be met only from the outside by the mother or her proxy. Here a different and more complex system of drives and protofantasies must be postulated for the understanding of subsequent development. Insofar as the ministering person is at first not reacted to as separate from the self, the facts of occasional total separation and the frequent focal (oral) separations are reacted to as if they were castrations and indeed probably constitute the essential substratum for the decisive castration complex. If we assume that the infant has a strong narcissistic-aggressive predisposition and episodic or chronic deprivation is a significant trauma, he will have an urgent need to bring about a situation as close as possible to the prehistoric intrauterine state, that is, to restore the original unity. One can only speculate on the protopsychic processes involved in such urges. It may be assumed that striving toward oral incorporation of the object or part-object is latent or potential in these urges or emerges from them. With the advent of teeth and growing awareness of the capacity to destroy food for more efficient ingestion, the primary destruction of the object becomes allied to the incorporative fantasy, and with it, as an intermediate step, there is awareness of the capacity to cause pain (sadism and its inhibitions).[8] It should be noted, however, such fantasies reach their peak long before they are connected with the idea of death. Finally, by a complicated circular route, the destructive or annihilatory fantasy constitutes a fulfillment of a latent original urge to reject the object as an outside and separate entity. Thus narcissism, in its evident biological corollaries, is linked with aggression that includes in its ultimate form the impulse to destroy the object.

The narcissistic principle in human social organization and its relation to aggression have certain remote extensions which are connected with narcissistic object choice. Besides the functional, traditional, and legal ties that maintain the family as the basic continuing group, the sense of physical resemblance and awareness of consanguinity are important in facilitating the first social displacement from relinquished individual narcissism. Intrafamilial hatreds, based essentially on sibling or oedipal rivalry, are originally of unparalleled intensity. But the cultural tendency is to displace manifest aggression outward concentrically to persons increasingly remote from the line of kinship or its complex psychic substitutes. Ultimately the violent forms of aggression become the exclusive prerogatives of the national state with which the individual is identified.

The sense of common national identity operates as a further extension of narcissism with aggression directed toward alien aggregates. Even within the nation there are innumerable peace-time group adherences which individuals require and use in the struggle to recapture lost narcissism. These carry with them varying degrees of hostility toward other groups. Freud's "narcissism of small differences" (1921), however, has been largely submerged or lost in this century of homogenized mass communications and pyramiding armaments of great nation states.

A countervailing consideration is the latent regressive tendency toward revival of murderous intrafamilial aggression. Civil wars, especially in nations homogenous in language and race, are often noteworthy for their fratricidal ferocity. Also great revolutions appear to unleash a tendency to wanton vengeful slaughter, sometimes followed by the recrudescence of intense nationalism or even imperialism. The tension between internecine war and war with the foreigner sometimes seeks a combined target. In the Western world, the Jews of the Diaspora provide the ideal scapegoat as citizens who can readily be viewed as alien. Thus they are especially liable to mass expulsion or slaughter. Those whose racial difference is more conspicuous, for example, the Negro, are more frequently subjected to chronic oppression and segregation than liquidation.

Except for such regressions, the tendency is to move the narcissistic barrier farther and farther from the self. To kill an animal for food is not conventionally held to be an aggression except by vegetarians. Vegetarianism, however, is not widespread. Most men prefer to eat an animal, one somewhat like themselves, but not too close in resemblance or in the sense of emotional ties. This is connected with the taboo on incest by way of the totem feast (Freud 1913). Incest remains taboo, but miscegenation is also the subject of mild and variable, although diminishing, taboo.

There is a dialectical relationship between the immunities granted by kinship and the intense hostilities provoked by the prolonged intimacies of early life in the family. The former is allied to group narcissism and aggression, the latter to the proverbial "wolflike" relationship of man to man. However, it must be noted that in the present stage of organic and geologic evolution man is the only creature who can seriously and immediately rival his fellow man for the good things of the earth and therefore challenge him to the only conflict regarded as decisive. This principle, I think, must be added to the principle of "domestication" stated by Von Bertalanffy (1965), in which the lack of interspecific danger permits the doubtful luxury of intraspecific murder: war.

If thus far no evidence has demonstrated or supported the existence of a primary (i.e., unmotivated, noninstrumental) destructive or lethal drive, this cannot be offered as proof that such an underlying drive or drives do not exist. Even when the aggressive activity seems clearly instrumental, it may still remain true that such putative drives in some subtle way motivate or facilitate these activities or the selection of aggressive techniques. We cannot, however, infer this solely from the phenomena, for the aggression is often appropriate in its own context of technology and morality. Federn, who sought to demonstrate the reality of the death instinct (1931), set aside striking examples of impulsive childhood aggression, for instance, the sudden killing of a small moving animal, as nondemonstrative of primary aggression because these examples have other possible motivations. It remains necessary at least to examine certain immediately relevant aspects of known human instinctual life itself in the further effort to understand the origin of aggression.

AGGRESSION AND HUMAN SEXUALITY

It is an interesting paradox that the sexual life of the human adult is the activity which most nearly resembles primitive combat between human adversaries. The intrinsic nature of coitus is similar to combat, and the small child's conception of the primal scene is often fraught with frightening violence, although such impressions vary with age and individual circumstances. This concept of the child's often has defensive elements; yet it still testifies to the important mechanical and physiological resemblances that facilitate the widespread illusion of violence. (The defensive element has been emphasized by Gero [Panel 1956].)

Defloration frequently involves actual pain and bleeding. This passing token experience of suffering and the actual lesion can, of course, have far-reaching unconscious implications. The fact that for many adults the infliction or suffering of some degree of pain can be part of the pleasure of foreplay and the sexual act testifies to the integral relation of protoaggressive behavior to the consummation of love. One may include the elements of grasping, bodily pressure, violent thrusting, and often biting, which are not perceived as pain or discomfort at all under the circumstances. However, it is clear that the motive is to gain pleasure and (under reasonably healthy circumstances) to give the partner pleasure. The point at which the partner feels distress or pain rather than pleasure or suffers injury other than defloration, manifest to the perpetrator as directly due to his acts, is the point at which aggression in the true functional sense occurs. If the active partner experiences sexual pleasure in his partner's pain or distress, the process is sadism in its original sense. Complementary reaction of the passive partner is masochism. These phenomena, even the intrinsic motor elements of coitus itself, are ordinarily accounted for by the fusion of the two great drives, libidinal and aggressive. However, the situation suggests more strongly the old but still valid instrumental view of aggression proposed by Freud, or else a deep intrinsic relatedness, perhaps continuousness, between what later must be regarded as two separate drives. Such a profound relationship or continuum would give way to dichotomy with the growth of object love, structure formation, and the increasing perceptual awareness of and empathy with the fact of untoward impact on the object.

The coital cruelty of other male animals can be much greater than that of the human; hence we cannot regard this behavior as a human psychological quirk. One may also note that although Freud and others, including Hartmann, Kris, and Loewenstein (1949), emphasized the relation of aggression to the muscular apparatus, little attention has been given to the instinctual importance of the muscular apparatus in coitus although it is of equal or greater frequency than is intraspecific aggression, even in primitive man. Inspired by Freud's remarks in the discussion of Little Hans (1909a, pp. 140–141), one might ask what would remain of sex as an instinct if there were no body, no musculature, and no aggressive movement to implement it? The movements of harmful aggression are in general much less stereotyped than those of coitus are and are more closely allied to ego activity. Saintliness, expressed in the withholding or suppression of aggression along with affirmative acts and tendencies, is practically always accompanied by the renunciation of sex. Biologically, there is more than fragmentary evidence of a correlation between the excess or lack of male gonadal hormones and corresponding fluctuations in pugnacity (Beach 1949). Without explicitly stating this, Durbin and Bowlby (1950) quote Zuckerman regarding the "battle royal" among male baboons for possession of the females, noting the shocking number of females killed in the process. The number seems far too great to be accounted for by accidents or mistakes. The submissive — sometimes masochistic — element in male homosexuality, at times overdetermined by reaction against violent aggression, is another striking link between two apparently opposing drives. Among animals this may take the stark and somewhat ritualistic form of the mounting of the defeated male by the victor (Kawamura 1967). Lorenz (1966) described the "pestering" of the victor by a defeated baboon, which continued until the victor carried out a perfunctory mount. The same author, quoted by Peto (1968) also stresses the importance among animals of the ritual transformations of aggression as a bond more powerful than the sexual alliance itself. A conspicuous example is the "triumph ritual" of certain wild geese. Lorenz generalizes: "Thus intraspecific aggression can certainly exist without its counterpart, love, but conversely, there is no love without aggression" (1966, p. 217).

It must be borne in mind that in man, whose prolonged infant-mother relationship is biologically obligatory, close bodily opposition — a type of violent "clinging" — is intrinsic to coitus and also to the most primitive (weaponless) forms of combat. One may infer that both have an important relation to infantile experience and the urge toward its renewal, that aspect of sexuality which, as Freud and others have emphasized, is "in the service of reproduction," but, like the conjugation of primitive forms, has its own independent functions. Again, it is refreshing to refer to the discussion of Little Hans for an early insight of genius in this connection (Freud 1909a, p. 111).

The idea of the female as the original victim of male attack or coercion, an attitude embodied in certain cultural taboos (Freud 1918), leads us to germane problems of infantile sexuality, culminating in the Oedipus complex.

AGGRESSION AND THE OEDIPUS COMPLEX

Whether or not there is a latent primary aggressive drive, the prolonged helpless state of human infancy may be viewed as especially conducive to the mobilization of aggression. Certainly the prolonged dependency on a maternal object provides an inevitable prototypic target. The devouring fantasies that are early diverted to the prey in nonhuman forms can only surge toward the indispensable object. Whether the immediate instigations of aggression are the repeated states of frustration in the broad and inclusive sense of Dollard and his coworkers (1939), or chronic and acute traumatic states of helplessness cannot be said with certainty. My own conviction is that aggression arises in the drive to master actual or threatened traumatic helplessness. In this sense, the objective awareness and conception of death as the ultimate state of helplessness achieves a special and terrifying meaning to be considered with the formulation proposed by Freud. If we pass over other infantile solutions for helplessness, largely in the sphere of pathological omnipotent fantasy, an important and consistently available alternative solution is found in specifically aggressive tension and fantasy.

Sophocles's version of the tragedy of Oedipus contains certain hidden or peripheral elements usually regarded merely as necessary devices in the ingenious plot. Essentially these are the details of Oedipus's mother's abandonment of the hero to his presumed death in an effort to circumvent the dreaded prophecies regarding his patricidal destiny, an abandonment about which the hero exclaims his horror on hearing of his mother's participation. The emphasis is not only on the psychic continuity from earliest anaclitic need through hopeless sexual love, mastered in fantasy by parricide, but also on the cruel and specific experience of infantile helplessness in abandonment and the murderous destiny thereby intitiated. (I take the liberty, in interpreting the plot, of reversing the causal relationship between the abandonment and the parricidal destiny.) That the mother is the latent object of such aggression seems implicit in Sophocles's tragedy and accords with the usual genetic facts I have inferred from analytic experience with adults (1967, pp. 13–14, n.).

There is reason to believe that all children experience, in varying degrees and with variations dependent on sex, the travails of Oedipus, from at times feeling abandoned to die to the ultimate tragic triangle of love. The murderous thrust originally awakened in the earliest experiences of helplessness may provide an Anlage of hostility, rage, and aggression resembling "drive." However, this cannot be drive in the inborn, constant, autochthonous sense of psychoanalytic usage. In the boy's displacement of raw, unneutralized aggression to the father, the libidinal impulse toward the mother may be freed of all aggression save that intrinsic in normal sexuality, i.e., compatible with the preservation and pleasure of the object. In reversing this displacement in a more complicated process, the girl accomplishes an essentially equivalent developmental tour de force.

AGGRESSION AND SUICIDE

So far as we know, suicide is confined to the human species and is a common mode of death. One may speculate that its limitation to man is connected with (1) the severe human sanctions against outward violent aggression in everyday life, (2) the great range and variety of possible symbolic gratifications that may be required by the human individual (see Von Bertalanffy 1965), and (3) the highly developed human capacity for introjection and identification. Thus one is often impressed with the existence of two, sometimes three, participants in the suicidal tragedy: the self as such, the introjected early object (usually the mother), and an implacable superego. In the strange phenomenon of "running amok" (Burton-Bradley 1968, Clifford 1896), the players may be externalized. The psychological content, however, does not vitiate the dramatic fact of literal self-murder, of the coexistence in one organism of the impulses to kill and to die in an apparent unitary drive, despite the great variety of motivations for the act that can be demonstrated or inferred (Kubie 1967). It is, of course, theoretically conceivable that such a drive exists as a truly unitary phenomenon prior to the participant self- and object-representations. Furthermore, it is known that the violence of the superego does not necessarily derive from actual parental behavior, that more often it derives its energy from the individual's own infantile aggression, presumably inhibited from external conveyance against the parents who stimulated it.

While more suggestive than any other single phenomenon in the great spectrum of self-punitive and self-destructive behavior, suicide is not convincing evidence of the existence of a death instinct or primary aggression. It must first be demonstrated (1) that the infantile motivations, including specific phase and erogenous zone conflicts (for example, the drinking of phenol or other painfully corrosive and destructive substances) and the functional importance of the self- and object-representations are, in fact, secondary; and (2) that the phenomenon, suicide, is truly a variant or elaboration of a universal tendency rather than a pathologic qualitative deviation from usual behavior.

PSYCHIC REPRESENTATIONS OF AGGRESSION

Certain literal experiential representations of aggression in the mind, not the concept of aggression as a distinctive form of psychic energy, are outlined below.

1. In relation to both sex and aggression, hallucinatory gratifications — using the term in its broadest sense — are readily available, both in endogenous form and as externally presented. The latter are abundantly present in the mass entertainment media as well as in the theater of current history. Since aggression, in contradistinction to sex, has no specific physiological apparatus and constant urge requiring specific physiologic satisfaction, it is thought that the degree of vicarious satisfaction attainable in the purely mental sphere is correspondingly greater. In the case of sex, while stimulation is often pleasurable, the remainder of the cycle must be consummated physiologically to provide adequate gratification. The contrast in the entertainment media between the traditional prevalence of stark violence and the rarity and fragmentary character of primal scene presentations must be noted, despite the current cultural revolution. The average healthy person may not kill at his own initiative or even fight too frequently, but he can usually establish adequate outlets for his sexual urges as an adult. It is true that curiosity about the sexual scene involving others often persists, and in some there is the special wish to witness perverse activities. To these wishes, as well as the general Zeitgeist of sexual freedom, the current trend in the cinema responds. However, all but the severely perverse will seek full satisfaction with living partners, and it is said that the current trend in the cinema is beginning to evoke boredom in those segments of the general public most consistently exposed to it.

2. The various conscious executions and potential executions of aggression, including subtleties, nuances, and omissions of action, are held to be connected with persisting unconscious representations of primitive aggressive acts or omissions to act. A simple paradigm is the failure to greet a neighbor, which may be bilaterally connected with literal "cutting" in the unconscious, as suggested by the widespread colloquialism. A failure to act in an emergency of uncompli-

cated and unequivocal nature may constitute an act of murder. Except in rare perverse instances, sexual satisfaction cannot thus be obtained.

3. The external accidents of life can provide vicarious but important aggressive satisfactions, notably disease of the object, sudden death (for example, automobile or plane crashes), or economic disaster. Hostile wishes of this character, often directed toward intimate objects, provide abundant chronic or transient symptom-formations, largely anxious reactions directed against such wishes. *Schadenfreude* is a more nearly ego-syntonic and exceedingly widespread variant.

4. The analytic transference occasionally provides striking expression in certain personalities of the preponderance of early omnipotent hallucinatory solutions, obviating manifest aggression. For example, the analyst is already castrated; he is stupid; his voice, a high-pitched falsetto, has been heard through the door; he is obviously and manifestly effeminate. Thus competitive envy and aggression may, to some degree, be obviated. Except by displacement to real objects, in autoplastic solutions, or in the sphere of germane aggressive or self-punitive fantasies, literally sexual elements cannot be manipulated to fantasy consummation without, for example, masturbation.

5. These facts may contribute to the principle that whereas violent aggression has been largely delegated to the state, at least in an "official" sense, sex has remained, with certain ritual exceptions such as the *droit du seigneur* or the *ius primae noctis*, the right and commitment of the individual.

AGGRESSION AS EGO FUNCTION

Waelder, in his 1956 *Critique*, outlines various motivations and purposes of aggression, including those derived from the ego, for example, "the mastery of the outside world" or "the control of one's own body or mind." In the Panel of 1956, Waelder, among other provocative questions, asked if aggression were an ego function. Having long held certain quasi convictions in this direction, I believe that this question should not be avoided.

In Freud's early classification, the ego instincts, as opposed to the sexual instincts, included the instinct of self-preservation. Aggression was assumed to be an integral part of the self-preservative complex. One might have to fight to preserve one's life or to get what was necessary to sustain it. Moreover, both the aggressive implementation of sex and the integration of aggression in sexuality were recognized. Indeed, in the same year (1909b) in which he spoke of the importance of hatred in obsessional neurosis, Freud, in refuting Adler's point of view, spoke of the indispensability of aggression for the implementation of any or all instinctual urges. The ego is the essential executive organ of the mind. Just as Hartmann has emphasized the importance of the human ego for the implementation of instinctual drives—not only for defense against them—as opposed to the stereotypes of traditionally conceived and literal instincts, one must still think of aggression as playing an important role in the system of ego functions. The variety and plasticity of aggressive movement, in relation to purpose are striking, as compared with the relative stereotypes of coitus. Certainly the ego aspect holds true if one speaks, as Freud did of the instinct for mastery, *Bemächtigungstrieb* (1924), as a manifestation of primary aggression—that is, if one does not quibble about the *trieb* part of the word. The impulse to mastery is an integral part of even the most complex ego activity, even in solving a problem in calculus. The alliance of such concepts to aggression, in its broadest sense, is tenable. This extends even to ideas of work as implementations of instinctual need. Greenacre (1960) and Anna Freud (1949a) speak of the aggressive sucking of the infant. Bell, in the 1956 Panel on the Theory of Aggression, mentioned the latent aggression involved in the infant's respiration, albeit in a nondestructive sense. Such conceptualizations are independent of the pragmatic consideration of harm to the object.

These functions are, of course, devoted to living. To ally work or mastery with impulses to destruction as such or, in the sense of the death instinct, with killing or dying requires the tour de force concept of fusion or a bold view, like Simmel's (1944), in which the instinct of destruction (if we except regression) is placed directly in the service of the life instincts. A somewhat startling and imaginative conception is that of Weiss (1935) who conceives of his *destrudo* as providing much of the energy for the ego functions but susceptible to being withdrawn, leaving these functions weakened as, for example, when the destructive energy invests the psychic representation of a trauma. Rosen, in the Panel of 1956, mentioned the problem implicit in the different terminological constructions of the concept of aggression. The problem persists and transcends the purely semantic, for such basic concepts as destruction as such and death (or killing) are not even approximately congruent ideas in their original and essential meanings.

In any case, aggression in its broadest sense can implement complicated ego strategies, whether by persuasion, or shrewd bargaining, or killing, and also a variety of frankly instinctual needs in the sense that these can be mediated only by the ego. It is an important question whether mastery is a tamed version of the impulse to death or destruction (waiving the difference for this question) or whether death or destruction appear as regressive variants when mastery or gratification or both falter or fail. Empirically, the latter seems more probable. For an infant to experience the impulse to chew up and swallow a frustrating or rejecting object may be his only conceivable representation of mastery. This is also true of his simple need for the ingestion of food. Such impulses are later assimilated to the developing conceptions of death, killing, and destruction. Then, later in development, when current and appropriate modes of mastery fail, the primitive modalities, with their implicit destructiveness, may reassert themselves. Waelder (1956), Fenichel (1953), and Reich (1933) have expressed similar views in connection with the question of aggression and libido (i.e., the shift in preponderance and in maturity of impulse), Waelder and Fenichel in specific relation to the question of "defusion."

It is also worthwhile to consider certain intrinsic elements of aggression, as ordinarily construed, in their role as primitive ego functions. There is no doubt that behind the barriers erected by progressive ego development, by object love, and by the superego, there persists in most human beings a primitive urge toward prompt, self-decided, and summary solution. A great segment of aggressive behavior represents primitive or, in the civilized adult, regressive instrumental or adaptive function which in its place and time can be appropriate and effective. In an undeveloped state, either ontogenetically or phylogenetically, the "straight-line-shortest-distance" principle of Euclidean geometry finds humble and understandable representation in behavior. You want something? Grasp and take it. It belongs to someone else? Bite it off, rip it off, cut it off. Increase the force, if necessary. A person is in your way? Knock him down or push or kick him out of the way. You want his "kill" or his woman? Stun him with a blow. The woman resists? Hit her on the head, pick her up, and carry her off. You are hungry? Kill, tear off a piece, put it in your mouth. And so on, endlessly. That this tendency persists, often in highly developed adults, is easily verified, subject, of course, to the restrictions of object love and structural conflict. When frustrated, highly intelligent men can break off doorknobs if something in the mechanism is stuck. Note the mechanically simplistic and sometimes amusingly ineffective behavior that may supervene when an individual tries to remove soap stuck in a dish. The same essential tendency may, of course, appear in the intricacies of personal relationships (man-wife, parent-child).

Looming large in the gamut of aggressive behavior is that element that reflects the direct effective musculoskeletal responses of the primitive ego. It is all too readily available in a regressive sense, but it is at times still appropriate. In an emergency, a good sailor will sometimes cut a line rather than untie it. If one has a gun, one shoots an armed and immediately threatening assailant. Alexander apparently saved himself for a time by cutting the Gordian knot. However, in the light of steadily increasing cultural complexities and demands and corresponding changes in psychic structure, it is the moral and adaptive nature of things to rely more and more on techniques equivalent to the untying of knots, Gordian or otherwise. That the quality of relationships with one's intimates and one's neighbors profits thereby goes without saying. That this may be at the cost of assignment of the right of individual aggression to the organized military activities of the State, should be recognized and accepted as a further problem.

The Dual Instinct Theory and Aggression

The derivation of libido theory from known biological facts seems, on the face of it, reasonable, although some do not agree (Klein 1969, Panel 1968). The theoretical problem is in the nature of aggression and its relation to the sexual instinct and to the now almost déclassé instinct of self-preservation or, as currently preferred, the "self-preservative instincts" or functions and corresponding ego functions (Hartmann et al. 1949, Schur 1966). Freud once assigned this instinct, or group of functions, to the ego, as pitted against the libido. In this self-preservative grouping, aggression (also flight) inevitably played an important role. In the later theory, the wish to live and the wish that others live became part of the vast complex of Eros, permeating all structures and functions to varying degree and opposed by Thanatos, the death instinct, whose turning outward via the muscular apparatus through the early intervention of the libido constitutes aggression toward the outer world as we know it. In a minor paradox or inconsistency even primary masochism is viewed as bound in the organism as a remainder, through its fusion with libido. Thus, some of the basic impulse to die or, potentially, "to die someone else" remains *in situ* in its own operational dynamics and provides the basis for erotogenic masochism.

My occasional use of "to die" in a transitive sense expresses a semantic-conceptual problem of the death instinct theory which, I believe, has received little attention, probably because of the scalar view of psychic energy that obviates such a problem. Although this view lends itself to elegantly facile metapsychologic manipulation, I am far from convinced that it answers the problems of motive, object relations, conflict, and other decisive human considerations. When a pathologically aggressive child (Rank 1949) receives tender care from a maternal woman and shows some diminution of aggressiveness, one may imagine his using this supply of libido for fusion in order to neutralize his aggression. Or one may think that being given what he has always needed, he is no longer driven to try to extort it, or punish the depriving woman, or even destroy her. I prefer the latter view, although I do not underestimate the resistance to enduring structural change (Beres 1952).

If we put aside the intellectual convenience of a manipulatable store of psychic energy, there is an additional problem: the nature of the transition from the immanent drive to die to the drive to kill. An immediate system of basic alternatives appears. Freud believed that this transition occurs first into musculoskeletal behavior (presumably fighting and, most primitively, the effort to kill). But what is meant? Is one merely "dying" someone else, so to speak, instead of oneself, projective identification, as some might have it? Or is one killing someone else so that one will not die, because one takes his food or usurps the libidinal gratification that his woman provides? There is a vast difference. Killing someone is the struggle to live and to seek gratification in living; "dying" someone is a killing of oneself "in effigy," employing the strange human capacity to merge or interchange or even confuse oneself and the object. Even when one is killing oneself in effigy it is presumably so that one may live, at least in the sense of avoiding the biologic consummation of the drive to die. This would otherwise be merely a blind and purposeless shift of direction. What is the catalyst that initiates the change? Presumably the slight contribution of Eros. I say "slight" because the difference must be postulated as being only this: that the object, who represents the self, dies instead of the actual self—hardly a loving act except in a literally and biologically narcissistic sense. There are, of course, sudden, apparently "senseless" murders, which may be, or at least seem to be, of this type.

Waelder[9] (1956) tends to regard such behavior, or parallel suicides, as indicative of the existence of "essential" aggression. Without detailed understanding of the personalities of such pathological individuals, this remains unconvincing. Most human killing has a discernible motivation of another sort. In the light of aggression theory one might still say that were this path not chosen, the individual would die. But this is self-evidently not true. For example, countless soldiers go home after prolonged periods of active combat. On the other hand, I believe most direct observation would tend to sustain Freud's earlier idea that aggression, however derived, under certain conditions can be turned on the self, for a variety of reasons and through a variety of mechanisms. This idea, as a secondary mechanism, Freud never abandoned.

Whereas aggression was once thought to subserve other impulses such as hunger or sex, it was later viewed as an alternative or equivalent to the wish to die and as consistently opposed to the wish to live, to unite with others, and to reproduce, and as opposed also to the theoretically adjacent or derivative impulses to love in a constructive way. In this very broad sense, to live and to try to live and the corresponding affirmative attitude toward others would be "at war" with the impulse to die (thus kill) and its various derivatives. This conflict has also been conceptualized as the antagonism between the impulse to bring particles together in ever-larger units versus the tendency to break larger units down into smaller units, most specifically to reduce living organisms to their inert elements.

It is, of course, explicit in the dual instinct view that the two drives are of separate origin, even within the cell itself, that they often fuse in various contexts or situations and "defuse" in other situations. This explains many clinical phenomena and provides metapsychological explanations for others. However, there is a special problem in the idea of fusion of two literally and radically opposed drives, because one would expect that they would cancel one another to varying degrees. Especially insofar as destructiveness is thought to be comprehended in aggression, the concept of fusion offends imaginative logic (if one may risk such a rhetorical fusion!). Some technical concept nearer to a compromise would be more acceptable and this would have to include quantitative concessions on one side or the other, not required by the concept of fusion. If a wish to kiss tenderly encounters a wish to bite painfully, one can imagine a compromise issue: a more gentle biting or a more savage kissing. The issue becomes more difficult if one thinks of an underlying libidinal urge toward the lips (to gain and give pleasure, to be in apposition, etc.) versus an essential wish to destroy the lips (the ultimate destruction being, of course, annihilation). In any case the basic theoretical question would remain as to whether aggression is indeed a primary drive of separate origin or whether it is, in its separate manifestation, an instrumentality (albeit one of primitive power and *élan*) subserving various functions including sex. Further, one must ask whether its frequently demonstrable and important relationship to sex — sadism, in the original sense — is not necessarily a fusion but rather an original continuousness, subject to separation as an epiphenomenon of critical importance evoked by the conflicts of object relationship.

Freud based most of his final arguments on the grounds of fundamental biology (1920), although his starting point or inspiration for these arguments was a group of well-known clinical phenomena: the traumatic dream, the traumatic neurosis, the repetition compulsion independent of the pleasure principle, and allied phenomena. The relation of the latter phenomena to the death instinct, as proposed by Freud, has been dealt with in repeated clinical psychoanalytic or metapsychological critiques.[10] While these phenomena may have served to inspire an intuition of genius, they can in themselves be adequately or, in the view of many, better explained by more accessible and demonstrable mechanisms.

Nor is the theory of the death instinct, in its broad and inclusive sense, a pragmatically useful explanation of the clinical phenomena which, while often formidable, are not always relentless (Fenichel 1953). Freud relied heavily on the primary biologic tendency to reject outer stimuli. In regard to more complex organisms in which an essential stimulus is internalized, he relied on the "conservative principle" in instincts: the tendency to strive to restore an earlier condition, a state of reduced tension. This is clearly demonstrable in the sexual climax or in the satisfaction of hunger or thirst. It is much less clearly demonstrable in manifestly and unequivocally aggressive acts, except in the sense of physical exhaustion, most often experienced as disagreeable, or when a specific motive such as vengeance, implemented by the aggression, has been gratified. In the postulated death instinct, the fundamental drive is to reduce all tension to the ultimate state in which the very capacity to develop tension disappears altogether (i.e., in death); here the direction is toward the breakdown of organic compounds into their constituent elements.

The arguments are engaging and sometimes formidable, for they have a broad and general explanatory validity. However they do depart widely from the realm of observable human psychology and behavior, and their position in this sphere is regarded as largely extrapolated from biology.[11] This last fact, as mentioned earlier, does not exclude, but rather obliges, further consideration of relevance in the new setting. Insofar as ordinary observation establishes the fact that there is a tendency to die, that in fact all do die, one is impelled to infer that there is a biological "drive" toward death. But, such a drive would still not necessarily have an equivalent psychological derivative or parallel. And then the fact of regularly occurring, i.e., apparently inevitable death, does not necessarily mean a biological "drive" toward death. We do not know how much of the tendency is essentially ecological or due to other factors to which there are alternatives at least in principle. If air pollution were to continue to increase with predictable effects, I do not believe that these effects could be adduced in support of increased tension in the individual's death instinct. More mundane and accessible factors are obviously of critical importance.

Finally, there is the question whether any type of remote biological principle can be regarded as decisive, even in a metapsychological sense, unless subjected to exhaustive empirical testing. It seems a matter of common sense that the crucial evidence for a basic "wish to die" (and thus "to kill" as related to it), if taken seriously and not just as a theoretical abstraction, should come from the grand panorama of man's development and history, from his actual activities and expressions, and from the detailed and relatively controlled observations of his mental and emotional life afforded by the psychoanalytic situation. While both, in certain references, lend plausibility to Freud's views, neither establishes the fundamental validity of the postulated nature of aggression in either of the primary forms. Historical phenomena can be otherwise explained. The psychoanalytic situation can at times demonstrate accessible reasons (Federn's "rationalizations") for, and mitigations of, suicidal impulses or outwardly directed aggressiveness. At times there may be drastic quantitative reductions of such phenomena and occasionally clinical abolition of their pathologic forms. But these are not always to be explained by fusion or defusion, although an increase in available object libido is usually concurrent. Resolution or reduction of anxiety, resolution of conflicts, increase in control and direction by the ego, and radical changes in motivation are more readily demonstrable.

I have mentioned some of the complexities and obscurities, sometimes fragmentary, and synthetic origins of the very concepts to kill (or to die) or to destroy in their genesis in human psychic life. These considerations can, of course, all be bypassed by assuming that to kill or to die are instinctually "known" concepts in a global sense and correspond to their sometimes instinctive or intuitive recognition in primitive conditions of nature, or what has been so regarded (Lorenz 1966). In other words, the postulated primordial store of aggressive or destructive energy would have primary "knowledge" of the varied and elaborate and sometimes contradictory or contingent directions of the evolution of aggressive behavior or, in a somewhat less platonic view, participate predominantly and decisively in their genesis. However, I do not see convincing evidence to this effect. This is not to exclude the possibility that like other intuitions of genius, this theory may some day be established even in the light of empirical criteria. For some reason the "instinct of self-preservation" is increasingly denied the type of innate "knowledge" that is readily accorded to the concept of primary aggression, at least by implication. I understand the critique (Hartmann et al. 1949, Loewenstein 1940) of the former concept and what is probably the legitimate empirical pluralism implicit in the currently preferred terminology. However, the a priori claim of an "instinct of self-preservation" to holistic organismic construction would surely be at least as impressive as that of an instinct of aggression, or destruction.

Whereas Freud originally viewed sadism and masochism in their descriptive and quite specific meanings, he departed from this ultimately and, in effect, spoke of sadism as the equivalent of aggression or destructiveness (1924), and of masochism as the complementary tendency. True, he never ceased to invoke the fusion with some quantum of libido as a necessary condition of their functional existence, although he recognized the possible existence of quanta not "tamed" by Eros (1924). Freud continued to use the original meanings at times, sometimes mixing the two usages, but the two words sadism and masochism have taken on a dual semantic significance as a result of his later theory. Furthermore, although we have spoken of several possible meanings of aggression that do not, in all instances, form a clear continuum, I think that there is at least room for doubt as to whether a *destructive* impulse, in the strict sense, is the *central* nonlibidinal impulse involved in sadism and masochism, although it does manifest itself as such, at least as a by-product, in the more severe forms of these perversions. The central issue is the causing or seeking of pain or of other forms of suffering as the necessary condition for sexual pleasure. This Freud specified.[12]

Pain is usually a threat to life, however remotely, apart from its immediate significance as experience. However in what is only a seeming paradox, it is also a guarantee of life to both sufferer and perpetrator: only the living can suffer. This is related to the common sadistic "tying" fantasies and impulses: the dead person does not require to be tied. Thus there is something in sadism and masochism as perversions that tends to avoid death. But this could be ascribed to the admixture of libido, which is an essential ingredient. In other words, is the pleasure in another's or one's own pain or suffering a compromise, the acceptance of a way station on the path to destruction? Or is there a specific pleasure in the suffering, perhaps linked to coercion or mastery, which means life? Certainly, the inflicting of pain or its equivalents with the deliberate preservation of life, i.e., torture or threats of torture, is an old and traditionally powerful mode of exploiting living submission. One's theoretical position must certainly influence one's answer. It is quite conceivable that the sexual drive in its essential nature ranges from tenderness through active sexual impulses and behavior, through heightened sadistic or masochistic behavior, to violent destructiveness whose sexual component, as usually construed, is not clearly discernible. The entire series is based on the irredentist urge to reestablish primal unity with the object apart from the reproductive functions or to establish whatever form of mastery most nearly approximates it, up to and including the killing of the object. The phenomenon of clinging, emphasized by Bowlby (1960, 1964) and by Bak (Panel 1956), would be an integral component of this tendency. Any recognizable component or phase of such a series may of course be separable and capable of an independent functional existence, as they usually are in the lives of most healthy adults.

I mentioned earlier certain considerations regarding the profound physiological change involved in birth and suggested that the prototypes of all major strivings are, in that situation, incorporated in two great drives: to live under "terrestrial" conditions and at the same time to restore certain features of intrauterine life as nearly as the situation will allow. One route is by way of the executive instincts: to breathe, eat, evacuate, and thus to achieve "repose." The external amniotic aspects of this need would have to be provided entirely by the hands and bodies of others, primarily the mother. The other route is to refuse the instinctual "challenge" without psychic representation of such refusal: not breathe, not suck, and thus, in effect, die. The difference in relation to the object with regard to the respiratory and nutritive functions, respectively, has been mentioned earlier.

In both instances a libidinal gratification is a corollary of the fulfilment of an urgent life need, aggressively implemented: respiration, essentially narcissistic, and nutrition, object related from the outset. In regard to both, there is evidence that the "drive toward life" under new conditions is not always absolute, total, and unequivocal. This could well be a corollary or partial corollary of Freud's conviction that indifference or hatred toward the object antedates the libidinal orientation. In such prototypes may lie the first dim representations of an urge to die, later a wish to die. Even here, while death may result, the impulse is not clearly toward death except as one postulates the type of innate organismic "knowledge" mentioned before. It is also true that over a much longer period, the failure of adequate overall "supplies" in the sense of holding, handling, voice, and the like, can produce reactions which may represent remote parallels (Ribble 1965). Here, however, there must be a specific etiologic factor, the external failure of a needed gratification that might reawaken the drive to return to an earlier state in which all was gratified automatically. At least, in the intrauterine state, no active effort is required; and the milieu is not full of shapes and forms and noises, changes in temperature, and other stimulating ephemeral or particulate phenomena. The mastery of this mass of sensory stimuli is another form of "work," which under certain unsatisfactory conditions may excite the preference to relinquish consciousness or to return to that relatively homogeneous stable condition experienced in a total organismic sense before birth.

Under "normal" conditions, such wishes play a cyclic role in everyday life. Sleep is both a physiologic and psychologic necessity. Days of rest and passivity and vacations play an allied role. But are these related to the wish to die? Perhaps, for some features of avoidance or relative control of stimuli and the cessation of active effort. These "retreats" are an integral part of life rhythms whose enjoyment greatly depends on the assumption of continued or renewable consciousness, if we judge them to be manifestations of the wish to die, we postulate compromises with the forces of the libido. We cannot, with the data now at hand, convincingly establish that they are indeed such manifestations. If we view them hardheadedly, it is difficult to avoid the fact that like the satisfaction of hunger, such "retreats" are necessary to life. In any case, to view them as directed ultimately toward death is no more or less convincing than our so regarding the tension-reducing end phase of any instinctual striving.

As to the question of aggression (as it is usually construed) in relation to the impulse to die or the acceptance of death, it is a fact of general observation that if a critical biologic balance is tipped, extreme tends to the opposite extreme. Note, for example, the agonal struggle, then death; mania and depressive stupor; catatonic excitement and catatonic stupor; the epileptic convulsion, then sleep; the intractable manic sleeping in a wetsheet pack. The commmon defensive pattern of everyday clinical experience, in which activity or aggressiveness is a defense against excessive passivity, and vice versa, may well be a part of this general phasic pattern. It is not incredible that the decision to live may involve frantic aggressive effort—for example, when one is in a state of near suffocation—or that an agonal struggle against death from disease may resemble combat, without a discernible corporeal adversary. The "death grip" of the drowning man may kill his rescuer without intending other than to save himself, if indeed even this wish is clearly experienced as such.

Do such struggles represent a critical and violent effort by Eros to divert the impulse to die into musculoskeletal behavior, i.e., into "dying others" or, better, having others die instead of oneself? Or are they the archaic prototypic movements from which the purposive efforts to wrest from the environment the wherewithal for life ultimately developed, augmented by the need to overcome a latent impulse to "give in," to die? This is a critical theoretic issue. Certainly there is little if any empirical evidence to support the former supposition, although the theoretical formulation on which it is based has a certain elegance that is intellectually attractive. The latter is, of course, in line with the clearly demonstrable role of aggression in the everyday lives of most human beings.

CONCLUDING REMARKS

I do not regard as proved or as pragmatically useful the concept of primary or essential aggression. The same is true of the origin of aggression in a death instinct.[13] It is, however, my conviction, based on the fragmentary evidence appearing in occasional neonates, with subsequent clinical parallels, that the rejection of the instinctual obligations of extrauterine life can become, in effect, an inclination to die. This latent inclination may reassert itself in the future; for example, in the severe psychotic stupors. Both manifest aggression and libidinal striving represent the urge to live and to gain repose by satisfaction of instinct. Thus they are in effect directed against this inclination, as they are against threats to life and instinctual satisfaction originating in the outer world.

Unlike sex, itself a primary and powerful motivating force, aggression is, with rare pathological exceptions, usually clearly and extrinsically motivated. Motivations are numerous and various. Aggression is often integrated with basic and unequivocal instincts such as hunger (where killing is archaically inevitable) and the various phases of sexuality. In addition it may bear a clearly instrumental or implementing relation to them. In this sense, as well as in its role in the primitive exploration, manipulation and mastery of reality (not to speak of its occasional role in complex intellectual activities), often serve as an important ego function.

Aggression can and does employ primitive preformed somatic and central nervous system patterns, including the powerful affect of rage[14] which confers on it a drivelike quality even when it remains essentially reactive. But it can also be executed in a planned, purposive sense for remote and complicated ends. Indeed, it can be carried out in its most primitive form under orders, as in war or in a legal execution.

Where origins, somatic and symbolic contributions, manifestations (including negative manifestations), and motivations are so numerous and complex, it is difficult to feel intellectually secure with a general and inclusive unitary explanation of individual aggression, assuming that one rejects the concept of a separately originating instinctual drive. Frustration (Dollard et al. 1939) is surely of great importance, and strikingly so in the instinctual sphere. Beyond this, the concept can be adapted to almost anything. To me, the condition of actual or threatened traumatic helplessness, beginning in earliest infancy, seems somewhat deeper and, in some references, of more genuine explanatory value. The two concepts are not mutually exclusive. The conditions of traumatic helplessness include a range from the inner or outer threat of death or castration or overwhelming instinctual or exogenously painful stimulation, to such complex matters as the experiencing of profound insult or humiliation and the need for vengeance.

The role of the drive toward mastery (*Bemächtigungstrieb*) merits a separate and extended discussion. It is mentioned by Freud as one of the major alternative modalities of aggression. In my view, it lies close to the functional center of the aggressive complex in the sense of implementation of any form of wish, by whatever form or degree of force may be required. "Negative" force, e.g., the withholding of food or water, may also be extremely effective and of prototypic significance for a vast category of aggressions equivalent in importance to direct and violent bodily attack. Whereas pain, death, and destruction can be, and too often are, the results of aggression, there is little reason to assume the existence of a primary drive to bring them about for their own sake. It seems rather that they represent ultimate efforts toward mastery. In some instances, where more complex and appropriate activities fail to secure gratification, aggressive solutions are clearly regressive. In others, they may be the outcome of considered judgment as to the most efficient instrumental solutions of a problem. These may be regarded as the "applications upward," so to speak, of the lessons learned from more primitive experience. Needless to say, the latter alternatives, except in a criminal sense, are now the exclusive prerogatives of the state.

NOTES

1. Some of my suggestions in this paper may have been made previously by others. If so, I gladly yield priority. I do not attempt to summarize the work in this vast field, nor to review its literature, in either text or bibliography.

2. I prefer this simple, inclusive, yet unambiguous English word to more technical ones. Buss (1961), for example, speaks of noxious stimuli; he also sets aside the problem of intent in a strictly behavioral approach.

3. Brenner (1971), has a different comment on this passage.

4. Hoffer (1949) notes how seldom infants bite their own hands. I assume that this is a result of experience rather than a primary tendency. Also, see Spock (1965) regarding early control of aggression.

5. In this connection, note Bak's remarks in the Panel Discussion of 1956.

6. Many years ago a gifted patient with a severe oral-narcissistic neurosis had a fragmentary dream: a baby with a placenta in place of a head.

7. The traditional use of pungent smelling salts against fainting suggests the importance of respiratory-olfactory stimulation in establishing or restoring consciousness. No doubt the first postnatal inspiration is in itself a powerful stimulant. However, there is probably considerable individual variation here: smelling salts may operate chiefly as a repetition of this primordial stimulus, the first respiration, or they may be effective because they are like olfactory perceptions of the mother's body. In this connection, see Marcovitz's interesting contribution on addiction to cigarettes (1969).

Worthy of at least brief mention is the phenomenology of the epileptic convulsion with its profound disturbance of consciousness, frequent disturbance of respiration, traditional cry, primitive motor discharge, and at times, more elaborate motor automatisms. (See Freud's 1928 paper on Dostoevski, and numerous other psychoanalytic contributions on epilepsy.) At a higher level of integration, closer to "normality" but still a regressive ephemeral bid for narcissistic-aggressive omnipotence, is the tantrum of childhood (Gellerd 1945). Even more strikingly relevant is the sometimes equivalent phenomenon of breath holding (Kanner 1966).

8. See Freud's pithy summary of erotic mastery in the oral phase, quoted above.

9. Waelder also refers to the behavior of remorseless tyrants like Hitler and Stalin. Again there is no consideration of the detailed personality data, the general importance to human beings of the "symbolic universe" (see Von Bertalanffy 1965), and the corresponding stupendous instrumentalities of destruction available to the individual who attains dictatorial power in a modern state.

10. See for example, Schur's critique in his 1966 monograph on the id.

11. Note Bernfeld's interesting reservation (1935) to the effect that Freud's theory is really an idea brought *to* biology rather than derived *from* it.

12. Freud speaks of the capacity of pain, with other varied experiences, to occasion sexual excitation in early development (mentioned originally in the *Three Essays* [1905, 1924]). He thought of this capacity as the probable physiologic basis for masochism.

13. See Fenichel's view regarding the usefulness of the new theory (1953).

14. The presence of rage usually indicates the primitiveness of provocation and response tendency. It does not, in my view, disestablish the instrumental nature of the potential aggression. See Buss (1961) for a different view. Nor do I separate predation from aggression in the human (Delgado 1967).

REFERENCES

Adamson, J. (1960). *Born Free*. New York: Pantheon.

Barnett, S. A. (1967). Attack and defense in animal societies. In *Aggression and Defense, Neural Mechanisms and Social Patterns*, ed. C. D. Clemente and D. B. Lindsley. Berkeley and Los Angeles: University of California Press.

Beach, F. A. (1949). *Hormones and Behavior*. New York: Hoeber.

_____ (1955). The descent of instinct. *Psychol. Rev.* 62:401–409.

Beres, D. (1952). Clinical notes on aggression in children. *Psychoanal. Study of the Child* 7:241–263.

_____ (1968). The humanness of human beings: Psychoanalytic considerations. *Psychoanal. Q.* 37:487–522.

Bernfeld, S. (1935). Über die Einteilung der Triebe. *Imago* 21:125–142.

Bibring, E. (1941). The development and problems of the theory of the instincts. *Int. J. Psychoanal.* 22:102–131.

_____ (1943). The conception of the repetition compulsion. *Psychoanal. Q.* 12:486–519.

Bovet, P. (1923). *The Fighting Instinct*, trans. J. Y. T. Grieg. London: Allen & Unwin.

Bowlby, J. (1960). Separation anxiety. *Int. J. Psychoanal.* 41:89–113.

_____ (1964). Note on Dr. Lois Murphy's paper: Some aspects of the first relationship. (With reply by Dr. Murphy). *Int. J. Psychoanal.* 45:44–48.

Brenner, C. (XXXX). Some problems in the psychoanalytic theory of aggression.

Burton-Bradley, B. C. (1968). The amok syndrome in Papau and New Guinea. *Med. J. Australia* 1:252–256.

Buss, A. H. (1961). *The Psychology of Aggression*. New York: Wiley.

Cannon, W. B. (1915). *Bodily Changes in Pain, Hunger, Fear and Rage*. New York: Harper & Row, 1963.

Clemente, C. D., and Lindsley, D. B. (1967). *Aggression and Defense, Neural Mechanisms and Social Patterns. Brain Function*, vol. 5. Berkeley and Los Angeles: University of California Press.

Clifford, H. (1896). The amok of Dato Kaya Biji Derja. In *In Court and Kampong*. Singapore and London: The Federal Rubber Stamp Co. and The Richards Press Ltd., 1927.

Darwin, C. (1871). *The Descent of Man, and Selection in Relation to Sex*, vol. 2. New York: Collier, 1902.

_____ (1872). *Expression of the Emotions in Man and Animals*. New York: Philosophical Library, 1955.

Delgado, J. M. R. (1967). Aggression and defense under cerebral radio control. In *Aggression and Defense, Neural Mechanisms and Social Patterns*, ed. C. D. Clemente and D. B. Lindsley. Berkeley and Los Angeles: University of California Press.

Dollard, J., Doob, L. W., Miller, N. E., Mowrer, O. H., and Sears, R. R. (1939). *Frustration and Aggression*. New Haven, Conn.: Yale University Press.

Durbin, E. F. M., and Bowlby, J. (1950). *Personal Aggressiveness and War*. New York: Columbia University Press.

Eibl-Eibesfeldt, I. (1967). Ontogenic and maturational studies of aggressive behavior. In *Aggression and Defense, Neural Mechanisms and Social Patterns*, ed. C. D. Clemente and D. B. Lindsley. Berkeley and Los Angeles: University of California Press.

Federn, P. (1931). Die Wirklichkeit des Todestriebes. Zu Freuds "Unbehagen in der Kultur." In *Almanach der Psychoanalyse*. Vienna: Internationaler Verlag, pp. 68–97.

Fenichel, O. (1953). A critique of the death instinct. In *The Collected Papers of Otto Fenichel, First Series*, ed. H. Fenichel and D. Rapaport. New York: Norton.

Freud, A. (1949a). Aggression in relation to emotional development: Normal and pathological. *Psychoanal. Study of the Child* 3/4:37–42.

_____ (1949b). Notes on aggression. *Bull. Menninger Clin.* 13:143–151.

Freud, S. (1905). Three essays on the theory of sexuality. *S. E.* 7.

_____ (1909a). Analysis of a phobia in a five-year old boy. *S. E.* 10.

_____ (1909b). Notes upon a case of obsessional neurosis. *S. E.* 10.

_____ (1913). Totem and taboo. *S. E.* 13.

_____ (1914). On narcissism: An introduction. *S. E.* 14.

_____ (1915a). Instincts and their vicissitudes. *S. E.* 14.

_____ (1915b). Thoughts for the times on war and death. *S. E.* 14.

_____ (1918). The taboo of virginity (Contributions to the psychology of love III). *S. E.* 11.

_____ (1920). Beyond the pleasure principle. *S. E.* 18.

_____ (1921). Group psychology and the analysis of the ego. *S. E.* 18.

_____ (1923). The ego and the id. *S. E.* 19.

_____ (1924). The economic problem of masochism. *S. E.* 19.

_____ (1926). Psycho-analysis. *S. E.* 20.

_____ (1928). Dostoevsky and parricide. *S. E.* 21.

_____ (1930). Civilization and its discontents. *S. E.* 21.

_____ (1933). New introductory lectures on psycho-analysis. *S. E.* 22.

_____ (1937). Analysis terminable and interminable. *S. E.* 23.

_____ (1940). An outline of psycho-analysis. *S. E.* 23.

Gellerd, E. R. (1945). Observations on temper tantrums in children. *Amer. J. Ortho-psychiatry* 15:238–246.

Greenacre, P. (1941). The predisposition to anxiety. *Psychoanal. Q.* 10:66–94.

_____ (1945). The biological economy of birth. *Psychoanal. Study of the Child* 1:31–51.

_____ (1960). Considerations regarding the parent-infant relationship. *Int. J. Psychoanal.* 41:571–584.

Hartmann, H. (1939). *Ego Psychology and the Problem of Adaptation*, trans. D. Rapaport. New York: International Universities Press, 1958.

_____ (1948). Comments on the psychoanalytic theory of drives. *Psychoanal. Q.* 18: 368–388.

_____ (1950). Comments on the psychoanalytic theory of the ego. In *Essays on Ego Psychology. Selected Problems in Psychoanalytic Theory*. New York: International Universities Press, 1964.

Hartmann, H., Kris, E., and Loewenstein, R. M. (1949). Notes on the theory of aggression. *Psychoanal. Study of the Child* 3/4:9–36.

Hendrick, I. (1942). Instincts and the ego during infancy. *Psychoanal. Q.* 11:33–58.

_____ (1943). Work and the pleasure principle. *Psychoanal. Q.* 12:311–329.

Hitschmann, E. (1947). The history of the aggression-impulse. *Samiksa* 1:137–141.

Hoffer, W. (1949). Mouth, hand and ego-integration. *Psychoanal. Study of the Child* 3/4:49–56.

Kanner, L. (1966). *Child Psychiatry*. Springfield, Ill.: Chas. C Thomas.

Kawamura, S. (1967). Aggression as studied in troops of Japanese monkeys. In *Aggression and Defense, Neural Mechanisms and Social Patterns*, ed. C. D. Clemente and D. B. Lindsley. Berkeley and Los Angeles: University of California Press.

Klein, G. S. (1967). Peremptory idention: Structure and force in motivated ideas. *Psychol. Issues* 5:80–130.

_____ (1969). Freud's two theories of sexuality. Paper presented before the New York Psychoanalytic Society, March 11.

Kubie, L. S. (1967). Multiple determinants of suicide. In *Essays in Self-Destruction*, ed. E. S. Shneidman. New York: Science House, pp. 455–462.

Lehman, E. (1949). Feeding problems of psychogenic origin. A survey of the literature. *Psychoanal. Study of the Child* 3/4:461–488.

Loewenstein, R. M. (1940). The vital or somatic instincts. *Int. J. Psychoanal.* 21:377–400.

Lorenz, K. (1966). *On Aggression*. New York: Harcourt, Brace & World.

Marcovitz, E. (1969). On the nature of addiction to cigarettes. *J. Amer. Psychoanal. Assn.* 17:1074–1096.

Matthiessen, P. (1962). *Under the Mountain Wall: A Chronicle of Two Seasons in the Stone Age*. New York: Viking.

Moore, B. E., and Fine, B. D., eds. (1967). *A Glossary of Psychoanalytic Terms and Concepts*. New York: American Psychoanalytic Association.

Nunberg, H. (1932). *Principles of Psychoanalysis*, trans. M. Kahr and S. Kahr. New York: International Universities Press, 1956.

Panel on the problem of masochism in the theory and technique of psychoanalysis. (1956). *J. Amer. Psychoanal. Assn.* 4:526–538.

Panel on the theory of aggression. (1956). *J. Amer. Psychoanal. Assn.* 5:556–563.

Panel on psychoanalytic theory of the instinctual drives in relation to recent developments. (1968). *J. Amer. Psychoanal. Assn.* 16:613–637.

Peto, A. (1968). The aggressive sources of defenses and adaptation. Paper presented before the New York Psychoanalytic Society, June 11.

Porter, R. T. (1967). Sports and adolescence. In *Motivations in Play, Games, and Sports*, ed. R. Slovenko and J. A. Knight. Springfield, Ill.: Chas. C Thomas.

Rank, B. (1949). Aggression. *Psychoanal. Study of the Child* 3/4:43–48.

Reich, W. (1933). *Character Analysis*, trans. T. P. Wolfe. New York: Orgone Institute Press, 1945.

Ribble, M. A. (1965). *The Rights of Infants. Early Psychological Needs and Their Satisfaction*, 2nd ed. New York: Columbia University Press.

Rosen, I. (1969). A brief summary of the psycho-analytical views on aggression. Paper given at the Symposium on Aggression, International Congress of Psychology, University College, London.

Schur, M. (1966). *The Id and the Regulatory Principles of Mental Functioning*. New York: International Universities Press.

Simmel, E. (1944). Self-preservation and the death instinct. *Psychoanal. Q.* 13:160–185.

Spitz, R. A., and Cobliner, W. G. (1965). *The First Year of Life: A Psychoanalytic Study of Normal and Deviant Development of Object Relations*. New York: International Universities Press.

Spock, B. (1965). Innate inhibition of aggressiveness in infancy. *Psychoanal. Study of the Child* 20:340–343.

Stone, L. (1961). *The Psychoanalytic Situation. An Examination of Its Development and Essential Nature*. New York: International Universities Press.

────── (1967). The psychoanalytic situation and transference: Postscript to an earlier communication. *J. Amer. Psychoanal. Assn.* 15:3–58. *Reprinted in this volume, Chapter 4.*

Tolstoy, L. (1931). *War and Peace*. New York: Modern Library.

Von Bertalanffy, L. (1965). Comments on aggression. In *Psychoanalysis and the Study of Behavior*, ed. I. G. Sarason. Princeton, N. J.: Van Nostrand.

Waelder, R. (1936). The principle of multiple function: Observations on over-determination. *Psychoanal. Q.* 5:45–62.

────── (1956). Critical discussion of the concept of an instinct of destruction. *Bull. Phila. Assn. for Psychoanalysis* 6:97–109.

Weiss, E. (1935). Todestrieb und Masochismus. *Imago* 21:393–411.

Woolpy, J. H. (1968). The social organization of wolves. *Natural History* 77:46–55.

Chapter 12

Remarks on Certain Unique Conditions of Human Aggression (The Hand, Speech, and the Use of Fire) (1975–1979)

This paper, as the title states, crystallized one aspect of my continuing interest in the nature of human aggression. It probes the relation between the distinctively human development of the hand, speech, the use of fire and the origin and specific qualities of human aggression. This construct is enriched by the consideration that the three phenomena are, in my opinion, intimately interrelated both biologically and in their genetic and socio-psychological significance. Most striking is the idea postulated here that the discovery and utilization of fire was an important factor in the emergence of speech.

This paper is, of course, speculative in its most important statements. However, it is the product of years of thought. One can hope that its speculative elements may still bear fruit, by leading to research data of a more convincing nature.

S everal years ago I wrote "Reflections on the Psychoanalytic Concept of Aggression" (1971). In developing a critique of the concept of a primary destructive drive, I suggested an alternative view: that of an essentially instrumental pluralistic mode of behavior of protean character subserving a variety of impulses, including sex and self-preservation. (For a special order of motivations, see Von Bertalanffy 1958 regarding man's "symbolic universes.") That this instrumental complex might represent development from a central archaic ego function — or system of functions — was thought likely. If one viewed the latter as an adaptive distillate from countless millennia of natural selection in central nervous and other anatomicophysiological spheres and then in cultural selection, one would gain my unreserved assent. This, as an evolutionary adaptive phenomenon, I would differentiate sharply from the concept of a primary destructive drive. In the course of these "Reflections," which still represents my essential convictions regarding this important subject, I mentioned in passing three considerations that I regarded as uniquely human: (1) the remarkable functions of the hand, (2) the existence of speech, and (3) the utilization of fire. Obviously, the first two are only unique in a relative sense, i.e., in the sense of their extraordinary development and their indispensable role in the repertoire of human functions. The purposive utilization of fire is, without reservation, also uniquely human. While there are other phenomena which I would like to consider, these three have a special and fundamental importance and are furthermore, in my view, importantly linked with one another. They are of course in each instance dependent not only on local anatomicophysiological developments and even to some degree on ecological factors but — par excellence — on the corresponding developments in the human brain.

I am, from the outset, aware that imaginative reconstruction and synthesis sometimes play an important unifying role in this paper. However, I believe that such processes serve a useful if not indispensable organizing function in relation to clinical psychoanalytic observations, on the one hand, and important data originating in other scientific disciplines, on the other.

THE ROLE OF THE HAND

The critical significance of the hand in man's emergence needs no reiteration. Whereas the more advanced nonhuman primates can use primitive tools or weapons of a sort (the chimpanzee even improvises tools, but largely in captivity[1] and only for immediate gain), the purposive *manufacture* of tools (as against mere chance or ad hoc *utilization*) distinguishes man; and some have thought this faculty the decisive distinguishing trait of genus homo, who then goes on to manufacture tools for the purpose of manufacturing other tools. The remarkable sensory capacities of the hand (both protopathic and epicritic) are to be noted, especially stereognosis. This last, apart from the enriching dimensions it adds to visual inspection, adds immeasurably to the taste and inclusion experiences of the mouth, which continue, however, in the human infant long after the prehensile operations of the hand are established.

One can note, in passing, the relevance of this mouthing practice to John Horne Tooke's (presumed) theory of articulated words, as originating in imitating the forms of objects with the mouth.[2] In the motor sphere, the hand gradually takes over from the mouth all exploratory and aggressive functions except those involved in the actual ingestion of food. The erotic functions of the mouth persist in varying form and degree throughout life. By the same token, in man, the hand is gradually freed of all primitive locomotor function, its tremendously varied and subtle repertoire of movements devoted entirely to the independent exploration and manipulation of the environment. Of special importance is the highly developed capacity for opposition of the thumb, especially the "precision grip" (Campbell 1968, Napier 1962). In the background of this development is the anthropological inference (Oakley 1968) that the use of tools began with life away from the forest. With this ecological shift came a series of critical changes, although uncertain as to precise sequence: the increasingly rigid foot, diminution in tooth size, disuse of the teeth as weapons, and an increase in meat in the diet—the last in contrast to the predominantly plant and insect diet of forest-living anthropoids.

The important erotic functions of the hand need no elaboration; however, its aggressive functions are indispensable. Whereas other essentially carnivorous mammals kill largely with their mouths and teeth, their extremities crudely subsidiary, man relies on his endlessly skillful hands, ultimately armed with weapons, the more versatile substitutes for his teeth (Arlow 1955, Oakley 1968). This phylogenetic "delegation" of certain critical functions from mouth to hand is repeated in the ontogeny of the human infant, both in his bodily adaptations and in the development of his ego. To this last, Hoffer devoted an excellent brief paper in 1949, stressing the critical significance of the first deliberate purposive insertion of the thumb into the mouth. Curiously, this intentional gratification also heralds and epitomizes a major transition of functions. In a sense, the hand reaching out from the vulnerable but exigent body in prehension, perception, warding off, attack, and defense is, with the locomotor system and the special senses, an indispensable somatic contribution to the Anlage of that central psychic organ, the ego. (See Almansi 1964 for a view of the hand and its symbolism from a different approach.)

One may quite reasonably ask why I stress these rather simple facts of natural history. I do not wish to propose a psychogenesis of evolutionary mutations or natural selection, but I do believe that psychological phenomena as such must inevitably be influenced by physical structure and function, apart from the central nervous system, and that this influence includes the distribution of libidinal investment and its discharge as well as the neurophysiologic tensions and energies involved in the impulses, acts, and fantasies of aggression. Further, I think it not unreasonable to believe that psychological processes thus stimulated may significantly influence the development of individuals and, via cultural transmission and storage, find important expression in group behavior without genetic alterations. That natural selection may then operate in relation to the success or failure of individual or group adaptations, thus preserving or obliterating certain cultural instrumentalities (and the capacity for them) is a further not unreasonable supposition. Nor is this an idiosyncratic view (See Darwin 1871, pp. 196–199).[3] At the moment, I have in mind the considerable deployment of primitive aggressive physiological tensions and functions (with corresponding cathexes of the psychic representations of the parts and functions) from the mouth and teeth to the hand and the relative freeing of residual physiologic energies and corresponding cathexes for employment in another anatomically oral function — that of speech. That a highly developed cerebral center with correlated respiratory-laryngeal and hearing capacities is necessary for this function if it is to exceed that of the parrot in significance is obvious. These, however, are not the foci of our interest. By the same token, I do not include in my discussion the self-evidently important shifts in libidinal cathexis.

That cannibalistic fantasies exist in the helpless human infant, at least with the onset of teething (the exact timing, however, is a matter of controversial opinion — see Lewin 1950, pp. 129–134) and are perpetuated in dream, symptom, addiction, ritual, myth, folk-lore, and religion is, I believe, rather generally accepted in psychoanalysis. However, severe taboos attach to primary attack with the teeth, and at least equally severe to literal cannibalism.[4]

Insofar as we are members of the great mammalian class of vertebrates whose very name refers to the phenomenon of breast feeding, it is not surprising that the oral sphere makes fundamental and lasting contributions to human psychology. Its inevitable role in the concept of destruction of the object was recognized and stated by Freud (1905) and the cannibalistic impulse and fantasy related by him to the substratum of phallic sexuality (pp. 159, 198). The specific and obvious relationship of the oral function of eating to the phenomenon of destructiveness has since been stressed by other writers, for example, Anna Freud (1949a, 1949b) and later by Eissler (1971), most recently in his pessimistically prognosticative work "The Fall of Man" (1975). Worthy of special mention is Simmel's 1944 paper in which the devouring impulse is understood to be in the service of the instinct of self-preservation (thus of Eros), although subject to regression to "intestinal hatred." In my own paper on aggression (1971, p. 206), I noted: "The fundamental and concrete position of the oral urges in the concepts of destruction, annihilation, and death should be emphasized. Especially notable is the holistic quality of the oral urge; in it the life-preservative necessities, as well as aggression and libido are tightly integrated." Nevertheless, a "drive" toward destruction and/or death as such, as a primary motivation in this process, however basic the physiochemical and mechanical paradigm it provides, has been and remains, in my view, an ungrounded and unacceptable inference. To interpret the lusty sucking of the infant as a manifestation of "destructive drive" seems no more reasonable to me than to regard the reception of a seed in the earth or semen in the vaginal canal as a destructive process, because they will lose their original forms in new forms of life. That they, like the milk or other food, disappear from view, is not to be disputed. When the subject is aware of painful or destructive impact on an object emphatically perceived as such via complicated cognitive and identificatory processes, "aggression" in its true sense appears.

What is distinctive about humans in this sphere? First, we must note that an important neurophysiologic dichotomy demonstrable in both the natural behavior of other carnivorous mammals (Lantos 1958, Lorenz 1963, Scott 1973a) and in controlled laboratory investigations (Reis 1974) is not clearly evident—certainly not decisively evident—in man or, at the very least, is extremely modified and blurred. I refer to the manifest differences between predation and intraspecific fighting; the former, of course, for food and the second most often motivated by sexual or territorial considerations or problems of food sharing. Not only is behavior different (for example, rage is not integral in the "quiet" stalking and killing of the prey); different physiologic systems are demonstrable; and pharmacological agents that stimulate one system may actually inhibit the other (Reis 1974). I do not mean to suggest that archaic residues are absent in the human, only that the functional and evident facts are quite different.[5]

It is true that herbivorous ruminant animals also address themselves directly to the larger natural environment for food once weaning has been accomplished. This remains a fact even in domestication, where grazing always remains an important alternative source of food. Among carnivorous animals, the learning and then accomplishment of predatory consummation follows on weaning after a relatively brief period of intermediate nurturance. The human infant, as has often been noted, remains helpless for an unusually long period and even in prepubertal childhood, would be largely incapable of providing for himself in an unmodified natural environment.[6] We must also note that even in a hunting culture, where killing and eating remain in close juxtaposition, the food is *acquired* by the hands and their weaponry. The infant's prolonged immediate nutritive contact with his mother, then the remarkably prolonged nurturance within the family, we may assume, are integral with (probably dynamically related to) the intense cannibalistic fantasies and then the subsequent incest complex which characterize human development. (See Hockett and Ascher 1968 regarding the frontal copulative approach, in possible relation to the Oedipus complex.) These two profound impulses and basic taboos are interrelated in individual psychosexual development and in cultural development, the relationship finding circular climactic and conjoint (although developmentally altered) expression in the totem feast (Freud 1913). This is the triumphant celebration of the cannibalistic and incestuous urges and their aggressive symbolic consummation. However, we may assume that anterior to certain complex and mutative processes of development, especially the emergence of the father as a possessive rival and threatening authority, the mother is the first object of (multiply motivated) devouring cannibalistic fantasy and impulse, as she is of all other important strivings, and that she provides the primary flesh-and-blood model for all other living (and nonliving) displacements, maturational substitutes, and symbols. Rage appears in relation to her, inevitably, in the oral sphere and later in sphincter discipline and in varied, sometimes subtle, or nonobvious forms in relation to other, more complicated frustrations, for example, in relation to narcissistic needs or phallic urges or, ultimately, even in the more elaborate cognitive-communicative spheres.

It would be a serious deficit not to mention the prototypic elements and forms of destructive aggression contributed by the sphincter experiences in the reduction and homogenization of material, expulsiveness, violent retention contraction, offensiveness, and disposal as offensive waste. Apart from this content, the prototype of emissive behavior (with its urinary counterpart) would seem to contribute to the rapid development of speech in temporal relation to the beginnings of sphincter control[7] (see Sharpe 1940, Fliess 1939).

In the sense of phase-derived *patterning*, if not of motivation, it is the contribution of this (anal) sphere that now poses the critical danger to species survival. At the very least, omitting the remote reaches of the human (creative or destructive) imagination, the excretory functions provide the basis for those injuries to narcissism so important in later human aggression: insult, contempt, besmirching, soiling, humiliating, and similar activities. Perhaps the simplest expression of this anal motif, supreme in its vulgarity, is the so-called Bronx cheer or raspberry. It is furthermore an important fact that some form of weaning is accomplished in other species, sometimes via severe maternal aggression, as in certain primates (Rosenblum 1974),[8] whereas sphincter training, at least in its stringent and regulatory parentally imposed forms, seems specifically human. Thus, interference with this instinctual freedom adds a specific thrust of object-directed anger to the forms and patterns of excretory and antiexcretory behavior. Although certain animals show considerable spontaneous cleanliness, the cat, for example, the well-developed forms of "housebrokenness" originate unmistakably in their human masters. It is also true that, in the sphincter struggle externally originated by objects who are usually quite clearly differentiated as objects from the beginning of training (loved, hated, or both), the struggle to control impulse is clearly internal, unlike giving or withholding nutrition, and therefore of special potential significance in structuralization.

It would be fallacious, however, to ignore the continuum and overlapping of the anal-urinary and oral spheres in terms of symbolic superimpositions, as cognitive development proceeds (the anus as mouth, for example) or the actual functional continuum in terms of intake, retention, and expulsion. There is also, in my inferential view, reason to assume that sheer overlapping discharge gratification, as such, substitutive, where necessary, is important in the phase continuum, that, for example, free spontaneous evacuation of urine or feces may be augmented in importance if grossly traumatic interference with oral gratification occurs. The opposite may also occur. Such serial overlapping gratification may have an underlying energic significance in the common fantasies and occasional materializations of autofellatio, less common, urinary autofellatio, and coprophagia, apart from their significance in object relations and other more complicated spheres. These views are adjacent to, perhaps implicit in, Ferenczi's conception of "amphimixis" (1924) and the theory of genital orgasm. This, however, slights somewhat the primordial contribution of the oral sphere. Freud, of course, accepted a special place for the cannibalistic thrust in phallic sexuality (1905, pp. 159, 198). I recall very vividly a male patient with a severe oral neurosis who, engaging in *soixante-neuf*, withdrew his penis suddenly (against his partner's wish), in pain and projective panicky fear (indeed incipient larval illusion) that it would be bitten off at the point of his own orgasm.

There is no question of the clear biographical primacy of the oral sphere in the development of object-related aggression, even though certain sensorimotor manifestations in this sphere may occur, in prevailing theory, before clear differentiation between self and object is established. The intimate feeding relationship with the parent continues, however, far beyond this period. The first clear experience of actually biting the human object often occurs in this primary relationship; the mastication of food is inevitably related to mother, directly or symbolically; and the phenomenon of swallowing is, of course, intrinsic in the nursing process from the beginning. Thus, the earliest *pattern* of painful and/or destructive attack with powerful organismic impetus arises in this situation and also, by inference and retrospective reconstruction, the impulse and fantasy of ingesting or incorporating the object (thus causing it to vanish from the exterior world) in a gamut and wide range of possible metamorphoses, healthy or pathological. These may range from literal cannibalism, through melancholia, gluttony (or anorexia), or alcoholism, to the rite of holy communion, or even further to healthy conservative identification with a love object, or (as I see it) to an important (and related) participation in the drive dynamics of speech itself. Throughout this range, the clear-cut patterning provided by the oral sphere includes the current or potential components of organic need, love, and actual object-directed aggression (in the sense mentioned earlier).

Thus, in relation to a special pattern of early nurturance, through the inevitable vicissitudes of separation and training, the human infant finds not only his first love object but also his first object of aggression in the first and most nearly indispensable human object of his life. The aggressive complex includes the devouring impulse, which is then not displaced to prey but to food provided by the same mother.

In further development, it is, to repeat, the much more efficient hands and their weaponry, that take over the functions of attack and killing, even though the initiating impulse derives from hunger. We may assume latent surplus physiological energies and cathexes available in the mouth-teeth-tongue area. Furthermore, to return to an earlier remark, the killed and eaten animal is to some degree inevitably a displacement from the human object, whether in the sense of the multiply motivated cannibalistic infantile aggressions directed toward the mother (who is also the first disciplinarian and the first object of envious rivalry), in the ultimate totem feast, or in the intermediate forms of struggle with an actual adult rival or adversary.

Apart from the primacy of cannibalistic aggression directed ambivalently toward a primary love object and its persistent influence in later development, another factor militates against the clear-cut separation of predation and intraspecific aggression in the human. With the development of the hand and then the even more marvelous establishment of speech and language, the rapid evolution, phylogenetically and ontogenetically, of the larval ego, facilitated by the rich multidirectional associative pathways in the human brain, would tend to disestablish rigidly unified patterns of behavior originally necessary to the gratification of a given specific need (see Hartmann 1948) and render many of their derivatives available to other spheres or to the whole organism, whose multiple instrumentalities are, in turn, available to the first putative need. Thus the "artificial foodstuffs" mentioned by Eissler (1975, p. 597) in the sense of a potent vitamin capsule, may save the life of a starving (but trusting) avitaminotic aboriginal hunter; or the strangling of a small animal for food may enable the survival of a ship-wrecked nutritional chemist, or the successful strangling of an attacking aborigine may save the chemist from a death by violence and give him a chance to supplement a minimal diet with a waterproof case of vitamins salvaged from the surf. That this capacity may lead to a unique survival period of creative brilliancy, or to the destruction of the entire earth, is an evident system of alternatives whose outcome depends, I believe, on infinitely complicated factors, beyond the putative existence of a primary destructive drive.

There are other considerations that may enter into the blurring or disestablishment of the basic aggressive dichotomy. However, since these two considerations require much further thought and study, I shall only mention them at this moment: (1) the perennial character of human sexuality and its relationship to the total instinctual economy and (2) the question of whether a supposed anatomical (intestinal) predisposition toward herbivorous nutrition in earlier anthropoid forms left correlates in central nervous structures and mechanisms persistently different from those of originally carnivorous species.

THE ROLE OF SPEECH AND LANGUAGE

The proximal origins of speech remain obscure. Theories range from those based on mating sounds, on infant babbling, on infant sounds of need, comfort, or discomfort, on warning cries, on various "call" systems, including food (Hockett and Ascher 1968), to the psychoanalytically congenial theory of Sperber

(1912) regarding affective sounds elicited by the use of tools because of their resemblance to primal-scene recollections or fantasies. In any case, despite inborn equipment, speech must be learned by each human infant in the particular variant taught him by his parents. That an urge to communicate exists and is implemented to varying degree and in various ways in all higher (and most other) animals, is probable, although its precise nature and motivation in other animals has been questioned. (See Hockett's 1960 formal analysis and classification of characters (design-features) and modes of communication in man and other animals; also, Edelheit's 1969 detailed summary.) It should be emphasized that in this paper my concentration is on the general position of speech in the evolution and economy of drive psychology and human object relations.

I have mentioned the displacement of certain essential executive functions from the mouth to the hands, freeing the oral structure and its energies for the new adventure of speech. While specifically libidinal elements certainly contribute to this impetus, for example, the progressive renunciation of the pleasure of sucking, it is the aggressive mechanisms in the sphere of "surplus energy" that engage our interest at this moment. Unchanged libidinal elements, even when inappropriate to a given developmental period, more readily find some form of displaced or sublimated expression, manifest or covert, since they are not intrinsically injurious to objects. That the curbing of sphincter freedom, which is roughly concurrent with the rapid acquisition of speech, also contributes important impetus to this function, I have already mentioned. Here again, the angry, destructive, or sadistic tensions that, when excessively stimulated, find their way into clinical disorder give added impetus to the *relatively* free and general emissive gratification of speech, in its benign and orderly fragmentation, storage, and transmission to intact objects of the representation of psychically metabolized inner or outer worlds.

There is a further, larger connection of speech with the combined phenomenology of drives and object relatedness. Since I have elaborated this view in the past, especially in relation to problems of the psychoanalytic situation (1961) and, in passing, to some comments on the general conception of "drives" (1967, pp. 8-10), I shall make only brief mention of it here. This is the assumption that along with the maturational urge to separation and individuation (Mahler 1965), with exploration and incipient mastery of the larger environment, there is a continuing urge to resist this separation, to cling to, or to return to the state of original union with the primal object or to the nearest possible approximation or equivalent of this state. Of the several derivatives, vicissitudes, and implications of this urge, including incorporation, I shall not speak, except in our immediate frame of reference. In its benign representations, it is importantly involved in identification, thus structuralization; in its malignant forms, it contributes to the severest illness. It is basically inimical even to the development of language which, as a "bridge for separation" (Stone 1961), postulates some degree of "acceptance" of the phenomenon of separation. The "preference" would be for silent merger, unity, or incorporation, for which the oral sphere, though

by no means exclusively involved in perpetuity, furnishes the basic and enduring prototype. Speech, then, replaces by an exceedingly complex psychosomatic
function the gradually subsiding bodily intimacies with mother and then provides the most consistent and enduring bridge of communication with her and
with the remainder of the human world. The word *communication,* as I have
suggested in the past (1967), while most directly connected with the idea of sharing, extends in its etymologic affiliation to *communicant* and thus to *communion,* in whose religious meaning the sense of incorporation returns on an ex-
alted conceptual level. I have sought to explain that this continuum-antimony
is of profound importance in the dynamics of the psychoanalytic situation
(1961). (See especially pp. 87–111, including the reference to Fliess 1939.)

One can best express by renouncing the effort, the oceanic position of
language in human existence. In substituting alike for the renounced bodily intimacies and for their primitive incorporative alternatives, a self-elaborating process is initiated of unbounded potentialities in any or all directions, creative or
destructive. For when all is said and done, language is the very stuff of the human
mind, the basis for its social storage and for communication between individuals
and their groups. Edelheit (1969) has suggested that language is the essential
structure of the ego, and a colleague from the field of behavioral (particularly
animal) psychology, John Paul Scott, viewing psychoanalysis from the outside,
has made a closely related suggestion (1973b). I do not accept these proposals
uncritically, for it is clearly evident that the ego exists before spoken language;
but this does not disestablish the profound importance of language in its further development. We no longer regard "conscious and ego" or "unconscious
and id" as coextensive, still less synonymous; but there is a strong and intimate
functional relationship between the respectively compared conceptual entities.
In conceiving of the transition from the unconscious sphere to the preconscious,
Freud stated that there was a shift from the exclusive cathexis of unconscious
images of "things" to their linkage with word symbols (1900). There is also, and
concomitantly, an access to the voluntary (musculoskeletal) nervous system and
the corresponding potentiality (for good or ill) in relation to objects. It is the
"ill" from which they must assiduously be protected; and this in the postinfan-
tile human, in an ego-syntonic sense, would most likely be effected by the hands,
however pressing and unrequited the oral cannibalistic drive representations continue to be. Simmel's observation of many years ago (1942) deserves mention:
in somnambulism it is the locomotor apparatus, not the hands, that is activated.
Both the aggression and the anterior erotic urge toward masturbation are warded
off. Thus the ego and its defensive operations as well as myriad essential executive operations in relation to the outer world are allied with speech and, with
the hand as its principal effector organ against the blind emergence of the unruly
perennial id, more particularly the predatory devouring aggressions whose urgencies find no expression in the everyday economy of life, and remain (in the sense
of unconscious representations) essentially bound to the human object.[9]

Now, it is clear that aggression is not obviated by speech. Just as it is an instrument of love and a limitless multitude of other contents, it can and does mediate threat, provocation, many varieties of subtle attack, and sometimes devastatingly destructive substantive onslaughts. But, in an important sense, it always remains potentially true to one aspect of its original emergence. The Utku Eskimo (Briggs 1970) uses gossip, malicious teasing, and ridicule freely, yet in the course of his struggle with an always dangerous environment, manages to maintain a physically nonviolent community life. The very words *parliament* and even more specifically *parley* testify to a trend of opposition between speech and violence. The young child in our own culture in taunting his verbal perse- cutor, sometimes chants, "Sticks and stones may break my bones, but names will never hurt me!" Anna Freud, only a few years ago (1972) noted the aggres- sive (especially anal) speech tendency in children, remarking on the approxi- mately contemporaneous elaboration of manual aggression in the direction of tools and weaponry. She also noted the crucial pacific alternative historically implicit in speech.

Another aspect of language has found enduring allegorical representation in the Tower of Babel (Genesis 11:1–9). One of the fundamental expressions of group narcissism, entirely apart from its utilitarian expediency, is the fact of common language. Before the days when the world shrank and the "narcissism of small differences" (Freud 1930, p. 114) gave way to the rivalries of great power agglomerations, even a foreign accent aroused suspicion in the unsophisti- cated—or ridicule or, at least, arrogant amusement. If the individual delegates his narcissistic and germane aggressive strivings in concentric assignments, first to his family or clan and finally to the political nation-state, his participation in the official language is a uniquely important badge of "belonging." Where groups have struggled to achieve statehood, an early emotionally charged act of sovereignty is the establishment of an official language, sometimes the revival of an ancient language, as in Ireland and Israel. Sometimes there is intense con- troversy, even rioting, within a country about the official status of minority lan- guages (as in Belgium or Canada), not dissimilar to clashes over religion (and, indeed, not unrelated in the unconscious), even when economic intercourse and external affairs are not vitiated by maintenance of the official language and in fact may be heightened in efficiency by linguistic homogenization. In reference to this, one should note the inevitability of varying degrees of dialect formation, even when nationalistic historical motivations are minimal or nonexistent. Fur- ther, in response to the conception that linguistic differences hinder mutual un- derstanding and thus allow the breeding of irrational animosities leading to wars between nations, efforts have been made to create universal languages utilizing elements from the major existing languages. There have been several attempts; some still persist; I think Esperanto is the best known. There is no evidence, however, that such efforts have really taken root. Whatever practical advantages a synthetic language might possess, it will not be accepted by those who cling to their "mother tongue."

Universal languages have been adopted as *second* languages by those who needed them: Latin, at one time, by scholars and scientists; French by diplomats and elite "society"; at present, whatever major language best suits the occasion, often English. However, these are ad hoc matters, in no way contravening the repetitive spontaneous thrust toward differentiation of language, putatively imposed of mankind by the Lord (in connection with simultaneous dispersion) in punitive counterattack for the arrogant heavenward aspiration of the Tower of Babel. This growing symbol of mankind's united monolingual strength could reach into Heaven and there threaten divine sovereignty. In terms of manifest symbolism, the analyst cannot but interpret this as the counterattack directed against the conspiring brothers by the jealous father of the primal horde; indeed, I believe that this anthropological postulate is strongly in evidence in this sacred myth. The anticipated totem feast is confounded by the wily strategem of the deity. Furthermore, the aspiring phallic symbolism rests on the important consideration of linguistic unity, i.e., in the sense of earlier passages in this paper, on oral fellowship and on having eaten together. (Note the importance of "breaking bread" together; of the laws of hospitality; and also their hypocritical exploitation for murder!) To reduce this forthwith; brothers who have nursed at the same breast, experienced the same cannibalistic transmutation of impulse, and then integrated these impulses in their phallic oedipal strivings, the lethal violent aggression displaced from mother to that unregenerate rival, the father, must accept the incest taboo and rival one another—or in alliance with one another, kill and devour the tyrant (Freud 1913). In the sphere of language, evolved in part to protect essential objects against these catastrophic developments, (my apologies for the teleology, of course!), there remains the secondary narcissistic-aggressive pride of difference. "You and I have different mothers; we have not nursed at the same breast; we speak different languages (or dialects)!" Thus patricide is, at least for a time, warded off.[10]

Yet the fundamental, if warded-off hatreds take origin within the family, between those who have been suckled by the same woman (albeit usually at different times!) or who desire the same woman in the phallic sense. It is then perhaps not an accident that when insoluble tensions within the body politic lead to regression and civil war, the ferocity of fighting seems to exceed, if anything, that of international wars. Persons of the same language, sometimes ethnically identical, fight the primordial intrafamilial battles in primitive fury. The American Civil War, the Spanish Civil War, the Vietnam War all are relatively recent examples of this phenomenon. (By the same token, the fate of deposed rulers in revolutionary upheavals often has a startlingly summary or brutal quality. Note the fate of the last Russian tsar or of Mussolini.)

THE ROLE OF FIRE

The ubiquitous, perennial, and protean position of fire in human history (practical, symbolic, mystical) is so obvious and compelling that I shall not waste the reader's time with a catalogue. We are interested in its role in human aggression, more particularly its functions in the psychology of aggression. Fire is, of course, an explicitly cultural phenomenon in its purposive sense. There is no evidence of a native readiness to learn the techniques of its genesis, as in the case of language. Aboriginal methods are indeed extremely laborious. Yet its use goes back into the dim recesses of antiquity; and it is so widespread that there is now no reason to believe that there are any human groups who do not use it, although it is said that certain very primitive groups "keep it," while not knowing how to produce it, for example, until recently, certain Andamese Islanders (Reclus 1910, Freud, 1932, Spier 1971). It is evident that whether the employment of fire spread transculturally or arose independently in many different parts of the world, it has been integrated into human individual and social processes in a manner and degree that give it a psychological position of a rank second only to the actual organic functions and equivalent or nearly equivalent to that of its symbolic complement and antithesis, water. Some inquiry[11] regarding fire, in readily available sources (for which I am indebted to Professor Ralph Holloway of Columbia) would suggest that all Upper Palaeolithic peoples were fire users (Oakley 1961, 1968). Earliest Palaeolithic users probably obtained it from natural sources (even spontaneous coal fires, likely in the case of Sinanthropus) and then sought desperately to preserve it. Much earlier use (Dart's "Australopithecus Prometheus") has not been substantiated by more detailed chemical examination (Oakley 1961, pp. 176–177). Regular hearths appearing in Middle and Upper Palaeolithic remains indicate that *most* Neanderthal and *all* Cro-Magnon peoples were fire producers, with the necessary devices a part of their regular equipment. It seems reasonably reliable to suppose that these men were largely carnivorous (evidences, for example, in the animal bones found with Peking Man). One thing seems reasonably certain: that fire making followed on tool production, probably at the outset from the accidental sparks in the use of stone. The developments beyond this very slight effective, highly undependable method would take us too far from our immediate purposes (not to speak of our sphere of competence).[12]

Freud's early remarks on this subject (1932) stressing the intense urinary seductiveness of fire for the male, including "homosexual competition" and deriving from this premise the woman's role as "guardian of the hearth." Freud's wit, scholarship, and acuteness were, as usual, present, but they left more room than usual for a deeper understanding of the subject at hand. Freud saw the stolen gift of Prometheus as conditional on the control of the urinary urge. (Let us, however, also note that Prometheus' punishment was to have his liver eaten by vultures.)[13] That this view was later elaborated by an insight into the representation of sexual passion by fire (including, specifically, the phenomenon of erection), the (regressive) equivalence of enuresis to masturbation, and finally, the idea that the individual extinguishes his sexual arousal with his own water brought us closer to our habitual plight of having little more to say. That "little more" is, however, worth opening for consideration.

First, a thought about the actual everyday use of fire: ranking high among its many functions is its use for cooking. This, in its general capacity to soften food, serves to diminish the necessity for the violent effort involved in the mastication of raw food, and — in line of our interest — specifically raw flesh (Stone 1961, pp. 90–91). It has also been mentioned that man's migrations were facilitated by his ability to cook and eat otherwise indigestible food[14] (Wallace, quoted by Darwin 1871, p. 195). (This would strongly complement the special carrying capability of the hands — so necessary to family life and further social extensions.) There is also, with cooking, an alteration in the taste, texture, and appearance of flesh and blood from those of the raw state. Perhaps the frequent wish that the food be warm represents a paradoxical (disguised) clinging to the love of freshly killed animal food (see Oakley 1961, p. 185, who also refers to Coon 1955, Frazer 1931, and Hediger 1950; also in reference to sun drying, Lévi-Strauss 1964, p. 71). I recognize that raw beef is sometimes eaten as a delicacy in the West, as are raw clams and oysters, that the Japanese are fond of raw fish, and that certain peoples, notably the Eskimos, often eat raw flesh. Yet all cook animal food much of the time, and most cook it all of the time. ("The exception proves the rule?") Since variations in taste are the rule in human gastronomy, it is not illogical to assume that other deeper, more nearly universal elements are involved, for example, that the disinclination to fragment food violently with the teeth and jaws and simultaneously the wish to alter its raw flavor are related (whether anteriorly or concurrently) to (1) the relinquishment of the direct aggressive utilization of the mouth and teeth; (2) the increasing delegation of such functions to the hand, in immediate or remote representations or expressions (in this case, following the hunt and its immediate operational sequellae, fire and cooking); (3) the increasingly severe and spreading taboo on cannibalism, with displacements to include certain domestic animals; and (4) the concomitant increasing elaboration of the faculty and function of speech in relation to the prodigious development of manual functions and the food-altering uses of fire.

Fire is, par excellence, a destructive force of awe-inspiring effectiveness. Before he ever committed it to his own purposes, the occurrence of forest or grass fires due to lightning or the existence of volcanic lava or other uncontrolled agents may well have terrified primitive man and created panic, as it still does in other animals. (I would not rule out the fear-stimulated relaxation of the urinary sphincter on this basis!) Thus rage — devouring, destructive rage — is a significance of fire, different from, if not totally unrelated to, sexual passion. In the latter, including the phallic thrust, it may well be integrated in a sort of "change of function" (Freud 1905). (Also, see my 1954 study of a linguistic correlate of this process.) Alongside its myriad benign uses in cooking, heating, lighting, metallurgy, and other arts, the application of fire's destructiveness appeared not only in individual incendiarism but in the burning of crops and dwellings in warfare and in the use of incendiary missiles before the advent of gunpowder. Ultimately, the direct application to human flesh in the burning alive of heretics, witches, and other putative malefactors completed a circle to which the canons of righteousness could give enthusiastic assent. For there is no unconscious human impulse to which fire gives symbolic expression so thoroughly as it does to the ravenous oral, devouring impulse. Almansi (1953), Arlow (1955), and Joseph (1960) have written of the oral symbolism of fire, with illustrative case material and/or material drawn from religious ritual.

Certain important factors (and inferences) can be mentioned again: There is a residual phylogenetically strong propensity toward the devouring of flesh (*fressen* vs. *essen*) in humans. The human infant is exposed to the breast for a relatively long period, and his earliest intense frustrations, ranging from an irreducible ("ideal") minimum to very severe, occur in this connection. Further, he continues to receive food from maternal hands for several years, and in a not inconsiderable fraction of instances is exposed to the spectacle of a succeeding nursing infant. Still further, he is thereafter not only not committed to the predatory hunt with mouth and teeth but also suffers severe punishment for the aggressive use of his teeth. That he is himself the possible target of (unconscious) adult oral ravenousness we sometimes overlook (see Rascovsky 1972). Note certain sacrificial folkways of "practical expedients" (for example, female infanticide) or, on a high level of literary achievement, Swift's "Modest Proposal" regarding the children of the poor (1729). Or, as possibly related, the Utku Eskimos' dental execution of white fish, eating of live warble-fly larvae and neurologically alive fish that "jump in the mouth" (Briggs 1975, p. 150).

My hypothesis is that the cannibalistic devouring impulse (varying in intensity) is one of the earliest and most powerful dynamic forces of the human unconscious, that indeed it may have constituted one of the fundamental conditions (if not *the* decisive condition) for its development, with the concurrent establishment of speech and the verbal preconscious in the setting of progressively exigent social organization. (See Lantos 1958, p. 119 for a related, although not identical, interpretation.) I wish to mention certain facts — or "quasi facts" — which must be brought into juxtaposition with such a hypothesis. It has been suggested (Oakley 1961) that man, emerging from the forest, had small teeth (before or after tool making?) better suited to a plant diet: further, that, to this day, his long intestinal tract would seem better suited to such a diet. Yet gorillas, it is mentioned, change to a flesh diet in captivity, with corresponding change in intestinal flora and fauna, and begin to prefer it (Oakley 1961, p. 190, referring to Reichenow 1920). It is also hypothesized that man's emergence from the forest was in hunger, probably because of drought affecting the vegetation, with a correspondingly increased orientation toward animal food. With this emergence came the relatively rigid foot,[15] the erect posture, and the improved "precision grip" of the hand (Napier 1962). It has also been noted that the vegetable diet required much more time and energy spent in gathering and chewing than the devouring of a "kill" for comparable nutrition.[16] Yet the "kill," as a hitherto living animal "like oneself," different from the earlier vegetable diet, must have had a profoundly different psychological impact on early hominids, as it does on us, heightening the need for elaboration of massive defenses. There would then also be the exigent problems of the hunt itself, followed by the problems of skinning and dismemberment. The latter, in some instances, would be even more stimulating to the elaboration of tools than killing as such. Carrying, so important in social development ("sharing"), as mentioned before, in itself depended on the progressive development of the hand. In any case, I think it is fairly generally agreed[17] that the emergence of true homo sapiens was conditioned by his emergence from the forest, with the use of and then manufacture of tools, with the use of and then actual making of fire, with an omnivorous (but, importantly, *carnivorous*) diet, and, of course, at some time still obscure in relation to these phenomena, the appearance of speech. In this connection, I think it important that our psychoanalytic knowledge of modern man, while it should be used cautiously, should not be renounced or disqualified in trying to reconstruct or understand remotely past events or to contribute to hypotheses, any more than one should dispense with chemistry in trying to determine whether bones were indeed burned a few hundred thousand or more years ago (even granting that the chemist's material is somewhat more tangible!).

Fire as an existing destructive force subject to human control could readily take its place as the materialization of a universal projection, investing a real and potentially terrifying external threat alongside the oral monsters of folktales, of childhood (sometimes adult) fantasy and dreams, of dragons, and deities demanding sacrifice. This could coexist with and reinforce the even more primitive terror, awe, and need to placate the prepurposive, uncontrolled natural force (possibly an ingredient of sun worship?). Flaubert's detailed description of the live sacrifice of children in *Salammbô* (1862), set in ancient Carthage, is a brilliant literary presentation of horror. Thus the "burnt offering," the sacrifice in fire, is integral in the conception and construction of ancient alters, the very word thought by some to be akin to the Latin *adolere* (to burn up).[18] The symbolism of fire in this reference has been abundantly studied, including the papers of our colleagues mentioned before (Almansi 1953, Arlow 1955, Joseph 1960).

To return to the more strictly psychoanalytic realm: there is little doubt that the most common dreams connected with fire are enuretic dreams. Yet enuresis itself has several known determinants, probably some that are not well understood. And there is a priori difficulty, at least for me, in accepting—beyond the concise formulation of a common clinical fact—the idea that dream urination is merely the metaphorical dream extinction of a sexual impulse. It surely is often a regressive infantile substitute satisfaction. For practical purposes, this is often the useful view. In some instances, however, it is possible that the impressive physical phenomenon of fire is invoked solely as a dream mechanism to "permit" the urination based on other than sexual causes—for example, the rebellion against harsh sphincter training or the regression invoked by rivalry with a baby sibling or the girl's penis envy expressed in urinary freedom. In these last instances, however, one skirts closely the implicit elements of oral rage. Further, it should be mentioned that dreams of fire can occur without enuresis, with the destruction of property and the danger to life the clear and essential references. I have seen this in a few patients, for example, two in connection with infantile oral rage dealt with principally by reaction formation or projection, another in a patient with more than moderately severe depression, and still another in a situation of intense extramarital temptation stimulated by "sibling rivalry" (with the subject's own children!).

In any case, there are important indirect connections between urination and the fire of orality, beyond the frequent dream phenomenon and proximal assumptions. Long ago, Abraham (1924) spoke of the frequency of urination often observed in oral characters and, with it, the tendency to conspicuous talkativeness. Also, the fantasy of urinary autofellatio does occur, although rarely in an undisguised conscious form. For reasons unknown to me, the manifest fantasy, not to speak of the fact, is less common than coprophagia (except possibly as an object-related frank perversion). One may postulate quite reasonably, that it often has a warded-off antecedent relationship with the very frequent seminal autofellatio fantasies of male adolescence, for which masturbation is a phylogenetically prepared successor (again, the mouth-hand sequence). I have no clinical knowledge of any phenomenon equivalent to autofellatio, i.e., autocunnilingus, in the female. Occasionally, kissing or sucking of the arm, less often the breast, may be inhibited equivalents. Tasting or smelling the masturbation finger is not infrequent. The dream of urinary autofellatio is rarely manifest and usually disguised in terms of beer or wine (occasionally, "homemade") or their equivalents. There were two males in whom such dreams were common. One suffered from a chronic peptic ulcer and had had severe enuresis in childhood, and the other suffered from (coital) ejaculatio reservata (Bergler's 1937 oral aspermia?) and a history of manifest aggression on the breast in infancy. I believe that urination, especially enuresis, can also "put out the fire" of ravenous oral rage and aggression and probably, in an anticipatory sense, by invoking a self-feeding or thirst-quenching fantasy, seek to obviate the "fire" in the first place.[19] Probably, most addictions have certain parallel elements, except that the actual problem of "supply" in relation to hard drugs tends to repeat the original vicissitudes of deprivation in horrible pathological form. In the case of smoking, which still remains a socially accepted addiction almost universally, the self-placation of one's oral destructiveness is probably very important, the more since one carries a supply in one's own pocket and, further, destroys with fire and inhales (then exhales) the object in alien and expendable form over and over again. (For emphasis on the respiratory elements as such, see Marcovitz 1969).[20] That one also risks destroying oneself as an end result of the repeated process is a relatively new confrontation.

SUMMARY

I have tried to single out for study, from the limitless complexity of human physical and mental life, three decisively fundamental elements that, individually and synergistically and in biological and psychological spheres, have contributed importantly to the distinctiveness of human aggressive behavior and psychology and their transformations. These are (1) the remarkable development of the human hand, (2) the primordial role of human speech, especially in drive economy, and (3) the purposive utilization of fire. The pervasive dynamic importance of human orality and its vicissitudes in relation to its phylogenetic background, has been stressed throughout. In this connection, the revolutionary role of fire has been brought into drive-economic relationship with the other two critical human instrumentalities. It is suggested that in its myriad roles, ranging from cooking to the prodigious function of sacrifice in human history and psychology, the decisive position of the role of fire in the emergence and development of homo sapiens may conceivably include a significant, "overdetermining" position among the multiple elements conditioning the appearance of human speech and language.

NOTES

1. The occurrence in captivity is thought associated with being on the ground, thus freeing manual energies from locomotor functions (Oakley 1968). This energic element in initiating or stimulating functions is relevant to the general thesis of this paper.

2. I say "presumed" in self-reference, because I have not, to this date, been able to verify this theory in examination of Tooke's published work, nor indeed in a few biographical studies or appropriate commentaries of his time. However, I may still find it in a quotation by one of his contemporaries. Tooke's idea was mentioned to me in casual conversation many years ago by that formidable scholar, the late Dr. Bertram Lewin.

3. It is frequently stated that the greatest (adaptive) growth of the brain occurred from the time of Pithecanthropus to about forty thousand years ago. Since that time, there has been no significant anatomical change. Yet the efflorescence of human culture has been prodigious in that period. This is most reasonably attributed to cultural rather than biological factors. See, for example, Vallois 1961 or Hockett and Ascher 1968.

4. This statement applies to our culture and to those which resemble it in certain basic essentials. The exceptions, reservations, rituals, mythologic representations, and detailed specifications are numerous and extremely interesting. However, we can not deal with the subject here; and the exceptions do not invalidate the fundamental and general importance of the taboo.

5. Dr. John Flynn of the Yale Medical School, an authority on this subject, told me some time ago (in response to my inquiry) that this dichotomy has not been satisfactorily demonstrated in the human or in monkeys; however, he believes that it probably exists. There has not been sufficient work. In any case, he feels that social factors could strongly influence such functions in humans. Because of the complexity of this subject, I recently made further inquiry to which Dr. Flynn responded as follows:

> There are two aspects to the matter you raise. One has to do with the difference between predation and intraspecific fighting. I maintain, and I believe the literature increasingly supports my position, that similar mechanisms are operating in the case of intraspecific fighting, particularly killing without eating. It seems, further, that the influences

of hunger on killing even where there is eating are not simple but rather complex. While starvation can influence the incidence of killing, once killing has been undertaken, the further increase brought on by hunger is not the major determinant of the behavior.

With regard to the second matter, whether or not the same mechanisms are present in human beings and in lower animals, as I indicated, there is very little evidence supporting the presence of such central nervous mechanisms, either in the human being or in the monkey. The work with reference to the mechanisms in monkeys has been carried out by Adrian Perachio and Marjory Alexander. Again, while I assume that these mechanisms are present in Man, I would see them as subject to much greater control in Man as a result of the social inhibitions imposed on Man and probably also his cognizance of the dangers he experiences in behaving in an unrestrained fashion [Personal communications 1975, 1977].

In still further explication by telephone, Dr. Flynn, whose classifications of behavior are more complex than most, said that he thought the similarities between the two broad categories of behavior definitely outnumber the differences, especially in the occurrence of killing without eating. Furthermore, based on his extensive laboratory investigations with cats, it is his opinion that "rage" is associated with "defensive attack," i.e., attack occurring in response to threat. (Author's note: See germane observation in Lorenz 1963).

One might infer from these observations and opinions that the blurring of a classical dichotomy in primates may have a longer evolutionary history than is usually supposed. Findings in other fields, in other references, may have a similar thrust. See, for example, the observations of predatory behavior with meat eating in chimpanzees, which I shall mention again later (Teleki 1973, Marler 1973). Or note the evidences of pebble tools with the oldest known "ape-man," discovered by the Leakeys at Olduvai (see Washburn 1960, Napier 1962).

6. The interplay between evolutionary biology, sociology, and psychology is exquisitely illustrated and expressed in this phenomenon. The earlier birth of the human infant (which cannot cling as ape babies do) is attributed to narrowing changes in the maternal pelvis associated with increasingly efficient bipedal locomotion, while ultimately larger brains are required for tool use (see Washburn 1960, pp. 179–180; Napier 1967, pp. 121–122). Further, then, the prolonged period of nurturance not only exacerbates the conflicts of which we speak, for good or ill, but also establishes the augmented period of education, for example, in speech (see Hockett 1960, p. 190).

7. As an "interdisciplinary" fragment, even though it does not include the specific dynamic formulations on which I base my views, note Hockett and Ascher's (1968, p. 225) mention of a hypothetical anal alternative in the evolution of speech.

8. Dr. Leonard Rosenblum (primatologist, Downstate University Medical School) also told me, in response to my question some four years ago, that sphincter training as such achieves little or no importance among other primates because of the intrinsic avoidances provided by arboreal existence. On further—more recent questioning—Dr. Rosenblum added the following statement: "To the best of my knowledge, although some suggestion appears in the literature that some types of monkeys can, under human control, be toilet-trained I know of no systematic work in this area. Furthermore, under wild conditions although some minor constraints on elimination might exist, these have never been documented, and indeed there is little reason to believe that they play an important role in the life of nonhuman primates. Furthermore, this fact appears to apply equally to those primates leading a primarily arboreal or terrestrial existence" (Personal communication, 1977).

9. It may be objected, at this point, since I speak of the ego, that speech is an autonomous ego function, arising independently of conflict (Hartmann 1939). I do accept this with regard to the participation of the central and peripheral nervous system. But I still incline to the original psychoanalytic view (Freud 1923, p. 25) that the ego is a partially derivative development from the id; and I do not view the "structures" as discretely bounded from one another, under ordinary circumstances. I would call attention, as a matter of interest, to Waelder's footnote quotation from Freud (1960 p. 84), expressing a preference for Rembrandt's style, for "more darkness," in this particular reference. Waelder himself emphasized that clear differentiation of structures was manifest only in conflict.

10. Throughout this brief passage, I have followed original psychoanalytic tradition in that the sexual references follow the basic pattern implicit in the Oedipus Complex. This is simply a matter of brevity and rhetorical simplicity. Needless to say, in the sense that we nowadays refer (loosely) to a girl's "oedipal conflict," both sexes are included in the broad pattern of child-parent and sibling struggle. We know that the mother is also the girl child's first object; and that — for a complicated series of biological, psychological, and sociological reasons — the father usually emerges as her principal love object and the mother as her rival.

11. It would be elegantly supportive (although not essential) to my own hypotheses to establish the use of fire as antecedent to the appearance of genuine speech. One may of course only speculate that this was so. Two complementary quotations from Darwin (1871, pp. 278–279), one a reference to Sir. J. Lubbock, could be interpreted in this direction. Lubbock believed that the art of making fire was probably already discovered before man wandered from his original birthplace. Wallace too (Darwin, p. 195) included fire-making among the techniques permitting mastery of colder climates. On the other hand, as if in complementary dialectic, Darwin himself (p. 279) states: "From the fundamental differences between certain languages, some philologists have inferred that when man first became widely diffused, he was not a speaking animal; but it may be suspected that languages far less perfect than any now spoken, aided by gestures, might have been used, and yet have left no traces on subsequent and more highly developed tongues. Without the use of some language, however imperfect, it appears doubtful whether man's intellect could have risen to the standard implied by his dominant position at an early period." (See Hockett 1960; Hockett and Ascher 1968; and Kolata 1974 for references to the importance of "duality" for true human speech, the human laryngopharyngeal sound tract as opposed to that of the ape, possibly to that of the earliest manlike forms [Australopithecus?] and the recent controversial research regarding the Neanderthals.) Efforts to time the appearance of speech, inferentially, through the anatomical study of cranial cavity configurations have apparently led to conflicting results. One scholar (Vallois 1961) asks: "Must it be inferred from this that Neanderthal man, like us, had articulate speech, while the australo-pithecines, like the apes, did not speak?" I would wish to say "yes". But this would reflect only speculative enthusiasm rather than knowledge! Vallois (1961, p. 221) is keenly aware of and explicitly states the serious limitations of research conclusions based on the scrutiny of endocranial casts. The fact is that even the meager outline sketch presented here concerning probabilities in the prehistory of fire is subject to reservations at every point. Demurrals regarding relatively accepted ideas concerning prehistoric man continue to appear in current scientific literature. The lineages of early hominids have been reinterpreted, with controversy as to whether they were a single stock or were two, of whom one increased only in total size then died out, whereas the other, with increas-

ing proportionate brain size and diminishing size of teeth, became the ancestor of man. Only their very great antiquity and the very early use of primitive tools seems generally accepted. (Kolata 1975). (For Bed I at Olduvai, a maximum date of one and three quarters million years is seriously proposed [Hockett and Ascher 1968].) The homogeneousness of the Neanderthal group has been questioned, and the problem of their extinction related to their putative *lack* of language, in the sense that characterizes modern man (Kolata 1974—a paper drawn to my attention by Dr. Norman Margolis—discussing the work of Lieberman and Crelin). This is based on anatomic reconstructions thought to establish the inadequacy of the continuous vocal tract for the formation of certain vowel sounds necessary for complex speech. (Also, see Hockett and Ascher [1968] regarding the sound tract in apes.) One must leave the evaluation of such reconstructive research to experts in the field.

In any case, the assumption, beginning at least with Darwin, that hominids had some primitive form of vocal communication, supported by gesture, when they began their wanderings, although it was probably not langauge in the sense that characterizes homo sapiens, is reasonable, since a type of communication of this sort appears to exist in the anthropoid apes.

12. I offer the following mixed reference, because I believe the three special themes of this paper to be intimately interrelated. A paper about the origin of speech, which I believe has been somewhat neglected, is that of Hans Sperber (1912). After reviewing the essential theories of the time, Sperber gave an important place to the mating call (*Lockruf*), but then even further, to a phenomenon which, he thought, lent itself to the great variety of directions, and the inclusiveness of the functions of speech. He referred to the sexually tinged affective (vocal) ejaculations of primitive man in his utilization of tools, based on the resemblance of these processes to coitus. In relation to the discovery of fire-making, I have always been fascinated by a passage in Melville's *Typee* (1846), in which Kory-Kory makes a fire with a stick in a grooved wooden board to ignite the author's pipe. The violence of exertion, the rapt attention, and the orgasmlike climax are striking. Perhaps this detailed description of a great author has something to tell us about the inspiration and form of efforts, directed to a practical end, thousands and thousands of years ago. The passage may be found in any edition of *Typee* so I do not quote it here.

13. I am indebted to Dr. Vivian Fromberg for directing my attention to a story concerning the childhood of Moses and for providing the reference to it. Moses, suspected of dangerous ambitiousness in relation to Pharaoh because he placed Pharaoh's crown on his own head, was subjected to a trial of childish innocence, at the initiative of the court advisors. On presentation of a gold cup (in another version, an opal) and a live coal, Moses was about to reach for the gold cup; but the angel Gabriel guided his hand to the live coal, which he grasped, burning his hand. He then put it into his mouth, burning it. He was thus "acquitted"; but he was left with the speech impediment, well known in his biblical career. This story of one of our greatest culture heroes juxtaposes and combines the three elements with which I deal in this brief essay. Whether of vague and anonymous folk origin or of individual creation, it is in my view based on profound intuitive perception of certain archaic psychic relationships (Ginzberg 1910; Midrash 1951).

It is also true that Moses' final punishment (to die without having entered the Promised Land) is assigned to his having *struck* the stone to bring forth water, instead of having *spoken* to it as directed by the Lord (Numbers, 20; Deuteronomy, 34). (In this connection, please note the association of stammering with the outbreak of tragic violence in Melville's *Billy Budd* [1924].) Both Moses' childish usurpation of the crown and his final punishment are mentioned by Freud (1939). However, the "ordeal of fire" does not appear. This was not, of course, Moses' last confrontation with fire. (See his first meeting with the Lord, in the burning bush [Exodus, 3:2].) Are such cornerstones of our elaborate culture entirely dissociated from the Bushman's fire dance? (See Van der Post, quoted by Oakley, [1961, pp. 185–186n].) Note especially the scooping up of burning coals into his mouth, with the attempt to swallow, by one frenzied dancer.

14. On hearing this paper, the late Dr. Sidney Kahr mentioned to me the idea that cooked flesh could be carried longer than raw flesh and still maintain its edibility. It is my recollection that Dr. Kahr referred this to Levy-Bruhl. Although I have not yet found the passage, the idea nevertheless retains its intrinsic merit.

15. This minimal passing reference does scant justice to the studies of this evolution from the bipedal jog of certain anthropoid apes, possibly early hominids, to the striding gait of modern man (see Napier, 1967).

16. It has been mentioned that the relative "idleness" of the mouth resulting from this change may have led to experimentation with speech. That such change may have given an impetus to the development of speech prior to the conditions I have emphasized may indeed be true. However, the energic consideration is related, and this hypothesis does not exclude the further crucial development of which I speak.

17. The expression, "fairly generally agreed," though restrained, may not be sufficiently guarded. In his recent fascinating study of killing and meat-eating by the Gombe Chimpanzees (Teleki 1973; Marler 1973) Teleki introduces an incipient question about this, based on the partly arboreal life of his subjects and the suitability of this environment for their hunts. This does not, of course, justify a generalization which would disestablish all previous observations. (See Napier's suggestion [1967] regarding the woodland-savanna as the origin of bipedalism; the open savanna as stimulus for the striding gait.) However, it is demonstrated that, unlike the sporadic spontaneous killing and eating by baboons, the hunts by chimpanzees seem of fairly regular occurrence, sometimes with an aspect of planned purposiveness, even involving the group, followed by singularly unaggressive, usually unviolent (although capricious) sharing. The sharing is conspicuously a matter of "taking." A few special features should be noted: (1) The state of surfeit (with bananas provided by the investigators) does not disestablish this practice; also this feeding is not a necessary condition, since similar attacks occur outside this area. (2) The occurrence in surfeit suggests either (a) an obscure dietary deficiency or (b) a "psychological" premium in the killing and eating. (3) Whereas baboons often mingle freely with the chimpanzees in the same area, the most frequent objects of attack and devouring are very young baboons! Can it be that this represents a compromise with the very general "taboo" on cannibalism among apes? That the baboon is attractive because "like themselves" (the opposite of the "spreading" taboo among humans)? That this would be an occasional safety valve for the envy and "filicidal" hatred of their young? (The author himself speculates that the infant selection is a result of social contact with the older baboons.) (4) Whereas the *coup de grace* may sometimes be given by the teeth, essential killing can be accomplished by clumsy flailing against a hard surface, or throttling, or live dismemberment. (5) The amount of time consumed in the dismemberment and devouring of a very small baboon is impressive — six and a half hours in one instance (p. 102) with a considerable group participating. The total dismemberment involves the synergistic use of both hands and teeth. (6) The total proportion of meat in the diet is very small (less than 1 percent) (Teleki 1973, p. 124).

18. While this etymology is not frequently given, the reference to burnt offering is usually an integral part of the definition. Ancient alters (for example, the great bone and ash alter of Pergamon) were usually made of incombustible material. As the Christian church developed, wood became the substance of choice. (In England, note "God's board," "holy table," and other variants, subject to theological dispute.) However, underlying this development came the central rite of communion, symbolizing the voluntary (vicarious) sacrifice of the god himself. It is, of course, striking that in this lofty (highly sublimated) ritual there is a frank return to the literal origin of sacrifice, obviating the actual use of fire. The important role of incense and the censer in certain churches provides a connecting link with fire. Perhaps the dual meaning of the word "incense" is not entirely accidental.

19. In this connection, note M. Katan's paper "The Role of the Word in Mania" (1940, 1971). In this interesting and complicated paper, speech (especially in the sense of "flight of ideas" as a means of maintaining contact with the world), urination as a special feature of mania replacing the anal features in depression, and Freud's concept of the fire-urine complex are tightly integrated in an exceptional psychopathologic study. From my own theoretical position, I would view certain emphases differently: the urinary episodes in two instances as reflecting inhibited urinary autofellatio, the word phenomenon in mania as representing the "razor's edge" desperate cathexis of word representations as against the manifest regression to biting oral destructiveness. It goes without saying that Katan is much more liable to be right in his more complicated interpretation, in relation to his own material. However, apart from detailed interpretation, the important dynamic series involving orality, speech, urination, and fire, are, I feel, significantly—if only indirectly—related to some of the ideas I present in this paper.

20. In Marcovitz's rich paper on this addiction, there is a thorough review of the subject and its literature. The author places special emphasis on the respiratory aspects of the addiction (for details one must consult the paper). This is indeed an even more archaic consideration than oral destructiveness; and it was the respiratory consideration (in a different sense) that first engaged my interest in Marcovitz's paper (Stone 1971, p. 213). However, while accepting most of the author's interesting material and interpretation—and the self-evident fact that the central mechanism is respiratory, I do not relinquish the importance of the oral sphere (the operation is, after all, initiated at the lips by sucking), to which the respiratory-pulmonary phenomenon may be regressively and defensively related. Note the traditional fear of smokers that they will become ravenously hungry if they cease to smoke. One cannot eat all day, except at great risk. Chewing lacks the important gratification of ingestion. Smoking (except for its remote consequences) can continue endlessly. This is not to set aside the special dimensions which Marcovitz so skillfully emphasizes but rather to reiterate the persisting importance of the oral impulses and fantasies inherent in the addiction, although these like the other several elements may vary in importance from individual to individual.

REFERENCES

Abraham, K. (1924). The influence of oral erotism on character-formation. In *Selected Papers on Psychoanalysis*. New York: Basic Books, 1953, pp. 393–406.

Almansi, R. J. (1953). A psychoanalytic interpretation of the Menorah. *J. Hillside Hosp.* 2:80–95.

_____ (1964). Ego-psychological implications of a religious symbol: A cultural and experimental study. *Psychoanal. Study of Society*, 3:39–70. New York: International Universities Press.

Arlow, J. A. (1955). Notes on oral symbolism. *Psychoanal. Q.* 24:63–74.

Bergler, E. (1937). Further observations of the clinical picture of "psychogenic oral aspermia." *Int. J. Psychoanal.* 18:196–234.

Briggs, J. L. (1970). *Never in Anger*. Cambridge, Mass.: Harvard University Press.

_____ (1975). The origins of nonviolence: Aggression in two Canadian Eskimo groups. *Psychoanal. Study of Society*, 6:134–203. New York: International Universities Press.

Campbell, B. (1968). Evolution of the human hand. In *Man in Adaptation, the Biosocial Background*, ed. Y. A. Cohen. Chicago: Aldine.

Darwin, C. (1871). *The Descent of Man*. London: John Murray, 1898.

Edelheit, H. (1969). Speech and psychic structure. The vocal-auditory organization of the ego. *J. Amer. Psychoanal. Assn.* 17:381–412.

Eissler, K. R. (1971). Death drive, ambivalence, and narcissism. *Psychoanal. Study of the Child*, 26:25–78. New York: Quadrangle Books.

_____ (1975). The fall of man. *Psychoanal. Study of the Child* 30:589–646. New Haven, Conn.: Yale University Press.

Ferenczi, S. (1924). *Thalassa: A Theory of Genitality*. Albany, N.Y.: Psychoanal. Q., 1938.

Flaubert, G. (1862). *Salammbô*. Cambridge, Engl.: Cambridge University Press, 1960.

Fliess, R. (1939). Silence and verbalizaton: A supplement to the theory of the analytic rule. *Int. J. Psychoanal.* 30:21–30.

Freud, A. (1949a). Aggression in relation to emotional development: Normal and pathological. *The Writings of Anna Freud* 4:489–497. New York: International Universities Press, 1968.

_____ (1949b). Notes on aggression. *The Writings of Anna Freud* 4:60–74. New York: International Universities Press, 1968.

_____ (1972). Comments on aggression. *Int. J. Psychoanal.* 53:163–171.

Freud, S. (1900). The interpretation of dreams. *S. E.*, 5.

_____ (1905). Three essays on the theory of sexuality. *S. E.* 7.

_____ (1913). Totem and taboo. *S. E.* 13.

_____ (1923). The ego and the id. *S. E.* 19.

_____ (1930). Civilization and its discontents. *S. E.* 21.

_____ (1932). The acquisition and control of fire. *S. E.* 22.

_____ (1939). Moses and monotheism. *S. E.* 23.

Ginzberg, L. (1910). *The Legends of the Jews*, transl. H. Szold. Philadelphia: Jewish Publication Society of America 2:272–275.

Hartmann, H. (1939). *Ego Psychology and the Problem of Adaptation*. New York: International Universities Press, 1958.

_____ (1948). Comments on the psychoanalytic theory of instinctual drives. In *Essays on Ego Psychology*. New York: International Universities Press, 1964, pp. 69–89.

Hockett, C. F. (1960). The origin of speech. In *Human Variations and Origins*, introd. W. S. Laughlin and R. H. Osborne. San Francisco and London: W. H. Freeman, pp. 182–190.

_____, and Ascher, R. (1968). The human revolution. In *Man in Adaptations, the Biosocial Background*, ed. Y. A. Cohen, Chicago: Aldine, pp. 215–228.

Hoffer, W. (1949). Mouth, hand, and ego-integration. *Psychoanal. Study of the Child*

3/4:49–56. New York: International Universities Press.

Joseph, E. D. (1960). Cremation, fire, and oral aggression. *Psychonal. Q.* 29:98–104.

Katan, M. (1940). The role of the word in mania. *Bull. Phila. Assn. Psychoanal.* 22:4–34.

———— (1971). Addendum to above. *Bull. Phila. Assn. Psychoanal.* 22:35–41.

Kolata, G. B. (1974). The demise of the Neanderthals: Was language a factor? *Science* 186:618–619.

———— (1975). Human evolution: Life styles and lineages of early hominids. *Science* 187:940–942.

Lantos, B. (1958). The two genetic derivations of aggression with reference to sublimation and neutralization. *Int. J. Psychoanal.* 39:116–120.

Lévi-Strauss, C. (1964). *The Raw and the Cooked. An Introduction to a Science of Mythology*, vol. 1. New York: Harper & Row, 1970.

Lewin, B. D. (1950). *The Psychoanalysis of Elation*. New York: Norton.

Lorenz, K. (1963). *On Aggression*. New York: Harcourt, Brace & World.

Mahler, M. S. (1965). On the significance of the normal separation-individuation phase: With reference to research in symbiotic child psychosis. In *Drives, Affects, Behavior*, ed. M. Schur. New York: International Universities Press, pp. 161–169.

Marcovitz, E. (1969). On the nature of addiction to cigarettes. *J. Amer. Psychoanal. Assn.* 17:1074–1096.

Marler, P. (1973). Meat eating in primates (Review of Teleki, 1973). *Science* 182:572.

Melville, H. (1846). *Typee; or a Peep at Polynesian Life*. London: John Murray.

———— (1924). *Billy Budd*. London/Bombay/Sidney: Constable. (Written 1891)

Midrash, R. (1951). *Exodus*, ed. H. Freedman and M. Simon. London and Bournemouth: Soncino Press.

Napier, J. (1962). The evolution of the hand. *Scientific American* 207:56–62.

———— (1967). The antiquity of human walking. In *Human Variations and Origins*. San Francisco and London: W. H. Freeman, pp. 116–126.

Oakley, K. P. (1961). On man's use of fire, with comments on tool-making and hunting. In *The Social Life of Early Man*, ed. S. L. Washburn, Chicago: Aldine, pp. 176–191.

———— (1968). Man as tool-maker. In *Man in Adaptation, the Biosocial Background*, ed. Y. A. Cohen. Chicago: Aldine, pp. 130–134.

Rascovsky, A., and Rascovsky, M. (1972). The prohibition of incest, filicide and the sociocultural process. *Int. J. Psychoanal.* 52:271–276.

Reclus, E. (1910). Fire. *Encyclopedia Brittanica*, 11th ed. New York: Encyclopedia Brittanica, vol. 10, pp. 399–401.

Reis, D. J. (1974). The chemical coding of aggression in the brain. In *Neuro-humoral Coding of Brain Function*, ed. R. D. Meyers and R. R. Drucker-Colin. New York: Plenum Press, pp. 125–150.

Rosenblum, L. A. (1974). Maternal aggression and infant attachment (monkeys). Second Colloquium on Aggression. Meeting of American Psychoanalytic Association, December.

Scott, J. P. (1973a). Personal, social, and international violence. First Colloquium on Aggression. Meeting of American Psychoanalytic Association, December.

———— (1973b). Rough draft of concluding remarks concerning Colloquium on Problems of the Psychoanalytic Theory of Aggression. Date and occasion as above.

Sharpe, E. F. (1940). Psycho-physical problems revealed in language: An examination of metaphor. *Int. J. Psychoanal.* 21:201–213.

Simmel, E. (1942). Symposium on neurotic disturbances of sleep. *Int. J. Psychoanal.* 23:65–68.

―――― (1944). Self-preservation and the death instinct. *Psychoanal. Q.* 13:160–185.

Sperber, H. (1912). Über den Einfluss sexueller Momente auf Entstehung und Entwicklung der Sprache. *Imago* 1:405–454.

Spier, L. (1971). Fire. In *Collier's Encyclopedia*, vol. 9. New York: Crowell-Collier Educational Corp.

Stone, L. (1954). On the principal obscene word of the English language: An inquiry, with hypothesis, regarding its origin and persistence. *Int. J. Psychoanal.* 35:30–56. *Reprinted in this volume, Chapter 13.*

―――― (1961). *The Psychoanalytic Situation: An Examination of Its Development and Essential Nature.* New York: International Universities Press.

―――― (1967). The psychoanalytic situation and transference: Postscript to an earlier communication. *J. Amer. Psychoanal. Assn.* 15:3–58. *Reprinted in this volume, Chapter 4.*

―――― (1971). Reflections on the psychoanalaytic concept of aggression. *Psychoanal. Q.* 40:195–244. *Reprinted in this volume, Chapter 11.*

Swift, J. (1729). *A Modest Proposal.* New York: Penguin, 1977.

Teleki, G. (1973). *The Predatory Behavior among Wild Chimpanzees.* Lewisburg, Pa.: Bucknell University Press.

Vallois, H. V. (1961). Social life of early man; the evidence from skeletons. In *The Social Life of Early Man*, ed. S. L. Washburn. Chicago: Aldine, pp. 214–232.

Von Bertalanffy, L. (1958). Comments on aggression. *Bull Menninger Clin.* 22:50–57.

Waelder, R. (1960). *Basic Theory of Psychoanalysis.* New York: International Universities Press.

Washburn, S. L. (1960). Tools and human evolution. *Scientific American* 203:169–181.

Chapter 13
On the Principal Obscene Word of the English Language
(1954)

At the time of its original presentation and publication, this paper evoked considerable interest among many colleagues because of its nuclear linguistic hypothesis and psychoanalytic implications. For certain others, the sheer phenomenon of a dignified inquiry into the "obscene" offered a sort of non-specific attraction, without much intellectual curiosity about the essential hypothesis. No doubt, the former interest was augmented by both the rapidly accelerating incursion of the word *fuck* into the language of polite society and the increasing acceptance of oral-genital sexual practices into the repertoire of nonperverse heterosexual relationships.

This paper is remembered by those who have heard or read it. I fear that the more labored and serious content has had less impact than the amusing and titillating appeal of the basic "fuck-suck" rhyme that originally inspired the study. Perhaps the republication will engage more serious consideration in light of the increasing current interest in the psychoanalytic linguistic borderland.

I must, of course, leave the detailed etymologic inquiry and formulation to the judgment of scholars. I remain as firmly convinced of the central significance of the basic rhyme and its unconscious reverberations as I was a few decades ago.

The word under discussion is known from childhood to most persons born to the English language, despite the severity of the taboo connected with it. Those who learn English later in life seem to learn this word promptly, regardless of their speed of acquisition of other words. Often it is known to people in remote parts of the world, whose remaining English vocabulary is negligible (Read 1934). Furthermore, the word has a recorded history of almost four and a half centuries, beginning with its forthright use by distinguished Scottish poets, or less by half a century, if we distinguish between English and Scottish. While our current use of this word demonstrates how little printed language may reflect popular speech, this national difference in literary usage may have some significance, especially when considered with the fact that our word has in general been used more freely and boldly by Scottish than by English writers. The possible significance of this will be mentioned later in relation to my hypothesis.

Since language is the chief instrument of psychoanalysis, and sex a major field of its scientific and therapeutic interest, the investigation of an obscene word would seem a natural psycho-analytic undertaking, especially when it is considered that obscene language, as a special variant of slang, lives and thrives in relation to conventional language, without official notice, in much the same sense that infantile sexuality lived and throve—in child and adult—before Freud brought it to scientific attention. Freud wrote of obscenity in *Wit and its Relation to the Unconscious* (1905b), explaining its function as a substitutive sexual aggression, which derived its effectiveness from the peculiarly evocative character of the obscene. Ferenczi (1916) explained the significance of obscene language in terms of the uniquely vivid character of the words, their capacity to evoke a type of regressive hallucinatory perception, as opposed to the relatively pure intellectual message of conventional words. (We may wonder if this quality is related to the special character attributed to the hypothetical "roots" of philology.) Ferenczi explained this quality by the association of the obscene words with the childhood period of learning, observation, and theorizing about sex and the intense feelings of the Oedipus complex, all subject to repression before the secondary acquisition of sexual knowledge and vocabulary. He postulated a period in which the use of obscene language represented a last stronghold of infantile sensual pleasure before true latency began. Bergler (1936) later reviewed the ideas of Freud and Ferenczi, presented his own case material, and emphasized the importance of the varying anal and oral gratifications to a given individual when obscene words were uttered by him or by his sexual partner. Bergler felt that the oral factor had been neglected in psychoanalytic literature. Another paper of Freud is especially relevant to this study, though it had no immediate connection with obscenity. In "The Antithetical Sense of Primal Words" (1910), Freud wrote an appreciation of the significance of Karl Abel's little book of the same name (1884). Abel's observation is relevant to the hypothesis to be discussed later. Furthermore, it led Freud to state his own early conviction regarding the potential value to psychoanalysis of the understanding of intrinsic language dynamics. In our present undertaking, it is rather a mutual illumination between word and psycho-analysis that is hoped for, in somewhat the same manner that the recovery of the past and the scrutiny of the present illuminate one another in the acutal work of psychoanalysis.

The views of the psychoanalytic writers already mentioned relate to the experience of the obscene in general rather than to specific words or phrases. Communications regarding the determination of such fixed expressions have appeared in psychoanalytic literature, although infrequently. Blau (1943) has sought to explain the absence of a slang term for the clitoris as a manifestation of denial of the organ, because of the unconscious attitude of both sexes toward it. Kanner (1945) later sought to supply the missing terms without rejecting Blau's observation of relative infrequency compared with other sexual terms. Bunker (1943), utilizing the concept of body-as-phallus and the striking memory of a terminological confusion in a patient, called attention to the resemblance between a Middle Gaelic term for penis (*Bod*) and the English word *body* in relation to the obscurity of the latter word's origin. Of special relevance to the present study is the very brief communication by Vivian Thompson on the expression "Irish toothache" for erection (Partridge 1950, Thompson 1932).

The present inquiry into the genesis and vicissitudes of the word *fuck* was initiated by the clinical observation of a distinctive use of the term by a female patient. The special interest is focused on the word itself rather than on the general problem of obscenity, on comparative sexual terminology, or on the word's various figurative uses.[1]

It should be noted at the outset that scholarly information about this important word is remarkable for its scarcity, although spoken communications about pseudoauthoritative etymologies or personal opinions are extremely abundant. No reliable American or English general dictionaries now current contain the word. Furthermore, and somewhat more surprising, one may examine, as I have done, a considerable number of dictionaries devoted to vulgar language without finding it (Barrère and Leland 1889, Hotten 1865, Irwin 1931, Jackson 1915, Partridge 1933, Ware 1909). It is interesting that the first French work on English vulgarisms I consulted does define the word (Manchon 1923). However, the French term *foutre*, thought by some to be the immediate souce of our word, does not always appear in French dictionaries.[2]

The redoubtable Mencken does not print our word (1923, 1949). Even the great Oxford Dictionary (1933) does not mention it.

In the *Dictionary of the Vulgar Tongue* of Captain Francis Grose (1788) the term is defined, and in Partridge's edition (1931) and later in Partridge's own dictionary (1937), it is thought possibly to be derived from French *foutre*, (Greek *phuteuo*, Latin *futuere*), the medial *c* and the abridgement being ascribed to an unspecified Teutonic radical and an Anglo-Saxon tendency.[3]

The first lexicographic appearance (1598 originally?) is assigned to John Florio's Italian-English dictionary (1611) in which it appears with four other words used to define the word *fottere*. The practical disappearance from the language of the other words, *jape, sarde, swive, occupy* should be noted in relation to the tenacious vitality of the word we are studying. In the copy (1611) I examined, *fucke* follows *jape* and is followed by *sard* and *swive*. *Occupy* appears several times in the definition of compound or derivative words.

In Partridge's dictionary (1937, 1950) there is reference to a paper by Alan Walker Read (1934) whose Teutonic etymological theory is thought to be more probably correct than the *foutre* derivation. Read's paper is invaluable as a summary of the general history of the word and its vicissitudes of status, in literature and in dictionaries. Read mentions the Scottish poets, William Dunbar (about 1460–1513) and Sir David Lindsay of the Mount (1490–1555), as the first writers in whose works the word appears and refers to the examples given by Farmer and Henley (1893) as evidence of the generally greater linguistic boldness of Scottish writers. Outstanding in Read's historical survey is the fact that the attack on obscene words in literature began even in Elizabethan times and apparently increased in severity thereafter. Our word does not appear in Shakespeare (*foutre* appears twice) (Bartlett 1894), and it is absent from certain old dictionaries (Blount 1674, Cockeram 1623, Levens 1570, Phillips 1662). The earls of Rochester (1647–1680) and Dorset (1638–1706) were the last English poets to use it; yet the word appears about 1790 (?) in Burns. A sort of attempted revival of the word may be ascribed to Joyce and Lawrence. However, this type of purposive and self-conscious employment of a word that is generally taboo is different from its original natural place in the vocabulary of writer and audience. Such a phenomenon and its effects are still difficult to evaluate in history. The same is true of the present vogue of the word.

In discussing the etymology of our word, Read vigorously denies that it has any connection with the Latin *futuo* or Greek *phuteuo*, which he feels are related to *fui* and thus to the meaning "to be." Our word, he feels, belongs to the original stock of native words, as can be seen from its cognates in other Germanic languages and from its original meaning "to knock." Referring to Kluge, Grieb and Schröer, and Brynildsen, Read gives as cognates Old Dutch *ficken* (*schlagen*), late Middle High German *vicken*, and German *ficken*. The first appearance of the word in its obscene sense is ascribed to Michael Lindener's *Rastbüchlein* (1558).[4]

The presumptive Latin cognates are thought to be *pungo* (to prick or puncture) and *pugil* (boxer), from the root *pug* (to thrust or strike). Probably because of the word's obscene character and the consequent paucity of reliable documentary material, Read's strong opinion about a unilateral etymology is stated somewhat arbitrarily, without documentation of intermediate sources. In such a situation the obligation of critical judgment is heightened, as is the impulse to investigate the matter directly, with due regard for the difficulties inevitable in seeking to understand the material of a separate and highly developed field of learning. The etymological problem will be resumed later in this paper.

My own clinical experience was as follows: Mary S., married, usually in sudden pauses of her free association, would state that there came to her mind, without affect or impulse, the phrase "I want to fuck the analyst." This was usually entirely out of context, at first gave rise to mild conventional embarrassment, and later came to be reported with slight bored irritation as a sort of recrudescent mild nuisance. (Descriptively, the phenomenon included an obsessive element.) Once, on leaving the analytic hour, the patient paused at the door to say: "Now the phrase comes to me—I want to rape the analyst," and on one occasion there was instead the phrase: "I want to kill the analyst." It should be noted that infrequent frightening hostile thoughts about her near relatives were among the patient's minor symptoms. Her principal complaints lay in a tortured, oversolicitous anxiety about the health and general safety of her husband and child and a generally coercive, supervisory, and protective participation in their lives. The morbid significance of the latter attitude assumed greater proportions in her insight as time went on, as the oversolicitude diminished in intensity. With more time, there emerged with increasing clarity an exacting, demanding, impatient, and querulously pessimistic attitude toward husband, child, and analyst (reflecting historical experience in the family), with a remarkable repetitive need to find herself "disappointed" and a reactive violent hostility whose force found some direct expression only in occasional outbursts against her child and in critical nagging of her husband.

The patient was largely, although not constantly, frigid in her marital relationship. She had married as a virgin after many years of successful executive work in business, rather ephemeral and highly self-conscious social relations with men, and a long history of devoted attachments to women friends and colleagues. There was abundant analytic evidence of preponderant unconscious homosexual orientation, violently denied, with intense acquisitive penis envy, also severely denied.

The patient's original sexual solution in her marriage was an exaggerated histrionic sexual compliance, *preceded* by orgasm, secretly induced by pressing her thighs together during the sexual play. In this maneuver, she epitomized sexually what occurred in the broadest manifestations of her character and interpersonal relations, including the transference. She rendered herself free of need and of any possible danger of disappointment. Whenever possible she went further. She sought to make everyone dependent on her and grateful to her, often in fact and *always* in fantasy, as in the transference fantasies, where she would become a greater benefactor to the analyst or emotionally indispensable to him. On one occasion, when at home with a somewhat equivocal illness, she spent a great deal of time speculating on whether the analyst missed her, with no conscious emotional reaction on her side whatsoever. She took pains to emphasize that one of the reasons for her choice of analyst was her initial impression that she would not fall in love with him. The patient had grown up with an ignorant, capriciously abusive mother who smothered all strivings toward maturity in her, even in connection with learning routine housewife's skills, and who violently attacked her pubertal sexuality by pathological accusations of incest between her and her father. The accusations were perhaps overdetermined by what the patient thinks was early developing impotence in her father. What the mother gave the patient was the type of forceful overprotection and supervision which the patient later manifestly thrust on the people around her and which she continued to seek for herself from those about her, with no, or minimal, awareness until the analysis intervened. The one respect in which the mother manifestly and grossly failed the patient was in connection with the general knowledge and the social techniques that would have facilitated her external development. The patient's sister, her "second mother," was gentle and helpful to her but left the home to marry while the patient still needed her and had her own babies, against the patient's remembered anxiety and inner protest. Her older brother, the second sibling, was the apple of the mother's eye, early evoked the patient's admiration and attachment over her hostile envy, yet also disappointed the patient whenever her expectation or dependence were strong. The father was a gentle, affectionate man, ill from the patient's earliest years, overtly awakening a strong attachment in the patient, but definitely stimulating in her the first remembered instances of extreme and guilty oversolicitude, with anxious, obsessive concern of such intensity as to vitiate seriously her adolescent social life. The father, partly because of his serious illness and partly from a character defect, kept the family in a state of constant anxiety and borderline poverty, vividly remembered by the patient. After he died, just as the patient became an adult, she entered business life and soon attained a position whereby she could support her mother, help her married sister, and fantasy offering help to her brother. When she married into a prosperous business family, although she renounced her own business career for the role of housewife (with many resultant problems) her own position of power in relation to friends and relatives was greatly augmented. Nevertheless, in her husband she managed to find a complete father surrogate, even at times evolving subtle complicated reasons for feelings of financial insecurity, although she actually was wealthy.

As the analysis progressed, viewing the movement in broad outline, there was a progressive appreciation of the depth and intensity of the patient's own dependent receptive (oral) demands, against whose exquisite vulnerability to disappointment and the related latent rage there had been erected an inveterate attitude of independence, need to provide for others and to dominate them, and to avoid at all costs the position of needing what another person could provide, whether the requirement was in terms of money, sexual gratification, or affection. From the point of view of unconscious infantile processes, an aggressive phallic attitude was predominant, at times with the castrated male as object.

The breast was rarely evident in analytical material, although food and eating were common themes. It was as though the dynamic attitudes originating with the disappointing breast had become incorporated and fixed in the attitude toward the phallus and the inveterate wish to return to a female object was to be expressed or implemented by securing and bringing to the latter a phallus.[5]

In the years before her marriage the patient acted out a role of this general nature in substitutive symbolic terms, although her acquisitive phallic aggression toward the male was reflected until her marriage largely in her frigid sexual attitude toward him. An anal phallus that her mother admired was accepted as a basis for overt competition until this incentive was also disavowed under the combined and overdetermining stress of unconscious competitive guilt and the conscious determination to marry, as befitted a woman. It should be noted that the patient was an attractive woman, thoroughly feminine in appearance and overt behavior and (in special connection with the linguistic phenomenon that interests us here) definitely careful, almost precious, in her choice of words and in her accent, in strong and generally successful reaction against the painful illiteracy of her early environment.

With this brief sketch of the patient's personality in mind, we may return to her repetitive phrase. The striking aspect of the phrase was the reversal of the usual masculine-feminine direction of the word, from the point of view of all my observation of everyday usage and all that is available of lexicographic authority on this particular point (Ash 1775, Bailey 1700, 1730, Partridge 1937). This the patient readily accepted as a problem when it was first pointed out to her. Curiously enough, much later, when the broader character resistances had been to a great extent analyzed and her own infantile passive needs and their vicissitudes were well developed in her awareness, she once undertook to argue that the phrase had no significance, that she had not learned this grammatical distinction when she learned the word (although the process of learning was never specified as to incidents). She did admit, however, that "to rape" a man was unusual[6] and that equality of activity — an intransitive "to fuck with" had not occurred to her.[7] To me, this sudden (and evanescent) resistance was contingent on the threat of awareness of the direct connection between her phrase and the intense oral conflicts underlying it. In a still later phase of the analysis, when the chief problem was the effort to bring the patient's exacting oral transference attachment to resolution, the phrase reappeared only rarely, usually in a demonstrably unconscious relation to its context.

Since only one aspect of the clinical-linguistic problem is being stressed in this paper, it is well to mention at this point that more than one factor indubitably entered into the patient's choice of expression. Omitting the consideration that at certain points it became a quasi-conscious, evasive device for expressing sexual fantasies, there was no doubt that from the beginning one determinant of the spontaneous symptomatic form was the simple feminine heterosexual incestuous wish, which found naïve and short-lived expression in early dreams. Next and closer to the long-standing functional adjustment of the patient's personality was the expression of the strong phallic impulse with masculine identification, in positive relation to a woman or occasionally in hostile relation to a man. In this latter connection and touching on the phrase "kill the analyst," as well as the oral consideration to follow, I may mention a dream about a male neighbor who died after a long illness during the patient's chronic anxiety about her husband's health. The dream was that it was necessary to test his death by "fudging" him, the actual maneuver remaining unclear. The only thought the patient offered was that "fudge" resembled "fuck." Another general conflict that found some focal expression in the patient's use of this "dirty" word, especially in its paradoxical aggressive direction, was in the anal sphere of her sexuality, which permitted every inference of severe early training—in the character of management of aggression or emotional display, in connection with money, in the actual sphere of dirt and cleanliness, in her ritualistic toilet habits, in a few early memories, and in many manifest dreams regarding the excretory functions. This verbal displacement of excretory impulses has justly been accorded an important place in the general problem of pleasure in obscene language.[8]

However, the connection which seemed crucial and especially challenging to me was with the patient's receptive oral wishes, i.e., with her impulse to *suck*. If her character had been built around the denial and actual reversal of such wishes, could not the striking reversal of usage of a primitive sexual word have an allied determination? Furthermore, might not the structure, i.e., the spelling and sound of the word itself, so obviously similar to the basic word for her deepest repressed impulses, participate importantly in this mechanism?

The literal importance of the sucking impulse in this patient found definite verification with the passage of time. Early her only reference to this theme was her pleasure in having her husband suck her breast as part of their foreplay. In the same period she spoke of the fact that her husband and she "ate too much, because of their unsatisfactory sex life." Later she began to mention the occasional fleeting wish for fellatio or cunnilingus or both during intercourse. There were also a few brief but unequivocal references to fellatio wishes toward the analyst. Quite late in the analysis (during her attempt to devaluate her rhetorical idiosyncrasy) she mentioned a social situation in which her usual inner shyness and somewhat strained social elegance and vivaciousness were much relaxed. On this occasion she had frequent fleeting ideas about sucking the penises of men with whom she had pleasant conversations, especially those of advanced years. In the context of this patient's rigid character defenses, the unsolicited emergence of literal, if nonspectacular, sucking fantasies was thought to be especially important.

Two fragmentary recollections early helped my effort to understand my patient's expression. One was a rhyme quoted to me many years before by a colleague, from the analysis of a male patient about whom I knew nothing else: "I wonder when I'll quit sucking and start fucking." The other was a transitory expression by a female patient who, partly from external psychoanalytic rumor and partly from actual interpretation, was painfully impressed by her inability to become aware of and thus to express hostile attitudes toward the analyst. The patient's transference was of a deeply dependent oral character, with marked inhibition of latent oral rage. Her slangy and wistful expression of the difficulty was: "I certainly would like to be able to sock you." The choice of word as such was not interpreted. Nevertheless the analyst's immediate intuitive reaction was that this choice, aside from its appropriate and manifest meaning, also included the latent resemblance to the word *suck*, i.e., to the unconscious impulse which was still predominant in the patient's interpersonal orientation, which in its disappointment generated most of the unavailable rage to which she referred and which in circular fashion, lest even the inhibited relation be placed in jeopardy, contributed largely to her inability to attack. (In this connection, notice the overlapping etymology of *suck, soak,* and *sock,* the last in secondary substantive meaning, which in fact includes an obsolete variant of the word suck itself, as well as a dialect meaning closer to soak.) (*Oxford English Dictionary* 1933) The secondhand rhyme of the male patient merely drew attention to the dynamic conceptual antithesis between the words whose obvious rhyme is used with what seems to me remarkable rarity, even in the ordinary obscene jingles of the day. This may well be because of the intense and complicated feeling latent in such a juxtaposition of words. It should be noted that the word suck itself was at one time among those threatened with ejection from the polite vocabulary (Read 1934).

From these impressions, I devoted the preliminary idea that the rhyme with the word suck might have been an important unconscious determinant in the linguistic fixation and taboo of our word in general usage, regardless of its origin. The participation or prior operation of many other factors, including those within the scope of known linguistic laws, would be assumed. The formulation was felt to be important enough to merit investigation, not only in its own right, but also because of its implications. What will be given below is devoted to the establishment of this preliminary idea as a reasonable scientific hypothesis. It is hoped that the effort itself, independent of its degree of success, will prove of heuristic value.

We may assume that there is an important reason for the persistence of this word longer than all other modern English coital terms, in both usage and taboo. If *jape* and *sarde,* given by Florio, are now unknown, and (Chaucer's word) *swive,* which has a much longer printed record in English than our word does, is a rare literary affectation or archaism, and *occupy* was returned to the language in the second half of the eighteenth century, without sexual meaning (Read 1934), why is *fuck* so vividly alive in the language?

The word fuck is distinguished among coital terms, whether slang, literary, or scientific, by its consciously absolute and exclusive explicitness. (The ambiguity connected with the existing or potential unconscious rhyme may be a part of the word's rich evocative capacity.) The word has no other primary meaning; all other meanings are figurative or (at the present time) consciously derivative. When a man says, "I got my day all fucked up," he is fully aware of the primary sexual meaning of the word. (That this awareness may disappear in the course of centuries, as in the evolution of actual sexual words traced by Sperber [1912] may well be true.) Certainly all other common and current slang words for copulation are secondary or derivative and of exceedingly varied determination, ranging from highly ambiguous or euphemistic expressions, such as the popular "to sleep with" to the mechanical, focal, and somewhat sadistic "to screw."[9] It may be objected that certain terms from the scientific or legal vocabulary, such as *coitus* or *fornicate*, are now quite precise in meaning. This is true, but not to the same extent psychologically or in the same exclusive sense as to fuck. To the group who uses such terminology, the sense of derivation from another language is usually a conscious matter and often the precise meaning of the etymological words of origin. The same distinction may be made with regard to the other so-called four-letter words and their elaborate equivalents. Related to the specificity of the word is another important feature, and that is its rich, many-faceted communicative capacity. While it may be used without or with slight modification as almost any part of speech in a sentence, it has all the implications of any form of sentence in itself and can easily be used as such, in a primitive sense, *without* other words. In this it fulfills conspicuously the criteria sometimes described for the postulated root words of primordial speech. (See Baker's [1950] opinion regarding the central linguistic position of obscene language.)

This archaic quality in the word fuck, in its hypothetical relation to suck, is anachronistically (or cyclically?) (Bodmer 1944) relevant to Abel's demonstration of the frequent antithetical sense of primal words based largely on the ancient Egyptian (Abel 1884). (with an appendix based on other languages, prominently Arabic.)[10] If the same primal word could mean strong and weak or light and dark or if words of equivalently opposite meaning could differentiate from an original stem by a slight sound alteration, it seems a tenable hypothesis that fuck and suck bear a relation to each other similar to that borne to one another by the slightly differentiated primal words (without considering the genesis of the coupling at this moment). The general etymological question is not fully explained by Abel.[11] If we assume the reasonableness of the hypothesis that the words fuck and suck have a general unconscious association in English-speaking people (at least because of the inevitable latent rhyme), we have one tentative dynamic basis for the general understanding of the antithetical sense of primal words, in that the verbal correlate of the first focal expression of the fundamental object relationship of extrauterine life (i.e., sucking) finds persistent representation in the very structure of another word (or in the unconscious obligatory rhyme association with that word), which represents a reversal of the original situation in the second great biological expression of object relationship, that is, in sexual intercourse.[12] If we think of the f and s sounds in this context as differing largely in terms of a modification of the sibilant sound corresponding to the appearances of the actual letters in German (and in earlier English) typography, the f representing emissive and intromissive activity and the s receptivity and some form or degree of passivity,[13] breast, or penis on one side, mouth or vagina on the other, a tentative and oversimplified but concise diagrammatic formulation may be attained. The differences in linguistic application in the respective sexes are consistent with other psychological differences and do not vitiate but rather support the importance of the putative verbal relationship. The important genetic link is the common experience in infancy of externally given gratification and externally imposed deprivation in the oral sphere.

The proposed hypothesis, insofar as it permits general and tentative inferences, can contribute a greater psychoanalytic consistency to the ingenious theory advanced by Sperber [1912] in his scholarly essay on the origin and development of speech. Sperber recognizes the importance of the infant's hunger call to the mother as a motive for individual speech. However, since the infant must learn conventional speech from the adult and since certain repetitive conditions for the standardization and propagation of speech can be met only by the adult, Sperber assigns the preponderant role in speech genesis to the adult mating call and then to the exclamations from secondary sexual tensions aroused by the coital fantasies implicit in the use of various tools. The tendency is to separate adult genital coitus as sexual from other forms of libidinal object relationship. The differences are obvious and important. However, the urgent need for the object is a common denominator. There is also a continuum between the infant's cry and the mating call in terms of libido or sex in its broader sense. From the point of view of indispensability of response of the object (hence relative intensity of the urge to communicate), the greater urgency must be accorded the infant's cry — aside from its vast genetic priority in time, the augmentation of communicative need by motor helplessness, and the probable proximal importance of oral (and anal) libido and aggression in the speech phenomenon. It is reasonable to assume that the call to the mother, however minimal its immediate role in the details of learned speech, remains of basic importance in the impulse to communicate and that it has a definite psychological share in the mating call itself and thus in the exclamations generated by the tool fantasies.[14] (Note the many oral fantasy interpretations of the primal scene.) Between the infant's cry and the mating call, although much closer to infancy in time, lies the period of infantile phallic primacy with its intimate relation to its pregenital substructure.

We may now temporarily relinquish the words as such to seek broad parallels in unconscious dynamics. The penis-as-breast, the vulva-as-mouth are common unconscious fantasies in both sexes. The same is true of oral impregnation. That the male often seeks food or drink to stimulate or replenish semen; the loving female often fulfils this fantasy for him. That oral problems may find expression in disturbances of erectile or ejaculatory potency in the male or in frigidity in the female, is also well known. The impulse toward (even the very attempt at) autofellatio in the pubertal male is common. Both statistical study (Kinsey et al. 1948) and psychoanalytic experience support this. The instances in which dreams reveal the autofellatio fantasy implicit in masturbation, especially and more frequently in males and less frequently and more subtly in females, are so impressive that I have often wondered whether adolescent masturbation as a transition phenomenon does not quite generally include the effort to find physiological genital satisfaction while maintaining an oral fantasy in relation to a parent with whom the masturbator is identified, under conditions resembling the earliest autoerotic sphincter gratification. A related fantasy is carried out with an external object in the practice of *soixante-neuf*. Here it should be noted that "69" or its components, fellatio and cunnilingus, have in the last few decades among the intellectually emancipated classes practically lost their aura of taboo, as long as they are part of forepleasure and are not homosexual. (See Freud's reference to them as "perversion.") We may assume that this very literal juxtaposition and blending of oral and genital sexuality was unconsciously present in a widespread sense in the period when the general taboo and individual repressions were stronger. We may venture the crude estimate that the recent diminution of intensity of the taboo on the word fuck corresponds in time to the general diminution of the taboo on oral-genital practices. In the pathological jealousy of the alcoholic where oral addiction is linked with pathological rivalry in genital terms, there can be no doubt of the profound contribution of the oral sphere to the entire syndrome, whose proximal basis in homosexuality is generally accepted. Again, the increase in drinking in our time and place of observation must be noted.

Speaking in broad and mixed generalities, the woman who may be said to have a genital mouth is liable to envy the male's activity and his protruding emissive genital organ. In the male the passive cravings and corresponding envy are powerful, but usually more severely denied and reacted against, both because of stronger cultural sanctions and the unconscious threat to bodily integrity usually involved in such fantasies. Male passivity is an important general factor in the neuroses, and while it has many determinants, surely the problem of male orality is an important one. In the case of the woman patient whose phrase first stimulated this study, it was as though she had unconsciously become a man in her fantasy development, and her own pressing oral needs, fraught with painful memories of disappointment, could now only threaten her fantasy phallus, her new basis for satisfactory object relations. Hence the impulse to suck was best defended against by the intensification of a drive opposite in direction which still included a hidden fraction of the search for the older gratification. This is analogous to the well-known hypererotic defense against passive male homosexuality. Viewed genetically, the homosexual defense is a sort of caricature of normal male genitality.

The tendency or need to give a phallic or active coloration to a passive receptive libidinal activity is striking and has long been evident in the cultural attitude toward drinking alcohol. Talents such as being able to drink a great deal, drink it straight, drink hard liquor, hold one's liquor, and even boast about how drunk one gets carry with them a certain masculine pride.

In inverse proportion to the degree of individual maturity, these tendencies compete in the mental life against moral or medical insights. Smoking, a specifically sucking act, was until recently permitted only to the strong mature male. To "inhale" was a matter of greater danger and greater manliness.[15] Furthermore, for this obvious sucking-inhaling activity, we have had to adopt a partially evasive and certainly specific usage of the word *smoke*. This also is true of *puff*.[16] There also is in drinking an aggressive cannibalistic drive (Simmel 1948) more important than the simple unambivalent *passive* wish is less widely emphasized than understood. This may be connected with the aggressive pride in drinking and with the fact that this indulgence is found most often in, or at least most thoroughly permitted to, those who are most thoroughly weaned and thus most understandably aggressive. This now includes increasing numbers of women.[17]

Overtones indicating the persistence of the original unconscious tendency appear in some of the phraseology of sexual relations. In the sexual act, certainly it is the male who is intromissive, usually more active, and specifically emissive. Yet the woman "gives herself to the man," or he "takes her." In vulgar language, the matter is often more narrow and more nearly explicit. The man may seek, find, or get a "piece of tail" or a "piece of arse." "Cherry" for virginity and "taking her cherry" for defloration are deeply rooted in American slang; the connection is apparently not explicit in English slang, although there is a connection with girl or woman (Partridge 1950). Certainly in the etymology of the word *rape*, the implication of plunder looms large. In especially ribald or rough moods, expressions such as "tore off a piece" or "ripped off a piece" have appeared in American slang. Note the currently popular use of *wolf*, which has classical connections for the psychoanalyst. In these the fantasy of (oral or prehensile) anatomic attack is strongly suggested. This may also have a part in "jerk off" or "pull off" for masturbation. Currently, and, I think, with some historical significance, one often hears a different trend, as when a man speaks of "getting laid." These verbal tendencies are felt to support—albeit indirectly—my further tentative conception that the words fuck and suck may be related dynamically in the English vocabulary, anterior to putatively accidental rhyme. Insofar as obvious aggression is implicit in the words, one thinks of the aggression of original oral deprivation.[18] Melanie Klein's interpretation of the sensations originating in the development of teeth as connected with primordial phallic sexual attitudes and would be relevant to this hypothesis, as it is to the well-known castration and masturbatory symbolism of teeth in dreams. The interference with sucking ascribed to the eruption of teeth was mentioned early by Freud and Abraham. Ferenczi (1938) stated strongly the conception of the tooth as "Urpenis." Halverson (1938) has observed that male infants in states of frustration and rage at the breast frequently develop erections. Thus in the deepest layers of experience there is a relationship between a *disturbance* of sucking and the physiological corollary of the impulse to fuck.

In trying to evaluate his remarkable observation, Halverson—despite the citation of considerable collateral evidence for the importance of the rage itself—concludes that increased abdominal pressure is the most likely cause of the tumescence, on a purely physiological basis. I maintain a large reservation about this particular inference in this otherwise excellent contribution. See Freud's early remarks (1905a) regarding heterogeneous internal factors as stimulants of sexual feeling. Pain and rage are included.

Since erections are often associated with the urinary impulse, we may mention Abraham's observation regarding the substitution for sucking by oral "giving" in certain oral characters, in the sense of interminable talking, with a related neurotic urinary urgency (1927).

The myriad historical factors that were playing on the English language at the time our word appeared are certainly beyond the systematic scope of this paper and of its author's competence. However, two matters have struck me by their contemporaneousness and their possible dynamic relevance to the linguistic problem.

Smoking was brought to England from America in 1586[19] (*Encyclopedia Brittanica* 1910). The special position of the pipe in the American Indian rituals of war and peace is consistent with the fundamental position of orality in the problem of aggression. It is known that the addiction spread with amazing rapidity through all countries in the seventeenth century, against the violent resistance, threats, and severe sanctions of political and ecclesiastical authority (*Encyclopedia Brittanica* 1910). It is conceivable that the introduction of widespread adult sucking, with its constant threat to repressions, may have heightened acutely the conflict about the word whose resemblance (at least) to suck was already unconsciously important. During the period of the rapid spread of smoking, the word fuck disappeared from polite usage.

Another interesting fact is that rhyme, which had largely supplanted alliteration as the chief ornament of English verse for a few hundred years, was in this period subjected to major critical attack.[20] Criticism had begun earlier in the same period (*Encyclopedia Brittanica* 1910). This may be purely coincidental, but it is a striking coincidence, which bears further scrutiny. The possible connection receives some support from the fact that the well-esteemed Scottish poets, in whose printed works the word appeared considerably before and much later than a corresponding appearance in English, did not labour under the same unconscious difficulty. The word for suck was *sowk*.[21] Thus in an amorous poem by Dunbar, which curiously enough has in a small space several references to sucking and weaning, and in one place the word *fukkit*, there is no attempt to rhyme fuck and sowk.[22] It is conceivable that the greater freedom in the other Germanic languages (*ficken* and variants) includes a similar negative factor. Two other historical details may be added at this point. While the editor for the Scottish Text Society (Dunbar 1885 and 1893) definitely includes this erotic poem in Dunbar's work, differences of opinion are mentioned. In Farmer and Henley (1893) the poem is attributed to Clerk and dated much later. It is therefore worth mentioning that the word also appears in a compound, *wan-fukkit* (impotent) in *The Flyting of Dunbar and Kennedie* (Dunbar 1885 and 1893), which is, beyond dispute, Dunbar's work. The use of *fycket* in another poem will be mentioned later. In Sir David Lindsay (1490–1555) it is worth passing mention that, in one of the two instances where the word was directly observed (Lindsay 1931–1936), the modern spelling was used—i.e. "fuck." The power of prosody is also illustrated in that the still current *swyfe* appears where assonance and alliteration favour it. ("They swyfe ladies, madinis, and uther mens wyfis.") The same is true of our word. ("Ay fukkand lyke ane furious Fornicatour.") Again a possible minor contribution to our hypothesis appears in *Ane Satyre of the Thrie Estaitis* of Lindsay, where the enviable situation of bishops is mentioned. "For they may fuck their fill and nocht be mareit." (Could the figurative use of "fill" be related to the unconscious association with "suck"?)

We may now return to further details regarding the word itself. Is there a possibility that, if not in the demonstrable outer phenomenology of linguistic history, there is a latent psychological relation between the words fuck and suck antecedent to the perfect rhyme between the words (in this case, the actual identity in all but one letter?) I feel that this may be true. In the history of English, an alternation between *f* and labiodental *th* has occurred even in the upper classes and even in writing, for instance, *erf* for *earth* (Wyld 1920). This can of course be observed today in the distortions of childhood speech and also occasionally in the speech of the unlettered. In the lisp of later childhood, the substitution of the *th* sound for *s* is common. Earlier *f* may be substituted for *th*. At times *f* and *s* may be perversely substituted for each other.[23] The coincidence (?) that the experiential correlates of the English words suck, thumb, and finger have a profound dynamic connection in childhood may also play a part in the structure of our word, especially since the hand is already reflexly involved in nursing (Freud 1905a) and is the preponderant active organ in masturbation, at least in the male.[24] Also, *f* can change to *s* in permanent usage in our language. In Anglo-Saxon (Stratmann 1891) the word *fneosan* means "sneeze." That this evolved into our word *sneeze* can hardly be doubted. In the linguistic area of popular psychology and psychopathology, there is further evidence. Certainly baby talk is common in the intimacies of adult lovers, although the details may vary. Children rarely use the word suck and usually without affect, except in deriding other children. This is surprising, considering the recent and sometimes current powerful importance of the phenomenon in their lives. This may be contrasted with the pleasure and (often guilty) excitement with which they shout the word fuck for its own sake, sometimes *before* its meaning is known. Here it may be objected that the unconscious association with sexual intercourse is already present, in addition to the specific taboo on the word itself. This is certainly true in most instances. However, as in the general hypothesis under consideration, it is suggested that the tremendous and complicated affect associated with the meaning of the word suck, whether by word-to-word displacement or by the role of the older word in the genesis of the new word, or both, has a considerable part in the excitement. It is, in any case, certain that the woman associated unconsciously in childhood with the word fuck is the mother who was once sucked.

I cannot say statistically how often frankly effeminate male homosexuals lisp or tend toward a lisp. But what is even more important in the study of a general linguistic phenomenon is that persons whose conscious orientation is hetersexual include the *th* for *s* very frequently in their mocking imitations of the homosexual. One more critical step and the conventional imitator, like some children, would say; "You must come up and fee me some time." But then he would jeopardize his self-satisfaction with his own sexual performance. I feel it conservative to say that the mocking attitude, which is a variant of the manifestly violent attitude toward the homosexual, is heightened in the individual when the passive homosexual components in the personality press especially strongly for recognition. It is a special form of defense, with broad cultural support in certain quarters. I believe that at such times the free use of the aggressive word fuck plays an equivalent role. Note its exaggerated use in the armed forces and in other male communities.

Since the etymology of our word is by no means established, it is reasonable to evaluate certain immediate elements in prevalent assumptions before turning to a deeper consideration of the presumptive words of origin or cognates. If the word came into English from another Germanic tongue in, or shortly before, the sixteenth century, it presumably came from *ficken* or a close variant. The general trends of intrinsic vowel change in English (Wyld 1936) do not account for the evolution from *ficken* to fuck. Lacking incontrovertible proof of the exclusive *ficken* origin, it is not obligatory to exclude entirely the word *foutre* from a position at least of influence in the formation of our word. Aside from the obvious massive impact of the Norman invasion on English culture and on the formation of Middle English, the French influence in its broadest sense was powerful in England to a remarkable degree over several centuries. It is noteworthy that the use of English (instead of French) in courts was eventually a matter of official decree. With regard to *foutre*, which may have participated with *ficken* (or a variant) in the formation of fuck,[25] the same doubt about spontaneous vowel change exists.[26] As to whether or not some obscure primitive quality (i.e., onomatopoeic) of the short *u* sound is involved, we cannot be certain. It is noteworthy that the word *cunt*, which (allowing for variation in spelling) has a longer printed history in English than our word (see Chaucer) and certainly rivals or exceeds it in low repute, contains the same sound.[27] Again, I would suggest that the word "suck" played a part in the evolution of our word from either of its putative predecessors or their effective resultant by fusion, outweighing the spontaneous intrinsic vowel tendencies.

It is, of course, possible that the word or its Anlage existed in the period of Middle English, without printed record, or even in the Anglo-Saxon period, under the same conditions. Such putative word ancestor may have had a vowel sound identical with, or genetically better related to, that in our word than either *foutre* or *ficken*. The assumption is widespread among people of education that "fuck" is an Anglo-Saxon word, a matter about which one can only say that there is no evidence whatsoever. There are, of course, numerous Germanic words whose relationship to our word seems superficially likely (see Grimm 1862); even the very word (in spelling and with divers meanings) exists in German. *Fuchsen* has an explicit obscene coital meaning. Grimm, however, directs the reader's attention definitely to *ficken*, specifically away from *fuchsen* which is sometimes given in older English dictionaries, with Flemish *fuycke* (Bailey 1700?, Bailey 1730, Skinner 1668). Another possibility suggested by the grossly known facts is that the word which first appears in print in Scottish poetry came into English from Denmark[28] through Scotland and was transformed there. See the essay on the intimate relations between Denmark and Scotland in Dunbar's time in the Scottish Text Society's edition (1885 and 1893). See Danish *fik, fikke, fu, fok, fokke, fyk, fyke* (Brynildsen 1927). In this period, shortly before Scotland ceased to be a separate kingdom, she was at odds with England and very intimate with both Denmark and France, the latter also in a strained relationship with England. In this case, since we have seen that "sowk" is the word which appears in Dunbar's poetry, we could not regard it as influencing the formation of our word, except in the negative sense previously mentioned. However, we may take into account the linguistic pressure and attraction from the expanding English power below the border, remembering in relation to *suck* what Ferenczi pointed out about the uniquely obscene power of native words (Ferenczi 1916) and at least consider the possibilty that a northern Teutonic root, with the French *foutre*, with the peripheral English *suck*, entered into the formation of our word, leaving the Scots somewhat less disturbed by the word because of the relative foreignness of the nonetheless influential English rhyme-word *suck*, in relation to their own word *sowk*.

At this point, two isolated special observations from earlier English usage may be mentioned. In Grose's dictionary (1788) we find the expression "sucking the monkey" (now obsolete) for the stealthy tapping of a barrel of wine. This involved a straw or similar implement, and is thus conceptually related to the idea of the phallic vehicle for unresolved oral receptive wishes. In other dictionaries, we find the word suck for plough-share (Levens 1570 and 1867, *The Oxford English Dictionary* 1933). This word apparently has a different etymology from the common basic word. (*Soccus* Gallic vs. *Sūcan, sūgan*, A. S.), yet it is probable that something more than linguistic accident reduced the words to the same spelling and pronunciation. This is mentioned, because of the fundamental position which the plough holds in phallic symbolism (Sperber).[29] Another fact which should be noted here is the state of English in the period preceding the recorded appearance of the word fuck. This was a period of extreme laissez-faire, when the decay of flexions was practically complete and Modern English was in process of being born. Great liberty was exercised in using passive verbs actively and in even more remote adaptations. ("To happy one's friend," for instance). In this state of lingistic flux, the potentiality of the verb *to suck* being used in a reverse sense (to give suck, to suckle),[30] if not actively and directly exploited, may be assumed to have existed latently as part of the general linguistic tendency and thus as one of many forces in linguistic change.

Inquiry into the remote origins of our word's putative ancestors was motivated by the feeling that such ancestry might in itself be illuminating. Needless to say, what is here offered is taken from conventional authoritative sources. Interpretations are, of course, my own.

With Italian *fottere* and other Romance language equivalents, the derivation of *foutre* is usually assigned to the Latin *futuo*. There is discussion about the etymology of *futuo*, and some authorities favour the relation of the word to *fui*, and thus to the Indo-Germanic root *bheu* (to grow, to be, to become, to arise from). However, stronger opinions place it with *bhaut-?*: *bhit*—to hit, push (adjacent to *bhāt-*: *bhắt*) (Ernout 1939, Walde 1910 and 1935) and thus in relation with Latin *battuo*. In this sense, the importance of "hit, knock, strike" in our word, as suggested by Read, would be paradoxically supported. (*Foutre* itself includes such meaning as *thrust* and *stick*) (Passy and Hempl 1904). Aside from the occasional sexual slang expression to *bang* and the much more widely used *knock up* and *knocked up* (to make pregnant, to be pregnant), also *knockers* (testicles), this connection has apparently long been felt in our language (see Read's reference (1934) to Keats's letter (1931). In Florio's dictionary (1611), the word *cunno* is defined as a "woman's nocke or privy parts," and *cunnuta* as a "woman well nocked." The past participle is somewhat ambiguous to the latter-day reader (parallels *well hung* for the male?) *Nocke* is mentioned because both the use of *knock* or *strike* for sexual intercourse and the possible relation of the substantive for vulva to the active verb may have special theoretical importance.[31] Sperber stresses the fact that the root words for vulva are often related to words for coitus, and like the verbs, undergo remote and varied elaboration into other meanings, whereas this is definitely less true of words for penis. Occasionally words for penis are derived from those for vulva. See *fydill* and *vudeslecke* from *Fud* (*Fut*), which also means Podex (Grimm and Grimm 1862).

In this connection should be mentioned the frequency in Germanic dialects of the use of vulva terms in contemptuous or hostile references to the mouth (Sperber 1912). This usage is remote from but obviously of the same origin as the scientific terms *labia majora* and *minora*. In the borderland of speech and interpersonal relations, it should be noted that while the maternal breast dominates the infantile oral situation, the process of sucking is active (although receptive) in its own right, the rhythmic effort corresponding more to coital activity than the role of the breast. It may be for this reason that oral male homosexuals sometimes refer to the role of fellator as the "active" role. This may be an additional factor in the shift of the active verb form from the receptive organ (suck) to the emissive organ (fuck). *Ficken*, the word with which the Grimms (and more recently, Read) associate our word, is also of obscure origin. The Grimms feel that the word has probably a longer history than its printed record, because of its great importance in popular speech for a few centuries. (There are no unquestionable printed examples before New High German). The chief meaning given is that of rubbing (*fricare*), scratching, sliding, and several variants in terms of repetitive small movements. A blow, as with a whip, is mentioned as a secondary meaning. A Latin derivation is rejected. A relation to *fegen* (*schön reiben*) (currently sweep or cleanse) is suggested, thus to *fügen* (see Kluge 1921 and 1934). The alliterative *Fickfack*[32] (blow with a switch or rod) is mentioned in this connection, also *Ficke* (pocket, small sack, or purse). The derivation of *Ficke* from *ficken* is rejected by Grimm. Grimm and Klugge suggest the relation of *ficken* to *Fach* a remarkable German word of multiple interesting meanings, especially in the older language, but with a basic original meaning of snare, related to *fangen*, to seize probably from the Gothic *Fahan* (suggesting again the primary role of the receptive function). See English *fang* (*Oxford English Dictionary* 1933). Actually *Fach, fügen,* and *fegen* may all be traced back to the Indo-Germanic *pāk* and *pāg* ("to make fast by ramming or joining together" and related concepts).

Kluge (1921) under *Ficke* mentions as "unclear" the adjacent forms *fudk, fobke, fuppe.* Sperber (1912) derives *Ficke* (= *Tasche* = vulva) from the general Germanic root *Fud* (Vulva or Podex) through the Low German *Fuddik.* (See *Fud* in English and Scottish dialects (The English Dialect Dictionary 1900; Halliwell 1852, Jamieson 1912). (Relation to "a piece of tail"?) Sperber regards *Fud* and *Fub* as variants of the same root, and close to the Germanic root *Fug* or *Fuk*, with the central meaning "vulva". The related words for sexual intercourse he finds distributed through the whole Germanic language province. Among these, he includes the English word fuck, referring to Grimm in relation to *ficken*. Meanings such as *to beat* or *to move to and fro*, in accordance with his theory, are regarded as derivative. Kluge (1921 and 1934), defining *ficken* under *Fickmühle* mentions *reiben, jucken*, MHG. *vicken, reiben*, but mentions the meaning *schlagen* for *ficken* in Old Dutch (*älter ndl.*). Grimm mentions a relation to English *fidget* (similar to Scottish *fike, fyke, feik?*)(Jamieson 1818). (See *fycket* above). The relation between the "small movement" theme and the "beating" theme has considerable importance, since both seem implicit in our word. (Note German *streichen*, English *stroke* and *strike* in this connection.) We have already seen that more than one authoritative source assigns *futuo* to a line of derivation involving the concept of attack. In discussing the derivation of *ficken*, Grimm mentions that *fechten* (AS. *fechtan*, Eng. fight) seems to "touch on it." The origin of *fechten* is found in the Indo-Germanic root (Walde 1926) *pêk-* ("to pluck or fleece, or pull about, wool or hair; wool animal, sheep; small cattle, first particular, then in general; wool (*Fliess*) also hair") Derivatives include words for cattle, money (*pecunia*), and allied concepts. However, we are struck by the mention of the other words which may belong to this group, OHG. *fehōn* (*verzehren, essen*), and Lat. *pectus, pectoris* (breast or chest). That this juxtaposition may be dynamically meaningful gains some support in the root origin of the Germanic words for breast. This is found under *bhreus* (Abel 1884) "to swell, or to sprout" (as for the shorter *breu*). For *bhreus* (Abraham 1927) the definition is "zerbrechen, zerschlagen, zerkrümeln u. dgl." (Regarded as an extension from *bhreu-* (*bher-*) "mit scharfem Werkzeug schneiden, hauen u. dgl.")

Here it is difficult to avoid the impression of linguistic connection which parallels the psychological connection between the origins of certain components of destructive aggression and the original relation to the breast. It should be further observed that the emphasis on *kauen* and "mit *scharfem* Werkzeug scheiden" would seem to bear some relation to the frequency of the coitus-related words for *stumpf schneiden* (Sperber 1912). (Grimm, under *fickeln*). One may note in passing the secondary slang meaning for 'toothache'—that of a loose blade in a knife (Partridge 1950). See Hoffer (1949) regarding the rarity of infants biting their own hands. Under *bhreus* (Abraham 1927) among other words germane to the root concept, should be noted (AS.) *briesan*, and its mild English derivative *bruise*. Under *bhreus, bhrŭs* (Ash 1775), the defining words are more complex and numerous, with the words so used still suggesting certain relevant transitional concepts, in my opinion.[33] The next root given is *bhreg* (= brechen.)

If we investigate the roots immediately anterior to *bhreus*, we find: "1) *Bhreu* (*spriessen, schwellen*) 2) *Bhreu* (extension of *bher*—cut with a sharp tool, etc., especially *zerschlagen, brechen*)." These are discussed, with possible antecedent longer and shorter root forms, and their derivatives. It is noteworthy that the rhyme between the two Old Indic words, *cárvati* and *bharvati*, is accorded special significance in the discussion (Wyld 1920). *Carváti* means "zerkaut, zermalmt," *bharvati*, "kaut, verzehrt." The influence of the rhyme is felt to be of such possible power as to introduce a question regarding the exact derivation of *bharvati*.[34] Next is *bhreu bhrū* (Kante, scharfer Rand), then *breu q-, k-*. The latter immediately precedes our *l.bhreus* and is defined as "schabend über etwas drüber streichen," "über etwas hinfahren u. dlg.," apparently related to *bhreu- bher* ('mit einem spitzen Werkzeug (z.B. Schaber) schneiden oder kratzen u. dgl.') Here the semantic relation to the older German meanings of *ficken* is striking.

Much further back in the series of roots beginning with "b" sounds is *bu* ("Schallnachahmend für dumpfe Schalleindrücke, z.B. Uhuruf, dumpfer Schlag u. a.") 2) *Bu* ("Lippe, Kuss") Onomatopoeic, lips inward. 3) *Bu, bhu* ("aufblasen.") Expulsive sound of the inflated cheeks, like *pu. phu*. From this latter conception are derived more complex and varied meanings ("aufschwellen, rundlich aufgetriebenes (dann auch eingewölbtes) verschiedenster Art, auch durch Einfüllen von Heu u. d.gl. anschwellen machen, stopfen" und "blasen, husten u. dgl."

It is also mentioned that the root *bheu* ("werden, entstehen") may well have been involved through connections with the conception "schwellen." See Read's *fui* in relation to the rejected *futuo*. Among the extensions of this root are the Latin *bucca*, and the (NHG) *(p)fauchen*. The latter, Grimm brings into relation with *Focke* (foresail), one of the several German words whose obvious sound relationship (aside from symbolism) makes it difficult to exclude them altogether from at least some direct or indirect *influence* in our word's genesis or persistence (also see Sperber). In the derivatives of extensions from these onomatopoeic roots are also the series of words meaning sack, pouch, purse, including (AS) *pohha, pocca* and (Engl.) *poke*. These words are mentioned by Grimm in relation to *Ficke*. Noteworthy in relation to our main theme is the current and increasing vernacular preponderance of the "thrust" significance of the word *poke* over its pouch meaning. (The two words are of separate derivation.) Under this same root comes the English word for a sprite, *Puck*. A linguistic-historical curiosity is the relation of *poke* and *puck* (evidently from an American-Indian word or words) to tobacco-smoking in early American Colonial speech. (See *Oxford English Dictionary* under *Poke*). Under another extension of the same root the possible relation of (Old Irish) *bot* (Middle Irish) *bod, penis*, is mentioned (see Bunker 1943). Under extensions of the same root are several words meaning vulva and sack or pouch. The essential summary impression from these deeper linguistic data is (1) the preponderant or primary character of the receptive organ (mouth, then vulva) in formation of sexual words; (2) the latter's capacity to become or to be conceived of as expulsive and (3) the evident language potentiality to evolve active or extrusive words paralleling the development in concepts of mouth utilization. This primordial tendency may be reflected in the later relation of the words suck and fuck. From the point of view of libido theory, the question of the role of anal impulses in an oral (specifically speech) phenomenon may be mentioned.

Read, in rejecting what he regards as the mistaken French-Latin-Greek derivation of fuck, mentions Skinner's *Etymologicon Linguae Angelicanae* (1668) in which, it is said, much is taken from Junius about the "unrelated" Gothic word *fodr* (*Foder*, in tracing *fuchsen*). The *Etymologicon*, while it mentions *fuycken* or *focken* and *fuchsen*, lists *foutre* first.

It is worthwhile to examine the word family of which *fodr* is a member. This brings us to a consideration of the German word *Futter* (Germanic *fodr, fothr*) which for a long time has had two distinct series of meanings: (1) Something that nourishes; (2) lining of clothes. (See Grimm and Grimm 1862 for variations and details.) Sperber discusses the latter meaning as the older, recognizable in the Gothic *fodr*, "sword sheath," related to French *fourreau*, and preceded by the earlier general Germanic meaning of "inner or outer covering of an object." The two meanings (following Falk and Torp) are thought to be only remotely related, originating in the Indo-Germanic root *pa* meaning (1) to graze, tend, feed, (2) to feed, (3) to protect, shelter. The related Nordic *föda* (*fôdjan*) has the dual meaning of "nourish" (*ernähren*) and "to give birth to" (*gebären*) (see Grimm regarding *füden* Old Norse *foeda*, "to beget, give birth to, nourish"). Sperber feels that an original *fôdr* was related to the second meaning of *föda* (*fodjan*) (i.e. meaning vulva), and supports this by mentioning the Swedish dialect term *födsla* (vulva). A similar double (antithetical?) meaning is illustrated by *Fuder* (waggonload), whose basic meaning is given by Falk and Torp as *Korb* (basket). That such root-like primitive inclusiveness, derived from the same source, appeared in English is illustrated by the Middle English *föder* (the precursor of modern *fodder*) (see Stratmann 1891), which meant "food, fodder; child, offspring." Note (older)

Scottish *Fude, Fuid* = (third meaning) "A child, a person, or man" — only in alliteration with "frely." Also see Lewin's case (1950, pp. 114–115).

In Grimm's extensive discussion of *futter*, he mentions also a *presumed* Gothic *fôdr* (related to *fôdems* — food) in the "food" line of descent, and a *known* Gothic *fôdr* (sword-sheath, vagina) for the "sheath" line. He mentions the borrowing by Middle Latin of German words to form *fotrum* (case) and the return to German in the word *Futteral* (from Middle Latin *fotrale*). We may at least raise the question, pending further investigation, whether this journeying of the *fôdr* series between the Germanic and Romance languages might not have played some part in the intermediate development of *foutre* and *fottere*. A more explicitly relevant feature of the Grimm discussion is the fact that one meaning of *Futter* (in the "food" series) is "fleischliche vermischung, coitus." The use of *Esel* for penis with corresponding terms for the female genital (*futterbarn, futterwanne*), in its assignment of the eating impulse to the penis symbol, is connected with our central hypothesis.

While other sources, for instance Kluge (1934) Feist (1923), and Walde-Pokorny (1926) are not as explicit as Sperber in stating the originally common origin of the two words *Futter*, the inference of at least intimate primordial relationship may be drawn from the discussion. In Walde-Pokorny, the adjacent roots *pōi*; (*pəi?:*) *pī* and *pā* are given; The first is defined as: "Vieh weiden, hüten; daraus allgemeineres schützen, auch durch Bedecken," the second as "Vieh weiden, hüten, woraus füttern, nähren," with relevant cross-references, and discussion. If only because of identity of spelling, we are led to inquire whether the "Gallic twist" (*futter*) of the word fuck ascribed to Sir Richard Burton by Partridge (Grose 1931) may not be over-determined by this important German word. Again, to summarize briefly, the outstanding implications of this word would be (1) the intimate early linguistic relationship, perhaps common origin, of now identical words meaning respectively that which receives and covers, and that which is given internally, i.e. food, and (2) its clear-cut place in German sexual vocabulary.

If we now seek the remote root of the word *to suck*, whose immediate etymology presents no problem, it is found with intermediate and related words under *seuq, sŭq*, and *seuq, sŭg*, gutteral extension of (1) *seu-* (which covers a broad field originating in juice, sipping, sucking, wine-pressing and obviously related concepts, and extending into more remote areas, such as dung and mud). *Seu-, sŭ* (II) means to "give birth to" (*gebären*); derivatives include closely related concepts, such as beget, pregnancy, son, etc. For *seu* (1) the definition is "biegen, drehen, schwingen, in lebhafte Bewegung, versetzen." *Seu* (2) has the basic meaning "in Bewegung setzen," "antreiben." With *seu* (3) the semantic change is more conspicuous: "sieden, heftig bewegt sein," with many derivatives related to the meaning of "sieden." The meaning of the root *suei* is "biegen, drehen, schwingen, lebhaft bewegen." This is followed by *sueik-* and *sueig* ("nachgeben, nachlassen" and other meanings.) The next root is *sûeip*, which holds special interest for us. Among its derivatives is (AS.) *swifan*, whose meaning is given as "bewegen, fegen, umherschweifen" and related to the English *swift*. For some reason, the clear and unequivocal relation to the principal Middle English verb (with derivative persistence in Modern English) for sexual intercourse is not mentioned. (Also see Scottish) (Lindsay 1931–1936). The important issue from these considerations is the apparent tendency to a parallelism between the continuity of phonological modification in a root and a corresponding semantic change which in itself suggests at least a relation to the evolution of infantile impulses. Furthermore, in this instance, the direction of change is from the root for suck to the root for *swifan*, the principal English coital term for many centuries.

Before passing on to some additional briefly stated clinical observations which are thought to sustain the hypothesis of the unconscious relationship between the linguistic symbols fuck and suck, it is worthwhile to test the applicability of the hypothesis to a sphere of symbolism that is widely understood and accepted, both in the special technique of psychoanalysis and in general folklore. The snake is an ancient and generally employed phallic symbol, and it seems that the general configuration of the snake is connected with this. However, the chief functional significance of the snake in human mental life (dwarfing by far the benign role of certain species) is that of danger and implacable mutual hostility, principally expressed in its venomous, potentially lethal, bite. In its primordial relation to man, its cannibalism in total bulk was undoubtedly also observed.[35] The injection of venom may be interpeted genitally, yet retains its strong connection with the symbolism of the breast (in terms of projected hostility). Needless to say, the serpent as a benign symbol of fertility is directly related to the penis and semen, but the relation of the serpent-phallus to medicine would seem to be a residual of the positive relation to the all-healing breast. In the alcoholic, where serpent symbolism plays such a large part both in folklore and clinical fact, it seems appropriate to recall that severe problems of oral ambivalence underlie the homosexuality to which such phenomena are usually directly attributed.

In relation to the general hypothesis under discussion, the serpent as a phallic symbol gains its importance (like the word fuck) from the ambivalent aggression engendered by separation from the mother, principally at an oral level. The serpent itself, paradoxically, is always close to the symbolic mother, Earth, a fact which is subject to multiple construction. We must mention in passing other pregenital or nongenital potentialities of this extremely important and pervasive symbol, for example, anal implications of dirt, holes in the ground, or the traditional hiss, or the symbol of projected hatred for a crawling sibling rival. In the story of Antony and Cleopatra, whose fascination for mankind persists through the centuries, the mode of Cleopatra's suicide holds a climactic place. It is my opinion that the application of the snake to the breast finds its vivid meaning in its expression of original oral hostility to the breast, possibly also the picture of an infant rival at the breast, anterior to the manifest tragedy of adult sexual love and its oedipal prototype.

In the powerful and enduring narrative of mankind's fall in Genesis, we may also test some of the implications of our hypothesis. The concept that God made Eve from a rib taken from Adam's side may be seen as a summation of the separation experiences from the mother (beginning with birth) and the crystallization of the mother as a separate object. The reversal of the birth fantasy is only an apparent paradox, since the phenomenon is described as the subjective infantile experience, i.e., that a part of self (the mother) becomes a separate object. (See Nunberg's different interpretation [1947]). In this connection, the original Adam can also represent the female infant in primordial relation to her mother. In the seduction of Eve by the serpent, then of Adam by Eve, certainly the incest fantasy is represented. However the explicitly oral character of the symbolism[36] and the nature of Adam's punishment (which included the tilling of the soil) suggest strongly that it is the biologically predestined displacement of unambivalent sucking at the breast (or the postulated still earlier bliss of intrauterine life) by chewing, relative separation, and the mobilization of latent hostility, which is deeper than the genital implications. The tilling of the soil for food is, of course, continuous with ploughing and sowing as coital symbols. (Is the "punishment" the *child* instead of the food from mother?) In the Oedipus layer of this fantasy, the threatening and punishing God represents the father; in the deeper fantasy, he is the depriving mother herself. In this connection, one may recall and think on the fact that in naming the great incestuous complex of childhood, Freud chose the name of the hero who returned to parricide and incest with his mother *after having been separated from his mother since early infancy* (whose father, incidentally, struck at him with a *toothed stick.*) This raises the question of whether there is not *always* a latent prehistoric transference relation to the father which gives him a (hostile) role in resolving ambivalence toward the mother, before his actual relation to the child is strongly felt. In her regression from female genitality, the patient originally mentioned reactivated at a phallic level this early complex.

At this point, we may return to clinical material that became an object of special attention after the linguistic problem was posed by the patient originally described. The importance of the direct psychodynamic relation between unconscious oral impulses and genital impulses may be dealt with very briefly, since such data are common in general clinical experience.[37] Two experiences may be mentioned, because of their striking clarity and explicitness. A man, while giving his infant daughter her bottle (while his wife rested), suddenly ejaculated in his trousers. The patient, a restaurateur, had a long history of emotional privation, experienced and represented unconsciously largely at an oral level; and there was considerable evidence that his children, toward whom he was in fact a very good father, had the unconscious meaning of sibling rivals. In this man, orality and unconscious feminine identification were severely denied by multiple mechanisms of defense. It should be noted that direct factors such as genital friction were not present.

In another striking example, the patient had been seen irregularly in psychiatric interviews, for special situational reasons. She was a young woman with two younger sisters, in whose dream material the importance of severe oral rivaly was unmistakable, yet completely repressed. There had been a history of very close friendships with girls, hectic "petting" with boys, and an intense affectionate attachment to an older woman who was later denounced as a "lesbian" by others under circumstances which shocked the patient and terminated the attachment. When the patient married, there was considerable difficulty in establishing satisfactory sexual relations, the difficulty ranging from prolonged avoidance because of fear of pain, through dyspareunia, to simple failure of orgasm. The dreams pointed to the preponderant fear of separation from maternal figures. The patient went to a remote point with her husband to help him in work with an underprivileged and poor group of families. After a few months, the patient wrote the therapist a long letter. In general, she had been quite happy, both with her husband and with her work. From great infrequency of sexual intercourse, they were now having intercourse two or three times a day! One of the special features of her experience was the constant forced observation of the poor mothers unashamedly nursing their babies at the breast. She was becoming accustomed to this sight, which had always occasioned great revulsion in her in the past. The immediate occasion for writing was a disturbing dream. In this dream, her mother was constantly engaged in nursing babies, and as a result of this constant expenditure of her strength and substance, she was deteriorating physically and becoming progressively demented. With due regard to the many other factors of varying importance undoubtedly involved in the immediate episode, the focal and explicit importance of the oral-genital complex is unmistakable. What is especially interesting is that the hypererotic phase required the cooperation of the husband, who had not previously shown an inclination to such sexual frequency. Possibly, he too was stimulated by the nursing observation; the sexual relations included a "great deal of breast sucking."

Except in an unmistakably receptive atypical instance, such as the case originally cited, the use of the word fuck in analytic sessions would be assumed a priori to be more likely due to any number of other factors rather than to specific relation between its sound or spelling and a profound unconscious drive. Furthermore the proof that this factor is decisive is extremely difficult. However, if the immediate cultural-linguistic factor is carefully evaluated, and the cases referred to are only those in which the use of the word may be regarded as extraordinary in its qualitative or quantitative aspects, or both, we may regard the material as at least deserving of thoughtful scrutiny.

In retrospective consideration of adult women patients over more than a decade, only three (aside from the patient originally mentioned) are recalled who used the word with positive pleasure in its use or more than ordinary frequency. (In most women patients, this means from "not at all" to "very rarely.") In none could this be regarded as largely due to cultural factors past or present. In fact, the three were university graduates actively involved in intellectual or aesthetic pursuits. (It is, of course, likely that this often provides a fractional motivation in itself, akin to the "highbrow" interest in slang, slumming, jazz music, etc.) In no instance was the usage as frequent as in male patients. In one, the utilization of the word was largely nonsexual, in slangy phrases and compounds, practically confined to the opening of her analytic experience with a male analyst, following two women analysts. The opening period was one of stormy hostility and rivalry, and the word seemed largely a manifestation of her own masculine strivings. The patient's capacity for orgasmic vaginal gratification in this period was very poor. Anal and oral infantile trends both were strong; however, a basis for direct correlation with the word is lacking. In a second patient, there was also a disturbance of vaginal orgasm. Hostility and rivalry toward the male and strong unconscious homosexuality predominantly associated with breast fantasies (although anal and urethral fantasies were also numerous and strong) were conspicuous, in an overtly childlike character structure marked by high intelligence and exceptional artistic talent. In this patient, a general pleasure in "dirty" words was above the average. In a third patient the word was used with its direct sexual significance, sometimes in the transference, with occasional teasing references to the analyst's "proper" speech. In this patient, who had a long analysis in which the struggle with the oral dependent attachment to the mother (exacerbated by rivalry with a younger male sibling) was the main skeletal theme, the violent denial of oral attitudes in "independent," often phallic homosexual attitudes (on a characterologic level) was a manifest struggle within and outside the analysis, a more plastic version of the rigidly structured mechanism evidenced by the patient described in the beginning of this paper. This patient also fantasized about the analyst as dependent on her and occasionally fantasized about raping him.

In none of these instances was the patient overtly masculine or homosexual. All were capable of clitoral orgasm from the beginning, although one had anxiety about manual masturbation of such severity that the clitoris was stimulated only in cunnilingus by her husband. In two of the patients, fellatio (often simultaneous with cunnilingus by their husbands) was a regular part of their sexual life. All were smokers. In all, some conflict in relation to sucking became manifest in the transference situation at one time or another: in one, nausea with a fellatio fantasy, and in another, conflict about the wish to smoke during the hour. In one instance, the patient came to the analytic hour smoking a freakishly long cigarette in a holder at a time when her dual problem with the male, represented respectively by the father who possessed mother on a genital level and the baby brother who sucked her breast, was close to the surface. Of the three patients, two drank alcoholic liquors quite steadily, and frequently to excess. All were married: only one did not pursue a career, having renounced it at the time of marriage. Curiously, perhaps only a coincidence, the three women were the oldest among their siblings: all had younger brothers; and in two of the three, there were no other siblings.

Since these are positive instances, the important question may be raised whether the rather widespread mechanisms mentioned for the three women (of differing manifest character structure and neurosis) may not have been present in many others who did not use the word fuck. This question also applies to the larger problem of choice of neurosis. Admittedly factors other than a broad theme of unconscious conflict are involved in the use of this or any other word. For instance, the word was never used by a schizophrenic girl with an exceedingly active and varied heterosexual life, in which panicky flight from homosexuality was one of the important motives. However, the patient had been born and reared in a part of the country where the training of girls in its moral severity and separateness from that of boys is quite different from that of the larger urban centers. Here it is conceivable (although by no means certain) that the word was not learned in early years. Another schizophrenic girl (usually not distinguished by vulgar speech) once suddenly stated that the reason she envied the male his penis was because she would like to "fuck all the nice girls." The patient was not overtly homosexual, but her paranoid episodes were repeatedly stimulated by increasing ambivalent tension when her originally affectionate attachments to maternal female friends continued. Conspicuous among them was a female employer whose imposing bosom was attractive to the patient, even though she was tormented by paranoid attitudes towards her. In general, I would maintain the impression from the retrospective review of my own experience with female patients that the significance of the nonappearance or rare use of the word may be due to a variety of reasons or may not be demonstrable; that when the word *is* used in its ordinary sense *frequently* and with *pleasure*, as a preference from an adequate vocabulary, its use may be linked with pregenital fixations that seek a genital conveyance and denial in the word (often corresponding to phallic homosexual fantasies), and that within this framework, the intense oral ambivalent attachment to the mother, highly colored by disappointment in sibling rivalry, may play a large part.

At this point, it may reasonably be asked how certain observations of the use of the word by patients in a narrowly defined clinical setting may be brought into relation with the widespread use of an obscene word under everyday circumstances, and its one-time more respectable historical position. We might respond that the rule of free association in a sheltered situation, since it frees language (relatively) of the usual social imperatives and sanctions, is more likely than ordinary conversation to bring out effective determinants in relation to the intrinsic structure and sound of the word itself. The real and transference aspects of the psychoanalytic situation are dynamically operative, but these are recognizable and demonstrable, as in other psychoanalytic phenomena, to a degree rarely possible in ordinary conversation.

As to the difference between "neurotic" and "normal" people, I can only submit my conviction (following psychoanalytic tradition) that the differences are rather of intensity than essential quality and that this problem of proportions must be considered in correcting errors of inference in exchange for the valuable clarity of perception that neurotic intensity and the psychoanalytic situation permit.

For example, the very existence of this word in the vocabulary and its occasional use, like the existence of certain optional somatic expressions or certain social rituals, may be sufficient to gratify widespread basic and conflicting unconscious drives of low intensity, whereas such "institutions" are not adequate to enable the neurotic person to maintain repressions or other satisfactory defenses. In the special use of the "institution" — in some instances — the very distortion may tell or at least suggest something about the relatively conventional, which would otherwise remain quite inaccessible.

There were six psychoanalytic patients who utilized our word with noteworthy frequency or in a distinctive manner. (Among males, it is, I believe, the rarest exception who does not use the word occasionally. I can recall only one male with whom I had prolonged clinical experience who — as far as I remember — never used it. I omit one man whose use of the word was practically exclusive and whose psychological problem was strikingly relevant to our study because his current social milieu and background weighed too heavily — almost spectacularly — in his manners and habits.) Again, all were university graduates, and all were engaged in essentially intellectual or scientific activities, although one was directly in the service of the business world. (It should be mentioned here that not *all* the author's patients were university graduates and some of the other males had business[38] and social lives whose general language might much more naturally have included occasional obscene and slang expressions. However, figures are not offered, because there is no attempt to establish a *statistical* basis for this observation.) Again, one feels at the outset that the intellectual or the "aesthete" is more liable to be drawn to the mode of expression of the polar group than is the great mass of people between them. All were native-born Americans except one (the man employed by a corporation), who had been brought to this country in infancy. All came from homes which were of comfortable economic status, except the same man. All were married except one. Two drank excessively, to an extent bordering on the pathological, and one gave a pathological position in his life to quantitatively moderate drinking. All were smokers, though one smoked little. Three had manifest conflict about smoking, related to matters of health. In one, the smoking conflict was extremely intense, carrying with it all the qualities and considerations of earlier adolescent masturbation conflict (see Brill 1922). Geographical or religious-cultural factors did not seem influential. All save one had seen service in the armed forces. However, a man whose military service involved no traditional military life used the word continuously and with extreme frequency, and another with long service overseas used it largely in only one period, in a special way. Other men who had served in either the First or Second World Wars did not use it with special frequency. (The importance of military service as a current cultural pressure in language may not be of equal influence on all men, and this inequality of influence may become increasingly evident with passage of time.) One man (the man of exceptions, who, also, had not seen military service) exhibited his interest in this word differently from the others. He did not use it with special frequency in the analytic hours. He occasionally spoke of his delight and guilt in uttering the word to his wife during sexual intercourse and his wish to have her repeat the word to him.

Roy F. had a notably varied sexual life, marked by strong unconscious homosexuality, severe demands and hostility directed toward women, and intense orality pervading his overt character reactions and his masturbation fantasies. Masturbation was often employed as a sedative, with fantasies of a woman performing fellatio on him. (Later material supported the original impression that the "woman" was also himself.) This patient, as did three others in this series, had occasional nonstructural bowel symptoms and many other less tangible evidences of unconscious anal conflicts. (It is conceivable that severe and premature sphincter training may greatly augment and perhaps infuse anal elements into the need for oral gratification.) Considering these factors and allowing for the investigative bias established by the original conception, it still is true that all six patients in varying ways and through varying experiences struggled most severely with the impulse to suck a breast or penis (in the proximal sense, the latter). Furthermore, in several instances, the immediate setting in which the word appeared strengthened the impression of its focal relation to the struggle with oral impulses. The man of oral inclinations, who at times uninhibitedly performed cunnilingus when his potency was disturbed, used the word with a sort of wistful idealization of its rough masculinity. It occurred most wistfully and most often in an hour in which he was lamenting a recent episode of impotence with a woman who was a complete mother substitute and at the same time expressing his growing insight into one of the several important factors that contributed to his impotence, i.e. his wish to be mothered, nursed, to be given things by the woman, and his anger that this was not forthcoming, that she actually required things from him. In this case, the wistful desire to "just go ahead and fuck" certainly expressed and denied its opposite. Also, it included his hostility to the woman. (When this factor spreads beyond the capacities of the word's ordinary structure, audible prolongation of the f sound may appear.) That the opposite verbal tendency could also more subtly express a relation among the words that appeared in the patient's description of his extreme self-consciousness when he took a woman markedly older than himself to the theater. He felt that everyone was looking at him, that he must have looked "abnormal, like a cocksucker." On one occasion, the word *soccer* appeared in a dream in which the qualifying adjective *French* elicited the associations latent in the sound of the word for the rough masculine game.

Robert F. experienced much marital trouble, based largely on his own unconscious homosexuality, intense narcissism, and intense hostility toward women. The latter, rationalized in many ways, was based largely on feelings of oral deprivation and rage, which only after a long period revealed themselves consciously in their anatomical associations. The patient's powerful fellatio impulses were violent denied for a long time, often occasioning obvious severe physical symptoms or appearing in inverted form in actual practice with his wife or in dreams with the analyst as fellator. The patient's erectile potency was good; sexual intercourse was frequent, at times with a literally compulsive quality. This patient delighted in our word—used it all the time. He played with it, experimented with new compounds, but above all seemed to relish its very sound. That this man envied his wife's not infrequent role as fellatrix and also her role in intercourse, while enjoying his own role, was demonstrated by abundant material. On two occasions in puberty, this patient had masturbated, using foods as lubricants. The masochistic solution of intense hostilities contributed a large part to his passive feminine envy and identification. Whether this tendency expressed itself in oral or anal or castrated genital fantasies, the usual mode of response included heightened coital activity and a corresponding augmentation in the pleasure utilization of the word fuck.

William W. had a considerable flair for words, and a severe neurosis involving multiple and complex social anxieties. In this patient too, the denial of castration anxiety was especially prone to be expressed by hypererotism. Again there were obvious disturbances in both the anal and oral spheres. It was my impression that the violent reaction to oral disappointment and the identification with the disappointing mother were the central issues in the multiple complicated problems in this case. This patient did not utilize the word with unusual frequency, but with strong focal relation to the unconscious trends presented at a certain time. For instance, the word appeared conspicuously when a vacation interruption of analysis was expected, when dieting for weight reduction was under way, and when a (temporary, but long) cessation of smoking had been effected. Both the pronunciation of the word (the prolonged *f* sound) and the context indicated a strong hostile component in its employment.

The fourth male differed from the others in that a special preference for the word seemed to be confined to the coital situation, and here it was only sporadic. His wish to have his wife say the word was largely aborted by the same intense guilt evoked by his own utterance of it. This man was the oldest sibling in a large family of the laboring class, with considerable early deprivation. The unmistakable evidences of severe unconscious sibling envy were dealt with largely by reaction formation; i.e., the patient early became the conscientious protector of his siblings and the pride and counselor of his humble parents. Unlike the other patients, although the patient had a routine job of an intellectual nature, he was unpretentious and unaspiring intellectually and conventional in his outlook and habits. His sexual morality was very strict, both in external adherence and in its structural role in his personality. He had numerous phobias, largely in intimate personal or social situations, and an alarming tendency to sudden syncope (related to unconscious passive fantasies). He had masturbated during puberty, with overt fantasies of intercourse with his mother. (This is not the man mentioned previously in connection with the snake symbol.) His wife, with whom he had relatively normal sexual relations, occasionally stated that he "seemed to need a mother instead of a wife." This perception must have been based on exceedingly subtle data, for excepting a morose (not demonstrative) hypochondriasis, the patient was excessively reserved and controlled, overconscientious, with no *overtly* childlike attitudes. Although it played no conspicuous part in his monogamous sexual life, the patient showed a greater than average interest in the breast; for instance, his exceedingly guilty extramarital impulses frequently found exciting expression in looking at women's breasts when their clothing became scantier in the summertime. This patient had occasional bowel symptoms among others; and there was good ground for assuming that severe sphincter training had at least contributed to the lack of spontaneity, the excessive sense of hazard in self-expression, and the general cautiousness in many spheres that characterized his personality. This probably contributed to the pleasure and guilt in the sense of a "dirty word." Yet the essential experiential core of this patient's character and illness lay in the tremendous structure evolved to repudiate, distort, hide, and yet gratify—through many intricate devices— his intense passive, specifically oral wishes, and the violent hostility to siblings evolved from them. When his girl baby was born, his tendency to identify himself with the child in all her infantile difficulties with her mother was truly remarkable.

In this instance, it should be mentioned that his hostility to women (mothers) was not the demonstrably intense and decisive personality problem that it was in the preceding three male patients. Nor, correspondingly, was his use of the word fuck tinged as much with violence as with shy guilty pleasure. I would infer, since the word was used in a satisfactory genital situation in preference to words of explicitly anal reference, that it appeared largely as an emissive oral gratification and demand, in which the phonetic relation to the word suck played a partly determining role. One may raise the question whether this patient's overt pubertal incestuous fantasy was not a reaction to the violently denied oral fixation to the mother, a striking exaggeration of the unconscious Oedipus complex, and speculate whether the universal remnants of oral fixation do not thus contribute an important factor to the normally occurring Oedipus complex, parallelling the relation of the words fuck and suck. This would not be too surprising, insofar as it is sucking and suckling that distinguish the entire vertebrate class to which we belong.

If the reciprocal phenomenon of regression connected with disturbances at the genital level is not stressed in this paper, it is not from lack of appreciation of its great importance. It is rather that the chief interest in the study lies in the relation of the genetically older phenomenon to its later integrated representation. I do not wish to subscribe to another "genetic fallacy." To the extent that genitality is soundly organized and unobstructed, it exists in its own right, with its own pecularities, like a true stable chemical compound. The same is true of the word we are studying. However, neurotic genitality may be compared with an unstable compound or even a readily separable physical mixture. To the extent that "normal" individuals share small proportions of the same traits that distinguish neurotic individuals, the existence of multiple reflections of such traits in cultural institutions may be of special assistance to them in maintaining their normality.

In the two remaining male patients (added long after this study was originally conceived), severe pregenital fixations were also striking. In both, oral demand, envy, and rage directed at women were of remarkable intensity. Both had younger sisters and amalgamated their rage toward the disappointing mother with the hatred and envy of the little girl rival. Both employed a variety of masochistic solutions for their passive wishes and hostilities. Both employed the diffusely pejorative adjective "fuckin'" (which seems largely a degenerative form of the present participle) with great frequency, apparently to give greater scope to the sheer sounding of the word. In both, the fellatio fantasies (and homosexuality in general) were close to the surface. In one, the man referred to in connection with the cannibalistic snake symbol, there had been naïve adolescent wishes that his mother should solve his sexual problem. In the other, incest fantasies had been severely repressed.

SUMMARY

Based on inferences from clinical observation, the opinion is established that the important and taboo English word *fuck* bears at least an unconscious rhyme relation, possibly an actual genetic linguistic relation, to the word *suck* within the framework of considerations that determine the general phenomenon of obscenity, including the anal emissive pleasure in speech. Toward the establishment of this opinion and impression as a scientific hypothesis, I investigated the known linguistic facts. From this, I adduced certain clinical psychoanalytic phenomena and a few broad historical observations in indirect support of the hypothesis. The controversy as to the origin from *ficken* or *foutre* was stated, with a subsequent effort to resolve the conflict, to trace both words to their respective origins in Indo-Germanic roots, and to demonstrate the probable important influence of the word *suck*. The deeper root data indicate that the oral receptive attitude of sucking may provide the conceptual and linguistic Anlage that ultimately eventuates in basic words for sexual intercourse in English, and that the evolution in roots shows a tendency to correspond to a putative psychic evolution through predominant oral aggression, toward (with later incorporation in) the active phallic sexual attitude, most clearly manifested in the normal male role. The male sexual role is the manifest structural opposite of the original sucking experience (except in the active rhythmic movement). Possible anal considerations were mentioned. The whole is thought to be relevant to Sperber's theory of speech origin (or more directly to an "oral" hiatus in it) and also to Abel's demonstration of the "antithetical sense of primal words." In general, the investigation was felt to support the hypothesis that the words fuck and suck have a general unconscious relationship, perhaps expressed only in the rhyme and latent conceptual relation of the corresponding drives, but possibly implicit in the actual structure of the words.

The questions that arise for further study in relation to this hypothesis and investigation are: (1) the general action of large unconscious trends, as conceived in psychoanalysis, on the more specifically linguistic factors in word formation;

(2) the psychological significance of rhyme; (3) the significance of specific sounds in word meaning; (4) the further investigation of the role of inevitable primordial object relation and separation (especially in the oral sphere) in the development of aggression in general, the role of such aggression in the nature of normal genitality, and in the normal and pathological Oedipus complex; and (5) further consideration of the role of language itself as a highly structured convention of object relationship, perhaps the most important instrument of the mastery of separation, fulfilling a role corresponding to the anatomic-physiological stereotypes, differing as they do from varied and fluid elements in individual emotional and psychical life, yet always in a continuous dynamic relation with these more labile components of personality.

NOTES

1. One element in numerous figurative uses should be mentioned. With the frequent tendency to utilize the word in one of its many forms in neutral compound intensification—for instance "the best (or the worst) fucking day"—the *preponderantly* hostile or pejorative meanings of these expressions should be noted. This tendency is connected with the central hypothesis of this paper. Also see Sperber 1912.

2. *Foutre* has apparently lost its sexual importance in French, preserving some pejorative significance.

3. Would this be analogous to a possible *foutre-ficher-fichtre* series in French? (Bloch 1932, Gasc 1941).

4. It is interesting, although not scientifically available, to note that the story in which the word appears involves (1) the banishment of sexual references from the dinner table and (2) a list of equivalent words among which a few involve intrinsic rhymes and two others rhyme with one another. The second consideraton is germane to the material which follows. The quotation is: ("Stropurtzlen, ficken, nobisen, raudimaudi, schiri-miri, nullen, menscheln (footnote *merscheln*), zusammen-schrauben, pirimini (footnote *pirimiri*) leuss imm peltz, pampeln, strampeln, feder-ziehen, auf den hackpret schlahen, pfefferstossen, imberreiben, fleyschlen, holtzhawen, und schleiterklüben, etc.").

5. An interesting analytic fragment reflecting this metamorphosis occurred in the long period in which the detachment from the analyst as mother was the principal problem. The patient, whose concern with the cosmetic aspects of her teeth was always hypochondriacal, acquired a transitory breast pain, with corresponding cancer anxiety, after hearing a patient in her dentist's office discuss the early detection of breast cancer. In the week of this preoccupation, the patient dreamed of her astonishment at the sudden appearance of her mother with a conspicuous beard.

6. In connection with the word *rape*, one may mention Devereux's study of Mohave orality (Devereux 1947), where the denial of orality is necessarily so severe that an attempt at rape is thought to have been provoked by an implied taunting offer of the breast.

7. For intransitive preponderance, see older Scottish *fuk, fuck* (Craigie 1937).

8. The relationship between this phenomenon and the investment of the entire system of free association in the analytic relationship with similar or related energies is an important theoretical problem beyond the scope of this investigation. See Fliess (1949). The

same is true of the important position of metaphor in language, as conceived by Sharpe (1940); also the problem of words and preconscious function (Kris 1950).

9. When I mention current everyday usage without qualification, it should be understood that I speak of American slang, which may or may not coincide with English slang.

10. Among the Arabic words, in my view, are noticeably a large number connected with the oral sphere. Can this be due *only* to the importance of the desert and the camel? See the word *wean*, which is now used largely in the sense of the deprivation of sucking. Its original meaning was the complementary and — in a sense — opposite one, i.e., to *give* solid food (*Encyclopedia Brittanica* 1910, Skeat 1912).

11. Abel refers to the views of the philosopher Bain and the etymologist Tobler in this connection. Bain postulated antithetical words, without reference to linguistic facts, as a logical necessity, based on "the essential relativity of all knowledge, thought, or consciousness." Tobler mentions that such double meanings are already present in the same roots in the first speech formations. He does not believe that one springs from the other, but rather that the basic meaning has its true existence in this polarity, analogous to an electro-magnetic field. Apparently Abel's views are not acceptable by all linguists today (Herzog 1951), presumably because of etymological considerations. However, the existence of individual words or almost identical couples of antithetical meaning in various languages, regardless of deviation, cannot be doubted (Abel 1884, *Encyclopedia Brittanica* 1910, Grimm and Grimm 1862, Skeat 1912). I myself occasionally stumble on new ones. In Persian, for instance, the word *tond* means swift, *kond* means slow (Haim 1936 and 1943). (Note that *t* and *k* have a relation in infant speech) (Jakobson 1942, Lewis 1936). In the same language, the word *fara* may mean ahead or behind, front or back, far or near, etc. It is possible that such word or its progenitor was originally accompanied by a gesture, as suggested by Abel for certain Egyptian words. Where words are of different etymology, it is hardly likely that purely phonetic attraction would tend to approximate them, against semantic contradiction, were there not at least an unconscious acquiescence or possibly an actual drive in this direction. Aside from other considerations mentioned before or elsewhere (as in the case of *wean*), psycho-analysis provides analogies for such a phenomenon, ranging from demonstrable antithetical representation in dreams or symptoms to the fundamental dual instinct theory. Certain basic "confusions" in the early phenomenology of speech provide a possible additional element in this tendency. The problem of learning the difference between the words *you* and *I* is often manifest in children, a matter which, like the existence of the actual personal mirror image (and the complementary organic phenomenon, strepho-symbolia), must become connected with the depth-psychological representations of "subject" and "object." That the "you-I" confusion in a child can be solved in a manner analogous to compulsion was suggested by a little girl exhibited to me by an amused mother. The child could not utter the letter "u," except when it was isolated, in immediate mimicry. If asked to spell the word *cut*, immediately after it had been spelt for her, she would say "c-me-t." A similar milder problem exists later in life with regard to the grammatical distinction between subjective and objective cases in the pronouns. Certain individuals, who have overcome with effort the tendency to say "me" for "I" will consistently, with a self-conscious air of correctness, substitute "I" for "me" after prepositions, i.e., "for you and I." The urge to mastery of an object may conceivably play a part in approximating opposites. A child less than two was observed commanding the household cat repeatedly and urgently to "sit down!" When the cat refused to obey, she shouted "Stamm up (stand up), pussy!"

12. In omitting the sphincter impulses, no depreciation of their importance is intended.

However, they are not primarily and immediately dependent on objects; hence they are originally more intimately related to autism than to communication. That autistic (specifically auto-erotic) anality contributes to the peculiar effect of basic obscene words, entirely aside from the association with primitive emissive relief, is my conviction. The pleasure in uttering obscene words lies not only in the communicative effect on the object but in the simultaneous autistic pleasure of utterance. The latter then heightens the importance of the most primitive fraction of object relationship and thus of communication, the fantasy of mutual identification.

13. The problem of frequent conventional linguistic confusion in psycho-analytic usage is one which must be accepted as an impediment and implicit reservation in any condensed formulation throughout this paper. In sucking, for instance, the mother's "activity" is essential to the establishment of the entire breast-mouth complex, yet there is no doubt that sucking as such is the *infant's* "activity." The question of protrusive versus recessive or emissive versus receptive is without this confusion. In the adult sexual act, the total role of the individuals is less easily categorized, except in statistical convention; the immediate anatomico-physiological realtionship more clearly involves activity in the male, receptivity and relative passivity in the female, although even in this connection there are variations which increase in possible degree with the remoteness from the zone of genital conjunction.

14. In this assumption, which merely parallels and particularizes the general trend of thought of this paper, I am extrapolating to the theory of communication a conception which is firmly rooted in the history of psycho-analytic theory. In this basic formulation of observations and ideas concerning sexuality (Freud 1905a), Freud repeatedly gives evidence of his conviction regarding the importance of the nursing relation to the mother as the basic prototype of object love, and clearly accepts the possibility of a direct dynamic psychological continuum between the phases. The phase of genital primacy is conceived of, when normal, as a "firm organization" including earlier phases, rather than as something essentially new. We may also refer to Brunswick's important paper on the pre-oedipal phase (Brunswick 1940). I believe that some linguistic evidence reflexively supports the conception of the enduring dynamic importance of the pregenital organizations in adult sexuality. Of the series "active-passive, phallic-castrated, masculine-feminine," it would be reasonable to assume that all find some representation in the putative linguistic transition from suck to fuck.

15. On the other hand see *fag*, occasionally used in American slang for cigarette, the same word for a fellator.

16. Both are now established in the dictionary. See *blow* in current American slang for "to perform fellatio," the same word in English slang, among varied uses, for *smoke*. Partridge for the last.

17. The destruction of numerous cigarettes, while less spectacular than the "killing of a quart," can provide a similar satisfaction.

18. An interesting piece of indirect evidence in this connection lies in the curious implicit pairing of the words fuck and suck in a relationship as silent as their obvious rhyme. In slang, the derivatives of suck are largely pejorative, and they usually involve contempt—as for one who is easily exploited, or for one who has already been exploited (*sucker*). The element of reversal of direction is present even in this usage, for it is often applied to one who has given too much or who gets too little or both. What is more interesting is that fuck is often used in the complementary sense. To *get fucked* is to be made a *sucker*. To fuck (even secondarily, to screw) someone is to make him or her (more often

used for the male) a *sucker*. To be *sucked in* tends to turn again in the original direction. Partridge's (British) collection (Partridge 1950) gives "suck-and-swallow" for *pudendum muliebre* (19th and 20th centuries, but (questionably) obsolete). *Suck* is an old word for strong drink. *Fuck* is assigned an additional substantive meaning by Farmer and Henley (Farmer and Henley 1893) and Partridge, i.e. semen.

19. It is interesting to note that tobacco on its earlier arrival in Spain (1558) was thought to have miraculous healing powers.

20. See Campion, 1602.

21. The word *sowk* was probably not, it should be observed, pronounced as it might be in modern English. Scottish pronunciation is and was admittedly highly variable; (Jamiesen 1912) spellings were very variable; dictionaries often do not indicate pronunciations of individual words. I have tried to ascertain probable pronunciations from good authorities — by specific or general statement, by comparison and inference, by rhymes (Baildon 1896–1900, Craigie 1937 and 1949, Jamiesen 1818, Murray 1873 and 1870–72, Reeves 1893, Wilson 1923). The impression persists that *owk* would not be a satisfactory, certainly not a compelling rhyme with *uck* or *uk*. The closest possible approximation which I can infer would be the long *oo* sound as in *boot* for *owk*, the short German "u" sound or the French "u" (as in *une*) for *uck* or *uk*. Probably the difference was greater. The tendency is towards separate systems of rhyme for the two systems of spelling.

22. *Fukkit* is rhymed with *chukkit* (Chuckled, as a hen to her chickens). *Sowk* is rhymed with *bowk* (body) and *owk* (week). One is tempted to reproduce this poem in its entirety because of the *multiple* oral references. Two striking lines are: "My chype, my vnspaynit gyane (Big soft fellow, unweaned giant). With moderis milk zit in your mychane" (machine, *membrum virile*).

23. It is apparent even from my own limited and casual field of observation that various combinations may occur. Recently, in successive sentences a little girl was heard to say that she "sought so" (thought so) and then to refer to "frowing" (throwing) something away. Aside from certain organic linguistic considerations it is conceivable that important sound-affect associations are involved, in addition to the broader childhood resistance to the adoption of adult speech conventions. (Is the Cockney transposition of *h* and *non-h* sounds allied to this? Or the New York *foist* for first, *kern* for coin?) For comparative linguistic data regarding infant speech and a detailed study of the systematic development of basic elements in language see Jakobson (1942).

Whether or not the typographical resemblance between the *f* and *s* in German is related to this phenomenon is a question about which at this moment I have no data. In earlier English printing, for instance in Florio's dictionary, this resemblance is striking. See also Bailey (1700? and 1730) and Skinner (1668). That the leap from *s* to *f* can occur in auditory errors with normal hearing is evidenced in a letter observed by me, between two intelligent adults in which the recipient is reproved for having heard "Cossingham" for "Coffingham." That the recipient is a person who occasionally and amusingly says "stove" instead of "icebox" or vice versa, adds, within the limits of persuasiveness of an isolated instance, to the conception that certain tendencies to variation of sounds and meanings respectively are liable to be importantly connected.

In noting the continuous and alternative relation of *s*, *f*, and *th* in English, we may think of *th* as interpolated — psychologically — between the other two sounds. From the point of view of chronology, it should be noted that *th* is acquired later than either *s* or *f* in children, and in aphasia tends to disappear in favour of *s* (Jakobson 1942). Also note the *th* delay in (child) K in Lewis's material (Lewis 1936). Actually, both published observations and my own casual experience support the fact that none of these three sounds appears very early in childhood efforts to talk. *F seems* to have a somewhat firmer place in general in English-speaking children, yet I know a child who — although he can utter the *f* sound — consistently and invariably replaces it with *s*. The special early problem with (*purposive*) "th" cannot be doubted, yet note the later lisp mentioned elsewhere. The word suck, despite the profound importance of the act to which it refers, is to be regarded as essentially an "adult" word, primarily symbolic and referential, objectively communicative in character. Where linguists connect early word-formation with sucking — especially the hunger cry (discomfort) — it is the "front" consonants, nasal and oral, which are involved. The wish to suck, expressive and evocative, is thus (from this point of view) included in the almost universal nursery word *mama*. (See Lewis 1936. This book in general provides a broad psychological context for language phenomena.) It is only a rare child for whom the word suck carries a strong conscious affect. Conceivably some of the primitive language function may reappear with this word in certain adult bucco-genital situations. It may have an aura resembling that of *fuck* to certain homosexuals. See *suck* in Partridge (1950) as "the homosexual v. (i. and t.) and occ.n." etc. The tremendous evocativeness and expressiveness of *fuck* have already been discussed. Possibly the hunger affect is latently associated with the largely referential word *suck* (in repression), and reappears with the linguistic transmutation into the obscene *fuck*. It should be mentioned that not all linguists accept the importance of sucking movements in front consonants (Jakobson 1940–1942).

24. Also, see Hoffer (1949) on the hand as an early "competitor" with the breast or bottle.

25. See Grose-Partridge (1931).

26. The preponderant tendency of the French "ou" sound in English was to become dipthongized into our present *ow* sound. However, insofar as the word followed another trend, common in native words of similar sound (109), it might tend towards shortening and "unrounding," i.e. towards our present short *u* sound. *K* and *t* sounds are sometimes interchangeable in childhood speech (Jakobson 1940–1942, Lewis 1936).

27. Note the phrase "to come" for "to experience orgasm" (paradoxically also to "go off," the latter meaning also "to die" — Partridge), also *come* as a noun for semen. (Also *scum* for semen, also *spunk*). The word *buss* for kiss is very likely related to the explicitly oral *baiser*, now a French obscene verb for sexual intercourse. See the juxtaposition of "fuck-beggar" and "buss-beggar" by Captain Grose (1931). The word *hump* for intercourse was very popular. The stereotyped grunt sound is *ugh*! While this sound has sexual (genital) as well as anal implications, it is conventionally associated with disgust, even horror. Curiously enough the patient who stimulated this study described her remembered early attitude towards sex as expressed by this word (in the sense of disgust).

28. In *The Dance of the Sevin Deidly Synnes* of Dunbar (1885) a possible transitional word appears in the lines: "All led thay vthir by the tersis (Penis)," "Suppoiss thay fycket with their ersis (Fundaments)." The glossary gives the meaning of *fycket* as "v.pt.t., moved from side to side or backwards and forwards." This is close to one of the primary meanings given for *ficken* (allied to English *fidget*) (Grimm and Grimm 1862). Furthermore, a close scrutiny of the lines leaves us with the strong impression that the author may possibly have intended the same meaning as *fukkit* (fucked). Apparently no similar transitional word has been observed, or at least mentioned, in English. Judging by spelling and occasional rhymes there is apparently some alternative relation between at least the letters *u* and *i* in Scottish. (See *sucker* rhymed with *bicker* in Burns.) Curiously enough the word *fuck* (not fukk-) also appears in Dunbar in a nonobscene sense: "And sic fowill tailis (dirty

dress trains), to sweep the calsay (causeway) clene // The dust vpskaillis (is thrown up); so mony fillok (giddy young women) with fuck sailis // Within this land was nevir hard nor sene." ("Devorit with Dreme, Devysing in my Slummer." (Dunbar 1885). "Fuck sailis" means "with ample-skirted dresses, like sails, hanging in folds." Fuck means "fold," "plait," also "in the shape of plaid." Two things must be noted, first the probable connection with the word *faik* (plaid) (Sw. *veck*) and the striking resemblance of the compound to the North German *Fock-Segel*. The latter is one of the several Germanic words of the wind and sea, which might conceivably have sexual linguistic connections. In *faik*, there is a connecting link with the protean German *Fach* (Grimm), which may be connected (Kluge 1934) with *Ficke*, a word probably of separate origin from *ficken*, but possibly influenced by it in its later development. ("Das Wort klingt uns heute gemein und kann nur in nachlässigem komischen stil gelten") (Grimm and Grimm 1862). *Fach* and *fegen* (connected with *ficken*), may be striking examples of the descent of versatile and respectable words, with the popular sexual words, from common ancestors.

29. Also see Walde-Pokorny for the common root origins for plough-share and pig-snout (Walde 1910).

30. "To suckle" would, of course, represent the direct antithesis of "to suck," thus accurately representing the infantile identification with the "active" mother. Incidentally, so strong is the latent impulse to confuse the "direction" of these words that we may, without difficulty, find examples of *suck* implications in the use of "suckle" by cultivated people. It is not surprising that the verb "to suckle" is regarded as a *possible* back-formation from the substantive *suckling*, and that the little-used substantive *suckler* is used both for the one who *gives* suck and for the one who sucks (*Oxford English Dictionary* 1933). It is important to point out that *fuck* is not in the line of *simple* antithesis, in the sense that the *actual* relation (apart from unconscious psychological factors) is in a different sphere; also, of greater immediate psychological relevance, that the word possibly includes in its structure the correlates of residues of profound emotional experience attendant on the frustration of the sucking impulse, and the ultimate forced renunciation of the practice.

31. This despite the fact that the origin of the word *nocke* (for vulva) is obscure, not necessarily the same as *knock* (ME. *knocken*, AS. *cnucian*). In fact, it may find origin as a cognate of *notch* (*Nock*, from OD. *Nocke*). In that case the relation to the word "knock up" as an active development from a receptive (in a sense) passive concept would be even more striking. It is not likely, in my view, that the approximation of the two words *knock* and *nocke*, even if of different etymology, is based *purely* on sound confusion. See *suck* (in the ordinary sense) and *suck* (plough-share). *Nock*, which can also mean buttocks, was, in the past, a transitive masculine coital verb. In a word such as *lick*, including current colloquial usage, we see the range from the oral infantile ("passive") attitude to aggression and conquest, the latter usages decidedly secondary. In a more remote sense, in English dialect, see *Fud* as (1) tail of a hare, (2) to kick with the feet (Halliwell 1852). Also, *tuck* equals "a kind of sword; a net" (Walker 1824).

32. Scottish *ficks-facks* (Craigie 1949, Jamieson 1818), "trifling and troublesome affairs" suggests the meaning given for *foutering* (in English) (Farmer 1893) and now frequently associated with fuck, as in "fucking around."

33. It is well to state my awareness that, while the facts reproduced are accurate, and my conviction about their interpretation strong, others investigating the same text without my hypothesis might conceivably find support for another trend of thought. The roots studied are, of course, those which I found in a relation to the words whose origins I sought. The huge accumulation and maze of interrelated meanings in a collection such

as Walde-Pokorny (Walde 1926–1932) would merit exhaustive and separate study in itself, from a psycho-analytic point of view. My impression, from incidental wide persual, is that this would be a most productive undertaking.

34. That rhyme is a profound influence in language development and change cannot be doubted (Sperling 1947, Walde 1926–1932, Wood 1907–1908). Secondary series of derivatives from words engendered by rhyme or assonance may occur as though a nonexistent common root had existed (See F. A. Wood 1907–1908). That the question of a special tendency to loss or addition of the initial *s* sound has been a matter of discussion and investigation, even though viewed with conservative reservations in the paper consulted (1907–1908), is of special interest in relation to the word "suck". Conceivably, an allied (unconscious) process might have some relation to the intermediate position of the English dialect word *yuke* (itch). (In an old rhyming dictionary spelled *yuck*) (Walker 1824). Note how often young children use the verb *itch* for *scratch*, even when assigned to another person: "Itch my back, mummy!" The potentiality for rhyme, of course, exists in the putative antithetical primal words, still more in the primordial cries of early infancy, from which Anlage all later language develops. The profound drive to reconcile contradictions, to restore the unity of sound and meaning, while still preserving the differentiation so necessary to aspiring life, may be important in poetry. In a brief paper, Sapir (1920) notes how — in the fortunate poetic line — the effort to establish a rhyme seems to have *contributed* to the accuracy of expression. Clinically, the regressive variant of the same process may be seen in the occasional *clang* associations of the manic. These may be regarded as sustaining my hypothesis, in the light of Lewin's work on the intimate relationship between elation and the complex of oral gratification and sleep (68). In the more immediate relation, see *Buck* = "to wash clothes; to copulate as bucks" (Walker 1824). Also see (Scottish) "Blind Buk" = Cupid (22), (Buk = male deer or he-goat); also Bailey's obscure reference to a "term used of a goat" in relation to fuck (Bailey 1730).

35. In one of my male patients, a snake in a dream was associated with his wife, and then spontaneously with a childhood fascination in watching snakes swallow small frogs whole.

36. In Róheim's interesting comparative study, "The Garden of Eden" (1940), the oral (nipple) symbolism of the apple and the variant female symbolism of the snake are mentioned. References are made to female snake goddesses. While Róheim devotes most of his paper to the oedipal content of the narrative of the fall, he points out towards the end the importance of the separation trauma and oral aggression. He does not however stress the hostile oral symbolism of the serpent as such. The plucking of the apple is also mentioned in relation to the trauma of birth (Rank). (See "fruit of the womb," the relevant old words previously given, the expression of Keats, Lewin's patient, and the relation of the woman's punishment to her crime.) Róheim refers to one part of the serpent's punishment — the *eating of dust* — as evidence that he is a "chthonic being, a denizen of the underworld."

37. See for example, the recent paper by M. Sperling, in which the oral fantasy in genital exhibitionism is conspicuous (Sperling 1947).

38. The male who — in my recollection — never used the word, was in the business world. He was of excellent formal education, of highly conventional tastes and ideals, of great propriety in his social life. This man had a severe oral disorder. Why then did he never use the word? The following may be suggested: (1) His relative lack of reaction against the characterological manifestations of orality; (2) A strong compulsive tendency against spontaneity, which allied itself with his social ideals, which even militated strongly

against the spontaneity of his free associations. Vulgarity or even the "rough" aspects of masculinity were held in low esteem in his circles throughout his life.

References

Abel, K. (1884). *Über den Gegensinn der Urworte.* Leipzig: Friedrich.

Abraham, K. (1927). Oral erotism and character. *Selected Papers* 393–406.

Ash, J. (1775). *The New and Complete Dictionary of the English Language, etc.* London.

Baildon, H. B. (1896–1900). On the rimes in the authentic poems of William Dunbar. *Transactions, Royal Society of Edinburgh* 39:629–665.

Bailey, N. (1700?). *English Dictionary. An Universal Etymological Dictionary, and an Interpreter of Hard Words.* London.

———— (1730). *Dictionarium Brittanicum.* London.

Baker, S. J. (1950). Language and dreams. *Int. J. Psychoanal.* 31:171–178.

Barrère, A., and Leland, C. G. (1889). *A Dictionary of Slang, Jargon, and Cant*, vol. 1. London: Ballantyne.

Bartlett, J. (1894). *A New and Complete Concordance . . . to . . . Shakespeare.* London and New York: Macmillan.

Bergler, E. (1936). Obscene words. *Psychoanal. Q.* 5:226–248.

Blau, A. (1943). Philological note on a defect in sex organ nomenclature. *Psychoanal. Q.* 12:481–485.

Bloch, O., and von Wartburg, W. (1932). *Dictionnaire Etymologique de la Langue Française.* Paris: Presses Universitaires de France.

Blount, T. (1674). *Glossographia, or a Dictionary, Interpreting the Hard Words, etc.* London: Newcomb.

Bodmer, F. (1944). *The Loom of Language*, ed. L. Hogben. London: Allen and Unwin, p. 199.

Bosworth, J. (1882). *An Anglo-Saxon Dictionary.* Oxford.

Brunswick, R. M. (1940). The preoedipal phase of the libido development. *Psychoanal. Q.* 9:293–219.

Brynildsen, J. (1927). *Norsk-Engelsk Ordbok.* Oslo: Achehoug.

Bunker, H. A. (1943). Body as phallus: A clinico-etymological note. *Psychoanal. Q.* 12:476–480.

Campion, T. (1602). *Observations in the Art of English Poesie.* With S. Daniel, *A Defense of Rhyme.* London: Lane, 1925.

Cockeram, H. (1623). *The English Dictionarie of 1623 by Henry Cockeram.* Pref. by C. B. Tinker. New York: Huntington, 1930.

Craigie, W. (1937). *A Dictionary of the Older Scottish Tongue (A-Futher).* Chicago-London: University of Chicago Press.

Daniel, S. (1603). *A Defense of Rhyme.* London: Lane, 1925.

Devereux, G. (1947). Mohave orality, an analysis of nursing and weaning customs. *Psychoanal. Q.* 16:519–546.

Dunbar, W. (1885). *The Poems of William Dunbar, Part II*, ed. J. Small. Edinburgh and London: Blackwood.

———— (1893). *The Poems of William Dunbar, Parts 4 and 5.* Notes by W. Gregor. Edinburgh and London: Blackwood.

Encyclopedia Brittanica (1910), 11th ed., s.v. "Rhyme," "Tobacco," "English Language," "Philology," and "Pipe."

The English Dialect Dictionary (1900). Ed. J. Wright. London: Frowde. New York: Putnam.

Ernout, A., and Meillet, A. (1939). *Dictionnaire Etymologique de la Langue Latine, Histoire des Mots*. Paris: Klincksieck.

Farmer, J. S., and Henley, W. E. (1893). *Slang and Its Analogues Past and Present*, vol. 3. London: Harrison.

Feist, S. (1923). *Etymologisches Wörterbuch der Gotischen Sprache*. Halle (Saale): Niemeyer.

Ferenczi, S. (1916). On obscene words. In *Sex in Psychoanalysis*. Boston: Gorham.

_____ (1923). *Thalassa: A Theory of Genitality*. Albany, N.Y.: The Psychoanalytic Quarterly, 1938.

Fliess, R. (1949). Silence and verbalization. A supplement to the theory of the analytic rule. *Int. J. Psychoanal.* 30.

Florio, J. (1611). *Queen Anna's New World of Words, or Dictionarie of the Italian and English Tongues, etc.* London.

Freud, S. (1905a). Three essays on the theory of sexuality. *S. E.* 7.

_____ (1905b). Wit and its relation to the unconscious. In *The Basic Writings of Sigmund Freud*, ed. A. A. Brill. New York: Modern Library, 1938.

_____ (1910). The antithetical sense of primal words. *S.E.* 11.

Gasc's Dictionary of the French and English Languages. (1941) London: Bell.

Grieb, C. F. (1869). *A Dictionary of the English and German Languages*, vol. 2, 6th Amer. ed. Philadelphia.

_____ (1911). *Dictionary of the English and German Languages*, rev. by A. Schröer, 11th ed. Berlin-Schoneberg: Mentor-Verlag.

Grimm, J., and Grimm, W. (1862). *Deutsches Wörterbuch*. Leipzig: Hirzel.

Grose, F. (1788). *A Classical Dictionary of the Vulgar Tongue*, 2nd ed. London.

_____ (1931). *A Classical Dictionary of the Vulgar Tongue*, ed. E. Partridge. London: Scholartis.

Haim, S. (1936). *New Persian-English Dictionary*. Teheran: Beroukhim.

_____ (1943). *The Larger English-Persian Dictionary*. Teheran: Beroukhim.

Halliwell, J. O. (1852). *A Dictionary of Archaic and Provincial Words; Obsolete Phrases, Proverbs, and Ancient Customs, from the Fourteenth Century*, 2nd ed. London: Smith.

Halverson, H. M. (1938). Infant sucking and tensional behavior. *J. Genetic Psychol.* 53:365–430.

Hatzfeld, A., and Darmsetter, A. (1900). *Dictionnaire Général de la Langue Francaise, etc.* Paris: Delagrave.

Herzog, G. (1951). Personal communication.

Hoffer, W. (1949). Mouth, hand, and ego-integration. *Psychoanal. Study of the Child* 3/4:49–57.

Hotten, J. C. (1865). *The Slang Dictionary*. London: Hotten.

Irwin, G. (1931). *American Tramp and Underworld Slang*. New York: Sears.

Jackson, L. E. (1915). *A Vocabulary of Criminal Slang*. Portland, Ore.: Modern Printing Co.

Jakobson, R. (1942). Kindersprache, Aphasie, und allgemeine Lautgesetze. *Uppsal. Universitets Arsskrift 9*.

Jamieson, J. (1818). *An Etymological Dictionary of the Scottish Language*. Edinburgh: Constable.

———— (1912). *Jamieson's Dictionary of the Scottish Language*. London.

Kanner, L. (1945). A philological note on sex organ nomenclature. *Psychoanal. Q.* 14:228–233.

Keats, J. (1931). *The Letters of John Keats*, ed. M. B. Forman. Oxford, Engl.: Oxford University Press.

Kinsey, A. C., Pomeroy, W. B., and Martin, C. B. (1948). *Sexual Behavior in the Human Male*. Philadelphia and London: Saunders.

Kluge, F. (1883). *Etymologisches Wörterbuch der Deutschen Sprache*, 2nd ed. Strassburg: Trübner.

———— (1921). *Etymologisches Wörterbuch der Deutschen Sprache*, 9th ed. Berlin and Leipzig: W. de Gruyter.

———— (1934). *Etymologisches Wörterbuch der Deutschen Sprache*, 11th ed. Berlin and Leipzig: W. de Gruyter.

Kluge, F., and Lutz, F. (1898). *English Etymology*. Strassburg: Trübner.

Kris, E. (1950). On preconscious mental processes. *Psychoanal. Q.* 19:540–560.

Le Roy, O. (1935). *A Dictionary of French Slang*. London: Harrap.

Levens, P. (1570). *Manipulus Vocabulorum: A Rhyming Dictionary of the English Language*, ed. H. B. Wheatley. London: Pub. for Early English Text Society by Trubner and Co., 1867.

Lewin, B. D. (1950). *The Psycho-Analysis of Elation*. New York: Norton.

Lewis, M. M. (1936). *Infant Speech*. London: Kegan Paul.

Lindener, M. (1558). *Michael Lindener's Rastbuchlein und Katzipori*, ed. F. Lichtenstein. Tübingen: Bibliotek des Litterarischen Vereins, 1883.

Lindsay, D. (1490–1555). *The Works of Sir David Lindsay of the Mount*, ed. D. Hamer. Edinburgh and London: Scottish Text Society, 1931–1936.

Lucas, N. I. (1863). *Englisch-Deutsches u. Deutsch-Englisches Wörterbuch. Bermen: Schünemann.

Manchon, J. (1923). *Le Slang, Lexique de l'Anglais Familier et Vulgaire*. Paris.

Mencken, H. L. (1923). *The American Language*, 3rd ed. New York: Knopf.

———— (1949). *The American Language*, 4th ed. New York: Knopf.

Meyer-Lubke, W. (1911). *Romanisches Etymologisches Wörterbuch*. Heidelberg: Winter.

Murray, J. A. H. (1873). The dialect of the southern counties of Scotland: Its pronunciation, grammar, and historical relations, etc. *Transactions of the Philological Society* 2:1–251.

Nunberg, H. (1947) Circumcision and problems of bisexuality. *Int. J. Psychoanal.* 28:145–179.

Oxford English Dictionary (1933).

Partridge, E. (1933). *Slang To-day and Yesterday*. London: Routledge.

———— (1937). *A Dictionary of Slang and Unconventional English*. London: Routledge.

———— (1950). *A Dictionary of Slang and Unconventional English*, 3rd ed. New York: Macmillan.

Passy, P. E., and Hempl, G. (1904). *International French-English and English-French Dictionary*. New York: Hinds, Hayden and Eldredge.

Phillips, E. (1662). *The New World of English Words: Or a General Dictionary*. London.

Read, A. W. (1934). An obscenity symbol. *American Speech* 9:264–278.

Reeves, W. P. (1893) A study in the language of Scottish prose before 1600. Ph.D. dissertation. Baltimore.

Róheim, G. (1940). The garden of Eden. *Psychoanal. Rev.* 27:1–26, 177–199.

Sapir, E. (1920). The heuristic value of rhyme. *Queen's Q.* 27:309–312.

Sharpe, E. F. (1940). Psycho-physical problems revealed in language: An examination of metaphor. *Int. J. Psychoanal.* 21:201–213.

Simmel, E. (1948). Alcoholism and addiction. *Psychoanal. Q.* 17:6–31.

Skeat, W. W. (1910). *Etymological Dictionary of the English Language*, 4th ed. Oxford, Engl.: Clarendon.

_____ (1912). *The Science of Etymology*. Oxford, Engl.: Clarendon.

Skinner, S. (1668). *Etymologicon Linguae Anglicanae, etc.*, ed. T. Henshaw. London.

Sperber, H. (1912). Über den Einfluss sexueller Momente auf Enstehung und Entwickung der Sprache. *Imago* 1:405–453.

Sperling, M. (1947). The analysis of an exhibitionist. *Int. J. Psychoanal.* 28:32–45.

Stratmann, F. H. (1891). *A Middle-English Dictionary*, ed. H. Bradley. Oxford, Engl.: Clarendon.

Sturtevant, E. H. (1917). *Linguistic Change, an Introduction to the Historical Study of Language*. Chicago: University of Chicago Press.

Thompson, V. (1932). Toothache and masturbation. *Int. J. Psychoanal.* 13:374.

Waelder, R. (1929). Sexualsymbolik bei Naturvölkern. *Die Psychoanalytische Bewegung* 1:73–75.

Walde, A. (1910). *Lateinisches Etymologisches Wörterbuch*, 2nd ed. Heidelberg: Winter.

_____ (1926). *Vergleichendes Wörterbuch der Indogermanischen Sprachen*, ed. J. Pokorny. Berlin and Leipzig: de Gruyter.

_____ (1935). *Lateinisches Etymologisches Wörterbuch*, 3rd ed. Heidelberg: Winter.

Walker, J. (1824). *A Rhyming Dictionary, etc.* London: Baynes.

Ware, J. R. (1909). *Passing English of the Victorian Era*. London: Routledge.

Wilson, J. (1923). *The Dialect of Robert Burns, As Spoken in Central Ayrshire*. Oxford, Engl.: Oxford University Press.

Wood, F. A. (1907). Rime-words and rime-ideas. *Indo-Germanische Forschungen* 22:133–171.

Wyld, H. C. (1920). *A History of Modern Colloquial English*. London: Fisher Unwin.

_____ (1936). *A History of Modern Colloquial English*, 3rd ed., Oxford.

Chapter 14
The Assessment of Students' Progress
(1974)

This brief paper was delivered as the opening address at the Pre-Congress on Training, an I.P.A. meeting held in Vienna in 1971. It is my only effort devoted entirely to problems of psychoanalytic training. (A 1979 paper, also delivered at a Pre-Congress on Training, was on the theoretical and clinical relationship between psychoanalysis and psychotherapy.) The title of the paper adequately indicates its content. The only provocative issue is the traditional "reporting" on the candidate by his or her training analyst. Here my position was vigorously against such a flagrant breach of one of the basic conditions of the psychoanalytic situation. Needless to say, I had predecessors in this position, especially Kairys and F. McLaughlin in their respective papers and in an incidental but pointed remark made by Robert Waelder. In any case, this view is still disputed although many have adopted the "nonreporting" position. My own view and its supporting arguments remain unchanged, more firmly held than ever.

I do not presume that these brief remarks constitute a systematic review or even outline. I merely wish to state a few individual opinions and debatable convictions about problems inherent in the evaluation of psychoanalytic students. My hope is that these comments, whether idiosyncratic or totally unoriginal, will serve heuristic or catalytic purposes better than would loftier observations.

A few general and essential considerations should provide a framework for the discussion:

First, the operational principle of "syncretism" (emphasized by Lewin and Ross 1960), which is intrinsic and inevitable in psychoanalytic training, should be carefully reevaluated in terms of its optional and purposive applications. It so permeates our training system that therapy threatens to crowd out the art and obligation of teaching as well as the objective extratherapeutic assessment of candidates.

Second, it is obvious that we assess a candidate's progress in order to evaluate his potentiality for graduation. All too often, however, the companion purpose of determining what help he may need in an individual sense (i.e., in terms of selected courses, reading, conferences, or a particular supervisor) may too readily be overshadowed by the "qualifying" estimate or may be disposed of by way of the traditional and somewhat reflex panacea "more analysis" or by its more explicitly didactic counterpart "more" supervision." Certainly, these two classical recommendations are of fundamental importance. It is my impression, however, that our reliance on these, especially on "more analysis," has achieved a certain automatic quality, which tends to sidetrack careful specification of indications and their nuances.

Third, I believe that we should add to the principle that the "unfit" candidate should be eliminated as soon as it is possible to make a valid and decisive judgment about his candidacy (this is usually done in some relation to supervisory observations), there should be added the principle that once this critical point has been passed, every resource of the institute should be marshaled in order to help the candidate to attain that base-line competence which will justify his graduation. The rational elimination of the student from candidacy, in my view, shows that the admissions committee was mistaken, that certain basic qualities and aptitudes are, in fact, not present. The second principle of action would be based on the assumption that given certain fundamental intellectual and emotional qualities, an absence of disqualifying illness, good motivation, and an adequate personal analytic experience, we should be able to teach the candidate to do acceptable analytic work. We should be alert lest we confuse common pedagogical difficulties with fundamental inadequacies of original endowment.

Fourth, we should remember that our opinion about a candidate, in most localities, whether qualifying or disqualifying, is after all just that. Although we should continue to train and assess candidates as an "elite corps" according to our best understanding and abilities, it would probably be an expression of our breadth of philosophic tolerance, and a mitigating influence in the crises of assessment, both for candidates and for ourselves, if we removed from our statutes (and our spirits!) such principles as the undertaking by the student not to represent himself as an analyst until "allowed" to do so. This is especially important (in the sense of rationale) if the practice of "psychoanalytic psychotherapy," which should rest on psychoanalytic competence, is regarded as his natural right, from the beginning. The mark of the graduate analyst should be his excellence rather than his certification, as it is construed in a literal proprietary sense.

Rather than list our usual "stations of progress," not to speak of their varying requirements and specifications, I shall proceed to a discussion of certain selected substantive considerations that are applicable to specific aspects of analytic training.

THE PERSONAL ANALYSIS

As far as I know, the requirement of experience as an analytic patient is now a universal keystone of training. Freud's own stated requirement in this sphere (1937) remained quite modest, providing essentially for the candidate to become directly acquainted with the technical aspects and the impact of the psychoanalytic method, as well as with some presenting aspects of his own unconscious life, leading to genuine conviction regarding the existence of the unconscious. That this brief and "incomplete" experience would initiate a spontaneous self-analytic process was essential. That the vicissitudes of the analyst's professional life would lead to later difficulties led to the recommendation that the analyst have repeated further analyses ("at intervals of five years or so"). Freud (1937) stated that the "main object" of this first "short" analysis was to enable the teacher to form a preliminary judgment as to the candidate's suitability for training. What was originally a modest requirement has, in my opinion, undergone enormous overgrowth in many psychoanalytic communities.

In many psychoanalytic groups, it has long been the tradition that the analyst — even if a "teacher" only implicitly — was an officer of the institute. He has usually been consulted about each critical step in training: the beginning of classes, the beginning of supervision, the contemplation of graduation. This fact, of course, has been known (and properly) to candidates, and has constituted an integral, "built-in," gross distortion of the psychoanalytic process, with obvious conscious and unconscious ramifications in transference, countertransference, and the freedom and reliability of communication, which need not (at least, cannot) be detailed here.

The continuation of this practice — despite frequent references to its adverse influence (see Kairys 1964) — may be ascribed to the "overdetermination" of sheer routinized habit, the quiet, inadvertent, and self-hypnotizing security of authority, and — in an affirmative sense — to the prevalent opinion that no one else can provide judgements about the candidate which could even approximate in value those of his analyst. Indeed, some think of a candidate's ability to do analytic work as best measured by his own analyzability. This was the opinion of one of the groups in the Pre-Congress Conference on Evaluation of Applicants, International Psychoanalytic Association, in Copenhagen (1967).[1] In contrast with this is the effort of my Paris colleagues to exclude the analyst entirely from such judgments (Pre-Congress Conference, Copenhagen 1967). While one may regard meaningful subjective analytic experience as of inestimable value to the potential analyst (and I do hold this opinion), it remains an inexorable fact, apart from pragmatic-empirical principle, that the carrying out of analytic work is an altogether different sphere of activity from the experience of being analyzed and therefore must be taught and tested in its own right. Apart from questioning the value of the entire institute principle (by Bernfeld, for example, 1952), there is a detailed critique of this particular aspect of the institute curriculum, with a review of the literature by Kairys (1964), later supported by F. McLaughlin (1967). I am in full sympathy with the view that the candidate's analysis should be completely separate from the evaluative process, though this is apparently still a minority conviction. (See, for example, Minutes 1965, Pre-Congress Conference, Amsterdam 1965).

The essential issues as I see them are as follows: If the analysis is the keystone of training, it should be as adequate as possible, both as therapy and as model, the former, of course, of preponderant importance. No analysis that lacks full confidentiality and suffers from the even more massive impediment of the analyst's power over the candidate's career, can be really satisfactory (although such analyses have been very helpful to many). I must emphasize that the latter consideration, the literal exercise of power by the analyst, whether it actually materializes in an interference in academic progress or remains silently in the realm of potentiality, is even more fundamentally inimical to sound analytic process than the dilution of the principle of strict confidentiality. Although the latter is self-evidently of critical importance to the "climate" of analysis, it could, in abstract principle, be waived by the candidate. The problem with this "waiver" is that it would not often be, in a genuine sense, voluntary (as in a clinical consultation). The fact that the analyst might decisively intervene in the candidate's career, a gross materialization of universal transference fantasy, cannot in any way be deprived of its vitiating effects. It is a severe distortion of one of the ultimate essentials of analytic process.

Apart from complicated emotional factors that might motivate a possible bias of judgment in either direction (and I have observed spectacular instances of both), it is also a fact that, while the analyst does know his patient in a uniquely penetrating sense, his field of observation is, by the same token, special in character, and severely limited in scope. The case of the "dead man," discussed in the Pre-Congress Conference in Rome (1969), is an example. Here the analyst overlooked a severe and incapacitating personality distortion. With due regard for the gross elements of fallacy in the analogy, there is still some potential illumination in the fact that a skilled orthopedic surgeon might not be the best judge, based only on his operative field, of the patient's capacities as a ballet dancer or a baseball player. I do not mean to suggest that the analyst's special field of observation (with these pragmatic limitations in mind) does not, or should not, produce uniquely significant data, especially with regard to pathology and its prognosis. But we still have to choose between two alternatives: offering the candidate a vitiated, basically distorted form of his chosen instrumentality, as therapy and model, which is for the analyst himself a complicated "mental hazard" of which even he may not always be fully aware; or risking some possible deficit in our knowledge of the candidate.[2] One can, as is now the practice in the New York Psychoanalytic Institute, leave this to the discretion of the analyst, according to his convictions. Nevertheless, apart from subtle difficulties which may be introduced into analyses by varying practices among analysts (Minutes 1965), the obligation to try to determine dialectically what is, in sum, the better alternative, continues.

There is understandable concern that abandoning this unique source of inforation may occasionally pose serious problems. What of the psychosis, the psychopathy, the sociopathic perversion, which may manifest itself in the course of the analytic work and which may have totally eluded the admission interviewers? There are, of course, rational alternatives to reporting the facts to an administrative committee, procedures carried out essentially between analyst and student, which may, in many instances, lead to voluntary withdrawal from candidacy. In more tenacious problems, private clinical consultations with the consent of the student may be invoked. In extreme (truly emergency) instances, which are in fact very rare, in which the candidate does not voluntarily withdraw, he may be withdrawn or discontinued. Although such an ultimatum is, by its nature, inimical to further progress with the same analyst, it remains closer to the spirit of the analytic situation than does reporting to a committee which then takes the responsibility for further administrative steps. The latter procedure sometimes takes on (without individual intent) a disingenuous, evasive quality, which can culminate in a reprehensible form of actual double-dealing, in which the unofficial communication of "smile" or "raised eyebrow" or "tone of voice" pretends to maintain "full confidentiality" while betraying it. This phenomenon was also mentioned to me by my colleague Dr. Pfeffer, who has observed it in his committee experience.

In any case, the possibility of emergency situations can be vastly exaggerated. It is true that one is sometimes forced to take extraanalytic action in nonacademic clinical practice. Equivalent crises can also occur in academic work, although they are even rarer. But that does not mean that the solution (or the substitute) for the agonies of highly personal professional responsibility and decision is the group-supported specious comfort which derives from routine reporting.

Let me, for the sake of argument, accept the idea that an analytic situation provides indispensable information regarding an analysand's progress as a student. One might accept this important contribution, even at the inordinate cost which we have already mentioned. An undistorted, voluntarily motivated analytic experience would then usually occur, if at all, after graduation. But I believe that we can consider a more satisfactory situation: Freud's own concept of training is more appropriate, less wasteful, and more just than the current one — that is, that training analyses not be long or profound and that their diagnostic, prognostic, implicitly didactic aspects and their limitations be bilaterally accepted. The student is then able to find his way (soon or late, as the case may be) to a deeper experience, independent of the curriculum, if he and his personal advisers feel he needs it. The old requirement (at my home institute) that the candidate have "at least 300 hours of analysis," is perhaps less naïve in retrospect than it seemed at one time. Surely, difficulties persist: the question of ambition-motivated concealment, even of *unconsciously* mediated or reinforced deception, as in *hypocritical dreams* (Freud 1900, 1920) and, of course, the establishment of tenacious transferences, distortions notwithstanding (or even contributory), which may prolong such primary analyses to a degree that has too often become the accepted custom nowadays. I strongly favor the complete dissociation of the analysis from all evaluations or assessments in the training process. But the older form of *didactic analysis* would to some degree be an improvement on the present ambiguously hypertrophied and internally contradictory procedure.

SUPERVISED ANALYTIC WORK

If the personal analysis is the keystone of analytic training, supervised analysis is a close second in indispensability. The supervising analyst is a clinical teacher. He is inevitably a clinical consultant. In either function, in keeping with the inevitable "syncretism" of analytic work, he may have to point out interference deriving from the candidate's personality. To assume the role of adjunctive analyst beyond this is, I believe, a grave mistake, leading to multiple confusions and inadequacies of role and relationship, not to speak of interference with another ongoing or indicated analysis. The supervisor is the person in the best position to make objective judgments about the candidate's capacity — and potential capacity — to do actual analytic work (as well as to advise on immediate practical questions of further supervision and of readiness for graduation). Furthermore, unlike the analyst, the supervisor can function in this role without intrinsic impediment. Beyond this, in a prolonged one-to-one relationship, there is usually an excellent opportunity to observe many nuances of the student's reaction to teacher and teaching, to patient, and to his professional work in general, not to speak of possible gross manifestations of psychiatric disorder.

The relations between students and supervisors are sometimes spectacularly varied, including occasional crises of sheer "incompatibility." This is not necessarily an emotional matter, although such is frequently the case. Orientations of experienced teaching analysts do vary, even in the application of the same generally accepted basic principles of technique. Students are sometimes legitimately confused, and not all are as promptly capable of handling such didactic conflicts as others. The sifting, evaluation, organization, and summation of report data by uninvolved teachers (i.e., faculty advisers and their parent committees) are essential. The tolerant acceptance of occasional severe pedagogic incompatibilities, with contingent transfers, without prejudice, would be a necessary corollary.

CONFERENCES WITH FACULTY ADVISOR

Conferences with a faculty adviser can be extremely useful, not only in the "advisory" sense, but in conveying the judgments of others, formulated by a teacher-analyst thoroughly and objectively familiar with the candidate's career, yet relatively uninvolved with him in the intensive ongoing sense that promotes tenacious transference and countertransference attitudes. Apart from conveying summarized academic data to (and from) a students' committee, the faculty adviser can establish thorough psychiatric estimates of the student's personality and of relevant elements in his developing professional and general life situation. Searching and extended interviews by this officer, sometimes with the aid of a consultant, could, with tremendous advantage, replace the controversial reports by the analyst. As the more highly organized institutes try to individualize their teaching and experiment with more flexible curricula, faculty advisers (and their assistants) should also assume increasing tutorial functions, with corresponding increase in the acuteness of assessment.

TRADITIONAL ACADEMIC METHODS: CLASSROOM, SEMINAR, COMPREHENSIVE EXAMINATION, AND GRADUATION PAPER

Reports from classroom and seminar can provide valuable information about both the intellectual development and the behavioral evolution of the candidate. Not only are these presented to the instructor in their obvious individual sense, but they are also significant in their dynamically important group context. I shall not elaborate these clear-cut sources of information further.

It would seem desirable, as the curriculum becomes freer and more flexible and the tutorial aspect becomes stronger, that the graduation paper and the final comprehensive examination, both as integrating experiences and as decisive intellectually qualifying communications, assume increasing importance so that they supplement the estimates of immediate clinical performance. These methods have been or are used at various institutes, but they are not universally employed. Their intrinsic intellectual appeal recommends them for further study and possible wider application.

Miscellaneous Extracurricular Data: Observation, Rumor, and Personal Opinion

This is a vague but inevitable (sometimes "unavoidable") body of data, which can sometimes be strikingly influential in the assessment of progress, for good or ill. Where reports do not meet serious and just criteria, they should, of course, be excluded, although they inevitably influence the opinion of at least one person (the originator) and sometimes that of others, in a subtle way. The result is similar to the effect of evidence which is technically excluded by the judge after it has been already given in court. In any case, it should be a rigidly maintained principle that no one's career should ever be injured or cut short on the basis of unsubstantiated, unconfronted rumor alone, however distinguished the source.

The Substance of Assessment

When we think of a candidate's progress and its "stations," we may try to specify crucial points in the candidate's development, from his admission as a student to his graduation as a qualified independent analyst. An example of the thoughtful schematization of such progress, which sees developing capacities in relation to "parts" of the analytic process itself, is the report of the Chicago Institute, made available a few years ago (1968). A recent statement from my own institute is simpler and more general (Loomie and Pfeffer 1971).

It is my impression that, in the intricate and subtle emotional-intellectual complex that makes for good analytic work, the intellectual-technical aspects receive the most attention because they are the most accessible. This, despite the fact that Freud would have been the last to underestimate the importance of more explicitly personal qualities (1937). Apart from personal kindness, total moral integrity, and allied general traits, I mention a few examples of specific psychoanalytic requirements in the emotional sphere. Certainly, the analyst must have a capacity for extreme discipline and self-control, which will enable an individual of lively feeling to sustain the exacting emotional requirements of the analytic personal relationship and its exaggeratedly sedentary context. Related to this capacity is another requirement, a high degree of patience. By this I mean not only interpersonal tolerance but also readiness to renounce the spectacularly evident for the long-term good. With this, one values the ability to accept and utilize personal passivity consciously, as part of a necessary technical complex, rather than experience it as a perennial personal frustration or a deep submissive — even masochistic (occasionally sadistic) — personality change, a sort of overdetermined occupational illness. Clearly, apart from the prior gift of necessary ego qualities, the successful analysis of the latent countertransferences participating in the candidate's neurosis will be important in these spheres.

We should not, I think, honor the slavishly ingratiating mentality that offers so-called orthodoxy as a gift for patriarchal (or matriarchal) approval. We need the adventurous spirit which is alert to new discovery, new understanding, yet can study and value and "hold fast" to what is enduring and perennially useful in the great contributions of the past, including their own evolutionary potentialities for "change of function." In a scientific field where unequivocal data and demonstrable processes are difficult to come by, there is all too much room for passionate conviction or rebellion initiated and sustained by nonscientific or parascientific spheres in human personality, including the transference. The importance of new discovery, stressed originally by Freud, has been reemphasized repeatedly in recent times. One can not overestimate the importance of research and new discovery. However, in clinical psychoanalysis, these must be byproducts of its therapeutic goal. Fortunately, there is an infinite storehouse for further discovery in the course of this activity. I would look askance at the candidate who places his research interest before his therapeutic commitment to individual patients. In short, while strong scientific interest is a desirable quality in the young analyst, it would be disastrous, apart from its immediate implications, if this were just a more subtle representation of a partially sublimated egosyntonic oral character tendency, a tendency which appears quite frequently in the general view of the patient as an individual who, in a sense, exists for analysis, indeed for the analyst.

Closely allied to such considerations are others, more explicitly technical. Whereas we seek teaching cases that do not deviate too far from the traditional norms, we do not always find them; furthermore, there are few, even of the "best cases," who do not at some point tax the analyst's ingenuity and flexibility. It is not a virtue to be unwilling to meet such crises, to cry "unsuitable" at the first difficulty. One hopes that the candidate can exercise the degree of detachment, neutrality, and objectivity necessary for good analytic work, including the facilitation and reduction of the optimum transference neurosis, without the vitiation of exaggerated aloofness, rigidity, coldness, or ritualization. We hope that he can employ the phenomenon of abstinence, as an indispensable analytic dynamism, but with discriminating understanding of its meaning, function, and proper limitations. He must be capable of productive awareness of his own involvement in the analysis, his personal likes and dislikes, his transferences and countertransferences to the patient; he must be able to utilize them to understand, to correct for them in his interventions and to analyze them (or have them analyzed) as necessary. He should understand both the potentialities and the general inherent economic limitations of analysis, in its neodevelopmental aspects. This would include not only the necessary recognition of the unanalyzable patient but also enough circumspection to recognize with humility that "unanalyzable" by one person (even one of competence and experience) does not always mean "unanalyzable" by another person.

These considerations, like many others, are not only matters of pretraining character endowment, of individual training atmosphere, or specific personal analytic experience. It is my conviction that they are also an important reflection of the variations in the general countertransference potentiality related to the authoritarian "reported" training analysis and the analyst's idealization, especially the training analyst.

There are certain simple—almost commonplace—considerations in the intellectual sphere which, I believe, may sometimes be overlooked, from the point of view both of instruction and example and of evaluation. I shall not specify them in detail. Those traits of mind we associate with any intellectually superior human being, in any field, whatever his origins or his ideological persuasions, must, above all, be preserved or augmented rather than subverted. The would-be analyst must have a sense of proportion about the great realities of the human situation and human history, the enduring importance of certain essential values and instrumentalities, moral, aesthetic, intellectual, and, of course, the perennial and ineluctable importance of common sense. In short, the awe-inspiring pageant of human existence must not be subjected to the reduction and pseudo mastery of glib interpretations.

A thorny question is that of specific aptitude for the work of psychoanalysis. One tries to assess this, before admission to training, on the basis of a constellation of qualities that are believed to foreshadow it. It is incontrovertibly true, in this sphere, that the "proof of the pudding is in the eating." Yet, it is important that this question of demonstration of aptitude not be submerged too readily in proliferating mystiques, employing (qualifying or disqualifying) clichés such as a "natural grasp of the unconscious," or its putative lack, or "too psychotherapeutic (i.e., in aptitude and propensity), not really analytic," as though such considerations—given certain basic personal endowments—were independent of training, discipline, adequate dissolution of neurotic impediments, and genuine intellectual grasp of principles. Indeed, the "natural grasp of the unconscious," when too conspicuous, must be scrutinized carefully, lest it reflect personal illness or a technical-intellectual failure to understand the relationship of genetic infantile factors to the adult ego, to the total personality, and to the formidable realities of life. The same is true of the verbal glibness of certain individuals, often intellectually seductive to the listeners, but occasionally matching too well, in ultimate significance, the overfluent associations of a not infrequent type of profoundly resistant and deceptive personality type among patients. Certainly, if the psychological intuitiveness (or even verbal giftedness) are genuine and sound (a question not easily settled in a few interviews), they do, with other necessary qualities, hold out promise of superior analytical potentiality. It is, of course, conversely true that sheer blindness or deafness to psychological meaning and motivation, if clearly established, should be disqualifying. However, this last is not really frequent among intellectually gifted and empathic individuals, if they are unhampered by overrigid defenses. In general, my view of these matters would be similar to that expressed by Waelder (1961). It is my impression that if a candidate truly has certain basic qualities[3]—the profound wish to master his discipline and the help of reasonably adequate analysis—the burden is largely ours: to teach him sound analytic method. Not every well-coordinated, well-motivated, intelligent, and conscientious young doctor, relatively free of disturbing sadistic conflicts, can be an Ambroise Paré or a Harvey Cushing; but he can learn to do adequately competent surgery.

Whereas, inevitably, I have my own picture of an optimum or ideal constellation of qualities in the graduating analyst, it is both realistic and just to remain aware of the idiosyncratic and fantasy elements that may participate in such standards. The opinions of experienced analysts who are called upon to judge progress, dealing with admittedly obscure, sometimes equivocal considerations, where all data are necessarily filtered through the minds of intermediaries, may rest not only on widely accepted principles necessary to the intellectual structure of a given institute, but sometimes, inadvertently, on strong individual convictions and preferences and the propensity to quick but tenacious intuitive conclusions. This is evident in the Report of Group II of the Conference on Training (Pre-Congress Conference, Copenhagen 1967). Of the series of wise questions, I quote only one: "Or do we expect of our trainees what we failed to achieve ourselves?" Or, at Group III, Rome 1969: the question "What is a good analyst?" was asked. "We are good analysts," was the immediate answer (Pre-Congress Conference, Rome 1969).

With this recognition, it is also necessary to give cognizance to the considerable gulf that may exist between the ideal, or even the attainable but remotely high standard and the practical level of competence necessary for graduation and to accept inevitable variation in particular endowments and skills and the likely variation in effectiveness with types of patients, even with individual patients. Both considerations require awareness, humility, self-correction, and a concession to the practical realities of our problems, implicit in the idea of consensus, including occasional compromise. What can we actually expect of the young men and women, so carefully selected, who have committed so many years of hard training to this complex competence? We might expect that they have passed a certain base line (hard, indeed, to quantify!) in each of the directions specified or emphasized by our respective institutes and that they can reasonably be expected to move with varying speeds toward the more far-flung goals, with increasing experience, study, and reflection. To give a simple example: we may assume that a successful candidate understands the significance of transference interpretations and their correct applications. There may be great variations in sensitiveness to emergent transference material and in the mode and timing of interventions (sometimes, indeed, reflecting the example of the candidate's own analyst and the teaching of various supervisors), yet still within the acceptable scope of effectiveness. But we would not, I think, pass a candidate who permits the intercurrence of destructive acting out, following a long period in which urgent and quite transparent transference material has remained inexplicably uninterpreted.

We must also bear in mind, in judging "base-line" capacity in this far-from-ideal world, that we are training highly educated persons in rigorous fashion, to enter a therapeutic sphere where half-trained and untrained therapists are elbowing their way into competition in increasing numbers. This does not mean that we should "lower" our standards. It does mean that these standards should be reasonable and attainable by well-endowed, carefully selected individuals and that they should not too readily express our intensely individual ideals or preferences, much less our idiosyncratic intuitions. A concept such as "base-line professional effectiveness" is of course relativistic in its very nature. Furthermore, it must also be construed with due regard for the endless "becoming" that is inherent in the idea of psychoanalytic competence.

At the outset, I mentioned in passing certain basic steps in the progression of training. These no doubt vary with each locale both quantitatively and qualitatively. Witness the informal setting and procedures described by Swiss colleagues a few years ago (Pre-Congress Conference, Copenhagen 1967). These seemed to approximate Bernfeld's (1952) noninstitute ideal. To some of us, this situation would seem enviable. However, most of us work in highly organized settings with highly structured academic progressions and the conscious and unconscious complications which they engender (Lewin and Ross 1960, Greenacre 1966). It would seem best that these be modified as much as possible, somewhat in the direction of the Emersonian ideal of government, toward less scheduled rigidity and more individual tutorial instruction, rather than in the direction of liquidating the highly developed facilities of our institutes. Even though I find it most interesting and would very much like to see it in operation at first hand, I find it difficult, in *a priori* principle, to reconcile a strictly demarcated step-like assessment of students' progress, still less a quantitative rating system (granted its administrative convenience) with this most desirable spirit. Both have apparently been tested at the Chicago Institute for Psychoanalysis (1967, 1968). While there is an inevitable chronological sequence of experiential learning in the student's first clinical cases, it is difficult for me to separate, in terms of clearcut priority of order, competence in initiating a psychoanalytic process and a working alliance, or rather the capacity to learn such techniques, from a later (but latent) competence to understand and to handle the transference neurosis. They seem to be phases of a holistic grasp of technique and theory, in which the particular qualities of the cases, the temporal order of appearance of problems, the supervision, and, of course, inner emotional and intellectual processes in the candidate, will highlight one or the other aspect of giftedness or deficiency. It would seem to be principally a matter of the deepening, and at the same time the broadening, to greater concentric inclusiveness, of an original and general rudimentary grasp of the total analytic process. That this learning through experience is proceeding toward reasonable base-line competence is a matter of judgment, which, I believe, in its application defies literal objective quantitation beyond such broad concepts as "satisfactory" or "unsatisfactory" or their extreme conceptual extensions. In my view (always subject, of course, to revision), it would be better to try to recapture some of the advantages and methods of the old informal tutorial days within the greatly augmented resources of our institutes, to search out specific pedagogic needs (given adequate basic endowments), and to "prescribe" accordingly — rather than adopt the "shot-gun" panaceas of "more analysis" or (without qualification) "more supervision."

To make the necessary pragmatic judgments, we need all the modalities previously mentioned, relying most heavily on the reports of supervisors and, increasingly, the intensive contacts of the students with faculty advisers or tutors. Perhaps ultimately we should also have more searching comprehensive examinations. Inasmuch as the ability to carry out effective clinical psychoanalyses remains our central and essential training goal, whatever the particular framework in which such analyses will be carried out, the consensus of supervisors in the summation and careful review of others will remain the primary and indispensable basis of judgment. These and other sources of data must always be scrutinized as to better implementation or utilization. I am impressed, for example, with the value of later conferences with original examiners (as described by French colleagues and also utilized in Chicago), to add perspective to the usual "horizontal" observations; also the presupervisory "colloquia" at the Los Angeles Institute (Lewin and Ross 1960) and some issues will, no doubt, continue to be argued, for example, the role of the training analyst in assessment. Two things are certain. In this most complex, intangible, and humanly inclusive of intellectual-technical disciplines, we need desperately to maintain the balancing role of consensus in all important judgments. Even more, in a discipline where the struggle for understanding and improved competence continues throughout professional life, those who make judgments regarding candidates need the old-fashioned and not spontaneously abundant virtue of humility.

SUMMARY

The sequestration of the training analysis from the evaluative process is urged and the reasons are stated. The reevaluation of the general principle of "syncretism" in its optional and purposive applications, is recommended. The author's own (rather broad) views on desirable qualities in the young analyst and the evaluation of their progress in training are given. The desirability of the importance of faculty advisors or tutors and the need for greatly augmenting their functions is supported. Lessening of academic rigidities and automatic responses, individualization of training whenever possible, assumption of greater responsibility for pedagogical problems by the institute, and realistic perspectives regarding "base-line competence" are urged. A position against cliché "mystiques" and idiosyncratic standards of judgment is taken. The importance of consensus, of tolerant understanding of personal incompatibilities, of respect for the essential "endlessness" of analytic training, and (finally) of sheer humility in assessing students is strongly urged.

NOTES

1. In my original presentation, I reported my impression that the analyst's opinions were important in the judgments of the Chicago Psychoanalytic Institute, especially in initiating "matriculation." I had gained this impression indirectly, from mimeographed statements understood to have originated in Chicago. Dr. George H. Pollock, Director of the Chicago Institute (personal communication, October 15, 1971) has since made

it clear to me that at that institute reports from the candidate's analyst are, in fact, optional.

2. Note Waelder's opinion (1961) in this connection: "On the whole, I would rather see an occasional ill-suited candidate being graduated from an Institute than see the basic climate of psychoanalysis changed for all—the climate in which the analyst is analyst only and does not at the same time have to play an important role in the patient's professional environment." There is much else in this brief and unostentatious paper with which I heartily agree.

3. One could specify or describe these in endless detail. Instead, I list a few essential qualities: superior intelligence, intellectual breadth and tolerance, capacity for human sympathy in its ordinary sense, empathy, imagination, absence of serious ego pathology. I have mentioned my opposition to cliché "mystiques," especially where they depend largely on highly personal intuitive responses in examiners.

REFERENCES

Bernfeld, S. (1952). On psychoanalytic training. *Psychoanal. Q.* 31:456–482.
Chicago Psychoanalytic Institute (1967). *Selection Research.* (Mimeographed report.)
_____ (1968). *An Outline of Steps in Progression.* (Unpublished.)
Freud, S. (1900). The interpretation of dreams. *S. E.* 5.
_____ (1920). The psychogenesis of a case of homosexuality in a woman. *S. E.* 18.
_____ (1937). Analysis terminable and interminable. *S. E.* 23.
Greenacre, P. (1966). Problems of training analysis. In *Emotional Growth.* New York: International Universities Press, 1971, pp. 718–742.
Kairys, D. (1964). The training analysis; a critical review of the literature and a controversial proposal. *Psychoanal. Q.* 33:485–512.
Lewin, B. D., and Ross, H. (1960). *Psychoanalytic Education in the United States.* New York: Norton.
Loomie, L. S., and Pfeffer, A. Z. (1971). Outline of student progression. *The New York Psychoanalytic Institute.* (Unpublished.)
McLaughlin, F. (1967). Addendum to a controversial proposal. Some observations on the training analysis. *Psychoanal. Q.* 36:230–247.
Minutes (1965). New York Psychoanalytic Institute Faculty Meeting, May 19. (Mimeographed.)
Pre-Congress Conference on Training (1965). Amsterdam International Psychoanalytic Association. (Mimeographed report.)
_____ (1967). Copenhagen. International Psycho-analytic Association. (Mimeographed report.)
_____ (1969). Rome. International Psycho-analytic Association. (Mimeographed report.)
Waelder, R. (1961). The selection of candidates. *Int. J. Psychoanal.* 43:283–286.

Chapter 15
The Influence of the Practice and Theory of Psychotherapy on Education in Psychoanalysis
(1982)

This lengthy discussion is based on the opening address given at the summer 1979 Pre-Congress on Training meeting of the International Psychoanalytic Association in New York. While its content and general direction are in keeping with its title, based on the Pre-Congress theme, it also represents a distillate and systematization of many years of thought on the relationship between analysis and related forms of psychotherapy.

In keeping with the predominant theme of this volume, the centrality of transference and the technical approach to it are not only stressed in their dynamic importance, but are also the basis for my classificatory distinctions. This is based on my own special view of these considerations. However, this view is not imposed on the facts, but based on long experience and reflection on the phenomenology. Others may prefer the intellectual convenience of a purely free intuitive approach to psychotherapy, or to view it as an effective "miniature" of psychoanalysis, or from other more personal angles. However, I do think that a hard-headed effort to systematize the problem of distinctions in technique based on the evolution of the transference has much to offer, even if not totally and invariably applicable or explanatory in every instance.

I have accepted the full title of the Pre-Congress as my own, perhaps because its spiral (if not corkscrew) intellectual quality evokes a certain resonance in my own mental predispositions. It is clear that most of our thinking has always gone in the opposite direction and that — title or not — this same direction must necessarily guide at least our theoretical orientation at this time. For without psychoanalysis there is no general theory of psychotherapy. Psychotherapeutic practice, however, is abundant and usually antedates the individual's practice of psychoanalysis, so that we cannot ignore the importance of the specific topic, apart from its inevitable presentation once again of the more general problem of the relationship between the two fields.

First, we should try to clarify what we are discussing; in other words, we should delineate the difference between psychoanalysis and psychotherapy. I think that for practical reasons I shall not take up your time with a comprehensive definition of psychoanalysis. Beginning with Freud, whose discoveries and corresponding formulations provide the essential foundation (in one instance, by far the most liberal [1914][1]), there have been stated or implied definitions by many authors (among them, Bibring 1954, Eissler 1953, Gill 1954, Gitelson 1951, Rangell 1954, and Stone 1954). While these may vary in strictness, or detailed comprehensiveness, or in their interpretation in various locales, I believe that we can assume a general current agreement about the broad outlines of the setting, technique, dynamics, and process of psychoanalysis, at least as differentiated from the vast, intellectually inchoate field of psychotherapy that surrounds it.

Now, what is psychotherapy? Were it not for our pragmatic obligation, this would be all too easy. Psychotherapy comprehends all forms of treatment utilizing principally psychological means. Psychoanalysis itself is indeed within its purview. Freud, who was inevitably aware of this, wrote about psychotherapy in its general sense (1905) and expressed his (quite natural) preference for what he called "the analytic method of psychotherapy," selecting the word "analytic" in preference to Breuer's "cathartic" (p. 259). It is of historical but also of current intellectual significance to quote Freud in regard to future potentialities: "Owing to the insight which we gain into mental illness by this method, it alone should be capable of leading us beyond its own limits and of pointing out the way to other forms of therapeutic influence" (1905, p. 260).

In current fact, most analysts (certainly in the United States) use the term *psychotherapy* quite naturally, as something self-evidently different from psycho-analysis, even though certain forms of psychotherapy are directly derived from it in essential principles, rationale, and technology. This relationship is often attested to in the term *psychoanalytically oriented psychotherapy*, or a close variant. Indeed, it is this general category to which analysts usually refer when using the unqualified term *psychotherapy*. We must therefore devote our principal attention to this form of practice.

Interestingly enough, it is the formal aspects of the therapeutic situation which most often determine the designation, i.e., whether the patient is sitting up or whether he is seen less than four times a week—even more pointedly and decisively if the frequency is less than three times a week. At times, the question of whether the treating physician is a fully trained analyst or at least an advanced student may be given weight in classifying a given treatment project. These peripheral elements constitute, to be sure, easily available and relatively certain data and therefore lend themselves to a certain classificatory convenience. However, no one of them is in itself decisive if the central substantive dynamic considerations are omitted from the classification, e.g., the rule of abstinence, the centrality of the transference neurosis, and the hierarchical primacy of the free association–interpretation dialogue, which—with certain ancillary considerations—characterize analysis.

As Freud (and others following him) have pointed out, psychotherapy is a very old and protean form of therapy, sometimes not knowingly or consciously applied as such, sometimes implicit in treatments thought to be specifically physiological in their impact, or in cures attributed to the intervention of supernatural powers. Faith healing, laying on of hands, the cures by the shaman or medicine man, exorcism, the relinquishment of alcoholism in "getting religion," and the administration of placebos whether in a sophisticated purposive sense or in the primitive potions of the fraudulent or naïvely believing witch are time-honored remedies and still resorted to by a good portion of the world's multitudes when desperate. In the minds and armamentaria of scientific physicians, the power of suggestion ultimately became recognizable as a significant psychological force, implicit or obvious in these cures, which could be assimilated to therapeutic discipline in various forms. In the form of hypnosis, because of the suspension of conscious controls in suitable individuals, it reached, and in skilled hands still reaches, its peak of dramatically effective influence.

When Freud ultimately relinquished suggestion as essential therapy, and then catharsis as such, having become aware of the formidable nature of the resistances and their implicit neglect in hypnosis, he began the method of waking free association and thus created psychoanalysis. With this advent, the purpose of insight and understanding became the leitmotif of psychotherapy, replacing the central role of the direct interpersonal authoritarianism of suggestion. The prodigious affirmative importance of this step and the extreme complexity of its implications cannot be overestimated. But two points of scientific reservation should not be ignored: (1) that while different goals (and appropriate techniques) became established in the psychoanalytic and neighboring psychotherapeutic consciousness, the power of the primitive interpersonal transactions (including suggestion) was not thereby disestablished. Indeed, in a paradox more apparent than real (although the "false connection" had been discerned very early in Freud's work), it was in the course of this more sophisticated practice that Freud was able to isolate and develop a sound understanding of that most powerful dynamic force, the transference, which is, among other things, the origin of suggestion; (2) that with the advent of psychoanalysis, the goal of insight (into hitherto unconscious processes) and the operational primacy of interpretation (in the strict sense of Bibring [1954]) have tended to displace, or at least overshadow to the point of near extinction, all other modes of therapeutic interpersonal influence, regardless of the nature of the patient or the problem. This has developed to a degree which is not always advantageous and does not always do justice to the therapeutic potentialities of our vast reservoir of knowledge of personality structure and dynamics. Interpretation is not the only or necessarily preferable mode of initiating psychotherapeutic process, and of engaging the patient's transference potentialities. For teaching (and its derivative techniques, of which interpretation is one unique variant!) and the far from simple phenomenon of "support" remain important dynamic modalities that can form a viable background for specific interpretation when such need arises. This is not to question the superiority of psychoanalysis, or proximal interpretative psychotherapy, or indeed the unique value of self-understanding in general for the strong, sophisticated, and committed individual of adequate financial resources with appropriately accessible illness. But there are a multitude of individuals to whom the "elite" forms of treatment are inaccessible or to whom (for various reasons) they are inapplicable. There are also certain patients who, while "suitable" (even in an economic sense), deserve a trial of a less arduous form of treatment than psychoanalysis. There is, further, corresponding to our knowledge, a vast reservoir of counseling, quasi-guidance, supportive, and integrally interpretative techniques to which psychoanalytic thought can make seminal contributions, and whose practice can be enormously enriched by psychoanalytic knowledge and understanding. I have often thought that this would be true, for example, of the psychobiological methods of Adolph Meyer (Lief 1948), at one time so influential in American psychiatry.

Let us return briefly to the central matter of the transference, certainly one of Freud's most fundamentally mutative discoveries. I shall not review its history. Suffice it to mention certain major and relevant elements in Freud's specific views on this decisive phenomenon: (1) that effective analytic work required that the major conflicts be fought out on this (battle?) "field" (1912); (2) that an essential dynamic element in this process was the emergence of the "artificial neurosis," the transference neurosis, which tended to replace the clinical symptomatic neurosis and to recapitulate the central infantile conflicts in interpersonal condensation within the psychoanalytic situation; (3) of quite early statement, but of fundamental importance, that interpretative work is premature, indeed futile, and possibly inimical to the progress of treatment until there is evidence that the patient is emotionally bound to the analyst, i.e., shows evidence of what is usually called a "positive transference"[2] (Freud 1913, pp. 139–140). I stress this fact because it represents the sophisticated conceptual reincarnation, yet also the actual archaic point of origin of that homely (often consciously despised) phenomenon "suggestion," which enables the patient to enter a hypnotic trance and give up normal sensation or pathological paralysis on command. I mention this in regard to interpretation because, in its very nature, interpretation does not deal with the self-evident or logical; the very concept of the unconscious excludes such qualities. Only when some "learning" has occurred, with incipient identification of the observing ego with the analyst and with the mounting pressure of unconscious elements toward the verbal preconscious is the acceptance of interpretation more than an act of faith, akin to the child's willingness to learn from mother before he is himself aware of the sense or practical applicability of what he learns. Only then is "instruction" in the true cognitive sense, accepted and appreciated as such. Now, when Freud speaks of the "gold" of analysis (in contrast with the "copper" of suggestion), he means that this element of suggestion is no longer the authoritarian curative element in itself. But it continues to function as a component of a facilitating interpersonal vehicle, the transference, to launch the new adventure of insight, self-understanding, and confrontation with conflict, ultimately itself to be subject to the analytic scrutiny intended to dissolve it, especially in the multipotential, drive-propelled resistance forms that usually evolve with time.

Freud (with one or two somewhat ambiguous exceptions — e.g., 1915, pp. 168–169 or 1937, p. 231), in common with other pioneer analysts, and indeed with many analysts of today, spoke of transference as a purely spontaneous phenomenon, essentially universal, and different in its analytic evolution only in the way it was treated. With its universality, at least as a potentiality, one can heartily agree. With the idea of its essential sameness in all situations, I must firmly disagree. The pioneer contribution in this direction was that of Macalpine (1950), a contribution whose place is secure but whose profound implications have by no means been fully appreciated. Macalpine stated (in effect) that the abstinences of the psychoanalytic situation, cognitive and emotional, in default of ordinary human responses, evoked a regressive adaptational response in the patient toward a situation and an object with which he could not otherwise cope emotionally. This was, essentially, the transference, based on the original early relationships with parental figures. The wishes, fantasies, and impulses thus derived invest the passive, unresponsive analyst to varying degree — ranging from ego-dystonic wishes indirectly expressed, through powerful affects variably rationalized, to outright misperceptions, and extending even to physical appearances. Broadly speaking, the qualities of such phenomena depend on the initial balance between the integrity and firmness of the ego perceptual apparatus and the intensity of drive. This balance is, in turn, upset by the regression-inducing deprivations of the rule of abstinence, which Freud stated in Spartan terms at the Budapest Congress (1919).

This regression, crystallizing in the transference neurosis, is regarded as an indispensable development of true psychoanalytic process, its interpretive reduction the actual crux of the process. I have no quarrel with this principle. Despite certain criticisms of its application, with corresponding theoretical positions (Stone 1961, 1967), I believe the law of abstinence to be fundamental and indispensable in psychoanalysis. In regard to our immediate purposes (as mentioned earlier) we can accept the classical psychoanalytic situation as it is broadly and usually understood, regardless of certain nuances of difference in point of view. For the broad outlines and goals remain essentially the same, in comparison with the various forms of psychotherapy. The (manifestly) nonpurposive, nonselective emphasis on breadth and spontaneity of communication, with the built-in deprivations of the process, is calculated to produce a sweeping exposure of the personality and, by the same token, a sweeping and deep transference regression, culminating in a broad, multifaceted transference neurosis. The entire depth and breadth of personality are potentially available on a day-to-day basis. Therapeutic effect is, so to speak, a by-product, a result of spontaneous adaptive thrust.

How can this psychoanalytic model or paradigm be modified to produce a technique that can be considered a rational psychotherapy? This is to be sure not identical with the question of how it is usually modified. These would comprise an endless gamut of ad hoc, or intuitive, or faute de mieux improvisations. In proposing my own conceptual schema, I realize that there are many others and that many practices may not be essentially different from what I describe. But these are not frequently stated except in terms of lacks, or defaults, or omissions in regard to analysis. Thus, my own statement may at least stimulate others to offer comparable or alternative affirmative formulations. We must recognize that intuitive and ad hoc variations of the psychoanalytic model must of necessity occur in default of consistent theoretical structures and that in the hands of experienced analysts, they may often be surprisingly effective. There is thus no reason not to assume that such practices will always have a certain place (Knight 1949). And, we must also recognize that this state of affairs may lead to the nihilistic view that analytic psychotherapy as such cannot really be taught. Such a view was recently expressed in a workshop by an experienced colleague, unusually gifted in the use and description of therapeutic tours de force (see, for example, Reider [1944, 1955]). Insofar as our concern is education, however, we must think of rational methods organized around recognizable theoretical concepts. These may, of course, be multiple.

If, to begin, we grant the imperfections of preliminary reconstruction and the inevitable necessity of augmenting knowledge derived from the process itself, a preliminary dynamic diagnosis worked out from adequate anamnestic interviews is an indispensable orientation for the psychotherapist. From this is derived not only the general selection of method but also the initial tentative orientation of interventions, interpretive or otherwise. Thus the original communicative dialectic of psychoanalysis is tilted more heavily in the direction of the therapist's early perceptions and reconstructions in psychotherapy. This shift, however, when overwhelming, is, I believe, an ultimate disadvantage; and thus may constitute too severe a handicap in certain forms of tendentiously brief psychotherapy.

What is often called "psychoanalytically oriented psychotherapy" is sometimes viewed as essentially a lesser variant of psychoanalysis. Indeed, when the frequency of sessions is as high as three per week, and if the basic interpretive system is that of psychoanalysis (which it usually is, regardless of quality), it may enter a gray area as to differentiation. In his extensive review (1969), Wallerstein mentions in passing a frequently held position, one that is also invoked by Rosen (1971) in summarizing a brief discussion of the problem: (in effect) that, in analysis, the suitable patient is one who can adapt himself to its strict requirements; in psychotherapy, the method is adapted to the patient's needs. But while there is some pragmatic truth in this aphoristic statement, it is more simply stated than rationally practiced. There are usually certain actual or potential substantive differences between the methods that become more marked as the planned frequency of visiting diminishes. Also, every technical improvisation, certainly every situational alteration, introduces a dynamic variation which must be reckoned with. Some patients may be seen once a week; rather often, in this area (New York), twice a week. It has become a preponderant convention that the patient sits up in such treatment, usually facing the analyst. This variable is in itself of great importance, since perceptual feedback tends to inhibit or at least limit the evolution of fantasy. While some colleagues encourage free association under these conditions, it does not invariably (and, in my view, should never) assume the routinized, obligatory position that it holds in psychoanalysis; more desirable is an understood full freedom of communication, whatever the rhetorical form or forms it may take. Free association, in my view, may be invoked for temporary ad hoc purposes, e.g., in regard to a dream. Extreme analytic passivity is usually set aside, and the therapist's active participation is an accepted feature of the work, whether it be in the form of guiding questions, active discussion of realities, or, at times, the suggestion of certain directions of discourse and inquiry. While the strict boundaries of the traditional doctor-patient relationship must always be maintained, certain traditional analytic elements are relaxed: Anonymity (except in highly personal spheres) is less rigorously maintained, and expressions of therapeutic interest of a reasonable and restrained physicianly nature are permissible, as is true of a general interest in the patient's life and career. In short, the psychotherapist remains avowedly a physician, employing a specialized psychological technique; whereas the analyst, in his technique, sets aside the manifest physicianly attitudes except as they remain implicit in the long-term goals and purposes of the treatment. The current and archaic importance of this continuum of identity I have dealt with at length elsewhere (1961).

The therapist's activity, instead of taking a reductive direction toward the genetic-infantile environment or its currently unconscious representations, tends to preserve the patient's cathexis of his real and immediate environment—his cathexis of persons, of problems as such, and conflicts as such—and (very importantly) his cathexis of the essential realities of the patient-doctor relationship. Within such a framework, interpretative activity of a special type does play an important role. But instead of orienting itself to facilitating the spontaneously evolving transference neurosis of the basic psychoanalytic situation, it is usually based on the therapist's conception of what constitutes the major and currently active conflict or conflicts in the patient's presenting illness or disturbed adaptation and the relationship of such conflict or conflicts to his actual objects. Such a conception is based on the careful reconstruction mentioned earlier, deepened or modified by additional material elicited in the therapeutic process itself. Interpretations, moreover, tend to be holistic and integrative (Stone 1951), minimizing the distinctions between defense and impulse, infantile and current, emphasizing large, accessible, and readily intelligible personality dynamisms, except as more detailed elements present themselves unequivocally for such understanding.[3]

Now, what is the basic differentiating element that emerges from this non-authoritarian but firm maintenance of the central position of current reality in all references and from the marked diminution of the specifically and uniquely analytic abstinences (e.g., from the maintenance of the critical sensory input of visualization of the doctor, the communicative give-and-take of discussion, and the evident physicianly role of the therapist)? The adult representations of the basic positive child-parent longings of early life (nonerotic, nonaggressive, in the usual sense) are gratified in integrated form; the tendency to regression and manifest fantasy formation is diminished; and the ungratified transference assumes a less diffuse, more selective form. The irrational demand or wish that is most urgent, most current, and cannot be gratified in the doctor-patient relationship as such will tend to manifest itself in the material—consciously, or in dreams, or in any of the expectable modes of expression with which we are familiar. There is thus another decisive consideration in this pattern of treatment: the economy of transference distribution. If we assume that all relationships are compounded of current reality elements and varying degrees of transference, these are—except in the very ill—usually in a relatively stable state of integration, unless disturbed by overstimulation, regression due to everyday or iatrogenic frustrations, or the "cognitive" pressure of persistent interpretation. Thus, in the psychoanalytic situation, several factors (e.g., cognitive and emotional deprivation, with intensiveness of contact)—factors comprising what I have elsewhere called "deprivation-in-intimacy"(1961)—combine to concentrate transference in the person of the analyst and relevant "auxiliary" personages. These transferences may then flow back into the environment by way of simple displacement or the more formidable phenomenon of "acting out." In the psychotherapeutic situation as described, some concentration of libidinal and aggressive transference cathexis ultimately *tends* to occur, but in a relatively minimal and usually selective or segmental sense. This introduces an important and central difference in interpretative thrust. Whereas in the analytic situation, transference interpretations in relation to the analyst are central, and ultimately decisive and anticipatory interpretation based on valid material legitimately employed, the situation in psychotherapy is different. Interpretations remain largely "in situ," so to speak, in regard to the individuals involved in the patient's actual daily life or their representations in dreams and related material, because the principal libidinal and aggressive investments reside, in fact, in these relationships. The physician, up to a certain point, is but one of the patient's "objects," although—by virtue of his actual functional role and the inevitable parental transference integrated in it (in the sense of "resemblance" [Stone 1954])—a singularly important and central object. And certainly, the patient may, and usually does, exhibit special and characteristic personal reactions to the therapist from early on. Insofar as these include transference elements, they are most often those integrated in quite firm character tendencies. These usually lend themselves best, in an immediate sense, to ad hoc clarification and reality testing. One may expect, in most instances, that those transference conflicts most active and pressing in the patient and not gratified or expressed in the physician-patient relationship will begin to appear as such, in the manner with which we are familiar in analysis. At this point, the therapist's maximum analytic acumen must be invoked and concentrated on this fragment of transference neurosis, including his judgment as to the required depth and breadth of interpretive work and the distribution of the transference between himself and environmental objects. With the interpretative resolution (or reduction) of this confronting and (relatively) isolated transference conflict, assuming reasonably mature personality organization, one may hope for a return of attention to the patient's extratherapeutic life and problems and the spontaneous orientation toward termination.

I prefer this "spontaneous orientation toward termination" to the "primary" time limitations which have currently achieved a considerable adherence and a sizable body of literature. Note, for example, the work of Malan (1976a, 1976b), Mann (1973, 1974), Marmor (1979), and others. (In regard to Malan, see also the book notices of Horowitz and Hoyt [1979] and Wallerstein [1979].) Sifneos (1972), who qualifies his method as "anxiety provoking," is less specific about the exact time limitation, while Mann, whose proposed time limitations are most severe (twelve sessions), attempts to develop a special theory based on the opposition between the "timelessness" of the unconscious and the inexorable time requirements of adult reality. I can consider these methods only briefly, as a group, in their shared common factors. While I am keenly aware that the pressure of time can in a general sense be implicit in the psychological context of brief psychotherapy, and can, when kept within reasonable limits, have an affirmatively stimulating effect (Stone 1951), I feel that the absence of a *primary* and explicit limitation provides a more natural and generally favorable climate in both the emotional and cognitive spheres. The arbitrary limit may be experienced as coercive, whatever the manifest response (which may include "emergency" recovery or improvement), and the likelihood of new data, sometimes of critical importance, can be reduced to the vanishing point. In this sense, I am affirmatively wedded to my analytic background in that I believe that directions (with the general "climate" and modes of expression) should, as much as possible, arise from the patient and from a discriminating observation of the patient and his "material." If these methods do find some inspiration in Freud's early time limitation with the Wolf Man, which followed considerable analysis (1918, p. 11), there is nevertheless a very fundamental difference. If Freud (1937, p. 219) believed that "a lion only springs once" (and not all of us adhere even to this principle!) this is still very different from springing before the prey is in view! I recognize, though, that my preferences do not determine scientific history. And, in any case, an open mind is essential and integral in the scientific attitude. The general motivation for the development of such techniques is clear and well founded, especially in the practice of overburdened clinics. The effort is worthwhile and engaging. Yet the actual clinical process and material, with the sometimes rigid adherence to a preestablished "central issue" (Mann 1974), while based on psychoanalytic thinking, do not impress this particular reader as effectively utilizing this analytic origin, except in a rudimentary sense. These efforts should nevertheless be recognized and encouraged. The study of nonanalytic therapeutic factors which may participate in these efforts can also prove informative and valuable in the long run. At the present time, however, I regard any of these methods as justified in my personal practice only by the most exigent and unmodifiable external realities or by the demonstrably sheer circumscription and accessibility of the presenting problem.

That problems of separation will assert themselves in the form of psychotherapy which I have outlined above is of course to be expected. But in view of the lesser cathectic concentration in the situation and in the therapist, and the lesser and less diffuse transference regression, one may expect less intense problems of termination than in the psychoanalytic situation. In the paradigmatic group, sufficient help may be given to render certain individuals comfortable and viable for long periods; in others, return for further consultations or periods of treatment will occur; in still others, the psychotherapeutic effort will prove to have established the motivation, the desirability, and the suitability for thoroughgoing analysis.

If we avoid the absurd pretense of encyclopedic "coverage," what are some of the other representative forms of treatment to which a similar basis of understanding might be extended? Many years ago Knight (1937, 1949) spoke of "suppressive" psychotherapy in severe cases, in contradistinction to uncovering or exploratory or expressive psychotherapy. Many others have made a similar distinction. The essential idea is that the therapist aligns himself with the patient's defenses, fostering them rather than seeking to weaken them. While this is conceptually and schematically reasonable, it does not lend itself readily to technical specification; and I would feel some doubt that it can often be achieved in a direct and purposive sense. That the negative side of the same coin—the avoidance of the literally analytic type of interpretation, especially defense interpretations—may be feasible and useful, as the therapist's informed interest in and support for the patient's current and potential adaptive struggle in his real environment may itself be beneficial.

In general, I believe that the useful aspects of this concept have been subsumed in the broader (if still somewhat ambiguous) concept of "supportive" psychotherapy, also employed by Knight and others. Here, whether the issue is one of acute situational distress in reality or chronic emotional illness in an individual burdened by old age, forbidding physical illness or another formidably oppressive situation, rigidity, lack of intelligence (or imagination), or (by inference) sheer threatening severity of underlying conflict, the effort is to provide a sense of friendly and reliable alliance in the therapeutic situation, involving the ordinary modalities of sympathetic listening, rational encouragement, and sometimes simple advice and guidance. To a varying degree, there may be added whatever modicum of broad understanding of the patient and his environment that may seem to contribute directly to the patient's greater comfort and effectiveness or that is required by the emergence of confronting conflict. This type of supportive effort should be taken very seriously. For one thing, it can be a powerful instrument against human suffering. The transference, again, invests the analyst with an authority of almost magical proportions. And, after all, in the treatment of severe borderline illnesses or psychotic remissions, the choice of method does not disestablish the patients' ambivalent transference capacities by silent fiat. Now it is true that this mode of treatment, providing as it does much gratification of child-parent cravings and minimal cognitive exploration, tends to obviate fulminating transference developments. However, with regard to the more severe illnesses, there is sometimes the insistent "pressure from below" against defenses, and the concomitant fact that such treatment sessions are usually less frequent than in exploratory or interpretive psychotherapy. This latter condition often diminishes the tempering gratifications of contact and of speech expression, in a quantitative sense. The continuum-paradox of impact of treatment frequency should be noted: Greater frequency yields greater gratification, but also greater cathectic concentration—and corresponding expectation. Which variable is critical in a given instance can only be specified by clinical knowledge of the case. When in supportive therapy signs of transference urgency—direct or in the form of acting out—begin to manifest themselves, psychoanalytic interpretive acumen adapted to the situation must be speedily mobilized and applied. Here, however, instead of heralding a possible end of treatment, the professional expectation may be for a change to "psychoanalytically oriented psychotherapy," begun under emergency or quasi-emergency conditions. In general, it is my conviction that such developments may often be anticipated if the schedule of visits is more frequent than the usual minimum, and if the material, including dreams, is monitored carefully, even if not for ongoing interpretive purposes. That broad clarifications deriving from such sources may often be usefully translated into the patient's language and utilized in support and guidance as an integral part of such therapy is also true. Indeed, the too-rigid avoidance of what may occasionally clamor for understanding can contribute to trouble just as surely as an unrestrained interpretive eagerness can do the same. In general, with regard to active borderline illness where the pressure against defenses is liable to be urgent at all times, it is probably best that a judicious interpretive approach be invoked from the beginning, as against the purely supportive approach (see Kernberg et al. 1972). However, interpretation always remains distinctively and often critically useful, even in essentially noninterpretive contexts. Thus the relationship between interpretation and other psychotherapeutic modes (even those apparently opposite) is often truly dialectical. While I agree with Kernberg (1982) that psychotherapy (in his sense of the definition) is most often the treatment of choice in borderline illness, I do not believe that support and interpretation are intrinsically and inevitably opposed, except perhaps in the choice of intervention with respect to a given specific issue.

A few summary words about the transference in psychotherapy: Many years ago, an older analyst whom I greatly respect, said that in psychotherapy one "used" the transference as opposed to "analyzing" it. The treatment can, of course, be "used," that is, manipulated, for good or ill. (For "good," there is the example of Aichhorn in his work with delinquents [1925].) But that is not what we — or I should say I — have in mind for psychotherapy. I do believe that it can be controlled, to a reasonable degree, as to its speed and/or intensity of emergence, with the severity and depth of illness as a limiting (possibly disqualifying) condition of such control. Since I conceive of the transference as decisively intrinsic in the pathological process, as surely as it is in the therapeutic process, it must be accepted that certain transference urgencies may overturn such assumptions of control, the more startlingly when they are unanticipated. But in individuals whose constitutional givens and very early vicissitudes have not crippled them too severely, one expects a reasonable capacity for positive attachment, wish, and expectation, with aggressive-destructive impulses of manageable degree, largely deployed in current adaptations. In such individuals, as mentioned before, the give-and-take of everyday life and the maintained realities and reality orientations of the physician-patient relationship tend to minimize regression and the efflorescence of diffuse transference fantasy, both of which are facilitated by the special nature of the psychoanalytic situation. However, insofar as pathogenic transference separates itself from its adult integrations, I believe it should be dealt with precisely as an analysis, by interpretation along analytic lines. Thus, one does not "use" the transference in psychotherapy as I would practice it. It "uses itself," so to speak, in a continued struggle for integrated, sometimes sublimated, satisfaction and adaptation, until, in the frustration of specific ego-dystonic urges which usually supervenes (even in the controlled and benign psychotherapeutic situation), it makes its clamor known, and calls for interpretative help.

In most instances, the existence of active psychosis has usually required, at least initially, a different approach to the transference: one form or another of special interpersonal involvement to the degree necessary to penetrate the patient's narcissistic world, his substitute (by virtue of hallucination or delusion or manifest withdrawal) for actual "object-relations." In some instances, this approach has been conservative, relying on prolonged and patient contact and empathy, with a relative preservation of neutrality and interpretations based on the therapist's particular intellectual convictions (e.g., Fromm-Reichmann 1952, Rosenfeld 1955). Schwing (1940), Sechehaye (1951), and Rosen (1953) present active methods of striking individual distinctiveness. These are all, of course, only examples from an extensive literature.

A few words in summary will have to suffice with respect to Alexander's experiments of a few decades ago (1956, chapter 4). If Ferenczi (1931) failed in his attempt to reduce resistances by giving adult patients the love he felt they had lacked in infancy, his failure had more than one reason. Even if he had succeeded, however, we must wonder as to the ultimate fate of such paternal love from a physician. Would it not ultimately lead to disappointment, frustration, rage, relapse? For a physician is not a parent; treating the patient as a baby is thus a double make-believe that cannot be maintained. A physician can only give that form and degree of love that is integrated in and compatible with his enduring and dependable professional role, a measure of love which can always be available to the patient should he need it. Less conspicuously perhaps, but no less genuinely—this applies to *any* posture assumed by a therapist other than that professionally assigned to him. When it impinges on the patient's transference, gratifying it or frustrating it, it is either felt as "fake," or, if successful for a time, leads to negative reactions thereafter. What the patient's transference invests the therapist with is part of his own inner world, which he can come to understand as such. There is thus always a "corrective emotional experience," the correction of infantile distortions of the object by increasingly correct perceptions of the present object, aided by interpretive work.

I shall limit myself to a single brief paragraph about noninterpretive therapies, including behavior therapy, which has been enjoying a sort of heyday. The transference in all nonanalytic therapies operates silently, investing verbal instructions or other activity with authority and effectiveness, as the communications of a loving, permissive, and omniscient parent. It is more than likely that the therapist's training methods or guidance also speak to underlying unconscious conflicts, albeit in a language different from that of purposive interpretation. They instruct, permit, forgive, foster, and so on. Here, too, when transferences are more complicated and more intensely ambivalent, disturbances may occur, recognizable to the informed perception and susceptible to benefit from interpretive intervention.

The same transference effects can even occur occasionally in the administration of psychotropic drugs. It is my conviction, perhaps largely (although not entirely) theoretical, that the principles we have been discussing are essentially valid for all the myriad forms of counseling and psychotherapy. The more the problem is largely and genuinely situational, subject to voluntary cognitive examination and control, the less intensive the contact, the shorter its duration, assuming appropriate responses by the consultant, the less will the governance of the transference be apparent, its influence residing largely in the facilitating sphere we have mentioned. The exceptions are (1) when deep illness underlies the immediate motives for consultation and (2) sometimes, when the consultant assumes an analytic attitude in an entirely inappropriate situation. The most severe transference regression I have observed in psychotherapy was in a clinic many years ago when a woman patient (more deeply ill than was apparent) was seen once a week for half an hour, lying on the couch, in free association.

Now, I have told you my own preference among the various methods of interpretive psychotherapy. It is a preference based on my experience and theoretical convictions, evolved over the years, and colored by the fact that I have mainly been a practitioner and teacher of psychoanalysis for the last decades, one who has nevertheless not lost interest in and respect for the potentialities of informed psychotherapy. There are indeed many ways to practice this art. Many years ago, when I led a study-group clinic consisting of a few advanced candidates and a majority of graduate analysts, one in which everyone was encouraged to follow his own convictions and inclinations (with the hope of sorting out our methods thereby), I was startled at the variety of approaches that emerged—ranging from methods roughly like my own, to one resembling Sechehaye's "symbolic realization," to efforts to conduct miniature psychoanalyses, and one which included early primitive transference interpretations. Something similar appeared (naturally, a highly attenuated experience) when a long time ago I participated in a group that met annually for a few years at the meetings of the American Psychoanalytic Association. Other approaches have been mentioned in the literature, some of which I am familiar with directly, others not. All are worthy of examination and discussion. While we do not have the great ocean of potential discovery available in analysis, a patient and sensitive ear on the part of the therapist and his patient's preserved sense of freedom may permit the "unexpected" to emerge even in a rationally guided psychotherapy. Although, as you have seen, I believe that the immediate technical procedure can vary considerably from interpretation (certainly in the strict sense of Bibring), interpretation remains the ultimate trump card for the therapist, who is always monitoring the process from a psychoanalytic point of view. To the extent that one must inevitably be selective, not only on the basis of ongoing material, but also as one is guided by pretreatment diagnostic reconstructions, including the mode of precipitation, it is my preference to select broad dynamisms or broadly outlined elements of conflict within the personality at the outset, rather than specific early personal relationships or specific events of the past. The reaction to precipitating events (and the events themselves) may be of immediately illuminating importance, representing a clear "known" in regard to a personality one is coming to know. There is less likelihood of misunderstanding or error in stressing the confronting dynamic issues; and there is a more dependable radiation from these into persons, places, and remote events than there is in working back to such confronting issues on the basis of remote factors.

If we omit the statistically very important considerations that are based on "economic determinism," i.e., time and money, what are the indications for psychotherapy as opposed to psychoanalysis? More than twenty-five years ago (1951) I listed these indications based on my own experience at the time and on the available writings on psychotherapy by analysts. I would not wish to bore you even with a revised list, for I believe that certain generalizations would, in this instance, be more informative or at least a better basis for discussion. Anyone can usually benefit from judicious psychotherapy, some a great deal and some to a limited degree. The situation in considering analysis is far more complicated so that it seems more practical to reverse at least the initial direction of our consideration. The original indication for analysis was the chronic transference psychoneurosis. This prime indication persists. Yet it is quite likely that many such cases, of milder grade, especially when incipient, would do well with a proximal form of interpretive psychotherapy. Where this seems likely from a careful preliminary study of illness and personality, I would think that a trial of psychotherapy in skilled hands would be entirely in order. A further indication for psychoanalysis is a character disorder of reasonable severity, with good initial insight into the disorder and strong motivation for treatment. Here I feel that psychotherapy (except as the distinction is largely nominal) is not indicated. It may be indicated, where the disorder is so severe that modest and limited goals are more realistic. In the case of deep-seated perversions (or addictions), granted their general refractoriness to treatment (for a variety of reasons), there is hope for help in psychoanalysis; whereas I doubt that much can ever be accomplished by a more limited psychotherapy. Again, in certain individuals who seem too ill for the abstinences of classical analysis, some amelioration and better adaptation may be achieved through psychotherapy. Or, in the hands of a skilled and interested analyst, modifications of analytic technique may make even the latter analytically accessible if motivation is strong and personality resources are impressive. I still adhere to my earlier conviction (1954) that if the ultimate and intermediate purposes and goals of analysis and its basic methods are adhered to, the procedure should be regarded as analysis, regardless of temporary emergency modifications. But I do not think the hair-splitting debate about nomenclature in this area is other than a diversion. With severe borderline cases or psychotic patients (if the latter are at all accessible psychologically), the same considerations obtain. "Modified" psychoanalysis or the "proximal" type of psychotherapy (depending on the threat of regression envisaged) are the treatments of choice. If we think of depression as a separate category, neurotic depression is an indication for analysis, with the proximal form of psychotherapy as an alternative, especially when the need for activity may be exigent. Borderline (and nonspecific psychotic) depressions are candidates for analysis, often greatly modified, with what may be necessary interludes of active psychotherapy. For "true" manic-depressives, despite the grand tradition of Freud and Abraham, I would be wary of the traditional analytic approach, except possibly in highly selected cases — with the immediate adjacency or context of hospital facilities. Such patients can, however, benefit from judicious psychotherapy at intervals, with considerable "educational" admixtures regarding the structuring or restructuring of their ongoing lives.

For acute fresh neurotic conditions, panics of uncertain nature, situational entanglements, problems of transition, and personal crises of varied nature, it seems to me that psychotherapy represents the treatment of choice, sometimes to be followed by analysis in the future, a transition which can be managed, even by the same therapist, in some instances to special advantage (although I realize that many have held otherwise).

A special problem is presented by the patient who has had many years of analysis, or multiple analyses, with unsatisfactory results or with later relapse. In cases in which the motivation to "try again" was still strong and where there seemed to be some hope for a further trial, I have undertaken reanalysis. In other cases, however, especially where there has been a certain passive, nonparticipating magical expectation in the prior analysis, I have found a more active "sitting up" psychotherapy, which sometimes invokes and integrates material from the past, to be more stimulating to the patient's own activity and more likely at least to encourage the bilateral hope for improvement. In a few instances, improvement has been demonstrated. Such alternative I have tried in the last several years. A final opinion about the differential indications and the complicated differences in process in this at best very difficult situation is still in the making.

A few words in conclusion: In addition to having proposed a single reasonably clear-cut pattern of psychotherapy, I have, I think, suggested some of the gradations and the sometimes more striking differences from the basic paradigmatic situation and process of analysis in those other modes of treatment that are nevertheless related to its fundamental dynamics by the pervasive and inevitable phenomenon of transference. I omit that extreme extension of the latent continuum at the analytic end—the computer model—because I have regarded it as *reductio ad absurdum* and not at all innocuous, in a pragmatic sense. The polar, although not precisely antithetical end of the continuum resides in the give-and-take of the ongoing friendly mutual "psychotherapies" of everyday life. To achieve or to try to accomplish nodal crystallizations of techniques along this continuum is, I think, a most important project, worthy of the sustained and energetic attention of our professional community.

Now having used much of my time discussing the nature and inner relationships of our subject matter, it is fitting to turn again to the problem it poses for training. I said earlier that there is no general theory of psychotherapy as such. What theory exists consists in the nature of the particular therapy's derivation from psychoanalysis or remote, even superficially opposing or contrasting, therapies, in the application of basic psychoanalytic theory (in all of its dimensions, even including technology) to the understanding of their clinical phenomena and processes. For if one has a profound conviction regarding the basic validities of psychoanalysis, one must regard all methodologies, to the extent that they are effective, as in large part consonant with these validities and subject to understanding in their light. This is not to say that additional and distinctive factors in the various psychotherapeutic modalities — factors the effectiveness of which cannot presently be understood in terms of our psychoanalytic convictions — will not also repay study, those, for example, of behavior therapy or group or family therapy. That the potentiality for theoretical feedback to psychoanalysis is real and possibly important cannot be doubted. If, for example, my own view regarding the alteration in transference evolution under the conditions described above were to be widely confirmed, this could ultimately impinge on psychoanalytic theory and practice. Similarly, the observations in behavior therapy (and to some degree, in everyday phenomena like the cessation of smoking) that symptoms presumably originating in conflict can be brought to manifest resolution without demonstrable substitute formations could also stimulate important theoretical questions, perhaps revisions.

But there is little doubt that, while other forms are largely practiced in their own proximal theoretical contexts, the practice of "psychoanalytically oriented psychotherapy" rests almost universally on a more or less adequately understood conception of psychoanalytic theory and technique. It follows that instruction in psychoanalytic theory and technique should precede the effort by analysts to teach psychotherapy and to construct theories for it. This view I have held for many years. I am pleased to note that a related view as to curriculum was expressed by Anna Freud in her paper on the "ideal institute" (1971). Now, ideal or not, there is no reason why such instruction should not be offered as an advanced or even postgraduate course by our institutes. It seems to me that only an old prejudice or a supercilious view of psychotherapy as self-evidently inferior can permanently impede such a development. In my own home institute, the New York Psychoanalytic Institute, and in the one other with which I have had a working relationship at different periods of my career, Columbia, courses were offered very early in the curriculum, certainly preceding supervised analytic work and consisting of supervised clinical work in psychotherapy. At the New York Institute, the course was continued for several years as a "Pre-First Year Course" and then discontinued by the educational committee. Currently, there is instead a course in clinical evaluation of patients as to their suitability for analysis. I note that Columbia has also discontinued the introductory work in psychotherapy. I have made no extended inquiries in this general sphere, still less a statistical investigation. But I have no doubt that many of our representative institutes can bring their specific experience to our discussion groups. What is important to me at the moment is that two representative institutes followed tradition in viewing psychotherapeutic work as elementary, indeed introductory, and then, after a considerable period, abandoned this instruction without offering regular advanced work in its place. Moreover, psychotherapy is now no longer offered to patients by the Affiliated Staff of the New York Institute (a group of younger graduate analysts) as an alternative primary treatment modality, as it was years ago. In the past, I did have a most gratifying experience with a voluntary group of advanced students and younger graduates (largely the latter) for a few years.

This experience strengthened my conviction regarding the appropriate curriculum position for this work.[4]

So much—in rather dogmatic brevity—for the question of theoretical and clinical instruction in psychotherapy in the formal psychoanalytic curriculum. But what is the situation in clinical practice or in hospital work, the alternative or twin situations from which our candidates emerge? The vast majority of our candidates, until "permitted" to practice unsupervised analysis, practice psychotherapy in various forms, with other elements of clinical psychiatry (e.g., drug therapy), for several years before and in the period of candidacy. Indeed, in the present era of psychoanalytic history, this practice looms large in the schedules of many analysts for many years after graduation, if not indefinitely, because of changing patterns of "demand." But this is a problem separate from that of training. The practice of psychotherapy is, of course, stimulated by the enormous need for it. In the case of psychoanalytic candidates, however, it is also dependent on the candidates' commitment not to practice (unsupervised) analysis until authorized to do so by their respective training committees. Thus, candidates are in the anomalous situation of practicing what should be a variation or derivative or special application of a rich and complicated discipline with a well-defined body of traditional and written precepts while adhering to a pledge not to attempt to practice the basic method to which they are devoted, which they are studying intensively and in which they are obviously greatly interested. I made pointed comment on this situation about thirty years ago (1951). Whether on a statutory or traditional basis, this restriction (to my knowledge) remains one of the keystone rules of formal psychoanalytic training. It has, on a guildlike basis, protected a hierarchical structure which still enjoys wide respect and acceptance even among those nonanalytic psychiatrists who value the psychoanalytic contribution to practice and theory.

The question of what this small excerpt from the vast ramifying world of psychotherapeutic practice means in our scientific and educational schema merits deeper consideration, regardless of how far we get with it. For small—but pointed—instance: Certainly, it exalts the convenience (sometimes the subterfuge) of arbitrary, nonrational distinctions: "Of course I am not analyzing the patient—I see him only twice a week" or "He has neven been on the couch!" Yet the practice may not include any of the other important adjustments necessary to changed conditions. But why fuss? The "appearance of evil" has been avoided! In the rare and extreme instance of devotion to the Word, the practitioner may simply call what he is doing "psychotherapy" rather than "analysis."

What does the indisputable fact of candidates' practice of psychotherapy contribute to (or detract from) psychoanalytic training (that is, if we omit further discussion of the tacitly accepted distortion that I have just mentioned)? First, the practice of psychotherapy includes the experience of numerous variations from the classical psychoanalytic pattern, in all spheres, from variations in the manifest emotional orientation to the patient, to variations in the entire gamut of technical interventions. This provides a rich experience, whether consciously or preconsciously sorted out and stored, in the nuances of impact and of patient or process response. These, regardless of the considered attitude toward them, remain as a latent reserve armamentarium for emergency and other atypical situations in analysis. They also provide a basis for comparison, whether in ongoing simultaneous practice or in retrospect, between the impacts of classically psychoanalytic situations and maneuvers and the infinitely diverse single or combined modalities of psychotherapy, both as to their immediate and remote effects. I believe it to be true that the conscious, organized utilization of such rich experience is, unfortunately, minimal on the part of analysts, because of their sense of practicing an inferior craft, faute de mieux; but this does not obliterate the preconscious, perhaps even unconscious, traces of such experience. There is little doubt that the hierarchical personal element in training also invests the respective modalities of practice with corresponding valences, independent of the questions of actual intrinsic merit. Psychotherapy has most often been viewed as a method that does not have an independent dignity and value of its own. In the days when it was taught as an introductory course at the New York Institute, a good friend and colleague of mine who taught it for years told me that he interpreted the essential purpose of the course as the demonstration to the students of "what was *not* analysis." Fortunately, however, most individuals do learn by experience, whether the learning is consciously organized or not.

Further, the candidate, whether in his current or past practice (indeed, in his future practice as well!), observes the general therapeutic effectiveness of psychotherapy, as well as its limitations and failures. These he can compare with those of psychoanalysis, again in a considered, attentive way or in an inadvertent and inevitable but nevertheless important way. Obviously, complexities enter into such judgments, under the best of conditions, and they are subject to many qualifications. But apart from the fact that such clinical judgments are ultimately necessary in the establishment of rational indications, they are inevitable psychic responses under the conditions of dual practice. While such responses are often holistic, intuitive, and hardly scientific, it is unlikely that they are entirely devoid of meaning. They are burdened in two conflicting directions: (1) the innate preference for demonstrable and swift therapeutic change, which is more often seen in psychotherapy (the magical aspect referred to by Zimmermann (1982) and (2) the strong counterbalancing "belief" in the a priori and universal superiority of psychoanalysis, which may require years to temper. It is as if each analyst must repeat for himself the experience of Freud. In any case, it is only the continuation of dual practice that can lead to ultimate clarification and scientific specification of this important issue.

Finally, it is often thought and said that there is an inherent conflict between the practices of psychotherapy and psychoanalysis. It is even thought that high competence in one field is inimical to, if it does not exclude, high competence in the other. Were this true, it would follow that insofar as the superior practice of psychoanalysis is our central goal, it would be incumbent on us to discourage the practice of psychotherapy, most certainly among our candidates; or at least, since exclusion from private practice would hardly be practicable, that it be excluded entirely from consideration in training. Sandler extends this possible option to its extreme representation (1982).

It is my impression, however, that these last propositions are based on misunderstandings and on longstanding, rather arbitrary traditional clichés. If psychotherapeutic practice is conceived of as a "do-as-you-please" relaxation from the strict analytic discipline, there might be merit in discarding it from training altogether. But, insofar as it is an honest, disciplined effort to utilize psychoanalytic knowledge in a variably different setting, it is difficult to see how this effort can have other than an enriching effect, in the references mentioned earlier. Now, it is true that the rule of abstinence, intelligently construed, is fundamental in psychoanalysis; by the same token, its considered and judicious modification is usually implicit in psychotherapy. There are also—or usually should be—germane and rationally based differences in setting and interpretive method. But to the extent that in both instances a satisfactory rationale is followed, deriving from a common intellectual source, it seems to me to belittle the technical adaptability of analysts and candidates to assume that the invocation of different (although related) technical modalities is beyond their effective capacities, indeed their capacity for gain from both directions. For these options are, or should be, expressions of autonomous ego functions. It is my purely personal impression that the fear of cultivating "bad habits" (with authoritative endorsement) weighs heavily in such intellectual attitudes. I do not believe that rational elections of technique need become "habits," even granting the ubiquitous tendency to minor structuralizations of behavior. And it is not desirable, by the same token, that the ideal version of the classical analyst be fostered by authoritative exclusivity as a system of automatized "correct" reactions. Irrational responses in either direction are to be assigned to the original personality or to its interaction with personal analysis. This is my impression from years of supervisory experience. Certainly it was true of the one conspicuous case I have witnessed, that of a tenacious didactic psychotherapeutic trend in analytic work that was for a long time resistant to supervision. Far more common in my experience was the "fear of doing psychotherapy," and the "bending over backward" in excessive passivity or stereotypy of response. What is not to be questioned is that "practice" is necessary in any technical discipline. Thus, a case load weighted too much in one direction will naturally lead to correspondingly greater facility in the favored discipline. Too often, nowadays, for "environmental" reasons, this is psychotherapy.

I realize that I have gotten myself onto the horns of some dilemmas, even contradictions, albeit benign; and it is best that I try to resolve them rather than give unswerving fealty to the hobgoblin of consistency. If, in principle, psychotherapy should be an advanced subject in the psychoanalytic curriculum (and it is my firm conviction that it should be) and if such teaching is to be most effective and creative, what are we to do for our beginning students to help them

cope with the everyday facts of their practices? Even if this is not our "responsibility," it should be part of our concern about their intellectual development.
(Naturally, in training them thoroughly in psychoanalysis, we are giving them
the best possible foundation for evaluating—and, yes, understanding—their
psychotherapeutic work, ultimately to bear fruit in better designed psychotherapeutic maneuvers. To this, however, we must append an important reservation:
that candidates not carry certain literally mimicked psychoanalytic methods directly into their psychotherapeutic efforts. Insistence on this reservation is in itself
an important pedagogical obligation.) In their psychiatric residencies nowadays,
our candidates of the future all receive supervision in individual psychotherapy,
at times from analysts, along with inpatient work and contact with such special
therapeutic methods as pharmacotherapy, group therapy, behavior therapy, and
family therapy. They are usually, furthermore, taught the basic contributions
in psychoanalytic literature—and sometimes far more—which may be beyond
their capacity to absorb and integrate with ongoing experience. Thus, they are
not really "without help." (It is, of course, an obvious fact that many psychiatrists
who do not go to psychoanalytic training have no more education than this [or
even less]. While this is a handicap, many may nevertheless do good therapeutic
work.) Candidates are, furthermore, able to arrange for private psychotherapeutic supervision if they wish. Finally, to be thoroughly inconsistent, there is no
impediment to offering candidates occasional consultative help on a group or
seminar basis, or even a few orientating lectures on the general subject, early
in the curriculum, neither intensive nor extended in character. These should be
offered as a "stopgap," in recognition of possible current perplexities and largely
to establish a tentative rational sense of dynamic differentiation from psychoanalysis, beyond "what is not analysis," and more useful than the prevailing
cliché conceptions which are usually prevalent. In any case, the important points
are: (1) Since there is little or no clear-cut psychotherapeutic theory and the methodology remains thoroughly dependent on the psychoanalytic framework, the
learning and discussion of psychotherapy will be undertaken most usefully and
creatively when a reasonable degree of mastery of the parent discipline has been
established. (2) Preanalytic therapeutic experiences, apart from the informed
comparisons mentioned earlier, are part of the candidate's general experience
in clinical psychiatry, like drug therapy or electroconvulsive therapy, or his experience with more remote psychotherapeutic modalities, or his direct contacts
with major psychoses. Whether or not his practice is well supervised (better, of
course, if it is), it creates a stock of clinical experience against which to acquire
and measure the carefully taught and carefully delimited psychoanalytic situation, method, and process. (3) I have mentioned that there may even be important theoretical feedback from psychotherapy if we are not afraid to open our
ears and eyes (and minds) and those of our students to it. This, of course, refers
to the impact of variant experiences on rather well-established psychoanalytic
concepts and methods. When a young doctor (in good—not excessively frightened—judgment) "sits up" a patient who threatens to slip away from his moor-

ings in reality, he carries out what is by now almost a convention; but the maneuver is probably related nevertheless to this stock of earlier experience with psychotherapy.

I do not believe that classical psychoanalysis has exhausted its possibilities for progressive change in its own right (1975). But apart from currently offered revisions of the basic model or far-flung expectations from neurophysiology or pharmacology, it is not utterly inappropriate or futile that we remain alert to what humble and earthy neighbors may have to offer. We should recall that the great Ambroise Paré began as a barber surgeon; that Withering learned of foxglove from an old woman in Shropshire; that the botanical forerunners of quinine and cocaine were found in use among aborigines. Language, music, and even morals often accept gifts or loans from a freer, less formal world of behavior than that of polite and cultivated society. Even in that (antithetical) haughty and most traditional sphere, military science and practice, what troops would now march in attack, brightly uniformed, bodies erect, with colors flying and band playing? The guerrillas and aborigines have taught us something there too—how to avoid getting killed, if possible. And a modern, well-trained commando would make a gutter street fighter appear like the Marquis of Queensbury himself. I trust that you will not misunderstand me. The primacy of psychoanalysis in the world of psychotherapy is not to be questioned (at least by me!); nor is the indepensability of its theory to all rational psychotherapies. However, like all scientific disciplines, psychoanalysis requires nutriment, and we should seek it from all sources. In spawning and feeding the psychotherapy with which we are most familiar, and taking it seriously, it may indeed find enrichment for itself.

Thus, our advanced students, in learning to apply psychoanalytic knowledge to psychotherapy, to create independent technical tools, and to respect these tools and their indications should not only benefit by the general and detailed widening of clinical and process experience which it brings but may also chance on experiences and observations that require further elaborations of psychoanalytic theory, or even revisions of established views, or possibly entirely new formulations. That new illumination might derive from such spheres as family therapy or behavior therapy is, if we could take the time to look at them hard and straight, certainly possible. It is for even better reason, then, that we recognize that such good fortune of feedback is not to be excluded categorically from the experiences and observations of "psychoanalytically oriented psychotherapy," our closest and most devoted intellectual stepchild.

NOTES

1. Referring to transference and resistance, Freud (1914) states: "Any line of investigation which recognizes these two facts and takes them as the starting-point of its work has a right to call itself psychoanalysis, even though it arrives at results other than my own" (p. 16).

2. Freud did not distinguish between (positive) "transference" and what is now called

"therapeutic (or working) alliance." Regarding *positive transference*, note the interesting suggestion of Lagache (1953) that the meaning of transference be examined as to its positive or negative influence on the psychoanalytic process (i.e., "on the learning of the fundamental rule") rather than its immediate affective content.

3. A remarkable, intuitive adumbration of the idea of integrative interpretation, reflecting Freud's genius, occurred in one of his early hypnotic adjurations (1892–1893, p. 120). Attention was drawn to this recently by Blum (1979, pp. 62–66).

4. When the "elementary" course was established with the founding of the Treatment Center at the New York Psychoanalytic Institute, I decided not to participate in the teaching, because of the didactic principle involved, even though I had directed the first volunteer (pre-Treatment Center) clinic of the institute. When I wrote Dr. Heinz Hartmann, the first director of the Treatment Center, of my view, he invited me to form a group of advanced students and graduates to test and study individual methods of psychotherapy. This group treated patients and met for discussion over a few years before it was dissolved, for several extrinsic reasons. While its research mission has not been fulfilled (the material is still on file), there was no doubt of the productiveness and mutual stimulation of the discussions and their lasting intellectual imprint on those who participated.

REFERENCES

Aichhorn, A. (1925). *Wayward Youth*. New York: Viking, 1935.

Alexander, F. (1956). *Psychoanalysis and Psychotherapy*. New York: Norton.

Bernfeld, S. (1962). On psychoanalytic training. *Psychoanal. Q.* 31:457–482.

Bibring, E. (1954). Psychoanalysis and the dynamic psychotherapies. *J. Amer. Psychoanal. Assn.* 2:745–770.

Blum, H. (1979). The curative and creative aspects of insight. *J. Amer. Psychoanal. Assn.* 27 (suppl.): 41–67.

Eissler, K. (1953). The effect of the structure of the ego on psychoanalytic technique. *J. Amer. Psychoanal. Assn.* 1:104–143.

Ekstein, R. (1962). Introduction to S. Bernfeld's "On Psychoanalytic Training." *Psychoanal. Q.* 31:453–456.

Ferenczi, S. (1931). Child analysis in the analysis of adults. *Int. J. Psychoanal.* 12: 468–482.

Freud, A. (1971). The ideal psychoanalytic institute: A utopia. *Bull. Menn. Clin.* 35:225–239.

Freud, S. (1892–1893). A case of successful treatment by hypnotism. *S. E.* 1.

——— (1905). On psychotherapy. *S. E.* 7.

——— (1912). The dynamics of transference. *S. E.* 12.

——— (1913). On beginning the treatment. *S. E.* 12.

——— (1914). On the history of the psycho-analytic movement. *S. E.* 14.

——— (1915). Observations on transference-love. *S. E.* 12.

——— (1918). From the history of an infantile neurosis. *S. E.* 17.

——— (1919). Lines of advance in psycho-analytic therapy. *S. E.* 17.

——— (1937). Analysis terminable and interminable. *S. E.* 23.

Fromm-Reichmann, F. (1952). Some aspects of psychoanalytic psychotherapy with schizophrenics. In *Psychotherapy with Schizophrenics*, ed. E. Brody and F. Redlich. New York: International Universities Press.

Gill, M. (1954). Psychoanalysis and exploratory psychotherapy. *J. Amer. Psychoanal. Assn.* 2:771–797.

Gitelson, M. (1951). Psychoanalysis and dynamic psychiatry. *Arch. Neurol. Psychiat.* 66:280–288.

Horowitz, M., and Hoyt, M. (1979). Book notice of *The Frontier of Brief Psychotherapy* by D. H. Malan. *J. Amer. Psychoanal. Assn.* 27:279–285.

Kernberg, O., Burstein, E., Coyne, L., Appelbaum, A., Horwitz, L., and Voth, H. (1972). Psychotherapy and psychoanalysis: Final report of the Menninger Foundation's Psychotherapy Research Project. *Bull. Menn. Clin.* 36:3–275.

Kernberg, O. (1982). To teach or not to teach psychotherapy: Techniques in psychoanalytic education. In *Psychotherapy: Impact on Psychoanalytic Training*, ed. E. D. Joseph and R. S. Wallerstein. New York: International Universities Press.

Knight, R. (1937). Application of psychoanalytical concepts in psychotherapy: Report of clinical trials in a mental hygiene service. *Bull. Menn. Clin.* 2:99–109.

———— (1949). A critique of the present status of the psychotherapies. *Bull. N. Y. Acad. Med.* 25:100–114.

Lagache, D. (1953). Some aspects of transference. *Int. J. Psychoanal.* 34:1–10.

Lief, A. (1948). *The Commonsense Psychiatry of Dr. Adolf Meyer*. New York: McGraw-Hill.

Macalpine, I. (1950). The development of transference. *Psychoanal. Q.* 19:501–539.

Malan, D. (1976a). *The Frontier of Brief Psychotherapy*. New York: Plenum.

———— (1976b). *Toward the Validation of Dynamic Psychotherapy*. New York: Plenum.

Mann, J. (1973). *Time-Limited Psychotherapy*. Cambridge, Mass.: Harvard University Press.

———— (1974). The experience of time: A model for brief psychotherapy (abstracted by R. A. Lobin). *J. Phila. Assn. Psychoanal.* 1:183–186.

Marmor, J. (1979). Short-term dynamic psychotherapy. *Amer. J. Psychiat.* 136:149–155.

Rangell, L. (1954). Similarities and differences between psychoanalysis and dynamic psychotherapy. *J. Amer. Psychoanal. Assn.* 2:734–744.

Reider, N. (1944). Remarks on mechanisms in non-analytic psychotherapy. *Dis. Nerv. Syst.* 5:1–4.

———— (1955). Psychotherapy based on psychoanalytic principles. In *Six Approaches to Psychotherapy*, ed. J. L. McCary. New York: Dryden Press.

Rosen, J. (1953). *Direct Analysis: Selected Papers*. New York: Grune & Stratton.

Rosen, V. (1971). Is it possible to have a distinctive methodological approach to psychotherapy? *Bull. N. J. Psychoanal. Soc.* 3:14–18.

Rosenfeld, H. (1955). Notes on the psycho-analysis of the superego conflict in an acute schizophrenic patient. In *New Directions in Psycho-Analysis*, ed. M. Klein, P. Heimann, and R. Money-Kyrle. London: Tavistock.

Sandler, J. (1982). Psychoanalysis and psychotherapy: The training analyst's dilemma. In *Psychotherapy: Impact on Psychoanalytic Training*, ed. E. D. Joseph and R. S. Wallerstein. New York: International Universities Press.

Schwing, G. (1940). *A Way to the Soul of the Mentally Ill*. New York: International Universities Press, 1954.

Sechehaye, M. (1951). *Symbolic Realization*. New York: International Universities Press.

Sifneos, P. (1972). *Short-Term Psychotherapy and Emotional Crisis*. Cambridge, Mass.: Harvard University Press.

Stone, L. (1951). Psychoanalysis and brief psychotherapy. *Psychoanal. Q.* 20:215–236. *Reprinted in this volume, Chapter 1.*

——— (1954). The widening scope of indications for psychoanalysis. *J. Amer. Psychoanal. Assn.* 2:567–594. *Reprinted in this volume, Chapter 2.*

——— (1961). *The Psychoanalytic Situation*. New York: International Universities Press.

——— (1967). The psychoanalytic situation and transference. *J. Amer. Psychoanal. Assn.* 15:3–58. *Reprinted in this volume, Chapter 4.*

——— (1975). Some problems and potentialities of present-day psychoanalysis. *Psychoanal. Q.* 44:331–370. *Reprinted in this volume, Chapter 16.*

Wallerstein, R. (1969). Introduction of panel on psychoanalysis and psychotherapy: The relationship of psychoanalysis to psychotherapy—current issues. *Int. J. Psychoanal.* 50:117–126.

——— (1979). Book notice of *Toward the Validation of Dynamic Psychotherapy* by D. H. Malan. *J. Amer. Psychoanal. Assn.* 27:276–279.

Zimmerman, D. (1982). A View from South America. In *Psychotherapy: Impact on Psychoanalytic Training*, ed. E. D. Joseph and R. S. Wallerstein. New York: International Universities Press.

Chapter 16
Some Problems and Potentialities of Present-Day Psychoanalysis
(1975)

This long paper was written largely in response to the atmosphere of crisis which prevailed in the psychoanalytic community at the time. Unfortunately, this is still the mood of many. I did not then and do not now believe that psychoanalysis is moribund, whether as a scientific discipline or a therapeutic method. The effort was to defend a considered, rationally optimistic point of view about our work, with consideration for its numerous difficulties and impediments. With this essentially optimistic orientation, the paper is also a critique of attitudes among psychoanalysts as a group which tend to "outlaw" (or at least segregate) radically new ideas and their exponents and to cling to rigidly interpreted precepts of classical psychoanalysis as immutable articles of faith. This is thought to be one of the major obstacles to the normal and expectable evolution of psychoanalysis along lines ordinarily inevitable in the growth of any scientific discipline. There is also an effort to consider analysis in its social–historical context, in its relationship to drug therapy, and in its development of rational psychotherapeutic methods.

This paper has occasionally been cited by subsequent writers, but I cannot feel certain that its arguments have been widely influential. However, I do not, at this time, disown any of them!

If, in this presentation based largely on personal experience and reflection, I sometimes speak as if hitting straight from the shoulder, it is because I believe that this bluntness is a more useful contribution to dialectic than more restrained utterance. Furthermore, there is hardly a tendency I criticize of which I have not sometimes been guilty myself. On the other hand, I do not wish to minimize the strength of my current convictions. With several authors who have recently made reflective statements in varying contexts (e.g., Arlow 1970b, Bak 1970a, Anna Freud 1969, Rangell 1967, Ritvo 1971), I have often felt agreement on selected issues even when there are large and important areas of disagreement; and there are sometimes differences in specific references or in focus or emphasis in relation to writers with whom many ideas are held fully and strongly in common. Thus, it seems worthwhile to speak my own piece.

THE PSYCHOANALYTIC METHOD

To define the nature and limits of the psychoanalytic method is more challenging than to speak of what is comprehended in the inclusive word and concept, *psychoanalysis* (method, process, data, and theory). What is the method (with responsive inner process) which remains central in our work and thought? Many have defined it in at least partial response to a specific historical context. Freud's own definition of 1914, brief and deceptively simple, singles out the recognition and management of the phenomena of transference and resistance ("takes them as the starting-point of its work") as the indispensable criteria for the valid use of the term, even if, mind you, the process leads to data and conclusions different from his own. This definition has often been repeated, including the important reference to it by Anna Freud (1954a). Although many of Freud's epigones would not be as broad minded as he, this definition remains of decisive importance because of the breadth and openness of scientific spirit which it expresses, and because of its selection of two dynamisms operative in, and demonstrable in the dynamic psychoanalytic field. Unlike even the historical references of emergent memories (a priori unreliable as data except in the fact of their statement) with which psychoanalysis came into antenatal existence, these powerful phenomena can in a sense be "seen" by at least one observer, and we hope in the end by two. Both include implicitly another indispensable conceptual bul-

411

wark, the idea of the unconscious. This type of definition, furthermore, remains one of those perennially refreshing wellsprings of thought to which we can return when in danger of coming to regard outer phenomenology as essence, of really beginning to believe that "clothes make the man."

Under the combined demands of historical change, it has seemed pragmatically necessary to make the definition of psychoanalysis more strict, more limiting. These demands have included the consolidation of technical tradition, crystallizing group identity and, very importantly, the weedlike growth of psychotherapeutic practice variously deriving from psychoanalysis. (I do not speak of the overdetermining, not always rational or noble considerations, such as dereistic displacement from essentials to words and forms, the comfort of ritual, the sheer power of tradition or even habit, considerations of group narcissism, and trends toward guild exclusiveness.) With the passage of time the facilitation of a full-blown transference neurosis and its reduction to critical elements of the past as basic vehicles of analytic change and the goal of structural change as an expression of thorough improvement or cure have achieved increasingly important positions in definitions. About these movements and changes cluster the mechanisms and the technical expedients which are devoted to bringing them about. Whether explicit or implicit in such definitions, the topographic change, the bringing of that which was hitherto unconscious into consciousness—although the early luster of this essential process has been dimmed in many minds—remains an essential and integral part of the psychoanalytic process in all important references.

I shall not take time to group, in the order of essentiality, the principles and the routinized technical measures which characterize analysis, ranging peripherad from the basic rule of free association or the general principle of abstinence, to those about which there may be wide differences of opinion or emphasis, or variably flexible practices such as "never answering questions" or "not interpreting the transference until it becomes a resistance." It is not necessary to describe to analysts the hierarchy of principles and techniques and the interpersonal and procedural format which constitute the psychoanalytic situation—a complex gestalt which some of us believe has an organic meaning far beyond the sum of its parts and in which the individual parts themselves may also have functions different from, or in addition to, those historically assigned to them (Stone 1961). It is hoped that the psychoanalytic world always keeps in mind the basic functions and purposes of this organic complex and its various functional components, although there is some evidence that this is not as universal a tendency as one would like. If the picture of an undistinguished but rigorously schooled person sitting behind a reclining patient—the latter speaking only in free association, the former murmuring occasional oedipal clichés or telling the patient he is "resisting," during fifty-minute hours, five times a week, and insisting that bills be paid on time "no matter what"—does not constitute a satisfactory presentation of analysis to informed minds, there is nonetheless an important intellectual warning in this *reductio ad absurdum*, this intellectual horror. For, to a not inconsiderable number, the formal modalities of analysis have preempted the authority of its conceptual core to a surprising degree. And this is conspicuous where simple mechanical description or specification of numbers, so easy intellectually, are the foreground considerations. Even the taboos[1] emerge largely in this sphere. The honest psychotherapist, especially if he is a candidate, dreads putting a patient on the couch or seeing the patient every day. (The candidate who is adjured not to practice psychoanalysis, while feeling free to practice psychotherapy based on psychoanalysis, is an unhappy epitome of this intellectual grotesquerie.)

I do not intend to derogate the current technical modalities which characterize psychoanalysis or the important and autonomously significant gestalt ensemble which they constitute. Each of the elements, including their sometimes complicated history and certainly their formidable synergistic organization — the psychoanalytic situation — hold my deep respect for their dynamic power as well as my perennial scientific interest about their nature, mode of operation, interrelationship, and potentialities for advantageous modification, individually or as an ensemble. Also, I believe them to offer currently the most effective available instrument for profound observational access to the mental and emotional life of the human individual in a specified and relatively controlled setting and, at the same time, the most effective means, however imperfect, of bringing about modifications, sometimes profound alterations, in that life by purely psychological means in a rationally purposive way.

Yet this is not a *confessio fidei*. My loyalty includes a constant latent, sometimes manifest, questioning of each part and the whole of the structure. I do not regard it, and I do not think it should be regarded, as perfect even for our time. To regard it as "perfect" is, to my mind, the widespread paradoxical blasphemy of our psychoanalytic era. While there is general agreement that we need new data and new discovery in our field (A. Freud 1969, Bak 1970a, Arlow 1972), "our field" by implication often appears to include its current instrumentalities and theoretical structure as taken for granted. Kurt Eissler's paper of 1969 is a brilliant example of this trend of thought. These givens are, of course, necessary for the orderly day-to-day progress of our work so long as they are rationally interpreted — hence the primary qualification "latent" at the beginning of this paragraph in relation to "questioning."

It is also true that we have only scratched the surface with regard to new genetic and dynamic data that may be available by way of and in relation to the present framework. In this too, I differ from some who are more devoted to the status quo. These new data are to be valued, if not barrenly exegetical in implication, both in their present meaning and for their potential change of function should there be shifts in our basic frames of reference. But it is my conviction that the more urgent, the far more difficult need, and the larger potentiality for scientific and therapeutic progress lie in the constant examination and reexamination of our basic procedural assumptions and our related theories regarding psychoanalytic process and personality dynamics. It is in this sphere that, stated or unstated, the greatest resistance in the psychoanalytic community appears, and in a manner which to me, whether as general observer or as participant in discussion, betrays an unscientific (sometimes antiscientific) nonrational component. This I regard as the greatest single obstacle to the progress of psychoanalysis and as far more important than our selection of patients or even of candidates (Bird 1968, Bak 1970a), or the antiadaptive rebellious attitudes of young people (A. Freud 1969), or putatively excessive analytic preoccupation with the earliest period of life (A. Freud 1969, Arlow 1970b), or lack of adequate research facilities or endowments — granted the great practical importance of the latter consideration.

What are some examples of the important issues I have in mind? I list a few: the general validity of the dual instinct theory and a host of germane questions; the dynamic role of attachment and separation phenomena and their relationship to drives; the concept of psychic energies, indeed the entire structure of our metapsychology and its seductive or coercive effect on our thinking beyond its usefulness as a shorthand language and a tentative scaffolding of ideas; the nature and origin of transference; the nature and origin of resistance; the basic dynamics of the psychoanalytic situation and the psychoanalytic process beyond manifest structure, clinical purposes, and phenomenology; the dynamic functions of various forms of abstinence, including their quantitative aspects; the relationship of various modalities of abstinence, including their quantitative aspects, to the genesis of the transference and the transference neurosis; the theory of our technical procedures and their effects, including their comparative study in relation to alternatives; the further study of the genesis and functions of the oedipus complex; the actual functional role of spontaneous recollection, of reconstruction by the analyst; the relationship between cognitive and affective exchange; the dynamic position of free association beyond its cognitive-communicative role in relation to the recumbent posture and frequent visiting; the dynamic and economic interrelationships between reality and transference; and the general role of speech as such in the psychoanalytic process.

Of course, these problems have been discussed and written about from the beginning, but not nearly often enough. I shall not undertake here to list the distinguished contributions to these subjects, past or recent. The latent or manifest reaction to "heresy," however, exists in a subtly persuasive sense all too often, in contributor as well as audience.[2]

PSYCHOANALYTIC PRACTICE

I shall turn now to certain current actualities of psychoanalytic practice. I have mentioned the complicated evolving definition of psychoanalysis as a procedure. To this I must add a further multifaceted dimension, which I deal with as a unit only for purposes of rhetorical simplicity and condensation: the importance of organizational hegemony in defining and regulating formal (i.e., institute) training accordingly; further, the derivative fact of a central and elite corps of psychoanalysts who regard themselves as authentic and authoritative (not to speak of authorized) in their work and who, to a varying degree, are similarly regarded by many others. The preeminent organizing authority in the United States has been the American Psychoanalytic Association. Even among its own institutes there are sometimes notable differences of orientation, but certain minimal requirements are met and the sense of a trained and elite corps is pervasive. This elite corps, however, exists not only as an island in an uncharted ocean of psychotherapeutic practice but in a growing archipelago of psychoanalytic institutes, clinics, and practitioner groups of mixed, variable, and sometimes uncertain origin as to the training and background of their faculties.

How many, or which, would be included in a general view of psychoanalytic practice and would vary with individual capacity for tolerant acceptance and, occasionally, with knowledge of individual merits. The unsophisticated public is prone to regard anyone who talks with patients frequently (i.e., as much as once a week, especially if he charges high fees) as a psychoanalyst. In the view of a member of the officially trained and recognized elite, however, the number deriving from the "outside" would not be considerable.

Thus, psychoanalysis is in this view a very narrowly delimited specialty with, relatively speaking, but a handful of thoroughly trained practitioners. There are still large areas of the country, even populous cities, where none exist, even though the distribution is gradually proceeding. We must acknowledge that the vast problem of the specialized care of the neuroses is, in overwhelming preponderance, in the hands of psychiatrists and psychotherapists whose thought and methods are variably influenced by psychoanalysis, pro or contra (more often pro in this country), and in ways or degrees beyond classification. And this is the state of affairs in a country where "Freud," "Oedipus complex," and "dream interpretation" are often household clichés; also, where the pompous omniscient practitioner of the mass entertainment media, with his empty grandiloquent diagnoses and his magical cures, sets the image and the hopes of the naïve public, engendering groundless expectations and an ambivalent mixture of wonder, awe, and fear.

To boil down detailed scrutiny of the distribution and socioeconomic availability of officially qualified psychoanalysts, one might say that in our private work we are, willy-nilly, if not devoted only to the rich and well born, largely doctors for the prosperous and sophisticated. Through our clinics we reach an additional small number of those relatively adjacent to them. Blue-collar workers or their families are rarely seen. It is only through psychotherapy that we reach effectively the so-called masses.

That there is an important reaction to this peculiarity of psychoanalysis is an unequivocal fact, whether it be expressed in certain doctrinaire ideologies, in deficiencies of financial endowment, or in the less formal bitterness and criticism of nondoctrinaire but socially concerned individuals within and outside the medical profession. (Note the recently quoted remarks of APA President Alfred Freedman in *Psychiatric News*, September 5, 1973; also those of Judd

Marmor, March 21, 1973.) It would be my strong interpretative hunch that this feeling, in a time of almost revolutionary change (by American standards) in the general position of health care, lends an important affective thrust to the currently mounting tide of criticism of psychoanalysis, both as to its scientific status and its therapeutic usefulness.

While not without earlier precedents, sometimes augmented by economic hard times, possibly a contributing factor in recent complaints regarding analytic practice, a gloomily ruminative view of the general situation among analysts themselves seems to me more common recently than in the past, including past periods of extreme economic or international turmoil. Apart from the practical anxieties of some, we must also notice the more frequent intellectual contributions regarding the scientific and therapeutic position of psychoanalysis. There are, of course, predecessors to those references cited earlier: Knight (1953), Gitelson (1955, 1964) among others, not to speak of Freud himself. But I do believe that more recent writings reflect and often express a more intense theme of perplexity regarding the nature of our commitment than in the past. In our organizational life, national and local, there is a ferment of mind searching, largely in an affirmative direction, regarding methods of training, research, and allied matters.

Let us return to the problem of the availability of analysis, which I believe plays a part not only in the ambivalence of our environment but in our own state of mind, whether guilty, reactively defensive, unconcerned, or disappointed in a failing material cornucopia, or impelled to reflective concern about the general problems of our commitment. I believe this problem of availability to be formidable and irrefutable, and essentially insoluble so long as the status quo (in a comprehensive sense) is maintained. How can we confront this problem? So long as our technology retains its present rationale, we cannot arbitrarily alter it, even to meet a legitimate social need. Nor can we by magical fiat bring about changes in psychodynamics that would enable such changes. In default of legitimate (i.e., sound and rational) changes, we must continue as we are, however limited the number we reach. This would leave us with a sort of trickle-down philosophy, *faute de mieux*. But what can we reasonably hope for, indeed offer, in establishing a more affirmative psychological orientation, assuming that we do not deny the problem or view the "service minded" from a stance of aristocratic or ivory-tower hauteur? Granted that the ultimate problem is in the hard statistical sphere, a change in orientation toward the problem could in itself be productive in several ways, even if at the outset largely in the psychological sphere.

1. Legitimate and fundamental changes may yet develop in the essential framework of our present procedures, enabling its wider application. It is unlikely that analysis will thus become freely and easily available; but any improvement in its effectiveness or any diminution in required time will be significant. To the present time, radical innovations with this explicit or secondary purpose

have not taken root, largely for sound and adequate reasons. These efforts have sometimes been valuable and instructive even in their failures, but further efforts need not be failures.

2. The theories and techniques of psychoanalysis may contribute further, more profoundly and extensively, to the establishment and improvement of other rational forms of psychotherapy. The study, practice, and research of such psychotherapies can be given dignity and importance in psychoanalytic groups, including a graduate, or at least advanced, position in institute training. I note with pleasure that Anna Freud (1966) mentions this important consideration in her sketch of an ideal institute. The issue of such training and study will often be utilized effectively by nonpsychoanalysts. While the creative responsibility can be assumed with maximum advantage by those who understand the parent discipline thoroughly, the broad outlines and principles of derivative techniques can thereafter be taught to those without this advantage. Not every good medical practitioner has intimate knowledge of virology or electron microscopy, or even of much less recondite but relevant fields. Further, a "bit far out" but not beyond serious consideration, psychoanalysts can try to extend their informed understanding, not only to deviant analytic and quasi-analytic views, but to remote forms of therapy (myriad, at this time), even those of a nonanalytic or putatively antianalytic frame of reference. They can thus sometimes contribute better rationale to these methods, and in this effort expand their own horizons, i.e., learn more about the varied dynamisms of personality change, whether brought about by analysis or by other as yet ununderstood personality processes.

3. The derivatives of our limited field of therapy can further enrich other intensely practical fields, for example, education and child care, and many other less proximal scientific and scholarly disciplines, outstandingly sociology and political science. In the latter spheres, indeed, the indication for serious psychoanalytic study seems urgent. The hazard to be guarded against, strikingly in relation to the study of creative effort but present in all remote applications of psychoanalysis is the temptation of the child with his toy microscope: the overenthusiastic pleasure in the surface facilities of psychoanalytic thought, the fun, and the spurious sense of omnipotence and universal intellectual superiority. This is opposed to the humble and serious application of the profundities of psychoanalytic method and thought to grave problems, in adjacency to and with full consideration and respect for the myriad nonanalytic considerations entering into all-important human behavior, and the multiple frames of reference in which even the fate of unconscious motivation and conflict can be viewed.

4. Finally, of course, there is the question of broadening and diffusing psychoanalytic training, including the "front door" training of nonmedical candidates, of giving up the exaggeratedly elite, guild-like status of organized psychoanalysis and in a sense legitimizing the tendency implicit in "wildcat" institutes. This would also mean simplifying admission criteria, as well as the requirements for training analyst status, while still maintaining certain reasonable but hard minimum standards.

With regard to the maintenance of certain reasonable minimal standards, some qualifications are important: by keeping requirements for admission, graduation, or training analyst status as much as possible in the hard, i.e., demonstrable sphere — as to education, clinical and teaching experience, intelligence, character, and scientific achievement — requirements could in some respects be even more rigorous than they are now. Yet, by removing or minimizing the elements of idiosyncratic personal approval or rejection by those in power (Stone 1975), especially in relation to cliché mystiques ("a natural grasp of the unconscious" or its putative absence, for example) or the charisma of psychoanalytic ancestry or adherence, a considerably broader base of candidacy qualification and faculty growth could be established. For example, lay analysts, who, I believe, should be systematically and overtly trained, could be required to offer evidence not only of adequate and structured advanced education in relevant fields but of an adequate minimum of training in the biomedical, especially psychiatric, sphere. The latter training could be a required preliminary phase of their psychoanalytic training. On the other hand, thoroughly trained analysts with a certain number of years of clinical experience should be automatically qualified to conduct analyses of candidates, if no important ethical or other professional misbehavior or inadequacy is validly demonstrated in relation to them. This last step in the prolonged initiation ordeal mentioned by Arlow (1970a, 1972) should be available to the colleague of mature years on the basis of interested and conscientious work, rather than on the basis of unclear intangibles. This would be to his and the psychoanalytic community's advantage.

Thus, anticipating the inevitable retrospective judgments of history, we could leave the elite aspect to the achievement of those individuals and institutes whose gifts and efforts earn such distinction. Such tendency must, of course, be considered carefully and in detail as to its ultimate results, specific methods of implementation, and presumptive hazards. But it finds some ancestor in the noninstitute trends vigorously expressed by Bernfeld (1962), and even in Freud's own rather modest views regarding psychoanalytic training. Again, these steps would probably not in themselves make psychoanalysis freely or generally available so long as its essential features do not change. But for those who want it and will make the necessary sacrifices for it, these steps would vastly increase the statistical opportunity for treatment by trained analysts.

RESISTANCE OF ANALYSTS TO CHANGE

I put aside with regret the extended discussion of my several personal observations and opinions regarding the origins of analysts' resistance to change in fundamental tenets of technique or theory. Perhaps this merits separate communication. Rather than omit this important subject altogether, however, I speak dogmatically.

It is worthwhile at least to mention at this point topics which might be considered in such extended discussion.

1. The inevitability of intellectual uncertainty in our field and the role of a rigidly maintained, narcissistically invested fiction of certainty in countering latent intellectual malaise.

2. Hostility toward the malefactor who threatens this defense, sometimes augmented by the ambivalence underlying the defender's own overwrought loyalty (see Arlow 1970a, 1972; Reik 1919).

3. The role of shared group convictions in the subtleties of transference analysis (criteria of acting out, for instance) and their potential influence on the later tenacious adoption of parental attitudes and sometimes irrational revolt against them.

4. Factors hindering the spontaneous self-analysis of our own zealot potential: (a) binding group solidarity with mutual approval and support; (b) the tendency to establishment mentality paralleling the success phase of revolutionary cycles in other spheres of human history; (c) the fact that the political struggles which sometimes achieve a repellent character in our groups tend to offer a premium for one direction or another of alignment and conformity, whereas these struggles, beyond the sheer question of literal personal power, are in themselves colored by the polytheistic authoritarian aspects of our training system, intrinsically inimical to original thought beyond certain limits; (d) within this framework the outstanding and critical role of the reported training analysis, which deprives the candidate of the first and indispensable rights of any analytic patient, i.e., absolute and inviolable confidentiality and immunity from intrusion into his extraanalytic life by the analyst. (If the candidate is a good boy he may some day be a training analyst and do the same to others!); (e) the dangers of a not too infrequent lack of humility in those in power, the acceptance of whims and caprices of judgment about other individuals as definitive and authoritative.

5. In a broad historiographic sense, which does not exclude psychoanalysis, the fluctuating decline of influence of literal religion among the intellectual elite of the world, with the consequent need for displacement of this universal transference to other spheres. Psychoanalysis, which tends to undermine the irrational factors in such phenomena, wherever they appear, tends by inadvertent paradox to leave only itself as a suitable object for such investment.

6. Finally, the tendency to displace away from the analyst or his method the reasons for therapeutic disappointment or failure. This supports rigid idealization of the method and secure rigidities of belief, rather than the open and receptive mind.

With due regard for the pragmatic necessity of intelligent primary adherence to convictions and the rational conservatism which may follow, the quasi-religious, irrational determinants of a doctrinaire sense of certainty (where uncertainty is inevitable, whether in so-called orthodoxy or revolutionary dissidence) are formidable obstructions to possible progress and deserve our serious self-analytic scrutiny, as well as our conscious, objective intellectual attention. Since my own convictions lie decidedly in what I regard as the classical orientation and since I feel that the greatest intellectual promise still lies in this orientation,

I am less concerned about the stormy irrationalities of militant dissidence than the prevailing rigidity in my own intellectual community. This resistance to change is the more important because its nature, involving the synergistic interaction of both individual and group needs and defenses, makes it less accessible to rational argument than other problems. The resistance is not often explicit or a matter of stated principle, in fact not frequently conscious, only rarely impolite, although it may be snide and, when expressed by superior minds, may achieve an indubitable elegance and scholarliness of expression.

The more crude or blatant form of rigidity manifested by the individual who cannot, or at least does not, think for himself is a serious problem, but it does not influence others importantly. The views of the gifted polemicist who combines scholarship, acuteness of intellect, and sound conservatism with the magical and subtle matrix of historical and current group narcissism and irrational sense of certainty are at one time the far more effective guardians of affirmative tradition and the far more effective watchdogs against creative change. It is therefore even more poignantly the burden of the intellectual leader to examine, if necessary, to analyze the irrational elements in his commitment to psychoanalysis. The tendency to resistance to change may be expressed in simply ignoring contributions, in attributing them to personal neuroses (see Keiser 1972, Arlow 1970a, regarding this phenomenon in organizational problems), in the emotional temper of discussion, in joking or supercilious generalizations, or in an endless variety of modalities for the summary disposition of intellectual disagreement without confrontation.

There is, of course, a simple and self-evident alternative to all this, and in the functional acceptance of this obvious truth lies the affirmative intellectual future of psychoanalysis: that intellectual convictions on rational foundations not only occur spontaneously and inevitably but are necessary for productive action, so that their existence requires no defense or apology; that such convictions are nonetheless compatible with open-mindedness not only toward new and even disconcerting data, but toward new or variant theoretical constructs; and that the maintenance of this open-mindedness must be a commitment transcending at any emotional cost, the narcissistic and other primitive considerations, mentioned earlier.

PSYCHOANALYSIS AS THERAPY

Now I shall turn to the question of psychoanalysis as therapy, without reference to statistics but rather from the point of view of observation and reflection derived from my own clinical experience and that of others to whose experience I have had access. Statistical studies are, of course, to be welcomed. The recent summary of the long study by the Menninger Foundation Group (1972) is thoroughly admirable. However, I do not believe that in a field of such extreme complexity—as to the definition of forms, diagnosis, technology, criteria of change, and the tremendous variations in the personal equation regarding analyst, patient and their matching—the general situation is as yet ripe for the dismissal of individual experience and reflection.

In the treatment of the moderately severe chronic neuroses (and sometimes considerably beyond these) and the milder, sometimes somewhat more severe, character disorders, there is not the slightest doubt in my mind that psychoanalysis is highly effective. Skillfully applied, it yields a high degree of improvement in an impressive proportion of cases, amply justifying the sacrifices of those willing to undertake them. Its scope extends outward from this core indication through various more severe nosologic groups, the application increasingly selective, the effectiveness progressively less dependable and increasingly contingent on extranosological individual and environmental factors as the nosologic periphery is approached. That analysis may occasionally be spectacularly effective with milder neuroses, in the sense of historically early tentative experiences and expectations is still true. But this is based largely on certain early experiences in my practice with rather naïve patients, usually young adults with relatively uncomplicated neuroses not treated previously and unencumbered by oppressive, fixed life situations or by complicated and tenacious aspirations unlikely to be achieved. That some of these were in part transference cures is probably true. However, the line of distinction is sometimes unclear in these cases.

Furthermore, the question of loss of motivation in patients relatively quickly relieved of suffering, with exigent and hopeful lives to get on with, with ample simple social displacements for residues of fundamental transferences, is inevitably important in the total emotional economy of treatment. Also, we should note that such transferences, maintained in a state of "clinical cure," usually of benign idealizing quality, do not have the malignant potentiality of the sometimes euphoric premature improvements of the more malignant neuroses, for example, those characterized by profound and intense oral ambivalence. Whether these simple and milder cases are actually less numerous than in the past, I do not know. They are not now frequent in the schedules of experienced practitioners, nor do they seem too common anywhere, including the applicants to psychoanalytic clinics (see Lazar 1973). Perhaps they still appear among the patients in hospital outpatient departments. The economic reasons which quickly come to mind may exist but are sometimes largely spurious. The fee gap between old and young analysts may be slight or nonexistent or, in some instances, inverted. It is also true that such patients are often accessible to a variety of forms of treatment, some of them ideal indications for a proximal form of interpretative psychoanalytic psychotherapy, in the sense which I have mentioned in the past (see Stone 1951, 1954).

As to the first-mentioned group—chronic neuroses in the middle range of severity and equivalent character disorders—they remain the core and backbone of psychoanalytic practice, conceived as ideal for therapeutic effectiveness. Such patients still appear occasionally in my practice, but definitely as a small minority. With the advance of years, apart from the analysis and reanalysis of colleagues, the increment of older patients in complicated life situations with long-standing severe illnesses and often with multiple past treatments including more than one analysis is quite formidable. Such patients often have special claims on the limited time of the older analyst and tend to crowd out those with moderately severe neuroses, not to speak of the highly responsive milder cases.

Are there observations in analytic practice, apart from changes in the constituency of individual private practices, which suggest intrinsic change in the neuroses and the patients' accessibility to analytic treatment? The special reactions of young people, discussed by Anna Freud (1969), have been verified as vividly stated points of view in a few consultations in my own office in the last few years. How enduring this reaction will be I cannot say. The recession in importance of traditional nonrational bulwarks of morality and the current cultural interim characterized by moral vacuum or chaos or impulsive groping are conspicuous in the present psychological climate. Such historic context does, I believe, favor a movement toward impulse, behavioral, identity, and addictive disorders, rather than symptom formations (see H. Lowenfeld 1969, H. and Y. Lowenfeld 1970). The diminution of attachment to the idea of God in terms of vivid personal imagery, even to diminished and unreliable secular equivalents, diminishes the facility of solution by displacement of residual basic transferences (Stone 1961, 1967), thus augmenting problems of separation from the analyst. Intensely relevant ideologies, for conspicuous example, Women's Liberation, notwithstanding rational affirmative constituents, can implement tenacious resistances in their irrational overflow. These are, of course, facts of cultural history to which analysis must make technical adaptation.

One old problem—the resistance called intellectualization, most formidable in the professionally sophisticated—has been disseminated and multiplied by cultural change. I refer to the wide diffusion of psychoanalytic knowledge and half-knowledge. Despite Freud's (1910) own somewhat equivocal and guarded optimism regarding this impact, largely in its broader societal implications, it is like the frequent anxiety-denying sexual freedom of this time, rather an obstacle to analytic process than otherwise. It is as though everyone from early on is subjected to diffuse premature interpretations with corresponding increases in resistances in central spheres—for example, the Oedipus complex. How to disarm this knowledge and gain genuine access to these critical spheres of feeling is more than an individual problem of traditional resistance interpretation. It calls for more general technical changes. The principle of *reconstruction upwards* (Loewenstein 1951, 1957) is an important move in this direction. The growing importance of the transference neurosis as the ultimate crucible of analytic work is a safeguard against glib "book-and-mouth insights," which are a substitute for, and defense against, true analytic experience and understanding.

What can we expect by way of therapeutic results in analysis? Certainly the patient hopes to get well in an ordinary sense, to overcome his suffering or disability. That is why he comes to us. This hope is met to varying degree, with occasional failures, the outcome dependent on a variety of interlacing factors which elicit many papers in themselves. Complete recovery, in this sense, is not as frequent as I and many others would like. It can occur with due regard for semantic relativism and prognostic fallibility, in the optimal type of patient mentioned earlier. Clinical cures can also occur for practical purposes in the more favorable range of moderately severe neuroses. What is more frequent is a significant reduction in the number and severity of symptoms and their interference with viability and the general capacity for happiness. With this is a capacity to abort recurrent symptoms in statu nascendi, sometimes by a sort of self-analysis but more often by a rapid spontaneous mobilization of awareness of the old factors involved in new situations. At times a visit or a few visits to the analyst may be invoked to facilitate such process. (I omit the question of reanalysis in this context.) With a generally greater sense of self-understanding, adaptability, and freedom of options, one may hope for a greater sense of overall well-being, sometimes expressed even in the somatic sphere (see Menninger 1958). One may certainly hope for decisive improvement in the sexual life and, importantly, in the larger general complex of personal relationships. This pattern of improvement has sometimes been greatly valued even by patients whose symptomatic results have not been striking. But the proof of the pudding, in my humble opinion, is that in many years of analytic practice, including a larger than average proportion of severe clinical problems, I can recall only a negligible number of patients who stated regret or disappointment over ever having had analytic treatment (regardless of the factors involved in such attitude).

Some years ago, in my strictly personal impression, a colleague of importance in early American psychoanalysis was subjected to a certain amount of subdued and covert criticism (at times, mockery?) for his blunt and insistent interest in psychoanalytic failures. This is in paradoxical relationship to a growing tendency to pessimism (or, to be exact, what I regard as pessimism in the light of my views of possible future progress) regarding psychoanalysis as therapy, sometimes among colleagues of unmatched intensity of commitment and devotion to the field in general (see, for example, Eissler 1969). Or a similar trend may appear in a high evaluation of the unique psychologic validities of the psychoanalytic process (along with an appreciation of its training and research value) with what one may call a special paradoxical correlate of its therapeutic limitations—the moral philosophical superiority of the tragic over the romantic view of life (see Klein 1973 and his reference to Schafer 1970).

We have reacted to therapeutic failures in many different ways—for example, Oberndorf (1950) and in a fundamental sense Freud's (1937) classic contribution in this sphere. One can legitimately wonder if the therapeutic limitations of psychoanalysis are connected with the occasional tendency to play down the therapeutic function of analysis altogether, possibly to find some obscurely tacit authority for this in Freud's original disinclination toward medicine or his apparent or putative later waning of therapeutic interest, and to substitute for its function as a therapy the broader view of the position and the role of analysis, beginning with its status as a general psychology.

On the whole, it seems to me that if one's expectations of psychoanalysis are rational and circumspect, it stands up as a powerful and exceedingly effective therapy, even "as is." If relapses, rare dramatic breakdowns, and occasional long and minimally fruitful analyses have confronted us with increasing vividness with the passage of years, we must react not only to this clear and unequivocal challenge but also to the simplistic view of neuroses which could originally have contributed to our feeling that we did have a magical panacea. Long ago Freud (1913) met the request for a short treatment for obsessional neurosis with a gently but appropriately sarcastic counterattack (p. 129). It remains true that to be able purposely to change human personality at all is something marvelous in itself, something like changing the leopard's spots. I use this commonplace metaphor advisedly, for constitutional biological elements, to varying degree, undoubtedly do confront us in our work, and only the infinitely plastic potentiality of human psychic life renders even this confrontation tenable without total despair. Neuroses are illnesses built into human development from the earliest days onward. They are adaptations to powerful inner dynamic forces and germane conflicts with the infantile environment — often self-compounding as the years go on, in the sense of multiplying pathological adaptations in large components (for important reasons [Stone 1973]), intrinsically resistant to change in the only radically effective therapeutic modalities known to us at this time and always vulnerable, even during treatment, to the pathological impact of environmental forces.

Instead of realizing these facts, physicians are still prone to view them as pseudoillnesses or nonillnesses masquerading as illnesses. Patients may bring to treatment the same attitude, compounded in varying degree by the magical expectations and demands of the transference. In the early days our own excited therapeutic optimism may well have fed such attitudes to mutual disadvantage. Even Freud was not entirely free of this enthusiasm. Witness his early comparison with the clear-cut therapeutic offering of the surgeon (1913, p. 131) or his understandable sense of decisive achievement in the outcome of the first *Wolf-man* analysis (1918 [1914]). I believe that there has been much salutary intellectual retrenchment and a growing sense of proportion. Freud's own work has dealt largely with the limitations inherent in human personality (1937). Perhaps there has not yet been sufficient appreciation of the contextual aspect of personality and process (although Freud was at least larvally aware of this, certainly in relation to the family). In analyzing an individual, we not only deal with him and his whole life history, including his future, but to some degree with the entire dynamic setting of his immediate and remote environment. In any case, I believe that the reaction to early excessive therapeutic optimism has swung in the other direction to an unjustified degree.

With regard to the medical origin and orientation of psychoanalysis and the medical model, and germane to its persisting therapeutic commitment, there is another incipient, if hesitant and equivocal, swing of the pendulum, at least in the intellectual sphere (see Eissler 1965, reviewed by Keiser 1969). There is now a growing tendency to disparage the physician as potential analyst. Such general attitude I reject entirely and regret that I cannot elaborate on this subject at this time. I must rest with the stated hope that the sheer lack of the degree of Doctor of Medicine will not one day become in itself the invisible badge of authentic talent, inclination, and education for the practice of psychoanalysis. This, I submit, would be quite different from the legitimate defense of *properly qualified* lay analysis, which began with Freud (1926).

Now as to the therapeutic purposes of psychoanalysis: I cannot give serious recognition to any conception of psychoanalytic practice in which these purposes are not the primary and central consideration of the analyst, however highly developed his other interests, including scientific interest, may be. The therapeutic obligation would remain even in the remotely hypothetical instance that the analysand too was motivated by scientific interest. Our knowledge and our methods were born in therapy. I know of no adequate rational motivation for turning to analysis—and persisting in it through its deeper vicissitudes—other than the hope for relief of personal suffering. Certainly, it is for therapeutic help that our patients remunerate us, giving us our livelihood. With regard to the training analysis, any colleague of some experience knows that its distinction from therapy is essentially fictive. It is usually a prolonged therapeutic analysis in which the professional aspiration is a special and complicating condition; the training aspect is an incidental by-product.

If there was a shift of preponderance in Freud's interest as time went on, this was in part due to the challenge of applying psychoanalysis to the broader canvas of human history, a challenge which persists at this time. It is no doubt true that there was also increasing awareness of the formidable obstacles to successful therapy, in many cases the confrontation with relapses and failures. Yet I am not aware of any explicit disavowal of interest by Freud in the therapeutic process and its problems, nor of any implication that Thanatos holds the clear ascendancy within the structure of all, or even most, neuroses. Be that as it may, I am inclined to interpret a recent mood in the psychoanalytic intellectual community as heralding a movement in the direction of therapeutic nihilism coupled with an increase in scientific emphasis. Thus recently Bak (1970b), while emphasizing "our ideal that medical service and scientific investigation coincide," suggested in effect that following a trial period we reject or terminate cases which are scientifically or therapeutically unproductive and leave their treatment to nonanalyst colleagues, "unfettered by the rigors of the psychoanalytic method" but trained for this purpose with aims "predominantly to alleviate suffering."

Granting that there are patients with whom a continuation or even initiation of traditional technique is contraindicated, the suggested alternative (while it may be applicable in some instances and is certainly consistent with the author's general views) seems to me somewhat vaguely conceived as to method and implementation—apart from the fact that it removes both the pathology and the subsequent process from our scientific scrutiny. There are both theoretical and statistical reasons (see Menninger Foundation 1972) to doubt the effectiveness of purely supportive therapy with borderline cases. The hostile transference does not always respect our categorizations of technical indication, and highly developed psychoanalytic skills may be necessary at critical junctures. Perhaps the so-called *flexible analyst* will in some instances find challenging interest in continuing with such patients by applying the analytic method with well-considered variations of traditional techniques, rather than by "dilution and contamination" of the method. In extreme instances he may indeed utilize his skill and experience in what would be called psychotherapy, whose challenges may sometimes be greater than those of the classical procedure and possibly even circle back eventually to a more strictly defined analytic situation. As to the scientific productivity of a given patient, there may be much room for discussion and probably for disagreement. I, for one, would defend the scientific productiveness of many of the more difficult patients who stretch the limits of our conceptual and technical framework. Fluent and interesting free associations or recollections are not our only scientific data. Furthermore, I have genuine confidence in the vitality of the conceptual and technical core of psychoanalysis, so that I do not believe it has to be guarded by rituals and shibboleths which define and protect its boundaries.

Further, regarding therapy: only the hope for help, expressed initially in the hope for relief of symptomatic suffering but involving ultimately the hope for help in resolution of the transference neurosis against its own complex of reactivated and exigent infantile demands (the "second chance"), will motivate an individual to expose those elements in his personality which permit true analytic process and which can at times constitute genuine contributions to analytic science. Thus, science, insofar as it is directly derived from psychoanalytic process, is inextricably involved with therapeutic considerations. In my view, then, the recent frequent distinction between professional school training and selection and training for research is largely specious (see Bird 1968). Actually, of course, there is no need to go beyond the manifest rights of patients to justify the primacy of therapy in our work, but I have thought it worthwhile to mention these other aspects of the therapeutic effort insofar as they are additionally and importantly significant.

INDICATIONS FOR PSYCHOANALYSIS

The question of therapy in a general sense leads quite naturally into consideration of the scope of indications for psychoanalysis. Some years ago (Stone 1954), I presented the opening paper of an Arden House Conference, sponsored by the New York Psychoanalytic Society, devoted to the Widening Scope of Indications for Psychoanalysis. This conference, in which Edith Jacobson (1954), Anna Freud (1954b), and other experienced colleagues participated, was a response to clinical actualities which had been making themselves felt for a long time and to which, indeed, some of our colleagues had begun to respond more than a decade earlier (e.g., Cohn 1940, Greenacre 1941, Stern 1938). Among the thoughtful analysts who have considered this general subject in more recent years (see Symposium 1967, Bak 1970b), however, a not infrequent tendency has been in the opposite direction, at least in a conceptual, i.e., a "paper", sense. A "narrowing scope" of psychoanalytic indications is thought desirable by some for scientific, didactic, and even clinical reasons (see Kuiper in Symposium 1967). As in many other spheres of psychoanalytic thought, conceptualizations or abstractly conceived principles or purposes do not always reflect very closely the realities of psychoanalytic process or practice. Recently, a misleading "slogan-building" potential was attributed to the title of my paper by Bak (1970b), although the author exempted the content from similar criticism.

In our field, more so than others, there are always grounds for legitimate disagreement and derivative dialectic. However, insofar as the *narrowing scope* represents a visible swing of the historical pendulum, I am impelled to try to understand psychological aspects of the historical trend. Certainly, in a general substantive way there are the following aspects: the painful problem of relative clinical frustration for group or individual, the great demands on time and emotional tolerance involved in treating the more severe disorders, the burgeoning of other forms of psychotherapy (which, however inelegant intellectually, are often clinically effective), and of course the dramatic clinical effectiveness of certain drugs. But it is possible that such reactions, seen in the light of multiple function, are in part manifestations of the deep general currents of concern and conflict about the therapeutic aspects of psychoanalysis and of the struggle with a tendency to give up on analysis as a therapy — beginning logically of course with the more difficult problems? Even the most devoted sometimes utter or imply strikingly pessimistic forebodings about the future of psychoanalysis as a science and therapy. Ultimately, one may speculate, is psychoanalysis to be led further from a traditionally narrow scope into a sort of genteel quasi retirement: a type of practice where patients who are prosperous, intelligent, gifted, and articulate, not really very sick, but genuinely curious about themselves, are to be treated by scholarly and scientifically committed analysts, unimpeded by intrusive therapeutic responsibility?

I have referred elsewhere (Stone 1975) to a type of candidate who regards the patient as in effect "made for him." I hope that this subtly expressed oral character tendency does not become generalized and authoritatively integrated in the further development of psychoanalysis. One who is unwilling to accept the unique travails of treatment efforts with borderline cases, for example, is more just to these patients and to himself if he does not knowingly undertake such analyses. This would be a legitimate expression of free choice of commitment, just as unassailable as any other reasonable election regarding the general scope and emphasis in one's practice. Whatever commitment reflects an honest evaluation of one's interests and capacities, with corresponding gratification in work and willingness to spend and concentrate energies, probably promises the best that one can give to the patients seen in this context and, I believe, establishes the greatest likelihood of genuine scientific contribution.

There are many brilliant contributors (too numerous, of course, to mention) whose work derives from a relatively invariant technical, theoretical, and general clinical context. Yet, from early on analysts have also explored remote areas. The recent valuable contributions of Kernberg (1967, 1968) and Kohut (1971), more systematic than earlier writings, are examples of the productiveness of less constricted applications of our methods within or deriving clearly and proximally from the classical frame of reference. Regarding therapeutic effectiveness in the treatment of more severe illness, I have little to add in the sense of summary remarks to my general impressions of 1954. Given certain personal resources in the patient and the analyst—the willingness and capacity to modify the rigidly conceived analytic instrumentality rationally in both emotional and intellectual spheres and the analyst's willingness to sustain greater travail than usually envisaged in the analytic routine, sometimes for very long periods—individuals can often be helped when this would have been thought extremely unlikely, if not impossible, according to narrowly conventional criteria.

Certainly, there are some futile experiences—more rarely, crushing disappointments. But even these sometimes loom less large when measured against the frequent alternative of prolonged hospitalization, withdrawal from life, invalidism, or suicide. And there are also, occasionally, the uniquely enlivening experiences of helping to an important degree worthwhile persons who may have been given up, even by colleagues of unequivocal competence. With increasing age and fatigue, the tolerance of some for the severe demands of such work may well decrease, and the attractions of work with relatively uncomplicated and highly responsive neuroses become correspondingly highlighted. Possibly, if one may risk a generalization, the optimum period for carrying a heavy schedule of borderline patients is in middle life when there is an adequate backlog of experience but vigor is not yet conspicuously diminished.

When my 1954 paper was given, it was discussed by Anna Freud (1954b), who—while she was in some respects more than generous in evaluating its content—expressed some regret over the amount of analytic time and energy spent in treating such patients, as against the greater therapeutic effect, the greater number of patients who might be reached and the more rapid improvement of our conventional techniques which might occur if we spent more time with more accessible patients. This view has a simple plausibility and commonsense validity which must be weighed carefully, especially since in any case we can reach so few people. However, certain germane questions persist. Is it the nature of productive human aspiration—whether in surgery, mountain climbing, or psychoanalysis—to confine interest and effort to areas where success is certain or highly probable? Is it wise to impose limitations on such aspiration? Who are the patients who present themselves for treatment, in private practice, in general, and in relation to specific analysts? Should eminently worthwhile men or women, sometimes persons of considerable distinction, creativeness, and current or potential productivity be denied access to the therapy which in many instances has most to offer them?

To reach into the scientific sphere, the more deeply ill patients do have something of unique importance to teach us about the fundamental organization and development of personality, about the most profound aspects of transference and resistance. And reflexively, such efforts can also lend new and improved perspectives to the treatment of the transference psychoneuroses. One may, of course, prefer to call many such efforts *psychoanalytically oriented psychotherapy* of a *modified analytic procedure,* as does Kernberg (1968). To me this is a terminological rather than a substantive issue, about which my own view remains the same as that which I expressed in 1954.

I am aware that the preverbal nature of certain profound experiences has been regarded as a formidable impediment in relation to a treatment process which relies preponderantly on the instrumentality of speech (see A. Freud 1969, Arlow 1970b). Certainly, this is another major difficulty in such work. However, I cannot accept it as comprehensively disqualifying. That which has no words can still find words—or be given words—in the reenactments of the tranference neurosis. This is allied to the establishment of "memories" via reconstruction, often a decisive process in psychoanalytic work.

More important, I believe, than the problem of verbalization as such is the depth and power of the early disturbances which enter into the very foundations, the warp and woof of the basic personality, the character traits, the quality and power of transferences, the relative strength of the ego, and similar matters. I would be the last to question that there are limiting factors in regard to a therapy which is, after all, neodevelopmental at best and thus has its own intrinsic limitations. But my emphasis at the moment is again, as in 1954, on the inappropriateness of arbitrary limitations, on the importance of estimates of the total patient personality and its resources, and on the analyst's orientation, as more nearly decisive than conventional nosology—granted that the latter is not without a certain time-tested statistical significance. With this principle Bak (1970b), a proponent of the narrowing scope, at least in part, agrees.

It is in this special sphere (i.e., the treatment of so-called borderlines) that conservative colleagues are usually most willing (if they approve of this sphere at all) to countenance modifications of technical method. A general reluctance to admit of possible changes in technology or theory—thus of considered experimentation—manifests itself most tenaciously in the outlines of traditional method and its application to those neuroses which are thought to lend themselves optimally to its operations. Nevertheless, analysis may, and probably will, change, not only in the sense of intrinsic new discoveries and ideas but with the evolution of medicine and science in general and with cultural change. Affirmative contributions should not be regarded as contaminations or threats to identity. Is the surgeon less or more a surgeon if he avails himself of the advancing contributions of cardiology, hematology, and other germane fields? Modern pharmacologic therapies, for example, if not used as total alternatives to or as evasions of fundamental confrontations and if used with appropriate consideration of their psychological role, may indeed contribute importantly to the feasibility of treating certain severely ill patients with essentially psychoanalytic methods (see Freud's contiguous idea, 1940 [1938], p. 182). In this sphere neurophysiologic research may ultimately make an important contribution. Elasticities of technique carry a potentially important secondary gain, the possibility of rational carry-overs of technical insights into the more general theory and practice of psychoanalysis. It was in the treatment of "borderlines" that I was originally stimulated to reexamine the rigors of the psychoanalytic situation in general (Stone 1961). One may by the same token achieve insights into the deeper nature of the neuroses from the treatment of "borderlines" in the sense that exploration and treatment of neuroses opened the understanding of so-called normal or healthy personality.

Beyond this, as mentioned earlier, is the continuing and urgent need to elaborate psychotherapies, frankly different from the classical analytic procedure, although with an admitted gray area in regard to the informed practice of interpretative psychotherapy (see also Bak 1970b, A. Freud 1966). Much work, of course, has been done, but important tasks remain, especially in creating new technical formats (and their more thorough investiture with psychoanalytic thought) and with regard to the respective unconscious structures of such formats, especially as related to the economic position of the transference and contingent phenomena. I have in mind the deeper understanding of the transference potentialities (and expectable responses) in a range of situations beginning with simple consultation and advice and extending to the classical psychoanalytic situation—with variants including interpretative or noninterpretative interventions, interview frequency, and the general formal and affective structuring of such nodal situations. Such methods, seriously applied, may prove specifically indicated in a primary rather than a socioeconomic sense for some of the more severe cases and for very mild cases and also as practical alternatives for those cases traditionally considered ideal for psychoanalysis. Such techniques, especially if we include the *gray area* methods, may ultimately compete for certain of the optimum cases on the basis of intrinsic therapeutic merit. Furthermore, through the observation of phenomena in variant modalities, the study of psychotherapy may well enrich psychoanalysis. What do sitting up, or low frequency of visiting, or "integrated interpretations," or quasi-conversational exchange instead of free association really mean in their impact on the patient's unconscious life?

Why do I trouble to make these assertions, to ask these questions, which many analysts would regard as self-evident or superfluous, like the excellences of peace or brotherhood or science? Because in many important quarters they are not living realities. Classical psychoanalysis to its great disadvantage has been invested with a group narcissism of an inflexible and grandiose sort. Psychotherapy is viewed as a sort of bastard derivative convenience, all right for *hoi polloi*. "This is not psychoanalysis" (an implied definition of psychotherapy) has been told to patients not as a scientific distinction, but to make sure that the patients, who are concerned with suffering and help, did not have an inflated idea of what they were getting. Unsophisticated patients ignore the distinction; sophisticated patients suffer with it. Another intellectually distressed by-product of this value system is its effect on analyst's teaching and supervision of psychotherapy by analysts. In many instances the result is a watered down, often grotesquely inappropriate transposition of the psychoanalytic method and, even worse, of the psychoanalytic attitude, sometimes in caricature, to situations where large-scale thought-adaptations, either ad hoc or in terms of preconceived general patterns, should be applied. This does no justice to the therapeutic challenge, to psychoanalysis, to psychotherapy, or to the professional development of the young colleague. Again, the special interest of analysts in psychotherapy is a matter of personal option. But the general mood and attitude of the psychoanalytic world is powerfully influential in the choice of such options.

PROGRESS IN PSYCHOANALYSIS

I shall apply some closing words to the question of progress in psychoanalysis. While I regard therapy and science as intertwined in the sphere of clinical data and psychoanalytic process, it is self-evident that the science as such has an independent existence supported by the many important paraanalytic fields inspired by psychoanalysis and now contributing richly to its great body of reliable data—the objective study of infant and child development, the neurophysiologic studies of dreaming, sociologic and anthropologic observations, various studies of perception, memory, and other functions. There are also the methodologically oriented studies regarding *parts* of psychoanalysis—interpretation and its sequellae, predictive possibilities, agreement between trained observers, and so forth. Obviously, processes such as free association can be excerpted for experimental procedures or as analytic material utilized for statistical word studies and similar investigations. It is conceivable that psychoanalytic therapy could cease to exist without entirely disestablishing the science or the manifold germane investigations which are already under way. Some of these fields have already shown, or promise to show, great productiveness. They lend themselves relatively successfully to conventional scientific methods. With some this is less clear, and the productiveness more questionable. However, even in these instances one cannot question the legitimacy and possible ultimate usefulness of these efforts. One can only hope however that the new growth of trees will not obscure the deep and mysterious forest or render it a matter of little interest.

If all the parts and aspects of psychoanalysis hold promise for science, their integrations in the psychoanalytic situation and process remain distinctively important. Understanding may be stimulated, enriched, and controlled by the type of study now increasingly in vogue: charts, numbers, tape recorders, multiple observers, one-way screens, etc. Clinical statistical studies may yet come into their maturity. Possibly, indeed, an important breakthrough may originate in such work. It would be a part of the antidoctrinaire principle, which I support unequivocally, to welcome such efforts—provided they have the informed assent of patients and, of course, that the investigators consider thoroughly the fragmentary focus of such studies and their own important factors of error.

But we must still look to that part of the working analyst's mind which remains adequately objective for the scientific evaluation of the long-term movement and meaning of analysis, even where his emotional responses are, to varying degree, involved. Indeed, sometimes precisely because of this important fact, the movement and meaning of the analysis may be inaccessible to all others (Meissner 1971). For it is in the sphere of transference, countertransference, resistance, their pervasive interrelationship with the detailed processes and data of analysis, and the central functional position of speech that the further larger problems requiring elucidation lie. If such individual observation and inference are unsatisfactory to the scientific ideologist, their results will by virtue of their substance, in the long run satisfy or dissatisfy other observers. The data and the derived theories will be tested and sifted out with time and by the responses of multiple observers. This has indeed occurred with Freud's own earliest findings, reflected conspicuously in his own critiques and revisions. There have also been the efforts of other gifted analysts to introduce important revisions, new paradigms, if you wish. Some, even in their bold failure—for example, the more striking ideas of Ferenczi—have taught us (or at least, suggested) more than many exegetical studies or carefully planned but uninspired investigations.

(If I may exaggerate for straightforward clarity a maverick role,) I am not overly impressed with the importance of formal scientific methodology. Without facetiousness, I concede that it has its place and can on its merits become an important interest, a specialty, if you wish. At times, no doubt, it can make its own important contribution by way of critique. But one would not wish it to become a new form of constricting intellectual authoritarianism[3]. The word, *paradigm* (Kuhn 1963), for example, should not begin to exert the same unintended hypnotic fascination in scientific discussion that *parameter* (Eissler 1953) holds for many in discussions of technique. If new and better paradigms are established, well and good. But tremendous scientific changes can occur without revolution and without the inevitable rejection of currently essential paradigms. It is only when rigid primary adherence to theory as such, or to putatively inseparable techniques inhibits the spontaneous testing of new ideas (Greenson 1969) that intellectual upheaval (scientific revolution) must precede every important advance[4]. If not all analytic contributors can "disturb the sleep of the world," as did Freud, one may still expect important work within and in relation to the basic paradigms Freud established. Greenson is certainly right that new creative work does not necessarily cancel out the major contributions of the past. Normal science can indeed produce radical innovations. Certainly this was true of Newtonian physics for more than two centuries, and, in many spheres it seems to me, its basic contribution is still very much alive. Needless to say, I do not propose an idiot nihilism in this methodologic sphere. But hardheaded common sense and good grounding in essential principles usually provide sufficient critique to avert significant dangers. The scientific spirit and scientific method find their most effective expression and control in supreme honesty, in unflinching observation and inference, in openness to new and sometimes disconcerting data and theory, and in informed common sense.

One derivative of the common-sense point of view is a requirement that observational method be reasonably adapted to what is significant in the field of inquiry. One could use a microscope in analytic research, for example, to examine the cross-sections of the hair of analytic patients, correlate the incidence of obsessional neurosis in blond and black-haired patients, and cross-reference the range of hair diameter in microns. There is, after all, very likely a constitutional factor in obsessional neurosis. Many would think such a study idiotic. I would be more temperate and suggest that it would probably not be productive. This is the sort of thing people sometimes actually do. But the reference to the man who knew that his girl friend had the two most beautiful legs in the world because he had counted them is much funnier (see Harrison's excellent paper, 1970).

Thus I can be interested, in an unsophisticated way, in the dispute and dialectic regarding the scientific aspects of psychoanalysis, but they do not create in me either dismay or enthusiasm. Any body of significant observations, gathered by credible and honest and informed observers, subjected to discriminating critique and evaluation, then organized and classified, and utilized toward rational theoretical constructions (which render the data more meaningful and productive, yet are never invested with rigid authority) is, in my modest view, scientific. I agree that we should try to make our data available to others whenever it is reasonably possible (Brenner 1968, Harrison 1970, Joseph 1973).

Before even primitive scientific astronomy appeared, human beings had to observe the rhythms of night and day and the seasons. They had to observe the sun, the moon, and the stars and to initiate simple correlations between them and the basic rhythms. Before the concept of gravitation as a specific measurable force could be developed, it had to be part of the everyday folk heritage of a genius to take it for granted that unpropelled and unsupported objects fell down.

If we are not quite in the position of primitive man in relation to his environment, we are closer to him with regard to the current data in our specific epistemological field than we are to mathematical physics or physical chemistry. I might add, to avoid feeding the arrogance of modern science, that we are much closer to the science of the modern scientific elite than they are to absolute knowledge. While we should welcome, try and test anything which promises to tell us more about our field or open the view of our data more satisfactorily to one another and to other scientists, it would be the ultimate in folly to leap to methods and methodologies appropriate to other fields in the eagerness to please a new establishment and to abandon the tradition of personal reflective natural historical observation, which still holds great promise in our own science. This is, of course, not an exclusivistic view. We can accept the potential value of modern methodologically oriented research approaches (Wallerstein and Sampson, 1971), participate in them or cooperate with them when they seem worthwhile, and yet refuse to withdraw from our natural, and still critically important, methods before an intellectual stampede. Nor is this view, in any case, incompatible with our listening critically, but avidly, to the invaluable hard data from related scientific disciplines—anthropology, ethology, experimental neurophysiology, for specific examples.

Conclusion

A few words in conclusion. I do not believe that the present complex crisis in psychoanalysis threatens its position as an independent and productive profession and science, whether our future lies in university or medical school affiliations or in independent institutes. The crisis is a compound of escalating outer attack, of intense and literal therapeutic competition, of the disappointment in unfounded dreams of panacea, and of reactive bristling orthodoxy and sometimes reactive inadvertent submission and anticipatory mourning within our own group. The scientific group, like the individual whose sense of self and essential worthwhileness are well founded and secure, need not fear contacts with others nor confrontations with new ideas and new methods. Nor indeed need it fear evolution, modification, or in fact possible improvement deriving from other contemporary sciences. Cross-fertilization is not to be equated with contamination. The crisis can stimulate a more profound than usual individual and group self-examination.

The relinquishment of residues of a priestly omniscient taboo, insusceptible to criticism from within or without, will be in no sense a regression or a loss. It will be indeed a prodigious advance. Psychoanalysis in its present form still has a plenitude of untapped resources to offer as science, as therapy, and as the parent to other therapeutic methods. It will probably remain the optimum treatment for certain individuals in the foreseeable future and a valuable basic training experience for all psychotherapists. In its present strictly delimited form, it provides a source of data and a model for comparative study and experimental variations of incalculable value. But it would be fundamentally wrong to assume that it cannot change or should not be changed, if adequate reasons for such change are developed. Well-considered efforts in this direction should be welcomed and even encouraged, examined critically to be sure, but with an open and tolerant mind. A vivid, still young instrumentality of therapy and science should not be forced, in a scientific sense, to settle into the function of a source of interesting data, related always and exclusively to a fixed frame of reference or—more sadly—into the unintended function of an exegetical tool. In its therapeutic function there is no adequate reason for a rigidly, permanently defined mold to which varied expressions of human psychopathology adjacent to, but not precisely congruent with, its traditional indications must be uncompromisingly adapted if they are to be offered its unique potential benefits.

NOTES

1. Taboos are, of course, not invulnerable, especially to economic considerations. The forty-five minute hour has made headway in the United States, at least in New York, and is not often debated openly in the sense that the four to five hour-a-week schedule was once a *cause célèbre*.

2. In discussing my paper (Stone 1954), in reference to the real relationship, Anna Freud (1954b) said: "I wonder whether our—at times complete—neglect of this side of the matter is not responsible for some of the hostile reactions which we get from our patients and which we are apt to ascribe to 'true transference' only. But these are technically subversive thoughts and ought to be 'handled with care'" (pp. 618–619). Even a jest testifies to the intellectual climate of the time.

3. Richard Sterba (1972/1973), in the course of discussing this paper, mentioned a remark of Freud's at one of the Wednesday meetings in the early 1930's, then wrote me about it in response to my inquiry. This (without specifying the verbatim accuracy) was translated by Dr. Sterba as: "Methodologists remind me of people who clean their glasses so thoroughly that they have no opportunity to look through them." I am greatly indebted to Dr. Sterba for this relevant and excellent example of Freud's wit.

4. For differing ideas or implications, see Gitelson 1955, 1964, A. Freud 1969, Eissler 1969.

REFERENCES

Arlow, J. A. (1970a). *Group psychology and the study of institutes.* (Address to Board of Professional Standards, Amer. Psychoanal. Assn., by the outgoing chairman.)

———— (1970b). Some problems in current psychoanalytic thought. In *The World Biennial of Psychiatry and Psychotherapy*, vol. 1. ed. S. Arieti. New York: Basic Books, pp. 34–54.

———— (1972). Some dilemmas in psychoanalytic education. *J. Amer. Psychoanal. Assn.*, 20:pp. 556–566.

Bak, R. C. (1970a). Psychoanalysis Today. *J. Amer. Psychoanal. Assn.* 18:3–23.

———— (1970b). Recent developments in psychoanalysis: A critical summary of the main theme of the 26th international psycho-analytical congress in Rome. *Int. J. Psychoanal.* 51:255–264.

Bernfeld, S. (1962). On psychoanalytic training. *Psychoanal. Q.* 31:456–482.

Bird, Brian (1968). On candidate selection and its relation to analysis. *Int. J. Psychoanal.* 69:513–526.

Brenner, C. (1968). Psychoanalysis and science. *J. Amer. Psychoanal. Assn.* 16:675–696.

Cohn, F. S. (1940). Practical approach to the problem of narcissistic neuroses. *Psychoanal. Q.* 9:64–79.

Eissler, K. R. (1953). The effect of the structure of the ego on psychoanalytic technique. *J. Amer. Psychoanal. Assn.* 1:104–143.

———— (1965). *Medical Orthodoxy and the future of psychoanalysis.* New York: International Universities Press.

———— (1969). Irreverent remarks about the present and the future of psychoanalysis. *Int. J. Psychoanal.* 50:461–471.

Freud, A. (1954a). Problems of technique in adult analysis. *Bull. Phila. Assn. Psychoanal.* 4:44–70.

――― (1954b). The widening scope of indications for psychoanalysis. Discussion. *J. Amer. Psychoanal. Assn.* 2:607–620.

――― (1966). The ideal psychoanalytic institute: A utopia. *Bull. Menninger Clin.* 35: 225–239.

――― (1969). *Difficulties in the Path of Psychoanalysis. A Confrontation of Past with Present Viewpoints.* New York: International Universities Press.

Freud, S., (1910). The future prospects of psycho-analytic therapy. *S. E.* 11.

――― (1913). On beginning the treatment. (Further recommendations on the technique of psycho-analysis I) *S. E.* 12.

――― (1914). On the history of the psycho-analytic movement. *S. E.* 14.

――― (1914). From the history of an infantile neurosis. *S. E.* 17.

――― (1926). The question of lay analysis. Conversations with an impartial person. *S. E.* 20.

――― (1937). Analysis terminable and interminable. *S. E.* 23.

――― (1938). An outline of psycho-analysis. *S. E.* 23.

Gitelson, M. (1955). Psychoanalyst, U.S.A. *Amer. J. Psychiat.*, CXII, 1956, pp. 700–705.

――― (1964). On the identity crisis in American psychoanalysis. *J. Amer. Psychoanal. Assn.* 12:451–476.

Greenacre, P. (1941). The predisposition to anxiety. Part II. *Psychoanal. Q.* 10:610–638.

Greenson, R. R. (1969). The origin and fate of new ideas in psychoanalysis. *Int. J. Psychoanal.* 50:503–515.

Harrison, S. I. (1970). Is psychoanalysis "our science"? Reflections on the scientific status of psychoanalysis. *J. Amer. Psychoanal. Assn.* 18:125–149.

Jacobson, E. (1954). Transference problems in the psychoanalytic treatment of severely depressive patients. *J. Amer. Psychoanal. Assn.* 2:595–606.

Joseph, E. D. (1973). *Science, research, and twin studies.* (Address of past president before Plenary Session of Amer. Psychoanal. Assn.)

Keiser, S. (1969): Psychoanalysis—Taught, learned, and experienced. *J. Amer. Psychoanal. Assn.* 17:238–267.

――― (1972). Report to the Board on Professional Standards. *J. Amer. Psychoanal. Assn.* 20:518–539.

Kernberg, O. (1967). Borderline personality organization. *J. Amer. Psychoanal. Assn.* 15:641–685.

――― (1968). The treatment of patients with borderline personality organization. *Int. J. Psychoanal.* 69:600–619.

Klein, G. S. (1973). Is psychoanalysis relevant? In *Psychoanalysis and Contemporary Science. An Annual of Integrative and Interdisciplinary Studies, vol, II,* ed. B. B. Rubinstein. New York: Macmillan, pp. 3–21.

Knight, R. P. (1953). The present status of organized psychoanalysis in the United States. J. Amer. Psychoanal. Assn. 1:197–221.

Kohut, H. (1971). The analysis of the self. A systematic approach to the psychoanalytic treatment of narcissistic personality disorders. (The Psychoanalytic Study of the Child, Monograph no. 4.) New York: International Universities Press.

Kuhn, T. (1963). *The Structure of Scientific Revolutions.* Chicago: University of Chicago Press.

Lazar, N. D. (1973). Nature and significance of changes in patients in a psychoanalytic clinic. *Psychoanal. Q.* 62:579–600.

Loewenstein, R. M. (1951). The problem of interpretation. *Psychoanal. Q.* 20:1–14.

_____ (1957). Some thoughts on interpretation in the theory and practice of psychoanalysis. In *The Psychoanalytic Study of the Child*, vol. 12. New York: International Universities Press, pp. 127–150.

Lowenfeld, H. (1969). The decline in belief in the devil. The consequences for group psychology. *Psychoanal. Q.* 38:455–462.

Lowenfeld, H., and Lowenfeld, Y. (1970). Our permissive society and the superego. Some current thoughts about Freud's cultural concepts. *Psychoanal. Q.* 39:590–608.

Meissner, W. W. (1971). Freud's methodology. *J. Amer. Psychoanal. Assn.* 265–309.

Menninger Foundation (1972). Psychotherapy and psychoanalysis. Final report of the Menninger Foundation's psychotherapy research project (O. F. Kernberg, E. D. Burstein, L. Coyne, A. Appelbaum, L. Horwitz, H. Voth). *Bull. Menninger Clin.* 36(1/2).

Menninger, K. A. (1958). Theory of psychoanalytic technique. (Menninger Clinic Monograph Series no. 12.) New York: Basic Books.

Oberndorf, C. P. (1950). Unsatisfactory results of psychoanalytic therapy. *Psychoanal. Q.* 19:393–407.

Rangell, L. (1967). Psychoanalysis—A current look. (*Bull. Amer. Psychoanal. Assn.*, 23[1], April 1967.) *J. Amer. Psychoanal. Assn.* 15:423–431.

Reik, T. (1919). *Ritual: Four Psychoanalytic Studies.* New York: Grove Press, 1962.

Ritvo, S. (1971). Psychoanalysis as science and profession: Prospects and challenges. *J. Amer. Psychoanal. Assn.* 19:3–21.

Schafer, R. (1970). The psychoanalytic vision of reality. *Int. J. Psychoanal.* 51:279–297.

Sterba, R. F. (1972/1973). Personal communications.

Stern, A. (1938). Psychoanalytic investigations of and therapy in the borderline group of neuroses. *Psychoanal. Q.* 7:467–489.

Stone, L. (1951). Psychoanalysis and brief psychotherapy. *Psychoanal. Q.* 20:215–236. *Reprinted in this volume, Chapter 1.*

_____ (1954). The widening scope of indications for psychoanalysis. *J. Amer. Psychoanal. Assn.* 2:567–594. *Reprinted in this volume, Chapter 2.*

_____ (1961). *The Psychoanalytic Situation. An Examination of Its Development and Essential Nature.* New York: International Universities Press.

_____ (1967). The psychoanalytic situation and transference: Postscript to an earlier communication. *J. Amer. Psychoanal. Assn.* 15:3–58. *Reprinted in this volume, Chapter 4.*

_____ (1973). On resistance to the psychoanalytic process: Some thoughts on its nature and motivations. In *Psychoanalysis and Contemporary Science. An Annual of Integrative and Interdisciplinary Studies, vol. II*, ed. B. B. Rubinstein. New York: Macmillan, pp. 42–73. *Reprinted in this volume, Chapter 5.*

_____ (1975). The assessment of students' progress. In *The Annual of Psychoanalysis. A Publication of the Chicago Institute of Psychoanalysis, vol. II.* New York: International Universities Press, pp. 308–322. *Reprinted in this volume, Chapter 14.*

Symposium (1967). Indications and contraindications for psychoanalytic treatment (S. A. Guttman, E. R. Zetzel, P. C. Kuiper, A. F. Valenstein, R. Diatkine, A. Namnum). *Int. J. Psychoanal.* 69:254–275.

Wallerstein, R. S. (1969). Introduction to panel on psychoanalysis and psychotherapy. The relationship of psychoanalysis to psychotherapy—Current issues. *Int. J. Psychoanal.* 50:117–126.

———, and Sampson, H. (1971). Issues in research in the psychoanalytic process. *Int. J. Psychoanal.* 52:11–50.

Source Notes

The Psychoanalytic and Psychotherapeutic Situations. *Psychoanalytic Quarterly* 20: 215–236. Reprinted by permission. Presented at the panel on Psychotherapy at the meeting of the American Psychoanalytic Association, Montreal, May 1949, and at the meeting of the New York Psychoanalytic Society, June 1949.

The Widening Scope of Indications for Psychoanalysis. *Journal of the American Psychoanalytic Association* 2:567–594. Reprinted by permission of International Universities Press.

The Psychoanalytic Situation. Excerpted from *The Psychoanalytic Situation: An Examination of Its Development and Essential Nature.* New York: International Universities Press. Copyright © 1961, The New York Psychoanalytic Institute. Reprinted by permission of International Universities Press.

The Psychoanalytic Situation and Transference: Postscript to an Earlier Communication. *Journal of the American Psychoanalytic Association* 15:3–58. Reprinted by permission of International Universities Press. Presented at the Sunday morning plenary session of the Annual Meeting of the American Psychoanalytic Association, Atlantic City, May 8, 1966.

On Resistance to the Psychoanalytic Process. *Psychoanalysis and Contemporary Science* 2:42–76. Reprinted by permission of Macmillan Publishing Co., Inc. Presented in its essential content as the John B. Turner Lecture of the Psychoanalytic Clinic for Training and Research, Columbia University, April 29, 1970. Presented before the Baltimore–District of Columbia Society for Psychoanalysis, November 21, 1970, and before the Atlanta Psychoanalytic Group, January 7, 1972.

Notes on the Noninterpretive Elements in the Psychoanalytic Situation and Process. *Journal of the American Psychoanalytic Association* 29:89–118. Reprinted by permission of International Universities Press. Based on a presentation at the panel on "Contemporary Problems of Psychoanalytic Technique," American Psychoanalytic Association, December 16, 1979. Presented in a paper before the Baltimore–District of Columbia Society for Psychoanalysis, March 22, 1980.

Some Thoughts on the "Here and Now" in Psychoanalytic Technique and Press. *Psychoanalytic Quarterly* 50:709–733. Reprinted by permission. This paper was presented before the New York Psychoanalytic Society subsequent to its submission for publication.

Some Thoughts on the "Here and Now" in Psychoanalytic Technique and Process. *Psychoanalytic Quarterly* 50:709–733. Reprinted by permission. This paper was presented before the New York Psychoanalytic Society subsequent to its submission for publication.

Transference sleep in a Neurosis with Duodenal Ulcer. *International Journal of Psycho-Analysis* 28:18–32. Reprinted by permission.

Two Avenues of Approach to the Schizophrenic Patient. *Journal of the American Psychoanalytic Association* 3:126–148. Reprinted by permission of the International Universities Press.

Refections on the Psychoanalytic Concept of Aggression. *Psychoanalytic Quarterly* 40:195–244. Reprinted by permission. Presented as the Brill Memorial Lecture, New York Psychoanalytic Society, November 26, 1968, and before the Western New England Psychoanalytic Society, January 11, 1969.

Remarks on Certain Conditions of Human Aggression (the Hand, Speech, and the Use of Fire). *Journal of the American Psychoanalytic Association* 27:27–63. Reprinted by permission of International Universities Press. Presented in abbreviated form at the special meeting of the New York Psychoanalytic Society, January 14, 1975, in honor of the eightieth birthday of Dr. Phyllis Greenacre.

On the Principal Obscene Word of the English Language. *International Journal of Psycho-Analysis* 35:30–56. Reprinted by permission. Presented before the New York Psychoanalytic Society, May 15, 1951.

The Assessment of Students' Progress. *Annual of Psychoanalysis* 2:308–322. Reprinted by permission of International Universities Press. Based on an introductory statement made at the plenary session of the Pre-Congress Conference on Training, International Psycho-Analytic Association, Vienna, July 23, 1971.

The Influence of the Practice and Theory of Psychotherapy on Education in Psychoanalysis. *Psychotherapy: Impact on Psychoanalytic Training*, ed. E. D. Joseph and R. S. Wallerstein. New York: International Universities Press, pp. 75–118. Reprinted by permission. Presented as the opening address of the Pre-Congress on Training, International Psychoanalytic Association, New York, July 26, 1979.

Some Problems and Potentialities of Present-Day Psychoanalysis. *Psychoanalytic Quarterly* 44:331–370. Reprinted by permission. Presented in abbreviated versions before the Michigan Psychoanalytic Society, October 7, 1972; the Washington Psychoanalytic Society, April 13, 1973; the Cleveland Psychoanalytic Society, October 19, 1973; the Mexican Psychoanalytic Association, March 18, 1974; and the New York Psychoanalytic Society, May 28, 1974.

Review of Franz Alexander's *Psychoanalysis and Psychotherapy: Developments in Theory Technique, and Training*. *Psychoanalytic Quarterly* 26:397–405. Reprinted by permission.

Index